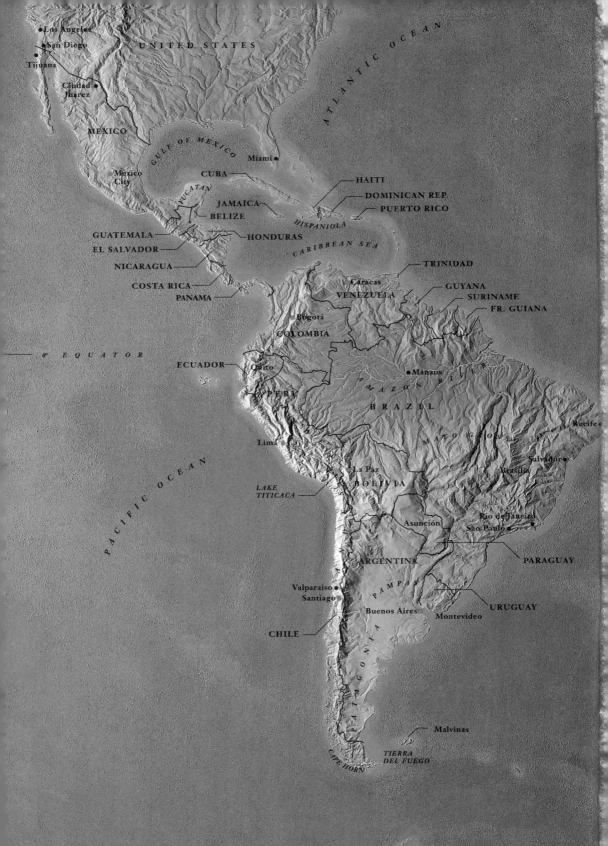

Americas

Americas

The Changing Face of Latin America and the Caribbean

Peter Winn

Pantheon Books, New York

Grateful acknowledgment is made to the following for permission to reprint previously published material:

Excerpt from *The Gaucho Martín Fierro,* translated by C. E. Ward, copyright © 1967 State University of New York Press. · Excerpt from a poem by Sor Juana, translated by Robert Graves, from *Chicana Literature,* edited by Joseph Sommers, copyright © 1972 Prentice Hall. · Excerpt from "Is It Utopia?" copyright © 1988 Grupo Olodum. · Excerpt from "One Hundred Years of Freedom: Reality or Illusion," from *Blacks and Whites in São Paolo, Brazil 1888–1988,* by George Reid Andrews, copyright © 1988 The Board of Regents of the University of Wisconsin System. · Excerpt from "La Guerra de los Callados," by Alvaro José Arroyo, copyright © Edimusica Ltda. · Excerpt from *Omeros,* by Derek Walcott, copyright © 1990 by Derek Walcott. · Excerpts from "Get Up, Stand Up," written by Bob Marley and Peter Tosh. Copyright © 1974. All rights for U.S. and Canada controlled by PolyGram International Publishing, Inc.; and excerpts from "Redemption Song," written by Bob Marley. Copyright © 1980 Bob Marley Music Ltd. All rights for U.S. and Canada controlled by PolyGram International Publishing, Inc. Reprinted by permission.

Library of Congress Cataloging-in-Publication Data

Winn, Peter.
    Americas : the changing face of Latin America and the Caribbean / Peter Winn.
        p.   cm.
    1. Latin America—History—20th century.   2. Caribbean Area—History—1810–1945.   3. Caribbean Area—History—1945–   I. Title.
    F1414.W56   1993
    980—dc20   92-54114
ISBN 0-679-41169-0

Book design by Fearn Cutler

Manufactured in the United States of America
First Edition

To my mother, Esther Winn,
who showed me that there were worlds beyond my own horizon
and other horizons from which to view the world.

Contents

Preface

*A*t the close of the Columbus quincentennial year, readers need no reminder that the history of the "Americas"—that unique outcome of the encounter among Europeans, Africans, and "Indians" in the Western Hemisphere—began five centuries ago. The *Americas* project does not go back quite as far, but it too has its history. The project—of which this book is an outgrowth—began a decade ago, when Mark Rosenberg and colleagues at Florida International University developed the idea for a television series and college telecourse about the Caribbean. During the years that followed, the project expanded in scope to include all of Latin America and in participants to include a score of scholars in seven disciplines at more than a dozen universities. Alfred C. Stepan, a leading expert on Latin American politics, then Dean of Columbia University's School of Public and International Affairs, became Chair of the Academic Advisory Board in 1985 and asked me to join it as Academic Director the following year. I was pleased to participate in a venture that offered a unique opportunity to present to a broad public a vision of contemporary Latin America and the Caribbean that went beyond the usual tourist clichés and crisis headlines.

The outlines of what we wished to convey to our television and student audiences were hammered out at several intense marathon meetings, where experts in one discipline had to defend their ideas against critiques by specialists of equal stature in others—anthropology, comparative literature, economics, history, political science, religion, and sociology. These ideas have continued to evolve during the years that we have worked together on this project.

But ideas and expertise do not by themselves make a television series. We had to find partners with the production skills and creative ability to translate our ideas into effective documentary films and the organizational capacity to fund, develop, and distribute a project of this magnitude. All roads led to WGBH, the Boston public television station with a long list of production credits that includes some of the most celebrated PBS series. Dr. Jean Mayer, then President of Tufts University, my own institution, and a trustee of the board that oversees WGBH, helped us make the initial contacts. Meetings with Henry Becton, President of WGBH, and Peter McGhee, its Vice-President for National Programming, led to an agreement for *Americas* to be produced for PBS by WGBH and by Central Television Enterprises for Channel 4 (UK), in association with the School of International and Public Affairs at Columbia University, the Latin American and Caribbean Center at Florida International University, and Tufts University. Judith Vecchione, a prize-winning documentary filmmaker who was finishing her work as Series Senior Producer on the acclaimed *Eyes on the Prize: Americas Civil Rights Years, 1954–1965,* became Executive Producer.

Several years of funding and development of the project followed, with both private and public funders playing critical roles. In the end, major funding for *Americas* was provided by the Annenberg/CPB Project, with additional funding from the Carnegie Corporation of New York, the John D. and Catherine T. MacArthur Foundation, the Rockefeller Foundation, the Corporation for Public Broadcasting, and public television viewers. Special thanks are due to Avery Russell of Carnegie, who championed the project from the start and helped it through its darkest hours.

In 1990 production on the first of ten hour-long documentaries began. During the three years that followed, producers from Latin America, the United States, Britain, and Australia contributed their talents, guided by scholars who acted as principal advisers to films in their areas of expertise and jointly as a critical audience for rough versions of the documentaries. Since *Americas* was also conceived of as an Annenberg/CPB Project college-level television course, an array of print materials was prepared to accompany it, including a volume of original essays, written by the advisers and edited by Alfred Stepan; an anthology of readings, edited by Mark B. Rosenberg, A. Douglas Kincaid, and Kathleen Logan; and a revised edition of their popular textbook *Modern Latin America* by Thomas E. Skidmore and Peter H. Smith.

Also in 1990, I was selected to write the companion volume for *Americas,* and at the end of that year Pantheon Books agreed to publish it. The idea was to create a book that would share many of the qualities of the television series—its thematic organization, its use of "small stories" about people's lives to convey its larger points, and its focus on the areas and dynamics of change in contemporary Latin America and the Caribbean. This book also shares the series' determination to present Latin America and the Caribbean through the eyes and words of its own people, while reflecting the best current scholarship.

At the same time, I wanted to expand on the television series by offering readers complementary information and analysis that were beyond its scope. This book begins, therefore, with an overview and history of the region largely absent on the screen. It also presents more stories in more countries—twenty-four in all—while setting them in a broader comparative context. My goal was a book that would enhance a viewer's understanding of the television series but also stand on its own as an introduction to contemporary Latin America and the Caribbean.

During the course of my research, I visited more than a score of countries and interviewed over a hundred people, in addition to the many with whom I talked in a less formal setting. Most of the interviews used in this book were conducted during the past three years, but I have drawn as well on interviews I have done during three decades studying the region. Occasionally, I have incorporated interviews by other writers. Unless otherwise noted, the interviews used in this book were conducted by myself or by the producers of the *Americas* documentaries.

A project of this scope inevitably incurs many debts of gratitude, only some of which I can acknowledge here. First, I would like to thank Alfred Stepan, Judith Vecchione, and Karen Johnson, Executive Director of Publishing at WGBH, for the opportunity to write this book. Second, I want to thank Erroll McDonald, Vice-President and Executive Editor at Pantheon, for his faith in the book while it was merely an idea and his continued support throughout the process of bringing that idea to fruition.

I am deeply indebted to the many people in the Americas who shared their words, ideas, lives, fears, and hopes with me. My debt to those whose names and words appear in the pages of this book is clear. Occasionally, I have changed their names to protect them or in deference to their wishes, but I have retained the names of public figures. In some cases, I have used only first names, particularly when drawing on anthropological sources which follow that practice.

There are many others whose names and words do not appear, yet who also helped me to gain an understanding of the region and to make contact with people who extended and deepened that understanding. It would be impossible for me to thank all of them here. But certain names stand out whose contribution to my enterprise has been too great for me to omit.

My colleagues on the Academic Advisory Board of the *Americas* project generously shared their ideas, writings, and experience with me, beginning with Alfred Stepan and including Cynthia Arnson, Margaret E. Crahan, M. Patricia Fernández Kelly, Albert Fishlow, Cornelia Butler Flora, Jean Franco, Franklin W. Knight, Anthony P. Maingot, Marysa Navarro-Aranguren, Alejandro Portes, Mark Rosenberg, Rubén G. Rumbaut, Helen Safa, Peter H. Smith, Marta Tienda, Kay Barbara Warren, and John Womack. Albert Fishlow, María Patricia Fernández Kelly, Anthony Maingot, Cornelia Flora, Jean Franco, Franklin Knight, Cynthia Arnson, and Rubén Rumbaut were also kind enough to give critical readings of individual chapters on short notice. Margaret Crahan, Peter Smith, Alfred Stepan, and Kay Warren generously read more than one chapter. The contributions of my colleagues to individual chapters are acknowledged in the endnotes. Their collective wisdom informs the pages of this book.

I am also indebted to many on the production side of the *Americas* project for their help in making this book possible, beginning with Judith Vecchione, who placed the considerable resources of the production staff behind the book. Adriana Bosch Lemus, the series editor, shared her ideas and comments from the start of the project and read draft chapters along the way. The production teams of the ten documentaries—David Ash, Marc de Beaufort, Peter Bull, Yezid Campos, Tania Cypriano, Andrés DiTella, Rachel Field, Juan Mandelbaum, Rebecca Marvil, Elizabeth Nash, Marisol Navas, Lourdes Portillo, Jane Regan, Raymond Telles, Joseph Tovares, and Veronica Young—generously made available to me the interviews they conducted in fourteen countries and the scripts and treatments they wrote; they discussed their interpretations and answered my questions. Almost all of them also commented on drafts of the chapters that related to their films. Many chapters rely heavily on their interviews and story lines; some would have been impossible without their assistance. Their contributions to individual chapters are specified in the endnotes.

Both advisers and producers have saved me from errors of omission and commission. Those mistakes that remain are mine alone, as are the opinions expressed in the pages that follow.

Others in the *Americas* project and in the Publishing Department of WGBH who play largely unsung roles also deserve recognition here. Margaret Carsley, Andrew Gersh, and Virginia Jackson helped me obtain materials that I needed in order to write the book. Elizabeth Buxton has been a sympathetic project manager and Marianne Neuman a skillful financial manager. At Tufts, Aida Higuerey and Alison Donahower aided my research.

But many people not associated with the *Americas* project were also generous in their support of this book. My research would not have been possible without the assistance of friends and acquaintances in many countries, who shared their knowledge and their contacts. I am grateful for their help, although I do not have space to acknowledge all of them. Some friends went further, setting up interviews for me and helping me to avoid some of the pitfalls of too rapid research. In Argentina, I am particularly indebted to Marcelo Cavarrozzi, Daniel James, Geoffroy De Laforcade, Miguel Sánchez, and Orlando Torrado; in Brazil, my research would not have been possible without the generous aid of Malak and Pedro Paulo Poppovic, Paulo Sergio Pinheiro, Rosiska Darcy de Oliveira, and José Serra, and I owe a special thanks to Ralph Della Cava, Mary Ann Mahoney, and Betty Mindlin. In Chile, I am particularly grateful to Sergio Bitar, Gonzalo Fallabella, Eugenia Hirmas, and María Angélica Ibáñez. In Colombia, my research was much indebted to the assistance of Francisco and Magdalena Leal and Mark Chernick; in Ecuador, to Jorge León, Rayda Márquez, and Melina Selverston; in Peru to Julio Cotler, José Luis Renique, and María Luisa de la Rocha; in Bolivia to Osvaldo Rivera and Jeffrey Himpele; and in Panama to Roberto Mendes and Andrew Zimbalist. Robert Duval and Rachel Beauvoir-Dominque greatly aided my research in and understanding of Haiti, as did Frank Moya Pons and Abraham Lowenthal for the Dominican Republic. In Jamaica, I owe a special thanks to Andrea McKay, and in Cuba to Santiago Díaz and Rafael Hernández. Mark Chernick, Lorraine Roses, and Thomas Skidmore made valuable comments on drafts of individual chapters.

The support of several institutions helped me to write this book, but the contributions of two stand out. I am grateful to my colleagues at Tufts University for their understanding during the years that I was working on this project. And I owe a special thanks to Douglas Chalmers and the Institute of Latin American and Iberian Studies at Columbia University for their hospitality in offering me a supportive New York base for *Americas*.

Writing—and rewriting—a book of this scope in the short time span allotted to such companion volumes is a formidable task, and one that is heavily dependent on the assistance of fine editors. Nancy Lattanzio at WGBH began that process and oversaw it to the end, with the assistance of Moira Bucciarelli. At Pantheon, Altie Karper shepherded the book through its stages and crises with skill and sympathy. But it was Sarah Flynn, my principal editor at WGBH, who bore the brunt of what was the always daunting and at times seemingly impossible task of editing the manuscript. It is to her "tough but kind" editing that I am particularly indebted. This book owes much to her talent and efforts, and I am grateful as well for her commitment and generosity of spirit.

If the hundred illustrations that enhance this book are each worth a thousand words, my debt is clear to Martha Davidson for her photo research, which was completed with the able assistance of Marta Garsd in Argentina and Deborah Paddock at WGBH. The many photographers and artists whose work fills the book's photo essays are credited for their contributions, but I have been inspired in particular by the photos of Sebastião Salgado and Susan Meiselas, who taught me that images can teach as much about Latin America as words.

I am also grateful to the many friends who supported me in this enterprise, at times against their better judgments. Richard Locke and Wendy Nicholson gave me excellent advice at the outset. Martin Sherwin and Donnah Canavan offered perceptive encouragement at times of trouble. And I owe a special thanks to Martin Garbus for his counsel, support, and assistance throughout.

Lastly, I want to thank my family, particularly Sue Gronewold, my life's companion and in-house editor, who took too much time away from her own writing to help with mine, and who took over a disproportionate share of our household's burdens so that I was free to shoulder what often seemed an endless task. And to Ethan and Sasha, who showed so much love and understanding during a year when I was too often unavailable to them, my thanks—and apologies. I hope that what they will learn from reading this book will compensate them for the school papers I did not read for them and the stories I did not read to them during the time that I was writing it. The people of Latin America and the Caribbean are their neighbors, too, and will play a growing role in their lives and those of their generation. This book presents the voices and visions of these hemispheric neighbors.

P.W.

August 1992

Americas

Chilean artist Alfredo Jaar's provocative forty-five-second computer animation, "Logo for America," was installed on the Times Square lightboard in the heart of New York City in 1987.

A View from the South

*I*N April 1987, strollers in Times Square who looked up to read the neon news headlines were startled to see a computer animation map of the United States across which was written: THIS IS NOT AMERICA. As they watched, the images changed. The word AMERICA expanded to fill the screen, and the "R" became a rotating map of both Americas—North and South. For Alfredo Jaar, a conceptual artist from South America, his forty-five-second "broadcast" was an effort to shock U.S. citizens into realizing that "this country has co-opted for itself the name 'America' and even our everyday language forces us to picture only one dimension of America."[1] Many North Americans forget that we share "America" with thirty-three other sovereign nations and their nearly half a billion people.

What makes the equation of "America" with the United States particularly ironic is that the name first appeared on sixteenth-century maps identified with *South* America, whose northeast coast had been explored by Amerigo Vespucci, the Florentine navigator. His accounts, which exaggerated his own role, were widely read. It was Vespucci's facility with his pen more than his maritime feats that got his name attached to the "New World" Columbus had "discovered." Only with the founding of the United States would "America" also be used for the northern part of the "Western" hemisphere. As Mexican intellectual Edmundo O'Gorman has stressed, America was *invented*, not discovered. Its invention began with the first

European chroniclers, who often projected onto their "New World" the Old World's fantasies of the exotic, and continues to the present day.

"Latin America" is equally an invention, devised in the nineteenth century by a French geographer to describe the nations that had once been colonized by "Latin Europe"—Spain, France, and Portugal. The Caribbean, a region named after the sea it encloses, and the almost extinct "Indians" who used to inhabit its smaller islands, is even more complex in its origins and polyglot in its peoples. There, beginning in the seventeenth century, England and Holland added their colonies and cultures to those of Spain and France. During the nineteenth century, they also added "East Indians" and Chinese to the descendants of the Africans brought in by Europeans to replace the declining "Indian" population of the "West Indies."

My own interest in Latin America and the Caribbean began in 1959, as a college freshman, when a thirty-three-year-old revolutionary who had just overthrown a corrupt dictator in a Caribbean island better known for its dance rhythms came to speak at my university. We were a study in contrasts: Fidel Castro sported a beard, long hair, and olive fatigues; I was clean-shaven, with a crew cut and a button-down collar. He was then a young rebel with a cause, who spoke the language of humanism, democracy, and social justice. I was part of a generation on the cusp between the monochromatic fifties and the psychedelic sixties, between social conformity and political engagement. Castro was convinced that his revolution marked the beginning of a new era for Latin America and the Caribbean. I was unaware that the decades that followed would be as filled with change for the United States as for the lands to the south of our borders. Two years later John F. Kennedy announced the Alliance for Progress, United States support for Latin American reforms intended to make revolutions such as Castro's impossible. Together, these events sparked an interest in Latin America and the Caribbean that quickly deepened, leading me to spend the last three decades studying the region.

This has been a period of far-reaching change for the people of Latin America and the Caribbean, changes that have transformed their countries and reshaped their lives. A largely rural region has become a continent of city dwellers, the result of one of the most massive migrations of modern history. In Brazil alone, thirty million people left the countryside during the 1970s. The child born to a peasant family in 1962 is likely to be an urban worker in 1992. This epic migration has produced some of the world's most populous and least livable cities. Mexico City's twenty million inhabitants give it the dubious distinction of being the globe's largest metropolitan area. By the year 2000, seven out of ten people in Latin America and the Caribbean will live in towns and cities.

During the past thirty years, Brazil, which occupies half of South America, grew from "an economy of desserts"—coffee, sugar, and tropical fruits—into an industrial nation that exports commuter planes to the United States and armored cars to Canada, as well as soybeans to China and orange juice to Florida. In the Caribbean thirteen new independent nations were created out of former British and Dutch colonies. In much of Latin America the Catholic church, long regarded as a bulwark of the status quo, emerged as a force for change. In El Salvador the murdered archbishop Oscar Romero became a martyr to this new cause.

Americas, the companion volume to the public television series of the same name, spotlights the dramatic changes of the last three decades in Latin America and the Caribbean. Like the series, it does not set out to be encyclopedic in its coverage. Instead, it focuses on areas where change has been most striking and on stories that reveal these changes most graphically.

The notion that the United States is "America" is not the only misconception that its citizens have about "their" hemisphere. So is the stereotype of Latin America and the Caribbean as lands of fiestas and siestas where nothing changes. *Americas* is the story of those changes. It is also the story of the people of Latin America and the Caribbean. Wherever possible, I have let them tell it in their own words. Like Alfredo Jaar, my goal is to offer North Americans views from the south.

"It is all a question of perspective," a Chilean philosopher explained to me in 1972, as he spread the map of the hemisphere on the sand near the

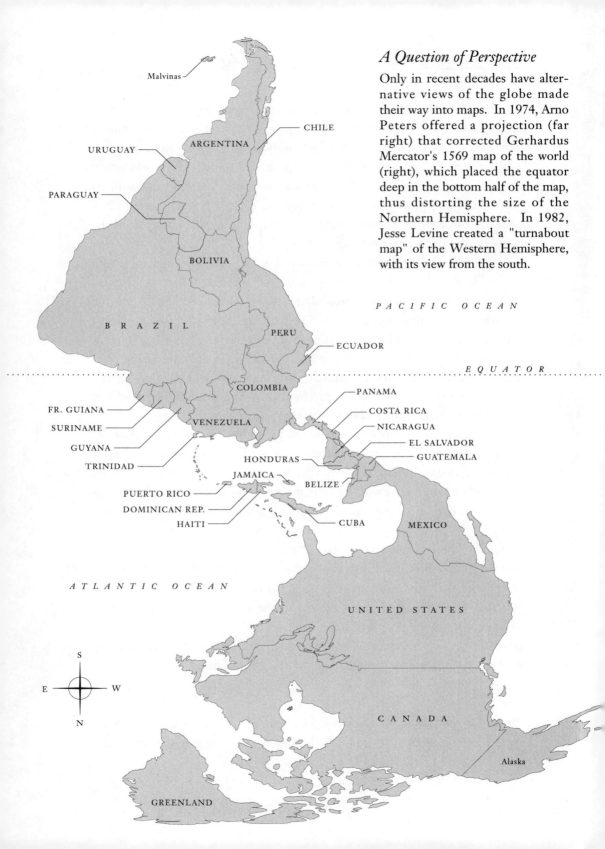

A Question of Perspective

Only in recent decades have alternative views of the globe made their way into maps. In 1974, Arno Peters offered a projection (far right) that corrected Gerhardus Mercator's 1569 map of the world (right), which placed the equator deep in the bottom half of the map, thus distorting the size of the Northern Hemisphere. In 1982, Jesse Levine created a "turnabout map" of the Western Hemisphere, with its view from the south.

Malvinas

CHILE

ARGENTINA

URUGUAY

PARAGUAY

BOLIVIA

B R A Z I L

PERU

ECUADOR

PACIFIC OCEAN

EQUATOR

COLOMBIA

PANAMA

FR. GUIANA

SURINAME

GUYANA

VENEZUELA

COSTA RICA

NICARAGUA

EL SALVADOR

GUATEMALA

HONDURAS

TRINIDAD

JAMAICA

BELIZE

PUERTO RICO

DOMINICAN REP.

HAITI

CUBA

MEXICO

ATLANTIC OCEAN

U N I T E D   S T A T E S

S

E

W

N

C A N A D A

Alaska

GREENLAND

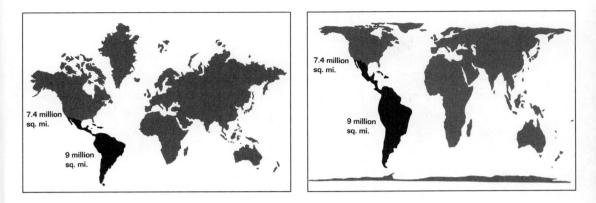

Mercator Projection   **Peters Projection**

crashing waves of the Pacific. "Like you, we have been accustomed to viewing our country from the north, and feeling our isolation and subordination as 'Chile,' which means 'the land at the end of the world' in the language of our Mapuche Indians. But, once you realize that our north is south," he exclaimed, turning the map on its head, "everything changes! Suddenly, Chile is at the *top* of the world, not the bottom. It is important to see us from the south."

The world has indeed been accustomed to viewing the Americas from the north, and to regarding the difference between North America and the rest of the Americas as a measure of the latter's inferiority. European cartographers reinforced this vision of the world by creating maps projected from the north, which exaggerate the size of the northern hemisphere and understate the scale of the southern half of the globe. We have all been brought up with this reduced image of Latin America and the Caribbean. In reality, with an area of nearly nine million square miles, the other Americas are larger than the United States and Canada combined. Viewed from the south, the geography of Latin America and the Caribbean takes on a different dimension.

The mountain chain of changing names that forms the Pacific spine of the continent from Chile to Alaska is the dominant geographic feature of this vast region. In South America the Andes rise from Antarctica to form the highest mountains in the hemisphere, with dozens of snow-capped peaks that scrape the sky at over twenty thousand feet. The snows of the Andes feed the Amazon, the Orinoco, and the Plata rivers, which together drain over three-fifths of the continent. The parallel ranges of the Andes enclose the valleys and plateaus where much of the region's people live. Its mountain walls ensure that the continent's major rivers flow to the Atlantic and that rainfall is concentrated in the lowlands to the east. As a result, the Amazon is the world's mightiest river, containing a fifth of the earth's fresh water, and flows through its largest rain forest, covering 2.7 million square miles of South America—an area equal to 90 percent of the contiguous United States. To the south the Plata river system waters the fertile pampas, the region's largest plains and one of the world's breadbaskets. The Pacific strip to the west of the Andes is mostly arid land, which requires irrigation to bloom. The coast of Peru and Chile contains one of the world's driest deserts, including areas where no rainfall has ever been recorded.

This pattern of a mountain range enclosing populous valleys and plateaus, and separating a dry Pacific fringe from a larger expanse of humid tropical lowlands, continues north into Central America and Mexico. Viewed from the south, the Rockies are just a less lofty extension of Latin America's mountain chain. The same is true for the Caribbean, an arc of islands stretching some twenty-five hundred miles from Venezuela's Orinoco to Mexico's Yucatán, the visible tips of a submerged mountain range.

Latin America and the Caribbean formally end at the Rio Grande and the Florida Straits. Viewed from the south, these are political boundaries but porous borders, which have not stopped the flow of people or culture. Since World War II more than five million people have migrated from the Caribbean to the United States. Altogether the twenty-five million people of Spanish American origin in the United States make it the world's fifth largest Spanish-speaking country. Latin America and the Carib-

Highways have opened up previously inaccessible rain forest areas to a tide of landless peasants and miners. Today more than three hundred thousand *garimpeiros,* or prospectors, search for precious metals in the Brazilian Amazon. At Serra Pelada, some thirty thousand miners sift the mud for gold in a barren landscape.

During the 1980s, some forty-five thousand gold prospectors invaded the lands of the Yanomami Indians, isolated hunters and gatherers. The mining poisoned the rivers with mercury, turning the once virgin rain forest of the northern Amazon into a wasteland, and the Yanomami into a malnourished people vulnerable to the diseases the miners spread.

Indians are not the only people whose way of life is threatened by the destruction of the Amazon rain forest. Chico Mendes, a leader of Brazil's rubber tappers, became world famous for his efforts to defend their example of sustainable development. His murder by a rancher's gunman in 1990 was deeply mourned.

The June 1992 Earth Summit brought
the world's leaders to Rio de Janeiro to
deliberate on proposals to protect the
environment while promoting development. It also featured a nongovernmen-
tal Global Forum, in which indigenous
peoples like these Amazon Indians
presented their concerns about land
and hunger as well.

bean continue deep into North America, uniting the Americas in a shared culture as well as a shared hemisphere.

Changes in the Land

"Geography has shaped our history," affirmed Ricardo Arias Calderón, Panama's vice president. It has molded the lives of the region's people in the past and continues to influence their future possibilities. Tourists are struck by the beauty and grandeur of the landscape of Latin America and the Caribbean, but for those who live there, nature has a more vital significance. Much of the land is geologically young and seismically alive. Tremors shake Chile each day, and in 1985, an earthquake left twenty thousand dead and one million homeless in Mexico. Yet its geology has also helped the region, forming rich deposits of metals and minerals, as well as petroleum and gas reserves that are among the largest in the world.

Most of the people of the other Americas live either close to a coast, as in North America, or in densely populated valleys and plateaus that range from four to twelve thousand feet above the sea. Nowhere else in the world do so many people live at so high an altitude. In Latin America, where three quarters of the land lies in the tropics, altitude moderates latitude. Throughout the Andes and Mesoamerica (Mexico and Central America), the majority of the people live in mountain valleys and table-lands whose cooler climes belie their proximity to the equator. In Ecuador a monument that marks "the middle of the world" is located at a chilly eight thousand feet, and natives wrap themselves in thick wool ponchos once the equatorial sun sets. Mexico's equally high central plateau has been the most densely inhabited area of the other Americas for millennia, and remains so today, containing its capital, Mexico City, and half of its eighty million people.

In most of Latin America, nature has dealt humans a harsh environment of mountains, deserts, and jungles, but the region's people have adapted with striking creativity. In the Andes, where only 2 percent of the land can be farmed, and what you can grow and graze depends upon altitude and rainfall, indigenous ethnic groups utilized every "ecological niche" for what it could provide, creating a unique "vertical" pattern of settlement, with "colonies" at different altitudes, in order to secure a complete basket of goods. Indigenous peoples also made full use of the region's plants and animals, many of them—including maize and manioc, potatoes and llamas—unique to this hemisphere.

The flora and fauna of Latin America and the Caribbean changed dramatically with the arrival of European colonists, who brought their animals and plants with them, and so did the ecology. Cattle and sheep altered both the landscape and the diet of much of the region. Wheat fields replaced cornfields, and sugar and coffee took over large tracts of land. Mules and donkeys replaced llamas and people as beasts of burden. European oxen were yoked to American plows. Between them, the horse and the steer transformed the Argentine pampas into ranches, while the coming of the railroad in the late nineteenth century turned it into farmland as well.

Although the landscape of Latin America and the Caribbean has been changing for centuries, in recent decades the transformations have accelerated and their impact on the environment has been intensified by the advance of technology, the stress on economic growth, and the multiplication of populations, which have more than doubled in the last thirty years. Economic development and population growth have exacted heavy environmental costs. Pollution now sullies once idyllic beaches with oil and sewage and poisons the atmosphere of cities with toxic smog from factory smokestacks and automobile exhausts. Today, Mexico City and Chile's Santiago rank among the world's most polluted cities, and Brazil's São Paulo is not far behind.

The changes in the seemingly immutable Amazon rain forest, long a symbol of unspoiled nature, are the most striking example of these changes in the land. To many North Americans, it is also the most disturbing example. Saving the rain forest has become an international ecological cause—and with good reason. But for the people who live there the issue is far more complex, and those who would save the rain forest need to understand its inhabitants' experiences and points of view.

From the air much of the Amazon still seems a carpet of green stretching from horizon to horizon, a two-thousand-mile canopy of two-hundred-foot-high trees from the foot of the Andes to the Atlantic. On the ground it is still possible to go for days along wild rivers through virgin forests that evoke Joseph Conrad's vision of "travelling back to the earliest beginnings of the world, when vegetation rioted on the earth and the big trees were king."[2]

Yet, even in the heart of the continent, the impact of "civilization" on the rain forest is now all too apparent. Downstream from Manaus, the capital of Brazil's Amazonas State, some sixteen hundred kilometers from the sea, the blue-black waters of the Rio Negro and the yellow waters of the Solimões—both several kilometers wide—come together to form the Amazon. This junction, with its distinct, banded colors running side by side for miles, symbolizes the majesty of nature in the earth's largest rain forest. But the river bank that stretches from Manaus to the "meeting of the waters" is lined with industries, including such heavy polluters as oil refineries, metal works, and lumber mills. In the swift current that flows past their steel structures, iridescent blue fish float belly up in the dark waters, innocent victims of "progress." João Andrade, whose family has fished these waters for generations, talked with me on his boat about the changes he has witnessed. His brother now works in a local refinery. "We need the jobs," he said, "but we also need the river."

The watery highway that makes these industries possible is no longer the only way into the rain forest. Today roads traverse the once trackless jungle, cutting its green carpet with ribbons of red dust, which miners, ranchers, and farmers have followed with devastating effects. Almost nine hundred kilometers southwest of Manaus lies the once remote state of Rondônia, which forty years ago was a sylvan wilderness on the border of Bolivia, whose largest population was some thirty-five thousand tribal Indians. But a decade ago a road was completed to Rondônia from southeast Brazil, and landless peasants were encouraged by the military regime to use it to colonize the undeveloped rain forest. More than half a million Brazilians embraced their government's offer of free land, followed by miners, ranchers, and lumber companies, each with their own ideas of how to exploit the natural resources of the Amazon. One quarter of Rondônia's rain forest was clear-cut for its hardwoods or burned down to make room for farms and cattle, while mining companies poisoned its rivers with mercury. But the tropical soils of the Amazon proved less fertile and more fragile than the settlers imagined, unable to sustain more than a few years of cultivation. Today, abandoned farms scar the landscape and nearly three quarters of Rondônia's population is urban.

Hundreds of miles to the northwest, the rain forest crosses Brazil's frontiers into Peru and then Ecuador, but the human assault on the Amazon does not stop at international borders. In Peru impoverished peasants are clearing the jungle to grow coca leaves for traffickers who are poisoning the headwaters of the river with the chemicals that transform coca into cocaine. In Ecuador foreign agribusiness corporations have cut down the forest for plantations of African palm and petroleum companies have polluted the rivers with their drilling.

Yet the changes in the Ecuadorian rain forest have also had some positive consequences. Although many indigenous groups have suffered, some have prospered. The Shuar used to be notorious for their blood feuds and head shrinking. Today they are better known for their self-government, cattle exports, and experimental education. When landless peasants followed the new roads down from the Andean highlands to colonize their "empty" lands, the Shuar stopped feuding and united in a federation that purchased livestock, secured titles to their land, and established an innovative bilingual education program in the middle of the rain forest. Shuar children now go to jungle schools where they are taught in their own language by radio. Many of them have gone on to secondary school and some have even earned university degrees.

The threat to the environment that sustains their way of life has also prompted the region's indigenous peoples to set aside ancient rivalries and overcome language barriers to form a federation that lobbies in Quito, Ecuador's capital, and sends leaders to present their case to international audiences and agencies, such as the World Bank. These pressures recently persuaded CONOCO, one of the largest oil companies in Ecuador, to stop drilling.

The Amazon rain forest has become a symbol of heightened global concern for the fate of the earth. It is the "lungs of the world," supplying one third of the earth's oxygen, and a "flywheel of climate," whose destruction would accelerate global warming with dire consequences for the rest of the globe. The Amazon is also a "library for the life sciences," stresses the Smithsonian Institution's Thomas Lovejoy, the most biodiverse area on earth, and the sole habitat of more than a million species of plants and animals. It is "the world's greatest pharmaceutical laboratory," whose organisms may contain cures for cancer and other diseases. For all these reasons, argues Lovejoy, saving the Amazon is "a matter of global destiny."[3]

For Brazil—with the Amazon regions occupying more than half its territory—the issue is more complex. Some Brazilians still regard the Amazon as so vast and so fecund that there is no need to be concerned if a dam submerges an area the size of Britain or ranchers burn down rainforest acreage larger than Belgium. Others resent being lectured on the environment by "the world's largest polluter," as one businessman termed the United States, "which slaughtered its own Indians to win its wild west" and is clear-cutting its own "last virgin forests." There are also Brazilians, not all of them military officers, who see the Amazon as "an issue of sovereignty," said Colonel Jarbas Passarinho, a veteran government minister, and worry that the current environmental concerns will be used as an excuse to "internationalize" the Amazon. Declarations by North American and European politicians that "the Amazon belongs to the whole world" have awakened Brazilian fears that the Amazon might become "a green Persian Gulf."

Increasingly, as signaled by Brazilian president Fernando Collor's hosting of the June 1992 Earth Summit, the U.N.-sponsored Conference on the Environment and Development, Brazilians do recognize the need for conservation of the Amazon. But in a country whose economy has not grown for five years and that is burdened with a $123 billion foreign debt and an equally onerous internal social debt—symbolized by its seven million street children and ten million landless peasants—there are other priorities that may seem more urgent than warnings that the rain forest may disappear by the year 2100.

"We need strategies that are *both* economically productive *and* environmentally sound," stressed Jacques Marcovitch, a respected University of São Paulo environmentalist. He is helping Brazil's state-owned Companhia Vale do Rio Doce design such a strategy for its huge Carajás mining and metals venture—including the world's largest deposits of high-grade iron ore—in the eastern Amazon. The company has devoted 12 percent of its multibillion-dollar investments to conservation in the past, and the result was an enormous mining and refining complex that did not itself pollute the surrounding river or atmosphere. But even that well-intentioned effort did not save the Carajás region—an area of 324,000 square miles—from environmental damage. The CVRD smelters were fueled by charcoal and the surrounding forest was gradually cut down to feed them. The discovery of gold at Serra Pelada in 1980 brought tens of thousands of prospectors to the district. Moreover, the railroad built to connect the project to the coast also attracted landless peasants from Brazil's impoverished Northeast, "which brought to its area of influence uncontrollable problems, such as land speculation and rural violence," as well as "deforestation" and "itinerant agriculture." "It is a complex problem," stressed Marcovitch. He was designing a solution that included a different fuel, but "sound technology is only part of the answer. We also need economic growth, political will, public understanding—and international support."

Eating Rain Forest Crunch ice cream or not eating a Big Mac will not save the Amazon. Nor will swapping virgin rain forest for foreign debt, as some environmental organizations have proposed, make a dent in either problem. These are well-intentioned but inadequate solutions. Viewed from the south, the need is for environmentally sound strategies that will help Brazil develop economically, and for policies that give the country's landless poor a better alternative than burning down the jungle to create a farm whose fragile soil will soon be exhausted. "You cannot talk about ecology," said Marcovitch, "to people who are struggling to survive."

Brazil's problems are shared by other countries of the region. The landscape of Latin America and the Caribbean will continue to change, as economic and social pressures grow. The task is to shape those changes so that they will not destroy the land—and the diverse peoples who live on it.

Lands of Immigrants

Alfredo Jaar, the artist who created "This Is Not America," is a Chilean of Dutch descent. He was shocked to be regarded as a "Hispanic" in the United States, a complaint echoed by Brazilians, who do not even speak Spanish. One of the misconceptions that many North Americans have about Latin America and the Caribbean is that it is a homogeneous region, whose people "all look alike." On the contrary, the diversity of its population, the result of immigration patterns as complex as those that formed the United States and Canada, is what gives the region its unique character. Most are of European descent, although roughly one quarter have Indian ancestors and perhaps an equal number African roots.

We think of Latin America as an area of Iberian colonization, but this is a simplification of its history and heritage, as a partial list of recent heads of state makes clear. Guatemala's Kjell Lagerud's Scandinavian heritage is evident in his name, as are the Slavic roots of Brazil's Kubitschek or the Italian and German lineages of his military successors, Médici and Geisel. Chile's Aylwin has British forebears, his predecessor Pinochet French origins. Nor are all of the region's heads of state of European descent. Argentina's Menem is of Arab ancestry. Peru's Fujimori campaigned for president dressed as a Japanese samurai. Yet names can also be deceiving. The roots of Grenada's Maurice Bishop and Trinidad's Eric Williams lie in Africa, not England, as do those of Haiti's francophone Duvaliers and Jean-Bertrand Aristide. Their names are a reflection of the colonial powers that brought their ancestors to the Caribbean.

Like the United States, the rest of the Americas are lands of immigrants. The first "Americans" were Asian hunters who crossed the Bering land bridge at the dawn of hemispheric prehistory and gradually made their way south. In time they evolved into the peoples Columbus mistakenly called "Indians," a name that has stuck even among many of these indigenous peoples. In 1492 there may have been sixty million of them, ranging from nomadic hunters and gatherers in the Amazon rain forest to the sophisticated urban civilizations of the Andes and Mesoamerica, where their more than 125 million descendants are still concentrated today. Most are now mestizos, people of mixed Amerindian and European ancestry, and anthropologists insist that only some twenty-five million are culturally "Indians"—a claim that prompted Francisco Calí, a Guatemalan Mayan leader, to retort: "Who are these foreigners to tell *us* who is an Indian?"

Europeans came next, beginning in 1492, to exploit the wealth of America: Spaniards pursuing gold and glory; Portuguese looking for tropical luxuries and elusive El Dorados; Northern Europeans seeking Iberian treasure and fertile lands; Catholic friars in search of heathen souls and American utopias. By 1800 some two million Europeans had migrated to Latin America and the Caribbean.

From the start, the Europeans brought enslaved Africans with them, first as personal servants, then increasingly as field hands to work the tropical plantations and mines of the Caribbean and Brazil. This wave of forced migration grew with time, cresting in the eighteenth century. Some ten million enslaved Africans were taken across the Atlantic in chains before this inhuman traffic was finally ended in the mid-nineteenth century. They are the ancestors of the more than one hundred million people of African descent who inhabit Latin America and the Caribbean today. Many of these are mulattos, people of mixed African and European origin, a separate racial category in Latin America and the Caribbean that is ignored in North America. Perhaps half of Brazil's 150 million citizens have African roots, as do most Caribbean islanders and many Panamanians and Venezuelans.

The late nineteenth century witnessed another massive influx of seven to nine million Europeans in search of land, jobs, and opportunities. Most were from Italy, Spain, and Portugal, but many were Germans and Slavs, and some were Britons and French. These European immigrants settled mostly in southern South America, changing the face of Argentina and Uruguay, as well as parts of Brazil and Chile. Asians came, too, during this era—Chinese and Japanese, Indians and Indonesians—mostly as replacements for African slave labor in the plantations of the Caribbean and Brazil. Arabs and Jews arrived in smaller numbers, but soon played significant economic and cultural roles as merchants and entrepreneurs, intellectuals and professionals.

As a result of these varied migrations, Latin America and the Caribbean is now a polyglot region with a diversity of races, ethnicities, and cultures. Mixing over the centuries has produced a racial spectrum and cultural kaleidoscope whose great variety and richness expresses itself in many ways, including language. In Latin America and the Caribbean people speak ten principal languages. Half of them are European tongues, with Spanish spoken by some 300 million people and Portuguese by another 150 million. English, French, and Dutch are used by significant numbers in the Caribbean, but in many islands a Creole patois that owes as much to Africa as to Europe is more common. Belize's Black Carib dialect combines the African with the Indian.

Once there were two thousand indigenous languages in the Americas, and even today some eight hundred are spoken, although many by small tribes that seem headed for extinction. Yet, five major language groups have survived the traumas of history and the assaults of modernity: Nahuatl, the language of the Aztecs, is still spoken by one million people in Mesoamerica, the numerous Mayan dialects by perhaps two million more. In South America eight million people speak Quechua, the tongue of the Incas, and another half a million highlanders, Aymara. Guaraní, once spoken through much of Brazil, is an official language in Paraguay, although most of its three million people are mestizos.

Like its landscape, Latin America's languages have changed with the shifting needs of its people. In many countries people of Amerindian and African ancestry are now bilingual, while in others indigenous peoples are losing their language as they migrate and assimilate. Yet change can also work in the opposite direction: In the northern Andes, Ecuadorian and Colombian Indians are learning Quechua as part of their reaffirmation of ethnic identity.

The foods of Latin America and the Caribbean, like their languages, reflect the varied people who migrated to their shores, as well as the tension between tradition and change. "It's not a Haitian meal unless it includes rice and beans," insisted Max Beauvoir, one of that country's leading Voodoo priests, as he added another savory dish to an already plentiful lunch. In Mexico the indispensable ingredient might be maize, in Argentina beef, in Brazil manioc. Throughout the Americas food and identity are intertwined.

Some diets reflected the shaping influence of geography. On the high plateau of Bolivia and Peru, where neither maize nor wheat can grow, the potato was long the staff of life, while along the Atlantic coast of Nicaragua that honor went to the banana. Other foods reflect cultural traditions or historical legacies. The maize tortillas and tacos of Mexico, as well as the flowers, herbs, and chili peppers that give Mexican cuisine its special flavors, are legacies of its indigenous cultures. On the streets of Salvador, the old colonial capital of Brazil, black women wrapped in African dress still sell *vatapá,* a paste of ground shrimp, cashews, and mint redolent with West African spices and palm oil, stuffed in *acarajés,* deep-fried bean cakes. Argentina's many beef courses go back to its gaucho heritage, while its pasta dishes and pastries attest to its Italian immigrants, and its afternoon teas to a British influence dominant a century ago.

Yet, throughout Latin America and the Caribbean, the foods people eat are no longer the same, a reflection of the changes that are transforming the region. Wheat bread is now as common in Mexico City as maize tortillas. Lamb and pork are more likely to be found on Andean tables today than llama or guinea pig, although the peppers and spices that flavor them remain resolutely Andean. Traditions of obtaining and preparing food are also changing under the augmented pressures and possibilities of modern life. When Rafael Pandam wants to eat meat or fish in his home in the Ecuadorian rain forest, the Shuar Indian takes the wooden spear that his brother emblazoned with carved snakes and goes out and hunts it. Most in the Americas once hunted, fished, and farmed for what they consumed, but few do today. Now they buy their food, although how they do it is also revealing. I remember villages in the Peruvian Andes two decades ago where potatoes were more readily accepted in the market than the national currency. Today, the overwhelming majority of Latin Americans are part of the monetary economy. The sound of maize being ground for tortillas on a stone metate is still heard in rural Mexico, but most Mexican women now buy their corn flour in a store and many purchase their tortillas as well.

Fast-food restaurants have spread throughout the region, bringing McDonald's to Managua and pizza to La Paz. Even the leisurely lunch eaten at home is disappearing in the region's busy cities. Yet, despite the pressures of modern urban life and the appeal of the international, the cuisines of Latin America and the Caribbean still retain their distinctive character.

The changing "traditions" of the other Americas also reflect their varied histories, expressed even in the sports that they now call their own. In South America, where European influence was strong, football—the worldwide game that only North Americans call soccer—is the national sport, and both their teams and players rank among the world's best. Argentina, Brazil, and Uruguay have all been world champions, and Brazil's Pelé is widely regarded as the finest player in football history. The South Americans have added their own personality to this European game introduced by British railway workers a century ago. Brazilians play with a fluid grace and elusive stylishness that has been traced to the Afro-Brazilian samba. When Argentina defeated England in football in 1950 it was hailed as a declaration of independence as important as Perón's purchase of the British railways.

In the Caribbean, the impact of British colonial rule is seen in the ascendancy of cricket, the upper-class English sport in which the descendants of British slaves now lead the world. The West Indians play with a Caribbean flair absent in Middlesex, transforming the game of their ancestors' masters in the process.

But most of the Caribbean basin is a zone of U.S. influence, and here baseball is generally the national pastime, a passion that transcends politics and international frontiers. When Nicaraguan Dennis Martínez became the first Latin American to pitch a perfect U.S. major league game in July 1991, both Contras and Sandinistas celebrated what President Violeta Bárrios de Chamorro hailed as "a feat that fills all Nicaraguans with pride."[4] Many players of Latin American and Caribbean origin have become stars in the United States, and Cuba's national team regularly wins the gold medal in the Pan-American games. On a street corner in Havana a young boy wearing a worn baseball cap overcame his shyness to ask if I knew José Canseco, the Cuban-born major league slugger; I confessed that I didn't, but promised to send him Canseco's baseball card. Though Cuba and the United States have been isolated from each other by ideology for three decades, baseball remains our common field of dreams.

Centuries of Change, Decades of Transformation

The nations of Latin America and the Caribbean may be diverse, but they have also shared a common historical experience, which continues to influence this changing region. This book will focus on the underlying dynamics of change that have shaped Latin America and the Caribbean in their current mold and that are reshaping it into the region of the future. The Americas began as European colonies, and their insertion into a changing world order according to the prescriptions of more powerful nations has marked their histories. It has created conflicts within their societies, over the loss of autonomy that this integration implied and over the division of its benefits and costs. The social unrest and political instability for which the region is notorious reflects these tensions. Yet they have also been creative tensions, which have stimulated the people of Latin America to innovate and experiment. Some of these attempts succeeded, while others failed, but all have had their impact, both within and beyond Latin America and the Caribbean. For five centuries the other Americas and the outside world have influenced each other, a two-way process of change that is still going on today.

It is a history that began with Columbus and an influence that reflects the imprint of colonialism. Tourists flock to the colonial monuments—the silvered baroque churches of Mexico, the elegant mansions of gold-rush Brazil, Nelson's Dockyard at Antigua's English Harbour—visible reminders of a vanished age. But the less visible legacies of European empire have lasted well into our own time.

In 1972 I was with a friend in Talca, a provincial town in Chile, which was in the midst of a sweeping agrarian reform. Inside the local basketball stadium, peasants dressed in their Sunday best sat in the stands to witness the expropriation of the large landed estates on which they and their forebears had worked for generations. When the name of an estate was read out, bursts of applause were heard from the section where its peasants were seated, along with the occasional shout: "Now the land is ours!" After the ceremony, an aging peasant with a broad mestizo face and leathery hands invited us into a bar to toast his good fortune. It was not just that his children would own the land, he stressed, but that they would no longer have to take orders from the old owners, bearers of an aristocratic Basque name, as he and his ancestors had done as far back as memory reached. Outside, a large sign proclaimed: TODAY THE LANDED ESTATE COMES TO AN END IN TALCA! My friend shook his head: "It is not just the landed estate that is coming to an end, but the whole structure of power that has dominated rural Chile for centuries."

No other region of the Third World was colonized for so long or penetrated so deeply by Europe. None shares its languages, religions, and values to so great an extent. More people speak Spanish and Portuguese in the Americas than in Iberia. Most of the world's Roman Catholics live in Latin America, with Brazil home to the largest national Church. Jamaica's parliamentary democracy, a British legacy, has sustained that new nation through years of economic crisis and polarized politics. The common experience of European colonialism is the starting point for understanding the region's unique relationship to the rest of the world.

Latin America and the Caribbean were inserted into a European world against their will. The Aztecs and Incas did not ask to be conquered by Spain. The Aymaras did not choose to do forced labor in the silver mines of Potosí. The Africans brought in chains across the Atlantic did not wish to be enslaved on the plantations of Brazil or the Caribbean.

Some accepted their subordination with a fatalistic resignation and tried to make the best of a world that they could not control. In Mexico there were Aztecs who helped the Spaniards conquer other Indians; in Barbados some slaves sought to improve their lot by proving their loyalty to an omnipotent master. Others tried to make their way in a colonial world of European design, whether as merchants or miners, servants or soldiers. There were "moneybags" Indians in Peru who bought substitutes to work in the mines; there were slaves in gold-rush Brazil who purchased their freedom with nuggets earned in the mines or bought by selling their bodies in the streets.

But many in Latin America and the Caribbean resisted the fate that others had decreed for them. In Guatemala, the Itzá withdrew deep into the Petén jungles and maintained an independent Mayan kingdom for two centuries after the coming of Columbus. In the backlands of Brazil, fugitive slaves created Palmares, a neo-African kingdom that lasted for most of the seventeenth century and included some thirty thousand people at its height. The eighteenth-century history of Peru was punctuated by Indian rebellions that culminated in the great Tupac Amaru revolt of 1780, which set the Andes ablaze, cost one hundred thousand lives, and took five years to suppress.

In the wake of the American and French revolutions, the independence movements of the early nineteenth century brought European rule to an end in most of the continent, but they did not end European influence. As the century wore on, another revolution—the Industrial Revolution—transformed Europe and drew Latin America and the Caribbean into a new world economic order as exporters of raw materials and importers of manufactures. The rich resources and markets of the region became newly valuable, and its elites were attracted by European ideas and luxuries—and the prospect of wealth on an undreamed-of scale. British investments, French fashions, and Italian immigrants flowed across the Atlantic, transforming much of Latin America. The pampas of Argentina were turned into modern ranches and farms. Buenos Aires became the "Paris of South America." Rubber barons built an elegant opera house in the heart of the Amazon. By 1890 British influence in Uruguay was so great that when Julio Herrera y Obes was asked how it felt to be that small South American country's president, he quipped: "It feels rather like being the manager of a big ranch whose board of directors sits in London."[5]

The twentieth century saw the rise of the United States as a global power that regarded the rest of the Americas as its backyard. U.S. interventions and investments were controversial in the other Americas, as were Washington's efforts to shape the politics and policies of Latin America and the Caribbean. The region's relations with the rest of the world became more difficult and attitudes toward the United States became more ambivalent. The United States was now the "Colossus of the North," regarded as both protector and threat, benefactor and exploiter, success story and cautionary tale. In much of the region, the United States is still viewed as both a model of liberal democracy to be emulated and as the source of foreign intervention to be opposed. "We love you, but we hate you," was the way a Cuban psychiatrist recently put it. "It is like an old affair."

The integration of Latin America and the Caribbean into a wider world has unsettled the region and worsened its internal tensions. The terms of this international merger have often reinforced the power and wealth of its elites, turning Argentine ranchers into cattle barons and Salvadoran coffee planters into oligarchs. But they have also clashed with the aspirations of the people of the Americas for democracy and social justice.

Uruguay offers a good example of these internal tensions. At the turn of the century, rural Uruguay was transformed into a landscape of modern ranches in response to Europe's growing demand for meat. Many of these *estancias* had elegant houses that reflected the new wealth and social pretensions of their owners. The ranches were separated by wire fences that enclosed branded cattle bred from prize imported bulls. There was no longer an open range for Uruguay's gauchos, the fabled "centaurs of the pampas," to roam. Nor was there as much need for their labor. Some became peons on the ranches, others rustlers on the range. Many became unemployed squatters in rural slums known as "rat cities." In 1897 they rose in a rebellion whose motto was "Free Air and Fat Cattle." When a delegation of ranchers came to their camp to press for peace, one rebel gaucho turned to a friend and said bitterly: "Here come those who would have us die of hunger."

The social unrest and political instability for which Latin America and the Caribbean are notorious still reflect such conflicts. "We needed a revolution," one Cuban peasant told me, "because Cuba was a rich country with too many poor people." Latin America has the most unequal distribution of land, wealth, and income in the world. In Brazil, the gap between the wealthiest state and the poorest is worse than in India. Moreover, many of the region's governments are unrepresentative and most of them are deeply in debt. "The result is an onerous double debt—a foreign dollar debt and an internal social debt," said a Brazilian publisher. "It is a struggle to pay off one, let alone both."

Yet their struggles to shape their own destinies in circumstances not of their own choosing have often prompted the people of Latin America and the Caribbean to innovate. During recent decades, in particular, they have responded to these external demands and internal tensions in creative ways. Their economists have devised new strategies and their religious leaders have embraced new theologies. Some have created a culture of migration: Barbados "exports" 10 percent of its people each year, whose remittances sustain their island families. Others have pioneered new grassroots movements, including women's movements whose union of professional and poor women differs greatly from their North American counterparts. Their writers have developed artistic voices of striking originality, reaching out to new audiences and blurring the lines between elite and popular culture. Puerto Rico's Luis Rafael Sánchez wrote a novel about a popular singer of boleros, romantic songs that he views as a defense of Hispanic culture against "U.S. cultural imperialism," in an innovative style that uses the words and forms of boleros. The tensions that afflict Latin America and the Caribbean have often proved creative tensions.

A common thread uniting many of these experiments is their democratic character. In October 1988 I was in Chile as an observer of that nation's plebiscite on General Augusto Pinochet's fifteen-year dictatorship. I saw elderly peasants with weather-beaten faces wait for hours in the hot sun to cast their ballots, and a pregnant young woman in labor insist on being carried to the voting booth before she was taken to the hospital. The following day people of all ages paraded past the dictator's headquarters demanding "Democracy Now!" while bewildered soldiers kept an uneasy guard. Chileans' desire for democracy had finally overcome the fear of repression that had held them in thrall for so many years.

Throughout Latin America and the Caribbean, the past decade has seen a surge of democracy in a region long known for its dictators. This movement for democracy has not been confined to national politics. The people of the other Americas have extended it to their churches, neighborhoods, and homes. In São Paulo's new suburban communities Brazilian migrants have formed Christian base communities as part of an effort to democratize the Catholic church. In the desert shantytowns of Lima, Peruvian women have organized themselves to press for neighborhood control of basic services, while Chilean feminists have demanded democracy in the home as well as the nation. In different ways, the people of Latin America and the Caribbean have sought to increase the participation and power of those who have been disenfranchised or marginalized. During these same years, leaders have tried to establish more equal relations between the nations of the hemisphere and some have pushed for social justice within their own societies by experimenting with diplomatic realignments and social revolutions. Not all of these experiments have succeeded, but most have had an impact on the region and many have influenced the world beyond.

Since the European "discovery" and conquest of the Americas, Latin America and the Caribbean have not only been shaped by the rest of the world; they have influenced it as well. During the initial period of mutual reconnaisance, the idea of a New World captured the European imagination, which peopled it with monsters and noble savages, and constructed its utopias on imagined American shores. In the centuries that followed, American treasure and trade helped Europe to dominate its economic relations with Asia and to construct the foundations for its global empires. "The gold and silver of the New World," concluded French historian Fernand Braudel, "allowed Europe to live beyond its means and to invest beyond its savings."

In our own era, too, the other Americas are having a major impact upon the rest of the world. Writers such as Gabriel García Márquez,

Octavio Paz, and Derek Walcott have won Nobel literature prizes and
focused world attention on the region's rich literature and art. Mexico's
revolutionary muralists were the first Latin American artists to win international acclaim. When I visited Mexico in 1967, I became friendly with
Luis Arenal, the brother-in-law of David Siqueiros, who along with Diego
Rivera and José Orozco was one of the "three greats" of the Mexican mural
movement. Siqueiros was painting a mural inside Cuernavaca's new helioport, and Arenal invited me to come with him to see the work in progress.
I was not alone. The helioport seemed filled with foreign visitors, many of
them artists from Europe or the United States who were there to learn from
this Mexican master, a politically committed innovator who painted futuristic forms with an industrial spray gun, and take the lessons home to apply
in their own countries. The paintings that cover the barrio walls of East Los
Angeles today are inspired by the Mexican muralists.

The vibrant popular culture of Latin America and the Caribbean has
also found an avid international audience in recent decades. Bob Marley
became a global pop icon and lambada a European dance craze. Reggae has
penetrated popular music in the United States and samba has shaped the
recent recordings of Paul Simon and David Byrne. Brazilian soap operas
are watched across the Atlantic, while their Mexican rivals have won
millions of devotees north of the U.S. border.

The "theology of liberation" developed in Latin America has influenced churches around the world, playing a major role, for example, in
the Philippines' democratic revolution. Its vision of a more activist and
democratic Church has challenged the Vatican's vision of Catholicism for
the third Christian millennium. Its stress on social justice has inspired
middle-class North Americans to risk jail in order to provide sanctuary for
Central American refugees.

Even the region's problems have had their impact on the larger world
order. The enormous debt owed by the nations of Latin America has forced
the international financial community to reconsider its policies. The accelerating destruction of the Amazon rain forest has focused global attention on the role that countries such as Brazil can play in promoting—or
preventing—global warming and the greenhouse effect.

Brazil is also a good example of the increased swathe that the nations of the other Americas are cutting in international circles. It is already the world's sixth most populous country and its eighth largest economy. Despite Brazil's current onerous debt and recent economic difficulties, during the coming century its size, rich resources, entrepreneurial dynamism, and industrial strength should make it an international force.

The same is true for Mexico, the largest Spanish American country. During the 1970s Mexico played a leading role in Third World demands for a New International Economic Order that would distribute the benefits of trade and investment more equitably. Its policies have changed, but not its significance. Mexico is the United States' third most important trading partner and its leading source of foreign oil outside the unstable Middle East. Currently Mexico is the moving force behind the creation of a North American Free Trade Association with the United States and Canada. This may prefigure a hemispheric common market that would reshape the Americas during the next century. In a world divided into trading blocs, the United States and the other Americas may well rediscover that they have a "special relationship."

Even smaller countries in the region have played outsize international roles. Over the past three decades Cuba has exerted an influence within the Third World far greater than its size would suggest. More recently, Costa Rica led the ministates of Central America in preempting U.S. military strategies in the region with negotiated solutions of their own. Colombia may be a nation of only thirty-four million, but its six billion dollars in cocaine exports has had a major impact on the United States and Europe. In the future, the growing number of independent Caribbean islands may increase their clout in such international bodies as the Organization of American States, where they will have a majority of the votes by the end of the next century.

In diverse ways, the nations of Latin America and the Caribbean are moving beyond their traditional roles as bit players on the world stage to claim leading parts in its economic, political, and cultural dramas. They are no longer, in García Márquez's phrase, "exiled from the memory of men" and "condemned to one hundred years of solitude."[6]

The people of the region are also having a profound impact on North America through their migrations. The flood of Latin American and Caribbean immigrants to the United States has altered its cities and labor force and challenged its educational system and notions of assimilation. There are already more than twenty-five million people of Latin American descent in the United States, and by the year 2000 there may be thirty million. In the next century Hispanic-Americans will become this country's largest minority, and one third of the nation's work force may regard Spanish as their mother tongue. They will exert a growing influence over the internal politics and foreign policy of the United States. The Cuban-American community already shapes Washington's policy toward Cuba, and the Hispanic caucus in Congress played a major role in designing the 1986 immigration law and 1990 census. In the future, Hispanic-American voters could act as a swing bloc in elections and their leaders will exercise increasing power in such major states as California, Florida, New York, and Texas. As their numbers and assertiveness grow, Latin American and Caribbean communities in the United States may well force that nation of immigrants to rethink what it means to be an "American."

The conquest of Mexico reshaped the history of the Americas in a European mold. This unusual view of the capture of the Great Temple of the Aztecs is through the eyes of Cortés's Tlaxcala Indian allies, whose tens of thousands of warriors helped the Spanish overcome the Aztec's numerical superiority.

Chapter 2

Legacies of Empire

chalchicue yca

This vision of the vanquished from a Maya drawing of the early colonial era shows the exploitation and oppression to which the indigenous people of the Americas were subjected by their Spanish conquerors—under the sign of the Christian cross.

The sugar plantation—with its cane fields and milling complex, enslaved Africans and white "Lord of the Mill," Big House and slave shanties—was first developed in sixteenth-century Brazil, but it spread through the Caribbean during the two centuries that followed, shaping economies and societies.

Spanish American society was mostly
urban and its public life centered
around ceremonies such as this ostentatious viceregal procession in the
main square of Mexico City, which
also served as a marketplace.

Spanish America boasted the hemisphere's first universities, but they were barred to women, whose sphere was restricted to the home. Women with intellectual aspirations like Sor Juana Inés de la Cruz, an elegant poet and precocious polymath, often had to enter a convent in order to pursue the life of the mind.

The greatest plastic artist of colonial America was Brazil's Antonio Lisboa, known as O Aleijadinho, or "The Little Cripple." A mulatto sculptor-architect who drew on his dual heritage, Aleijadinho created this baroque masterpiece of twelve prophets for his sanctuary of Cangonhas do Campo in the gold-bearing mountains of Minas Gerais.

Legacies of Empire

Hispaniola is marvelous. The mountains and the plains are so beautiful, and so perfect for planting and sowing, and for livestock of every sort, and for building towns and cities. The harbors of the sea you could not believe without seeing, and so too the rivers, many and great, and good streams that bear gold.[1]

With these words, Christopher Columbus described to the Spanish monarchs, Ferdinand and Isabella, the New World that he had "discovered" and taken possession of in their name. His account mixed wonder at its natural beauty with an awareness of its potential for European colonization.

It was on the island that Columbus called Hispaniola, after the Latin name for Spain, that it first began, the invention of the "Americas," that unique synthesis of European, Amerindian, and African. It was here that Europeans conquered their first "Indian," and to which they imported their first African slaves. It was here that Columbus established Isabela, the first European settlement in the New World, and here that his brother founded Santo Domingo, America's first European city. It was here that the Spanish built America's first churches and cathedral, convents and monasteries, schools and university, shops and foundries, port and fortress, hospital and plazas, private houses and government headquarters. Hispaniola was the first land Europeans conquered, and the first that they colonized.

European colonialism has influenced much of the Third World, but no region so profoundly as the Americas. The legacies of a colonial experience that lasted three centuries in most of Latin America—and has ended only recently in much of the Caribbean—continue to shape the region's economy and politics, society and culture in countless ways, both large and small.

The visitor to Santo Domingo, today capital of the Dominican Republic, will find that when dusk falls and the tourists leave, the restored Calle de las Damas, the first European street in America, looks much as it did in the early sixteenth century. Then it was called Fortress Street after the imposing fort, with its crenellated ramparts and towers, that still dominates its south end, lending it a strikingly medieval look. It was late medieval Castile that shaped Spanish America's society and stamped its culture with a set of values that were the product of Spain's long Reconquest of its territories from the Moors completed in 1492, the same year that Columbus "discovered" Hispaniola. They were crusader values, which stressed the role of the warrior and the Church, and assumed the inherent justice of European rule over people of darker hue, alien culture, and heathen beliefs.

News of Columbus's discovery of a New World excited the Old. Spain prepared to colonize Hispaniola, and in 1493 Pope Alexander VI granted it the "islands and firm land" in "the western parts of the Ocean Sea, towards the Indies," in return for Madrid's commitment to Christianizing its peoples. Portugal, which had spent decades pioneering a route around Africa to the riches of Asia, protested this papal donation and threatened war. Signed in 1494, the Treaty of Tordesillas divided the world between the two Iberian powers along a line that would give Spain most of Latin America and the Caribbean, but gave Portugal Brazil, discovered in 1500.

In 1493 Columbus returned to Hispaniola with fifteen hundred Spanish colonists. Hispaniola would be the first colonial laboratory in which the characteristic institutions of Spanish empire were tried and tested, modified and adapted to the special conditions of the New World. From here they were taken to the mainland by the conquistadors who earned their spurs in the Caribbean but would win fame and fortune in Mexico or Peru.

It was in Hispaniola that the idea of making America the private fief of its conquerors was tried and found wanting, and replaced by a more bureaucratic colonial government. At the north end of Fortress Street, the architecture of the Casas Reales, the first government headquarters built by the Spanish in the New World, symbolizes the counterpoint of powers that characterized Spanish rule in America. It has one wing of offices for the viceroy and an opposing wing of offices for the *audiencia,* a high court with administrative as well as judicial roles, which was used by the Crown to limit the pretensions of its viceroys, colonial governors whose executive powers were enhanced by their distance from royal authority.

Many of the economic and social patterns that would characterize Spanish colonialism in America also first appeared in the Caribbean. It was on Hispaniola that the first European gold mine and sugar plantation were created, establishing the stress on luxury exports that would be a central colonial legacy. It was here, too, that the refusal of Spanish colonists to mine the gold they sought or grow the crops they consumed was made clear, as was their expectation that non-Europeans of darker hue—Indians and Africans—would do that manual labor for them. "I have not come to till the land like a peasant," declared Hernán Cortés on arriving in the Caribbean, and the future conqueror of Mexico was not alone. Even Spaniards who had been peasants in the Old World refused to till the land in the New. They had made the fearful journey across the ocean to become noblemen, and Spanish nobles did not sully their hands with "the dishonor of work." Instead, Spanish conquistadors divided the Indians among themselves, seizing the women and forcing the men to mine gold in the mountains. When harsh treatment and epidemic disease decimated the Indian labor force, the Spanish imported African slaves to replace them. These patterns, too, the Spanish would take with them to the mainland, and their European rivals would emulate their example.

In response to clerical complaints and reports of an alarming decline in Indian numbers, Queen Isabella in 1503 ordered the introduction of a Reconquest institution, the *encomienda,* from the Spanish *encomendar,* to entrust. The *encomienda* granted the conquistadors most of the royal share of Indian labor and production, in return for their commitment to assure the welfare of their charges. In theory, the *encomienda* was a temporary stewardship of Indians; in practice, the colonists transformed it into a de facto grant of the Indians' land as well, which allowed them to fulfill their feudal fantasies. Soon, concerned clerics were attacking the *encomienda* as a new form of Indian slavery and campaigning for its abolition.

It was on Hispaniola that the Catholic church first revealed the conflicting priorities that would characterize it in the New World. On the one hand, it was an established Church, a partner in empire, justifying the conquest and seeking its share of the spoils in saved souls. On the other, it emerged as the conscience of the conquistadors, taking them to task for their mistreatment of the Indians and campaigning for a royal policy that would protect these new subjects from enslavement. It was in Santo Domingo in 1510 that the Dominican friar Antonio Montesinos warned the conquerors that they were "heading for damnation" for "destroying an innocent people." One conquistador, Bartolomé de las Casas, was so moved by what he had witnessed in the Caribbean that he gave up his *encomienda*, donned the Dominican habit, and devoted his life to protecting the Indians of the American mainland from similar depredations.

The impact of Spanish colonization on Hispaniola was not confined to institutions. The fields and forests of Hispaniola also became a colonial laboratory. It was here that the plants and animals of Europe were introduced to the New World, and their ability to adapt to American conditions tested. It was here, too, that the Spanish became familiar with the flora and fauna of the New World, and learned to add such foods as maize, manioc, and guavas to their diet.

In a broader sense Hispaniola saw the beginning of that diffuse and far-reaching process that later scholars would call "the Columbian exchange"—the sharing of plants, animals, and diseases that has transformed the lives of ordinary people in both hemispheres. From America, the Old World would receive new staffs of life, such as corn and potatoes, as well as some of life's guilty pleasures, such as tobacco and chocolate. In return, the Spanish brought over to the New World the characteristic plants and animals of Mediterranean Europe—grapes and wheat, pigs and chickens, horses and cattle. Over time they would enrich American diets and ease the tasks of New World farmers and porters.

But much of the Columbian exchange was not positive for the indigenous people of the Americas. European crops were often less efficient users of scarce arable land. The loosing of sheep and cattle on cultivated fields played havoc with the intensive farming that had supported dense populations and upset the delicate ecological balance of many regions. They contributed to famine, which made people more vulnerable to disease.

The most traumatic aspect of the Columbian exchange for the natives of the Americas was the least visible: the unintended transfer of Old World diseases, such as smallpox, measles, and plague, to an isolated New World population with no natural immunities against them. The result was the greatest demographic disaster in history. Waves of epidemic disease virtually wiped out the native inhabitants of the Caribbean within decades of their "discovery" and reduced the indigenous population of Central Mexico from over twenty-five million to less than one million within a century of their conquest. As a consequence, the Caribbean became a virtual tabula rasa upon which a European imperial design could be inscribed. The colonial legacy would be a plantation society ruled by an elite of European origin and based upon the labor of enslaved Africans. The countries of the Caribbean are still wrestling with this problematic legacy to their economies, race relations, and national identities. The deadly diffusion of microbes continues today in the Amazon, where tribal peoples such as the Yanomami are still being decimated by diseases brought by colonists and miners. This too is a contemporary legacy of European empire in America.

It was on Hispaniola then that the Spanish initiated the predatory pattern of colonization, with its cavalier disregard for indigenous human and natural resources, which later generations condemned. In the Caribbean, the Spanish exhausted the accessible precious metals and the "red gold" of Indian labor, then moved on to repeat the story elsewhere. From Hispaniola, the locus of Spanish colonization shifted to the nearby island of Cuba. It was from Cuba, in 1519, that Hernán Cortés set sail for Mexico on a journey that would inaugurate the "age of miracles."

For the Caribbean was also the launching pad of Spanish empire, from which the American mainland would be explored, conquered, and colonized. Two great arcs of conquest spread out from the Spanish Indies: one went north and west, traversing Mexico, Central America, and the territory now comprising the South and Southwest of the United States; the other curved down from Panama through the Andes to Chile. Together they would transform the "Indies" into the "Americas."

The Age of Miracles

We then set forth on the road to Mexico. . . . When we beheld the number of populous towns on the water and on the land, and that broad causeway, running straight and level to the city, we could compare it to nothing but the enchanted scenes we had read of in Amadis de Gaul, from the great towers and temples, and other edifices of lime and stone which seemed to rise out of the water. Many of us were not sure whether we were asleep or awake . . . for never before had anyone seen or heard or dreamed of anything equal to the spectacle which appeared to our eyes on this day.
—*Bernal Díaz del Castillo,* The True History of the Conquest of New Spain[2]

The story of the conquest of Mexico is one of the great epics of history, and this account by a Spanish soldier in Cortés's expedition poses its riddle: How could a few hundred European adventurers conquer a warrior empire of millions whose sophistication was greater than their own? For the Aztec emperor Moctezuma it was a divine judgment of his gods. For Cortés's admirers it was his military and diplomatic skill that won the day; for soldiers like Bernal Díaz it was their courage that prevailed.

Modern historians have stressed other explanations of the Conquest. For some, the key to Spanish victory was Cortés's ability to find allies among the Aztecs' oppressed subjects and traditional rivals, whose support offset the Aztecs' numerical superiority and sustained the Spanish in the hard fighting that followed Moctezuma's death. For others, it was the unequal military contest of steel weapons against stone, ships against canoes, European siege warfare against stoic Indian endurance. For many recent historians, Cortés's invisible allies—the disease microbes his men brought with them—played an equally important role in his triumph. Smallpox killed more Aztecs than Spanish swords and weakened those warriors who survived until they could fight no more. On August 13, 1521, Cuahtémoc, the last Aztec emperor—and modern Mexico's hero—surrendered to Cortés. The conquest of Mexico was history—and on its way to becoming myth.

To Spanish contemporaries, the Conquest was a medieval romance, like the tales of Amadis—or El Cid. It was an epic story of how a few hundred brave men, trusting in their Spanish steel and Christian god, conquered a heathen empire that commanded hundreds of thousands of warriors. It was a tale of Spanish superiority, and proof that God was on their side and the age of miracles was at hand. If Cortés could conquer Mexico against all odds, then anything was possible in this New World of their dreams.

With that vision emblazoned in their minds, Cortés's companions and rivals set out to find new worlds to conquer. Many would die in the attempt, and most would find at best the sunset mirage of "cities of gold" on the distant horizon. But, in 1530, after repeated failures, Francisco Pizarro found and conquered "another Mexico" in the heart of the Andes. In Peru, the treasure that Pizarro extorted from the Incas was so great that their share conferred riches on even the lowliest of his foot soldiers. Yet few enjoyed their ill-gotten gains for long. Many conquistadors died in the rebellions and civil wars that followed, or were executed for treason by Spanish officials, whose authority they refused to recognize. Others gambled away their gold or died seeking still more in the Amazon jungle or Chilean desert.

By 1570, the age of miracles was over. On the edge of empire, Spanish adventurers could continue to dream of an elusive El Dorado just over the next mountain or beyond the next river. But in Mexico and Peru, the conquest was complete and a colonial system had been imposed on both the conquered Indians and their unruly conquerors.

Victors and Vanquished

In 1978, workers excavating for Mexico City's new subway near the Zócalo, the cathedral square that was the center of the Spanish colonial city, uncovered the ruins of the Great Temple of the Aztecs, the heart of their capital, Tenochtitlán. Today the remains of the Indian temple and the European cathedral constructed with its stones stand juxtaposed, visible symbols of Spain's imposition of its culture and values on the ruins of the civilization it conquered.

The consequences of the conquest were profound and lasting. Spanish viceroys ruled where Aztec emperors had reigned, part of an imposition of European political institutions that has characterized the region ever since. In Spanish America, colonial rule was a paradoxical combination of centralized authority and local autonomy. In theory the power of the Crown over its subjects and possessions in the New World was absolute. It was exercised in Madrid by the Royal Council of the Indies, whose stream of laws and regulations would have made Spanish America the most governed colonies on earth—had they been implemented.

But America was far from Spain in an age without steamships or airplanes, telephones or fax machines. Councilors in Madrid might misunderstand conditions in Lima, and many months would elapse before a royal response to a colonial dispatch could be received. As a result, Spanish officials in America were allowed considerable discretion in carrying out their instructions. "I obey but I do not implement" became their credo, and a startling reversal of policy was often the result. "O sacred Majesty, how just and good are the royal orders that you send to this province," wrote Bernal Díaz del Castillo from his Guatemala *encomienda* in 1552, adding ruefully: "and how officials mold them here and do what they wish!"[3]

In America, royal authority was vested in a viceroy—literally a "deputy king." Normally a high Spanish aristocrat, he was surrounded by the pomp and ceremony of an imperial legate. The viceroy enjoyed extensive powers of appointment and the right to regulate many aspects of colonial life, from the siting of churches to the times of ferryboats. Until the late eighteenth century, there were only two Spanish viceroyalties, New Spain (Mexico, Central America, and the Caribbean), with Mexico City as its capital, and Peru (Spanish South America), with its capital in Lima.

Yet, because the viceroys' authority was so great and their powers so magnified by distance, the Spanish Crown hedged in their viceroys with checks and balances that undercut their authority and limited their power. In his capital, the viceroy was forced to share his authority with the judges of the *audiencia,* and often had to contend with Church officials as well. In 1624 the combined opposition of judges and clerics forced one viceroy of New Spain, the Marqués de Gelves, from office.

In regions distant from the viceregal capitals, captains-general and presidents ruled as mini-viceroys, with autonomy from viceregal orders. These smaller colonial administrative units—given even greater autonomy by eighteenth-century reforms—would form the territorial bases of today's republics, enduring legacies of imperial politics.

The imposition of European rule on the ruins of Indian empires was not the only consequence of the Conquest. In its wake, Castilian conquistadors soon replaced Indian nobles as lords of land and labor. Initially, the form this took was the *encomienda,* a grant of the royal right to Indian tribute introduced in Hispaniola. In the valley of Morelos to the south of Mexico City, noted for its perfect climate and fertile fields, Cortés received an enormous *encomienda* of over one hundred thousand Indians. It was here that his descendants later consolidated one of the region's largest private estates during the centuries that followed the Conquest.

Landownership began in the sixteenth century, when the Crown awarded grants of suburban farms to produce European foods for the new Hispanic cities. It took off in the seventeenth century with the decline of the *encomienda,* under the double pressure of royal disfavor and the dramatic drop in the Indian population due to epidemic disease. In its place emerged the hacienda, the landed estate of many names and varying character, most often a group of properties owned by an absentee landlord, which produced a variety of crops for local markets.

The typical hacienda was a low-risk investment that did not depend on a single crop or foreign markets, and spent little on labor and imported technology. Despite its low profit rate, it made sense in an uncertain economy. Owning land was a hedge against inflation, a diversification of risks for merchants or miners, and a largely self-sufficient refuge in times of economic trouble.

But the landed estate also reflected long-standing Iberian values, which viewed landownership as a sign of status, a cultural bias that has endured into our own time. On their estates Spanish colonists might become in fact the lords that they might not be in title. Owning a landed estate was a way for a merchant to overcome the society's prejudice against trade. It was an asset in the marital negotiations that cemented social alliances and made family fortunes. Lands were also acquired by royal grants, by purchase, by inheritance—and by encroachment on the communal lands of Indian villages.

By the eighteenth century landed estates dominated the Spanish American landscape and their owners had become the gentry of colonial society. They confronted Indian villages with reduced lands from which to feed populations rebounding from the demographic disaster of the initial encounter with the Europeans and their diseases. Unable to support their families on their tiny plots, many Indians became indebted peons on the local hacienda or worked seasonally for the low wages it offered, creating a complex of land and labor, of large estates and dwarf farms. "The maldistribution of land has been one of the principal causes of the people's misery,"[4] affirmed the bishop of Michoacán in 1810, the year in which a massive Indian rebellion detonated Mexico's struggle for independence. These inequalities and social tensions endured into the twentieth century. By 1910 only a few thousand families owned the lands on which the great bulk of Mexico's three million farmers lived and worked—an inequality reflected in the violent revolution that followed. Latin America's unequal distribution of land is an onerous legacy of empire.

A new social hierarchy also emerged in the wake of the Conquest, based on color but reinforced by class. It was a caste system, with whites of European birth at the top and people of darker hue at the bottom. Initially it was composed of the separate "republics" of Europeans and

"Indians," the racial category to which the Spanish reduced the many ethnic groups they encountered in the New World. (There was no word for "Indian" in any of their languages, but this Spanish imposition became its own reality. It remains so today.) It was a social order in which the Indians were subordinated in the lands of their ancestors to the descendants of the Europeans who had conquered them. They were compelled to pay tribute to the Crown and taxes to the Church, were subject to conscription for labor service, and were often forced by corrupt local officials to purchase unwanted European manufactures at outrageous prices and sell their own produce for sums inferior to their value. They could not bear arms legally or reside where they wished, and they were barred from most artisan and merchant guilds.

Over time, the ethnic identities that had loomed so large in pre-Hispanic Mexico became eroded, along with the local languages, the status of once proud nobles, and the city-states they had ruled. By the eighteenth century only the "Indian" village remained to confront the Spanish hacienda. In the Andes, a greater consciousness of ethnic identity endured, based upon region and reflecting its fragmented geography, with its isolated mountain valleys. In Peru, moreover, a nobility of Inca descent survived in the ancient capital of Cuzco. Yet the gradual replacement of local languages by Quechua, the tongue of the Incas, pointed to a leveling process similar to that which had taken place in Mexico. In the Andes, moreover, the Spanish even imposed dress codes of European design upon the Indians. *Polleras,* the layered skirts that Bolivia's Aymara women today consider badges of their ethnic identity, were derived from Iberian peasant dress and imposed by the Spanish authorities during the colonial era.

The native peoples of Latin America did not accept their subordination and exploitation with equanimity. On the contrary, during the three centuries of Iberian colonial rule, they did all they could to elude its burdens and evade its restrictions. In Peru, where those drafted for labor in the mines rarely returned, many Indians fled their native communities to avoid this fate. Some enserfed themselves to local landowners; others left the region to live as landless outsiders or migrated to the anonymity of Hispanic towns and cities where they might make their way as artisans, vendors, or servants. Still others remained in their villages and carved out middlemen roles as brokers of goods or labor for the white elites or Spanish authorities. Like many of their modern descendants, individual Indians found ways to evade their assigned roles in a system that was not of their design.

The same was true for many indigenous communities. In central Mexico, Indian villages learned to use the Spanish legal system to protect their remaining lands and rights. In the Yucatán, in southern Mexico, entire Maya communities fled beyond the frontiers of Spanish control. Today Guatemala's Mayas continue to resist attacks on their communities and culture, even fleeing into the mountains and jungles rather than submit to an army whom they regard as a continuation of the Spanish conquest.

The history of colonial Spanish America is also punctuated by periodic Indian rebellions, most of them the outraged response of a local community to a particularly grasping or tyrannical official. But others had a broader following and goal, and some a messianic character. In the Andes a half century of Indian risings culminated in the great Tupac Amaru revolt of 1780, in which hundreds of thousands of Indians rallied to the standard of a descendant of the Incas who promised an end to tribute and labor service, and a restoration of ancient rights. The rebellion, which took five years to suppress and cost more than a hundred thousand lives, left a legacy in Peru and Bolivia that is seen to this day in the names of ethnic nationalist movements and guerrilla groups. Throughout the Americas the inferior status of Indians within the colonial caste system left a legacy of racism and inequality that continues to plague its people.

In Brazil, the story was different but the social legacy was similar. There, colonial society was shaped not by conquest but by the sugar plantation, and the slave labor it required. If conquest was one great American confrontation between peoples of different races, slavery was the other. The first enslaved African probably arrived in America with Columbus, and as personal servants they were present throughout Spanish America, often as valued collaborators in the Conquest or as overseers of Indian labor. But African slaves were expensive to purchase, and what they produced had to justify the cost of their labor. As a consequence, it was the sugar plantation, developed in Brazil during the sixteenth century and then spread through the Caribbean during the two centuries that followed, which was largely responsible for the massive slave trade that brought more than nine million Africans to the Americas in chains.

Most were condemned to hard labor in the fields, mines, and mills of their masters, and confined to a place at the very bottom of the social hierarchy, with the stigma of slavery added to the stain of color. Their shortened lives were expended working in inhuman conditions and subject to draconian discipline. Their living conditions were equally harsh, with food so inadequate that theft was common and clothing so skimpy that observers often described them as naked. Family life was limited by a sexual imbalance dictated by the plantation's labor requirements, with its premium on adult males, and compounded by the appropriation of the most attractive female slaves by their white masters and mulatto over-seers—ironically, the origin of modern Brazil's image of itself as a racial democracy.

The tightly controlled lives of slaves offered them few chances of rebellion. But they did find ways to protest their oppression and some even managed to escape their shackles. In Brazil, significant numbers of slaves in mining zones or cities were able to earn enough to buy their freedom. During the eighteenth century, in gold-rush Minas Gerais, one African ethnic group even pooled their resources to purchase the liberty of their king, Chico Rei, who then led efforts to buy others out of slavery, an inspiration to Brazil's later black abolitionists.

For those slaves who could not win manumission, rebellion was rare but resistance common. The weapons of the weak included sabotage of machinery or production, or even poisoning of an oppressive overseer or master. But the most successful form of slave resistance during the colonial era was flight. Throughout the Americas, slaves fled their oppression to risk their freedom in the wilds beyond planter control, banding together with other fugitive slaves to form maroon communities. In Jamaica and Cuba they fled to the nearby mountains, in Suriname to the dense rain forest, in Panama to the pestilential jungles. But it was in northeastern Brazil that Palmares, the most extraordinary community of runaway slaves, was established. It lasted for most of the seventeenth century and engaged in trade and diplomatic negotiations with the Portuguese and Dutch. Palmares contained some thirty thousand people at its height, living in villages and ruled by an elected king and local chiefs along African lines. Palmares was an "African" kingdom within a European colony in America. Its legacy of resistance against oppression continues to inspire Brazilian blacks who struggle for equality and social justice.

Yet, over time, the racial dichotomies of this social order were blurred by another consequence of conquest and slavery: the appropriation of Indian and African women by European colonists. It was the beginning of centuries of racial mixing, whose largely illicit liaisons produced a growing population of *castas,* people of mixed descent. By the end of the colonial era, a complex process of miscegenation had overwhelmed the caste system with its growing numbers and permutations, with *castas* accounting for roughly a third of Spanish America's seventeen million people. In most of Latin America and the Caribbean, racial mixing is still reshaping society today.

In the end, the racial and cultural complexity of the region's people, who combined European, Indian, and African strains in varied and unique permutations, was itself a central colonial legacy. In many ways it is the *castas* who have defined the uniqueness of the region. Today, Mexico is only the largest of the many countries of Latin America with a majority of mixed racial ancestry. The formation of what Mexican intellectual José Vasconcelos called "the cosmic race" is one of the most profound colonial legacies.

Mestizos, children of mixed European and Indian descent (although the term is sometimes synonymous with *castas*), were not subject to tribute or the labor draft and were free to make their way in Hispanic society as best they could, subject to legal restrictions and popular prejudices. Many became artisans or merchants, and some became soldiers or landowners. In Central America, where the European population was small, mestizos even emerged as the local "Hispanic" elite.

Over time, subtler distinctions were made among people of mixed racial ancestry and "passing" for a caste of lighter hue became a common pattern, encouraged by the greater economic and social opportunities open as an individual climbed the social ladder of caste and color. "Manuel Hilario López, Spaniard as *he* says but of very suspect color" read a revealing eighteenth-century Mexican tax entry.[5] Although the Spanish authorities conceived of their caste system as "racial" in character, in practice it was based more upon physical appearance than parentage. The laws of genetics meant that two children of the same parents might have very different skin pigments and physical features. With passing, they might also have very different destinies. Passing, and the heightened consciousness of skin color and physical features that accompanies it, underscore the complexity of the region's racial attitudes, an important, if elusive, colonial heritage.

But physical appearance was not the only shaper of caste in colonial Latin America. "Money whitens" is an old saying in Brazil, where landowners of questionable racial purity were still known as "whites of the land." In Spanish America it was possible to purchase a higher caste status from a bankrupt crown or its corrupt officials. Legitimacy also could offset color, especially where a Spanish or Portuguese father was willing to recognize his mestizo or mulatto offspring. At a certain point, the very prevalence of passing made it easier. As one Spanish census taker in eighteenth-century Mexico confessed: "Nobody dares to classify the *castas*. This would imply the gathering of odious information and, if rigorously done, very dark stains erased by time would be uncovered in well-accepted families."[6]

Yet, passing had its limits, and they grew more rigid as an individual climbed the social ladder and legal restrictions were reinforced by white fears and popular prejudices. Indians, blacks, and even *castas* were generally excluded by law from government and church posts, while prejudice often barred them from universities, professions, and guilds. Royal efforts to admit a wealthy mulatto to university in late colonial Venezuela provoked a strong backlash by a creole elite who asserted that they were "justly proud of their pure Castilian blood."[7] Although there were exceptions to every colonial rule, elite social circles were reserved for people of European descent. In Brazil there were significant numbers of free blacks and mulattos at the close of the colonial era in 1822, but there were few mulattos and no blacks among the elite then—or now. They were confined to the lower and middle ranks of colonial society and condemned by the double "stain" of illegitimacy and racial impurity to remain there. At the end of the colonial era, people of African and Indian descent still made up the broad base of the social pyramid. In most countries of the region that is still true today.

At the top of this colonial social hierarchy were the Europeans and their American descendants. It was a distinction that had emerged with time. The conquistadors and the first settlers who followed them across the Atlantic were all "Spaniards." By the eighteenth century, their descendants had become "creoles," people of European descent born in America, distinguished from the smaller numbers of "peninsulars," who had been born on the Iberian peninsula. The top posts in the state and church bureaucracies were reserved for peninsulars, who also dominated the lucrative commerce with Spain. But most of the colonial elite were creoles, as were much of the middle sectors of colonial society. They were landowners and lawyers, merchants and mine owners, as well as lesser officials and master artisans, priests and shopkeepers.

Creole society centered on the extended family, which has retained its importance in Latin America to the present day. It was a patriarchal family, presided over by the oldest son of the eldest male line. In exchange, he had to manage the family's resources and use them to advance its interests and to care for its members. Younger sons and nephews had to be educated and found positions in the state, church, or military. Poorer relations were often maintained at his expense. Retainers also enjoyed his bed and board, along with slaves and servants. Daughters had to be dowried and found advantageous matches. The interests of future generations had to be assured by a wise stewardship of family resources, many of which were in trust for that reason and could not be sold. The Spanish American creole family was an institution that stretched through social space and time, incorporating relatives of differing degrees of wealth and status and generations both living and unborn. Its goal was to advance the family's fortunes and all its members were expected to do their part.

The extended family played many roles in colonial society. In an age without stock markets or limited liability, it was an economic organization composed of the only people you could trust: your relatives. In merchant families, sons and nephews were colonial junior executives who could run the branch offices along the major trade routes. In the strategies of creole elites, relatives were also assets to be placed in the state and church bureaucracies, where they could use their power and influence to promote family interests. This blurring of the lines between private priorities and public trusts remains a difficult legacy for the region's republics.

The extended family was not only the basic institution of Spanish American creole society, but also the model for others. It was extended further by the ties of godparents, the fictive kin whose responsibilities are still taken seriously in Latin America today, at all levels of society. It was also emulated in the occupational guilds that regulated the colonial economy and in the religious brotherhoods that loomed so large in its social life. Groupings of extended families, united by ties of marriage and godparentage, and common membership in guilds and brotherhoods, dominated colonial society and influenced its economy and politics. They continued to shape its course after independence, with a legacy of powerful patrons and dependent clients that retains its importance in much of the region.

Creole behavior reflected a lineage loyalty that placed the interests of the family over those of the individual. This hierarchy of concerns also shaped the lives of women, who were valued mostly as mothers and marriage partners. Within the confines of the home, the elite woman had a respected place as the bearer and raiser of legitimate children and the keeper of family ties and Hispanic cultural traditions. Outside its walls, her roles were restricted. She was unable to enter university or a profession, and dependent on the permission of her father or husband to sell property or sign contracts unless she was single and there was no male heir. The ideal of the patriarchal family was codified in law as *patria potestas,* which gave fathers total power over their children until they became adults. At marriage a woman exchanged the authority of her father for that of her husband. This patriarchal legacy has plagued efforts of Latin American women to win equal rights and opportunities to the present day.

Marriage occupied a central place in the "dynastic" strategies of elite families. Love had little to do with the choice of a partner, but the best laid family plans could be upset by a well-timed elopement with a man of lower station. At bottom, it was creole women who sustained the caste system. Creole men were allowed to indulge in sexual liaisons that crossed racial and social lines and violated the marriage vows, the origin, some argue, of the region's notorious machismo.

For the colonial woman, the respectable alternative to marriage was to enter a convent, where a wealthy widow could manage her own property and enjoy an autonomy absent outside, while living in an apartment whose luxurious furnishings had little to do with vows of poverty, and being waited on by the servants who had accompanied her into the nunnery. Either way, the wealthy creole woman was a protected being, chaperoned as a girl to safeguard her virginity, and secluded as a wife or nun to protect the family honor.

Poor women—and most Latin American women, then as now, were poor—were neither secluded nor protected. Poverty forced them out of the home and into the world, whether as landladies or servants, street vendors or streetwalkers, none of which were respectable pursuits. It also made them vulnerable to physical and sexual abuse, particularly as most also belonged to lower castes. Such abuse is still a common complaint of domestic servants in Latin America and the Caribbean, who are usually of darker color and lower status than their employers. Law and custom might give husbands power over women's lives, but few poor women were legally married and many headed their households, as so many do in the region today.

Cities were the center of Hispanic life in colonial Spanish America, where most people of European descent lived. But most city dwellers were poor, illiterate, and nonwhite. Their lives were a struggle for survival, not advancement. Their life-styles were characterized by monotonous diets, inadequate housing, and a heightened susceptibility to disease. It was little wonder that they indulged in alcohol whenever they could and celebrated religious holidays and patriotic events with abandon. They had little to look forward to and much to forget.

It was at the public celebrations for which Spanish American colonial society was famous that the disparities between rich and poor were most on display. The pomp and ceremony of a viceregal procession or the fireworks and theatricals that celebrated the awarding of a university chair underscored the wealth that could indulge in such conspicuous consumption. The elegant costumes of the peninsular officials and creole elites, and their retinues of liveried servants and slaves, attested to a life-style that contrasted starkly with the poverty of the artisans and street vendors watching them. By the close of the colonial era, Mexico City was as notorious for its beggars and cutpurses as it was famous for its rich merchants and ostentatious displays of wealth. Such inequalities have continued to be a source of social tensions and political upheavals in Latin America and the Caribbean during our own era.

Culture: A Triple Heritage

"The truly [Latin] American is the mestizo," underscored Manuel Moreno Fraginals, Cuba's leading cultural historian. The mixing of European, African, and Indian in America was cultural as well as genetic, creating an art that is uniquely American. The cultural heritage of the colonial era is as diverse as the peoples who created it. Creole Spanish America had the region's most developed academic culture, with universities that dated to the mid-sixteenth century and renowned creole intellectuals such as Mexico's seventeenth-century polymath, Carlos de Sigüenza y Góngora, a distinguished mathematician and historian, astronomer and archaeologist, philosopher and critic.

Mexico also boasted colonial America's finest poet, Sigüenza's friend Sor Juana Inés de la Cruz (1651–1695), who was equally at home in allegorical theater, philosophic sonnets, and popular songs. Her precocity and beauty enabled her to overcome her illegitimate birth to a rural family of low social standing to become the teenage star of the viceregal court. She was a child prodigy who could read at three and confound the learned at thirteen. Sor Juana retired from the court to a Jeronymite convent at sixteen, where for a time she was able to pursue the life of the mind barred to women in secular society. Her poetry, at times enveloped in Baroque allusions and personal enigmas, can be strikingly modern in its self-revelation, baring a divided, "confused soul, one a slave to passion, the other measured by reason."[8] Sor Juana's poems can also be delicately lyrical or caustically polemical, as in the verses that have led some modern feminists to view her as a precursor:

> *Which deserves the sterner blame,*
> *Though each will be a sinner:*
> *She who becomes a whore for pay.*
> *Or he who pays to win her?*[9]

In the end, Sor Juana was compelled by her religious superiors to sell her books and devote herself to social work, but her reputation as the pinnacle of Mexico's creole culture has grown with the centuries and inspired women writers and artists in our own time as well.

Yet where the arts were concerned, no European colony or ethnic group had a monopoly. Peru was home to the Cuzco School of the late seventeenth and early eighteenth centuries, the most original painters of the Americas, mestizo artists who rebelled against their Spanish guild masters and the imitation of European models. Instead, they formed their own workshops, found patrons in the Indian and mestizo elite of the ancient Inca capital, and created a syncretic style that combined the flattened perspective, primary colors, and Andean symbols of Indian culture with the techniques and themes of European painting, creating an innovative new art in the process.

Brazil could claim the hemisphere's greatest colonial sculptor and architect, the mulatto Antônio Francisco Lisboa, known as O Aleijadinho ("The Little Cripple"), who overcame a deformity that forced him to work with chisels strapped to his wrists to create transcendent art. Aleijadinho's powerfully expressive sculptures and airy churches combined Italian, Portuguese, and African elements in a personal artistic synthesis.

Classical music was performed throughout the Americas, but the finest composer was another mulatto, the French Caribbean's Chevalier de St. Georges, whose talents won him a warm welcome in eighteenth-century Paris as well as in the islands of his birth. Latin American elite culture generally imitated European models, although often styles that had already faded out of fashion in Paris, Madrid, or Lisbon. But even the most imitative art often incorporated American imagery, and the most memorable art produced in Latin America and the Caribbean synthesized diverse cultural influences into a unique art that could only have been created in the New World.

For most of the region's people, popular culture formed an even more important colonial legacy, one that could fuse the triple heritage of Latin America and the Caribbean. Throughout the region, music played a part in daily lives. In Mexico, popular *vilancicos* transformed the Spanish Christmas carol with witty verses that mixed colloquial Creole expressions with Indian and African words into what a bemused Sor Juana called a cultural "salad." In the Caribbean, dances combined the melodies of Europe with the rhythms of Africa and the gourd instruments of IndoAmerica into a vibrant musical mix. Only in the Americas could the European guitar, the African drum, and the Indian maraca or Andean flute play together, creating a new sound that was distinctively American. The salsa bands of the Caribbean and the *chicha* music of coastal Peru are their modern descendants.

In societies where literacy was confined to a small elite, oral tradition was often more important than books. In the Americas, these traditions were rich and varied. The myths of the Incas and the Maya live on in the festivals of their descendants in the Andes and Central America. Each year, in Bolivia's Aymara villages, masked dancers still retell the story of the Conquest from the viewpoint of the vanquished. The griot storytelling traditions of Africa were brought to the New World by slaves and survived in the Caribbean to influence the modern poetry of Derek Walcott. The medieval romances and religious legends of Castile and Portugal became part of the rural traditions of Colombia and Brazil, rich sources for the prizewinning fiction of Gabriel García Márquez or the innovative films of Glauber Rocha.

During the colonial era, plays and music were not only performed in private theaters and elite salons, but also in public squares, ancestors of today's park performances and street theater. Masquerades, in which hundreds paraded through the streets dressed up in allegorical costumes from literature, history, or religion, were a Mexican passion of all castes and classes. In 1621 Mexico City delighted in a creole display of chivalric heroes from Amadis of Gaul to Don Quixote. Six decades later the Indians of nearby Querétaro celebrated the dedication of a new church to their patron saint with a masquerade featuring the great Indian monarchs of the pre-Hispanic past wearing "crowns of turquoise . . . and shimmering golden green plumes of the Quetzal bird," wrote Sigüenza y Góngora.[10] Popular culture also found less formal expressions, including some that extended the idea of performance. The evening promenade around the main square or public park, such as the Zócalo or Reforma of Mexico City, was a theatrical spectacle that revealed much about colonial culture. The flamboyant clothes and colors that struck foreign visitors to Mexico City reflected an American sensibility very different from that of dour Madrid.

Saints' days and state holidays were marked by processions and pageants. In colonial Brazil, where lay brotherhoods celebrated the feast of their patron saint with elaborate parades, the artistry of the black and mulatto devotees of the Virgins of the Rosary and the Conception made their celebrations public spectacles. In eighteenth-century Rio de Janeiro, the colony's capital, the annual *congada* featured a procession in which blacks and mulattos danced the samba around litters in which a "king of the Congo" and his "queen" were carried to be "crowned" in a church and then to the square before the viceroy's palace, where they performed an allegorical play about the African experience in Brazil. The African rhythms, elaborate costumes, and creative fantasies of these displays are the ancestors of today's Carnival pageants. Throughout the Americas, these colonial celebrations, with their mix of traditions and forms, left a rich legacy which continues to influence the region's culture.

Religion: A Layered Tradition, A Divided Legacy

"Bear in mind from the beginning that the first aim of your expedition is to serve God and spread the Christian Faith," Diego Velásquez, the governor of Cuba, instructed Cortés as he departed for Mexico in 1519. "You must neglect no opportunity to spread the knowledge of the True Faith and the Church of God among those people who dwell in darkness."[11]

From the start, the sword and the cross advanced hand in hand. Clerics accompanied the conquistadors and sanctified their demands for Indian submission. Franciscan and Dominican friars followed soon after, taking their share of the spoils in saved heathen souls. But Cortés, who requested their presence, was well aware that the friars also helped pacify the Indians and consolidate his conquest with one of their own.

The first clerics to arrive in Mexico viewed themselves as "American apostles," and were imbued with an evangelical zeal and intolerant of idolatry. During the decade that followed Cortés's conquest, Juan de Zumárraga, the first bishop of Mexico, claimed to have destroyed more than five hundred heathen temples and twenty thousand idols. He credited the Franciscans alone with the conversion of more than one million souls in mass baptisms.

Yet these forced conversions were more apparent than real. To the Indians, accustomed to accepting the gods of conquerors into their pantheon, the request that they worship the Christian God was reasonable. But the demand that they cease to worship the gods of their ancestors, who assured them good harvests and fertile marriages, was not. The result was that the old gods went underground, and the Indians learned to cloak their worship in a Christian guise. Spanish clerics could smash Indian idols, but they could not prevent the site on which they had stood from becoming the focus of a Catholic cult whose saint was identified with the old Indian deity.

On a high hill north of Mexico City stands the Basilica of Our Lady of Guadalupe, Mexico's most sacred site. In December 1531 an Indian, Juan

Diego, claimed that as he was passing the hill the Virgin Mary appeared
to him in the guise of an Indian maiden and instructed him to tell Bishop
Zumárraga to build her shrine on that very spot. The Franciscan bishop
was skeptical, especially as that hill was sacred to the Aztec mother goddess, Tonántzin. But according to legend, the miraculous apparitions continued. A rosebush suddenly bloomed on the barren hillside, and when the
roses were brought to the bishop in Diego's cloak they miraculously turned
into the painting of the Brown Virgin that still hangs on the altar of the
shrine today. The Church eventually agreed to build the Basilica of Our
Lady of Guadalupe, in part as a strategy for winning the loyalty of Mexico's Indians to the Catholic faith.

The Brown Virgin of Guadalupe became the cult of central Mexico's
Indians, who worshiped at her shrine in ways that recalled the rituals of the
Aztecs more than the rites of Spain. One sixteenth-century Spanish cleric
who visited Guadalupe was shocked to see Indians "dressed in their ancient style, form a circle, bound together by ropes of flowers, dance in the
very middle of the church dedicated to the miraculous Virgin, while they
hummed a monotonous tune which doubtless reminded them of their
past."[12]

Yet for all its unease at these pagan survivals, the Church eventually
came to terms with their presence, both as a social safety valve and as an
aid to conversion. Christian lyrics were written to Indian melodies and
native dances were incorporated into Catholic morality plays. In the end,
the Church accepted a process of mutual adaptation, in which the Indians
embraced Christian symbols and forms, while the Church turned a blind
eye to the pagan content beneath the Catholic surface. This layering of
beliefs is typical of the complex colonial religious legacy in Latin America.

Ironically, when the creole descendants of the conquistadors in the
eighteenth century sought a symbol that would differentiate them as "Mexicans" from Spain, it was to Guadalupe that they turned. The Brown Virgin
was transformed from an Indian protectress into the patron saint of Mexico, under whose banner Mexicans of different castes and classes fought
together for national independence in the early nineteenth century.

Today, modern technology has mechanized the appearance of the

Brown Virgin's image and amplifies the prayers of the faithful. But the faithful of many hues who crawl to the altar on bleeding knees over ancient stones continue to fuse their mixed heritage into a uniquely Mexican cult, a fitting symbol for a mestizo nation.

A comparable process of adaptation took place among Latin Americans of African descent. In Portuguese Brazil blacks worshiped the warrior god Ogum as St. George and the sea goddess Yemenjá as the Virgin of Conception. They filled their churches with figures of black saints such as Benedict the Moor and paraded these images through the streets to African rhythms. This syncretism was encouraged by the Jesuits, who created Christian rituals in African languages, music, and dance as a way of reaching the slaves. Today, millions of Brazilians, including many with no African ancestry, are devotees of the Afro-Brazilian religions of Candomblé and Umbanda. In the old colonial capitals of Salvador and Rio de Janeiro, thousands gather on the feast of Yemenjá to throw flowers into the sea.

In French Caribbean Saint Domingue, the gods of Africa also found their Christian equivalents. The patron saint of France, Notre Dame d'Assomption, was identified with the powerful Dahomeyan goddess Ezili Freda and the Congolese mother goddess Manbo Inan, whose festivals were celebrated on the same day. Even today, a Dürer reproduction of the Madonna in a cloud of angels hung in a Haitian shrine is a cover that "deceives," a Voodoo adept explains. "Those aren't angels at all. They are children: Manbo Inan and her 101 children."[13] As one Jesuit father recently confessed, "The images they kneel before are Christian, but we never know to what deity they are praying."

In colonies as distant and diverse as Brazil and Saint Domingue (now Haiti) the gods of Africa remained alive in the fields, forests, and cities of America, a spiritual legacy that peoples of African descent, slave and free, sustained behind a Christian façade. This layering of religious beliefs continues to characterize the beliefs and rituals of Brazil and Haiti today.

The colonial era bequeathed other legacies that have influenced the Catholic church in more recent times. As an established church, it was closely linked to the colonial government, and at times exercised political

authority within it. Papal decrees in the early sixteenth century ceded to
the monarchs of Spain and Portugal Rome's power to appoint and discipline clergy, found churches, and collect tithes in their American colonies,
in return for their agreeing to defend the faith and evangelize the Indians.
This *patronato real,* or royal patronage, converted the American church into
a colonial bureaucracy, and was one of the Crown's most valuable attributes. Despite areas of tension and moments of conflict, the Catholic church
and Iberian empires worked out a mutually reinforcing relationship in
which church and state cooperated in shaping a colonial society molded by
Christian values.

The Church also emerged as a large landowner and repository of
wealth during the colonial period, and as the educator of the elites and a
patron of the arts. As their resources grew, the religious orders and hierarchy sometimes seemed more concerned about their own privileges than
the welfare of the faithful. By the eighteenth century the Church was
regarded more as a career for younger sons of the creole elite than as a
calling for the American apostles of Christ. Its kingdom seemed very much
of this world, symbolized by the resplendent gold leaf that decorated the
churches of Salvador, Brazil or Quito, Ecuador.

But the colonial Church left a divided legacy. From the first years of
the Conquest, there have always been voices within the Church—a minority perhaps, but a vocal minority—that sided with the oppressed and
protected the weak. The Dominican Bartolomé de las Casas in sixteenth-
century Spanish America and the Jesuit António Vieira in seventeenth-
century Brazil were only the most famous of the clerics who defended the
indigenous peoples from enslavement, using their moral authority, rhetorical gifts, and political influence. This moral commitment of clerics to the
just treatment of the poor and powerless would also be a legacy of European empire. So would the utopian vision that led Vasco de Quiroga to
create post-Conquest Mexican missions with communal ownership, labor,
and government.

During the eighteenth century, Jesuit intellectuals brought the ideas
of the European Enlightenment to Latin America and helped create a new
national consciousness among its creole elites and a questioning by some

of the divine right of kings. Although most of the Catholic hierarchies remained loyal to their imperial patrons during the nineteenth-century wars of independence, the bishop of Quito helped lead a revolt in 1809. The following year, Father Miguel Hidalgo, a cleric who believed that the Church had a special calling to help the poor, began a rebellion that was at once a movement for Mexican independence and a struggle for Indian liberation. His *Grito de Dolores* is still celebrated each September 16 as Mexico's Declaration of Independence. It is part of the complex legacy that the colonial Church left to inspire its modern Latin American inheritors.

The Golden Century's Silver Lining

"I and my companions suffer from a disease of the heart that can only be cured with gold," Cortés told Moctezuma's envoys. The Spanish did get some gold from the treasuries and streams of America, but they found far more silver in the mountains of Mexico and Peru that lay beyond the frontiers of dense Indian settlement.

The most fabulous of these silver strikes was Potosí, the Cerro Rico, or "Rich Hill," of silver sky-high in the Peruvian (now Bolivian) Andes. It was discovered in 1544 by an Indian servant, and a year later, the first mine was in operation. By 1600 Potosí was producing half the world's silver. The richest silver strike in history, it would yield sixty million ounces of precious metal during the colonial period alone.

With the stakes so high, Spain and its American colonists demonstrated an entrepreneurial drive and a capacity for technological innovation and effective organization that belied foreign stereotypes, which then as now question their capacity for economic development. To provide waterpower, they constructed twenty-seven reservoirs to capture the melting snows of nearby mountains and created an artificial river to carry the water to Potosí's 132 silver mills, where 66-feet-tall waterwheels helped grind the hard rock into a fine powder. The Spanish also developed an amalgamation process with mercury to refine the silver ore, and built a mountain road hundreds of miles long to bring the vital but toxic liquid by mule train from the mines of Huancavelica. They constructed a mint, built a port on the Pacific Coast, and organized the transportation of the precious metal from Potosí to Spain, via Panama, thousands of miles away across snow-capped mountains, barren deserts, pestilential jungles, and hostile seas.

When Indian resistance to work in the mines at an altitude where West African slaves did not thrive threatened silver production, the Spanish reinvented the Inca *mita* labor tax and conscripted one out of every seven adult males in sixteen highland provinces to labor in the mines and mills of Potosí each year. The drafted miners were compelled to endure "four months of excessive work in the mines, working twelve hours a day, descending to perpetual darkness where it is always necessary to work with candles, with the air thick and evil-smelling, trapped in the bowels of the earth," reported one appalled Spanish observer. It was a vision of hell, with the miners "cutting ore with bars weighing 30 pounds, at the expense of blood and sweat," or "crawling along like snakes, burdened with ore."[14] For this infernal labor the Indian conscripts were paid less than it cost them to support their families. It was no wonder they chewed coca leaves to still their hunger, exhaustion, and pain, or that they lacked the resources to make the long journey home when their time was up. Each year, the *mita* brought fifty thousand Indians, counting the miners and their families, to Potosí, swelling its Indian population to some one hundred thousand—an early, if coerced, example of the labor migration that continues to swell the region's cities today.

At its height in the early seventeenth century, Potosí had a population of one hundred fifty thousand, more than any city in America or Spain, exceeded in Europe only by Paris, London, and Amsterdam. What made this urban growth so remarkable was that Potosí was located 13,400 feet above sea level on a frigid and barren plateau where nothing grew and everything consumed had to be brought in, often from a great distance at considerable cost. But the silver of Potosí had become the life's blood of Spain's empire, and the economy of the viceroyalty of Peru was reshaped to meet its needs and desires. Its legacy was an economy so dependent on mining exports that all other interests were subordinated to its requirements.

Silver also shaped the rhythms of commerce, the contours of finance, and the distribution of wealth. In a world without credit cards, checks, or paper currency, silver coins were the essential medium of exchange. In Panama's Portobello it was traded for the manufactures of Europe, presaging that country's modern role as the crossroads of continents. In Manila, American silver was all Chinese merchants would accept for their precious porcelains and silks.

Great profits were earned on the silver and the commerce it spawned all along the silver route. Fortunes were made—and lost—in the mining itself, but trade was the surest road to riches. The great merchants made huge profits supplying the mines and selling their silver—150 percent profit was common on the European trade—and then used their possession of that rarest of colonial commodities, liquid capital, to make loans at usurious interest rates to miners and landowners. Fortunes of half a million silver pesos, a fabulous sum, were not unknown in Lima, and the great merchants became the viceroyalty's economic elite. Their self-regulating guilds, which enjoyed a monopoly of the official trade, are the ancestors of the powerful business monopolies of more recent times. Peru's government still talks about the need to dismantle monopolies that date from the colonial era.

The Spanish Crown, too, was among the great gainers from the silver of America. It was entitled to the royal fifth of everything mined and minted, to which was added the sales taxes and other levies and the profits on the sale of mercury, a royal monopoly. Income from American silver was among the most important sources of royal revenues, and was often used as collateral for vital loans. Government ownership of subsoil resources is still a powerful legacy in the region today.

Silver exports were the basis for Spanish America's initial insertion in the emerging international economy centered on Europe, and they would remain its chief link throughout the colonial period, with Mexico replacing Peru as the biggest exporter in the eighteenth century. But when the depleted mines of Potosí declined in the late seventeenth century, the city and the industries and regions oriented to its needs declined as well, revealing the costs of depending on so narrow and nonrenewable an economic base—another issue that Latin Americans have debated in more recent decades.

Peruvian silver—and the gold of equal value discovered in the mountains of Brazil at the turn of the eighteenth century—also illustrated the extraordinary impact of colonial Latin America on the rest of the world. American silver financed Spain's "Golden Century" (1550–1650), which gave the world the novels of Cervantes and the paintings of Velásquez. It enabled the Hapsburgs to fight dynastic wars that dominated a century of European history and their nobles to enjoy luxurious life-styles. But it also generated an inflation that made Spanish industry and agriculture uncompetitive. In the end, the abundance of American silver may have promoted Spain's decline, instead of enhancing its power.

Nor was the impact of American silver restricted to Spain. Most of the silver coins minted in Potosí passed through Spanish hands into Dutch, French, and British coffers in payment for the goods that Spain consumed but did not produce. The result was an eightfold increase in Europe's money supply in a century, and its concentration in nations that would make the most of these augmented financial resources. American silver enabled Europe to expand its commerce with Asia, reversing a long trade imbalance. It also put the profits in Dutch and British pockets, making possible the birth of capitalism in seventeenth-century Holland and the dawn of industry in eighteenth-century England, which received the lion's share of Brazilian gold as well. Precious metals from America helped place Europe on the road to industrial revolution and global empire. In short, American silver and gold altered the course of world history.

For Latin America and the Caribbean, this legacy of mining economies oriented to overseas markets has lasted into our own era, although the metals and minerals extracted have changed, and new mines have replaced exhausted lodes. In Bolivia, tin has replaced silver and newer mines Potosí, but the economy's focus on mining has remained. In Peru and Chile, copper has now claimed pride of place, and in Jamaica and Guyana bauxite. In Brazil, a dozen metals and minerals now compete with the gold still washed from tropical streams. But the colonial pattern of unruly miners pursuing the glitter of gold through the tropical wilderness, with scant regard for its ecology or indigenous peoples, continues in contemporary Brazil, where some three hundred thousand gold miners are scouring the Amazon in search of modern El Dorados. Throughout the region, however, oil has become the most sought-after subsoil resource, with Venezuela and Mexico the leaders, but countries as diverse as Ecuador and Trinidad also supplying lucrative overseas markets. What they all share is a dependence on mining exports that is a central colonial legacy.

Brazil's Bittersweet Crop

"He who says Brazil, says sugar and more sugar,"[15] wrote the Bahia planters to their king in 1662, with the air of men pronouncing a truism. The Portuguese had discovered Brazil by accident in 1500 and colonized it as an afterthought, to prevent European rivals from doing it instead. It was sugar, an Asian crop that Portuguese colonists brought with them from Africa, which transformed Brazil into one of Lisbon's prize possessions. What silver was to Spanish Peru, sugar was to Portuguese Brazil. Sugar was the spur to colonization and the economic pole around which the rest of the colony revolved, as well as the driving force behind its system of coerced labor. It was also Brazil's initial link to the outside world, its biggest export and major source of wealth.

Unlike the Spanish conquistadors, the Portuguese who landed on Brazil's tropical coast in the sixteenth century found no cities to conquer, treasuries to despoil, or mines to exploit. Instead they encountered virgin forests with the red dyewood that gave Brazil its name, tropical fruits, and naked Tupí warriors who resisted their encroachments. But the Portuguese colonists also found some of the most fertile lands in the hemisphere, whose well-watered virgin soils and proximity to the Atlantic made them ideal for the production of sugar for export to Europe, where it was a rare luxury prized for its supposed medicinal properties and evident sweetening powers.

Sugar was the first agricultural crop worth the costs and risks of transporting it across the Atlantic, the pioneer commodity of an American export agriculture that has shaped many of the region's economies. Then as now, foreign investment and markets played a central economic role. The Flemish and Dutch were willing to put up the capital needed to establish plantations and mills and to refine and market Brazilian sugar throughout Europe. The Portuguese had developed the necessary technology on the island of Madeira. The remaining obstacle to the world's first sugar boom was labor.

At first, the Portuguese tried to solve their labor problem by bribing or coercing the local Amerindian population to work on their sugar estates. But the Tupís, seminomadic hunters and farmers, were unaccustomed to regular hard labor and uninterested in earning a steady wage. They either sickened and died under the Portuguese lash, or else slipped away into the nearby forest. After 1570 Brazilian planters began to replace them with African slaves, an association that would accompany sugar throughout the Americas. By 1620 Brazil had become the world's largest sugar exporter—and slave importer. Both sugar and slavery would leave deep imprints on Brazil: It would remain an economy of agricultural exports for over three centuries, and today Brazil is the world's second largest "African" nation after Nigeria.

The plantation complex—with its Big House and slave barracks, sugar mill and chapel—would shape Brazil in a mold as distinctive as the conical shape of the sugar loaves it produced. Brazilian plantations were early agro-industrial complexes, which combined canefields, milling, processing, and packing and shipping on one site. They were forerunners of our own industrial age, whose inhuman rhythms of work and melding of men and machines shocked contemporary observers like Father António Vieira, who recorded his impressions of a night shift in a boiling house:

Anyone who sees in the blackness of night these tremendous furnaces perpetually burning; the flames leaping . . . through the two mouths or nostrils by which the fire breathes . . . the cauldrons . . . boiling lakes . . . vomiting froth, exhaling clouds of steam. . . . The noise of the wheels and chains, the peoples the color of the very night working intensely and moaning together without a moment of peace or rest; [anyone] who sees all the confused and tumultuous machinery and apparatus of that Babylon cannot doubt . . . that this is the same as Hell.[16]

It was little wonder that Brazilians regarded sugar as a bittersweet crop.

Unlike the typical Spanish American hacienda, the Brazilian sugar plantation was a capital-intensive operation, with a heavy investment in machinery and slaves. All of its valuable land was devoted to growing sugarcane. All of its energies were focused on producing this single crop for export to Europe.

Equally striking was the society it spawned. The "Lord of the Mill" was not only an agrarian capitalist, but also a rural seigneur, with virtually unlimited power over his slaves and dependents. Within his Big House he was a patriarch who could seclude his wife, send his daughter to a convent, and take slave mistresses at will. He ruled his plantation in patrimonial style, dispensing justice and favors, a stern disciplinarian but a paternalistic patron. He was not only master of all he surveyed, but also of much that did not meet the eye: the less wealthy white cane-growers without mills of their own; the mulatto subsistence farmers who grew the plantation's food crops on their marginal lands; the mestizo backlands ranchers who sold him their oxen, tallow, and meat; the itinerant priests and merchants who serviced the plantation; even the Portuguese officials charged with protecting royal interests but looking for advantageous marriage alliances of their own.

Brazil has remained a deferential society, a complex web of patrons and clients, where connections count for more than credentials. Even its politics still retains this character. The economic and social patterns created by the sugar plantation, with its dependence on a single crop and foreign markets, migrant labor, and an unequal society stratified by color as well as class, would be enduring, both for Brazil and for the islands of the Caribbean.

The European rivals of Spain and Portugal had never accepted the pope's division of the world between them. Francis I, a Catholic French king (1515–1547), rejected such monopoly claims with the observation that he "had never seen a clause in the last will of Adam conceding such control to the kings Charles and Manoel."[17] The Protestant monarchs of England and Holland had less reason still to accept papal authority and more cause to attack their Spanish enemies. After 1580, when Portugal came under Madrid's rule, its colonies, too, became targets of Dutch attacks. Madrid and Lisbon might defend their colonies with arms, but papal benediction would provide no protection.

Madrid enjoyed roughly a century in which the Caribbean was a Spanish sea. But during the seventeenth century Spain's Caribbean claims were contested by European rivals with greater naval and economic power—Holland, France, and England—who punctured its monopoly pretensions with ships and colonies of their own. Although Spain held on to the largest and most valued of its Caribbean possessions, by the eighteenth century it had ceded control of Jamaica to England, the western third of Hispaniola to France, and the smaller islands of the eastern Caribbean to all three of its European rivals—the origin of today's polyglot and politically fragmented Caribbean—retaining Trinidad until 1797.

By then, the Caribbean had replaced Brazil as the leader in global sugar production. In 1630 the Dutch seized twelve hundred square miles of northern Brazil, including some of its richest sugar lands, and held them for more than two decades. When they were expelled in 1654 they took the secrets of sugar production with them to their new Caribbean colonies. The British and French planters learned from the Dutch, but soon surpassed them in efficiency and production. Symbolically, it was in Saint Domingue, whose 1697 cession to France marked the formal end of Spain's Caribbean monopoly on the island of Hispaniola where it had begun two centuries before, that the Caribbean sugar colony would reach its eighteenth-century apogee—and, in 1791, generate the social explosion that signaled the beginning of the end of slavery in the Americas.

By then, sugar was no longer the only agricultural commodity whose value in Europe made it worth shipping across the Atlantic. It had been joined by tobacco and cacao, cotton and indigo, the last two in response to the beginnings of the Industrial Revolution in England. A century later coffee and bananas had emerged as major tropical exports, with Central America and northern South America added to Brazil and the Caribbean as producers, while the temperate zones of South America were shipping sizable quantities of wheat, corn, and flax, as well as wool, hides, and meat. More recently Brazil has become a leading exporter of soybeans and oranges. In the end, sugar pioneered the creation of the agrarian export economy that would become the way in which most of the Americas were inserted into the global economic order. But it also created an economy dependent on foreign markets beyond American control. The boom and bust cycles of colonial Brazil's sugar industry were a harbinger of things to come.

Imperial Economics, Colonial Politics

Throughout the region, European powers sought to shape the economies of their American colonies so as to maximize their exports of precious metals and agricultural commodities in demand in Europe. As a result, the concentration of labor and capital in export industries was a common theme and economies oriented to exporting the products of mines and plantations were a shared colonial legacy.

So were the efforts of imperial powers to compel their colonists to buy their manufactures. For much of the colonial era, European governments subscribed to mercantilism, an economic doctrine that favored state regulation of the economy and the protection of domestic industries and agriculture from foreign competition. Although its ideology and rhetoric would change, this economic vision has retained a resonance in Latin America to this day. In theory, mercantilism created a mutually beneficial relationship between a "mother" country and its colonies, one in which the imperial power supplied the manufactures its colonists desired, receiving in exchange prized natural resources and strengthening its navy by giving it a monopoly of the carrying trade. Together they would form a self-sufficient commonwealth. But neither Spain nor Portugal developed the industries that could supply their colonists' wants. Instead, the monopolistic merchant guilds that controlled colonial commerce imported these goods from northern Europe, added their own profits to the costs they passed on to the American consumer, then pushed up the price still further by keeping their colonial markets undersupplied. As a consequence, only the wealthy could afford these imported European goods.

One predictable result was a rise in smuggling, as merchants who were not admitted to the official commercial guilds moved to supply their American customers with the goods they lacked at prices they could afford. This contraband trade expanded alongside the legal commerce, and by the eighteenth century probably equaled it in value. Another consequence was that Spain's American colonists themselves began to produce what they needed, imperial regulations to the contrary notwithstanding. Giant manufactories, some with hundreds of workers, wove cloth in Quito, Ecuador, and shaped glass in Puebla, Mexico. Wine was fermented in Peru and liquor distilled in New Granada. By the mid-eighteenth century both Mexico and Peru were largely self-sufficient in the necessities of life, although their elites still looked abroad for the luxuries they consumed. This pattern would repeat itself in our own era, as would the debates over the economic policies it reflected.

By 1776 the annual silver fleets had ceased to sail and Spain's Bourbon rulers were willing to recognize the inevitable and reform their weakened imperial economic system. Their Bourbon Reforms created freer trade within Spain's empire, opening up ports all over Spain and America to transatlantic commerce and allowing the colonists to trade with each other. But they retained the monopolistic merchant guilds and stopped short of free trade. An end to state economic regulation and the promotion of free trade would be banners raised by liberals during and after the struggles for independence but opposed by local producers who feared their interests would suffer from European competition. As a result, both open versus closed economies and state regulation versus the free market would be conflictual issues during the nineteenth century, and they continue to be controversial today.

The colonial political legacy was also problematic. Creole experience of self-government under Spanish rule was limited and restricted to the very wealthy. Creole elites participated in the *cabildos*, local councils that at first were elected by the leading citizens of the municipality. But by the seventeenth century, a bankrupt Crown was selling off council seats to the highest bidder and allowing them to be inherited and sold like any other property. It was little wonder that the creole elites of Spanish America came to view such government positions as investments to be mined rather than as public trusts to be measured. Not having been elected, moreover, the *cabildo* member felt little sense of civic responsibility. In the absence of truly representative institutions the lineage loyalty of Spanish American elite society also shaped the political legacy of the colonial era. In Portuguese Brazil, whose proprietary colonies enjoyed greater autonomy and colonial elites greater influence, local legislatures had even more power and their self-interested character was even more apparent. This patrimonial approach to government might be compatible with the political style of the monarchies of the day, but it boded ill for efforts to establish republican institutions, and still plagues many of Latin America's nations.

Spain's attempts to reform this colonial political system in the late eighteenth century created more conflicts than they resolved. As with the economic reforms of the era, the goal was to revive a declining Spain and to save its American empire from being lost either to Madrid's European rivals or to creole elites. Although the upper levels of colonial government were reserved in theory for peninsular-born Spaniards, in practice wealthy creoles had been allowed to purchase seats on the *audiencias* and fill senior posts in the Church hierarchy before the Bourbon Reforms reimposed a stricter imperial rule. In local administration, the corrupt but creole *corregidores* were replaced by Spanish intendants. Creole anger at this reversal of their political gains after a century of benign neglect was clear, as was their resentment of Spanish carpetbaggers whose assertion of social superiority grated and self-interested displacement of creole officeholders seemed a second conquest of America.

As the Marqués de San Jorge, a creole aristocrat in Bogotá, capital of New Granada (today Colombia), wrote to his king:

*[T]he Viceroys here and their retainers . . . mock, humiliate and oppress us.
. . . The more distinguished the unhappy Americans are, the more they suffer . . . their
honor and reputations are attacked, insulting them by depriving them of any honorific
office of consequence.*[18]

This creole resentment fed a growing sense that they were "Americans,"
not "Spaniards." It would be reflected in creole leadership of the nineteenth-century independence movements.

The Bourbon Reforms were an effort to revive Spanish power by a
more efficient exploitation of American resources, and that was how creole
elites viewed them. As a result, the reforms helped undermine the very
colonial system that they were intended to reinforce. The economic reforms stimulated commerce on both sides of the Atlantic, but sacrificed the
interests of American farmers and manufacturers to those of their Spanish
competitors. The creation in the eighteenth century of two more South
American viceroyalties—New Granada in the north and La Plata in the
south—and the granting of greater autonomy to regional governments
were intended to establish a more effective imperial rule, but they also
promoted regional identifications, creating the geographic bases of today's
independent nations. The expulsion of the Jesuits, who had schooled the
creole elite and recruited many of their best and brightest into the order,
also fueled creole anger. The collection of back taxes and imposition of
new levies and royal monopolies alienated all castes and classes. At the
same time, the Bourbon Reforms did little to improve the position of
Indians or the opportunities of the *castas*. The results were riots in Quito,
an uprising in New Granada, and a massive Indian rebellion in Peru.
Madrid's imperial reforms did contribute to the prosperity of late-eighteenth-century Spanish America, when silver mining and agrarian exports
reached new heights and were joined by the expanded production of farms
and workshops oriented to the needs of an enlarged population. (This
demographic growth gave Spanish America some seventeen million people
by 1810—with another three million in Brazil and perhaps a million more
in the non-Hispanic Caribbean—beginning the accelerating population
growth that has lasted to the present day.) But the increased wealth of the

creole elites made them chafe all the more at their restricted political roles and inferior status.

At the same time the growing inequalities within late-eighteenth-century society exacerbated simmering social tensions throughout Latin America and the Caribbean. As a consequence, when the French Revolution brought the age of reform to a close in Europe, it also set off a Caribbean revolution that opened the era of independence in Latin America. In an irony of history, European colonial rule in the region would end first on the island of Hispaniola, where it had begun three centuries before.

The End of Empire

On a high mountaintop overlooking the northern plain where the Haitian revolution began stand the imposing ruins of the citadel of La Ferrière. Its massive stone walls symbolize the determination of Haiti's former slaves to defend their hard-won freedom. Today Haiti is a black republic, defiantly proud of its African identity and culture, but with an impoverished economy that never recovered from the destruction of the plantations that had made French Saint Domingue the most valuable colony in the Caribbean.

Haiti's social revolution was a direct result of Saint Domingue's economic advance. Between 1770 and 1789 its sugar industry took a great leap in both production and productivity, emerging as the most modern and efficient in the Caribbean, growing and milling almost as much cane as all the British islands combined. This economic progress was based on a virtual doubling of the colony's slave population and an intensification of the exploitation to which they were subjected. Saint Domingue became the colony where the black population was most dense and most African, and thus least accepting of their oppression. It was also a rigid society, divided by class and caste, as well as by slavery.

It was the French Revolution that detonated this Caribbean powder keg, and Napoleon, its imperial heir, who unwittingly set the stage for independence in French Saint Domingue, Portuguese Brazil, and the Spanish American mainland, although by divergent routes and with dif-

ferent outcomes. After 1789, revolution in France prompted dreams of
autonomy in colonial Port-au-Prince as well as debates over the Rights of
Man in Paris. In Saint Domingue poor whites and free mulattos struggled
for power with the planter elites, while black slaves watched—and waited.
It would prove a fateful combination.

August 15 is the feast of the Assumption of the Virgin, the patron saint
of France, and sacred as well to the African deities identified with her in
Haitian Voodoo. In 1791, that date was the occasion for a secret Voodoo
ceremony by slaves and maroons at Bois Caïman in the northern plains of
Saint Domingue. The use of Christian holidays as a cover for the celebration of African rites was normal in Saint Domingue, but this would not be
a normal ceremony. Instead, Boukman, the African-born Voodoo priest
who led the rites, would use them to launch the greatest slave rebellion in
the history of the hemisphere. (Today, Haiti's leading "roots music" group
calls itself Boukman Eksperyans.) African talking drums spread the news,
and within weeks, the prosperous plantations of the northern plains were
in flames, their white masters and mulatto overseers fled or massacred,
their once cowed slaves triumphantly in command.

Before the Haitian revolution was over, slavery would be abolished
in Saint Domingue, the plantation system destroyed, and French rule
brought to an end. Europe's most valuable Caribbean colony would be
transformed into the region's first independent state. This liberation would
take thirteen years of brutal combat, in which blacks fought against local
whites and mulattos, in addition to French, Spanish, and English troops,
under the inspired leadership of Toussaint L'Ouverture, the self-educated
former slave whom Napoleon called "the gilded African." Even Napoleon,
the conqueror of Europe, was forced to admit defeat in Haiti, after losing
an army of twenty-five thousand crack troops under the command of his
brother-in-law. In 1804, Jean-Jacques Dessalines, Toussaint's illiterate,
African-born lieutenant, could proclaim "Haiti" (after the Taino Indian
word for mountainous) an independent nation, one in which all citizens
were defined as "black" and all blacks were citizens.

The Haitian revolution was the handwriting on the wall for slavery
in the Americas, but it also delayed the independence it promoted, sending

powerful but mixed messages to the rest of the region. Its success demonstrated that colonial rule could be overthrown, and inspired revolutionaries elsewhere, particularly blacks and mulattos. In its wake, rebellions involving slaves, maroons, and Afro-Caribbean religion swept through the Caribbean, from British Jamaica to Dutch Suriname. But none would succeed in following Haiti's path to freedom, because its social revolution alerted slave-owners elsewhere in the region, who saw in the fate of the planters of Saint Domingue a presentiment of their own destiny. On the neighboring island of Cuba, where many of Saint Domingue's surviving sugar planters fled after 1791, the Haitian revolution helped persuade the creole elite to remain loyal to Spain. As a consequence, Cuba did not become independent until 1898, after slavery was abolished and the issue of political independence was separated from that of slave rebellion.

To the creole elites who led the struggles for Latin American independence on the mainland, the Haitian revolution, with its slave rebellion, race war, and social upheaval, was also a cause of anxiety. It allowed fearful loyalists to argue that political independence was a Pandora's box which opened the way to a social revolution that might end their own privileged positions, not just those of Spaniards and Portuguese. As a result, it would be left for Napoleon to create the context within which Spanish America and Portuguese Brazil would gain their independence. In 1808 he sent his armies across the Pyrénées, hoping to close Iberia to British commerce and bring England to its knees. Instead, he brought both Brazil and Spanish America to their feet.

As French troops neared Lisbon, Dom João, the Portuguese prince regent, boarded a waiting fleet with his court and treasury and sailed off to Brazil. Their ensuing years in Brazil convinced the Portuguese princes that it was the most valuable of their possessions. At the same time, the self-regard of their Brazilian subjects was enhanced by the experience of being the center of the Portuguese empire, and made them unwilling to return to being a colony. When a revolution in Portugal tried to reimpose the imperial authority of Lisbon and bade Dom João return home in 1821, he left Crown Prince Pedro as regent and advised him: "If Brazil demands independence, grant it, but put the crown upon your own head."[19] As a result, when Brazilian independence was declared a year later, it was the Portuguese crown prince who proclaimed it with broad Brazilian support. The result would be not an American republic but a New World monarchy. The continuity that this naturalization of a European dynasty afforded Brazil helped it maintain its unity and stability during the difficult decades that followed. Its modern legacy would be a nation with the size and resources to dream of greatness and a twentieth-century republic ruled by the aristocratic politics of deference.

Napoleon was also the catalyst of Spanish American independence, although that came by a dramatically different route. Napoleon kept the Spanish Bourbons captive in France while his brother Joseph replaced them on the throne of Spain. In the absence of a legitimate monarch in Madrid after 1808, Spain's American colonies had to decide for themselves whom to obey. It was a situation that brought to the surface the social tensions within their societies.

In Mexico, whose "monstrous inequality of rights and wealth"[20] shocked even European aristocrats like the widely traveled Alexander von Humboldt, a creole conspiracy detonated an Indian and mestizo rebellion against the oppression of centuries. It was centered in the northern provinces where silver mines and haciendas had expanded prodigiously during the preceding decades, increasing the pressure on the remaining Indian villages and the exploitation of landless mestizo laborers. On September 16, 1810, a radical creole priest, Miguel Hidalgo, gathered his Indian charges in the village of Dolores and urged them to fight for their country's freedom—and their own liberation. As word spread, some eighty thousand Indians and mestizos gathered under the banner of the Brown Virgin of Guadalupe and swept over northern Mexico, sacking haciendas and cities, and killing "Spaniards" without regard to their continent of birth. The social war unleashed by Hidalgo's political preaching frightened Mexico's creoles into remaining loyal to Spain, delaying its independence until 1821. Peru, where memories of the recent Tupac Amaru rebellion exerted a similar influence on creole loyalties, would not be liberated until 1824, and then by an outside army.

As a consequence, it would be on the edge of Spain's American empire—in the late colonial economic boom areas of La Plata (present-day Argentina) and Venezuela, where self-confident creole elites were restive under the restrictions of the colonial commercial system and the limitations on their political power—that movements for independence would first take root. In Buenos Aires a special open *cabildo* meeting in 1810 declared self-government in the name of the captive king; and in Caracas, in 1811, patriots seized the opportunity to declare the independence of Venezuela, the first independent republic in Spanish America.

Still, it would take fifteen years of hard fighting under the "Liberators"—Simon Bolívar and José de San Martín—before this independence was secure and Spanish South America was free. In the north, Bolívar, a wealthy Venezuelan creole planter with enlightened ideas, would have to learn how to win the support of mestizo cowboys and black slaves without frightening the creole elite in order to triumph, after many defeats. In the south, where color and caste played a lesser role, San Martín, a professional creole soldier of Argentine birth, Spanish training, and conservative views, would have to free his army from the regional and political rivalries of La Plata before he could liberate Chile in 1818 and use its resources to attack Peru, the heart of Spanish power in South America, where Bolívar won decisive victories in 1824 and 1825. In the end, it was the triumph of liberalism after 1820 in Spain—where troops ordered to America to suppress its independence mutinied and imposed a constitutional government on Madrid instead—that persuaded Peruvian and Mexican conservatives to support independence as a way of preserving their colonial privileges. As a result, the imperial state was destroyed in Spanish America, but colonial society was preserved. There would be political independence, but no social revolution. Independence would be the last legacy of empire.

The Aftermath of Independence

By 1825 Spanish and Portuguese rule had come to an end on the American mainland. The break with Europe left the new nations of Latin America free to shape their own destinies but in poor condition to take advantage of their hard-won independence. Fifteen years of fighting had left deep scars. Burned homes and depleted livestock herds, closed mines and abandoned farms were the most visible costs, but the dislocation of commerce and the decline in investment were equally problematic. Even where physical destruction was limited, the economic costs of war and insecurity were high. In Mexico, a late colonial economic success, silver exports had fallen by over 80 percent, export agriculture was in disarray, and a once dynamic economy lay in ruins.

The ravages of war, moreover, did not end with independence. In much of the region the departure of European armies was a prelude to new rounds of fighting. Some of these contests were wars of secession, others regional or partisan conflicts that grew out of the politics of the independence era. Too often independence had been secured by a compromise that left underlying conflicts unresolved. In Mexico, royalists became Conservatives and patriots Liberals, but the antagonisms between them remained the same. In Argentina, where independence had come by common consent, its achievement set off a regional struggle over the distribution of its gains—and costs. Throughout Spanish America, centuries of imperial peace were followed by decades of civil war.

With the decapitation of the colonial state, the center could not hold and things fell apart, beginning with the old viceroyalties and ending with the new nations themselves. Brazil, where a Portuguese prince had transformed himself into an American emperor, preserved its unity, but only after suppressing secessionist rebellions. Spanish America was less fortunate. Three hundred years of thin imperial rule combined with considerable local autonomy left Spanish America with little sense of shared nationality. Simon Bolívar might envision Spanish America as one big republic, but it was a profoundly unrealistic dream. In the end, he was unable even to sustain his vision of Gran Colombia, a republic uniting his native Venezuela with neighboring New Granada and Ecuador. Created by the force of Bolívar's will and prestige, it did not survive the Liberator's own premature death in 1830.

The four colonial viceroyalties soon split into eight Spanish American republics, which then broke into twelve unstable states, several of which were soon threatened by further divisions. Even smaller regions with a common colonial past, such as Central America, found the centrifugal pulls of local loyalties too strong to resist. First the Central Americans split from Mexico in 1823 and formed a federation that included the former provinces of the Captaincy General of Guatemala; but even this loose regional union could not survive the test of time, dissolving two decades later into five ministates. A century after the end of Spanish colonial rule, its four viceroyalties had become eighteen sovereign states.

But even those republics that held together were only nominally nations, with little power to command the loyalty of their citizens. The new "sovereign" states were often little more than a loose collection of courts, customs houses, and military units. They had neither the resources nor the power to impose their will on the great landowning families who controlled the provinces and identified the national interest with their own private concerns. In the absence of a king who ruled by divine right, governments lacked legitimacy and their officials authority. Spanish Americans found little reason to obey a president whose office was seldom won by the ballot box and whose election was rarely democratic. Constitutions were written—and rewritten—many of them based on that of the United States, but their guarantees were not worth the paper they were printed on. As a result, civil strife and unstable politics were the order of the day. It was little wonder that at the end of a life devoted to the cause of Spanish American independence, Simon Bolívar had lamented: "America is ungovernable. Those who have served the revolution have ploughed the sea."[21]

In the wake of independence, *caudillos*—strongmen who were often leaders of the landed elite—imposed a personalistic order on fractious societies. Juan Manuel de Rosas was a rancher and entrepreneur before he became dictator of Buenos Aires and master of Argentina from 1835 to 1852.

Chapter 3

The Perils of Progress

Argentina's mestizo gauchos once roamed the open range, living off its wild cattle. During the nineteenth century, landowners like Rosas converted the gauchos into peons on fenced-in ranches stocked with branded cattle, setting the stage for the export boom of 1880–1930.

Immigrants furnished much of the labor
for the export booms of the late nineteenth century, and they came from all
over the world. In Brazil, Japanese
contract laborers often replaced freed
black slaves in the coffee plantations
of São Paulo.

In Argentina, labor for the export economy was largely provided by immigrants from Italy and Spain. Most
settled in Buenos Aires, where they
worked as manual laborers and lived in
conventillos that housed as many as
one thousand slum-dwellers in single
rooms off a central courtyard.

The prosperity of the late nineteenth
century transformed Buenos Aires into
the "Paris of South America" and its
elite into "the oligarchy." This 1904
photograph of the National Race Track
in the upper-class suburb of Palermo
reveals the Argentine elite's Europhile
tastes and pretensions.

3   *The Perils of Progress*

I am a gaucho, and take this from me . . .
I was born as a fish is born
at the bottom of the sea . . .
It is my glory to live as free
as a bird in the sky:
I make no nest on this ground
where there's so much to be suffered,
and no one will follow me
when I take to flight again . . .

In my part of the land, at one time,
I had children, cattle, and a wife;
but my sufferings began,
they pushed me out to the frontier—
and when I got back, what was I to find!
a ruin, and nothing more.
—*José Hernández*, The Gaucho Martín Fierro[1]

*T*he *Gaucho Martín Fierro* is the great epic poem of Argentina's first century as an independent nation. It celebrates the free gaucho, the self-sufficient mestizo cowboy who navigated the great plains of Argentina by instinct and experience, equipped only with his knife and *boleadoras* (a weighted throwing rope), horse and lasso. It tells the story of life on the open range, of simple meals of grilled beef eaten by the light of the camp fire, of macho men facing off with guitars and knives at a rural *pulpería*, a combination bar and general store, settling their disputes by their own rough code.

But *Martín Fierro* is a nostalgic work, written during the 1870s, when the conditions that had made the free gaucho possible—the open range, wild cattle, and the Indian frontier—were fast disappearing, replaced by fenced-in ranches, crossbred livestock, and destroyed Indian communities. The free gauchos had become impoverished peons and the great ranchers cattle barons.

Alongside the Argentine gaucho appeared the Italian immigrant— the gringo "Papolitano" with whom Martín Fierro clashed in Hernández's poem. Yet together, the strength and skill of the Fierros and Papolitanos would make possible the "revolution on the pampas" that would transform Argentina from a primitive ranching economy into a land of modern mixed farming, whose exports of grains and meats, oils and wool, would make it one of the world's wealthiest countries by the 1920s.

This was the Liberal Era (1870–1930), when Latin American elites sloughed off their colonial traditions and embraced European ideas and fashions, including the ideal of progress and the life-style of Paris. In economics, they adopted liberal capitalism as their model and free trade as their gospel, accepting Adam Smith's argument that prosperity was best achieved by each nation specializing in producing those goods in which it had a comparative advantage.

Drawn into the orbit of the world economy by the magnetic attraction of an industrial Europe and United States, the countries of the region focused their efforts on exporting a narrow range of commodities in demand abroad. The products that they specialized in varied with their resources—meat, wool, and grains in Argentina, minerals and oil in Mexico, nitrates and copper in Chile, coffee in Brazil and Colombia, and sugar in Cuba and the Dominican Republic—but the results were similar: an economy oriented toward exports, a dependence on imported manufactures, and an era of economic growth and material "progress," but often at a high social cost.

Other countries in Latin America and the Caribbean also underwent major changes during these decades, but Argentina was the great success story of the Liberal Era. It is also the most dramatic tale of transformation, where the elements that shaped the reinsertion of Latin America into the world economy—political stability and a good investment climate, foreign markets and migrant labor, imports of capital and technology and exports from the region's mines and farms—are particularly clear, as are the tensions caused by the uneven division of its benefits and costs.

The Age of Rosas

The story of Argentina during the century of independent life that began in 1830 is also one of the building of a nation out of the fragments of a colony and the polyglot people who came to inhabit its territory. This is a tale as well of the struggle to define Argentina's identity between two opposed visions of the nation and its future: one stressing the "civilizing" influence of Europe, the other defending a notion of American autonomy. In many ways, the history of Argentina has been shaped by this continuing conflict of changing labels. Some would maintain that it has yet to be resolved, and that Argentina's xenophobic nationalism, yet weak sense of national identity is the result.

The largest country of Spanish America in area, Argentina is one of the few whose territory lies largely within the temperate zone. It is bounded by the high Andes mountains on the west—in whose valleys Indians who had formed part of the Inca empire produced foods and handicrafts for colonial Potosí—and the Atlantic Ocean in the east. But its geography is dominated by the vast pampas, a fertile plain the size of Texas, "a flat land, its horizon a perfect ring of misty blue . . . where the crystal-blue dome of the sky rests on the level green world."[2] For most of the colonial period, the pampas had been the domain of unconquered nomadic Indians. By its close, the land contained more cattle than people, the wild descendants of herds let loose by the early Spanish settlers. By then, these cattle were being slaughtered for their hides, which were in demand in Europe, in *saladeros,* the region's first processing plants, which also turned their tough carcasses into salted beef jerky for the slaves of Cuba and Brazil, and their fat into tallow for candles.

Buenos Aires, the capital of the Viceroyalty of La Plata and strategically situated at the mouth of the Rio de la Plata, prospered as the center of the *saladero* industry and as the chief port for its pastoral exports and the silver of Potosí, importing African slaves and European manufactures in exchange. By 1810, Buenos Aires was a burgeoning city of fifty thousand, and the home of a self-confident creole merchant elite who chafed at the restrictions of the closed colonial commercial system. It prevented direct commerce with England—the world's first industrial nation—the advantages of which had been made clear during the British occupation of the Plata delta in 1806–7. It was no wonder that Buenos Aires became one of the earliest centers of independence in Spanish America, nor that Argentina was the first nation in the region to embrace free trade. Yet, in Argentina, as elsewhere in Latin America, the conquest of independence would prove easier than the consolidation of nationhood, and the affirmation of free trade principles simpler than their application.

In Argentina, though independence had come by general accord, it was followed by half a century of civil war between Federalists and Unitarians. On the surface this was a contest over whether its provinces should be centrally governed, with Unitarians favoring central rule from Buenos Aires, Federalists a looser confederation of its provinces. At bottom, this fratricidal conflict was a struggle over who would reap the economic gains and pay the costs of independence. It pitted the merchants of Buenos Aires and their desire for a monopoly of free trade against interior provinces trying to protect their artisans from the competition of "the thin, showy, and low-priced goods of English manufacture."[3] Adding to these tensions were the weaknesses of postcolonial governments and the rivalries between local political leaders. The result was an instability that sometimes verged on anarchy, and a political vacuum filled by the caudillo, the proverbial Latin American strongman, sometimes the classic "man on horseback," but often a landowner. What these diverse caudillos shared was a disdain for institutions and due process, a personalist view of politics, and an impatience with opposition. In an age without strong parties or a civil service, the caudillo treated the resources of the state as his own, a spoils system that provided the cement for a political stability otherwise conspicuous by its absence.

Between 1829 and 1852 Argentina was dominated by Juan Manuel de Rosas, a man vilified by his enemies as a tyrant but seen by his supporters as saving the country from "anarchy." Rosas combined many of the archetypal caudillo's characteristics. He was a military commander, head of the provincial militia of Buenos Aires, the country's largest province, and a Federalist civil war hero. Rosas was also a leading landowner, who represented the province's ranching elite, mostly urban merchants like his cousins the Anchorenas, who had invested in land after independence, when British merchants began to dominate foreign trade and the silver of Potosí that had represented four-fifths of the exports of Buenos Aires ceased to flow down the Rio de la Plata. But Rosas was also a caudillo with a common touch, who could "outride, outfight, and outcurse" his gaucho followers.

The descendant of ranchers and military officers, Rosas (1793–1877) proved an able heir to both family traditions. He was one of the pioneers of the new ranching economy in the postindependence era, when the first large *estancias*, or ranches, were formed, as well as an adviser to the Anchorenas and the administrator of their ranches. Rosas emerged as a military leader during the civil wars between Federalists and Unitarians that followed independence, his route to political power capped by his being named governor of the province of Buenos Aires in 1829.

Rosas left office in 1833 to an ally and led the army of Buenos Aires in a war against the Indians on the province's southern frontier. He established control over the army and made it a key element in his consolidation of power. He also expelled the Indians from the fertile southern pampas, which were then divided among the great ranchers of Buenos Aires. This expanded the province's occupied lands by more than two fifths and solidified the domination of his rancher allies. Rosas himself received some four hundred thousand acres of prime pastureland and the support of an increasingly powerful ranching elite, which accumulated vast land holdings during this era, including their purchase of lands rented from the state under an earlier scheme. The Anchorenas led the list with over 1.8 million acres of land by the 1840s. By the 1850s, claimed Domingo Sarmiento, a Rosas critic, 825 people owned an area of Argentina the size of England. The Argentine landed "oligarchy" had been formed.

This giant land grab reflected the primitive character of Argentina's ranching economy during the age of Rosas. The *estancias* of the era were not yet fenced in and many of their cattle were still wild. As a result, ranchers needed large numbers of gauchos to round up the herds in daily rodeos (from the Spanish *rodear,* to ride around) and were always short of labor. This put a premium on reducing the free gaucho to an obedient peon, a transformation in which Rosas showed the way. It was an economy with low levels of technology and little incentive for improvements, in which the only way for ranchers to increase their profits was to expand their herds, which in turn required an extension of their landholdings. Rosas himself owned over three hundred thousand head of livestock by 1852, the Anchorenas far more, while in the province of Buenos Aires as a whole, there were more than three million cattle. The Argentine landed elite had become cattle barons. They had also become rural patrons, obeyed by gauchos who had become clients dependent upon their favor, ready to follow their patrons in war as well as peace. It was the gauchos of his ranches who formed Rosas's first troops, and the gaucho cavalry of Buenos Aires remained his most feared regiments during his more than two decades in power.

This expansion of the land, livestock, and military of Buenos Aires also solidified the ascendancy of Rosas nationally, aided by his able manipulation of Argentina's regional politics and personal rivalries. By 1835 he was not only once again governor of Buenos Aires, but also master of all Argentina, leader of a loose alliance of Federalist caudillos who would rule the country for the next sixteen years. As head of this Argentine confederation, Rosas handled its foreign affairs, but each caudillo ruled—or misruled—his own province with an iron hand, as Rosas did Buenos Aires.

As the governor of Buenos Aires, Rosas proved a shrewd but ruthless leader, capable of diplomatic compromises, but intolerant of opposition and unforgiving to his enemies. He decreed that all official documents begin with "Death to the Savage Unitarians!" and made Unitarian blue a dangerous color to wear in Buenos Aires. But Rosas was authoritarian by conviction as well as by personality. He might be a political demagogue, but he was no social revolutionary. On the contrary, Rosas was a conservative elite politician who idealized the social order of the colonial era and set out to impose an order of his own upon the anarchic Argentina of his time. As he explained in 1835:

> *Society was in a state of utter dissolution. Gone was the influence of those men who in every society are destined to take control; the spirit of insubordination had spread and taken widespread roots . . . no one was prepared either to order or to obey. In the countryside there was no security for lives or property. . . . The inevitable time had arrived when it was necessary to exercise personal influence on the masses to reestablish order, security and laws.[4]*

Rosas began on his own ranches, which were known for their obedient work force and efficient estate management, shaped by his detailed instructions to his managers and overseers. His central goal was "subordination," a respect for hierarchy, authority, and private property. For Rosas, the *estancia* was a miniature state—and the state was a ranch writ large.

As governor of Buenos Aires, Rosas demanded—and received—dictatorial powers. He used them to the hilt, dominating the legislature, interfering with the judiciary, and controlling the bureaucracy through a spoils system that rewarded his followers and purged his enemies. Rosas did not delegate authority. Instead he ran the government with a personal hand, down to its details, referring to his cabinet ministers as "my secretaries." He even supervised the Mazorca, his unofficial secret police, led by former security personnel, who terrorized his opponents and organized the cult of personality and displays of popular support that reinforced Rosas's power at moments of crisis. Rosas himself affirmed to a British envoy that he "wields a power more absolute than any monarch on his throne."[5]

Part of this power lay in the support that Rosas evoked among the lower classes, the result of a populist style that was in reality a calculated strategy of social control. "You well know the attitude of the have-nots against the wealthy and the powerful," he told the Uruguayan ambassador in 1829. "I have always considered it very important to acquire an influence over the poor in order to control and direct them; and at great cost in effort, comfort and money, I have made myself into a gaucho like them."[6] In return, they followed Rosas with a fanatical loyalty that sustained him in power for more than two decades, serving as his cavalry in uniforms of Federalist red ponchos. So did the urban poor, including the fifth of Buenos Aires that was black or mulatto, whose ethnic associations Rosas subsidized and whose Candomblé religious rites Rosas permitted and attended. The "Carnival of Rosas" was an unruly lower-class festival that honored the "Restorer of the Laws," while justifying his dictatorship to their social superiors. Even when his power was ending, the poor of Buenos Aires remained loyal to his memory.

It was the Unitarian elite, and especially the lettered Europhile intellectuals such as Domingo Sarmiento and Bartolomé Mitre, who proved Rosas's most enduring challengers. To them, Rosas was not only a murderous political rival, but also a tyrant who stood in the way of progress, which they identified with European ideas and models. To these, Rosas and his supporters opposed their "American system" with its protection of local industries and reflection of Argentine idiosyncracies that justified in their eyes the harsh measures he had taken. Between them was a fundamental debate over the character of Argentina and the shape of its destiny. It is a debate that has continued to this day, with Rosas remaining a storm center of controversy long after he had passed from the stage of history.

Yet, in retrospect, Rosas was a paradoxical figure. He was a leader of the rural lower class who worked for their subordination, and a Federalist caudillo who secured the ascendancy of Buenos Aires. He was a nationalist opponent of British influence, who resisted their intervention, but spent his last twenty-five years in exile as a gentleman farmer in England. He was a fierce enemy of centralized government who prepared the way for its imposition.

In the end, what brought Rosas's long reign to a close in 1852 was not the victory of his Unitarian enemies, although both Mitre and Sarmiento were present at the final battle, but the defection of his most important ally and best general, Justo José de Urquiza, the Federalist governor of Entre Ríos, an upriver province with rich lands and livestock herds. An Anglo-French military intervention of 1845–47 had failed to compel Rosas to open up the Rio de la Plata to free navigation. But it had awakened Urquiza, himself a rancher and entrepreneur, to the possibilities of direct trade with Europe—and aroused his resentment at Rosas's insistence on Buenos Aires's monopoly of foreign commerce. Urquiza formed an alliance with Brazil, which feared Rosas's expanding influence, and won a decisive military victory in 1852.

The fall of Rosas signaled the start of a new era, in which a younger generation of liberal reformers took the lead. The intellectual force within Urquiza's Argentine confederation was Juan Bautista Alberdi, whose dictum *Gobernar es Poblar*—"to govern is to populate"—inspired the promotion of European immigration and the settlement of the interior, along with the opening of the country to free trade and free navigation. During this era, sheepfarming made inroads on cattle ranching, with immigrant Irish shepherds on the cutting edge of change. By 1880, wool would be Argentina's most important export.

Bartolomé Mitre, who defeated Urquiza in 1861 and became president in 1862, continued these policies, while combating provincial caudillos and promoting foreign investment. A decade later the presidency was occupied by Domingo Sarmiento, who had spent the Rosas years in exile, studying public education with Horace Mann in the United States and writing *Facundo: Civilization and Barbary*, which viewed the caudillo, the gaucho, and the Indian as barbaric obstacles to the civilizing influence of Europe. As president, Sarmiento expanded public education, reformed the commercial codes, and established a national telegraph network. But his solution to the "Indian problem" was expulsion and extermination, a policy he justified by reference to the U.S. example. It was completed by Nicolás Avellaneda, his education minister and successor as president in 1876, who used the army to clear the Indians from Patagonia. This "Conquest of the Desert" was led by General Julio Roca, who became president himself in 1880. By then the foundations had been laid for the boom in immigration, investment, and production that would reshape Rosas's Argentina in a modern mold.

New Nations, New World Order

One Sunday morning before mass sometime in the late 1880s, a tall, well-dressed stranger appeared in a northern Italian hill town of the Veneto, the depressed agrarian mainland near Venice. He greeted the ladies politely and took a prominent seat in the church, provoking a flurry of curiosity. After the mass was over, he joined in the ritual promenade around the town square, doffing his top hat to those he passed. Then he sat down in the best café and waited until the curiosity of the young men got the best of them. When they approached he invited them to join him, ordered them a glass of wine, and told his story, pausing ostentatiously to check the local church bells on his own solid gold watch. He came from a village close enough so that they had heard of it, but far enough away so that they would not have any close relatives there. "Once I was just like you," he told them, "a poor peasant without past or future."

"How did you become so prosperous?" they asked. "I went to Argentina," he replied. "It is easy to do. You don't need money, only a willingness to work."

In reality, the elegant stranger was an agent for the steamship line that had been contracted to recruit indentured laborers for the new farming operations on the ranches of the Argentine pampas. Before he left town, he had signed up its young men for the long voyage to Buenos Aires. Only later would they learn they would travel in steerage compartments that were used to transport cattle on the return journey. Once across the ocean, the immigrants had to work off the cost of their passage as agricultural laborers on the estates of the interior before they would be free to *hacer America*—seek their fortunes—in Argentina. Italian immigrants would play a central role in the revolution on the pampas and the transformation of Buenos Aires that together reshaped Argentina during the Liberal Era.

It was the Industrial Revolution in Europe that impelled the dramatic changes in Latin America and the Caribbean that began in the late nine-teenth century. By then an increasingly industrial and urban Europe needed an expanding supply of foods and fibers to feed and clothe its urban workers, and raw materials for its multiplying factories. For Latin America, this represented an unprecedented opportunity. Europe was willing to provide not only the markets for its exports and the merchants to manage the commerce, but also the capital and technology needed to extract and process the resources it desired, as well as to transport them to distant overseas markets—provided the Latin Americans did their part. This en-tailed assuring European capitalists a good investment climate by provid-ing political stability, sound finances, a modern commercial code, and free trade.

In the aftermath of independence, when powerful landed elites had other priorities, similar European demands had fallen on deaf Latin Ameri-can ears. But now the wealth to be won from integrating into the world market was too great to resist. The building of railway lines would not only make marginal lands viable and farming possible. It would also multiply the value of the vast landholdings that elites like the Anchorenas had ac-cumulated during the preceding decades. A rancher could become fabu-lously wealthy overnight. It was an offer that even an Anchorena could not refuse.

By comparison, the elite feuds that had sustained civil strife now seemed less compelling. During the final decades of the nineteenth cen-tury, in country after country, warring elites patched up their quarrels and came together to provide the political peace that European investors and bankers required. In Argentina, after 1862, Bartolomé Mitre used the re-sources of the national treasury to reconcile provincial governments to their loss of autonomy and Federalists to the defeat of their cause. During the years that followed, the partisan politics that had fueled decades of civil war gradually disappeared. By 1880, both Unitarians and Federalists had passed from the Argentine political scene, replaced by a single elite party, the National Autonomous Party (PAN), which ran an oligarchic "democ-racy" with an iron fist in a velvet glove for the next thirty-five years.

In other countries, peace was imposed by military strongmen of more modest origins. Mexico, where civil strife had meant fifty governments in fifty years, now experienced thirty-five years of stable, if authoritarian, rule under the mestizo General Porfirio Díaz, whose motto—"A little politics and a lot of administration"—was endorsed by many rulers of the age, along with his elite advisers' ideology of "order and progress."

Throughout the region, elites set aside their differences, strengthened the state, and used it to promote immigration and control restive populations. They assured foreign investors the political stability and good investment climate they sought, reformed legal codes, and guaranteed loans. They banned unions, suppressed strikes, and limited the political participation of peasants and workers. They invested in land and mines, and they opened their countries to foreign capital and enterprise.

In return, Latin America and the Caribbean received ten billion dollars in foreign investment between 1870 and 1919. The lion's share came from Great Britain, but France and Germany accounted for substantial amounts and U.S. investments predominated in Mexico and Cuba after 1900. During the age of the "New Imperialism" in Asia and Africa, Argentina received more British capital than India. In 1889, half of English investment overseas went to Argentina. Most of these British capital exports were in the form of government loans or ventures that enjoyed guaranteed profits, such as railways or utilities, but large sums were also invested in banking and mining, and in plants for processing the raw materials of Latin America for export to Europe. British capital flowed not only to ventures whose promised profit rates seemed worth the risk, but also to areas with resources that were in demand in Europe, and to investments that would tie the producing areas of Latin America and the Caribbean to the global industrial economy centered on London and Lancashire.

In Argentina and nearby Uruguay, the key role in linking British capital and technology to American resources was played by "old River Plate hands" like George Drabble, who knew the region's productive potential. Drabble had begun as an importer of his family's Manchester cottons during the Rosas era, and then branched out into ranching and estate management in the 1850s. He became involved in railways and banking in the 1860s, tramways in the 1870s, and meat packing in the 1880s, heading some of the most important and profitable British enterprises in Argentina. Knowledgable entrepreneurs like Drabble still played a major role in the 1880s boom in Argentine investments, but increasingly it was the big investment bankers like Baring Brothers and Rothschilds who brought out the new issues of stocks and bonds until the international economic crisis of 1890 called a temporary halt to British capital flows. By then it was clear that a new era had begun in Argentina.

During the second half of the nineteenth century, the advance of technology brought Latin America and the Caribbean dramatically closer to Europe, speeding the transfer of goods, people, and ideas. In 1851 the first steamship line cut the sailing time between Buenos Aires and London from two months to five weeks. Twenty-three years later, the first undersea telegraph cable was laid between Brazil and Europe, bringing the latest news and fashions to South America at the speed of sound.

Equally important was the introduction of technologies that decreased the distances within the countries of the region. The most important was the railroad, which had already transformed both Europe and North America by 1860, when the railway age began in Latin America. Between 1860 and 1914, the advance of railway lines in the region was dramatic. Argentina led the way, laying its first track in 1857 and completing its first line, the Central Argentine, across the pampas in 1870. More than twenty-two thousand miles of railroad had been built by 1915, giving Argentina more track per capita than the United States. These lines were constructed by British companies, who sold the land along the track to ranchers and farmers. Wealthy Argentines were willing to invest in the land but reluctant to risk their capital on the iron roads that linked them to the coast. As a result, the nation's internal transport system was British-owned, an outrage to later generations of nationalists. Drabble himself bought the Argentine government's controlling share of the Central Argentine and headed other lines that traversed the southern and northern pampas. The railway lines radiated into the pampas like spokes on a wheel from the port and processing plants of Buenos Aires, the hub of a rapidly expanding commerce that exchanged Argentine wool, meat, hides, and grains for the best manufactures that Europe had to offer, integrating the pampas into the world economy.

The railroad was a key link in the transportation chain, but it was not the only technological innovation required. Equally important to the future of Argentina was the invention and application of meat processing techniques that could preserve the abundant beef and lamb of the pampas for the European dinner table. The first step was the creation in 1865 of commercial beef extract, an enterprise that involved a German engineer and Belgian merchants, British capital and Uruguayan cattle, which together transformed the discovery of Baron Justus von Liebig, the father of biochemistry, into a successful export industry: the bouillon cube. Canning, using a pressure process and vacuum tins, came to the region in 1871, although its debut was not auspicious. The meat decomposed and the sound of the exploding cans was heard for miles around, giving rise to rumors of yet another Latin American revolution.

In the end, it was refrigeration, perfected by French engineers during the following decade, that would enable South American meat to be transported across the Atlantic as the steaks, chops, and roasts that could enjoy an expanding market in Europe. In 1882, George Drabble founded The River Plate Fresh Meat Company to export frozen carcasses to Britain. The age of refrigerated meat was just around the corner.

The issue was whether the ranchers of Argentina would be ready for it when it arrived. The problem lay in the native livestock, noted for tough hides and ample fleece, not tender meat. Transforming these stringy steers and sheep into steaks and roasts of European quality required crossbreeding with imported bulls and rams, and new methods of rearing and feeding livestock. For ranchers accustomed to doing little more than allowing their animals out to feed on the rich grasslands of the open range, the investments and adjustments this implied were difficult to accept. The rural association formed in 1866 had promoted crossbreeding as the key to the future of ranching, and the Anchorenas had invested ten million pesos in barbed wire fencing in the 1870s. But it was not until the freezing plants offered a 50 percent premium for improved animals in the 1880s that most ranchers became convinced that such investments were justified. During the final years of the nineteenth century, the Shorthorn steer and Lincoln sheep, together with wire fencing, branding, and feedlots, began transforming the livestock of La Plata into the animals that would dominate the British meat market in the twentieth century—and make beef Argentina's leading export and the pampas a land of modern ranches.

But modern ranching was only one part of the revolution on the pampas that European capital, technology, markets, and immigrants spurred during the late nineteenth century. Railways also made possible the rapid expansion of grain exports, cutting transport costs and rendering agriculture profitable. The result was an epochal shift from ranching to mixed farming, in which the acreage planted increased, the number of farmers multiplied, and production and exports boomed. In 1870 fewer than one million acres of the pampas were cultivated and agricultural exports were unimportant in Argentina's trade balance. By 1900 more than ten million acres were planted, and agriculture accounted for half of Argentina's exports earnings.

Most of this wheat, corn, and flax was grown by tenant farmers, generally Italian immigrants like the Veneto contract laborers, who were brought in by ranchers to break up the hard sod, farm a five-hundred-acre plot for three to five years, and leave it planted with grain and the alfalfa needed to feed the rancher's newly refined livestock. It was a sharecropping arrangement that gave the landowner most of the harvest and all of the improvements made by his tenants.

This was an inexpensive and effortless way for the rancher to improve his land, increase its value, and prepare for the new ranching economy, while creating a hedge against low wool and cattle prices. From all this effort of others, he was the great gainer. This was also the method by which Argentina became one of the world's major grain exporters, rivaling the United States by 1914, and diversified its agro-export economy, the base of its growing wealth and power.

The physical and social landscape of Argentina was also transformed. Railways now bisected its vast plains and fences divided them. Agriculture now complemented ranching on the fertile pampas. The primitive *estancia,* with its open range and wild cattle, gave way to the modern estate, with wire fencing, imported breeding stock, and fields of grain. The transformation of the free gaucho into a dependent peon, begun in the age of Rosas, was completed in the era of Roca, who put an end to the Indian frontier with Remington rifles and railroads.

Argentina's ranching elite also took on a different appearance. In the early nineteenth century, European observers were surprised to find that even owners of large ranches lived simply, in brick houses free of adornments, sometimes receiving startled foreigners on furniture made of cattle bones and skins. By the century's close, a visitor to a large ranch was more likely to be received in an elegant French château or an English country house, and served afternoon tea on fine china. The paternalistic patron had become a rural capitalist, more concerned with the bottom line than with the welfare of his gauchos, whose numbers had shrunk with the introduction of wire fencing. The "prince of the pampas" had become a cattle baron, who lived in his French town house in Buenos Aires, was well known in the gilded circles of Madrid, and paid only occasional visits to his ranches; he left it to others to supervise the native-born peons and immigrant sharecroppers who produced the wealth that supported his extravagant life-style. In their own eyes the cattle barons were cultivated aristocrats, equally at home in Europe and America, in the salon and the stable. To the displaced gaucho and impoverished worker, though, they were the "oligarchy," a name that has stuck to the Argentine elite ever since.

For the Italian immigrants, however, sharecropping was a way to work off their passage and get a start in their new promised land. Word that Argentina was the land of opportunity was first brought back to Italy by *golondrinas,* the world's longest distance migrant laborers, named after the swallows, those other birds of transoceanic passage. Taking advantage of the difference in seasons between the northern and southern hemispheres, they would come to Argentina to harvest the maize and wheat of the endless pampas and then return to Italy in time to reap the crops there. They came home with tales of the rich land across the southern sea, where wages were higher and food was cheaper. Eventually, some stayed in Argentina, from where they sent word back to their friends and relatives to join them, creating networks of information and mutual assistance that stretched across the ocean and encouraged the young and adventurous to risk the journey. Recruiting agents, contract labor, and subsidized passages also helped promote the massive European immigration of 1870–1930.

Latin America and the Caribbean received seven to nine million transatlantic immigrants, with Argentina their favorite destination. Immigrants arrived in Argentina from all over Europe, including Irish shepherds and Spanish shopkeepers, Jewish artisans and Arab vendors, but most came from Italy. During the 1880s alone, 640,000 immigrants passed through the port of Buenos Aires. Between 1880 and 1930 the country had to absorb 2.5-million immigrants, in addition to the 50,000 to 100,000 *golondrinas* per year. The implications for Argentina were dramatic. Argentina ranked first in the world in the proportion of immigrants in its population during these formative years. As a percentage of its inhabitants this was double what the United States had to assimilate during that era of mass immigration.

Argentina, moreover, was not the United States. The indentured immigrants might be free to seek land of their own after several years as sharecroppers on an isolated pampas estate, but there was no Homestead Act until 1884, and by then the good pampas lands had been appropriated by the great ranchers. In the Littoral region, upriver from Buenos Aires, where land was cheaper, some European immigrants were able to purchase fertile farms and establish agricultural colonies that helped place grains and oils among Argentina's leading exports. But they were the exceptions that proved the rule. Few immigrants were able to acquire the land they sought, although some stuck it out in sod huts on dirt-poor farms. Most of the Italian peasants who emigrated to Argentina in search of land of their own spent some time as tenant farmers and then drifted back to Buenos Aires, where they could find work as unskilled laborers and the fellowship of Italian immigrants like themselves.

As a result, despite its agricultural boom, Argentina never developed into a country of family farmers. Rural towns remained small and undeveloped, country roads unpaved. Argentina, with its vast fertile plains, became the most urbanized of Latin American societies—and Buenos Aires, its capital, became the home of one third of its people.

The Paris of South America

At the turn of the century Buenos Aires was a city of foreigners. Its population, only 180,000 in 1870, increased tenfold during the six decades that followed, fed by the record flow of European immigrants. By 1890 most of its residents were foreign-born and three out of four workers were immigrants. Much of the city seemed more Italian than Argentine, with a diet of pasta, bread, and vegetables that set them apart from the carnivorous Argentines. It was also an overwhelmingly white population, a dramatic change from the Buenos Aires of 1810, in which four out of five people were of African or Indian descent. The overgrown village of 1870 became the continent's first metropolis. Towns became suburbs and suburbs neighborhoods. Streets were paved and engraved with tramway rails, underlain by sewers and illuminated by electricity.

The social geography of Buenos Aires was also altered in the process. White-collar and skilled workers followed the new tramway lines out into the countryside, looking for an affordable plot of land where they could build or rent their own tiny two- or three-room house, a step up from the tenements *(conventillos)* of their parents. Gradually, the artificial new towns created by the real estate developers evolved into working-class neighborhoods, the barrios celebrated in the tangos of the era.

The changes in the city center were equally extensive. Beginning in the boom years of the 1880s, a confident Europhile elite set out to make Buenos Aires the "Paris of South America." Diagonal avenues cut through the narrow streets of the old Spanish city on the model of Haussman's plan for the Paris of Napoleon III. Broad boulevards lined with trees, cafés, and restaurants were built to connect enlarged squares. The wide Ninth of July Avenue became the Champs Elysées of America, only bigger and bolder than the European original.

Patrician and pauper often lived within blocks of each other in a downtown area that revolved around the Plaza de Mayo, with its pink presidential palace—the Casa Rosada—and its neoclassic colonial cathedral, but their living standards and life-styles differed dramatically. In the emerging Barrio Norte that stretched from the Plaza San Martín in the city center to the cemetery of La Recoleta, where the elite patriarchs of the past were buried under ornate family monuments, a new oligarchic life-style took shape. Ostentatious "palaces" in the fashionable Beaux Arts style replaced stolid Spanish-style houses with their dull façades and cloistered patios. The social life of the Argentine elite mirrored their architectural pretensions.

Tea was now taken English style late in the afternoon, pushing the dinner hour toward today's midnight fashion. The Spanish *tertulia*, with its conversations about literature and philosophy, became an evening salon, with French the language of choice and the latest European fashions the favorite topic. When the Guerricos, leaders of high society, celebrated their golden anniversary in 1906 in their *palacio* on the Plaza San Martín, the twelve hundred invited guests dined in the garden, which hundreds of workmen had converted into a giant salon for the occasion, on a meal that began with woodcocks stuffed with foie gras and chestnuts and ended with the obligatory Moët & Chandon champagne.

The life-styles of the poor bore little resemblance to those of the wealthy. Where a one-family Barrio Norte mansion might fill an entire city block, one thousand Arab immigrants were crowded into tenements that occupied a comparable space a few blocks away. On the south side of the Plaza de Mayo was another Buenos Aires, which stretched to the port of La Boca, its streets teeming with stevedores, sailors, and prostitutes. This other Buenos Aires was a polyglot working-class area of decaying houses that had been subdivided into seven to eight single-room apartments, each occupied by a family or group of bachelors, who shared a patio, with its grill and latrine. Roughly a third of the population of Buenos Aires lived in such crowded and unhealthy conditions in 1910, and another third in the tiny houses of more established workers that afforded greater privacy but little more space. Frequently six to twelve people lived, slept, and worked

in a twelve-by-twelve-foot room, where women and children supple-
mented inadequate family incomes by sewing buttons or other home work.
It was no wonder that workers escaped these crowded tenements as soon
as they could afford better housing and an improved living standard.
Buenos Aires might be a paradise for the rich, but it was a purgatory for
the poor.

Other Argentinas

The unequal distribution of Argentina's prosperity evident in Buenos Aires
was even clearer in its interior provinces. The benefits of Argentina's
export boom were not only distributed unevenly among its classes, they
were shared unevenly among its provinces. There was another Argentina
in the interior, which felt excluded from its fair share of the "progress" that
was so conspicuously on display in Buenos Aires. Here the dominant
physical feature was not the endless pampas, but the soaring Andes and the
arid valleys whose lands are watered by its melting snows. During the
colonial era, the region had prospered supplying the mines of nearby
Potosí with food, mules, and handicrafts. Its decline in the late colonial era
paralleled that of Potosí, compounded by Bourbon Reforms that replaced
the wines and oils of Mendoza with those of Spain in the markets of Buenos
Aires, and the introduction of smuggled English textiles that were cheaper
and lighter than the woven goods of Córdoba. Independence and free trade
had completed the decay of the interior, which recovered slowly from the
ravages of civil war and lacked the fertile plains and easy access to the sea
that made Buenos Aires and the Littoral region targets of European investment and immigration. It had more in common with the Indian and mestizo
Andean nations to the north than with the rest of Argentina.

　　The elite politicians who controlled Argentina after 1870 were aware
of this disparity in development and the political problems it caused:
Sarmiento, Avellaneda, Roca, and Juárez Celman all came from the interior. They had pushed for the railroads that connected the interior with the
coast, in part to impose political order and discourage rebellion, in part to

integrate the interior into the nation by encouraging the development of local industries such as sugar.

Tucumán was the center of this other Argentina, and it was the centerpiece in development plans for the interior. Its tanning and cart-building industries had fallen on hard times by 1880. The arrival of the railroad in 1876 promoted the expansion of a sugar industry for Argentine consumption that was consolidated by the tariff protection promoted by Avellaneda and Roca, both natives of Tucumán. But within the region, the benefits of sugar production were as unevenly distributed as the export boom was in the nation. Other Andean provinces remained economically stagnant areas of subsistence farming, whose youth migrated to Tucumán for work. Within Tucumán sugar produced a small number of millionaires, but most of the seventy thousand people the industry employed were poor mestizos or Indians, whose low wages were paid in scrip redeemable only at the plantation store. As a result, during the twentieth century the Andean provinces would export more people than products to the rest of Argentina, and Tucumán would remain a province whose social and political tensions simmered just below its sugared surface. Sugar also created an economy dependent upon a single product whose cycles of boom and bust reflected those of the nation at large.

Argentina's export-oriented economy was also vulnerable to foreign events and decisions beyond even its elites' control. Its ups and downs had long followed the business cycles of European capitalism. A financial crack in London in 1865 had produced one Argentine economic crisis, the Panic of 1873 another. But the boom of the 1880s was unprecedented and Argentina's export elites acted as if it would go on forever, speculating in land and real estate, flaunting a life-style of extravagant luxury and multiplying their nation's public and private debt in the process. When inflation at home and recession abroad warned of a rougher economic road ahead, the elite used their political power to protect their own hard currency export earnings, while the rest of the nation was paid in paper pesos that depreciated with the country's accelerating inflation. Increasingly, the boom in Buenos Aires depended upon foreign credit, which in turn reflected British confidence in the prospects of Argentine exports and the profitability of English investments there. When Europe's downturn dampened international trade and a stock market scandal cast a pall over Argentine investments, British capital ceased to flow across the South Atlantic and the "boom of the '80s" turned into "the crisis of the '90s." In England, the resultant Baring Crisis bankrupted one of London's most powerful investment bankers and nearly brought down the Bank of England. In Argentina it brought down the government and nearly resulted in a revolution.

Since 1880, Argentina's elite had ruled the country through an oligarchic "democracy," complete with a president and congress in which decisions were made by the elite and imposed from above by a combination of force, fraud, and manipulation. But as the crisis intensified, along with inflation and unemployment, disgruntled army officers and dissident oligarchs came together with a discontented middle class to form the Civic Union reform movement. They demanded a more democratic political system, with honest elections and universal suffrage, and took to the streets to press their point. In the face of this threat, the elites patched up their differences, defeated the rebellion, and retained their monopoly of power. Still, as one senator put it: "The Revolution is beaten . . . but the government is dead."[7]

Out of the defeated "rebellion" of 1890, moreover, emerged the Radical party, which refused to participate in electoral politics until its demand for universal suffrage was granted. Its abstention and periodic failed attempts to take power by force kept Argentine politics on edge during the two decades that followed. The Radicals also organized an urban political machine that presaged the arrival of a mass politics that reflected the complex changes in Argentine society brought about by immigration and economic growth, one in which the middle class was a growing presence. So were urban workers, and by the turn of the century their growing organization and militancy had replaced the threat of Radical party rebellion as the elite's chief cause of concern. In the new century, this "social question" would reshape the politics of Argentina.

Anarchy or Reform?

By 1900, the economic crisis was over and prosperity was restored, but the social crisis had just begun. The unequal distribution of the profits of the pampas, so visible in Buenos Aires, lent credence to the critiques of capitalism by anarchism and socialism, ideologies which the immigrants brought with them from Europe. The more moderate Socialists, who had split off from the Radicals to form their own left-wing party, had considerable support among the more educated workers. But it was the anarchists, with their communitarian vision of class struggle, who won the strongest support among the immigrant workers of Buenos Aires, few of whom were eligible to vote. The combative mass meetings and strikes that they organized during the first years of the new century alarmed the Argentine elite, who tried repression, deportation, and cooptation, but without much success.

Juana Rouco Buela, who emigrated from Spain as a child and became an anarchist in Buenos Aires as a teenager, was a good example of the anarchists' appeal and persistence. In 1907 she helped organize a remarkable rent strike in Buenos Aires, where the cost of lodging had tripled in real terms since 1870, sharply reducing the value of the seemingly high wages that had lured immigrants across the sea. Their growing anger at high rents and crowded conditions boiled over in a tenants' strike that spread through the working-class barrios of the capital, involving 120,000 people and violent demonstrations that the anarchists fanned and the police repressed. In its aftermath Juana was deported to Uruguay along with other suspected anarchists, but she soon returned to Buenos Aires disguised as a widow, her face hidden by a black veil. She went on to found the seamstresses' union and an anarchist newspaper.

The growing social tensions in Buenos Aires came to a head in May 1910, the centennial of Argentine independence, which the elite intended as a celebration of their stewardship and their country's progress. For the anarchists, the centennial was an equally symbolic occasion, but one that called for protests to unmask the "bourgeois" character of this "progress."

The result was a violent clash between anarchist demonstrators and the police, against a backdrop of patriotic indignation which united the growing middle class with the elite that had excluded them from political power. In Argentina, as elsewhere in the region, the export economy expanded the middle ranks of society—professionals, managers, bureaucrats, shopkeepers—many of whom favored political reform, but few of whom wanted social revolution, and most of whom aspired to join the elite, not overthrow it. In 1910, the anarchists lost the battle in the streets of Buenos Aires, but their show of strength sent a shiver up the spine of the oligarchy and established the working class as a potentially powerful political force.

During the crisis of 1890 President Miguel Juárez Celman had rejected the demand for universal suffrage, calling it "the triumph of universal ignorance." His fellow oligarchs had sustained that view in the face of two decades of Radical party rebellion and electoral abstention. But with the emergence of the "social question," a majority of the elite changed its mind—and its political tune. In 1910 they chose as president Roque Sáenz Peña, whose program of electoral reform was intended to avert a social revolution by coopting both the middle class and workers. In 1912, the Sáenz Peña law brought universal male suffrage to Argentina. At the time, its effects were limited by the large number of unnaturalized immigrants, as well as by its exclusion of women. But the expansion of the electorate to include one out of four adults brought the victory of the middle class and its political expression, the Radical party. In 1916, Hipólito Yrigoyen, the longtime Radical leader, triumphed in the country's first competitive presidential election. A shaken elite hesitated, but then accepted his narrow victory—and their unprecedented political defeat.

The Argentine oligarchy need not have worried about the Radicals. They proved less of a threat to the status quo in power than in opposition. The Radicals exacted a larger share of the political pie for their middle-class constituents, but they did not challenge the agro-export economy that financed their political patronage or the elite's role in owning and running it. Moreover, despite their populist rhetoric and initial support, the Radicals responded to working-class militancy with a repression that differed little from the oligarchic governments of the past—as the "Tragic Week" of 1919 would demonstrate.

That year witnessed a time of troubles around the globe. Euphoria over the end of the First World War had faded in the face of economic recession, and social tensions had given rise to widespread political unrest in both Europe and America. In Chile, socialist leaders filled the streets of Santiago with hundreds of thousands of demonstrators protesting rising prices and unemployment. Across the Andes in Argentina, economic conditions were equally difficult. The remaining anarchists and their syndicalist allies, who believed in the general strike as a revolutionary weapon, were determined to take advantage of the opportunity.

"It started here in an iron foundry, the British-owned Vasena metalworks, which was a real hell, the conditions were so terrible," recalled the ninety-three-year-old Humberto Correale, in his younger days a silver-tongued anarchist leader in the port of Buenos Aires. The metallurgical industry had suffered from rising costs during World War I and its workers from deteriorating real wages. By the end of 1918 their situation was desperate. "So when we began to talk with the people at the entrance to the plant about how they had to raise their salaries, which were not enough to live on, and to improve their working conditions and reduce their working hours, they were all with us. By conversing with the people, we got them to go on strike."

The metalworkers' strike soon escalated into a major social and political confrontation. "When they went on strike, this set off a chain reaction of repression," Correale explained. After a policeman died in a clash with strikers, the police responded with an ambush in which five bystanders—"innocent people"—were killed. "So the workers movement and the FORA [the anarchist federation] responded with a general strike. That is how the Tragic Week started," Correale said. "It was almost a revolution!"

That perception on both sides of the conflict underlay the events that followed. Some of Correale's comrades believed that the moment had come for the great general strike that would destroy the "bourgeois state" and usher in the revolution of their dreams. On the other side, fears of "anarchy" and "revolution" were intensified by the Russian revolution and rumors of "Bolshevik conspiracies."

The Yrigoyen government had been sympathetic to earlier efforts at labor organization, in part as a strategy to win worker political support, but in 1919 it was persuaded by the armed forces, foreign companies, and Argentine elites to take a firm stand against this threat from below. When the funeral for the workers killed in the police ambush turned into a vengeful riot in which tramcars were overturned, a church was burned, and the British directors of Vasena were besieged within the struck metalworks by an angry crowd, the British envoy protested to Yrigoyen, who authorized military action. The result was the Tragic Week, in which armed police roamed the streets in fire trucks, shooting anyone they saw, as panic spread and the general strike brought Buenos Aires to a halt. The police were joined by the paramilitary forces of the rightist Argentine Patriotic League, who combined anti-Semitism with anticommunism and turned a witchhunt into a pogrom. They invaded Jewish neighborhoods shouting, "Death to the Russians," and dragged terrified immigrants from their homes. Before the violence ended hundreds had been killed, including many innocent bystanders and Russian Jews merely suspected of being "Bolsheviks."

The Tragic Week was a moment of truth for all concerned. The anarchists and syndicalists never recovered from their defeat and the persecution that followed. When labor organizations revived during the following decade, they were weaker and more moderate, and led by Socialists and Communists. For the Radicals, it meant an end to their plans for reform. Faced with a resurgent Right and menacing armed forces, Yrigoyen focused on a partisan populism that expanded the state bureaucracy and catered to his middle-class clientele. For the oligarchy, 1919 confirmed that the Radicals were less radical than their rhetoric and that they could be relied upon to oppose the working-class threat from below, leaving the elite to manage the agro-export economy.

A Return to Normalcy?

During the mostly prosperous decade that followed, this division of labor brought benefits to all concerned. The Radicals enjoyed the spoils of power, the agro-export elites profited from a period of unequaled prosperity, and workers found more jobs at higher wages. It was the roaring twenties, when the global capitalist economy recovered from its postwar doldrums to shine brighter than ever before.

As always, Argentina's prosperity reflected Europe's. Demand for its grains, fibers, and meat reached new heights. In 1925 Argentina accounted for half the world's meat exports, two thirds of its maize trade, and three quarters of its flax. The grain was visible on the docks of La Boca and in the warehouses of nearby Barrancas. Across the fetid Riachuelo canal, pungent odors announced the slaughterhouses and tanning factories of Avellaneda. But to comprehend the scale of the agro-export economy it was necessary to visit the great cattle market at Liniers, the world's largest, where seventy thousand animals were sold each day, or to travel by rail to Berisso, some forty miles to the southeast. There, U.S. companies had established huge *frigoríficos* that butchered, froze, canned, and shipped Argentine beef for the British meat market.

In its heyday during the 1920s more than ten thousand workers labored in the slaughterhouses and freezing chambers of the huge Swift *frigorífico* in Berisso, with almost as many working in the Armour plant a few miles away. Together they formed one of the largest concentrations of urban workers in early-twentieth-century Latin America. One of these workers was Oreste Sola, an Italian immigrant who described the Swift plant in a letter to his parents in Italy:

It's a gigantic factory . . . on an average 3,000 animals daily are put to sacrifice. . . . They begin slaughtering at 4 A.M., and by 8 P.M. everything is already canned or in frozen quarters. The bones, separated and carefully cleaned, are divided into sections. The remainder is processed, put into sacks, or packaged like fertilizer, and the blood gets the same treatment. The skins are cleaned, salted, and prepared for tanning. It's really an example of the North American system.[8]

The work was hard and demanding, in squalid conditions similar to those described in *The Jungle,* Upton Sinclair's exposé of the Chicago stockyards where Swift and Armour developed their industrial model. The hours were long, the wages low, the discipline tough, and the unions weak after the defeat of the long and bitter strike of 1917, which was repressed by the navy. But for those skilled workers with a steady job, it was a ladder to social mobility.

This was particularly true during the twenties, when Berisso workers made enough to be able to buy a tiny lot and a house. They were houses of corrugated-metal sheets, hot in summer, cold in winter, whose layers of bright pastel paint could not conceal their poor quality, but to the workers they were homes of their own, unlike the *conventillos* of Buenos Aires. They were concentrated in residential barrios, where workers found their friends and wives. Nearby were commercial avenues with cafés and bars and the ethnic clubs around which the social life of Berisso revolved—Croat, Italian, Arab, Lithuanian—reflections of the polyglot mix of immigrants who crossed the Atlantic to seek their fortunes in Argentina, and provided strong arms and backs for its new export industries. It was in these clubs that recent immigrants found the support that helped them cope with their new work and home. Here, too, they found the fellowship of friends who spoke their language and shared their culture. Yet, by the 1920s, many had children who were Argentines, and the music to which they danced was not the polka, but the tango.

By then the tango had replaced beef as Argentina's best-known export. The origins of the tango were as international as the city that had created it. Born at the turn of the century in the working-class barrios of Buenos Aires, with their mix of immigrants and Argentines, its music fused the *milonga* of the pampas with the *habanera* of Cuba, and combined the Spanish guitar with the Italian violin and the German accordion known as the *bandoneon.* Its lyrics interspersed *lunfardo,* the Italian slang of La Boca, with Argentine Spanish. Its greatest singer was born in France. Its sinuous and intricate dance, with its unashamed sexuality, owed much to the traditions of the city's blacks and mulattos.

By 1910, the tango had become a fixture both in the bars of La Boca and in the dance halls of the city center where young men of all classes went for excitement and entertainment. Argentina's elite considered the tango—that "reptile from the brothel"—lower class and disreputable—until it took Paris by storm in the years before World War I. Argentine tango bands alternated with American jazz bands in the clubs and dance halls of Montmartre. Although Europeans ignored the urban character of the tango and insisted on seeing in it "the melancholy of the pampas," they embraced Argentina's contribution to global popular culture with unfeigned enthusiasm.

"Tangomania" had swept over Europe by 1913. Paris was renamed "Tangoville" by one wit, and "tango teas" and "tango dinners" were all the rage. The pope condemned the tango as immoral, and the emperor of Germany forbade his soldiers to dance it in uniform, but this only seemed to add to its attraction. The musical hybrid that had been born in the barrios and brothels of Buenos Aires had become the world's first Latin dance craze.

The tango age survived World War I, and in the return to normalcy that followed, the whole world seemed to glide across the floor to the sensuous rhythms of Buenos Aires, from Rudolph Valentino on the silent screen to lovers in dance halls from New York to Tokyo. In Argentina itself, even the oligarchy now succumbed to its seductions, led by the aristocratic president, Marcelo T. Alvear. The *compadrito*, the slick but sentimental barrio tough with his tight-fitting suit and ready knife, his blend of mestizo macho and Italian lover, took his place next to the gaucho as an Argentine archetype. By the 1920s the tango had become equated with the quintessentially Argentine, and a divided nation had found its cultural synthesis, the musical key to its elusive national identity.

By then, the tango had also acquired its characteristic voice, the legendary Carlos Gardel, whose expressive baritone and evocative lyrics defined the tango for all time. With his pomaded hair, trademark smile, and eternal cigarette, Gardel incarnated the urban ideal of a self-confident Argentina. He was also its first pop idol, Argentina's gift to this century's popular music, who was applauded in Madrid and Montevideo, New York and Paris.

Argentine cattle barons were equally familiar figures in the high society of Paris—which they had begun to refer to as "a little Buenos Aires." So struck were the Parisians by the wealth of the Argentine playboys who spent the proceeds of the pampas in their casinos and dance halls, that "as rich as an Argentine" became a popular expression.

While the boom lasted, the international economy worked like magic. All an Argentine landowner had to do was pasture his cattle and sheep on the rich grasses and alfalfa of the pampas, and send them off to feedlots to be fattened for the British meat market. In return came the best that money could buy—English tweeds, French champagnes, Italian automobiles. "Argentina became rich almost by accident . . . not through effort," said Torcuato Di Tella, Jr., son of an Italian immigrant of that era who found his fortune in Argentina.

But its riches were still unevenly distributed. Poverty persisted in the Buenos Aires barrios the tango celebrated and many Andean provinces felt left out of the celebration altogether. Moreover, the Radical party, which had come to power with a promise of democracy, good government, and social welfare, had proved as autocratic and corrupt as its elite predecessors and no more willing to defend popular interests.

The Argentina of the roaring twenties, however, was an optimistic era. The children of immigrants born in poverty, who had worked their way out of the *conventillos* to their own little houses in a suburban barrio, could be forgiven the assumption that their children would live better than they, and would find in Argentina the American dream that had motivated yet eluded their parents. It was not surprising, therefore, that social protests remained muted, and that the Radicals were forgiven their political and social sins by the voting public, who returned the aging Yrigoyen to the presidency with a landslide victory in 1928. A year later, Wall Street crashed, setting off a chain of events that would lead to the Great Depression of the 1930s, in which international trade shrank and Latin American exports plummeted.

During the Liberal Era most of Latin America and the Caribbean shared Argentina's export orientation, and much of the region also enjoyed periods of growth and prosperity, which enriched local elites and justified their rule. But these were dependent economies, vulnerable to downturns in foreign demand for the products of their mines and fields. They had felt intimations of the system's mortality in earlier crises, but they were unprepared for the Great Depression. By 1930 it was clear that the gilded age was at an end, and a far harsher age of iron was at hand.

Immigrant entrepreneurs like Argentina's Torcuato Di Tella often led the way in the new import-substituting industries that developed after the collapse of international trade in the Depression of the 1930s.

Chapter 4

A Second Independence?

Populist leaders like Argentina's Juan Domingo Perón and his actress wife, Evita, held together coalitions that included both business and labor in support of nationalistic industrial and social welfare policies by the force of their personalities and the distribution of material benefits.

Peronism also exemplified the new mass politics of the postwar era. On October 17, 1945, a massive demonstration by workers in the heart of Buenos Aires saved Perón from prison and launched his presidential campaign. Three years later half a million supporters jammed the Plaza de Mayo to commemorate the occasion.

4   *A Second Independence?*

*I*t was 1968 and Uruguay was on the verge of its gravest crisis in four decades. The old man driving the taxi said mournfully: "Señor, you have arrived at a bad time."

"When would have been a good time to have arrived?" I asked.

His voice grew more animated: "Nineteen twenty-eight—now *that* was a good year!"

He was right. For Uruguay, Argentina, and a host of other Latin American countries that had bet their futures on the continued prosperity of the global economy, 1928 was the last golden year. In 1929, boom turned into bust on Wall Street and the downward spiral of international trade and Latin American production followed. Although prosperity would eventually reemerge, the blithe confidence of Latin Americans in the liberal economic model, with its stress on exports, free trade, and comparative advantage—and the elites who led them to depend on it—was never fully restored. The trauma of the Great Depression lingered for decades, coloring the worldview and politics of a generation.

A Decade of Depression

There had been crises before, but they had not hit Latin America with such force, a reflection perhaps of its greater degree of integration into the world market by 1930. Between 1930 and 1934, the value of the region's exports dropped by almost half, and in some countries by more than three quarters. As exports led the economies in most of the region, the consequences of this precipitous drop rippled through the rest of the economy, leaving a trail of bankruptcies and unemployment.

Throughout Latin America economic depression raised social tensions and generated political unrest. Virtually all the nations of the region were affected, many of them seriously. In response to the growing threat from below, export elites clamped down on political opposition and intensified their social control. In country after country, oligarchic "democracies" gave way to dictatorships, many of them headed by military strongmen who ruled on the elites' behalf. Where popular movements were strong, the repression was particularly fierce. In El Salvador, thousands of peasants and Indians suspected of participation in an abortive leftist rebellion were massacred, inaugurating three decades of military rule and a pattern of defeating popular movements by violating their human rights that has yet to end. In nations with a deeper involvement in the international economy, such as Brazil, the crisis led to the discrediting of the traditional export elites. There it brought to power a populist caudillo, Getúlio Vargas, ending the political dominance of the São Paulo coffee planters.

The Depression led to even more radical political shifts where economic liberalism was still contested terrain. In Mexico it undermined the authority of Plutarco Elías Calles, the revolutionary general-turned-political boss who had steered the revolution on a conservative course oriented to capitalism at home and the U.S. market abroad. He was succeeded by Lázaro Cárdenas, a radical populist, who revived languishing land reform, sided with Mexican workers against foreign enterprises, and nationalized the U.S.-owned oil industry, while organizing Mexico's peasant majority, laying the bases for industry, and promoting a "Mexican socialism."

At the other end of the continent, the Depression prompted an even more dramatic political reversal in Chile. There, General Carlos Ibáñez had ruled with an iron hand since 1925, riding roughshod over his opponents and imposing free market economic policies shaped by U.S. advisers and the country's booming copper exports. But the Depression hit Chile harder than any other country in the world. The value of its exports fell by 80 percent between 1928 and 1932, and Ibáñez's political stock fell with them. Unemployment soared and caravans of jobless miners made their way south to Santiago, the capital, where they added their class-conscious voices to the growing discontent. Ibáñez had no answer to the deepening crisis, and in 1931 the Chilean strongman fled in the night to Argentina.

A year later, an army air force colonel with the unlikely name of Marmaduke Grove seized power and proclaimed Chile the hemisphere's first "socialist republic." Although Grove's revolution lasted less than a fortnight and its socialism owed more to the welfare state than to Karl Marx, its initial appeal underscored the extent of Chile's disillusionment with liberal capitalism and the export elites whose policies had led the country into such dire straits. Significantly, even the conservative president who restored the old order in Chile, Arturo Alessandri, himself a mining entrepreneur, promoted industry as an alternative to the country's over-dependence on copper and nitrate exports.

Argentina: Depression and Industry

Argentina was not hit nearly as hard by the Depression as Chile, but its impact was still traumatic. Perhaps because Argentina had scaled such heights of success before the Wall Street crash, its fall from grace was all the more disillusioning. The decades that followed witnessed an intense struggle over economic strategy, out of which a commitment to government economic intervention and the promotion of manufacturing emerged.

Argentina became as classic a case of the new Latin American enthusiasm for import substitution—in which protected national industries produced the consumer goods that used to be imported—as it had once been of export economies and the laissez-faire state. During this new era it would also become a prime example of Latin American populism under the charismatic Juan Perón, who held together a contradictory coalition of business and labor by the force of his personality, the benefits distributed by his government, and their shared interest in industrial development. For nationalists such as Perón, this stress on the promotion of domestic industries had the larger goal of an economic autonomy that he viewed as a "second independence."

Argentina might not have been as affected by the Depression as its neighbors, but the decline in real wages and rise in unemployment raised the specter of renewed social conflict. The inability of the aged Radical president Hipólito Yrigoyen to deal with the crisis gave the elite enemies of Argentina's limited democracy—who resented their loss of political power—the opportunity to overthrow him.

In September 1930 a coalition of oligarchs and officers ousted Yrigoyen. At first they experimented with an Argentine fascism under General José Uriburu, who had the support of the younger generation of German-trained army officers such as Juan Perón. But Uriburu was soon replaced by General Agustín Justo, a more traditional officer with links to the export elites and a belief in the British connection. As president between 1932 and 1938, Justo restored the old rules of the game. Rigged elections, justified as "patriotic fraud," assured elite rule, and the repression of unions defused the threat of a renewed "social question." A deal with Britain, the Roca-Runciman Pact of 1933, rescued Argentina's export economy by preserving a reduced access to the British meat market in return for preferential treatment of British goods and investments that nationalists denounced as a sellout of Argentine interests. On the surface the oligarchy had turned back the clock to 1912, before universal suffrage or mass politics interfered with their ability to run Argentina according to their lights and in their own interests. But Argentina was changing in spite of their efforts to freeze it in time. The export elites might not be interested in promoting national industries, but the depression in international trade made them a necessity. Argentina's reduced exports yielded fewer dollars and pounds to spend on imported manufactures. The result was a natural protection for domestic industry and a market niche that local entrepreneurs were quick to fill.

Most of these industrial entrepreneurs were immigrants—Italians, Germans, Arabs—who had established small businesses during the boom years but now saw in the Depression the opportunity to become major industrialists. One of the most important of these immigrant industrialists was Torcuato Di Tella, who had come to Buenos Aires from Italy as a teenager in 1905; in 1910 he founded a small metalworks producing dough-making equipment for bakeries. After the First World War he added the production under license of a North American gasoline pump. Di Tella became an Argentine citizen and secured a lucrative contract to supply the national oil company (YPF) with pumps and tanks. He had established a thriving business that had outgrown his small workshops when the Depression hit.

Although a large new investment was risky during so deep an economic crisis, Di Tella pressed on with his expansion plans, building his first large factory in an empty area of Avellaneda, across the Riachuelo canal from the port of La Boca. He also branched out into new product lines, including household refrigerators, which would be the key to the future success of his company, SIAM Di Tella. Although Di Tella often utilized foreign technology and products, in his advertising he appealed to Argentine nationalism in an era of growing anti-imperialist sentiment. His refrigerator ads pictured a gaucho woman and a caption that read: "Argentine . . . and with great honor."[1] Mostly, Di Tella relied upon his salesmen to reach his middle-class consumers, a stress on personal relationships that reflected Latin American culture and stood him in good stead in other aspects of his business. It was personal relationships with government officials that had secured the YPF contract, and personal relationships with bankers that helped him ride out the contraction of credit during the Depression. They were also central in dealing with his workers.

Labor was cheap in the depressed Argentina of the 1930s, but skilled workers were scarce. Di Tella recruited mostly from the Italian immigrant community and practiced a paternalism calculated to maintain their loyalties. His wages were no higher than those of his competitors in this era of weak unions, but he pioneered an unusually generous company welfare system that included sick pay, death and maternity benefits, medical care, and paid vacations. As the Argentine economy recovered from the Depression, SIAM's market and profits grew. "At the outbreak of World War II," recalled Di Tella's son, Torcuato Jr., "my father's company was doing very well." So were other Argentine industries oriented to the national market. Like SIAM Di Tella, they had expanded in response to the Depression, and profited as the incomes of their Argentine customers grew with renewed prosperity.

Elsewhere in Latin America this substitution of national manufactures for consumer goods that had been imported before the Depression was winning state support and becoming government policy. In Brazil, President Getúlio Vargas threw the resources of his "New State" behind an ambitious effort to industrialize South America's largest country. In Chile, a Popular Front government that included Socialists and Communists lauded industrialists such as Juan Yarur, an Arab immigrant of Palestinian origin who had established a modern cotton textile industry that he promised would "promote the cultivation of cotton, solve part of the unemployment problem and produce a good savings for the country, which was now forced to purchase for itself in foreign markets what could be produced right here."[2] The Popular Front also created a government development corporation that would nurture infant industries and then sell them to local capitalists for further development.

By the late 1930s even the export-oriented Argentine elites were beginning to promote domestic industry to complement their shipments of meat and grain. Although Argentine exports had recovered, war clouds were gathering in Europe and imported manufactures and capital were in short supply. The alternative was to produce in Argentina goods that previously had been imported from Europe.

By the end of World War II a sizable manufacturing sector was in place, led by metals and textiles. Torcuato Di Tella "was among the biggest of the new industrialists in the metallurgical sector," Torcuato Jr. said. "The war provided an automatic protection and it was a boom time." By its close, SIAM had over four thousand employees, established product lines, and a solid financial position. Many of these workers were now migrants from the interior, part of a tide of internal migration that would have as great an impact on Argentina as the earlier wave of European immigration that had brought Di Tella to its shores.

The social changes set in motion by the Depression were as far-reaching as the economic shifts that the crisis impelled. With declining export markets for their produce, landowners began laying off laborers and expelling them from their estates. A veritable army of the unemployed streamed out of the dusty farms and towns of the interior of Argentina and headed for the cities of the coast. By 1947, 1.4 million internal migrants had settled in Buenos Aires, drawn by reports that there were jobs to be had in the new manufacturing industries. Between 1935 and 1946, half a million workers were added to Argentina's industrial labor force, which more than doubled in that decade.

Many of these internal migrants were mestizos from Andean provinces like Tucumán, who found jobs in the new textile mills and metalworks. But they also found that their low wages made it hard to make ends meet, and that weak unions and a repressive state made it difficult to improve their living and working conditions. In the factories of Buenos Aires and Rosario they encountered the children of European immigrants, heirs to a tradition of militant unionism, which influenced and was influenced in turn by these new arrivals. Out of this fusion of "the two Argentinas" a new working class would emerge and the country would consolidate its new identity, an urban identity infused with rural elements, speaking a Spanish with Italian rhythms and slang, eating both beef and pasta, singing milongas *and* tangos.

It was in 1935 that one of those poor rural migrants—a teenage girl with alabaster skin named Eva Duarte—left the provincial town of Junín in the heart of the pampas 150 miles west of Buenos Aires and headed for the capital. She was only fifteen years old, small, thin, and intense, with pubescent good looks, an empty purse, and a small-town dream of becoming a big movie star like the Hollywood actresses she had seen on the screen of the Crystal Palace on Junín's Rivadavia Street. She became an actress in soap operas, a world in which actresses made their careers by attracting male patrons who promoted and protected them; Evita's name was linked to several in the gossip columns of the day. By 1944 she had her own company, a good salary, and a small apartment in the elite Barrio Norte. When an earthquake struck the Andean town of San Juan in January of that year, she volunteered to appear at a Buenos Aires benefit for the victims organized by Colonel Juan Domingo Perón, the secretary of labor in the military government installed in June of 1943. It would prove a fateful meeting for both—and for Argentina.

Perón! Perón!

There was little in Perón's early life and military reputation to suggest his later career as a populist caudillo. His ethnic roots—Italian, Spanish, and Indian—mirrored those of the nation he would lead; his father was a small rancher, his mother a midwife. He had been born on the pampas and brought up in Patagonia before being sent to the military academy in Buenos Aires at fifteen. Perón became a soldier's soldier, who taught military history at the war college and was known for his skills as a teacher. He had supported Uriburu's coup and brief experiment in Argentine fascism, and spent part of the next decade in Europe as military attaché in Mussolini's Italy, which he admired. He returned to Argentina in 1940 determined to repeat fascism's success, but without Uriburu's key mistake: setting the army and organized labor against each other. This insight would lead him to a greater power than any Argentine had exercised since the reign of Rosas came to an end in 1852.

In the 1930s Argentina had been ruled by oligarchic governments under the so-called *Concordancia* of elite parties. It had shepherded Argentina through the Depression years without the upheavals of some of its neighbors, but its surface stability was an illusion, maintained by fraud and force. Behind the government stood the army, whose younger officers were increasingly unhappy with that role—and the oligarchy's rule. The older generation of officers, like President Agustín Justo, came from elite families and had British training and ties. The younger officers, like Perón, were often from more modest backgrounds and had received German training. They were highly nationalistic and resented British domination of Argentina's economy and the oligarchy's sacrifice of national interests on the altar of self-interest. Not that this made them friends of democracy. On the contrary, these younger officers viewed democratic politics with disdain. Most were authoritarian in their instincts, a common military trait in Latin America, and many admired the Catholic fascism of Franco's Spain. Some had supported Uriburu in 1930 but lost out to the more experienced officers around Justo in the maneuvering that followed. They had bided their time, moving up in the hierarchy of command, and forming a secret society, the GOU, which served as the center for their conspiracy against a discredited government. Juan Perón was a central figure in the GOU, which ousted President Ramón Castillo in June 1943 and installed a military regime.

Perón claimed a major role in organizing the coup, but his share of the spoils seemed quite modest. He asked only to be made secretary of the army, an administrative post, and secretary of labor, a job that nobody else wanted. But in Perón's shrewd hands these bureaucratic positions would be transformed into the twin pillars of his power: the army and the workers.

As secretary of the army he was in charge of promotions and postings, which allowed him to do favors and place his loyalists in key commands. When the struggle for power began among the disparate officers who formed the GOU, Perón could rely on their loyalty in return. By February 1944 he had become war minister, and by July vice president under his friend and patron, General Edelmiro Farrell. He was now within one step of supreme power. "In revolutions," said Perón, "men impose their will from the second row, and not from the first, where they invariably fail and are removed."[3]

But it was Perón's conduct as secretary of labor that best showed his political genius. Argentine workers were heirs to a tradition of militant unionism, but labor had suffered from the repression of what its leaders called "the infamous decade." When Perón began in 1943, barely a tenth of

Argentine workers were organized, most of them grouped in the CGT (Confederation of Argentine Workers), which was divided into rival Socialist and Communist organizations. Neither one was strong enough to prevent the sharp drop in real wages that workers experienced even in the midst of a wartime boom. Yet within three years Perón would transform these unions into the most powerful political force in Argentina. He used his authority to force businesses to give in to worker demands for improved wages and working conditions, while increasing his control over the unions and assuring business that he was really on their side. "It is necessary to know how to give up thirty percent rather than lose everything," he told an audience at the stock exchange in August 1944. "Modern experience shows that the better organized masses of workers . . . are those who can be best directed and led in a completely orderly way"—by leaders like himself.[4] It was typical of Perón's ability to seem all things to all people, as well as his attempt to reconcile the opposed interests of labor and business around a vague populist amalgam of nationalism, industrial development, and social justice. As one railway worker observed after a meeting with Perón: "He had the virtue of leaving his audience satisfied without promising them anything."[5]

Perón's handling of the meat-packing unions, which grouped together the workers of Argentina's most important export industry, was a pivotal example of how he operated. One of the military regime's first acts had been to dissolve the Communist CGT; but one of Perón's first moves as labor chief was to free José Peter, the Communist leader of the meat-packing union, from his Patagonia prison, and to force the companies to agree to collective bargaining and raise wages. Within a year, however, he had undermined Peter by throwing his support to Cipriano Reyes, an insurgent leader from Berisso, who had organized his own rival federation.

By 1943 nearly twenty thousand workers labored in the giant Swift and Armour meat-packing plants in Berisso. But the character of this labor force had changed since the 1920s. Many of the immigrant workers were now Argentine citizens, focused on the New World, not the Old. They might still play cards at their ethnic clubs, but that ethnicity had ceased to define them, and they had stopped teaching Serbo-Croat, Italian, or Lithuanian to their Argentine-born children, who often found their friends and mates in other ethnic communities. Many of these children now also worked at the *frigoríficos*. But they did not remember the repressed strike of 1917 and did not share their fathers' fears.

By 1943, moreover, they had been joined by a more recent group of migrants with a different character and experience—internal migrants from Tucumán in the Andes and Corrientes in the north, whose darker skin and broader features betrayed their mestizo origins and whose behavior revealed their rural background. They were part of the great wave of internal migration that had transformed Argentina's cities during the preceding decade. The oligarchy called them *cabecitas negras*—"little blackheads"—with a disdain at once racial and social.

In Berisso, these internal migrants were hired as day laborers by Swift and Armour, U.S.-owned companies producing Argentine frozen beef for the British meat market. Unlike the veteran "European" workers, they had no seniority or job security, and thus "nothing to lose," explained Manuel López, a Berisso Peronist activist. It was in their ranks that Reyes would find his most militant supporters when he began to organize the Berisso meat packers in the 1940s.

"The conditions in the *frigoríficos* here were terrible," Rafael Tata, a Peronist of Arab descent and a former Swift worker, recalled. "It was cold and damp. You had to work ten- to twelve-hour shifts in the freezing rooms. The work was hard, and they were constantly watching you, even when you went to the bathroom. The foremen were like little kings in their sections. They even forced the women to go out with them. The abuses were awful." Alberto Proia, another veteran Berisso Peronist, agreed: "The workers were like slaves here. . . . The people earned starvation wages. They didn't have social security, pensions, vacation pay . . . no benefits of any kind. Here the companies cared more about the animals than the people who worked on them."

It was Reyes who took this diverse labor force and molded it into a militant union. Then he led them in the first strikes in Berisso since the navy had crushed the anarchist-led movement of 1917, militant strikes that provoked government intervention. But with Perón in charge this government role took on a different character than in the past. Perón sided with the Argentine workers against the foreign companies, forcing concessions on everything from wages and benefits to job security. He also underscored his loyalties by appearing publicly with Reyes.

When one of Reyes's brothers was killed in a violent clash in September 1945, Perón attended the Berisso funeral, where he pledged that he "would always be with the workers," Rafael Tata recalled with buried emotion. By then Berisso's once passive workers had become militant and won improvements in their wages and working conditions. "It was with Perón that things began to change," one former Swift worker stressed. Although their own actions and leaders had much to do with these advances, Argentine workers were not wrong in attributing their gains to Perón.

The Berisso meat packers were not alone. Throughout Argentina workers had benefited from the policies of the man the Rosario railway union hailed as "Argentina's Number One Worker."[6] Perón established labor courts and extended social security benefits. In November 1944 he signed the "Statute of the Peon," which set a minimum wage, paid holidays, and medical care for the most exploited of Argentine workers. As secretary of labor, Perón helped unorganized workers to organize, and organized workers to strengthen their unions and secure their demands. In the process he bound the workers and their leaders to him with ties of gratitude and links of personal loyalty. Without realizing it they were becoming "Peronists." In June 1945 Perón boasted to Spruille Braden, the new U.S. ambassador: "I have the army with me to a man and more than four million laborers who recognize me as their leader and sole benefactor."[7]

But even as Perón was consolidating his position with Argentina's workers and soldiers, his political ambitions, labor policies, and personal life were provoking opposition. Intellectuals blamed him for the regime's interference with the freedom of the press and the autonomy of universities. For democratic opponents of the military regime "that demagogue" Perón was their main target, while business elites opposed his prolabor measures and promotion of unions. Communists and Socialists opposed Perón as their chief rival for worker loyalties. This unusual alliance of right and left was united by its antifascist banner. It was led by Braden, who seemed to regard his 1945 posting to Buenos Aires as the last battle of World War II. As the British envoy, Sir David Kelly, put it: "Mr. Braden . . . came to Buenos Aires with the fixed idea that he had been elected by Providence to overthrow the Farrell-Perón regime."[8] The Second World War was ending with the defeat of fascism in Europe and a wave of democracy in the Americas. Braden encouraged the opposition to what he termed "Fascist military control" by Argentina's elites and middle class.[9]

The oligarchy spoke first, with a June 1945 manifesto attacking the regime for "a long series of measures, attitudes, resolutions and speeches [that] have converted social agitation into the gravest question [and created] a climate of jealousy, provocation and rebellion, in which resentment and a permanent feeling of hostility and demands are stimulated."[10] In September, it was the turn of the middle class, who filled the streets of Buenos Aires in a "March for the Constitution and Liberty" that its organizers hailed as the largest demonstration in Argentine history. Perón dismissed the marchers as "foreign elements, reactionary spirits, politicians with terminal illnesses and egotistical plutocrats."[11] But this massive show of opposition support persuaded many army officers that it was time to return to the barracks. President Farrell promised free elections, and even Perón's military friends began to waver in their loyalties.

It was Evita who pushed them over the edge. Perón was already a forty-eight-year-old widower, with a weakness for girls so young that he had to introduce them as his "daughters," when they met in 1944. Evita first became his mistress and then his confidante. To the Argentine elite she was a "common prostitute," and Perón's association with her confirmed their low opinion of him. Army officers were less concerned with Perón's sexual tastes than with the damage to the institution's image from Evita's increasingly public displays of affection and influence. Rumors that she controlled—and profited from—the Government Press Office were compounded in military eyes by her pushing Perón to replace an army officer with a friend of hers as head of the post office. By October 9, the Buenos Aires garrison was up in arms and Perón was forced to resign his government positions. President Farrell, a figurehead buffeted by both sides, allowed Perón to make a final radio broadcast to "his" workers, in which he recounted what he had done for them and insinuated that his ouster would mean the reversal of their gains. He saluted them with *"Hasta siempre"*—"Until Forever!"—"because from now on I shall be with you, closer than ever."[12] It was a prophetic prediction. On October 12, the Day of the Hispanic Race holiday, Perón was arrested and imprisoned by the navy on the island of Martín García in the Plata delta. His fall from power seemed final.

One Day That Shook Argentina

What happened next is the stuff of legends, many of which have been spun around the events of October 17, 1945. The tale begins in the meat-packing plants of Berisso, although the story in factories elsewhere was similar. As word spread of Perón's ouster and arrest during the days that followed, the workers began to talk among themselves about doing something to force his release. "When we heard that Perón was a prisoner, the people stopped work spontaneously and came out in the street with sticks to defend Perón," Alberto Proia recounted. "We all gathered at the meat-packers' union, where Cipriano Reyes was working to get unions throughout the country to collaborate in this effort." The Berisso meat packers decided to go to Buenos Aires to demand Perón's release and sent representatives on ahead to factories in the capital to ask workers there to join them.

"We left for Buenos Aires that very day," Rafael Tata said. "When we started out there were hundreds of us. By the time we reached the road to La Plata [the provincial capital], there were thousands of us, marching and chanting, 'There is no work without Perón.' Berisso was the lance point, followed by Avellaneda."

In Avellaneda, the workers of that populous industrial belt had also walked off their jobs in protest. "The revolutionary movement has started," one SIAM Di Tella manager wrote in his diary for October 16, 1945. "Around three in the afternoon workers began to leave the factory and in one hour everyone had left."[13] It would be three days before they returned.

At the edge of Avellaneda, the government tried to turn back the Peronist tide by raising the drawbridge that led to the city center. It was like trying to stop the sea. "Somebody found a small boat and began to ferry people across, especially the women and children," one worker recalled. "Some of the young guys just jumped in the Riachuelo and swam across." Finally some sailors came and lowered the drawbridges and "the police gave us the sign that they were with us and let us go." The marchers gave a big cheer as they crossed the bridge into Buenos Aires and continued until they came to ·the Plaza de Mayo, where the coup leaders were gathered in the Casa Rosada, Argentina's presidential palace.

"When we arrived in the Plaza de Mayo, we found that there were thousands and thousands of workers like us, who had come to defend Perón," Rafael Tata said, as the images of that day flooded his memory. Their faces were dark, their clothes shabby, their hands calloused. Many carried Argentine flags or homemade signs or photographs of Perón. The Berisso workers had even brought their Carnival drums. They climbed trees and lampposts, rolled up their sleeves, and played in the elegant fountains of the Plaza de Mayo.

It was a social world turned upside down, in which those who normally knew their place invaded the space of their betters, streaming through the wealthy districts of the city, singing songs that mocked the "mad oligarchs" as they marched past their mansions. But it was the repeated chants of "Perón! Perón! We want Perón!"—at once a litany and a demand—that defined their purpose.[14]

All day and all night they kept coming, hundreds of thousands of workers, many with their wives and children, taking over the streets and squares of the capital, demanding the return of their leader. It was an extraordinary sight, unprecedented in Argentine history, one that shocked the elite who watched uneasily behind shuttered balconies, and paralyzed the army officers who had ousted Perón.

The reactions of the middle class were more complex. Felix Luna, then a young anti-Peronist intellectual, recalled looking "at them from the sidewalk with a feeling akin to compassion" and wondering, "So many of them? So different from us? Had they really come on foot from those suburbs whose names made up a vague unknown geography, a *terra incognita* through which we had never wandered?"[15]

All seemed transfixed by the drama unfolding before them, yet unable to do more than play out their assigned roles. The upper and middle classes felt a challenge to their self-confident view of their society: "Everything up till then was coherent and logical; everything seemed to support our own beliefs," Luna said. "But that day when the voices began to ring out and the columns of anonymous earth-colored faces began to pass by, we felt something tremble which until that day had seemed unmovable."[16]

The demonstrators filled the Plaza de Mayo in front of the Casa Rosada and refused to disperse until Perón was freed and himself told them to go home. By nightfall this peaceful demonstration of Perón's popular support had disarmed his opponents' military strength. Uncertain what to do in a situation they had not anticipated, Perón's captors brought him back to Buenos Aires to calm his loyalists. It was a confession of defeat.

After hours of negotiations Perón finally stepped out on the balcony of the Casa Rosada at 11:00 P.M. on October 17. He was greeted with thunderous applause. "When Perón appeared on the balcony, I cheered as never before," Rafael Tata recalled. "It was one of those moments that I will never forget." Neither would Argentina. It was a moment that changed the course of its history. Perón announced that he was resigning from the army "to put on the coat of the civil servant and to mingle with the suffering and powerful masses who build up with their work the greatness of the nation."[17] It was both a victory speech and a campaign address. By then the chant had become: "Perón for president!"

One week later a Labor party was formed to back his candidacy. Perón's campaign against a lackluster Radical politician backed by the oligarchy, the United States, and most of the Buenos Aires middle class was a political masterpiece. Its theme of social justice was symbolized in his first rally when he removed his own jacket, held aloft a pole with an Argentine flag and a shirt, and identified himself with the *descamisados*—shirtless ones—of Argentina. His speeches, studded with references to tangos, *lunfardo* slang expressions, and couplets from *Martín Fierro,* underscored

Perón's identification with Argentina's urban workers and rural migrants. His alliance with a faction of the Radicals and stress on nationalism and economic reform appealed to part of Argentina's sizable middle class as well. His endorsement of religious instruction in public schools and stress on his Catholicism brought him Church support.

Perón campaigned with Evita, now his lawful wife, in the interior, on a train dubbed *La Descamisada,* capitalizing on the regional resentments of marginalized provinces. "In Tucumán," recalled Raúl Bustos Fierro, one of Peron's speechwriters, "a little old man and his grandson rode on horseback all night and all day to present a bouquet of mountain flowers to Perón."[18] Near the Bolivian border, in Jujuy, an Indian delegation hailed him as "Perón, Indian leader."[19] When former ambassador Spruille Braden, by then assistant secretary of state for Latin America, publicly opposed his candidacy, Perón ran as a defender of Argentine sovereignty, telling the hundreds of thousands of self-proclaimed *descamisados* who filled the broad expanse of Ninth of July Avenue for his culminating campaign rally that "the choice at this crucial hour is this: Braden or Perón."[20] Running with a makeshift party against an alliance of all the traditional parties, Perón won decisively in the February 24, 1946, election, which even John Moors Cabot, the U.S. envoy, admitted was the "fairest in Argentine history."[21]

Perón the Nationalist, Perón the Populist

On June 4, 1946, the third anniversary of the military coup that had begun his rise to power, Juan Domingo Perón took the oath of office in a military uniform as the democratically elected president of Argentina. He had been elected with 52 percent of the vote, to 42 percent for his leading opponent, allowing Perón to claim a mandate for the changes he had advocated during his campaign. Moreover, his coalition had won two thirds of the Chamber of Deputies, giving him the power to pass legislation and enact reforms. The strong state of the Argentine economy, whose wartime export earnings, the fruit of its uneasy neutrality, remained unspent, gave Perón the resources with which to fulfill his promises and carry out his program.

There were many goals projected in the ambitious "five-year plan" that Perón presented to a joint session of Congress in two bound volumes, but their recurring themes were economic independence and social justice. His economic plan envisioned an Argentina whose strategic sectors were no longer under foreign control and whose prosperity did not depend upon foreign investors and markets. Perón's social reforms set out to humanize capitalism along the lines urged by the social doctrine of the Catholic church, with workers receiving an increased share of the nation's income and an equal power to participate in the country's political life. These two pillars of Perón's program were linked by a strategy for rapid industrial growth that would finance his social goals, without a massive redistribution of wealth, and by the formation of a populist coalition embracing both industrialists and workers around the goal of Argentina's "second independence."

Perón had risen to power on the shoulders of the workers and the army, and been elected with the support of the provincial middle class as well. He had appealed to industrialists, but his prolabor policies left many of them uneasy, and only a minority of entrepreneurs adhered to his standard before 1946.

Once in power, though, Perón was able to use its levers to form the populist coalition of industrialists and workers that had eluded him during his campaign. One of those who came to support Perón only after his election was Torcuato Di Tella.

The Italian-born industrialist was a strong democrat and longtime enemy of Mussolini. He had publicly opposed Perón and his labor policies as "fascistic" and "feared the indiscipline that might result" at his factories, according to Torcuato Jr. But once Perón became president Di Tella's position shifted. Perón's government controlled state contracts and labor relations, credit and imports. "To take a stand against Perón and Evita was to destroy everything that he had worked for during many years," Di Tella's widow stressed.[22] Moreover, Perón was willing to overlook Di Tella's past opposition, provided that he collaborated with him now. He could make or break a company. It was an offer that Di Tella could not refuse. He became a reluctant but public Peronist.

"Perón tried to win his support," Torcuato Jr. explained, because "he thought he was a very important industrialist." Di Tella was a leading figure in the Argentine Industrial Union, the manufacturers' association, which had forged an alliance with the nationalistic military, who were worried about the industrial progress of Getúlio Vargas's Brazil, Argentina's historic regional rival. But Argentina's industrialists had found no political expression before Perón embraced their cause.

Torcuato Di Tella might not have liked Perón, but "the Perón government benefited him," his son affirmed. Di Tella's business had progressed greatly during the war. Now he branched out into pipelines for oil, turbines for heavy industry, and oil extraction rigs, products with assured markets in state industries, such as the YPF petroleum enterprise. "The boom continued after my father's death in 1948," Torcuato Jr. said. By that time the company was a multinational corporation with subsidiaries in Brazil, Chile, and Uruguay. SIAM Di Tella's sales and profits had never been higher.

SIAM Di Tella was not the only Argentine manufacturer to gain from the boom that followed Perón's inauguration, nor the only industrialist to take advantage of the government's promotion of domestic industry. Perón established high tariff barriers, awarded lucrative contracts with state enterprises, and sold manufacturers foreign currencies at subsidized rates of exchange. One way or another, the success of Argentina's new industries depended upon the largesse of Perón's government.

The transformation of the Argentine economy during Perón's first presidency (1946–52) was striking. Between 1945 and 1948, manufacturing increased by more than half and industrial employment rose by one third. By 1950 domestic manufactures had virtually replaced imported consumer goods, which had declined to only a tenth of Argentina's import bill. Most Argentines now dressed in cloth, slept on beds, and cooked on stoves made in Argentina. Manufacturing accounted for nearly one quarter of the national income and had replaced agriculture as the engine of economic growth. Almost a quarter of the labor force, some 1.5 million people, worked in industry by 1951.

In Avellaneda, the sides of Pavón Avenue were lined with factories.

The once isolated SIAM Di Tella plant was now part of a booming industrial belt. The streets nearby bustled with commercial activity that revolved around its thousands of workers. Interior cities such as Córdoba and Rosario saw a comparable explosion of manufacturing. Even in Berisso, with its giant meat-packing export plants, the expansion of the YPF oil refinery pointed the way to an industrial future that responded to the rhythms of domestic, not foreign, demand.

The creation of an Argentine industry capable of self-sustained growth was the key to Perón's goal of economic autonomy, but it was not its most dramatic statement. With over $1.5 billion in wartime export earnings to draw on, Perón was able to pay off Argentina's entire external debt and buy back many of the foreign-owned investments that so offended Argentine nationalists. On July 9, 1947, the 131st anniversary of San Martín's declaration of Argentina's political independence in Tucumán, Perón journeyed to the same spot to sign his own Declaration of Economic Independence, in which he proclaimed the determination of Argentines "to break the chains of domination that have bound them to foreign capital, and to recover their right to control the sources of their national wealth."[23] Perón's goal was to put an end to Argentina's colonial economy. Although U.S.-owned enterprises such as the Argentine Telephone Company were among those purchased by Perón, it was the $1.5 billion in British investments that were the principal target of Perón's well-heeled drive for economic autonomy. Perón's obsession with the British was understandable, but it made more historical and psychological than economic sense. British capital was not as dominant in Argentina in 1946 as it had been half a century before, although it still represented some 60 percent of the $2.5 billion in foreign investments that made Argentine nationalists bristle. More than three fifths of this British investment was in a railway system that British companies had allowed to run down, adding the complaint of poor service to the critique of foreign control. But above all, the British-owned railways symbolized to millions of Argentines the continued domination of their country by "imperialism."

By 1946 the British goal was to exit with as much of their investment as possible, while most Argentines were equally eager to see them leave.

Perón satisfied both sides, although at a high financial cost, using 80 percent of the $750 million Argentine export earnings that the British were holding hostage in London to buy back what he reportedly complained was "out-of-date equipment."[24] On March 1, 1948, hundreds of thousands of workers filled the Plaza Britania in front of the Retiro railway terminal in Buenos Aires to celebrate the occasion, whose meaning was illustrated by an enlarged map of the railway system behind the speaker's stand that bore the legend: "Now they are Argentine!" It was this symbolic significance that one old Peronist railroad worker remembered when he recalled that demonstration: "I don't know if it was a great deal in economic terms," he admitted, "but the important thing is we were buying national sovereignty." It was Evita who articulated the meaning of Argentina's new economic independence best: "The days have passed," she proclaimed, "when our destinies would be settled thousands of miles from our own shores; today we Argentines are the architects of our own destiny."[25]

But Perón also offered the workers of Argentina concrete benefits. Between 1945 and 1949, real wages for industrial workers rose by more than half, the largest leap in Argentine history. The shift in the distribution of the national income was equally dramatic, with workers increasing their share by one quarter, although industrialists and the middle class also gained—at the expense of ranchers, farmers, and exporters.

In implementing his program of "social justice," Perón found an active collaborator in his wife, who abandoned her acting career and found a new vocation as the "Queen of Labor." Although Evita held no formal position in the government, she installed herself in an office in the newly created Ministry of Labor, and intervened actively in collective bargaining, pressing employers to grant large increases in wages and benefits. "During Perón's time, the only person who commanded was Eva Perón," asserted a top SIAM executive.[26] Perón might try to balance the interests of labor and business, but Evita's sympathies were clear. She had been born poor and illegitimate and never forgot—or forgave—the humiliations of her youth. She had learned as a child that "there were poor because the rich were too rich."[27] Once her husband was president she used her new power to redress this "injustice" and redistribute Argentina's wealth. "When I saw

Perón take the flag of the workers to carry it to victory," she explained, "I, a humble woman of the people, understood that it was my duty to take my place with the workers, with the *descamisados.*"[28]

With state support assured, unions became bolder in their demands, and workers pressed for greater control on the factory floor as well. This new sense of worker empowerment was seen even in paternalistic enter-prises such as SIAM Di Tella, where managers complained that "the laborers changed so much that in the factories one could not tell them anything."[29] As one port worker put it: "With Perón we were all *machos.*"[30]

Perón's political "revolution" from above loosed a social "revolution from below." In Berisso, the meat-packing workers won record wage in-creases, improved working conditions, and the job security that they had sought in vain before Perón. And Argentine workers not only received higher real wages, but paid vacations and social security as well. "For us, Perón's epoch was a golden age," reminisced Eduardo Novoa, a worker at the shipyards in Ensenada. "As a union member, for fifteen pesos, which was nothing, I could spend two weeks at the beach at Mar del Plata."

Perón's "gifts" to Argentina's workers seemed equally great outside the workplace. In Berisso they still talk of the time that Perón came for a visit and offered them the housing project they had wanted for so long. "One of our biggest problems was housing, particularly for the migrants recently arrived from the interior. So, when Perón announced that he was coming to Berisso, we decided to ask for new housing to be built on an empty lot," Peronist activist Manuel López recalled. "But the old fox beat us to it. Before we could say anything, he announced that he was going to build houses for the workers on that very spot." Perón also sponsored the construction of a clinic and a social center. "All of this we owe to Perón," López affirmed as we drove past the simple but solid one-family houses and clinic. It was a common sentiment in Berisso, where many workers had stories about how small wishes were granted under Perón or larger dreams came true. They have remained Peronists ever since.

Berisso was unusual in its association with Perón's dramatic rise to power in October 1945, but the benefits it received from him were not unique. Throughout the country housing projects, hospitals, schools, and

The Amazon's forest primeval is going up in smoke in Brazil, where an area of virgin rain forest larger than Massachusetts is burned down each year to make way for mining, farming, or ranching. North Americans charge ecocide, but for many Brazilians the issues are economic growth, landless peasants, and national sovereignty.

Peru's Machu Picchu, the "Lost City of the Incas", attests to the extraordinary achievements of the indigenous peoples of the Americas. Its sophisticated agricultural terraces and stone constructions were built at an altitude of seventy-five hundred feet on a mountain ridge above the steep gorge of the raging Urubamba River.

The snow-capped mountains behind La Paz beckon tourists to the "roof of the world", thirteen thousand feet above the sea. But it is the economic and educational opportunities of Bolivia's capital that draw Indian migrants from the densely populated high plateau to live in shacks clinging to the barren hillside of its "European" city center.

The giant statue of Christ the
Redeemer on top of Rio de Janeiro's
Corcovado is an eloquent symbol of
the imposition of European beliefs
and culture on an American landscape. Beneath its outstretched arms
lie both the luxurious beachfront
hotels of Copacabana and the
squalid shantytowns many urban
Brazilians call home.

A futuristic capital for the "country
of the future," Brasília, with its modern architecture and planned vistas,
expresses the aspirations of Latin
America's largest country. Built on
a wilderness plateau at the nation's geographic midpoint, Brasília
symbolized the determination of
Brazilians to occupy the country's
vast interior and exploit its rich
resources.

(*Right*) In Salvador, Bahia, the center of Afro-Brazilian culture and Brazil's first colonial capital, a street vendor in "African" dress offers foods of both the Old World and the New, seasoned with spices of African origin.

(*Below*) The gumbo pot of ethnicities and cultures that defines the West Indies is reflected in this cricket field in Port-of-Spain, Trinidad, where descendants of British colonists and the African slaves and Asian laborers they brought to the Caribbean to work their sugar plantations play this quintessentially English game.

Espanol con India. Mestizo.

Mestizo con Espanola Castizo.

Castizo con Espanola Espanol.

Espanol con Mora Mulato.

Mulato con Espanola. Morisco.

Morisco con Espanola Chino.

Chino con India. Salta atras.

Salta atras con Mulata. Lobo.

Lobo con China Gibaro.

Gibaro con Mulata Albarazado

Albarazado con Negra Canbujo.

Canbujo con India. Sanbaigo.

Sanbaigo con Loba Calpamulato.

Calpamulato con Canbuja Tente en el Aire.

Tente en el Aire. con Mulata Note entiendo.

Note entiendo con India Torna atras.

By the late eighteenth century, extensive miscegenation threatened to overwhelm Spanish America's caste system, which pretended to order society by race. Mexican paintings like *The Castes*, in which parents and their offspring were labeled by caste – "Spanish father & Indian mother = Mestizo child" – showed colonial officials how to categorize their subjects. But categories like *No te entiendo* – "I don't understand you" – revealed the system's absurdities.

Potosí's sacred mountain became the "Rich Hill" of the Spaniards in 1545, and by 1600 was the source of half the world's silver. *The Virgin of the Hill of Potosí,* an anonymous eighteenth-century painting of the syncretic mestizo school, portrays the Virgin Mary as both Queen of Heaven and Pachamama, the Andean Mother Earth. The Indian donor is joined in prayer by Pope Paul III and Spain's King Charles V, while an Inca is seen on the Virgin/Hill, which is flanked by the Sun and Moon, ancient Indian deities.

sports stadiums recall that era. Many of them bear the names of Juan Domingo or Eva Perón.

But beyond the material rewards that Perón gave to Argentina's workers was the restoration of their dignity after years of the oligarchy's disdain. He took the word *descamisado*—shirtless ones—the insult with which the elite ridiculed the Argentine lower class, and made it a badge of pride. Perón also gave Argentina's workers a sense of self-worth. "With Perón, I became *some*body," was the way many workers put it. Under Perón, *descamisados* became workers and workers became protagonists of their own destinies.

In the process, a new Argentine working class was born, one that united the descendants of the archetypal gaucho Martín Fierro with those of the Italian immigrant Papolitano under the political banner of the leader whom José Hernández had prophesied in his epic poem would someday come forth to rescue them from domination by the oligarchy—a prophecy that Perón made part of his political campaigns. This newly self-conscious and self-confident working class would survive Perón's own defeat and exile. It would prove his most enduring legacy.

Evita added her charity to Perón's largesse. In addition to her efforts on behalf of workers, she also headed the Eva Perón Foundation, which replaced the aristocracy's Society of Philanthropy as the quasi-official national charity—although she insisted that her "social aid" was really "social justice." Evita spent each afternoon there receiving petitioners. She embraced the sick, lifted up the poor, and granted their wishes, whether they were a hospital bed or a new house, a sewing machine or a chair. The foundation also built modern hospitals where the poor received free care, housing projects with subsidized rents, and a "Children's City," which symbolized Perón's claim that in his New Argentina "only children will be privileged."

By 1952 the Eva Perón Foundation was Argentina's biggest "private" enterprise. Its assets approached two hundred million dollars, with unions "volunteering" two days' wages of their members each year, Congress passing on a share of the lottery and vice taxes, and private businesses "donating" the rest. Although some of the foundation's contributions were obtained by methods that resembled extortion—one pharmaceutical company that refused to contribute was forced into bankruptcy and its directors jailed—and the luxury that surrounded Evita gave it the appearance of a show, her dedication to the poor was sincere. Even when weak with cancer, Evita put in long afternoons at the foundation listening to the plaints of each of the many petitioners who sought her help.

Novelist John Dos Passos visited Argentina in 1948 and captured the flavor of these audiences:

> *In a small office with red-damasked walls were rows of benches packed with ragged-looking women and children facing her desk. Babies squawked. Everybody talked at once. . . . Distinguished visitors were posed as an admiring group behind the Señora's handsome blonde head as she leaned over her desk to listen to the troubles of some poor women with their tear-grimed children. . . .*
>
> *At the end of each hard-luck story, the Señora reached with jewelled fingers under the blotter on the desk and took out two fifty-peso notes. Then she made out with a rapid scratch on a pink slip an order for a doctor or a doll for the baby girl. . . .*[31]

Evita would force the powerful who sought her favor to wait while she attended to the problems of the poor. It was no wonder that poor women felt a special kinship with Evita, who began to merge with the Madonna in their prayers as "The Lady of Hope."

Evita might be the most powerful woman in Argentine history, but she acted as "the bridge of love" between the people and Perón, their Conductor.[32] Evita was the political priestess at the shrine of his growing cult of personality. She was joined with him in the obligatory photographs in every public building and in the Peronist "hymns" of the era. But Evita was also the expression of Perón's commitment to Argentina's workers, and her days at the labor ministry and the foundation were intended "to show them that . . . the gulf which had separated the people from the government no longer exists."[33] Her speeches to "My dear *descamisados*" reminded them of their former exploitation by the oligarchy and that social justice had only entered their lives with Perón.

Evita was also Perón's chief political link to Argentine women. Although feminism had a long history in Argentina, it was Evita who persuaded Perón to give women the vote in 1947. She then organized the Peronist Women's party, which soon had half a million members and a group of female cadres that would influence Argentine politics for years to come. With women casting their ballots overwhelmingly for Perón, he was reelected president in 1951 with more than 60 percent of the votes. It would prove the peak of his popularity.

Perón the Dictator, Perón the Fascist

Not everyone in Argentina was as enthusiastic about Perón as Berisso's workers or Evita's women. Socialist and Communist labor leaders were hounded from their unions and sometimes jailed and tortured as well. But even independent labor leaders, like Cipriano Reyes, who had helped Perón gain power, were shunted aside after his election in favor of more compliant Peronists, as Perón moved to consolidate his control over the labor movement that had spearheaded his rise to power.

Former allies were not the only ones to feel Perón's wrath. The sizable urban middle class was never enamored of Perón. They might benefit economically from his policies, but they remained his political opponents. Their alienation grew as he purged their universities, censored their press, and harassed their political leaders. The autonomy of Argentina's public universities was violated, their faculties and curricula were "Peronized," and student protests were repressed by Perón's police. Press censorship had existed in Argentina since the 1943 military coup, but Perón took it several steps further, forcing the venerable opposition newspaper, *La Prensa*, to close, and creating a Peronist radio monopoly. Even the Congress, with its constitutional immunity, provided no sanctuary for opposition political leaders: Two were expelled from the Chamber of Deputies and tried for "disrespect of the government," under a law passed by the Peronist majority and sustained by Peronist judges. One of Perón's first moves as president had been to impeach the entire supreme court and replace it with his loyalists. Intellectuals called Perón "the dictator" and many democrats considered him a fascist. Although his first presidency witnessed more intimidation than outright repression and there were few political prisoners in 1951, Perón's disregard for constitutional checks and civil liberties, and his intolerance of political opposition and public criticism were harbingers of things to come.

The agro-export elites and their allies led the opposition to Perón. They had viewed him as their enemy from the start and everything he had done confirmed this belief. He had put an end to their political power and mocked their social pretensions. He had accused them of selling out their country and made the *descamisados* they despised the new symbol of Argentine nationality. He had made the oligarchy his rhetorical whipping boys and Evita had publicly humiliated their women.

Evita evoked an almost visceral hatred among the Argentine upper class. To them, her bejeweled beauty and designer gowns symbolized the vulgarity and corruption of the Perón regime. Jorge Luis Borges, Argentina's most celebrated writer, spoke for the country's elite when he called her "a whore." Another noted Argentine writer, Ezequiel Martínez Estrada, damned her as "a sublimation of vileness, abjectness, degradation."[34] But there was more to their distaste than disdain for her illegitimate birth, lower-class manners, and career as an actress. Evita also symbolized Perón's commitment to social justice, at once a critique of their values and an attack on their interests. And she never forgot a slight or forgave an insult. Borges's mother was once jailed in a cell reserved for prostitutes after participating in an anti-Peronist demonstration in the city center, while the writer himself was transferred from his post at the national library to a job inspecting poultry in public markets. When Evita was dying of cancer, graffiti appeared in the elegant barrios of Buenos Aires proclaiming: "*¡Viva el cáncer!*"

Perón had also prejudiced the elite's economic interests. A scion of the landowning elite like Tomás de Anchorena, a descendant of Rosas's cousins, might be willing to concede that "there was a lack of vision on the part of the ruling classes [because] we continued to be agro-exporters and didn't invest our wealth in industry." But Perón, Anchorena felt, had gone too far in the other direction. He had promoted industry at the expense of agriculture, and subsidized improved urban living standards out of the profits of the pampas. He had nationalized foreign trade, forcing the agro-export elites to sell their meat and grain to his government for depreciated paper pesos, taking away any incentive to increase their production. He had kept the prices of their produce low in Argentina as a subsidy to urban workers, whose increased meat consumption in a nation of carnivores had significantly decreased the quantity of meat available for export.

The agro-export elites were also critical of Perón's anti-imperialism. He had weakened Argentina's ties with Great Britain, whom they had long considered "the principal factor in the country's political, economic, and social progress."[35] From their perspective, this was a measure of irrational xenophobia, not healthy nationalism. "With Perón there was a sort of persecution," explained Alfredo Campanelli, a cattle buyer at the Liniers market for the elite Heguy family, and an admirer of Britain's contributions to Argentina. "He nationalized everything that the British had built: the railways, the ports, the telephones, . . . the services." He also diminished the profits of the *frigoríficos* by imposing increased wages and benefits and allowing a decrease in work discipline and productivity. As a result, concluded Campanelli, "the meat trade declined by half."

Perón and the oligarchy differed in their visions of Argentina, with Perón projecting Argentina as an industrial power, while the agro-export elites clung to their vision of Argentina as a great landed estate. Perón had clipped the oligarchs' political wings, but left them in control of Argentina's most valuable economic resources. When the time came they would have their revenge.

Decline and Fall

For a few years, Perón held together a contradictory coalition of labor and business through the force of his personality and the power of his state, and through a shared interest in industrial development and the resources that allowed him to give benefits to all his supporters at the same time. His

Peronist party of changing names was little more than an electoral vehicle. *Justicialismo,* the name he gave to his political philosophy, which combined nationalism with a commitment to social justice and a vague "third position" between capitalism and communism, was little more than an ideological fig leaf.

Evita's premature death from cancer in 1952, at the age of thirty-three, marked the end of Perón's social revolution and the beginning of his political decline. But there were more profound reasons for Perón's declining fortunes than Evita's demise. By 1952 the hard currency reserves accumulated during World War II were gone, and he lacked the resources either to distribute or to invest. Nor could he count on any new windfall in the forseeable future: The world prices that had favored Argentine exports in 1946 were now reversed. The agro-export sector—owned by his enemies, penalized by his policies, and hurt by drought at home and declining demand abroad—was not expanding its production or earnings. The cost of imported machinery rose and industrial production slowed. Taken together, these setbacks spelled a decline in economic growth and a rise in social tensions. As the economy faltered, his populist coalition broke apart on the rock of inflation and the conflict over who should pay its costs. With their real wages and living standards in decline, workers used their new power to protest, only to find their strikes opposed by Perón and repressed by his police.

With no resources left to distribute, Perón began to stress "a just distribution of spiritual and moral benefits" over the material rewards he had once championed, and criticized the concern with material rewards as the cause of "great misfortune and the decadence of nations."[36] With a desperate need for new investments, he began to favor capital over labor, and to invite back the foreign companies that he had expelled, even offering lucrative oil concessions to U.S. companies he had previously attacked as "imperialist." Faced by a growing balance of payments problem, Perón cut back on industrial growth, loosened state control over exports, and reduced food subsidies and wage supports. He even made a deal with Britain that resembled the Roca-Runciman Pact he had denounced in the past as a "sellout" of the national interest.

The increasing economic hardships made the corruption of his regime more glaring and less tolerable. Just when he needed it most, Perón's political touch deserted him. His cult of personality became more prominent, his manipulation of his *descamisados* more overt. He had never been gentle with his opponents or tolerant of dissent, but rarely had he relied so heavily upon repression. Peronist mobs sacked the Jockey Club, a symbol of his elite enemies, in 1953, and attacked the capital's cathedral, the sanctuary of his former allies, in 1955. His security apparatus filled the jails and tortured dissidents. During his last few years in power Perón's Argentina became the police state his opponents had always accused him of establishing.

His enemies multiplied and his support ebbed away. The Vatican excommunicated him, strikes increased in number and intensity, and so did conspiracies among Catholics and within the armed forces. By 1955 his power seemed vulnerable. On September 16, the aristocratic navy, traditionally close to the agro-export elites, began a revolt that soon spread to the army. Perón chose not to fight. Four days later, he resigned and left the country—only one month shy of the tenth anniversary of his dramatic rise to power. This time there would be no worker demonstrations in the Plaza de Mayo demanding his return. Instead a well-dressed crowd filled the square to celebrate their "Liberating Revolution."

Perón's Legacy

In 1950, Pavón Avenue in Avellaneda was the heart of a booming industrial belt that symbolized Argentina's economic progress. Today it is a rusty industrial ruin. The abandoned factories stand in rows like silent witnesses to a vanished past. A mile beyond in a quiet cul-de-sac is a vast field filled with weeds and decaying buildings. In a corner of the lot, a bright sign on a small but modern plant announces: SIAM-Aurora. This foreign venture is all that remains of the SIAM Di Tella industrial complex that once filled this enormous space. The refrigerators and automobiles that Argentines buy today are foreign brands. Despite its initial success, Perón's bid for economic independence was ultimately a failure.

Far from leaving a legacy of economic autonomy, Perón bequeathed to his successors a burden of inefficient industries that required state protection to survive and imported machinery and raw materials to produce. Worse still, they were light consumer goods industries, without the coherence or the heavy industry that might have served as the base for self-sustaining growth.

What made Perón's failure particularly poignant was the sense of lost opportunity. He inherited a treasure chest of over $1.5 billion in wartime export earnings and came to power in an era when the demand for Argentine exports was high. Had Perón invested this considerable capital in a concerted program of industrial growth, he might have been less popular politically but more successful economically.

Instead, the money was expended unproductively. The aging British railways he had purchased—and nationalized—at such high cost and with such fanfare ran at a loss and were a heavy charge on the resources of the state, as were its bloated bureaucracy and military and extensive social programs. Moreover, Perón understood too late that a strategy of accelerated industrial growth required the expansion of exports as well as the substitution of imports. He committed the same error as the elites he vilified—assuming that the fatted calves of the pampas could pay for it all. The consequence was a growing trade deficit that soon generated an expanding foreign debt and accelerating inflation. Perón's declaration of Argentina's "second independence" proved a hollow boast.

Yet Peronism survived Perón's economic shortcomings, political fall, and seventeen-year exile to triumph again at the polls in 1973. During the intervening years, his military and civilian opponents failed to solve the economic problems he bequeathed them or to win over the other Argentina that remained loyal to his memory. Perón returned to general acclaim in 1973 with a new program of economic independence, social welfare, and a "third position" between capitalism and communism that was similar to his old one. But Argentina's circumstances in 1973 were less favorable than in 1946, and Perón's second coming was even less successful than his first. When the aging caudillo died in 1974, Argentina was so polarized between left and right that its fragile democracy soon descended into a vortex of violence that culminated in a military coup two years later and a "dirty war" that made Argentina notorious for its violations of human rights. The regime's economic failures and military defeat in the Malvinas/Falklands War of 1982 doomed its political project of erasing Peronism from Argentina. Ten years later Carlos Saul Menem, a Peronist politician from an Andean province—elected in 1989 on a platform that resembled Perón's—was president, and the Peronist party once again controlled the Congress.

But by then the inefficient industries that Perón had spawned were in ruins, the Argentine national debt was so high that it could not be paid, and Menem was dismantling the protection of Argentine industries and subsidies of living standards that Perón had set up. President Menem was also selling off Argentina's state enterprises to mostly foreign buyers, including some, such as the national oil company (YPF), that were created before Perón.

In the Barrio Norte of Buenos Aires, where on a winter's afternoon men in leather jackets and women in fur coats sip tea and nibble Italian pastries in elegant cafés, Menem is newly popular. "I never thought that a Peronist would abandon Peronism," quipped a banker old enough to remember Perón's first regime. "It is like having a liberal as president, but one who can keep the workers quiet."

In Berisso, site of a major YPF refinery, where the invocation of Perón's name still opens doors and the memory of his death still produces tears, many workers are bitter. They had voted for Menem, believing his promises "to carry on the work of Perón," only to see him betray their hopes and his legacy. "I worked fifty years for Swift and the YPF, and I was a Peronist of the first hour," Alberto Luria proclaimed. "For the poor, for the workers, we have arrived at a Peronism that has nothing to do with Perón, because Menem is carrying out a policy that is the opposite of Peronism. My hopes were destroyed by Menem. . . . He betrayed Perón, he betrayed the party, he betrayed the workers, he betrayed everybody."

For Menem, the issue was not loyalty to the past but the need for change. "Those who want to hang on to an ideological past are completely mistaken. The world is evolving, and if your ideas and ideology don't keep pace, you will fail totally," he stressed. "I can't expect to succeed in 1992 with a program from 1946."

At Berisso's Club de Lote, a shed of galvanized metal, some thirty friends gather each Saturday to eat meaty barbecued ribs, drink rough red wine, sing tangos, and remember the old days. Most are ardent Peronists, many are middle-aged, and all are products of Perón's Argentina. "What is left of Perón's legacy?" I asked, quoting from Menem's campaign sticker, which pictured him with Perón and Evita, and the Peronist program: political sovereignty, economic independence, and social welfare. "Just us," one grizzled retiree replied. "Just us . . . and the memory of a different Argentina, where there was work for all, beef at every meal, and dignity for each Argentine." For them, this nostalgic memory is Perón's most enduring legacy.

Between 1964 and 1976, military regimes overthrew democracies in most of South America and tried to restructure their economies and politics. In Chile, the burning of the presidential palace in the 1973 coup symbolized the military's readiness to break with the past and presaged its neoliberal economic "shock treatment."

Chapter 5

Capital Sins

The unequal distribution of wealth in Latin America and the Caribbean can be seen in cities, where luxury apartment towers and squalid shantytowns are often uneasy neighbors, as in the Santa Marta area of Rio de Janeiro. Little of Brazil's economic "miracle" of 1968–73 "trickled down" to the poor.

The social costs of Brazil's "growth first" policies and 1980s economic crisis are poignantly evident in the estimated seven million children who live on the streets of its cities, surviving by begging and petty crime. Many have been victims of death-squad violence.

Grassroots social movements led the struggle for the restoration of democracy in South America. Benedita da Silva organized slum-dwellers in her Rio de Janeiro *favela,* or shantytown, and was later elected to Brazil's Congress, where she is a quadruple token—poor, black, female, and Protestant—but also a hopeful sign.

5   *Capital Sins*

*J*oãozinho Trinta is one of Brazil's leading Carnival producers. His broad face has decorated the cover of the country's magazines and he has appeared frequently on television. His Carnival pageants are famous not only for their creativity but for their social comment. In 1990 his theme was *Alice in Wonderland,* but as "a version of Brazilian history." For him, "Alice represents the consciousness of this great country, which sometimes is still sleepy, as in the story." His Alice is a giant figure who has just drunk the magic potion. "She is crying because all of a sudden she grew huge," he explains. "She can't even reach her feet. . . . She cries like Brazil, which is also a giant and cannot solve its enormous problems."

"Brazil is the country of the future—and always will be" is a popular saying in Brazil, one revealing of this vast nation's optimism and aspirations—and its sense of irony. The optimism comes with the country's vast territory, burgeoning population, rich resources, and vibrant culture. The aspirations follow suit, giving rise to the notion of *grandeza*—a vision of Brazil as destined for greatness, the United States of South America. The irony is a product of Brazil's recent history.

Since 1960 Brazil has experienced both an economic "miracle" that has vaulted it into the ranks of the world's ten largest economies and a deep crisis that has called its destiny into question. It has restored democracy after two decades of dictatorship, only to see its civilian leaders fail to solve the problems bequeathed them by the military regime. It has projected itself upon the world stage, yet failed to sustain its self-image as a great power.

A Different Destiny?

Brazil has always been different from the rest of Latin America. It is by far the largest country in the region, with a territory bigger than the contiguous United States and one third of Latin America's people. Brazil ranks fifth in the world in area and sixth in population. It is the only nation in the hemisphere whose predominant language is Portuguese, the product of its distinct colonial history. Nor did the differences stop with the end of empire. Where Spain's American empire was decapitated, Portugal's was naturalized: The Portuguese Crown Prince himself declared Brazil's independence and it remained a monarchy until 1889, the only one on the continent. Brazil was the last country in the hemisphere to abolish slavery, in 1888, and today it has three times more people of African descent than any other nation in the Americas.

Its unique history has given Brazilian society a different character and its people a distinct personality. Brazil emerged from the monarchy as a society ruled by elite consensus and shaped by deference. The monarchy also bequeathed to the republic that succeeded it a vast continental empire that it had held intact while Spanish America splintered—and a dream of *grandeza*. Modern Brazil is a nation that has believed in its uniqueness and in its destiny as "the country of the future."

But Brazil has also shared with the rest of Latin America and the Caribbean the boom and bust experience of being integrated into the global economy as an exporter of agricultural products and an importer of manufactures and capital. In Brazil, coffee was king and industry limited for the century that ended in the Great Depression of the 1930s. The Depression discredited the old coffee elites and brought to power Getúlio Vargas, a populist caudillo who scorned Brazil's "economy of desserts"—coffee, sugar, and tropical fruits—and placed the resources of the state behind a program of industrial growth a decade before Perón did it in Argentina, Brazil's historic rival for regional ascendancy. But President Vargas's goal of making Brazil an industrial power was still a distant dream when he died in 1954.

Juscelino Kubitschek took up the torch the following year. He reunited Vargas's populist coalition behind a program of promoting import substitution industries and set out to demonstrate that Brazil could succeed where Argentina had failed. Kubitschek had promised "50 Years of Progress in 5" and as president (1955–60) he delivered on this pledge. "He had set out thirty specific goals for his administration, and he achieved all of them," his daughter Marcia claimed. Steel output doubled, while automobile production increased by 80 percent. Much of this industrial growth was concentrated in São Paulo, which since the Depression had gone from being the center of Brazil's coffee economy to its industrial heartland.

Foreign car makers were largely responsible for the surge in automobile production, but their concessions were carefully regulated by the Brazilian government. Major U.S. and European companies such as General Motors, Ford, and Volkswagen were granted exclusive concessions for a class of vehicle, but on condition that a growing portion of that car or truck would be made in Brazil. This encouraged them to look for Brazilian parts suppliers and, unlike Argentina, to create an integrated industry that could serve as a base for future industrial growth.

Metaleve, a São Paulo enterprise that produced pistons and bearings, was one of the beneficiaries of this policy of import substitution. "We were favored by the fact that Brazil was being industrialized," José Mindlin, a founder of Metaleve, explained. "Engine parts were basic to creating an automotive industry, so we grew with the country—and helped the country to develop as well."

São Paulo might be Brazil's industrial center, where more than half its production and workers were concentrated by 1960, but it was Brasília, the new national capital that Kubitschek had built on a wild plateau in the middle of Brazil, which best expressed the vision of *grandeza* that underlay his industrial goals. The late 1950s was an era of rising nationalism and impatience for development. Brazilians saw their country as a sleeping giant that should awaken and assume its rightful place as a world power. Shifting the capital from coastal Rio de Janeiro to a new city in the heart of the interior signaled Brazil's determination to settle its entire territory and to exploit all of its rich resources, the only way that it could fulfill its potential and become a great power. The construction of the new capital was at the same time part of Kubitschek's strategy for accelerated industrial growth. Its roads and bridges, buildings and services became a major market for Brazil's industries. "Kubitschek was the first Brazilian president to have a coherent industrial policy," said Claudio Bardella, whose family metallurgical business benefited from Kubitschek's projects. Building Brasília was central to Kubitschek's economic strategy as well as to his geopolitical vision, affirmed Marcia Kubitschek, who in 1991 was lieutenant governor of the capital district: "He used to call Brasília the unification of all his goals."

This vision of Brasília as the capital of a continental power was clear in its design. It was constructed on a grandiose scale, a planned city of unwalkable distances and monumental vistas. Its buildings were created in an elegant international style that attested to the cosmopolitan character of the country and the sophistication of its elite. Even today, when its glass has lost some of its gleam and signs of wear have appeared on the steel and stone that face its towers, Brasília remains a strikingly modern city—a futuristic capital for the "country of the future."

At its inauguration in 1960 French writer André Maurois called Brasília "the city of hope," but by then the hopes that had launched it were being undermined by the costs of Kubitschek's economic edifice. His industrial strategy had overheated the economy. Inflation was accelerating and balance of payments problems were increasing. There was corruption in government and inefficiency in industry: The new automobiles rolling off the São Paulo assembly lines might look like German Volkswagens, but their quality was much lower and their cost far higher. Kubitschek left office before the house caved in, leaving it to his successors to deal with the economic collapse that followed.

They were not alone. By 1960 economic crisis, social unrest, and political unease were widespread in Latin America and the Caribbean.

Prices for the region's exports had declined, reducing national incomes and creating balance of payments problems. But those nations that had stressed industry were in no better shape. They suffered from balance-of-payments problems, rising inflation, and skewed prices, consequences of the economic model of import substitution they had all adopted. Even Mexico, the other industrial success story of the 1950s, whose economy had doubled in a decade, was now seeing its growth slowed, as demand for its manufactures had hit the limits of a national market that was restricted by a distribution of income so unequal that only a minority could afford them. In this situation of frustrated aspirations and dashed expectations, moderates embraced reform and radicals revolution, while the military waited in the wings with solutions of their own.

It was Fidel Castro who transformed concern into alarm. The Cuban revolution's turn to socialism at home and the Soviet Union abroad persuaded the United States to support the Latin American land reforms and industrial programs it had previously opposed. Kubitschek himself had proposed in 1958 that the United States lead a hemispheric reform movement that he dubbed Operation Panamericana. In 1961, just a month before the CIA-sponsored invasion of Castro's Cuba, President John Kennedy took up this idea and promised the Latin American and Caribbean leaders assembled in the White House an Alliance for Progress, the hemispheric Marshall Plan they had sought in vain since World War II. For Latin America's ailing economies, the Alliance proposed industrial growth within a regional free trade association that would expand their markets. The United States pledged twenty billion dollars in investments and loans; Latin America's entrepreneurs and governments would do the rest, investing billions of their own. For the region's impoverished peasants and hard-pressed governments, it promoted agrarian and tax reforms that would decrease rural inequality and increase government revenues. For struggling democrats, Kennedy offered support for their efforts to combat dictatorship. The Latin American military would receive special training to make them the nation builders and an effective barrier to the continental revolution that Castro called on the youth of the region to spearhead.

Brazil was one of the countries in which the Alliance for Progress soon lost its way, and where its contradictions became clear. After the resignation of Kubitschek's enigmatic successor, Jânio Quadros, Vice President João Goulart, head of the Labor party, took charge of the government. "Jango" Goulart was a disciple of Getúlio Vargas, but a more radical populist without the latter's political balance. In retrospect, the reforms he proposed were quite moderate: a limited land reform and restrictions on the repatriation of profits by foreign investors, extending the franchise to illiterates, and legalizing the Communist party. But within the context of the era and of Brazil—a nation with extreme inequalities of wealth and poverty, limited political participation, and an almost feudal society in the rural Northeast—these reforms and the popular movements that backed them seemed positively revolutionary. They alienated Brazilian businessmen and foreign investors alike, along with the powerful landowners of the Northeast and anticommunists in the Church, the armed forces, and the middle class.

Goulart's measures also antagonized the United States. Although many of the reforms Goulart proposed fit within the Alliance for Progress, Washington was angered by his refusal to break relations with Cuba, fearful of his economic nationalism, and suspicious of the popular movements his government promoted. As a consequence, U.S. aid was diverted from social reforms to the political campaigns of candidates who opposed them.

Foreigners ceased to invest and Brazilians sent their money out of the country. Inflation approached triple digits and consumer shortages began to appear. In an atmosphere of growing crisis, Goulart played the demagogue, compensating for his loss of control with incendiary rhetoric. His political and economic opponents organized a São Paulo march of half a million, mostly middle-class women, demanding Goulart's ouster. The conflict soon spread to the armed forces, where Goulart was accused of interfering with military discipline. In 1964, the armed forces seized power and installed General Humberto Castelo Branco as president, confident they had the support of middle- and upper-class Brazilians—and the United States.

Although President Kennedy had promised Latin Americans "an

abrazo for democrats" but only "a handshake for dictators," by 1964 he was dead and Lyndon Johnson was in the White House. Johnson was more worried about communism than dictatorship and less willing to give leftist reformers a chance to carry out the "peaceful revolution" that the Alliance for Progress had promised. When the Brazilian military overthrew Goulart, it was with the complicity of Washington. The United States then deluged their regime with the aid previously denied the civilian government.

There had been military regimes before in Latin America, a region notorious for its dictatorships. But this one was different. It was a government of the armed forces as institutions, not of an individual strongman. The military chose Castelo Branco's successors, and officers deliberated on government policy and ran state enterprises. Moreover, the Brazilian armed forces seized power with a mission that transcended the ouster of a suspect civilian leader: It was the first "national security" state, with a broad notion of national security that included economic development, social discipline, and political stability.

In time the Argentine, Chilean, and Uruguayan militaries would emulate the Brazilian example, leading analysts to speak about a new type of military government, a "bureaucratic authoritarian regime," in southern South America. Although they differed in their economic policies, they all repressed labor unions and popular movements and were virulently anti-communist, a label they applied to leftists of all shades. Many leftists found it expedient to go into exile, while others languished in jail or found early graves. José Serra, today a respected federal deputy for the moderate Social Democrats, was one of those who left Brazil in 1964. "I was president of the National Student Association [UNI] at that time and I had to leave the country," he recalled. "UNI was a very strong student movement and together with the CGT [labor confederation] was one of the main targets of the repression."

But the aspirations of the Brazilian military went beyond stopping the threat they discerned on the left. They took over with a determination to change Brazil's economic and political habits. For Castelo Branco, a moderate within the army, this was a temporary military tutelage before returning a "purified democracy" to civilian control. For hardline officers like General Oswaldo Oliva, who had studied "national problems" as well as military strategy at Brazil's War Academy, the goal was a Brazilian revolution that would fulfill the country's destiny to be a great power. "We often used the expression 'Brazil the great! Brazil the powerful!' " Oliva said. "Power in the world is a great nation that has territory, population, wealth, financial resources, technology, material goods, minerals. Brazil had almost all of these elements and we knew this. So we tried to develop Brazil using these comparative advantages."

In order to make Brazil a great power, Brazil's military leaders recruited skilled civilian technocrats and gave them a mandate to design and implement policies that might not have been politically acceptable under a democratic government. "We elaborated a great big document that was called 'Concepts and Strategies for National Security,' " General Oliva said. "The great objective was to make Brazil grow. It was a secret document that said what Brazil should do and how it should be done. We made sure that the ministers did not detour from these objectives. Within this context, the ministers had freedom of action," he explained. "To ensure that the economic part was well done, we put in the best economists of the time, men like Roberto Campos, who Castelo Branco made planning minister."

Campos, who had previously worked for both Kubitschek and Goulart, was an orthodox economist with U.S. training and conservative views. "We inherited a chaotic situation," he recalled: "High inflation, capital flight, an enormous budget deficit, a balance of payments crisis." His solution was to impose a harsh austerity program, which reduced real wages and government spending and gradually brought inflation under control. When workers protested, the military showed the fist within their starched gloves: Strikes were broken, leaders jailed, and activists fired.

Political opponents met with a similar treatment. First the leaders of the left lost their political rights, then it was the turn of the center, and finally of the right, despite their initial support for the military regime. If democracy was to be restored it would be under different parties and politicians. Even Kubitschek went into exile, his daughter explained, "because he felt there was no climate in Brazil for a strong believer in democracy."

Campos "persuaded the generals" of the necessity "to implant a modern capitalist system in Brazil." The government continued to play an active economic role, but as "a promoter of export-oriented growth, instead of the inward-looking strategy of import substitution." It was "unique in Latin America for that time," claimed Campos, and preceded Taiwan and Korea in adopting similar policies. "Our slogan was: 'The solution is to export.'"

Yet not until 1968 would international trade revive and these policies succeed in restoring the rapid growth that had made Brazil the world's fastest expanding economy between 1940 and 1960. Castelo Branco was dead by 1968, replaced by more hard-line generals, who expected the military to rule for an extended period and thought of democracy as guided by the armed forces. Roberto Campos was gone as well, replaced as economic czar by António Delfim Netto, an equally persuasive but less orthodox economist, whose goal was rapid growth and who inherited the ideal conditions in which to achieve it.

"He received an economy that was tight, lean, reformed, restructured, with an exchange system in order, fiscal reform in place, and ample stocks of commodities," said Campos, with pride in his own accomplishments. "We were the sowers of the Miracle, but not the reapers."

A Miracle—and Its Costs

Delfim Netto would reap the economic growth that Campos had sowed, with the aid of "a wave of international prosperity, from which he was wise enough to benefit," observed Campos drily. "It was a moment in which the world was moving quickly," Delfim said. "So we put our boat in the water and it moved very fast. Between 1968 and 1974 we grew at over ten percent a year." Industrial production expanded at an even faster rate, 13 percent, and the number of industrial workers doubled, from nine million to eighteen million. This surge was led by the automobile industry and its suppliers. During the decade that followed the 1964 coup the number of vehicles rolling off São Paulo's assembly lines quintupled, to nearly a million a year, while steel production tripled. Foreign investment poured in, attracted by Brazil's political stability, controlled labor force, and incentives that ranged from tax credits to subsidies. As one U.S. automobile executive said at the time: "In Brazil, we expect to get our money back in only two years." But public investment soared as well, concentrated in the basic commodities, such as steel and petrochemicals, required to manufacture consumer goods, but also in expanding the infrastructure of economic growth—energy, roads, communications. Brazil's private sector benefited from the economic boom, too. Claudio Bardella's metallurgical firm expanded into earth-moving equipment. José Mindlin's factory sold many more diesel engines. "Metaleve grew steadily after 1964," Mindlin said, "but for many Brazilian companies the nineteen seventies were a real miracle."

Unlike the earlier Kubitschek industrial surge, with its inefficient protected industries, this one was export oriented. In 1960 industrial goods made up only 3 percent of Brazil's exports; by 1974 Brazil's industries accounted for 30 percent of exports, underscoring their new competitiveness. Agricultural and mining exports also expanded, aided by favorable exchange-rate policies. Inflation remained under control, foreign currency reserves high, and Brazil's external debt low.

Between 1968 and 1973, Brazil's economy grew more rapidly than any other in the world. *The Economist* dubbed it the "Brazilian Miracle," confirming the belief of the country's military leaders that Brazil would take its rightful place in the ranks of the world powers sooner rather than later. "That's our nation's destiny," General Oliva said. Yet, even *The Economist* cautioned that the Miracle had its costs. "The Brazilian economy has grown over the past decade in much the same way as a Brazilian drives his car," it quipped: "Extremely fast, disregarding everyone else on the road, narrowly avoiding accidents and not stopping to consider whether his passengers have been left behind."[1]

The loss of political freedom was one of the costs of the economic miracle. "It was the time of the greatest repression," recalled Luis Inácio da Silva, who as "Lula" would become Brazil's foremost labor leader. "The repression of the union movement, the repression of political parties, the repression of the students, the repression of the intellectuals." Yet, he reflected, "it was exactly at this time of the biggest political repression that Brazil had its great economic growth."

This was no coincidence. The social "discipline" and political stability that attracted foreign investors was assured by an increasingly repressive military regime. Workers were not the only Brazilians to lose their rights during the years of the economic miracle. By 1969, General Emilio Médici, a former head of the national intelligence service, was president, and the hard-line military dominated the government. The congress was closed, the press censored, and the courts controlled. The universities were purged and student protests were crushed—all in the name of "national security." With democratic avenues of dissent closed to them, some opponents of the regime took up arms, in a weak guerrilla movement that one expert termed "a veritable 'Children's Crusade,' "[2] at once young, idealistic, naive—and doomed. This was the military's terrain and they declared an internal war. It was a dirty war in which torture became routine and disappearances commonplace. Military intelligence and the political police grew in impunity, and Brazil became notorious for its human rights violations, another area where it blazed a trail that military regimes in Argentina, Chile, and Uruguay later followed, and extended. The guerrillas were soon defeated, but the security apparatus remained, maintaining a grim surveillance of a cowed opposition.

For military hard-liners like General Oliva, a member of Brazil's powerful National Security Council during these years, it was a struggle against "communism," a battle between good and evil in which the ends justified the means. "It is good to remember that in the decade of the sixties, Cuba had been taken over, the U.S. had failed in the Bay of Pigs, and we were one of the goals of the communist movement that was spreading around the world," he said. "If Brazil had become communist, all of South America would have followed, and I don't know what would have happened to the United States," Oliva said, articulating the military's domino-theory view of the world. That was why Brazil's military government "gave such emphasis to security."

It was a struggle for the destiny of Brazil in which the university was as much a battleground as the jungle. "In that struggle, unfortunately, many young people became involved and turned against us," Oliva said.

One of them was his own son, Aloisio Mercadante. "I was in the university at the time, and I could not accept the violations of human rights or the social costs of the so-called Miracle," he said. "I had different values than my father. There were many arguments. It was very painful."

For many opponents of the military, the pain was not just emotional. Thousands were jailed and tortured, hundreds disappeared into unmarked graves. "When one fights with arms," responded General Oliva, "someone dies, someone suffers, someone pays." But most of those detained had nothing to do with the guerrillas. They were workers active in their unions, priests who were organizing community groups, or students who protested the military's denial of political rights and civil liberties.

General Oliva remained unapologetic. "If there were excesses, they were unintentional," he said. "They were errors that we would have liked not to have happened, but that is part of the process. I don't repent of anything that I did, not even my errors." He still maintains today that it was not a "military dictatorship" because "the press was only controlled where *subversive* writing was concerned." The military's definition of "subversive," moreover, was an expansive one—and the written word was not its only target.

"In the early seventies, all of Brazil suffered and the slums were no exception," recalled Benedita da Silva, then a community leader in Rio de Janeiro's Chapeu de Mangueira *favela,* one of the city's many shantytowns. "We didn't have the freedom to express what we thought. Almost all the community leaders were persecuted." When the military took power in 1964, "they said they knew what was good for Brazilians; that they would resolve the chaos of Brazilian society," she said. "But what they did was oppress the poor."

The Miracle brought increased prosperity to many Brazilians. Some became millionaires, while others increased their fortunes. "There was a great effervescence," recalled Sergio Andrade de Carvalho. "Delfim Netto used to say, 'Whoever stands still will be run over.' " Andrade's family had taken a small regional bank and within four years turned it into the fifteenth largest in Brazil before selling it for an enormous profit. But it was not just the wealthy who benefited. The middle class grew in numbers and income, able to enjoy the consumer society of their counterparts in the United States or Europe. Workers in the modern industrial sector also gained, but to a lesser degree. Lula described this as a time when an autoworker was "considered privileged because he lived in a reasonable house, he could buy a little car, he and his wife could go to the supermarket and fill up the fridge. He could eat out on the weekend and go to the beach once a month when it was hot. It was a reasonable life-style."

Yet, in 1974, at the end of the Miracle, Brazil had a more unequal distribution of income than India, and the worst poverty rate among the world's twenty-five largest economies. In part, this was because people in Brazil's upper income brackets had gained disproportionately from the economic boom. But the new prosperity had not "trickled down" to the rural and urban poor. Four out of ten Brazilians might live far better than before, but the lot of the majority had not improved significantly.

Delfim Netto was aware of the problem. At the start of the Miracle he had warned that "a cake had to rise before it can be sliced and served up," General Oliva said. "If there was no cake, what could be divided? So, we made the cake grow." Yet, even after the cake had risen to impressive dimensions, many questioned the way in which it had been sliced.

For Benedita da Silva, growing up black and poor in Rio de Janeiro meant that "life itself was a struggle. I worked as a maid, then I left and went to work as a cleaning lady in a school. I sold lemons and cosmetics, too. I've done everything you had to do so you didn't die of hunger." She also became a community leader in Chapeu de Mangueira and during the "Miracle" helped save her *favela* from being destroyed in the military's "slum removal" program. For da Silva and her impoverished neighbors, that was the "only miracle *we* saw."

They had started out believing in the military's promise of a share of the Miracle's benefits. "Everybody had to work a lot because they said, 'Let the cake grow and when it's really big everybody is going to get a piece,' " Benedita said. "But our piece of it was to continue without water, without electricity, without sewage." She was "a Fundamentalist Christian" who "believes in miracles," she stressed. "But this Miracle . . . happened for the military, for the big landowners, for the businessmen. . . . The rich became richer. The mansions grew." But the poor never received their promised share: "We didn't have even one slice of that cake on our table. You call this a miracle?" she scoffed. "It was Brazil's capital sin!"

Albert Fishlow, a leading expert on the Brazilian economy who headed a U.S. advisory group in Brazil until 1969, agreed that the military regime had missed a unique opportunity. "They had the resources to address Brazil's poverty problems, but they refused to do it. Instead, they said that Brazil was still poor, and that they needed another decade of growth before Brazil could afford the luxury of dealing with its unequal distribution of income."

As a result, even in São Paulo, the industrial heartland of the Miracle, a Catholic church study documented the widespread persistence of poverty. It was concentrated among the millions of Brazilians who had migrated from rural areas in the impoverished Northeast in search of a future. The inequality among Brazil's regions—between its industrial Center-South and its underdeveloped Northeast—was as dramatic as the gap between its rich and poor. São Paulo was twelve times as wealthy as Piauí, Brazil's poorest state, the greatest regional inequality among the world's major economies. The military had not created this geographic inequality, but they had halted the reforms that might have addressed it, and their own policies had exacerbated it. While São Paulo and other states of the Center-South were expanding their industries and modernizing their farms, the Northeast remained a drought-stricken region of large estates and dwarf farms, unemployed youths and impoverished peasants—like the aging Dona Biu, who scratched a bare living from the parched soil of Pernambuco. "The land in the Northeast is tired, because it doesn't rain here," she said. There were some farms that had irrigation and grew vegetables for the market, but "that was for the rich."

Thirty million people migrated from the depressed rural Northeast to the cities of the Center-South in the 1970s. Dona Biu had raised ten children, and all but one had left. "Who that is young would stay here with

a hoe and a sickle in this place where nothing grows?" she asked rhetorically. "The youth, they go to a place that has something."

During the Miracle, São Paulo had something that was the dream of
every migrant from the Northeast: industrial jobs. Dona Biu and her
husband had gone for a time, too, believing that in São Paulo "everybody
becomes rich," only to find that it was not so easy to succeed there,
although she and her husband "struggled all over the city." The new
migrants swelled the shantytowns that ringed the city, living in poverty
with other migrants from the Northeast and searching for a job. It was a tale
told by the *cantadores* in their songs:

> *You work and nothing comes of it.*
> *You leave the land that you planted*
> *To go and live in a slum. . . .*
> *The people don't have schools or hospitals.*
> *So we will go to São Paulo*
> *And suffer in the same way.*

For the desperate poor of regions such as the Northeast, the regime failed
to deliver its promised miracle.

Another three million migrants followed the new roads built by the
military into the Amazon rain forest. The military regime promoted the
colonization of the Amazon as a strategy to consolidate Brazil's frontiers
and to develop its economy. "Nearly four hundred years after its discovery," Delfim Netto declared in August 1984, "we will at last take possession
of our own country." For hard-line president Emilio Médici, colonization
of the Amazon was also a way to solve the problems of land hunger in the
Northeast without a "communist" land reform, by moving "people without
land to a land without people."

As the Trans-Amazon Highway cut through the rain forest, an army
of landless peasants followed, pioneers on an inhospitable frontier who
burned a clearing in the forest and squatted on the land as subsistence
farmers. Hard on their heels came big ranchers and corporate investors
with greater resources and better connections. They employed private

armies to drive the squatters off their farms and terrorize migrant workers into accepting low wages and unsanitary living conditions that left most diseased and many dead.

The tropical soils of the Amazon, moreover, proved less fertile and more fragile than the migrants imagined, and abandoned farms soon dotted the burned-out landscape. Mining ventures followed, to exploit the mineral riches that lay below the leached soils, poisoning them and the rivers with their chemicals and wastes and cutting down the forests to stoke their furnaces. So did the lumber companies, which clear-cut the ancient hardwoods and left a jungle wasteland in place of the sylvan wilderness.

The military had encouraged this "development" of the region, pushing the highways deeper into the rain forest without regard for their environmental impact. Today, Delfim Netto is willing to admit that the colonization of the Amazon was a mistake, although he still defends the highway. But, he argues, to criticize his government for ecocide is to apply the standards of today to the policies of the past. "Nobody talked about ecology in 1970"—or Indians.

The indigenous peoples of the Amazon, already much reduced by centuries of disease—but still the most numerous tribal peoples on the continent—found their lands and rivers invaded by squatters and ranchers, miners and lumbermen. Their efforts to defend their way of life were often met with a violence they could not withstand and by the spread of diseases they could not resist. The military failed to protect their lands or defend their reserves. The 321 Kreen-Akarores were ousted from the lands of their ancestors to make room for a highway. Only seventy-nine survived their resettlement in the Xingú reserve. The Indians of the Amazon, too, became victims of the "Miracle."

After the Miracle

Brazil's economic miracle was not only costly, it was vulnerable, dependent upon an international environment that Brazil could not control. "In 1973," Delfim Netto recalled, "our exports were six billion dollars, our imports were six billion dollars, our [foreign currency] reserves were six billion dollars, and our external debt was twelve billion dollars." Moreover, "inflation was running at only fifteen percent a year and our rate of growth was fourteen percent for the year." At the end of 1973, however, the Middle East war and the Arab petroleum embargo that followed sent oil prices skyrocketing. Despite its mineral riches, Brazil relied on imports for 90 percent of its oil requirements and depended on petroleum to run its factories and transport its goods. It was the biggest oil importer in the Third World. By the beginning of 1974 it was clear that the Miracle was over and that an era of hard choices had begun.

A new military president, General Ernesto Geisel, was inaugurated early that year. He had been head of Petrobras, the state petroleum company. One of his first major decisions was how to deal with the oil crisis. "The first oil crisis was devastating," said Delfim Netto, who became the new government's ambassador in Paris. "We went from spending seven, eight, or nine percent of our export earnings on oil to using almost half."

Brazil was not the only country that confronted this oil shock. The United States cut back on growth and fell into a deep recession. Like most of Latin America, Brazil looked for a way to keep growing, and found it in the loans offered by international banks awash in petrodollars generated by the same OPEC price hike. "Instead of curbing development and waiting for a solution to the oil crisis, they continued to accelerate on an absolutely unrealistic basis," charged banker Sergio Andrade de Carvalho.

"There was no choice," Delfim Netto said. "To reduce our oil imports by fifty percent would have meant a cut in our Gross Domestic Product of twenty-five to thirty-five percent. Brazilian agriculture depended on oil, so did industry and transport. The decision was either to increase our debt or else to decrease our economy dramatically." Brazil, like most of the region, chose to increase its debt, a decision that even economists who disagree with Delfim's doomsday scenario believe was a reasonable one at the time.

"There were important projects in Brazil that we wanted to continue," said Luis Bresser Pereira, a critic of the military regime and later a finance minister. Moreover, "the private banks, the World Bank, and the

IMF supported that decision and all wanted to lend us money. So it makes perfect sense that we became indebted at this time." It was an era of easy money, especially for a country with Brazil's record of economic growth and dynamism. "Every day we were almost begged by foreign bankers knocking on our door," said Andrade de Carvalho, then a director of the state-owned Bank of Brazil, "offering us as many dollars as we wanted—long-term loans at low rates"—in some cases as low as the rate of inflation.

Beyond these economic calculations lay both the vision of *grandeza* and more pragmatic political considerations. Geisel was a military moderate who came to the presidency with the idea of opening up the political system and beginning a carefully controlled transition to a new Brazilian democracy. The Miracle had made economic success the touchstone of political legitimacy. "Brazilians had come to expect economic growth as their divine right," Roberto Campos snorted. Geisel needed continued economic prosperity to rally support for his political opening. In Brazil the economic watchword would continue to be "growth first."

The Opening

"It was always our intention to restore democracy," insisted Colonel Jarbas Passarinho, a veteran of all the military governments, who had signed the decrees that curtailed democracy and those that restored it. "We never suspended the constitution, like the Chileans," he said. "Congress remained open except for a brief period." There was some truth to his claim, but it hid as much as it revealed. The military hard-liners may have maintained the constitution in form, but they had violated its spirit with their decrees and its letter with their torture and electoral fraud. The hard-liners anticipated decades of military rule before Brazil would be "ready for democracy," and the democracy they envisioned was one in which the military retained a tutelary role.

But the 1974 presidential "election" brought back to power the military moderates under General Geisel, whose brother was head of the army.

The new president returned General Golbery Couto e Silva, a military intellectual who had been Castelo Branco's political chief of staff, to his old position. They set out to ease the military grip on Brazilian society, restore the rule of law, end human rights violations, and return the "revolution of '64" to Castelo Branco's original vision of a military transition to a sanitized democracy.

It became known as the *abertura*, the Portuguese word for "opening," and was conceived by General Golbery as a controlled process of gradual liberalization that would lead to the restoration of democracy. There were reasons other than loyalty to their original vision that led Geisel and Golbery to initiate this political opening. By 1974 the necessity of military rule was less clear and its legitimacy was being called into question.

The original rationale for the military seizure of power in 1964—the threat of a communist revolution—seemed less compelling a decade later. The guerrillas had been defeated, the Communist party had been decimated, and the Cuban revolution had lost much of its allure and menace. The military had also succeeded in bringing order to the economic and political "chaos" that had been another motive for their intervention.

If the successes of a decade of military rule argued for the armed forces to declare victory and return to the barracks, so did growing criticisms of the regime's excesses and the effects of its policies. The Catholic church, which had supported the military takeover in 1964, had turned increasingly against it during the decade that followed in response to human rights violations and the social costs of the economic miracle. By 1974 prelates like São Paulo's Cardinal Paulo Evaristo Arns were coming close to challenging the legitimacy of military rule.

The end of the economic miracle created other reasons for the military to change their political course. "By then, what gave the regime legitimacy was not the fight against communism, but economic development," said José Serra, the former student leader who had become an economist during his years in exile. But the economic miracle of 1968 to 1973 had set a high political standard that the oil price hike and the global recession made hard to live up to. The military might be best advised to share responsibility with civilians for the harder economic times ahead. At a minimum, Golbery argued, it would be wise to allow the growing popular pressure for change to be released by what he called "decompression."

These rationales came together in the political opening that began in 1974 and continued until the restoration of civilian rule in 1985. But if this was a transition to democracy, it was one shaped by the military regime to avoid a return to the past. The old parties and politicians remained banned. In their place, two new parties were created—a government party and an opposition party—and new leaders were handed their reins.

Geisel and Golbery began the *abertura* confident that most Brazilians supported the "revolution of '64." When the first free elections revealed that this was not true, they continued the opening, but at a slower speed and with a manipulation of political rules and media access that would have made a U.S. political boss blush—from a Chamber of Deputies that greatly overrepresented conservative rural areas to packing the Senate with appointed "bionic senators" and allowing the opposition only one hour of television time a year.

The opposition's electoral success provoked a more serious threat to the *abertura*: repression from hard-line officers who controlled military intelligence and important army commands. In São Paulo they began a witch-hunt against alleged communists in government. In 1975 they arrested and killed Vladimir Herzog, a respected journalist who was news director for the educational television channel of São Paulo State, where the opposition had recently won elections. José Mindlin realized that "it was the first act in a right-wing military coup scenario." Mindlin was not only a successful entrepreneur, he was also a firm democrat and a man of great culture, whose private library was one of the finest in Latin America. When he was asked to become São Paulo's secretary of culture, he felt that he could not refuse to contribute to the political opening. It was a job that made him Herzog's boss and a target of the hard-liners. "They interrogated Herzog and other journalists they arrested about 'communist infiltration.' They considered me a 'communist' because I was outspoken in my support of democracy." Mindlin offered to resign, but São Paulo's civilian governor told him that if he did he would "weaken our resistance to the coup, because they want to arrest you, then arrest me, and then overthrow Geisel." Mindlin withdrew his resignation, Cardinal Arns rallied civilian resistance to this renewal of state terror, and Geisel used Herzog's murder and another death in custody in January 1976 to replace São Paulo's hard-line army commander and consolidate his position. The *abertura* was safe. "It was very gratifying," Mindlin recalled. "The Herzog affair was a turning point."

A year later José Mindlin was selected as one of Brazil's ten most respected businessmen in a poll of his peers. Eight of the winners then issued a manifesto calling for a return to democracy and for direct negotiations between business and labor. "It was the first collective statement by businessmen," Mindlin said, "and it made a major difference." Claudio Bardella, who had built his family firm into a booming business making everything from structural steel to earth movers, was another of its moving spirits. "After we began, others followed," he recalled. "Even the politicians of the government party began to speak about democracy."

Bardella also pioneered a new kind of labor relations in Brazil, where since the days of Getúlio Vargas, the government had controlled unions, regulated labor relations, and brokered accords. He had lived in Germany, where workers negotiated directly with their employers and "analyzing the results, I saw that Germany had a better idea." Foreign companies like Volkswagen and General Motors were used to direct negotiations. Brazilian businessmen were not. "In the beginning, other businessmen said I was crazy," he recalled, "but afterwards, many of them joined us."

The Geisel government was pleased at entrepreneurial support for their political opening, but it "was very afraid of our new vision of labor and business, and tried to stop our direct negotiations with labor," Bardella said. "But we were convinced that this was the best solution, so we went ahead without the government." Bardella saw himself as "a new kind of business leader, who did not look to the state for direction."

Neither did Lula. Luis Inácio da Silva was born in 1946 into a peasant family in the Northeast that migrated to São Paulo when he was a boy. He had gone to an industrial school and worked his way up as a lathe operator in the factories of the nearby city of São Bernardo do Campo, the center of Brazil's automobile industry. It was during the Miracle, Lula recalled, that he was elected to union office and became conscious that "the unions were not combative unions trying to organize the workers within the factory," but "mere medical assistance agencies" controlled by the government. Lula soon won a reputation as a leader "who fought for the workers." In 1975 he was elected head of the São Bernardo metalworkers union, which he turned into "a new kind of union," one which rejected government subsidies in order to be free to oppose its policies and "fight the drop in real wages."

"Lula," stressed Claudio Bardella, "was a new kind of labor leader. When Lula first started negotiating with me, he said, 'I have nothing to do with the state, with parties, with the Church. I just represent the workers.' " The two men's direct bargaining was a landmark whose symbolic significance transcended the wages and benefits they agreed on. In fact, Bardella said, those first negotiations "were not difficult, [because] in the beginning, Lula knew nothing about economics and neither did the people around him." But "Lula was intelligent and likable," José Mindlin pointed out, and he learned fast. By 1978, with wages falling behind inflation, he was ready to organize the first major Brazilian strike in more than a decade.

"Between 1975 and 1978, there was an effervescence in society," Lula said. "People began to demonstrate. Students and intellectuals began to struggle. Businessmen began to speak of democracy and the right to strike. The press spoke about the right to strike. Even people in government began to speak about the right to strike. So when we struck, they couldn't do anything." For Lula, it was an historic turning point: "I felt that from then on we could improve the living standards of the workers. I felt that from that instant the history of this country would begin to change. I felt from then on that we would reconquer democracy."

In 1979, Lula and his union set off a wave of strikes that involved three million workers, one of the biggest walkouts in Brazilian history. In 1980, there was another strike, in which Lula was jailed. But when the government cracked down on the strikers the Church opened its doors to them, and student associations, women's groups, and other grassroots organizations rallied to their cause, as did middle-class professionals. The political opening had promoted a rebirth of civil society, whose new social movements supported each other against the regime. "Lula played a very important role in this process," said Aloisio Mercadante, General Oliva's son, who had become an economist and adviser to the labor leader. "He expressed the social demands and the demands for a renewal of democracy that the military had tried to repress. He symbolized civil society's challenge to the authoritarian regime." By 1980, Brazil was confronting dramatic economic challenges as well.

Of Growth and Grandeza

At first the strategy of debt-led growth that the Geisel government had settled on as a response to the first oil shock seemed a success. While the United States was sliding into a deep recession in 1974, Brazil's economy grew by 9 percent, and it continued to grow by a remarkable 7 percent per year for the rest of the decade. "It encouraged the belief that the laws of economics did not apply to Brazil," Albert Fishlow recalled. "Brazilians even boasted that the United States could learn how to handle an oil price rise from their experience."

Foreign loans sustained the economic expansion that allowed the Geisel government to continue its political opening. The money borrowed from abroad, moreover, helped finance an enlarged public investment that compensated for the low levels of private investment. Although Geisel talked of the Brazilian economy as being pulled by a troika of foreign corporations, local entrepreneurs, and state companies, for him it was the public sector that was the lead horse. Geisel had been head of Petrobras, and he "was highly nationalistic and wary of foreign investment, unlike Delfim and myself," Roberto Campos said. "His ideology was: If they want to come they can, but if we borrow we will retain control and that would be better." The increase in the government's economic role was striking. By 1980 twenty-four of Brazil's twenty-six largest enterprises were state-owned, and foreign observers were talking about its "managerial state," while Brazilian businessmen complained about "state capitalism."

For Geisel, this increase in public investment was motivated not only by a continued commitment to growth, but also by a desire to make Brazil self-sufficient in capital goods—such as machinery. "After Kubitschek," said Claudio Bardella, whose business profited from government contracts, "Geisel was the only president to have a real industrial policy." In addition to "maintaining a reasonable rate of growth" and creating a capital goods industry, the Geisel government sought to promote exports and to undertake social programs that would begin to address Brazil's problems of inequality and poverty. "They were all good goals," said the respected opposition economist José Serra. "But to pursue them all at the same time was overly ambitious."

Brazil's ambitions were symbolized by the huge high-profile projects that absorbed much of the foreign credits, such as the Trans-Amazon Highway system and the gigantic Itaipú dam built to tap the Iguaçú Falls, the continent's largest, at a cost of fifteen billion dollars. Critics called them "Pharaonic projects," which had more to do with the military's vision of Brazil's *grandeza* than with their economic utility.

"Brazil has a mania of greatness, starting with its size," said Sergio Andrade de Carvalho, who left the government bank to return to his family business during the Geisel era. "I think that these eight million square kilometers give us a sense that we must be big in everything, and sometimes enormous errors are committed that are justified by this false sense of greatness." General Oliva was impatient with such criticisms. "Brazil is not a tiny country like Portugal. . . . Whoever thinks small cannot lead a large country," he argued. "A large country is large. Solutions must be on a grand scale."

Even Delfim Netto agreed that the government's nuclear energy program, which had only one problematic plant to show for billions of dollars invested, was a product of "imperial ambition," and the Brazilian military's concern "to keep pace with Argentina. Had we spent this money instead on finding and producing oil," Delfim admitted, "we could have solved our energy problem." But most of the post-1973 projects "were productive," he insisted, with economic value that repaid their costs. José

Serra agreed, pointing to the heavy investment in alternative sources of energy, from hydroelectricity to gasohol, in which Brazil now leads the world. Itaipú now supplies one third of São Paulo's electricity needs and most Brazilian automobiles burn gasohol or alcohol instead of gasoline. Another example was the ambitious investment in capital goods, Serra noted, "which represented a jump in economic development."

But these projects were expensive, and their considerable costs were financed with foreign credits, which greatly increased Brazil's external debt. By 1979 the foreign debt exceeded fifty billion dollars, and the interest on it accounted for one half of Brazil's balance of payments deficit. By then, oil accounted for one third of imports and inflation was accelerating. Still, stressed Delfim Netto, who took over as economic czar again in mid-1979, "the economic situation was manageable—until the Arabs raised the price of oil and the Americans increased the cost of money."

The Lost Decade

"The second oil shock was dramatically worse than the first," Delfim Netto explained, "because in 1973 oil increased from $2 to $12 a barrel, while in 1979 it jumped from $12 to $34 a barrel." For Brazil this meant the oil that had cost it $4 billion in 1978 would cost $11 billion in 1980.

What compounded Brazil's problems was the U.S. decision to deal with its own inflation by raising interest rates to historic heights. "Then they applied these higher interest rates to our loans as well," General Oliva protested. Like the rest of the region, Brazil had borrowed at an adjustable rate of interest and now that decision came back to haunt it. Brazil found itself paying interest rates of over 20 percent on loans that it had contracted at 4 to 7 percent a year. "The enormous elevation of interest rates for a country greatly indebted like ours was really tragic," Sergio Andrade de Carvalho said. It presented Brazil with a decision similar to 1973 but in far more perilous circumstances. Orthodox economists like Roberto Campos called for a slowing down of growth to adjust to the new international economic environment, but they were not heeded. "A nation can't be stopped like a train. Put on the brakes and *tccch* it stops," said General Oliva. "[A nation] doesn't stop. The process has to continue."

Brazilian entrepreneurs, whose own overextended positions were vulnerable to a contraction of the economy, agreed. Delfim Netto, the magician of the Miracle, was once again in control, and he exuded confidence that Brazil could grow its way out of this crisis as it had the last. At first it seemed to work; a new round of foreign borrowing enabled Brazil's economy to expand by 9 percent in 1980 while the rest of the world plunged into recession.

But this time it was an illusion. The old magic could not continue to work amid the gathering storms of the 1980s. Inflation soared over 100 percent in 1980 for the first time in Brazilian history, and the foreign debt approached sixty-five billion dollars by the year's end, while interest payments on it accounted for one half of the country's growing dollar deficit. By then, Delfim had conceded that the magic was gone and reversed his course, contracting the economy. The result was a steep recession, in which real per capita income fell 5 percent in 1981, the sharpest drop in a century. Yet inflation remained high and Brazil's foreign debt continued to mount, exceeding seventy-five billion dollars by year's end. Debt payments absorbed two thirds of the country's export income.

Brazil was not the only Latin American country with a heavy foreign debt burden. Most of the countries in the region had followed a similar policy of debt-led growth after 1973. By 1982 even oil-rich countries like Mexico and Venezuela were in trouble, as oil prices dropped in the global recession. When Mexico suspended payment on its eighty-billion-dollar external debt in 1982, the international banks suddenly realized their own vulnerability, and loans dried up, even for countries that had always paid their debts, like Brazil.

Delfim Netto was unwilling to admit defeat. Confident that he could beat inflation and turn the economy around if he could secure new foreign loans, Delfim did the unthinkable and went cap in hand to the International Monetary Fund. By 1983, he had reached an agreement on a stabilization plan with the IMF and an accord on Brazil's debt with the international banks. Loans coming due would be rolled over, but Brazil's foreign debt would grow, exceeding one hundred billion dollars by 1984. It was an agreement that sacrificed Brazil's dreams of *grandeza,* punctured its illusions of strength, and belied its claims of economic autonomy. There was worse to come. Despite the accord, the banks continued to shrink Brazil's credit lines. For the remainder of the decade, more capital would leave Brazil to pay its debts than would enter it as new foreign loans or investments—despite Brazil's having one of the most positive trade balances in the world.

With the possibility of new loans gone, Delfim Netto struggled to avoid a default on Brazil's debt by slashing imports and increasing exports. Export promotion had begun during the Miracle years, when Brazil began to export significant quantities of manufactured goods for the first time. It had continued under Geisel, with the expansion of mining and the emergence of Brazil as one of the world's leading arms exporters. After 1980, however, Delfim pushed exports with all the incentives and ingenuity at his command. Brazil continued to export more coffee than Colombia and more sugar than Cuba, but it now became the world's biggest exporter of orange juice and a major shipper of soybeans. The giant Carajás mining project, with its major deposits of iron and manganese, which came on stream in 1985, symbolized the intensified exploitation of the rich mineral resources of the Amazon—at great environmental cost. Brazil also became a major industrial exporter, selling everything from shoes to planes in North America, while using its political influence to establish itself in African markets and flexible policies to make its mark in the Middle East. Brazilians built dams in Egypt, prospected for minerals in Angola, and pumped oil in Iraq. By 1985, the country's exports had risen to twenty-four billion dollars, a testament both to government policies and enterprises, and to the creativity and dynamism of Brazilian entrepreneurs.

But the six-billion-dollar positive trade balance in 1983 was due more to the sharp drop in imports than to the expansion of exports. It reflected a deepening recession that cut per capita income by almost 6 percent and industrial production by 7 percent, as well as a halt to technology imports that would damage Brazilian industry. Government spending and real wages were reduced, but inflation soared to 233 percent in 1984. By then, despite the resumption of growth, it was clear that Delfim Netto's heterodox magic had exacerbated the economic crisis instead of conjuring it away.

Time had run out. Not only had the government's confident belief that the oil price rise was only temporary and that foreign money would flow to Brazil forever proved false, but so had the regime's assumption that they could control their people indefinitely through repression and manipulation. The deepening economic crisis provoked growing social unrest and political protest. With the luster of its economic performance dimmed, and its legitimacy questioned, the military began to pay the price for decades of ignoring popular needs. Grassroots organizations multiplied and grew in militancy. When the government cut food subsidies, riots broke out in major cities. Wages lagged behind prices and strikes increased in number and scope. The charismatic Lula emerged as a national labor leader, head of a combative Brazilian confederation formed in 1981.

The political landscape had changed as well. In 1979, General Geisel was replaced as president by his handpicked choice, General João Figuereido, the head of army intelligence. He continued the *abertura,* although without Geisel's skill and commitment. Still, under Figuereido, the political opening would reach its fruition in the restoration of democracy. In 1979 an amnesty for Brazilians imprisoned or exiled for political crimes was declared and the political rights of former leaders were restored. The same year saw the end of the compulsory two-party system, which produced a growing array of new parties. The government continued to manipulate the rules of the game in an effort to control the process, and managed to maintain a majority in the electoral college that would choose the next president.

But the economic crisis was much more difficult for the military to control—and so were its political consequences. After 1970, the military regime increasingly legitimated its rule by its economic success. When, after 1980, it could no longer deliver prosperity and growth, it was not only attacked by its opponents but also abandoned by its former civilian supporters. In 1984 more than four million people of different classes and political loyalties took to the streets to demand an immediate return to democracy and the direct elections that would assure the inauguration of an opposition president. In the end, the *"Direitas Já"*—"Direct Elections Now"—campaign failed to secure its goal, and it would be 1989 before a president would be directly elected in Brazil. But the depth of popular discontent displayed by the campaign helped undermine the regime's support in Congress, where the government party divided, allowing the opposition to elect Tancredo Neves, the respected governor of Minas Gerais, as president. But Tancredo died before he could take office, leaving the presidency to Vice President José Sarney, who until recently had been head of the promilitary party. There are many in Brazil today who believe that if Tancredo Neves had become president the history of Brazil would have been different.

Democracy and the Double Debt

In April 1985, José Sarney took the oath of office as Brazil's first civilian president in more than two decades. He inherited a country that was very different from the Brazil the military had taken over in 1964. It was a nation of 125 million people, of whom two out of three lived in cities. Many more than ever before were middle class, beneficiaries of the economic miracle but opponents of the political dictatorship. There were also over ten million more urban industrial workers, many members of unions that were independent of the government. Equally striking were the tens of millions of rural migrants who had settled in the shantytowns surrounding Brazil's cities. Many of them had joined grassroots organizations promoted by the Catholic church, which itself had played an important part in the resistance to the military regime. New social movements had spearheaded the campaign for democracy and represented a new factor in Brazil's political equation.

Businessmen had been among the chief beneficiaries of military rule, yet they too had turned against it in the end, in part for philosophical and in part for pragmatic reasons. They had embraced democracy but remained part of an elite that enjoyed the lion's share of wealth and power.

In Brazil, the richest 10 percent received half the national income and the wealthiest 1 percent—1.3 million people—received more than the sixty-five million poorest.

The economic changes in Brazil had also been dramatic. In 1985 it was the world's eighth largest market economy and fourth biggest food exporter. It was also a more industrial country, producing one million automobiles a year and manufactures that accounted for 55 percent of its exports. But the civilian government also inherited a double debt from its military predecessor—the world's largest foreign debt and an equally onerous social debt of postponed popular expectations, symbolized by the seven million children in its streets. Two out of three Brazilians earned less than $115 per year and only five countries in the world had a larger number of malnourished people. In addition, the military bequeathed to its civilian successors an inflation of over 200 percent, a bloated government bureaucracy, and an economy in which twenty-four out of the twenty-six largest Brazilian companies were public enterprises, many of them unprofitable.

It was a Brazil that might criticize the military for their infatuation with *grandeza* yet shared their vision of an industrial Brazil that had settled its vast territory and taken its rightful place among the powers of the world. The military had finally returned to their barracks, but they had left their mark upon Brazil and their two decades in power would prove a hard act for their civilian successors to follow.

José Sarney was not equal to the task. He was a politician of the old school from the Northeast, the country's most traditional region. In a situation that cried out for strong and visionary leadership, Sarney could provide only patronage politics and back-room deals. It was the old politics in the service of the new democracy and the results were disillusioning. Still, in 1991, Sarney looked back with satisfaction on having "presided over the transition to democracy," and took particular pride in having been president for the writing of a new Brazilian constitution, "which has solved the problem of institutions." "Our economic problems are transitory," he said. "It is the political problem that is definitive. The road to development passes through democracy."

Other Brazilians also took pride in having played leading roles in the country's restored democracy. Colonel Jarbas Passarinho, a veteran of many military cabinets, became a senator and a minister of justice; Luis Bresser Pereira served a turn as finance minister. Former supporters of the military regime, such as Roberto Campos and Delfim Netto, became deputies for conservative parties. They were joined in Congress by opponents of the military, who had helped lead the struggle for democracy. José Serra became a deputy for the centrist Social Democrats; Aloisio Mercadante, a representative of the leftist Workers' Party (PT).

More surprising have been the political careers of Benedita da Silva and Lula, both of whom became PT federal deputies. For Benedita, as her constituents call her, the only poor black woman in the Congress, her presence in the Chamber of Deputies signifies the beginnings of a change in Brazil. "A few years ago I wouldn't have dreamed that I would be here today," she reflected. "Not because it shouldn't be the dream of a little black girl, the daughter of a washerwoman from a shantytown, to become a congresswoman and consider that a natural course of events. That's how it ought to be, but it isn't. Yet, here I am after years of fighting, working in defense of the oppressed. . . . That's the way I got here and that is how many other Beneditas and Beneditos will get here."

The political trajectory of Lula has been the most extraordinary of all. As a result of his success as a union leader, this child of poor peasant migrants went on to become founder of the Workers' Party, a federal deputy, and then, in 1989, a presidential candidate. Lula came close to winning as the nominee of a broad center-left coalition that attacked Brazil's inequalities. To many Lula was the Lech Walesa of Brazil, and his trajectory symbolized the importance of the new social movements in Brazil's restored democracy. For Aloisio Mercadante, still one of his close advisers, Lula had demonstrated that he was not only "a great labor leader, but also a very important political leader, who expressed unmet social demands and represented the renewal of democratic political life in Brazil."

But the restoration of democracy did not solve Brazil's economic problems. The new civilian government was burdened with the largest double debt in the region—a $110 billion foreign debt and the most unequal distribution of income of any economy its size in the world—plus Brazil's fading but still compelling dreams of *grandeza*. It also took charge of Brazil at a time when rising international concern about the environment and indigenous peoples focused on the Amazon, adding new considerations— and costs—to Brazil's already difficult policy choices. Brazil's democratic leaders struggled to come to terms with these competing demands, as well as with the military legacy of high inflation and expectations of rapid economic growth. By 1992 five drastic plans to stabilize the economy had been tried—and failed, leaving the level of inflation and unemployment higher, and the rate of growth and investment lower. As a result, Brazil has endured the longest economic downturn in its history.

The most recent plans were named after Fernando Collor, the patri- cian populist who defeated Lula for president in 1989 on a platform of economic reform. A man of bold gestures, Collor froze private bank ac- counts, in addition to wages and prices, a shock treatment that brought inflation—and economic activity—to a momentary halt. Yet, within a year inflation was soaring again, heading toward a record 1500 percent level. Collor had promised to sell off state enterprises and reduce the federal budget deficit, but by late 1991 he had done little to fulfill this pledge. Still, Luis Bresser Pereira remained optimistic. "In the beginning, populist and nationalist ideas dominated," he argued. But "now things have changed and people believe that these reforms must be undertaken."

Brazil's civilian rulers proved as reluctant as their military predeces- sors had been to make the painful adjustments to a changed international economic landscape that were needed to place Brazil's economy on the road to recovery. "After the transition to democracy, Brazil should have thought about economic restructuring," said Bresser Pereira, as in Chile and Mexico, which were prosperous again by 1992. "Instead, we had a series of policy disasters," concluded Roberto Campos, with the air of a man who had told them so. "For Brazil, the nineteen eighties was a lost decade."

For most of Latin America, the 1980s were an era of economic crisis in which many of the social gains of the 1970s were reversed and newly democratic governments struggled with the onerous legacies of military rule. But for Brazil, whose economy had grown faster than any other in the world between 1870 and 1980, the "lost decade" was particularly traumatic.

The losses included the competitiveness of Brazilian industry after a decade without the importation of new technology. In 1970 Brazil had roughly the same size economy as Korea, and as late as 1984 the value of their exports was similar. In 1992 Korea's exports were double Brazil's and its economy was three times as large. Korea had become one of the new industrial tigers, while Brazil had become a paper tiger.

More difficult to quantify was Brazil's loss of self-confidence, the shaking of its conviction that it is destined for greatness. The congenital optimism of Brazilians seemed to be another casualty of the lost decade, as capital fled the country and Brazilians emigrated in large numbers for the first time. In 1992 Brazil still had the largest industrial sector in the region, but it also had the largest debt and the highest inflation. Its combination of accelerated growth and protected industries, with government playing a managerial role, had gone out of fashion. The price of growth had been too high, its gains transitory, and its *grandeza* a delusion.

After five years of the slowest economic growth in Brazil's modern history, it was hard to find Brazilians who were still confident that Brazil was "the country of the future." Even Delfim Netto had become more pessimistic. "The future is now past," he quipped. "Now we can see that it was a detour." General Oliva, however, still retained his faith in Brazil. "I believe in my people, I believe in my country," he affirmed. "We are at a moment of transition, a moment of confusion, but I don't doubt for a minute that we will come out of it, and that we will grow. It's our destiny—a destiny to greatness."

Lula was less certain. "When I hear these people saying that Brazil is the country of the future, I remember that I heard this when I was ten years old. It's already been thirty years and Brazil continues to be the country of the future—a future that is further away each year, because Brazil is walking backwards, because there is no investment in industry, in agriculture, or in education." Claudio Bardella shared Lula's diagnosis that inadequate education was Brazil's Achilles' heel in an age of high technology, and he was even more pessimistic about the country's possibilities. "Brazil seemed much more the country of the future twenty years ago than it does today," he reflected. "In the seventies we were catching up to the rest of the world, but in the eighties the gap between us and the world grew, and today it is so much greater. That is our problem—and there are no short-term solutions," he said. "We need a twenty-year plan."

Brazil might still be the country of the future, but that future seemed more remote in 1992 than it had two decades before. "In the seventies Brazil was the model to imitate and Chile was the *anti*model to avoid," said José Serra, who had lived in both countries. "Now, we are the *anti*model to avoid—and Chile is the model to imitate."

One of the Most Open Economies in the World

"For Chile to truly develop economically, it was necessary to implement a series of changes," explained Alicia Romo, who had supervised many of those changes as director of industry and commerce after General Augusto Pinochet's 1973 military coup. "To do this we needed a long time, and power had to be concentrated in a strong hand who could make changes without debate. That was the fundamental legacy of the military government."

Like Brazil, Chile had come under military rule after a period of growing economic dislocation, social conflict, and political instability. The crisis that led to the coup of 1973 was far more intense than the situation that prompted the Brazilian military to assume power in 1964, as were military fears of a "communist" revolution. As in Brazil, the Chilean armed forces seized power determined to carry out a revolution of their own. They also imposed an authoritarian regime that ignored the rule of law and violated human rights, and recruited talented civilian technocrats to design and run their economic policy.

But there the similarities ended. Chile, with a population of only twelve million, was a far smaller country than Brazil. It had rich mines and fields but a relatively small and inefficient industrial sector that enjoyed high levels of protection. "The government set prices, quotas, wages," said Daniel Platowsky, today president of Chile's Chamber of Commerce. "The best businessman was not the best manager but the best lobbyist." It was also an economy that depended for its prosperity on copper—long Chile's major export—accounting for three quarters of its export earnings. The principal mines had been nationalized during the preceding decade, and the country's large ranches and farms had been transformed into peasant cooperatives during this same era. Most banks and large industrial enterprises had come under government or worker control during President Salvador Allende's "democratic road to socialism," which began in 1970. The state-owned economic sector was enormous—and so was the budget deficit.

There were political and policy differences between the two countries as well. The military regime in Chile also began as a government of the armed forces, but General Pinochet gradually transformed it into a personal dictatorship. The technocrats he chose, moreover, were U.S.-trained "Chicago boys," neoliberals who implemented the doctrinaire free-market capitalism they had learned in the United States. Backed by Pinochet's bayonets, they imposed a harsh cure for Chile's economic ills. Overnight, prices were freed and wages frozen, leading first to soaring inflation and then to a deep recession. A rapid and widespread privatization of banks, factories, and commercial enterprises that were in government hands followed, along with the conversion of rural cooperatives into private parcels. A new labor code crippled unions already weakened by military repression, allowing employers a free hand with their workers. Government spending on education, housing, and health plummeted, reducing the budget deficit at the cost of social welfare. A deregulation of the financial sector completed the reduction in the government's economic role. Under Chile's military regime, unlike Brazil, there would be no "managerial state." "It was a completely new system for Chilean businessmen," said Platowsky. "Suddenly we were confronted with a government that said: 'Señores, from here on, you are on your own. The state won't regulate anything.' It was a big shock."

The full neoliberal "shock treatment" came in 1977, when protective tariffs were eliminated and Chile's high-cost import substitution industries were left to sink or swim on their own. In Chile, there would be no industrial miracle. Instead, lower cost foreign imports flooded Chilean markets, driving local firms into bankruptcy—or to import what they had previously manufactured. Daniel Platowsky's company had assembled radios and televisions from imported parts. Now they would have to compete with Japanese products. "We did a calculation and began shutting down our assembly lines," he said. "We decided to import Panasonics instead. From an industrial enterprise we became a commercial enterprise."

At first, the results seemed more negative than positive. There was a lot of speculation but little productive investment. There were many bankruptcies and soaring unemployment. When the deregulated financial sector crashed in the global recession of 1981–82, the Chilean economy collapsed. It was Chile's most severe economic crisis since the Great Depression. Bankruptcies multiplied and, by 1983, one third of the labor force was unemployed, with another tenth in government make-work programs. Protesters filled the streets and demanded the restoration of democracy. The neoliberal economic "revolution" seemed a total failure. Pinochet was forced to bail out the banks and to resume state management of enterprises he had once privatized.

But the crises had wiped out the speculators and bankrupted the inefficient. A new group of entrepreneurs emerged in their place, many of them, like Daniel Platowsky, from a younger generation that had been educated abroad and was aware of the new opportunities in changing world markets. Instead of investing in manufacturing for Chilean consumers, they put their money and expertise into new export lines in fruits, fish, and forestry. Together with more pragmatic government policies, these "non-traditional" exports reduced the country's dependence on copper and led the Chilean economy to renewed prosperity during the last half of the 1980s. As a result, Chilean grapes now grace Christmas dinner tables in the United States, and Chilean sea urchins crown the sushi in Japan. While the Brazilian economy went from crisis to crisis, Chile enjoyed six years of steady growth with low levels of inflation, declining unemployment, and an increasing trade surplus.

Although Chile's per capita foreign debt was larger than Brazil's, the country continued to attract foreign investment. Chile pioneered an aggressive policy of "debt-asset swaps," in which holders of Chile's debt could use it to purchase state-owned enterprises at a sharp discount. This not only reduced the external debt by one fifth between 1985 and 1992, it also helped restore foreign confidence in Chilean investments. By 1991 foreign capital was pouring into Chile and the value of its debt was so high that debt-asset swaps were dying a natural death.

By then, observers were hailing a "Chilean miracle," where they had once proclaimed a "Brazilian miracle." But the benefits of this Chilean miracle were even less well distributed than those of the earlier Brazilian one. Little of it trickled down to the poor, whose numbers had multiplied under military rule. "The rich got richer and the poor got poorer," charged labor leader Arturo Martínez. By 1988 opposition leaders like Martínez were accusing the military regime of dividing the country into "two Chiles," one "increasingly wealthy," the other "desperately poor." It was this maldistribution of Chile's prosperity that led to the defeat of General Pinochet in the 1988 plebiscite on his rule and to the loss of Hernan Büchi, his economic czar, in the presidential elections of the following year. "I voted NO to Pinochet, because my children are hungry," Luisa Torres explained at the victory rally after the plebiscite. "With a democratic government we will be better off."

The issue of poverty was raised during the campaigns by Alejandro Foxley, a Christian Democratic critic of neoliberal policies who held Pinochet and Büchi responsible for creating a nation in which 45 percent of the population were poor and one in four Chileans was destitute. By 1991, Foxley was Finance Minister in President Patricio Aylwin's center-left coalition government, the first democratic government in almost two decades, but there had been little change in economic policy—and Luisa Torres's children had little more to eat than before. "We have already paid the social costs of these neoliberal policies," said Foxley, "so we might as well reap their economic benefits."

There were other reasons as well for the continuity of economic policies between the military regime and its democratic critics and successors. Foxley wanted to demonstrate that a civilian government could manage the economy as well as—or better than—the military regime. In Chile, unlike Brazil, few businessmen had supported the restoration of democracy, and Chileans had learned during the Allende years that entrepreneurial hostility could undermine the country's economic and political stability. "This government had to convince business that they were really in favor of the economic system," Daniel Platowsky said. Foxley went out of his way to court the cooperation of his country's business elites, consulting them on proposed reforms and promising them continuity in economic policy and the rules of the game. A leading analyst of Latin America's past policy errors, Foxley, according to Assistant Minister Andrés Velasco, was also "determined to break the populist cycle, in which a government is elected on promises to satisfy unmet social demands but in doing this undermines its budget, generates inflation, erodes incomes, and is overthrown—two years of euphoria and fifteen years of penance!" For the Aylwin government, the lessons of Chile's past were critical: "We were not going to indulge in solutions that bring bread today and hunger tomorrow."

As a result, Chile's first democratic government resisted pressure from its supporters to fulfill their expectations of dramatic increases in real wages and government social programs. "This would have stimulated inflation, historically Chile's economic disease," Velasco emphasized. "Our message was clear: We are not going to make the mistakes of some of our neighbors and some of our predecessors."

Instead, Foxley designed a policy calculated to help the destitute through housing and utility subsidies, and the poor through increases in minimum wages and pensions, but relied on continued economic expansion to put the poor back to work. Only "increased productivity and skills will raise the wages of Chilean workers to First World levels," Velasco said. In the long run the government planned to address the problem of poverty through increased spending on education, housing, and health care, which had been cut back under Pinochet. They would be paid for by the increased tax revenues that the government's approach had led businessmen to accept and that an expanding economy would generate. In its first year, the center-left Aylwin government had raised five hundred million dollars in new revenues, "and every peso went to social programs," Velasco emphasized. The Aylwin administration also had to find the money with which to clean up Chile's polluted air and waters, another cost of the unregulated economic growth of the Pinochet years, and an area where government intervention was needed "to correct the failures of the market," he maintained. "But we are committed to avoiding the budget deficits that undermined the restored democracies in Argentina and Brazil. Our rule is not a peso spent without a peso earned." The restoration of democracy had led neither to inflation nor to dramatic changes of economic policy—but did lead to an increase in social spending and social welfare, Velasco explained. "If you want to help the poor you have to be hard-headed."

It was a quality that Chile's businessmen appreciated. They had been among the chief beneficiaries of the military regime and had "worried about what democracy would bring," recounted Daniel Platowsky. But, the Chamber of Commerce head admitted, "we have been happily surprised. Given the character of the government, a coalition which includes socialists who in the past criticized the capitalist system, we had expected a shift to a much larger state role, in the Latin American manner." There had been adjustments as well as tax reforms and labor reforms, but "the government has been much more responsible than we had imagined, and the results have been much better than we expected."

Labor leaders were less pleased with the limited gains in wages, benefits, and legal reforms. "We were the ones who started the struggle against the dictatorship, and it is hard for people who fought so hard and suffered so much for democracy to accept that their aspirations for justice have been postponed," asserted Arturo Martínez, now vice president of Chile's new labor confederation. "We didn't expect much more economically because we knew that the economy of this country couldn't give much more, but we *did* expect a greater political will to change Chile," he underscored. "It is hard to accept that the same people who persecuted us under the dictatorship are still ordering us around." But real wages were rising, unemployment was falling, and the labor law reforms would help Chile's unions rebuild their membership and strength for the future, Martínez said. "We unionists have learned that rather than have a bloody and ferocious dictatorship such as the one we suffered under Pinochet, it is better to assume this kind of cost and try to deepen the democratic process step by step. [The] aspirations of the workers could not be postponed forever," he cautioned, "but we are committed to democracy."

It was the poor who had expected the most from the restoration of democracy, yet so far have received the least. In a shantytown on the outskirts of Santiago, Elena Vargas used the sleeve of a frayed sweater to wipe away the tears streaming down her face from the onions she was cutting for the local communal soup kitchen. "For us poor people, not much has changed," she said. "We still need this soup kitchen in order to survive." But the military regime had been more repressive and more recent than in Brazil, and its abuses were still clearly etched in people's minds. "It is good to be able to say what you think without fear," Vargas said. "This is our government and we have to give it a chance."

Chile's democratic government was counting on this popular forbearance, but was well aware of the continuing plight of the poor. "Chile is a poor country," Andrés Velasco lamented. "The problem of poverty will be with us for a long time . . . but at least we have made a start."

By 1992 this new Chilean model was evoking the kind of interest in the rest of the region that the Brazilian model had commanded two decades before. "We are one of the most open economies in the world," Velasco said, "and we have demonstrated that it works—and *with* democracy too." It was part of a dramatic shift in economic thinking and policy that set Latin America and the Caribbean on a very different course than had seemed likely three decades ago.

For both Brazil and Chile—as for the rest of Latin America and the Caribbean—the crisis of the 1980s was a sobering experience. The challenge of the 1990s is to find a way to combine democracy and development with payment on the region's onerous double debt of foreign loans and postponed popular welfare. It is a difficult task, which even an economic miracle might not resolve, and which makes such a miracle far less likely.

In Chile, democratic political leaders with a broad vision have taken the first steps, enlisted the cooperation of both business and labor leaders, and persuaded their people to accept a more realistic economic strategy than many had predicted. In Brazil, that political vision and economic realism has yet to triumph, and the "lost decade" has stretched into the century's final decade. For José Serra, the key was leadership. "Brazil's elites—political elites, business elites, labor elites—have to reach a consensus on the nature of our problems and how to solve them. If we can reach agreement and control inflation, Brazil will begin to grow again."

By mid-1992, there were signs that Brazil's leaders were closer to this consensus, and that its economy had begun to recover its dynamism. Inflation and political disarray were still high, with the likelihood of a presidential impeachment trial on corruption charges and the prospect of a 1993 vote on shifting to a parliamentary system clouding the horizon. But a congressional majority supported the government's renegotiation of its $44 billion debt to foreign banks and sale of unprofitable state enterprises. Foreign investment and economic growth were returning to Brazil, and so were hints of the country's historic optimism.

In a Rio de Janeiro warehouse, Joãozinho Trinta explained the message of his *Alice in Wonderland* Carnival pageant. "In the garden Alice meets the Caterpillar, who asks her, *'Who* are *you?'* Alice doesn't know how to reply. She says, 'I no longer know who I am. First I was small like Brazil, underdeveloped, with many problems. Suddenly I grew, became a giant, a great power, but with many problems, a huge foreign debt. I don't know what else I can do. I don't know who I am.' But Caterpillar says, 'Pay attention. I am a caterpillar, but I turn myself into a butterfly'—which is the symbol of transformation. 'This could happen to you,' " the Caterpillar told Alice. "And this will happen to Brazil," stressed Joãozinho. "Of that we are certain."

During the decades since World War II, an accelerating tide of rural migrants has flooded the cities of Latin America and the Caribbean in search of economic and educational opportunities. New arrivals often create housing by invading vacant suburban lands, as in this 1983 *toma,* or takeover, in Santiago, Chile.

Chapter 6

Continent on the Move

Many migrants start out living in squalid conditions, as in this Mexico City shantytown, but gradually work their way up. Over time the shanty-towns themselves change, as residents find better jobs, build more solid houses, and win battles for urban amenities such as paved streets, sewers, and running water.

The economic crisis of the 1980s even afflicted oil-rich Mexico, prompting these unemployed construction workers to offer their skills in the cathedral square of their nation's capital. The "informal economy" of off-the-books businesses that hire these workers has created new jobs, but they are usually ill paid and often unsafe.

The decreasing job opportunities and increasing urban blight of Mexico City have led many rural migrants to look elsewhere. Tijuana, a border town with numerous *maquiladoras,* assembly plants for export, has attracted many single women, who are preferred as docile and dexterous workers by multi-national firms.

Many migrants from Mexico and Central America, like these Guatemalan refugees, cross the porous two-thousand-mile border between Mexico and the United States, the longest in the world between a Third and First World country, drawn by the enormous wage differentials between the two countries.

Continent on the Move

*A*s the dawn broke over Zapata canyon on the California border between Mexico and the United States, it revealed a strange sight. On the Mexican side of the frontier, a motley "army" of would-be immigrants— Mexicans, Guatemalans, Salvadorans—waited for the first light to cross the canyon and "invade" the United States.

On the other side of the desolate canyon a far smaller group of armed Border Patrol agents waited to repel the expected charge. When it came, they would capture some illegal aliens, interrogate them, and send them back to Mexico. But the agents were so outnumbered that their efforts were little more than a ritual act that underscored the futility of the policy that placed them there.

Hundreds would get through, while those the Border Patrol sent back to Mexico would try again the next night, or the next week, until they too reached the land of opportunity. By 1991, so many illegal migrants—generally rural people with no experience of superhighways—were making it across the border near San Diego, but then getting killed trying to cross Interstate 5, that special traffic signs were put up to warn motorists to slow down: signs equivalent to warnings of animal crossings.

The San Diego area is a zone of heavy illegal immigration, but it is by no means unique. Along the porous two-thousand-mile U.S. border with Mexico—the longest unguarded border between a First and Third World nation—are crossing points known to the "coyotes" who guide the migrants to the promised land for a fee. Thousands of "boat people" from Cuba and Haiti make perilous journeys across the Florida Straits to reach U.S. territory. Thousands more arrive by air as tourists in Miami, Washington, or New York, and then melt into the large Latin American and Caribbean communities already established in those cities.

In 1990 alone there were an estimated 400,000 illegal entries from Latin America and the Caribbean. Over the years this surreptitious flow of migrants has generated political debate in Congress and social conflict in U.S. cities. It has prompted restrictive legislation and revamped policies. It is what North Americans think of when they hear about migration in the Americas.

But the main story of migration in our hemisphere takes place *within* Latin America and the Caribbean. Viewed from south of our borders, the wave of immigrants to the United States is only a small part of the massive tide of migration that has transformed the entire Americas during the last half century. Since World War II over one hundred million people in the region have left home to seek their fortunes elsewhere. It is one of the most intense movements of people in modern times.

Most of this migration is internal, largely a movement of rural people to their nation's cities. It has turned a continent of farmers into a hemisphere of city dwellers, where four out of five will live in urban areas by the year 2000. It has also created an unprecedented population explosion in the great and small cities of Latin America and the Caribbean. During the past half century the population of Greater Mexico City has gone from 1.6 million to more than 19 million and that of São Paulo from 1.4 million to over 17 million. Four of the world's ten largest metropolitan areas are now in Latin America. But even smaller cities have experienced spectacular growth. Between 1970 and 1990 Lima's population zoomed from 650,000 to 6.5 million, Kingston's from 100,000 to 700,000, and Tijuana's from 110,000 to 1.5 million. Also common has been the concentration of a nation's people in one metropolitan area, an urban center of economic, political, and cultural power that acts as a magnet for migrants. A third of Argentina's population now lives in Greater Buenos Aires, two fifths of Peru's in Lima, and half of Uruguay's in Montevideo. Migration has caused a demographic revolution that has transformed the face of the region and altered the distribution of people within its nations.

Some of this migration spills over the borders and shores of the countries of Latin America and the Caribbean, a flow of people within the region that rarely makes it to our newspapers and television screens. West Indians have long migrated in search of work, whether to build the Panama Canal or to harvest sugar in other islands or bananas in Central America. In recent decades Guatemalans and Salvadorans have filled similar roles as seasonal workers in Mexico, as have Colombians in Venezuela. But it was Central America's civil wars of the 1980s that sent hundreds of thousands of Guatemalan and Salvadoran refugees fleeing across Mexico's southern borders in search of a safe haven.

Economic opportunities and political upheavals have also led Latin American professionals to leave their homes for others within the region. Argentine doctors have sought better opportunities in oil-rich Mexico and Venezuela than exist in Buenos Aires; Chile's military coup of 1973 produced a veritable diaspora of leftist intellectuals. Uruguayans had never left their country, known for its democracy and welfare state, in large numbers before a military regime took over in 1974. But during the decade that followed, one-quarter of Uruguay's population emigrated, mostly to other nations in the region. Each of these migratory flows has its own rationales and causes, but taken together, they amount to one of the major international migrations of our era. Only a small portion of those who leave home in Latin America and the Caribbean migrate to the United States, and of those who do, some 80 percent come to work for a season and then return.

Whatever their destination, most of the migrants are pursuing better jobs or educational opportunities. Some of these journeys are the first leg of a round-trip, a temporary stay for work or schooling in preparation for a return home with the resources to make it there; others are one-way tickets, even though the migrants themselves may leave their homes planning to come back. Taken together these varied migrations add up to a continent on the move.

Before 1930 the Americas were all lands of immigrants. Immigration to the hemisphere began with the prehistoric Asian hunters who are the ancestors of today's "Indians," and continued with the European colonists who began to arrive with Columbus, the enslaved Africans they brought in chains across the sea, and the Asian and European laborers imported after the abolition of slavery in the nineteenth century. The twentieth century saw new groups of immigrants cross the Atlantic, most of them in search of safe havens from political persecution: Christian Arabs fleeing the Ottoman Turks before the First World War, Spaniards escaping Franco's fascism during the 1930s, Jewish refugees from the Holocaust, and Germans escaping the Nazi defeat after World War II. Beginning with the Great Depression and increasingly after World War II, however, Latin America and the Caribbean became areas of net emigration. The few immigrants who arrived from other continents were outnumbered by those who left their homes within the region. By 1950 internal migration had replaced immigration as the movement of people that was reshaping the demographic map of Latin America, with rural migration to the region's cities the driving force.

Callampas

In 1930, the city of Santiago hired Karl Brunner, one of Europe's distinguished urbanists, to draw up a plan for the orderly growth of the Chilean capital. Brunner's master plan was a model of its kind, with industries sited in one area, offices and commerce in a second, elite homes in a third, and mass housing in a fourth. But Santiago did not grow the way Brunner expected. Within three decades Brunner's carefully constructed plan had been overwhelmed by the tide of rural migration.

There had always been migration from countryside to city in Chile, and it increased with the dislocations of the Depression. But there had never been rural migration as massive as occurred after World War II, nor had Chile's cities expanded so rapidly. In 1930, Santiago had half a million people and Chile was a mostly rural country. By 1990, 83 percent of Chile's thirteen million people lived in cities, almost five million in Santiago alone.

There were many reasons for this unprecedented movement of people from the villages and farms where their families had lived for generations, and they were similar throughout Latin America and the Caribbean. The postwar boom in commercial agriculture prompted landowners in Chile's fertile Central Valley to expel sharecroppers and tenant farmers from their estates as the plots they had tilled became too valuable to be used for subsistence crops. It also spurred a mechanization of farming that reduced the need for hired hands. At the same time, the size of rural families was growing, a result of the decline in infant mortality produced by the spread of modern medicine. Increased schooling persuaded rural youths that they would be able to make it in the city. Transistor radios and then television brought news of the abundance and excitement of city life, whetting rural appetites with the promise of higher education, factory jobs, and urban life-styles.

As a consequence, during the decades that followed World War II, an accelerating stream of peasants and their children left the starry nights of the farms and villages of Chile's Central Valley for the bright city lights in a migration that often proceeded by steps. The migrants moved first from a farm to a local town, and then along the railway and bus lines to a regional center, before ending at the central railway terminal in Santiago, the nation's economic hub as well as its capital.

The new arrivals joined thousands of others searching for a place to live. Prior to this massive influx, migrants to Santiago—whether from Europe or the Chilean countryside—found lodging in the decaying mansions of the city center. Each family occupied a single room around a patio, as in the *conventillos* of Buenos Aires. But the migrants who arrived after World War II were too numerous to be accommodated in these urban slums and lacked the steady income required to pay their rents. Instead, they began banding together and squatting on vacant lands on the outskirts of the city. Soon these shantytowns were even springing up in zones that Brunner had set aside for other purposes.

Throughout Latin America and the Caribbean, a similar spectacular growth of cities through the extension of squatter settlements was taking place during the postwar decades. In Lima the shantytowns were built out onto the desert hills; in Caracas they spread up the valley walls; in Rio de Janeiro they clung to the hillsides above luxurious beach districts; in Kingston they filled in the low-lying area along the bay. Their names varied from country to country. They were called *barriadas* in Peru, *favelas* in Brazil, *solares* in Panama, *colonias proletarias* in Mexico, and most descriptively, *villas miserias*—"towns of misery"—in Argentina.

In Chile, these squatter settlements were known as *callampas,* after the wild mushrooms that sprang up suddenly in the countryside after the rain. The earliest *callampas,* like those that lined the Zanjón de la Aguada, a fetid canal bordering the industrial belt along Santiago's southern rim, were spontaneous settlements. But Chile is a nation with a long tradition of social and political organization. Special associations representing the homeless were founded. Political parties of the left and center began to organize land seizures as part of their competition for the loyalties of recent migrants.

The *tomas* (from *tomar,* to take), as the land seizures were known in Chile, became ritualized. A group of squatters, usually recent migrants with a leaven of homeless workers, would invade a vacant suburban lot during the night with their wives and children. By morning they would have put up their tents. When the dawn broke and the police arrived to evict them, there they would be with their wives and children clutching the Chilean flag as if it were a talisman, daring the police to desecrate the national banner by attacking defenseless women and children. This drama was often enacted in full view of the press, who had been alerted by the sponsors of the *toma* that a confrontation was about to take place. Occasionally, the police would try to enforce a court eviction order sought by the owner of the land, or a conservative government would take a stand for law and order. The result would be a massacre, the sites of which—José María Caro or Puerto Montt—are inscribed in the social and political history of Chile. The popular revulsion and loss of political support that followed such slaughters of the innocent meant that they were few and far between.

An agreement usually would be worked out that would leave the squatters free to build their shacks of wood and metal. Then began the far longer struggle to press the government for paved streets, running water, electricity, sewers, schools, and buses—the infrastructure of city life. In Chilean fashion, the squatters formed neighborhood associations, organized public demonstrations, and allied themselves with political parties that promised to take up their cause. Gradually, they won their battle for urban amenities. The houses became more permanent—and more attractive. Extensions were added on for married children. The empty spaces in between were filled with other houses, sometimes on land rented from the original squatters. By then many migrants had gone on from initial jobs as day laborers to win coveted factory jobs in one of Chile's new manufacturing industries.

In the process, what had begun as a lower-class shantytown became a solid working-class neighborhood. By then, another group of squatters had seized an empty lot further out, and the process would began all over again. Although the *callampa*, with its self-built shacks, unpaved streets, and unkempt children seemed squalid to outsiders, to its residents it was a giant step toward realizing their urban dream.

Though the rhythms and details of city growth differed from country to country, its overall contours were similar. Chile's tradition of social organization was unusual, but not unique. In multicultural societies such as Peru, ethnic associations might be the basis of squatter organization. In Brazil or Mexico it might be region of origin. Everywhere the struggle for land and urban services was similar in its goals if different in its tactics. Chile's democratic politics lent themselves to a more public and political squatter strategy. But even in Mexico, where the ruling Institutional Revolutionary Party (PRI) rigged elections and did not allow rivals a shot at power, squatters often found it possible to get what they wanted from the state by appealing to the governing party's revolutionary rhetoric and populist past. Mexico was also proof that by the 1960s, even Latin American peasants who had land were finding it hard to make ends meet—and finding the appeal of urban opportunities too attractive to resist.

Land of Broken Dreams

Forty miles from the old colonial mining town of Zacatecas, in a dry valley nestled in the legendary Sierra Madre, lies the Hacienda Santa Rosa de Lima and the nearby village of Malpaso. The exhausted silver veins and soils of Zacatecas, the enormous hacienda, and the impoverished villagers symbolize the complex legacy of Mexico's past.

Mexico is the largest and most populous country in Spanish America, as well as the closest to the United States. It was Spain's richest colony, which Alexander von Humboldt predicted at the turn of the nineteenth century would be the great power of the Americas. But independence was accompanied by decades of civil war and foreign intervention, which cost Mexico half its territory and half a century of political instability. The thirty-five-year Porfirio Díaz dictatorship (1876–1910) imposed peace on warring political parties and fractious regional caudillos, while developing Mexico into a prosperous exporter of minerals, metals, and fibers in collaboration with foreign investment. But this progress came at a high social cost that fueled the Mexican revolution of 1910–17, the first great mass upheaval of the century, which cost two million lives. The revolution, fought largely by landless laborers, also challenged the large estates that dominated rural Mexico.

Once one of Mexico's biggest ranches, with a prosperity that reflected the silver mines it supplied, Santa Rosa is today the site of an agricultural cooperative, or *ejido*. Small farmers scrape a precarious living out of its parched soil, which is better suited for cattle than crops. María Luz Ojeda is over seventy, the matriarch of a peasant family that has farmed in the valley all her life, first as peons, then as *ejiditarios*. She still remembers the day Lázaro Cárdenas came to give the peasants of Malpaso the titles to their plots on the nearby hacienda. Cárdenas, a revolutionary general and reforming governor who became Mexico's president in 1934, set out to fulfill the Mexican revolution's promise of "Land for the Peasants" made two decades before. He pledged to distribute twenty million hectares during his six years in office, and by 1940 a third of Mexico's twenty million people had been awarded their parcel of land. "President Cárdenas was wonderful," María Luz recalled in a voice still filled with gratitude. It was from him that "we finally got our own plot of land." As elsewhere in Mexico, the land was deeded to the cooperative, but each family received a forty-four-acre plot to farm for themselves. For a brief moment it seemed as if the dream of Mexican peasants for a farm of their own had come true.

Cárdenas left office in 1940, and the governments that followed had a different development strategy. Instead of supporting subsistence farming, they promoted commercial agriculture for export to the United States, making use of irrigation, modern technology, and the "green revolution" in miracle grains and hybrid fruits and vegetables. Such policies helped wealthy Mexicans and foreign corporations create modern factory farms, which required expensive machinery but little labor. Instead of producing more maize and beans for Mexico's burgeoning population, they devoted more and more of the country's land to growing strawberries and tomatoes for New York's winter dinner tables.

Postwar presidents also did not share Cárdenas's concern for the rural poor. In the arid state of Zacatecas, the land required irrigation and fertilizers to make it bloom, but the government did not aid the peasants and they could not afford such large expenses themselves. In the course of time, the small *ejido* plots of Malpaso were exhausted by constant cultivation and subdivided to provide for Mexico's large families. It became more and more difficult for the peasants to support themselves on their tiny plots. Many gave up, rented them out, and left the area. The Mexican revolution, with its massive dislocations of people fleeing and following the fighting, may have loosened the ties that bound peasants to the villages of their fathers. But it was the failure of the revolution's agrarian reform and the mechanization of agriculture that pushed an accelerating stream of rural migrants out of the countryside.

María Luz Ojeda and her husband, Pedro, worked hard to hold on to their small parcel of land, but it was the money sent back by their children who had left Zacatecas for the United States and Mexico City that enabled them to make ends meet, a survival strategy typical of Latin America's farm families. Then Pedro died in an accident, and María Luz rented the land to a neighbor and moved to the nearby community of El Salto. Today she holds on to the land title in the hope that her daughter Marcela will return and farm it with her children.

But Marcela and her husband, Atanacio, left in the first place because the land could not support them. "We left because we were hungry, because of necessity," she said simply. "We couldn't make a living on the farm, and there was nothing else for us to do in Zacatecas." They were not alone. Since the mechanization of mining and agriculture, there were few jobs to be had in Zacatecas, where 40 percent of those who want to work are unemployed. More than half the people born in Zacatecas now live elsewhere, making it the Mexican state with the highest emigration rate.

Some of these migrants went north, to industrial Monterrey or the border towns, or to "the other side," as they refer to the United States. But as with other Mexican "sending" regions, most of those who have left Zacatecas since World War II headed for Mexico City.

So did Marcela and Atanacio. There are many reasons people migrate and they are usually mutually reinforcing, but the more she talked about their decision, the more complicated it became. In their case, Zacatecas's arid soils and high unemployment were only part of the story. Another theme was the tales of Mexico City jobs and schools brought back by friends who had migrated. There were also more personal reasons. Atanacio, who came from a more prosperous family, felt that he had been cheated out of his fair share of his inheritance and was determined to show his family that he could make it on his own. "He always wanted to work and achieve something," Marcela said. "He was proud that the people back home knew that when we left, we left hungry, but that one day he achieved something."

Atanacio was a man with entrepreneurial drive and a better-than-average education, who was convinced that he had what it takes to make it in "La Capital." In that he was a typical migrant. Those who migrate are usually not the poorest and least educated, but the more resourceful and better prepared, who have enough confidence in themselves and their skills to be willing to take the large leap into the urban unknown.

La Capital

When they left Zacatecas in 1972, Atanacio and Marcela were in good company. During the past half century, thirty million Mexicans have migrated and Mexico City has been their favorite destination. Mexico City now grows each year by an astounding eight hundred thousand, the equivalent of the entire population of San Francisco, with migrants accounting for two thirds of this demographic explosion. It squeezes 22 percent of Mexico into .02 percent of its area, stretching far beyond the boundaries of the federal district into the surrounding state, transforming farmlands into shantytowns and tilled fields into garbage dumps.

Today, Mexico City is the largest metropolitan area in the world, with a projected population of thirty million by the year 2000. It is a textbook case of what migration experts like Rafael Corona are calling "hyperurbanization." To him, the explanation for its unprecedented growth is not only the lack of viable rural alternatives, but also the magnetic attraction of city life: "People go to the great city, in this case, Mexico City, because . . . they are told that there they will find work. They will find entertainment. They will find a better life. They know this through the media, but mainly because there are people from their own families or their own villages who already live in Mexico City who stay in contact with them. They tell them that they can find a job and live better in Mexico City."

Government policies also contributed to the creation of this urban giantism. Industrial promotion, a postwar economic strategy in Mexico as elsewhere in the region, drew migrants to the city in search of jobs. The government encouraged this movement of cheap labor by controlling food prices for the urban poor and by concentrating such services as education and electricity in the cities, increasing their attraction for the rural poor in the neglected countryside. By centralizing its own activities in Mexico City, and making access to the state bureaucracy necessary for businessmen, the government also promoted the concentration of economic services in the capital, already the heart of the nation's political and cultural life.

The Mexican government then compounded the problem by abandoning any serious effort to regulate the results of its policies. The absence of environmental controls has made Mexico's capital one of the world's most polluted cities. In April 1992, the air quality was so perilous that the government was forced to take emergency measures, closing factories and limiting the number of cars on the roads. The lack of adequate transportation clogs its streets and crowds its buses. The low priority accorded social welfare means that most of its residents live in substandard housing and nearly half have no running water. The pervasiveness of corruption allows the wealthy to buy their way around regulations, while the poor suffer the consequences of their powerlessness.

To deal with the difficulties of urban life, in Mexico, as elsewhere in the region, the poor rely on each other. The informal networks of friends, relatives, and people from their village or area that spread the word about urban opportunities also help the migrants adapt to their new environment once they arrive in the city. It was such a network of neighbors that led Atanacio and Marcela to a *colonia proletaria* where other Zacatecan migrants had settled.

Like Chile's *callampas,* squatter settlements were a postwar phenomenon in Mexico, aided by the revolution's rhetorical commitment to "land for the people" and the state's reluctance to use violence to oust the "parachutists" who "invaded" a vacant lot at night and had thrown up cardboard, wood, and tin shacks by morning. The *colonia* where Marcela and Atanacio first settled was the result of such a land "invasion," and its conditions were still primitive. "When we arrived in Mexico City, we lived in cardboard boxes and foraged for food from the garbage dump," Marcela recalled. "I cried. This is not what I had dreamed of, but there was no return."

A friend from Zacatecas had promised to help them if they came to Mexico City, but when he did not make good on his pledge, Atanacio began scouring the streets in search of work. At first he worked as a day laborer, the typical entry-level job for male migrants. Finally he ran into someone from his hometown who got him a job in a Popsicle plant, a small "factory" in what is known as the "informal economy," where everyone works off the books. The wages were low and working conditions bad, but to Marcela and Atanacio the job represented a step up. This meant that they could move to a room in a nicer *colonia* and "were no longer poor. At least we could eat beans and tortillas and pay rent," she said.

Atanacio and Marcela were determined to make it in Mexico City. To supplement his meager wages, they did piece work at night. "I won the lottery when I married my husband," Marcela said. "He was a hard worker. He used to walk to and from work in the middle of the night because we didn't have money for the bus." It was a story typical of migrants throughout Latin America. Their next step, however, was unusual.

Many migrants leave their homes reluctantly, planning to return. They prefer to live in the countryside where they grew up and most of their family still resides. In the back of their minds as they board the bus that will take them to Mexico City is the idea that they will make their nest egg and then return home with the resources to buy that plot of land or improve their farm. Few are able to fulfill this dream. Atanacio and Marcela were among those who tried.

With the money they had saved in Mexico City and an offer of work from Atanacio's brother, they returned home to Zacatecas, where Marcela gave birth to a baby girl. "At first, it was wonderful to be back home," Marcela recalled. But their rural dream soon turned into a nightmare. Atanacio's brother did not pay him as promised, and Zacatecas still offered few job alternatives, even for so resourceful and hardworking a man as Atanacio. They were poor and hungry again, and when the baby got sick they could not get her the medical care she required. When their baby daughter died, Marcela blamed Zacatecas. Less than a year after they had left the capital, they decided to return to Mexico City. At least there Atanacio could earn a living and assure their children food and medicine. The city might be less appealing than the countryside, but its advantages outweighed its defects.

It was 1977 and La Capital was booming from the profits of the oil recently discovered in southern Mexico. Migrants were pouring into Mexico City at the rate of a thousand a day, attracted by the economic expansion and government programs financed by foreign borrowing. Mexico was rumored to be "another Saudi Arabia" and foreign loans were easy for it to obtain.

This time Atanacio found a factory job without difficulty. He knew his way around and was able to get work in a textile mill at a time of economic expansion. Marcela and her husband continued to work nights at home as well. They prospered along with the economy. Gradually they acquired the money to build a house in Loma Colorada, a *colonia* that had once been a shantytown but was now becoming a settled neighborhood, with concrete houses replacing cardboard and tin shacks and a mixed population of blue- and white-collar workers. Pointing to a new garbage-strewn shantytown on the opposite hill, Marcela said: "That's what this neighborhood used to look like. It's gotten better. Now we have water and gas."

Throughout the region there is a tendency for governments and elites to view the shantytowns that ring their cities as problems, hotbeds of unemployment, vice, and crime. In reality, shantytowns are symptoms of the society's problems rather than their cause. Unemployment is no higher in Latin America's squatter settlements than in the society at large, although its residents are more likely to work in the "backstreet" informal economy than in its modern industrial sector and to work harder yet earn a lower wage as a result.

For Benedita da Silva, the Brazilian shantytown leader and federal deputy from Rio de Janeiro, the prevailing view of the shantytown as "a problem" is exactly wrong. "The slum is not a problem, because the slum-dweller is a solution," she argued. "It is the slum-dweller who constructs the buildings and makes the furniture, who drives the buses and renders all the services necessary for the population." The problem of the slum-dweller is not unemployment but inadequate wages and benefits. Despite these "contributions" to society, "the shantytown is the only place he can live, [and] he doesn't have basic food or the security that other 'contributors' enjoy." The problem, in da Silva's view, is not the shantytown, but rather "the lack of public policy for the people who live in them."

This is as evident in Mexico City as in Rio de Janeiro. Moreover, not all migrants to Mexico City were as successful as Atanacio and Marcela, nor have all *colonias* progressed as much as Loma Colorada since their founding as squatter settlements. Adelaida and her husband, Felix, who arrived in the capital in 1980, seemed on a treadmill to nowhere a decade later. When Adelaida arrived from her native Oaxaca, like most Zapotec Indian migrants she found a place to live in Nezahualcóyotl, a lower-class area of the capital. With a population estimated at two to three million, "Neza" is probably Mexico's fourth largest city. It may also be the world's largest slum, as its residents claim with perverse pride. Named after the legendary philosopher king of ancient Texcoco, over whose drained lake it is built, Nezahualcóyotl has fewer amenities than its pre-Hispanic predecessor.

Eventually, Adelaida acquired a shack and land from her sister in Ayotla, one of the many "lost cities" of Neza, a slum without sewers, running water, or public telephones, whose unpaved streets are flooded in the rainy months and dust bowls in the dry season. She worked hard as a washerwoman going door-to-door and as an unskilled construction worker carrying sacks of cement on her broad back. Finally she settled for a job as a maid, the most typical work of female migrants. Most maids earn minimum wage, roughly three dollars a day at the end of the 1980s, not enough to meet even half a family's basic needs. Yet, together with the even lower wage that her husband received as a construction worker on the city's metro, this was all Adelaida had to support her five children. Although her employer, a foreign journalist, paid her considerably more than the legal minimum, it was still hard for her to make ends meet.[1]

The polluted air and lack of toilets in Neza breed disease, and diarrhea kills more people than cancer or heart attacks. When her children took sick, which was often, Adelaida had no medical insurance or nest egg to which she could turn. She worked in a house that was a three-hour bus and subway ride away, and arose at 5:00 A.M. to get to work on time. If the buses were too crowded, as was frequently the case, she had to pay more to board a private minibus, which could cost more than half her daily wage. Nor could her budget accommodate losing her roof in a storm, having her pocket picked in church during her daughter's confirmation, or having her husband mugged and beaten so hard that he was laid off from his job. In her native village Zapotec traditions provided communal assistance for those in need. In Mexico City she was forced to ask her employer to lend her the money to be discounted from her wages, which reduced her meager income even more in the future. If self-help and reliance on social networks is one typical migrant pattern, this dependence on a powerful *patron* for work, connections, and emergency loans is another.

Adelaida and Felix may have had a harder time making it in Mexico City than Marcela and Atanacio because they were Indians and uneducated, but they had also arrived in the capital at an inauspicious time. Before 1980, migration to Mexico City was an optimistic process and the relative success of those who made the journey fueled the hopes and dreams of those who followed in their footsteps. But the possibilities of migrants are affected not only by their own courage and creativity, and by the policies of their government, but also by world economic conditions beyond their control. The oil boom that had fueled the prosperity that drew migrants to La Capital at record rates during the 1970s came to an end in the global recession of the early 1980s, leaving Mexico with one of the highest foreign debts in the world, and Mexico City without the financial resources to maintain its urban infrastructure or extend social services to new arrivals. For a while, migration to the capital continued unabated, sustained by the memory of opportunities that were fading fast and the networks of friends and relatives who were already there.

By 1982, however, Mexico could no longer make payments on its debt. Foreign loans ceased and the economy plunged into a deep crisis, one that the rest of Latin America and the Caribbean shared. Mexicans now had reason to regret the heavy debts they had contracted during the easy money era of the boom, as well as the unproductive ways in which many of those loans had been expended. For Mexico City, this economic crisis was compounded in 1985 by a devastating earthquake, which left a million people homeless and a monumental task of reconstruction at a time of virtual national bankruptcy.

One of the other consequences of the crisis of the 1980s throughout

Latin America and the Caribbean was a rise in urban crime. In cities as distant and disparate as Lima, Santo Domingo, and Rio de Janeiro crime reflected growing unemployment and desperation. "Why do you think there are so many thieves?" an out-of-work carpenter named Tony asked rhetorically on a crowded Mexico City sidewalk. "Because there is no other way to make a living," he added with barely suppressed anger. It made Mexico City a more dangerous place to live and work, as Atanacio found out to his family's sorrow. He had continued to progress by dint of hard work even during the economic downturn, and by 1988 had saved enough money to buy a van and begin his own delivery service. Two weeks later he was killed, a victim of the crime that now seemed endemic to Mexico City.

Atanacio's death left his grieving family with a house and van, but soured on Mexico City and looking for a future elsewhere. Marcela, still mourning her husband and blaming Mexico City for his death, as she had once blamed Zacatecas for her daughter's, now wants to go back to Zacatecas. Her children are less eager to make the move. They have grown up in Mexico City, where they have friends and enjoy the action; they think they would be bored in the countryside. Her twenty-one-year-old son, Martín, did return to El Salto, but only to get married. One week later he brought his young bride, Lucía, back to Mexico City, where he uses his father's van to make a living for the whole family. His fourteen-year-old sister, Leticia, a single mother like many teenage girls in Loma Colorada, has added her own problems to the family's travails. The success that had once seemed within their grasp now seems to be slipping away. The city that had once represented progress and prosperity now offers only an uncertain and insecure future. Martín talks about going north, perhaps even to "the other side."

Marcela and Adelaida are not the only migrants who have soured on Mexico City. In recent years people have been leaving the capital in large numbers and looking elsewhere for their future. Instead of moving his family to the expensive and overcrowded capital from his native Michoacán, construction workers like Diego Santos have pioneered new forms of short-term labor migration that have turned the Observatorio bus station on the edge of Mexico City into an informal hiring hall for the construction industry. There workers like Diego wait each morning with their tools in hand, hoping to be hired for a week or a month, returning home when the job is completed. "The jobs are badly paid," Diego said, "but at least here in the city there *are* some jobs." For recent migrants like Diego, Mexico City is a place of temporary employment for minimal wages, not the city of his dreams.

The Informal Economy

But even amid the gloom and doom of the 1980s, there were signs of the creativity with which the people of Latin America and the Caribbean have responded to adverse circumstances. In Mexico City, when the government proved incapable of meeting the challenge of the earthquake, the people themselves took over, rescuing neighbors, rebuilding homes, and demanding state action. Pervasive bureaucracy and corruption also hampered the private sector of the economy, which was slow to recover.

In this crisis, it was the informal economy that filled the gap. Producing everything from shoes to candy, "microenterprises" employing up to fifteen workers mushroomed in the *colonias* damaged by the earthquake, owned by migrants who were used to uncertain conditions and able to respond to them with greater flexibility than bigger businesses that had to deal with the state bureaucracy.

Regino Ramírez, who started his shoe "factory" in a small storefront during the oil boom of the late 1970s, continued to prosper and expand even during the crisis of the 1980s. He is typical of the small businessmen who have made backstreet shops and factories Mexico's most dynamic economic sector. Ramírez is hardworking and hardheaded, but he is also incurably optimistic, convinced by his own experience that anyone can make it in Mexico City if he tries hard enough, "even if it's only setting up a small business at home, in the bedroom. You can start there, get the family working, and go forward from there." By 1990, this subterranean economy of workshops, artisans, and vendors accounted for more than a third of Mexico's national income. It was a share similar to that of the informal economy in Brazil, the region's other industrial leader.

For many of Mexico City's residents, moreover, it was the only economy they knew, as other jobs, goods, and services were beyond their reach. "The city is filled with street vendors because the minimum salary is not enough," Regino Ramírez explained. "To get workers, I don't need special ads. I just take a piece of paper, pin it outside, and the next day I get thousands of applicants." This underground economy might be informal, but it had a form of its own. Each craft and service came to concentrate in a street or district, like the souks of a Middle Eastern bazaar. If you needed a printer or a bookbinder you went to the Plaza Santo Domingo. If you wanted a carpenter or shoemaker you went elsewhere.

The dynamism and innovation of the informal economy during an era of economic stagnation has prompted a reassessment of its role throughout Latin America and a reevaluation as well of the importance of the shantytowns and migrants on which it is based. It has even led economists such as Peru's Hernando de Soto to tout the informal economy as an alternative development strategy for Latin America and the Caribbean, one now embraced even by such prestigious international agencies as the World Bank.

Such projections are premature and probably misplaced. The informal economy has proved a way for enterprising individuals to become small businessmen in economies dominated by large corporations, but it has yet to produce captains of industry. It has been a welcome source of jobs in an era of high unemployment, but its low wages and substandard working conditions make it little more than a survival strategy for the urban poor. It has provided low-cost goods and services to larger enterprises and to sectors of the population that cannot afford to acquire them elsewhere. Yet its ability to play more than a supporting role in the national economy and fill the gaps left vacant by big business and the state remains to be demonstrated.

What the success of the informal economy in the region does underscore is the creativity and determination with which the people of Latin America and the Caribbean are struggling to shape their own destinies. By

1990 shifting Mexican migration patterns attested to a flexibility characteristic of migrants throughout the region. Today, Mexico City has ceased to
be a mecca for the country's migrants. Its population is still increasing, but
at a slower rate. People continue to flow out of the countryside in search
of a better future, but increasingly they are heading for smaller provincial
cities, like Guadalajara or Aguascalientes, where the Mexican government
has begun to relocate state agencies in a belated effort to decentralize its
activities away from the overcrowded capital. The cycle of migration that
has made Mexico City one of the world's largest—and least livable—cities
is coming to an end.

The End of the Road?

Mexico City was not the only Latin American megalopolis to reach its city
limits during the 1980s. São Paulo, at the other end of the region, also
experienced a slowing of the spectacular growth that had made it South
America's largest metropolitan area.

"From nineteen-forty to nineteen-eighty, [São Paulo was] a very
strong pole of attraction for migrants," said Lucio Kowarick, one of Brazil's
leading experts on migration and urban growth. Both peaked during the
economic miracle of the 1970s, when thirty million Brazilians left their rural
homes to seek a better life in the country's cities. A booming São Paulo,
with half of Brazil's industrial jobs, was their most popular destination.

But during the economic crisis of the 1980s, to the surprise of the
pundits, the population growth of the areas on the edge of São Paulo
slowed by two thirds, while that of the inner city accelerated and surpassed
it. The poor, including the working poor, were leaving their suburban
shantytowns for inner-city slums. "It is a new phenomenon," Lucio Kowarick pointed out, but one that "you are beginning to see in Buenos Aires
and Montevideo as well. What you see in São Paulo today may be what
happens in the other large cities of the region in the next two decades."

It was, Kowarick acknowledged, a pessimistic forecast. "Before, living
in a *favela* in São Paulo, a family had to work hard, day and night, for ten

to twenty years, but at the end of that time you had your own house. But if you are renting a room in an inner-city tenement, at the end of ten years you will have nothing."

Today Greater São Paulo has more than seventeen million people, multiple centers, heavy traffic, and high pollution. It is a difficult city to live and work in, even for the professional with a car, phone, and maid. For a worker who lives in a suburban shantytown and has to commute to work four hours a day on crowded buses, it is a purgatory. For the unemployed poor, it can be hell. With a million workers unemployed, São Paulo is a hard place to look for a job, while the consolidation of *favelas* in its suburbs has made land expensive, squatting more difficult, and evictions common. In the inner city, at least there are jobs to be had in the service enterprises that have replaced industry as the leading economic sector, and it is possible to rent a tenement room cheaply and save time and money on commuting as well. It is little wonder that poor people are moving back to the center, returning to a pattern of lower-class housing that prevailed before 1930, but in far less auspicious circumstances. By 1990 it seemed as if the limits of São Paulo's urban sprawl had finally been reached.

Many others are leaving São Paulo altogether, heading for more dynamic industrial zones in the region, such as São Bernardo, or to smaller cities in the western part of São Paulo State like Campinas. New migrants are still arriving in São Paulo, but far fewer than in the past. Increasingly, they are bypassing São Paulo for greener pastures elsewhere.

This is particularly true for rural migrants, who in the absence of industrial opportunities are heading instead for the western part of the state or the adjoining regions of Mato Grosso, the new centers of export agriculture. There they can find work as *boias frias,* the "cold lunch" workers who are bused daily from *favelas* on the outskirts of small cities hundreds of kilometers away to harvest soybeans or cotton and return home at night. The work is hard, the pay is low, and the commute is long, but it is a job in a down economy and the cost of living is cheaper than in São Paulo. Significantly, Brazil's small cities—with twenty to fifty thousand inhabitants—grew faster in the 1980s than the large ones like São Paulo or Rio de Janeiro that had led the way before.

Working as a *boia fria* might put rice and beans on the table, at least for part of the year, but there was no future in it, unlike the industrial jobs São Paulo had offered in the past. There was no land available for squatters and "the landlords want everything for themselves," Avelino complained in a Campinas shantytown. Here he "just worked to be able to eat." For those with higher aspirations and greater resourcefulness, the agricultural regions of western São Paulo and southern Mato Grosso became a jumping-off point for a far more ambitious migration north through the Mato Grosso wilderness to Rondônia and Acre in the farthest reaches of the Amazon rain forest. When asked what he would do if he won the lottery, Avelino replied: "Ave Maria! I'd buy a farm in Rondônia."[2]

The draw of rain forest land was part of a new Brazilian migration pattern, a flow this time to the north of Brazil, into the vast expanses of its last frontier, the Amazon. During the 1980s more than one hundred thousand Brazilian families migrated from the south to Rondônia, attracted by the government's lure of free land. They burned down a quarter of Rondônia's rain forest, spread diseases that decimated the small remaining indigenous population, and helped turn the state into a wild west frontier. Yet, by 1991, Rondônia was looking like another illusory El Dorado. Its leached soils could not support the growing of rice and beans. Coffee prices were too low to feed a family and the rubber trees migrants planted often failed to produce. Today, abandoned farms dot the landscape and more than half of the cleared land is overgrown with brush and trees. Environmental concerns pressed on Brazil by international agencies have now limited lumbering and mining as well. As a result, migrants have gravitated increasingly to Rondônia's towns, turning them into cities. Its capital, Pôrto Velho, is even beginning to develop big-city problems. "People are abandoning the countryside," said Francisco José Silveira Pereira, the state's environmental chief. "In nineteen-eighty, Rondônia was seventy percent rural. Today, it is sixty percent urban." Hoping to escape São Paulo, the new migrants seemed to be re-creating it inside the Amazon instead.

In Mexico, too, migrants headed north during the 1980s, away from Mexico City and toward the frontier. But there the frontier they sought was not the Amazon rain forest, but the arid border with the United States, and their goal was not land to farm, but an industrial job in a border assembly plant.

From Border Town to Boom City

Since Prohibition, Tijuana has been synonymous with sleazy border town, where it was possible to find all the vices banned across the frontier in the United States. Then it was liquor and gambling that drew gringos across the border from San Diego to one of Tijuana's ninety-five bars, with their free floor shows and cheap prostitutes. Fifty years ago Tijuana's resident population was little more than one thousand and almost a fifth of those citizens were prostitutes. The ill-named Revolution Avenue is still lined with honky-tonk bars, dingy strip joints, and hot-bed hotels, but everything else about Tijuana has changed.

Tijuana is now a city of 1.5 million people, equal in size to San Diego on "the other side." Long a jumping-off point for illegal migrants to the United States, for many Mexicans it is now a more attractive destination than San Diego. During the past decade, Tijuana has become a center of industry, an island of prosperity in Mexico's sea of economic troubles.

They are export industries of a special kind, taking advantage of Tijuana's border location and an arrangement between Mexico and the United States that has created a duty-free manufacturing zone that has become the model for the proposed North American Free Trade Area. It may well become the model for the hemisphere. The new industries in Tijuana, Ciudad Juárez, and other border towns are *maquiladoras,* assembly plants that take electronic components or other parts imported exempt from Mexican tariffs, assemble them into finished products, and then reexport them duty free across the border to the United States. Along the industrial strip that lines the frontier near Tijuana appear many of the biggest names in manufacturing—Sony, General Electric, Panasonic, Xerox.

In the "global sourcing" strategies of these international corporate giants, Tijuana plays an assigned role as a low-wage site for their labor-intensive operations. It is a bit part in a far larger economic drama that spans many countries, but it is enough to make Tijuana Mexico's new boom town. Its *maquilas* employ one hundred thousand workers and are growing at a rapid rate, by more than 18 percent in 1989 alone. The assembly plants now range from food processing, shoes, and clothing to electronics, tools, and machinery. Industrial free-trade zones in the Dominican Republic and other countries of the region are experiencing a similar expansion. Tijuana, with 40 percent of Mexico's *maquiladoras,* looks increasingly like the cutting edge of economic change in the hemisphere.

It is the prospect of jobs in these border industries that has served as the magnet for migrants from other parts of Mexico, making Tijuana today a more attractive destination than La Capital, and over the past ten years Mexico's fastest-growing urban area. Most of the *maquila* workers are single young women from rural areas. They are preferred by *maquiladora* managers because they are paid less than men and are believed to be more dexterous and docile, as well as more tolerant of the assembly plant's monotonous work.

Carmen Moreno is a typical *maquiladora* worker. She came to Tijuana in 1989 when she was sixteen, from rural Michoacán, a state to the south of Zacatecas that traditionally sent its migrants to Mexico City but has now begun to send them to the border towns instead. She works at PPH Industrial, which assembles electronic pieces for a Chicago electrical equipment company. "I remember when I first got here," she said. "I came with a friend and we had to sleep at the bus station our first night. But the next day it was so easy to get work. They asked me three questions and I had a job." Tijuana has virtually no unemployment. "Here it's ugly, but there's lots of work," agreed Amalia Sánchez, a migrant from Zacatecas. "That's what's good about this place."

What's bad about Tijuana is the work itself, which is boring, and the conditions. Wages are as low as fifty-five cents an hour, and workers like Carmen Moreno have to live in rented shacks in distant shantytowns. Carmen has to get up at the crack of dawn to get to work, where she puts in long hours for low wages doing repetitive tasks. "I don't like the work and I am always feeling tired," she confessed. Not surprisingly, high turnover is one of the problems in the *maquila* industry. Others criticize the exploitation of low-wage Mexican workers, which has earned foreign companies billions of dollars in profits but given Mexico little back in return. "The *maquiladoras* pay no taxes, they pollute the environment, and their working conditions are often unsafe," complained one Mexican researcher, who preferred to remain anonymous. They also do not create a base for future industrial growth, nor do they leave a legacy of technological skills. Concha Pérez worked in a *maquila* for five years and at thirty-two is viewed as too old and too ill to be hired. "My eyesight was ruined working on the micromachinery. Then they put me in the chemical section, which hurt my lungs and kidneys. To get rid of me they kept changing my position. On top of that they give me a night shift. I had to say 'Enough.' They had won."

Ignacio Pérez, the owner of PPH Industrial and head of Tijuana's Maquiladora Association, has heard these criticisms before. He is willing to admit that the workers suffer from boredom and poor working conditions, and that "the turnover period of an employee in a *maquila* is very short." But he insists, "how else are we going to employ the people arriving in this city? I still remember Tijuana as a backward frontier town where people came only on the way to the other side. Now we have people from all over coming to work in Tijuana. Many are even arriving from Mexico City, both poor and rich, and all this is because of the 'terrible *maquiladoras*.'"

The Mexican government is well aware of the criticisms of policies that have given the *maquiladoras* free rein in Tijuana. But it feels that cracking down on the *maquilas* is a luxury that it can ill afford. The country is only beginning to recover from the economic stagnation of the 1980s, when the *maquila* border zone was one of the few bright spots in an otherwise depressed economy. When Carlos Salinas de Gortari became president of Mexico in 1988 he bet his own and his country's future on the creation of a North American Free Trade Area that, in effect, would turn all of Mexico into a *maquiladora* zone, bringing in foreign investment and creating Mexican jobs. It might also spread the migration now focused on border towns like Tijuana throughout the country, averting the creation of "another Mexico City." By 1992 Zacatecas itself had become the site of industrial parks—and sixteen thousand new industrial jobs. In the future, the poor peasants of the region may not have to migrate to find work. Tijuana is the showcase for this strategy, and Salinas is not about to jeopardize it by playing hardball on wages or working conditions with the foreign firms he wants to attract.

Nor would the workers who arrive in the Tijuana bus station with only the clothes on their back and the dreams in their head want him to. Carmen Moreno may not like her work or wages, "but I earn money and there are lots of things to do in Tijuana." The alternative would be to go back to rural Michoacán, and that was not attractive to her: "I don't want to return home," she explained with a seventeen-year-old's directness. "There's nothing to do there."

In Tijuana there are many things to do. There are also jobs to be had, and not only in the *maquiladoras*. The assembly plants shape an estimated third of Tijuana's economy, but their indirect impact is greater still. Another major source of business opportunities and employment is the commerce and other services that revolve around the *maquila* industry. Construction, which has been booming in Tijuana, is an example. The wealth created around the *maquila* industry has generated a construction boom that has transformed the face of the city. Today Tijuana stretches from horizon to horizon, and extends beyond its city limits. The boom has even spread down the coast, where condominiums and hotels for wealthy Mexicans and North Americans now obscure the shoreline in former fishing villages.

On a construction site in Rosarito, five miles from Tijuana, José Leyva is supervising the building of a new condominium by a group of stonemasons from his hometown of El Salto, the same Zacatecas community where María Luz Ojeda now lives. He is a middle-aged man with an open face, a thick moustache, and a look of contentment. "I came here in 1974," he said. "I was trying to be real macho and go to the other side to earn some dollars, and so have a fancy car and a smart house and get myself a wife back in Zacatecas, but 'La Migra' [the U.S. immigration agency] caught me the first time and then a coyote stole my money so that I had to get work in Tijuana. I haven't looked back since." He had begun as a construction worker and when he accumulated a bit of money and experience went out on his own as a contractor in the informal sector. Leyva saw that there was a need for good masons, a skill well developed in his native village, so he began bringing school friends from El Salto to work for him in Tijuana. It was a mutually beneficial arrangement. "I have brought over ninety families from my village to work here," he said with pride. "They all call me 'Tio' [Uncle] José, and all the men get good jobs as bricklayers. . . . I think this place ought to give me a medal!" What Tijuana has given José Leyva is material rewards and a sense of self-worth. "Now I have a car and a good wife, and I still go back to Zacatecas to get more workers. I need to get good ones because now I have a reputation to keep up."

This human chain stretching from Zacatecas to Tijuana is a good example of the social networks that shape migration in the Americas, spanning countries and often borders as well. Leyva's story also underscores the fact that it is skilled workers who are the most likely to migrate. For areas such as Zacatecas, this exodus of skilled workers is a double-edged sword. On the one hand, it means a loss of the people who have the skills to develop the region; on the other hand, their remittances help maintain the population that remains, and in some cases—as with the new apricot farms started by returned migrants near El Salto—provide the capital and experience that may yet rescue such declining rural areas.

One of Leyva's workers is Francisco Rivera, the husband of Marcela's cousin Guadalupe. While Marcela and Atanacio had migrated to Mexico City during the booming 1970s, in 1988 Guadalupe and her husband had chosen instead to move to Tijuana, where Francisco had been offered a job by Tio José. Two years later he was earning twice the going Mexico City wage, and they had a house in the Colonia Pancho Villa, a poor but lively shantytown, where other workers from El Salto also lived. There they re-created a community where traditional fiestas, news from home, and a stream of visitors keeps their ties with Zacatecas alive. Guadalupe visits El Salto less often than her Mexico City cousins but feels fortunate to be living in Tijuana, despite complaints about contaminated water, inadequate transportation, and the high cost of living—problems similar to Mexico City, as is Tijuana's increasing urban sprawl. The shantytowns that are multiplying on every cliff and canyon may be a city planner's night-

mare and a tourist eyesore, but to migrants such as Francisco and Guadalupe, they are hopeful signs. In a booming Tijuana they can earn enough
to send money back to their families and can dream of the day when, like
José Leyva, they too will set up businesses of their own.

Nor, despite the proximity of the border, do the Zacatecan masons in
Pancho Villa feel tempted to go to the other side. They are satisfied with
their life in Tijuana and, like José Leyva, have few illusions about the
American mirage that still beckons Mexicans with fewer opportunities.
"Once I went to the other side, like many of us poor people from the
village," Leyva tells an approving audience of his workers. "We were
always curious about going to the U.S. to earn dollars. People said that
things are very nice there. Some of them are lucky, but the majority get
there and realize that it's not like that. The U.S. is expensive. Yes, you earn
dollars, but you also spend them." Leyva had realized that despite its
higher wages, the United States is a difficult place to fulfill Mexican
dreams. "In the United States you can live for twenty, thirty years and
you'll never own anything, you're still renting. Here in Zacatecas, even if
you're only living on the cliffs, you have an opportunity to build yourself
a little house. It may be poor, but it's your own—and that's the most
important thing," he said. "For me the U.S. is not an option. I wouldn't like
to live there."

Neither would most Mexicans, although many young men want to
come to the United States to earn a nest egg and then return to set
themselves up in a business as José Leyva has done. It is when they cannot
find work in Mexico City, or in Tijuana, where the *maquilas* prefer to hire
women, or when the difference in real wages is too great, that the tempta-
tion to go to the other side becomes irresistible. Then they head for Zapata
canyon—or look for a good *pollero*.

"Don Sal" is a veteran *pollero,* or coyote. He makes his living guiding
illegal migrants, or *pollos* (chickens), across the border. It is midnight and
he has four nervous *pollos* "who just want to make a living and send some
money home" in his care. It isn't easy, and the floodlit fence that makes the
border here look like a war zone is the least of their problems. "To start
with, you have to have money, and lots of it," Sal explains. "A jump across

the border will cost you $150, but to San Diego it goes up to $300. L.A. is $450 and so on. Then you have to have connections on the other side, in order to stay and get some work." Four out of five migrants go to work, not to stay. "I see guys who have come and gone each year for years now," says Sal. "If you asked one of them if he'd like to go to hell, he'd probably say yes, if he could get work there." Few migrants would be willing to go to hell for a job, but throughout the Americas, they have demonstrated their readiness to go anywhere in the hemisphere in order to get ahead.

But with a booming Tijuana offering migrants jobs on the Mexican side of the border, Sal's own work is not what it once was. "I have seen this town grow and grow but I have not seen my business improve. In fact, these days it's getting hard for an honest *pollero* like me to make some money," he confessed. "Tell the gringos to relax. The Mexican invasion of the United States is still far away."

Throughout the Americas, so-called
"eternal Indians" are changing under
the impact of modernity, yet reaffirming their identities. The autumn equinox
ceremony at Bolivia's Tiwanaku, site of
the Aymara mother culture, attests to
the survival of ancient beliefs, but also
reflects the revival of ethnic nationalism and foreign tourism.

Chapter 7

Children of the Sun

Since World War II, many Indians have migrated from their rural communities to the region's cities. Some have sloughed off their "Indian" identities in an effort to assimilate, but many have retained its markers. In La Paz, Aymara women in *pollera* skirts and bowler hats sell electronic equipment.

Mauricio Mamani and his sons are university-trained professionals who wear Western dress but have retained their Aymara name and identification. But it is Dominga Mamani, an entrepreneur who continues to wear "Indian" dress and speak Aymara, whose business success has financed their studies.

Modern technology is changing the lives and possibilities of once isolated indigenous peoples, from Brazil's Yanomami—shown here listening to tapes of Indian leaders protesting the invasion of their Amazon lands by gold miners—to Ecuador's Shuar, who are educated by radio in rain forest schools.

Despite heavy repression, indigenous peoples have organized to defend their interests, increasingly linking their struggles across international frontiers. On Columbus Day 1991, Indian leaders from many countries gathered in Guatemala—where violence has created half a million refugees—to plan a counter-quincentenary for 1992.

The fate of the indigenous peoples of
Latin America has become a popular
cause in Europe and North America,
turning Raoní, a Kayapó chief from the
Brazilian Amazon, into an international
celebrity. He has toured the world with
the British singer-actor Sting as part of
their campaign to "Save the Rain
Forest."

Children of the Sun

*R*aoní seemed at ease amid the metallic forest of electronic equipment, moving in rhythm to the bossa nova that he had asked composer Tom Jobim to play for him "about that little forest bird." A closer look revealed the incongruity of this Kayapó chief in a New York recording studio. His words were muffled by the wooden plug that extended his lower lip several inches, his broad features were set off by straight jet-black hair worn long, and his homemade wooden pipe completed the picture. From the neck up he was a *National Geographic* portrait. But his wrestler's body was clothed in a designer T-shirt and jeans, and his sandals carried a discreet Pierre Cardin monogram that had nothing to do with the Xingú, his home in the Amazon.

Yet when Raoní talked about the rain forest the next night, at a standing-room-only benefit at Carnegie Hall with the British rock star Sting, it was with a simple eloquence that evoked its harmonies and moved his audience with pleas for help—for the endangered environment and for his people, whose way of life depended upon its survival. Raoní may have adapted to New York's concrete jungles, but his heart remained in Brazil's rain forest. There, with his painted body and minimal clothing, the Kayapó chief seems the "noble savage" for an age that celebrates Indians but insists on their remaining exotic. Still, even in the rain forest the noble savage has changed. When Raoní meets with Brazilian government officials, seminude

Kayapó warriors videotape their conversations to ensure that the promises made will be remembered.

Today, there are few "noble savages" left in the Americas—as if this romanticized European image ever reflected their reality. Some tribal peoples in the shrinking rain forests of the Amazon and Guatemala's Lacondón jungle continue to live like their ancestors; a few groups even avoid contact with outsiders, and some may still not have been "discovered." In isolated valleys of the high Andes the celebrated Brazilian photographer Sebastião Salgado has visited Indian communities where he was the first outsider in living memory to set foot.

But these are the exceptions that prove the rule. The outside world has encroached increasingly on the Indians of the Americas, transforming them, but being transformed in turn. As a result, the image of the "eternal Indian" is changing, and the "noble savage" is being replaced by a more complex figure who confounds our stereotypes and contradicts our categories.

During recent decades indigenous farmers have become city dwellers in unprecedented numbers, while rain forest hunters have become cattle ranchers and university-educated professionals. Some Indians have played with fluid identities, while others have reaffirmed their ethnic identification or experimented with a broader pan-ethnic nationalism. Indians have revitalized their cultures, revalued their pasts, and rewritten their histories. They have also organized themselves to defend their interests and reached out to other Indians in their region and nation, overcoming language barriers and ancient rivalries to form pressure groups that represent their joint interests.

Indians have become eloquent voices in national politics and international fora and have demanded a say in development policies and constitutional reforms. Some have even taken up arms to defend their people, but more often Indians have been victims of violence, not its perpetrators. Some have defined themselves as communities, others as ethnicities, still others as nationalities or even as nations. In diverse ways, the Indians of the other Americas have sought to become protagonists of their own destiny.

Peru, Bolivia, Ecuador, and Guatemala contain the great majority of the region's Indians. Their stories illustrate the dramatic changes that are taking place in the lives and identities of all the indigenous peoples of Latin America and the Caribbean.

"We have no need of the Christian god," said Margarito Esquino, heredi- tary chief of El Salvador's Nahuatl Indians. "We worship our father the sun and our mother the moon, like our grandparents before us."

When Columbus "discovered" Europe's "New World" there were perhaps sixty million children of the sun living in the lands that Europeans would call the Americas. Today there are some twenty million "Indians" in Latin America and the Caribbean, all but three hundred thousand in Spanish America, concentrated in the mountain spine that runs from the Rockies through the Andes and the adjoining rain forests.

Another one hundred million could claim Indian ancestry if they wished to do so. Most are mestizos—of mixed indigenous and European descent—but many are not. They have chosen not to identify themselves as "Indians" because of the prejudices against indigenous people and their nations and the disadvantages that Indians face in making their way in the non-Indian world.

Although their decisions to pass as mestizo reflect the burdens of being Indian in Spanish America, they also reflect the differences in the meaning of "Indian" in North America and Latin America. In North America "Indian" is a racial category and race is indelible: once an Indian, always an Indian. Latin Americans will often cite physical characteristics in describing "Indians," but, at bottom, "Indian" is an ethnic category defined by culture, not color.

Genetic "Indians" who shed the cultural markers of being "Indian"— who speak Spanish instead of Nahuatl, wear shoes instead of sandals, call themselves Matos instead of Moctezuma, move from their communal village to the capital city—are no longer viewed as "Indians." In Central America, they may be called *ladinos,* along with mestizos and people of purely European descent. In the Andes, they may refer to themselves as mestizos, but be regarded by others as *cholos,* a term used for Indians who are trying to pass as mestizos but cannot mask their origins. Yet, throughout the region, there is a fluidity that allows individuals to redefine their identities, along with a rigidity that subordinates Indians to non-Indians. Throughout Spanish America, a central colonial legacy is a social hierarchy based upon color and reinforced by class, in which the descendants of the vanquished Indians are subordinated to the cultural heirs of their Spanish conquerors. Yet it is also a society in which the growing number of mestizos enjoy greater social mobility, and where resourceful individuals can make their way up the social ladder by passing for people of higher status.

Independence changed little for the Indians of South America. In Peru, the heartland of both the Inca and Spanish empires, the Indian tribute was ended, but a tax of equal value replaced it. If anything, the removal of imperial restraints freed the creole elite to make even greater inroads on Indian lands and labor. During the century that followed, Peru's Indians were excluded from the republic's political life and viewed mostly as a source of cheap labor for its mines and farms.

Yet, despite their subordination and exclusion, the Indians were increasingly at the center of the debate over Peru's destiny. For most of its history, the nation's creole elites regarded the "backward" Indian as the major obstacle to its progress. They have continued to regard the Indian as a problem, but one that could be solved by assimilation, which would put an end to Peru's dual society. After the Mexican revolution, populist reformers like Victor Raúl Haya de la Torre and Marxist revolutionaries like José Carlos Mariátegui argued that Peru's Indians held the key to its future. Mariátegui, in particular, saw the Indian community as a model for a Peruvian socialism and the country's Indian majority as a potential mass base for a communist revolution. Today's Shining Path guerrillas, who regard Mariátegui as a guiding light, have sought to transform his prophecy into strategy, recruiting heavily among Peru's poor Quechua Indian peasantry.

This specter of Peru's Indians as a potential revolutionary force has haunted much of its recent history. In the wake of the Cuban revolution, Peruvian leftists tried to link their cause with that of oppressed Indian peasants. The army suppressed their guerrilla movements, but the experience persuaded influential officers that unless the inequalities of rural Peru were modified, the threat of an Indian-based revolution would grow. The solution of the Indian "problem" became a goal of the "Peruvian revolution" that followed the military's seizure of power in 1968, a preemptive reform from above to avert the danger of revolution from below.

Inti Raymi

On June 24, 1968, the sky was clear and azure over the ruined Inca fortress of Sacsayhuamán guarding the ancient capital of Cuzco. On the great boulders of cut stone that had once formed the fortress walls, Indian families in traditional dress spread their picnics and placed their transistor radios. They had come for the celebration of Inti Raymi, the Inca solstice festival, with its reenactment of the pre-Hispanic ceremony in which the Inca blessed the Four Quarters of his empire and assured their prosperity for another year. When the actor playing the Inca was carried to the four corners of the field in a covered palanquin, the rumor spread around me that it was not an actor, but an Inca returned to reclaim his kingdom. In reality, it was a show produced by the Peruvian government, which had declared June 24 "Indian Day" as a token of its concern for the otherwise neglected majority of its people.

The next Inti Raymi would be different. On June 24, 1969, the president of Peru's new military "revolution," General Juan Velasco, decreed the abolition of "Indian" as an official category. Henceforth, all "Indians" would be called "peasants," he commanded. Then, with the ringing pledge, "Peasants! The landlord will no longer eat from your poverty," Velasco proclaimed a sweeping land reform that would transform the country's large estates into producer cooperatives and end the domination of rural Peru by its creole elites.[1] By 1977 there were virtually no private estates left in highland Peru. On paper, the ethnic structure of power that had dominated rural Peru since the colonial period was no more.

But these military reform measures did not end social tensions or lead to an upsurge in Indian support for the military's "revolution." In part this was because Velasco's land reform benefited only one out of four rural families. It did little for the 40 percent who lived in Indian communities and continued to press their claims for lands taken from them by the old owners, and nothing at all for the millions of landless rural laborers. The new cooperatives, moreover, were generally run by government managers whose mistreatment of the Indian members differed little from that of the old landowners. Equally important was that the military's solution to the "Indian problem"—the latest in a long series of assimilationist "solutions"—ran counter to the strategies that Peru's Indians had devised for themselves.

Mario Vargas Llosa is Peru's most celebrated writer, the author of highly regarded novels and plays. He has also run for president, and lost to Alberto Fujimori, a Japanese-Peruvian agronomist, because he was regarded as the creole candidate in a country that Vargas himself has described as "an artificial gathering of men from different languages, customs, and traditions whose only common denominator was having been condemned by history to live together without knowing or loving one another." Although much of Vargas's work is experimental, his most controversial writing was probably a 1990 essay in which he defended the Spanish conquest and embraced assimilation as the solution to Peru's Indian problem and migration as its strategy. "Indian peasants live in such a primitive way that communication is practically impossible," he argued. "It is only when they move to the cities that they have the opportunity to mingle with the other Peru," a mestizo country with a Hispanic culture. "The price that they must pay for this integration is high," he wrote: "Renunciation of their beliefs, their traditions and customs, and the adoption of the culture of their ancient masters. After one generation they become mestizos. They are no longer Indians."[2]

Clearly Vargas Llosa has never been to Mayobamba, a rural community of some 450 people ten thousand feet up in the Western range of Peru's central highlands, near the provincial border between the mining zone of Cerro de Pasco and Lima, the nation's capital.[3] Its people grow potatoes and other subsistence crops on communal lands, and also herd cattle and sheep, producing milk and cheese for regional and national markets. Mayobamba was officially designated an "indigenous community" in 1935, which protected its communal lands from sale. The nomenclature changed to "peasant community" in 1969, but little else did.

In Mayobamba, however, the key question is not "Who is an Indian?" but rather "Who is a *comunero?*"—a recognized member of the local community. *Comuneros* share responsibility for needed public works, cultivating communal lands, caring for the community cattle herd, and administering community affairs. In return they can grow subsistence crops like potatoes on communal plots, draw on emergency food stocks in time of need, and participate in the local democracy, with its rotation of offices among adult male *comuneros*.

Yet, like most Andean communities, Mayobamba has not entirely conformed to this communal ideal for many years. Private landholdings began during the colonial era, and increased after independence. Enterprising *comuneros* and Indians acting as intermediaries between their community and the non-Indian government authorities, the mining firms of Cerro de Pasco, and the haciendas of the coast, took advantage of their roles and resources to acquire land and livestock and assume a preeminent position within their community. By the time the military seized power in 1968 almost all the good irrigated land in Mayobamba was in private hands, although the community retained the right to regulate the vital flow of water to these plots and pastures. Those who owned the land formed the local elite, who hired others to care for their lands and livestock. Many of these workers were poorer kin who depended on their richer relatives for their livelihood, offering them a loyal labor force in exchange. It was a class structure that cut across the community's ethnic homogeneity and extended families, making it difficult either to challenge from inside or to impose harshly from above.

Only men could become *comuneros* in Mayobamba and boys came first in family inheritance or educational strategies. As a result, women enjoyed greater economic opportunities in the cash economy of the nearby market town of Chiuchin, located in the valley below Mayobamba, which served as its link with coastal markets and authorities until the road reached

Mayobamba in 1968. The new road made it easier for Mayobamba families to go to the coast and establish networks of their own that stretched from the high pastures of the sierra to the shantytowns of Lima.

They were part of a far larger migration of Indians from the sierra to the coast that was largely responsible for the tenfold increase in the population of Lima between 1940 and 1990. This inundation of highland people transformed a provincial capital city of 645,000 into a metropolis of 6.5 million, whose shantytowns extended for miles over the barren hills. Some Lima residents saw this as an Indian "invasion," a threat to the Spanish character of Pizarro's "city of kings." But to the "modernizers" among Peru's creole elite, like Vargas Llosa, this massive migration was the way in which the Indians could be integrated into the nation shorn of their separate culture and identity.

To the Indian migrants themselves, however, moving to the coast was an opportunity to extend their communal networks, not an occasion to sunder their ties and shed their identity. They had their own "development strategy" and it was rather different from that projected by Peru's creole elites. Most of those who moved from Mayobamba to Lima were young and unmarried, in search of educational or job opportunities not available in their sierra community. Some were children of wealthy families looking to establish themselves on the coast. Esteban and Pilar, Chiuchin storekeepers, sent their sons to be educated in Lima, where they are professionals today.

Others, like Carlos, were young men with more enterprise than resources, for whom Mayobamba had little to offer. His family had little land, his father was dead, and his brother soon followed him to the capital. There Carlos studied nights and found a job at an urban poultry farm, little thinking that this would be his destiny. Once he had mastered the poultry business, he set up one on his own with his brother. As his business expanded, Carlos needed workers whom he could trust, so he returned to Mayobamba and recruited relatives to work for him, using the men as truck drivers and the women to sell in his market stalls. By 1975 he was employing over a dozen Mayobamba "kin," not all of them close relatives.

Carlos did not use his new wealth to distance himself from his home community. On the contrary, he donated the doors for Mayobamba's new school and the gates for its soccer stadium. He capped it off by serving as sponsor of Mayobamba's patron saint's day festival, itself both an honor and a great expense. For that occasion, Carlos returned home triumphantly with a ten-piece band and two truckloads of other migrants from Mayobamba. He used his coastal resources to win social prestige in his home community in traditional terms, albeit by nontraditional means. In Lima, Carlos may have seemed to creoles a *cholo* businessman—shrewd, aggressive, and ambitious. But in Mayobamba he was a respected community leader who occupied one of its most prestigious offices and offered coastal employment to its youth.

One of the relatives whom Carlos hired as a market woman was Concepción, the daughter of a wealthier Mayobamba family who had moved to Lima with her brother to be educated. When he returned to the sierra, she remained to prepare for her university entrance exams, living with a cousin and dreaming of becoming a nurse or a teacher. But after two years of university, Concepción married, became pregnant, and dropped out of school, intending to return. Four babies later, her husband suddenly died, leaving her to make her own way in Lima with what she had learned on the coast. Like many migrants, she turned to her family networks in the highlands. Concepción's two daughters were sent to live with her mother-in-law in Huaral. Her own father moved to Lima to help her, and her youngest sister stays from time to time to look after the children. Concepción's Mayobamba family helped her to build a solid house on the outskirts of Lima, where they could also stay when they visit the coast. She designed it to accommodate a small shop in the front, which could free her from working at Carlos's stall across town. It is a family investment in a strategy that encompasses the sierras of Mayobamba and the shantytowns of Lima.

Although each story is unique, Carlos and Concepción are typical of Mayobamba migrants in their retention of ties with their home community and their creation of networks of reciprocal exchange. These ties and networks are flexible, capable of accommodating changing needs. If extra labor is needed, they can be used to recruit a cousin to drive a truck or run a market stall. If a family needs more income, a grandparent or younger sibling can move to take care of children so that a mother can work. But it also works the other way. A child sent to be educated in Lima lives with a relative, bringing a share of the potato harvest as part payment for his bed and board. A young woman in search of a job is offered a base, advice, and moral support by her Lima kin, or a position by a successful relative. In times of economic downturn or family troubles, children can be sent back to the sierra, or the entire family can return home to ride out the economic storm on their communal plots or private pastures, which they held on to for such a rainy day.

Significantly, Mayobamba families almost never sold off their lands or surrendered their *comunero* status, even if it meant paying others to work their lands or fulfill their responsibilities. Instead they created a network of informal exchanges of goods and labor stretching from their sierra community to the coast, the modern equivalent of their ancestors' archipelago of producing colonies in diverse ecological niches. Far from being a way to integrate Indians shorn of their culture into a mestizo nation, modern migration is a flexible strategy of sierra families and communities to secure the resources they need to prosper without surrendering their identities.

Mayobamba is typical of the Indian communities of the Western sierra, whose relative proximity to Lima allows for a constant flow of people, goods, and information. This enables them to sustain ties so close that their Lima "colonies" reflect the character and structure of the home community and the migrants even organize labor and serve in festival offices back in the sierra. Not all communities can sustain such cohesion or replicate the patterns of the sierra. Indian migrants from more distant Asillo—on the high plateau near Puno where they had been peons on haciendas owned by mestizos—viewed their migration to Lima as a liberation from their highland oppression and refused to have anything to do with migrant Asillo mestizos once they got to the coast.

In general, the cohesion of highland communities within the chaos of Lima is remarkable. Their migrants invade vacant suburban lands together and build houses together, work together and celebrate their saints together. It is a cohesion reinforced by newcomers and visits home, and by a tendency to marry within their community. Individual migrants may also join neighborhood organizations and political parties. But the most striking feature of this migration of highland communities has been the formalization of their shared identity in social clubs based on place of origin—many with legal status, club houses, sports teams, and music groups. These associations also raise money to pay for improvements back home and serve as an aid to new arrivals.

Many clubs correspond to a single sierra community like Mayobamba, but others are broader in their geographic reach, embracing an entire region, department, or province—allowing migrants to define themselves as *serranos*, people of the highlands, or as *provincianos*, people from the provinces. In these regional associations, migrants create ties with each other that may not have existed in the sierra, yet which are treated with the same sense of "kinship." By 1985, there were seven thousand regional associations in Lima alone, more than the number of official Indian "communities" in Peru. It had become clear that far from serving as a creole strategy for Indian assimilation, the great migration to the coast had become what some experts have termed an Indian "Trojan horse."[4]

On the Roof of the World

In a village near Lake Titicaca on Bolivia's high plateau, twelve thousand feet above the sea, masked dancers whirl to celebrate St. John's Day with rhythms and movements that recall their Aymara ancestors. In the tin mines of Oruro, dark-skinned miners with electric lanterns on their helmets pour libations to statues of the old gods before descending into the bowels of the earth. Even in modern La Paz, revelers pour a few drops on the ground "for the Pachamama," the ancient Andean earth goddess, before beginning their fiesta. Throughout Bolivia, there are constant reminders of its pre-Hispanic past and Indian majority.

Around the shores of Lake Titicaca, the world's highest navigable waterway, the ancestors of the Aymara people built one of the earliest civilizations of the Andean highlands. In time, the Aymara kingdoms were conquered, first by the Incas and then by the Spaniards, who drafted them to work in the silver mines of Potosí and in the haciendas that they carved out of what had been Indian lands. Independence brought self-rule to the creoles of Upper Peru and the creation of a new state named after its Liberator, Simon Bolívar, but it brought little more than formal liberty for Bolivia's Indian majority. The century that followed saw increasing encroachments on communal lands by a creole and mestizo elite freed from imperial constraints.

"The Aymaras were the ones who suffered most," asserted Mauricio Mamani, a prominent Aymara anthropologist and leader. First it was the Incas, "and after that the Conquest, and then the Spanish colony, and then the republic, and after that, the hacienda bosses." In 1952 Bolivia was a classic example of Latin America's notorious rural inequality. Only 6 percent of the landowners owned 90 percent of the arable land, with estates that averaged over two thousand acres, while 60 percent of the landowners had only 0.2 percent of Bolivia's farmlands, mostly Indian peasants who eked out a living on dwarf farms of eleven acres or less. Unable to survive on their tiny plots, which were further subdivided with each generation, Bolivia's Indians were forced to work for the large landowners, receiving in return only the right to plant their crops on idle marginal hacienda lands. Most were serflike *pongos,* obligated as well to perform personal services for the generally absentee owners or their local overseers.

In rural Pasopaya, an aging Felix Zorrilla Martínez recalled the hacienda of his youth without nostalgia. "I remember how I suffered . . . how they beat us, how they made us work for free." He remembered, too, "how the sons of the owner abused the women when they went to get water." His voice choked with buried emotion: "These memories make me furious . . . and ashamed."

It was little wonder that the Indian peasantry became a major base of support for the Bolivian revolution of 1952. With the encouragement of the militant miners who spearheaded the revolution, and with the acquiescence of the urban middle-class reformers who led it, the Indians seized the lands that had been taken from their ancestors and destroyed the haciendas. They also formed peasant unions, whose political support was courted by the new generation of politicians, and celebrated the official abolition of the category "Indian" with which they had been oppressed for so long.

But formal discrimination proved much easier to change than social prejudice. In theory Bolivia's Aymara- and Quechua-speaking Indian majority might be equal to the country's creole and mestizo elites. In practice they found it difficult to make their way in the Hispanic world beyond their rural communities. Few Indians were literate or spoke Spanish; fewer still had received much education or learned technical skills. Those who tried to obtain them often found their way barred as "Indians." "For five hundred years, the Aymaras were oppressed by the same system of discrimination and suffering," Mamani said. It was "in order to avoid any further sufferings, any more discrimination, that the Aymara tries to hide his identity when he abandons his community and arrives at an urban center. In other words, they try to change their ethnic features so they will not be noticed."

Passing had been common in the Andes since the colonial era, but as Indian migrants flooded the cities after World War II, it assumed new dimensions and forms. In Bolivia, where almost everyone had some Indian blood in their veins and even "people with Spanish origins are dark-skinned," what determined discrimination was "not necessarily skin color," Mamani explained. "Andean people have straight hair, [so] to avoid being 'Indian' with straight hair, these people go to a beauty parlor to get a perm that will give them curls or at least waves." Although a young man in a La Paz hair salon might see his perm as affirming his place in an international youth culture, for Mamani it represented a denial of Indian identity.

But in Bolivia today a growing number of Indians—Aymara, Quechua, Guaraní—are reaffirming their Indian identities and revitalizing their culture. Mamani is defiantly proud of being an Aymara, and has made his way in Bolivia's ethnically divided society despite its burdens.

Mauricio Mamani is an Aymara success story. In a country where most Indians were illiterate, he has earned a university degree and become a respected professional. In a nation where Indians were usually excluded from political power, he has been a cabinet minister. In a society where the overwhelming majority of Indians are poor, even by the standards of one of the continent's poorest countries, he lives comfortably, and can afford to educate his children for professional careers. Ramiro is completing his medical training and Oscar his legal studies; Johnny and Clodomiro are engineers. Mauricio's wife, Dominga, is a successful businesswoman in La Paz and a major contributor to her family's prosperity and children's education.

Mamani had accomplished these goals in the face of great obstacles. He was born into a poor Aymara-speaking family, and almost not allowed into school because he was an Indian. At first, "they wouldn't allow him to go to the university" either, Oscar recounted. "Even at work he was not well received." But Mauricio persevered and became an anthropologist and a rural development expert, and was chosen in 1985 to be minister of agriculture. "It's incredible," Oscar concluded, "that he went from poverty to being a minister."

Even more remarkable was that Mauricio Mamani had done it his way. He retained his Aymara surname, which immediately identified him as Indian in a society where Mamanis on the make changed their name, which means eagle, to Aguilar, or some other Spanish-sounding equivalent. His wife still dressed in the bowler hat and layered *pollera* skirts that were visual symbols of Aymara identity, and spoke Aymara, not Spanish. Moreover, they still went back to the altiplano to harvest their potatoes and make *chuño,* the freeze-dried potatoes invented by their ancestors, stamping out the liquid with their bare feet in the time-honored fashion, "so as not to anger the spirits."

Yet these achievements came at a high personal cost, and the Mamanis bore the scars inside. Dominga Mamani had seen some of her friends become more distant as they exchanged their *polleras* for "Spanish" dresses, "because they want to be polished, like the ladies" of La Paz. Mauricio Mamani himself had faced discrimination throughout his career. Even his moment of greatest triumph—his inauguration as minister of agriculture— was clouded by prejudice. He arrived at the Plaza Murillo—"where before the revolution Indians were not even allowed"—in his black suit, and had difficulty talking his way past a colonel who could not believe that a Mamani "was going to take the oath" as a minister. The security guard at the government palace was equally skeptical and refused to let him in. "I was very nervous because they were going to call my name and I wasn't going to be there," Mauricio recalled. "Luckily, the president's secretary called for the diplomatic corps to enter the palace." Mauricio Mamani looked around at these foreign representatives to the land of his ancestors. "There were the British, the French, the Chinese, the Japanese." He had been to Japan and spoke a few words of Japanese, so he mingled with the Japanese diplomats and "got into the presidential palace as a member of the diplomatic corps" to take his oath of office. In Bolivia, even two decades after the revolution that "liberated" the Indian and abolished the category, it was acceptable to be Japanese, but not Aymara. "We are very different from these people, from this urban Bolivian elite," Mauricio reflected. "If I were one of them, I wouldn't have any problems." Because he was not, Mamani mistook his appointment—a token Indian in an otherwise creole and mestizo cabinet—as an opportunity to help his people, and was forced to resign a few months after assuming office.

Mauricio's sons, too, had suffered discrimination and confronted problems because of their Aymara name and Indian identity. Ramiro Mamani might be a doctor today, but he recalled that as "a kid at school, I had fights [because of] my last name." At the university, Oscar recounted, there was also prejudice, although there it was "certain professors" who were responsible. But it was their brother, Johnny, who had paid the highest price for being an "Indian."

As a teenager Johnny had fallen in love with Patricia, the girl who lived across the street in their comfortable La Paz neighborhood. Patricia became pregnant and they wanted to marry, but her parents wouldn't allow it, "because of my last name—Mamani—and also because my mother wears *polleras*. There was a social discrimination," Johnny explained. Before the affair was over there was much more than just "social discrimination." Patricia's family was from Chuquisaca, the old colonial capital, "and they think they are from the aristocracy, descended from the Spaniards," scoffed Mauricio—even though "they were peasants just like the Mamanis," Patricia revealed. When their daughter refused to end the affair, they "went to the police [and] put Johnny in jail. [Then] her parents sued us in court because they didn't want their granddaughter to have Mamani as a last name," Mauricio recalled. In the end, the families settled out of court. But when the baby was born Patricia's family gave her their name—Romero—pretended it was Patricia's sister and refused to allow Johnny to see his child. The Romeros and the Mamanis are still neighbors, but they "don't even say hello," passing each other in silence as if they didn't inhabit the same block—or mestizos and Indians the same country.

Bolivia is an overwhelmingly Indian nation whose non-Indian elite has largely ignored its rich pre-Hispanic past. Yet less than an hour's drive from La Paz lie the ruins of Tiwanaku, which many believe was the mother culture of the Andes. There, in a shallow valley near Lake Titicaca, in a treeless landscape above the maize line where only potatoes and quinoa can grow, the ancestors of today's Aymara Indians built one of the great civilizations of ancient America more than a millennium ago.

Tiwanaku was probably the first great metropolis of the Andean highlands. Centuries before the Inca empire, it was the center of an extensive economic network that crossed altitudes and ecological zones to assure its people a complete basket of goods in the vertical terrain of the Andes. Tiwanaku may also have been the capital of an empire, with an archipelago of colonies that stretched from the Pacific to the Amazon, many of them connected by paved roads. It was a creative civilization, which developed an innovative raised-field agriculture, and a religion symbolized by Tiwanaku's Gate of the Sun, whose radiant sun-god the Incas would make their own. "Our excavations are showing that many of the advances that have been attributed to the Incas were already present at Tiwanaku," said Osvaldo Rivera, until 1992 head of Bolivia's National Institute of Archaeology, which oversees a major archaeological and development project in collaboration with a group from the University of Chicago. "They were really accomplishments of the ancient Aymaras."

But the Tiwanaku project is not just changing our ideas about Andean prehistory and its ancient peoples. It is also altering the lives and consciousness of their modern descendants. All the workers on the project are local Aymaras and they have gained both new skills and new self-esteem. Mario Losa has become a surveyor through his work at Tiwanaku, but equally important for him has been his new sense of his origins—and himself. "Before, we were told that Aymaras were inferior," he said. "But when I see what our ancestors built at Tiwanaku I know that is not true." His new ethnic pride was shared by César Kalasaya, the local foreman, who has virtually "become an archaeologist," during his years on the project, capable of interpreting the finds. The Tiwanaku project has also experimented with the ancient Aymara raised-field agriculture, in which rich mud from irrigation channels is added to well-watered plots, and found that its yields are up to forty times higher than those of today. "At first the local peasants were skeptical," Osvaldo Rivera recalled with quiet satisfaction. "But now that they have seen the results, they all want to try it." By 1992, thousands of peasants in communities along the shores of Lake Titicaca were experimenting with the "new" farming techniques. International development agencies have also expressed interest. By the end of the century, Rivera projected, these ancient Aymara techniques could transform agriculture in the altiplano.

They have already transformed the consciousness of Aymaras who neither live nor work at Tiwanaku. In the Tiwanaku Museum in La Paz, a group of Aymara women in their bowler hats and layered *polleras* talked excitedly in Aymara while they looked at the exhibit of objects found at Tiwanaku. "I have been to Tiwanaku and I see that our ancestors knew more than we do," Elena Ibarra affirmed, while others nodded in agreement. She had seen the vast city they had built and "was filled with emotion. I not only feel admiration, but also pride. I feel proud of my ancestors, and proud to be Aymara."

Even the Bolivian elite, which for years denigrated anything Indian, used *cholo* as a term of contempt, and downplayed Tiwanaku except for tourists, seems to be changing its tune. Political leaders now want to associate themselves with the Tiwanaku project, and its Bolivian funding, some from private sources, has increased. A Tiwanaku park and museum have been set up at prominent La Paz sites. Part of the explanation is political: In a nation where three out of four people are Indian, Aymara votes are important, and in the current revival of ethnic awareness, Tiwanaku has become a symbol for the Aymara. But among the younger generation of educated mestizos, the elite of tomorrow, there is also a new interest in their indigenous roots. At the national university in La Paz, mestizo students have revived the celebrations of their Indian forebears, complete with costumed devil dancers, and made them a major annual event. It has even become chic for students to go to Oruro to dance La Diablada in its famous miners' carnival. "There has been a reevaluation of Bolivia's Indian culture," explained one student leader. "We realize that these are *our* cultural roots and that they are something to be proud of."

For Bolivia, a fragmented nation that has had difficulty in establishing its identity, consolidating its frontiers, or sustaining its sovereignty, the glories of its pre-Hispanic past symbolized by Tiwanaku have become a more compelling founding myth than the Spanish Conquest. The new Bolivian history being uncovered at Tiwanaku has been embraced as well by extremist Aymara nationalist groups such as the Tupac Katari Movement, named after the Aymara leader of a colonial rebellion. The Kataristas emerged out of university groups that focused on Aymara cultural identity to found a peasant union, two political parties, and a guerrilla group that has been rumored to have ties to Peru's Shining Path. From Mauricio Mamani's pride in his name and Tiwanaku's revival of ancient Aymara agricultural techniques to the many radio stations broadcasting in Aymara and the Kataristas' rejection of all that is not Indian, Bolivia's Aymara Indians are stirring.

On the morning of the autumnal equinox the first rays of the sun strike the sacred gate at Tiwanaku, illuminating its narrow opening with a magical star burst that looks like an inscription from the sun-god. For many who have kept vigil through the night to witness it, the rising sun symbolizes the reemergence of the Aymaras in the land of their ancestors.

The Uprising

In the wintry dawn of a June day in 1990, the Indian peasants of the region around Cayambe streamed into the small town in highland Ecuador, the women in their brightly colored pleated skirts, the men with their white pants and sandals. The traditional red flags they waved stood out against the snow-clad backdrop of the mountains. But the Quichua slogans they chanted underscored their increasingly assertive ethnic identity and political purpose. They had come from their highland communities at the behest of the Confederation of Indigenous Nationalities of Ecuador (CONAIE), in solidarity with the hunger strike of their leaders in Quito, the capital, and in protest against government rejection of the reforms CONAIE had demanded. Women surrounded the tanks sent to intimidate them and neutralized them with their numbers and unity. Armed with nothing but sticks and anger, they faced down the soldiers' guns. In the end, the soldiers retreated without firing a shot and the tanks turned away, leaving the Quichua peasants in possession of the "battlefield."

All across Ecuador, similar scenes were enacted. Roads were blocked by barricades and landed estates were seized by their peons. In Chimborazo, officials accused of abusing Indians were subjected to mock public trials. By the time The Uprising was over, the myth of Indian passivity had been shattered and Ecuador's Indians had established themselves as a powerful political force. "We had to show the government the depth of our support," said Shuar leader Ampam Karakras. "We were determined to take charge of our own destinies."

Ecuador is a small but densely populated Andean country of eleven million, of whom one out of three are considered Indian, and most of the rest have some indigenous blood in their veins. But these Indian numbers have not translated into Indian influence. As in Peru and Bolivia, since the Conquest, Ecuador's Indians have been excluded from power, shorn of their territories, and treated as inferiors in the land of their ancestors.

An exception to this subordination were the Amazonian Indians living in the dense rain forests beyond effective government control. Of these, the most famous were the Shuar, whom Ecuadorians knew as the Jívaro and feared as headhunters, notorious for their poison darts and shrunken heads. The Shuar were redoubtable warriors, who had forced the Incas to retreat and driven the Spanish out in 1599, leaving only one terrified colonist alive to tell the cautionary tale of how the governor had been killed by having "the tax of gold which he had ordered prepared" poured down his throat.[5] The Spanish withdrew from the area, and it was not until the late nineteenth century, when a road was built down from the mountains, that the Shuar faced sustained incursions from the outside world. Then Salesian friars created Shuar missions and over time helped convert the Shuar from their blood feuds and warring ways. The Shuar no longer shrink human heads, but they retain their redoubtable reputation among non-Indians—as leaders of Ecuador's Indian movement, one of the most militant in the continent.

It was the twentieth century's demands for land and natural resources that forced the Shuar to change their way of life and emerge from their rain forest isolation. During the 1960s, landless highland peasants began to settle in Shuar territory, encouraged by governments that sought to deflect peasant demands for redistribution of the large estates in the sierra by promoting colonization of the "empty" lands in the Amazon. In response the Shuar "colonized" their own lands more visibly by settling in centers of twenty-five to thirty families, which joined together in 1964 in a Shuar Federation, "the first of its kind in the Andes," said Karakras, and a model for federations elsewhere. They also sought to demonstrate that their lands were not empty by creating cattle ranches, an economic activity that even the creole elites had to recognize. The Shuar Federation secured legal titles for ancestral lands and loans with which to purchase the cattle to fulfill the legal requirement that the lands be "in use"—as if the ancient way in which their ancestors harvested the rain forest was not using its resources. In time, the Shuar Federation pioneered a system of bilingual education by radio for isolated communities, created its own police, and established direct marketing of its exports to Europe. "We were also the first to take back our Indian names," said Ampam Karakras, one of the first Shuar university students and a key leader of their efforts to reach out to other Indian groups.

By the 1980s, however, the pressure from colonists was growing, to which was added the discovery of oil in the Amazon and the penetration of lumber companies. To confront this increased threat, the Shuar turned to their rain forest neighbors, the Quichua, and proposed that they unite their efforts to protect their common interests. It was a revolutionary notion. The Shuar and the Quichua might live in neighboring territories, but they spoke different languages and lived separate lives—except for the sharing of magic by their shamans. It was left to the mission-educated younger generation, often the children of chiefs or shamans, to forge the link between the two nations. The missionaries had given them Spanish-language skills and knowledge of Ecuador and its laws as part of a strategy of assimilation, but now the Indians would use their education for their own purposes. "The Salesians called us ingrates," said Ampam Karakras, "but we were determined to use what we had learned for our people."

The lowland Quichua, like the Shuar, were a self-sufficient rain forest people who lived by hunting, fishing, and farming. For them, the central threat to that way of life came from the drilling of international oil companies. The discovery of oil in its Amazonian territory in 1972 was a boon for Ecuador, but it was the bane of the Quichuas, who saw their rivers polluted, their forests clear-cut, and a flood of migrants follow the roads built to the oil wells in search of jobs or land. Like the Shuar, the younger Quichua had been educated by missionaries, and some had attended secondary school. A few like Leonardo Viteri had gone on to university in Quito. The Quichua formed their own ethnic federation and then joined with the Shuar to confront the threat to their lands and cultures.

They decided to invite the other lowland peoples to form a Confederation of the Indigenous Nations of the Ecuadoran Amazon (CONFENIAE). It was a difficult task, as many groups were isolated and spoke no common language. Moreover, several of them were long-standing rivals. But they overcame these obstacles, and in 1983 CONFENIAE was formed, said director Eloy Likuy Shihuanco, "with the aim of combating the oppression of the large transnational companies, and to defend our lands, cultures, and traditional customs."[6] They insisted on self-government, the demarcation of their lands, and the right to rule on proposals to exploit the resources in their territories.

But these ambitious goals required political pressure in distant Quito, and for that the Indians of the Ecuadorian Amazon reasoned that they needed to unite with the more numerous Indians of the highlands. It was the Quichua, who were rain-forest Indians culturally but whose dialect could be understood by sierra Indians, who made the first contacts, through the Quichua-speaking merchants of Otavalo.

As dawn breaks over the dramatic mountain landscape that frames the marketplace of Otavalo, the first light reveals hundreds of Indians, sitting cross-legged behind choice ponchos, shawls, and sweaters of fine alpaca, llama, and lamb's wool, the product of many days of labor on hand-looms. For centuries the Otavalo Indians have been among the most celebrated weavers of the Andes, an area in which fine weaving was considered more precious than gold or silver. Today, in markets as distant as New York and Barcelona, the Otavalo Indians are a distinctive presence, selling their textiles at street corners and crafts fairs, the men with their characteristic fedoras, the women wearing the multiple strands of gold that represent the family bank account.

Fabián Muenala grew up in a weaver's family, in which "each child had his loom" that he worked at on returning from school. "My work as an artisan," he explained, "paid for my studies," which culminated in a rare university degree in linguistics. As a student he was acutely conscious of the prejudice against Indians by Ecuador's mestizos and creoles. "To wear the Otavalo hat to school was to risk being insulted by your teachers and having it knocked off by other students," he said.

But Fabián came from resistant stock. His grandfather had been the first Indian political head in his native Imbabura, replacing a mestizo boss who had controlled the community. Fabián's father had taken the lead in unifying twenty communities into a regional federation, the first in the highlands, which built irrigation ditches and roads and supported the struggles of the Otavalo peons on haciendas whose lands, as in Bolivia, had been taken from their ancestors by creole and mestizo elites. It was the 1970s, and a "stronger ethnic consciousness" was emerging among Ecuador's highland Indians, in part through the influence of leftist parties and progressive Catholic clergy. Fabián and his friends formed a youth club, which focused on culture and education, "because our fathers only stressed land issues." They created a Quichua street theater, whose plays dealt with such widespread concerns as exploitative landlords and abusive officials, and whose goal was "to get the people to identify with our struggle." The Indian movement in Imbabura elected the local prefect and carried out a successful land invasion, or "recuperation," of the large Quinchuqui hacienda. The Otavalos also played a leading role in uniting Ecuador's Quichua-speaking highland Indians in ECUARUNARI, the "Brotherhood of Indigenous Peoples," in 1972. By 1980, when Fabián Muenala joined fifty-two educated young Indians in a bilingual Catholic University program in Quito, Ecuador's sierra Indians were ready to unite their efforts with those of the Amazonian Indians about whom they knew little.

During the early 1980s, that bilingual education project, based in part on the Shuar experience, served as a frame within which Ecuador's Indians became familiar with each other's cultures and histories. They also spent these same years working out common positions on controversial issues. "It was a difficult process," Muenala said. "There were many outside influences that tried to bend our interests to suit theirs: The Marxists wanted us to be part of a class-based peasant organization, the Christians wanted us to be part of a religious movement, the *indigenistas* wanted us to become dependent on foreign aid agencies, and the *indianistas* wanted us to reject everything Western and re-create the Inca empire. [But] in the end, we developed our own positions, in accordance with our own criteria and experience." After studying the examples of the United States, the Soviet Union, Canada, and Switzerland, the Ecuadorian Indians decided that they were "nationalities"—each with their own language, history, and "cosmovision"—living in a country that should recognize it was a multinational state. In 1986, they joined together in the Confederation of Ecuadorian Indigenous Nationalities (CONAIE), the first organization in South America to unite highland and rain forest Indians despite the many differences between them. "In the Amazon, we are trying to defend the lands of our ancestors," said Leonardo Viteri. "In the sierra they are trying to recover the lands taken from their ancestors. We agreed to support each other's struggle."

The formation of such a confederation was an historic event, but it marked the beginning of their struggle, not its end. The 1988 election of a center-left reform government led by Rodrigo Borja sparked Indian hopes: Borja had agreed during his campaign to CONAIE demands for the recognition of Ecuador as a multinational state and Quichua as one of its official languages, as well as to bilingual education, agrarian reform in the highlands, and the demarcation of Indian lands in the rain forest. Once in office, however, Borja dragged his feet on fulfilling his promises to CONAIE.

As a result, CONAIE decided on a dramatic protest. It began as a hunger strike in Quito's Santo Domingo church by two hundred Indian leaders, "to protest the government's refusal to grant our demands or even to discuss them with us," Fabián Muenala explained. The government responded by sealing off the church with troops. It backed down in the face of Church mediation and international pressure, but then refused to recognize the accord. In response, CONAIE called for peaceful protest marches throughout the country. The result was the Indian Uprising of June 1990, which galvanized Ecuador's indigenous people in Cayambe and other communities in the sierra and the rain forest. CONAIE's leaders "hadn't realized what the magnitude of response to its call would be," Muenala said. "The people exploded against the injustices they were suffering, and their energy and force paralyzed the entire country."

The scope and effectiveness of the Indian protests took Ecuador by surprise. The Church was sympathetic and offered to mediate with the government. Support from labor, women's, and peasant organizations poured in, along with expressions of solidarity from ordinary Ecuadorians—including mestizo taxi drivers, *chola* marketwomen, and creole intellectuals. Only the government refused to recognize the popular rebellion for what it was, accusing the Indians of being "agitators without a sense of nationality who want to divide the country."[7] But after three days, "the cities were dying of hunger" and the government was forced to agree to a Church-brokered accord that committed it to negotiating Indian demands.

The Indian rebellion had brought the Ecuadorian government to the bargaining table, but had not persuaded it to compromise on substantive issues. As one official insisted on condition of anonymity: "The government can not allow a small group of Indians to control its development policies and oil revenues." Nor was the Borja government willing to confront the creole elite that controlled Ecuadorian politics over land reform in order to placate its Indians. A year later, CONAIE occupied the Chamber of Deputies to protest the slow pace of reform, the jailing of Indian leaders, and the failure to declare Ecuador a multinational state. In April 1992, a two-week march of seven thousand Shuar, Ashuar, and Quichua activists from the Amazon to Quito—retracing the 180-mile ascent of the Andes undertaken a century ago by indigenous chiefs for a similar purpose—dramatized the lack of progress on several of these issues.

By then it was clear that the struggle for indigenous rights in Ecuador was going to be a very long march. It was also evident that it was going to be an increasingly violent struggle. The government had intensified its repression, jailing leaders and harassing organizations. Even more ominous was the formation of paramilitary death squads by local landholders threatened with Indian land invasions. Kidnappings and murders of Indian activists confronted the movement with a new situation. "We do not want violence," Leonardo Viteri insisted. But neither he nor other Indian leaders would rule out violence in response to violence. "Indians have been dying for centuries," affirmed Shuar leader Rafael Pandam. "We are not afraid to die for our people." Viteri was conscious of the parallels to the experience of indigenous people elsewhere in the region: "We do not want another Guatemala," he stressed, "but it may not be up to us."

Valleys of Blood[8]

The northern highlands of Guatemala are achingly beautiful, verdant tropical valleys and majestic mountains wreathed in clouds, where Mayan Indian peoples have planted maize and cultivated their *milpas* for centuries. But between 1978 and 1985 these green valleys ran red with blood. In Tacaná, the army massacred forty villagers. At the Hacienda San Francisco, soldiers burned families alive in their houses. In Kaibil Balán, they "started with the men and then began to kill the women and children."

Rigoberta Menchú was forced to witness her fourteen-year-old brother being burned alive, after having his tongue cut out and fingernails ripped off. Juan López saw the soldiers string up his neighbor—"who hadn't done anything except farm his land"—and cut off his legs at the knees. Ivelia Lucas fled when "the army came and began killing everyone."

The roots of these modern massacres stretch back to the Spanish Conquest, with its wanton disregard for Indian lives and its subordination of the vanquished Maya to the *ladinos,* as the cultural heirs of the conquistadors are known in Guatemala. The *ladinos* controlled the national society and its institutions, but they also dominated the highland communities in which most Indians lived. The *ladinos* were the landowners, merchants, teachers, and officials for whom the Indians labored in their fields and homes, plantations and factories. Guatemalan racism was reinforced by this ethnic division of labor.

For five centuries the descendants of the Maya Indians who form a majority of Guatemala's population, and the largest surviving Indian group north of the Panama Canal, have resisted the efforts of the *ladino* elites to destroy their communities and appropriate their land and labor. They bent before the storm of the Conquest, the impositions of the colony, and the demands of the world market, but they did not break. Instead, the Indian communities turned inward, to their rich civil-religious culture, finding solace in its rituals and self-esteem in its offices. Their communal lands might be reduced in size, but they apportioned them and farmed their *milpas* as their fathers had. Their men might be forced to migrate seasonally to the south coast to earn money harvesting cotton for export, but they would return to their native village for the religious rites and fiestas that defined their culture and reaffirmed their community. The relative isolation of each community sustained its strong sense of ethnic identity and cultural unity, an inner strength that helped its members deal with their lack of power and resources in the larger society, where they suffered racial discrimination as well.

Ostensibly white, many *ladinos* are in fact mestizos. Moreover, in a country where "Indian" and *ladino* are cultural categories, "Indians" can become *ladinos* if they move to the city, speak Spanish, and adopt *ladino* dress and ways (though they may resume being "Indians" if they return to their native communities). As in the Andes, such an assimilation has long been the goal of Guatemalan reformers, and a strategy adopted by Indians seeking to improve their lot or escape the burdens of being Indian in a society that discriminates against them. After World War II, the cotton plantations of the coast and the factories of the capital became alternatives to the exhausted and shrunken plots of Indians' highland communities.

But the modern roots of La Violencia of the 1980s can be found in the aborted "revolution" of 1944–54, which challenged *ladino* control of Indian lands and labor, and in the brutal repression that followed. The military has dominated Guatemala ever since, in close alliance with its *ladino* elites. In the highlands the Catholic church was brought in to inoculate the Indians against the revolutionary virus. Its Catholic Action movement weaned many young Mayas away from their syncretic religious culture, with its brotherhoods and rites, but also helped the Indians form cooperatives and demand social reforms and more equal treatment. By the late 1970s, Indian grassroots organizations had strengthened, but had been met by an elite intransigence and military repression that dashed hopes of peaceful reform. This experience politicized many Indians, some of whom joined the *ladino*-led Guerrilla Army of the Poor, which claimed five thousand Indian fighters by 1980 but enjoyed far wider Indian support. The fear of a leftist revolution based on Guatemala's Indian majority detonated the ensuing conflict.

For the guerrillas, it was a war of liberation in one of the hemisphere's most inegalitarian countries. For the army, it was a dirty war against "terrorists" to be won at any social cost. But all were aware that there was also an ethnic dimension to the conflict, in a society where the lines of class and ethnicity often overlapped. As Army Chief of Staff General Benedicto Lucas put it in explaining the deaths of civilians that followed: "It is difficult to tell the guerrillas from the people." The Indian guerrillas targeted *ladino* landowners, while the army—*ladino*-led but, ironically, using mostly Indian troops—focused its overwhelming firepower on the Indian communities it believed were the elusive guerrillas' base of support, but which the guerrillas were powerless to protect. The result was a war against defenseless Indian communities, including many with little or no guerrilla involvement, that took on genocidal overtones. To many it seemed like a "reconquest" of the Mayas, whose demands for political participation and social reform had become too threatening to the *ladino* elite and their military allies.

During the counterinsurgency campaigns of 1978–85, more than four hundred communities were destroyed, their populations dispersed, their buildings razed, their fields burned. An estimated fifty to seventy thousand Guatemalans were killed, most of them unarmed Indians massacred by their country's own army. The litany of men tortured, women raped, babies murdered, and families burned alive filled the pages of international human rights reports with a numbing horror. "To the army," one Cakchiquel leader charged, "we were 'just Indians.' "

As a result of these atrocities, as many as one million Guatemalans— out of a population of only nine million—may have fled their homes. Most of them became political refugees in their own country. Many discarded the clothes and habits that identified them as Indian and tried to pass as *ladinos* in the anonymity of Guatemala's cities or coastal plantations. Others fled deeper into the mountains and jungles of northern Guatemala, where they joined with an estimated seventy thousand refugees from other towns and villages to form "resistance communities."

Still others fled Guatemala altogether, seeking safe havens abroad. Over 150,000 Guatemalan Indians trekked across the wild frontier that separates Guatemala from Mexico, some of them wandering for a year in the Lacondón jungle before crossing the border—exhausted, malnourished, and disoriented. "We did not want to leave our family land, it is all we have," Ivelia Lucas said. But in the end, "we had no choice but to go. We did not really know where we were going," she said. "When we crossed the border we looked like ghosts, hoping to start a new life in a different world." Another two hundred thousand Guatemalans did not stop until they had arrived in the very different worlds of Europe and the United States. Although the repression diminished after civilian rule was restored in 1985, military control in the Indian highlands continued, and most refugees have remained in exile to this day.

Those who survived the slaughter and stayed behind were often resettled by the army in special villages of military design, surrounded by barbed wire and with machine guns to "protect" them from the guerrillas. They were frequently forced to work at minimal wages building military roads into the mountains or jungles that served as guerrilla refuges, to act as military spies, and to go on "civilian patrols" under military command. Often people from other regions were brought in to repopulate villages whose inhabitants had fled, given the lands of the refugees, and indoctrinated against them as *metidos,* people with dangerous guerrilla sympathies. When Juan Lucas, Ivelia's father, tried to return to Kaibil Balán to recover his land, he found it given to newcomers who treated *him* as the intruder—and as suspect. He was forced to leave his village once again and to eke out a living in the shadows of the Playa Grande military base that had "pacified" the region.

But even communities that were spared the worst of the violence have felt its lingering effects. There were individual disappearances and mysterious attacks, but no massacres in San Andrés, a Cakchiquel town near Lake Atitlán, which was outside the major combat zones, and few of its people fled. But La Violencia still influences the way people talk and interact. One cost has been a veil of silence, out of a desire to deny the impact of what was clearly a traumatic era, but also because the violence sowed seeds of distrust. Abuses of power were so arbitrary, surveillance and punishment could come from so many possible directions, that it was difficult to know whom to trust. Yet it was necessary to depend on others for the information that would make it possible to survive a dangerous era of political uncertainty. For the Indians, one risk was the racism of the *ladinos,* with their ethnic hatred of the Maya. But after an attack on their homes, the leading *ladino* families left town. More troubling was the Indians' distrust of each other, the fear of betrayal by old enemies or envious neighbors to the army or the guerrillas. The army's 1982 imposition on the town's males of a civil patrol whose real task was to spy on their own neighbors was the visible symbol of coerced complicity in La Violencia. It was disbanded soon after civilian government was restored in 1985. But the internalized legacy of this violence and distrust was often more difficult to exorcise—and many communities lacked San Andrés's ability to combat it by drawing on a history of cooperation that transcended local animosities.

In the wake of La Violencia, Guatemala's Indians confronted an altered social and cultural landscape. Many communities had been destroyed, their people dispersed, their land given to others. The new military settlements mixed people from different communities who shared no common history or culture. With the support of the military and foreign funding, evangelical Protestants who opposed Mayan culture were making inroads among traumatized Indians. At the same time, the younger generation of Maya were being educated in schools that inculcated the national *ladino* culture and drawn to the international youth culture available on television screens and cassette players. The elders who had been the keepers of Mayan beliefs and values were dying without passing on their knowledge or skills. The survival of Mayan culture itself seemed at stake.

But the ethnic violence that weakened local communities also created an increased awareness of their common identity as Mayas. In Guatemala this has led to the emergence of a new ethnic nationalism. Until recently, "the Maya" as an ethnic group existed only for archaeologists, tourists, and historians. The descendants of the ancient Maya, speakers of twenty-three separate languages, identified instead with their community, or at most with their linguistic group—Quiché or Cakchiquel—while *ladino* society damned them all as "Indians." For centuries, Quichés and Cakchiquels have been enemies, but in the face of the violence both have suffered at the hands of the *ladino*-led army, these ancient rivalries have lost their strength. "In the resistance communities," said Francisco Calí, himself a Cakchiquel leader, "it makes no difference whether you are Quiché or Cakchiquel. You are all Mayas trying to survive together."

The emergence of a broader pan-Mayan identity that would unite both Quichés and Cakchiquels is a striking development of the past decade in Guatemala—one that is not confined to refugees or the isolated mountains and jungles. Since the return to civilian rule, Guatemala has witnessed a new Mayan studies movement created by *Mayan* social scientists, linguists, and teachers at universities and research centers. Some focus on the study of Mayan languages, others on the creation of a Mayan development strategy, still others on taping the aging bearers of Mayan traditions before they pass on. What all these groups have in common is an interest in revitalizing Mayan culture, encouraging pan-Maya identifications, promoting Mayan autonomy, and analyzing the racism of the national culture and its impact on Maya youth through school and the media. Particularly striking is their stress on transmitting a sense of Mayan culture and identity to the younger generation, subjected to the lures of modern *ladino* society, international popular culture, and evangelical Protestantism.

Today, the Maya cultural resurgence in Guatemala is palpable. Scholars are writing a counter-history to *ladino* accounts, stressing examples of Maya resistance to the Conquest and the centuries of colonialism and subordination that followed, in an effort to create a usable past. Even the Catholic church is promoting Mayan culture. Radio programs and educational materials in Mayan languages now abound. Tapes of lectures by Mayan scholars share adolescents' cassette players with rock music. There are tensions between the revitalization of local Mayan cultures and efforts to create a broader pan-Maya identity. But they are both part of the Maya ethnic revival that gained strength as 1992 approached—the year in which Maya activist Rigoberta Menchu would be awarded the Nobel Peace Prize for her work "for the rights of indigenous peoples."

Five Hundred Years of Resistance

"After five hundred years of oppression, exploitation, and discrimination, we Indians have little to celebrate in 1992 except our resistance, and much to protest," said Francisco Calí, the Mayan leader from highland Guatemala, to the approval of Indian activists from Colombia, Ecuador, and El Salvador. In preparation for the Columbus Quincentenary, representatives of indigenous peoples from all over the Americas had come together in a series of meetings to plan their response. They culminated in October 1991, when hundreds of Indian leaders and representatives of popular organizations met in Guatemala to plan a "Continental Campaign" using the celebration of the five hundredth anniversary of Columbus's epochal journey as the occasion to raise the consciousness of indigenous people throughout the hemisphere and bring the struggles of Native Americans to the attention of the world.

The Indian delegates had come from all over the Americas. They spoke different languages, dressed in different clothes, had different political loyalties, and reflected different experiences. But what they shared was a common commitment to their identity as Indians and to righting the wrongs of the past.

Many could report significant achievements. In Colombia, a relatively small but well-organized Indian movement had won their demand for dual citizenship and open borders for Indian peoples whose lands straddled international frontiers. In Ecuador, Amazonian Indians had pressured CONOCO into halting its oil drilling in the rain forest. The resolutions they passed were predictable: denunciations of violations of indigenous rights and lands; critiques of an anniversary that for the Indians of the Americas is more a cause for mourning than for celebration. So, too, were the debates—the tensions between *indigenistas* who wanted Indians to go it alone, and leftists who saw alliances with popular organizations and political parties as the correct strategy, a reflection of their differing experiences and struggles.

But above and beyond the words they spoke and the banners on the walls was the fact of their presence together five centuries after the coming of the Europeans to the lands of their ancestors. "It hasn't been all pain and suffering," affirmed a Campaign leaflet. "Our peoples still exist with pride and dignity: It has been five hundred years of resistance, of tremendous courage and heroism." For Shuar leader Rafael Pandam, the quincentenary's lessons for the future were clear: "We have been struggling for five hundred years—and we are prepared to struggle for five hundred more."

Although more than one hundred million people in Latin America and the Caribbean have African roots, only Haiti defines itself as a "black" republic. This market in rural Haiti is an image of Africa in America.

Although virtually all Haitians are descendants of enslaved Africans, tensions between a mostly mulatto elite and an impoverished black peasantry have shaped Haiti's history. In 1957, François (Papa Doc) Duvalier—shown here with his wife and bodyguards—won power with an election campaign that played on these conflicts.

The Dominican Republic, on the other side of Hispaniola, is a largely mulatto nation that has defined itself as "white" and "Spanish" to differentiate itself from Haiti. Dr. José Peña Gómez, who is of Haitian descent, has had to overcome this stigma in pursuing his political career. ▶

Most Dominicans are mulattos like taxi driver Carlos Pérez, but politics and prejudice have led many to deny their African roots in a country where they are labeled "Indians," not "blacks," and enjoy greater social mobility. Pérez was shocked to be regarded as "black" in the United States. ▼

Roughly half of Brazil's one hundred fifty million people have some African ancestry, and the region's largest nation thinks of itself as a "racial democracy." Yet its leading children's television star is Xuxa, a Nordic blonde role model for a racially mixed people.

In Salvador, Bahia, the center of Afro-Brazilian culture, *blocos afros* like Ilê Aiyê, shown here with its founder, Antônio dos Santos Vovo, have promoted a black consciousness movement that has transformed its Carnival into an expression of cultural politics, with pageants on African themes or Afro-Brazilian history.

Trinidad is a multiracial and multieth-
nic nation, with equally large communities of East Indian and African descent.
In 1990, a coup attempt by a Black
Muslim sect led by Abu Bakr (here
shown surrendering) failed to win the
support of Asian Muslims or black
Christians that it needed in order to
seize power.

A Question of Color

*C*arlos Pérez is a light-skinned mulatto who was "more or less a part of white society" in his native Dominican Republic. Then he paid his first visit to the United States, where he was shocked to find he was regarded as black. "From the minute I arrived at the airport I was treated like a black," he recalled. "Any mulatto, no matter how light, is a black in the United States. They are very racist."

Compared to Latin America and the Caribbean, the United States is not just racist, but color-blind: people are either black or white. In the other Americas, a more complex consciousness of color sees black and white, but also recognizes many shades in between. Nor do the differences stop there. In the United States, any degree of African ancestry makes a person black, while in Latin America and the Caribbean any degree of non-African ancestry means that a person is not black. As historian Eric Williams, Trinidad's first prime minister, observed half a century ago: "If in the United States one drop of Negro blood makes a man a Negro, in the [Caribbean] islands one is white or not according to the color of one's skin."[1] Many leaders of the African-American community in the United States would not even be considered "black" in the countries south of our borders.

For North Americans, moreover, race is biological and biology is destiny. In Latin America and the Caribbean, on the other hand, where the issue is color, racial mixing is prevalent, and "passing" is common, the laws of genetics mean children may appear to be a different "race" from their parents. Class and culture also play a part in a region where "money whitens," and "colonels are never black," no matter how dark their skin. This does not mean that there is no racial prejudice in Latin America and the Caribbean, but rather that it takes different forms.

Race is an historical construct that can only be understood within the context in which it was created. On Hispaniola, where Africans first arrived in the Americas, two nations with very different complexions and cultures share the same island. In Haiti, an overwhelmingly black country, African ancestry is a cornerstone of nationality. Next door in the Dominican Republic, a mostly mulatto people identify with their Spanish forebears. Brazil, a country where most people regard themselves as white but half the population is of African descent, has long regarded itself as a racial democracy—but this belief is now being put to the test. English-speaking Trinidad, on the other hand, is a multiracial society where blacks dominate politics, but the presence of large numbers of Asians has created a different mix of races and cultures—and examples of both tension and tolerance. Together, Brazil and the Caribbean account for the overwhelming majority of the region's more than one hundred million people of African descent. Their varied examples add up to a composite portrait of race relations in a region where race is a question of color, but color correlates with class and culture shapes their meaning.

Africa in the Other Americas

Africans came to the Americas with the conquistadors as personal servants and they have been an active presence ever since. But African slaves were expensive, particularly when compared to the minimal cost of coerced Indian labor. As a result, the massive trade in slaves from Africa to America was associated not with conquest, but with sugar, a highly profitable export crop that required a large labor force to work under conditions Indians proved unable or unwilling to bear.

It was in the Caribbean that this association of African slavery and sugar first began, during the early sixteenth century, and it was in the Caribbean that black slavery reached its height of intensity—and first came to an end—almost three centuries later. But wherever sugar went in the Americas, enslaved Africans followed, and the population of African descent multiplied.

Brazil received the largest share of the more than nine million Africans sold in the Americas during the three centuries of the Atlantic slave trade, and it was in Brazil that the dyad of sugar and slavery was consolidated and the plantation system was developed. From Brazil, the sugar plantation was taken by the Dutch to the Caribbean, where it was perfected by the English and the French, and then by the Cubans. Although it required processing machinery and skilled technicians, the sugar plantation and its milling complex was dependent upon large supplies of cheap, unskilled labor, which until the nineteenth century was provided everywhere by slaves of African descent.

The end of the slave trade came to most of the region in the mid-nineteenth century, and abolition followed soon after, with Cuba and Brazil the last to free their slaves, during the 1880s. By the end of the nineteenth century, slavery had ceased to exist in the Americas. Yet its legacies—racism, poverty, inequality—remain, a burden that the region's one hundred million people of African descent still bear today.

One Island, Two Worlds

Aboudja is a powerfully built black musician and radio personality who has promoted Afro-Haitian "roots music" and is also a *houngan,* or Voodoo priest. He dresses in robes of African design, and the sound that he extracts from his African drum echoes back to the land of his ancestors. "Mostly everybody in Haiti is proud of being the great-great-grandchildren of Africans," Aboudja said. The exceptions are "the Frenchified mulatto bourgeoisie," he said. *"They* think like Dominicans."

Carlos Pérez's face bears the evidence of a mixed European and

African ancestry typical of the Dominican Republic. "The Haitians, they're different than we are," he said. "They are black and we are not. They are African and we are Spanish. We are Catholics and they practice Voodoo. We may share the same island, but we live in different worlds."

The flight from the Dominican Republic to Haiti is a short hop, but the cultural distance seems immense. Santo Domingo, Columbus's capital, is identifiably Latin American in its faces, sights, styles, and sounds. By contrast, Port-au-Prince, Haiti's capital, seems African. Faces are of unalloyed ebony. The language spoken is African-inflected Creole. The market women, the Madame Sarahs, are wrapped in colorful African-style dress. The food they serve is redolent with the spices of Africa. Even the "tap-taps," pickup trucks turned into minibuses painted in Haitian Primitive style, with bright colors, vibrant designs, and protective Voodoo invocations, belong to a different world.

History has played a major role in shaping these neighbors in distinct racial, cultural, and social molds. In the western third of Hispaniola, the French made Saint Domingue the Caribbean's richest plantation colony in the late eighteenth century through the massive importation of African slaves and their harsh regimentation. The result was the great slave rebellion of 1791, which evolved into the Haitian revolution led by Toussaint L'Ouverture—a long and complex struggle among blacks, whites, and mulattos, as well as French, British, and Spanish forces. After Napoleon's effort to reconquer Saint Domingue failed, Jean-Jacques Dessalines declared the independence of "Haiti" in 1804 as the hemisphere's first "black" nation. By then, both rich and poor whites had been killed or fled Saint Domingue, leaving a small mulatto elite, some of whom had become educated and wealthy under the French, to struggle for power with the black leaders of the hundreds of thousands of former slaves.

Napoleon's invasion, with its threat of French reconquest and reenslavement, had united blacks and mulattos in a common struggle based upon racial identification. But if race united Haitians, color divided them. Despite Haiti's social revolution, which destroyed the plantation system as well as slavery, the colonial experience continued to shape independent Haiti in significant ways. The racism of French Saint Domingue left both blacks and mulattos with a clear sense of their African ancestry, but its caste distinctions—calibrated with pseudoscientific exactitude in degrees of whiteness—divided them along lines of color that were reinforced by class and culture. The mulattos, better educated and wealthier, would distinguish themselves from the poor, illiterate black majority by identifying with the culture of the former colonial power, speaking French instead of Creole and practicing Catholicism instead of Voodoo.

During the century after independence, urban mulatto mercantile and professional elites disputed power with rural black military leaders, although the mulattos often needed a black puppet president to reign and the blacks depended on mulatto ministers to rule.

Only in the face of another invasion by foreigners with racist attitudes—the United States occupation of 1914–34—would nationalist black and mulatto intellectuals make common cause and promote a national identity based on a shared African past. The result was a celebration of Afro-Haitian culture as a culture of resistance, and a defense of Voodoo as a religion, Creole as a language, and the poor black peasantry as the bearers of the country's African traditions. Jean Price Mars, a leader of the movement, urged Haitian mulattos to stop denying their African roots and to give up the " 'grandiose and absurd task' of becoming colored Frenchmen."[2]

At the same time, U.S. policies cut in a more divisive direction. The occupier's preference for the mulatto elite, coupled with the occupation's creation of the educational and economic preconditions for the emergence of a black professional middle class, strengthened the underlying antagonisms between them. This set the stage for the postwar emergence of a black politics that François Duvalier, an adherent of the ideology of *noirisme,* rode to power in 1957 with a call for "raising racial consciousness."[3]

Duvalier brought the new black middle class to power with him, but his fourteen-year dictatorship did little for Haiti's poor black peasant majority, who were oppressed by his officials and terrorized by his paramilitary Tontons Macoutes. A rural doctor with a shrewd understanding of peasant mentalities, Duvalier used this knowledge to keep their support, while ignoring their interests. He manipulated the culture of

Voodoo for his political advantage, claiming occult powers that few dared challenge. Under his son, Jean-Claude, who became president at nineteen on his father's death in 1971, the new black bourgeoisie mixed with the old mulatto elite to form a loose ruling class that looted the country and perpetuated its poverty.

As a result, when Haitians rose up in 1986 to overthrow the corrupt and repressive Duvalier regime, class replaced color as the defining conflict of Haitian society and politics. The presidential election of 1990 was not only the most democratic in Haitian history, it was also the first in decades in which color played no significant role. It was poor Haitians, virtually all Voodoo celebrants, who elected the Catholic priest Jean-Bertrand Aristide in a landslide—and it was wealthy Haitians of all colors and creeds who hailed his overthrow in a brutal military coup less than a year later.

"For the first time, Haiti has the opportunity to construct a society in which color will be neither a barrier nor a weapon," said one Aristide supporter in the wake of his election. Aristide himself hailed the many colors used by black and mulatto artists to create a collective mural celebrating Haiti's Afro-Caribbean culture shortly after his inauguration as "a good example of the way to build a New Haiti."

On a steamy Sunday in March 1991, a crowd gathered at the entrance to the art museum near the presidential palace in downtown Port-au-Prince to watch the creation of another collective mural on the theme of Haiti's national identity. Inside, seven artists with skin pigments that ranged from beige to black were hard at work on a vast canvas. Its colors were vibrant, its imagery reflected Haiti's African roots, and although the painters' styles varied, they were all identifiably "Haitian." Tiga, the light-skinned mulatto artist who was the guiding spirit behind both "collective creations," explained that "the artists here have very different styles— some abstract, others figurative, some naive, others international—but we all share the same African cultural roots. . . . We are all Haitians."

If Tiga's collective murals symbolized the need for Haitians of all colors to work together for a New Haiti, his Sun Center, a rural artistic community that turned peasants into painters, underscored the extraordinary creativity of Haitian culture. The rest of the world has discovered it in the prized paintings of the Haitian Primitives, with their luminous colors, dynamic design, and Voodoo themes. It is a creativity rooted in Haiti's Afro-Caribbean culture, anchored in Voodoo, which for many Haitians is a way of life as well as a system of belief.

"Voodoo," explained Max Beauvoir, a leading *houngan,* "establishes a harmony between the individual and the natural universe." It was rural in origin, but, he said, Haitians "had adapted Voodoo to urban life as well— even in New York City." Didier Dominique is an architect and the coauthor, with his wife, Rachel, of a prize-winning book on Voodoo written in Creole. They underline the central historic role of Voodoo among Haitians from the revolution of 1791 to the present day. "Voodoo," said Didier, is "the cornerstone of Haitian identity."

Aboudja, the Voodoo musician and radio personality, agrees but says that, although this cultural identity was strong among "the peasants, who form seventy-five percent of the population," it had been in danger of being lost by those "people who are living in the cities," where they were "subject to the influence of other cultures—French culture, American culture," and where the elite had "a color problem." But recently there has been an Afro-Haitian cultural revival in the cities as well. Creole is now an official language. The new popular Afro-Haitian roots music movement is reaching many among the black middle class and mulatto elite. Even "in the Catholic or Protestant churches," Aboudja said, "they are using the drums, chants, and dress of our ancestors."

Moreover, even members of the mulatto elite, "who think that they are not black . . . when they go to other countries, like France or the United States . . . realize that they are not white," he claimed. The result was a confusion out of which he hopes "they will regain their identity." But the thousands of Haitians who brave the rough seas in small boats are neither mulatto nor elite: They are poor blacks trying to escape their country's political violence and grinding poverty.

Haiti is the poorest nation in the Americas, with its weak economy further undermined by the corruption of past governments and the political instability of recent years. Its deforested hillsides and eroded soils can no longer support a rural population that has grown in numbers but not in resources. Three out of five Haitians do not have jobs, three out of four cannot read, four out of five are poor.

It is this poverty and unemployment that have led hundreds of thousands of Haitians to migrate to the Dominican Republic in search of work. Many of them were recruited to cut cane on sugar plantations where "they treated us like slaves and forced us to live like slaves as well," said Jean Larue, who spent twenty-three years in the Dominican Republic and had "nothing to show for it but an aching back." Others were illegal migrants who slipped across the loosely guarded border and found work at wages that Dominicans would not accept, as farm laborers or as unskilled workers in construction or the informal sector. All faced racial prejudice as blacks, in addition to a Dominican chauvinism that looks down on Haitians as "poor, dirty, and illiterate." Still, in time, many married and raised their families in the Dominican Republic, where they now form part of the estimated one million Dominicans of Haitian descent, many of whom, like Rosa María, "would not know Haiti if I saw it."

Yet they continue to speak Creole and to celebrate the Voodoo ceremonies of their ancestors. It was the eve of Good Friday 1991, in Alejandro Bas, an impoverished community of Haitian descent near the Dominican town of San Pedro de Marcorís, famed for its baseball players. The celebration by the local Ga-Ga, or Voodoo society, was "heating up." To the sound of African drums and bamboo "trumpets," a woman who had been "mounted," or possessed, by an ancestral spirit danced uncontrollably by the sacred fire. Around her a protective circle of celebrants chanted and sang in a shared moment of ecstasy and communion. Teresa, a single mother who worked in a local assembly plant, looked at her neighbors, whose worn clothes contrasted with their illuminated faces. The Dominicans "say that we Haitians are poor," she said. "But we have riches that they will never know." Across the island in Port-au-Prince, Didier Dominique agreed: "Haitians may be poor, but they have a dignity that comes from pride in their culture. Haitians know who they are."

· · ·

Dominicans are less certain about their identity, although you wouldn't know that from talking to historian Carlos Dobal. "The Dominican Republic is Spanish, Catholic, and white," he said, echoing the language of President Joaquín Balaguer. Yet a trip to the beaches near Santo Domingo, Spain's first colonial capital in America, reveals a population "the color of coffee with milk," as most Dominicans describe their compatriots. The amount of milk in the racial coffee cup, moreover, varies greatly, creating a spectrum of skin colors that ranges from creamy to espresso. "We are all mulattos here," said Carlos Pérez, the tan-skinned taxi driver whose awareness of race had been heightened by his visit to the United States. "We just don't like to admit it."

Three out of four Dominicans are of mixed European and African descent, making it the nation with the highest proportion of mulattos in the Americas. Yet, on the official identity cards that Dominicans are required to carry, the word "mulatto" does not appear, and only those of Haitian descent are defined as "black."

"We deny that we are mulatto, because we don't want to say openly that we have African roots," Carlos Pérez said. "Someone who is fairly light-skinned will say: 'I'm white.' A mulatto with medium skin like myself will say: 'I'm Indian.' And blacks themselves will say: 'I'm a dark Indian.' Blacks are treated badly in this country, so we don't want to be black."

Whites remain privileged in the Dominican Republic, as in most of the Hispanic Caribbean, a colonial legacy reinforced by subsequent U.S. influence and ingrained in popular prejudices. Want ads in newspapers ask for employees with "good looks," which Dominicans know mean a "white" appearance. "If a white and a black apply for a job, the white will get it, even if he is less qualified," said Pérez, adding that a light-skinned mulatto with "white" features "will pass as white. Looking white is your passport to opportunity in this country."

As a result, in a mulatto nation where racial boundaries are blurred and appearance counts more than ancestry, most Dominicans want to look as white as possible. Since little can be done to alter skin color or facial features, much of this preoccupation focuses on hair. "In our country, there are two kinds of hair: good hair and bad hair," explained Altagracia Sánchez, whose friends call her Tatika. "Good hair is straight hair, bad hair is kinky hair," she said, pointing to her own soft afro. When she was a teenager, a girl looked forward to "becoming fifteen," she recalled, "because at that age she was allowed to straighten her hair...in order to look like a European or American woman." But hair straightening was "a very demanding treatment that will damage your hair if it is not well done." "A poor woman who goes to a beauty salon will find that she has to straighten her hair at least three times a year." As a result, only the rich could afford hair straightening that made them "look good, refined." In the Dominican Republic, looking "white" is a matter of class as well as color. "It is expensive," Tatika said. "That's how you see the gap between rich and poor."

To be poor in the Dominican Republic is to be "black." Within this context, even dark-skinned Dominicans who want to identify themselves as black have found it difficult. Blas Jímenez is a poet who has lived in the United States and considers himself black. But when he wrote "black" on his passport application, "the lady who was writing the passport gave it back to me and told me to put 'dark Indian.' " When he insisted, "Look at me, I'm black," she replied: "You look like you're eating. You *can't* be black."

Dominican concerns with racial appearance are particularly strong when it comes to a choice of spouses. Then, family pressures are added to personal preferences, said Carlos Pérez's *mulata* mother, María Consuelo. Although she said she would accept anyone he chose, she preferred him to marry a woman lighter than himself "because then he'd improve the race, and the children would come out well. You have to think of the future," she explained. "A man like him with a black woman, imagine!"

Despite the intense racial feelings in her family, Carlos's sister, "a blonde with green eyes," had married a black man, "because she fell in love with him"—over the vehement objections of her mulatto father. "If you have a family member who marries a black, you have to worry about your social standing," María Consuelo explained, and "parents are afraid that a little black baby will be born." In white families, Carlos claimed, children who married blacks "could be disinherited."

Narcisa Tavares's family came from Moca, a hill town in the Cibao valley proud of its white families. "We have had cousins marry each other in order to avoid mixing," she said. Two of her siblings married cousins. But Narcisa fell in love with Enrique Berboda, a black medical student from a working-class background whom she had met at university, and she was determined to marry him. "When I first brought Enrique home, it was tough on my father. He said: 'Where are you going with that black man?' . . . But I went anyway." Her father had adamantly opposed her marriage to Enrique, but he came to accept it before he died. By then, Enrique Berboda was a doctor, "who took an interest in my father's health," and was respected for his high-status profession. Now he was no longer "that black man," but "Enrique, my daughter's husband," she said. In the Dominican Republic, class and culture can cast color in a different light.

So can desire and affection. Whites may win beauty contests, but among Dominican men, *la mulata* is the sexual ideal. In a mulatto country, moreover, the laws of genetics can confound even the most calculating choice of mates, producing children whose skin color and features vary among siblings and may differ from their parents. Carlos Pérez is one of four children. "There are two who are darker and there are two who have blue eyes," his mother said. "But I love them equally, because I have a motherly feeling for them." Her feelings were reciprocated, even where her children were "whiter" than she was. "My daughters do not resemble me," María Consuelo said, "but they love me a lot. . . . That's why we say: 'Love is repaid by love.' "

Racism is real in the Dominican Republic, but class and culture, love and desire, along with a pervasive racial mixing, blur its lines and modify its rigor. The result is a complex color consciousness and fluidity of identities that is uncommon in North America.

These are characteristics that the Dominican Republic shares with the rest of the Hispanic Caribbean. What distinguishes race relations in the Dominican Republic is the place of Haitians in its categories and the role played by Haiti in its history. In most of the Americas, new nations forged a sense of their identity in opposition to the European colonial power from which they had separated. In the Dominican Republic, a national identity was created in opposition to Haiti: The independence day they celebrate is not their separation from Spain in 1865 but their liberation from twenty-two years of Haitian occupation in 1844. In the Dominican Republic, as in Haiti, the construction of race and nationality have historical roots. But on the Dominican side of the island, the history is less clear, the categories are more ambiguous, and the construction itself is more convoluted.

Unlike French Saint Domingue, Spanish Santo Domingo never developed into a plantation colony. Few slaves were imported, and these prided themselves on being personal, not plantation, slaves as in Haiti. Most of the colonists were poor peasants engaged in subsistence farming, and racial mixing was common. A French diplomat described the Dominican population at the end of the colonial period as composed mostly of mulattos, "who say they are white … and had ended by being considered as such."[4]

Within this society, the Haitian occupation of 1822–44—a final expansive burst of the Haitian revolution—would have an indelible effect. Its abolition of slavery, confiscation of lands, and preferment of Dominican mulattos to administrative posts hit at the pillars of the white elite, some of whom fled, while others retreated to the mountains surrounding the Cibao valley. If white flight and Haitian migration during this era increased the black strains and African strands in the Dominican population, the need to rally all sixty-three thousand Dominicans, regardless of race, to defeat the more numerous Haitians led to a further softening of Dominican race relations. In this nationalist struggle, culture took precedence over race and the popular saying became "It does not matter if one is black, as long as one speaks clearly" and affirms one's Dominican identity. Blacks and mulattos played important roles in the struggle for Dominican independence. It was led by a weakened white elite who used the struggle to promote a national identity defined in opposition to Haiti: If Haiti was black, African, and Voodooist, then the Dominican Republic would be white, Spanish, and Catholic—strengthening their own claims to lead the new nation. The elite's weaknesses and fears of Haitian reconquest led some of them to invite Spanish recolonization in 1861—a sure sign that the Dominican sense of nationality was not consolidated.

Mulattos and blacks led the second fight for Dominican independence, and the flight in 1865 of many of the whites who had supported

Spanish rule helped democratize the republic's social structure and race relations. Military leaders of modest origins came to power, including Ulíses Heureaux, a black of Haitian descent. During this era, the white Cibao elite reinvented itself as a paternalistic aristocracy with genealogical ties to the Spanish conquistadors. They also intermarried with the new bourgeoisie of European immigrant origin that emerged around the sugar plantations established on the south coast. Black cane cutters were imported from the Anglophone eastern Caribbean and from Haiti. As a result, the elite was whitened and the lower class became more black, but without altering the predominantly mulatto cast of the population.

The U.S. occupation of 1916 to 1924 reinforced the white elite with its racism, but threatened their position by reforms that opened the way for a mulatto middle class led by General Rafael Leónidas Trujillo. A mulatto from a lower-middle-class provincial family, Trujillo came to power through his U.S. connections, over the objections of the white Cibao elite. He parlayed his appointment to head the new "apolitical" National Guard into a thirty-one-year dictatorship that began in 1930. During those three decades, the Cibao aristocracy would lose power to a new urban bourgeoisie, most of them mulattos linked to the dictator and the expanding capital city. Yet, paradoxically, it was under Trujillo that the construction of race and nationality forged by that white elite during the struggle against Haiti would be extended and consolidated.

Trujillo might have been looked down on by the white elite and blackballed from their clubs, but he shared their racial attitudes and Hispanophilia. Instead of redefining the Dominican Republic as a mulatto nation—as Mexico's postrevolutionary mestizo elite had redefined that country as a mestizo nation—he surrounded himself with white sycophants and Hispanophile intellectuals like Joaquín Balaguer, and transformed the white elite's identification with Spain into a national ideology of *hispanidad,* which defined Dominicans as "the most Spanish people of America."[5]

In Spanish America, it was not unusual for people of mixed descent to identify with the European side of their ancestry, in view of its greater power, wealth, and status since the Conquest. It was also common for mulattos to associate with whites and try to pass for white themselves.

What was peculiar in Trujillo's construction of Dominican identity was to
deny the existence of African strains in both the population and its culture.
In an overwhelmingly mulatto country, this required a reworking of racial
identities, a rewriting of history, and a whitening of culture. It also entailed
a massacre of Haitians and a whipping up of anti-Haitian hatreds.

Under Trujillo, Dominican mulattos and blacks were redefined as
"Indians," presumably descendants of the Tainos, who had been extinct for
nearly four hundred years. Enriquillo, a sixteenth-century Taino chief,
became the nation's founding father, and a noble Indian statue appeared
alongside that of a heroic European outside the natural history museum.
Even Hispanophile intellectuals who know better than to deny the presence of African slaves in Santo Domingo have attempted to justify this
racial myth. "Our slaves were not blacks from Sub-Saharan Africa as in
Haiti. They were Berbers from North Africa," claimed Carlos Dobal,
offering a revision of Dominican history with no documentary base. "That
is why our people have the skin color of Indians."

There was little that was Indian about the merengue, Trujillo's favorite music, which he made into the Dominican Republic's national dance
through his control of the airwaves. The merengue was a combination of
African rhythm and Spanish melody, but Trujillo purged the African hand
drum from the merengue band, where it had always been an essential
instrument. The merengue was also given a different genealogy: Despite its
similarity to the Haitian merengue and clearly African roots, the origins of
the Dominican merengue were ascribed instead to the independence struggle against Haitian domination.

Trujillo also banned Voodoo ceremonies, but that was the least violent of his acts against the fifty-two thousand Haitians living in the Dominican Republic, most of them as cane cutters or as peasants in the border areas.
In 1937, in an unprovoked act of genocide that Trujillo justified as "de-
Africanizing the country and restoring Catholic values,"[6] the dictator ordered the massacre of thousands of ethnic Haitians, many of them
Dominican-born children of families who had lived there peaceably for
generations. Trujillo then whipped up the anti-Haitian fears latent among
Dominicans to justify the massacre, and to reinforce his own position as the

defender of Dominican nationality against what his ideologues called a "peaceful invasion."[7] In the decades that followed, generations of Dominicans would be brought up on histories whose villains were Haitians and whose heroes were those Dominicans who fought them. Haiti became the linchpin in the construction of a Dominican national identity that defined the Dominican Republic as its opposite. If Haiti was black, then the Dominican Republic was white, appearances to the contrary notwithstanding. Race became a metaphor for the nation, and nationalism reinforced racism.

Trujillo's policies were a classic case of the official promotion of racism for political purposes. But in a country where racial distinctions depended upon subjective perceptions of color and physical features, what had begun as an official myth took on a life of its own. Trujillo's anti-Haitian racism outlived the dictator's assassination in 1961, aided by the political longevity of his Hispanophile collaborator and successor, Joaquín Balaguer. With Balaguer's support, the definition of the Dominican Republic as "Spanish, Catholic, and white" was consolidated. Dominicans of African descent remained "Indians" on their identity cards and "black" remained a term of disdain reserved for Haitians. The merengue recovered its African drum, but efforts by young musicians to recognize its African roots were denounced as "unpatriotic."[8]

For mulattos, particularly those with "white" features, many of whom have moved into positions of wealth and power during recent decades, this construction of race and nationality meant ideological support for their social ascent. Mulattos with white features may be defined as "Indians," but like Carlos Pérez, they are "more or less a part of white society." It is the darker mulattos and Dominican blacks who pay a higher price for their country's denial of its African roots. This myth may allow them to deny that they are black and to consider themselves superior to Haitians, but despite their public identity as "dark Indians," in private other Dominicans regard them as "black." As a result, they have to confront the racism that flows from prejudice in their daily lives and careers, reinforced by the nationalistic equation of black with Haitian. "People often call me 'Little Haitian,' " Tatika said. "They don't mean to offend me, but when someone is referred to as Haitian or black, it's never meant as a compliment."

The estimated one million Dominicans who are ethnic Haitians have paid the highest price of all. Not only are they defined as black in a society where "to call someone black is to humiliate them," but they are excluded from the Dominican definition of their nation. Some of them are migrants who came to the Dominican Republic as cane cutters or farm laborers. But many "Haitians" are second- or third-generation Dominicans, who work in construction and the informal sector, where they play important economic roles in jobs that other Dominicans refuse to take.

Even Dominicans who have won positions of power, such as José Peña Gómez, have had difficulty in overcoming the double burden of looking black and having Haitian ancestry. Dr. Peña Gómez has been mayor of Santo Domingo and head of the center-left Dominican Revolutionary Party (PRD), the nation's largest. He is widely viewed as the most powerful and qualified political leader of his generation. Yet his presidential ambitions have been hurt by the perception that "he is black and he is *Haitian*—that's the Dominican bogey man," Tatika stressed. His wife is white, Peña Gómez "does not admit that he is black," and he has "publicly demonstrated that he has no Haitian ancestry." He even had a campaign biography written proving his Spanish descent. But "his facial features, nose, mouth, and color point to Haitian roots," insisted Carlos Pérez, and most Dominicans believe that "he has a Haitian mother, but was an orphan who was adopted as a baby by Dominicans." In the 1989 election campaign, his party "made a huge poster where they showed Peña Gómez with thinner lips, rosy skin, and less curly hair," Tatika recalled. When "the PRD won more votes than in the previous election, everyone said it was on account of the poster."

The casting of Haitians as the ethnic "other" has enabled the racially diverse Dominicans to unite around a negative definition of themselves as *not* African and *not* black. But it has also legitimated racism in the name of nationalism. "The majority of the people will tell you, 'No, I'm not a racist,' " Blas Jímenez said. Yet these same people will defend being anti-Haitian as "patriotism." For Blas, the situation will not change until Dominicans "grasp our negritude" and say, " 'Yes, this is what I am.' We haven't been able to look at ourselves in the mirror."

But the identity of that face in the mirror is a portrait shaped by history, politics, and culture. Blas's own view of himself and his people has been influenced by his U.S. experience, and follows a U.S. definition of race. For Dominicans of mixed ancestry, Blas's insistence that they identify themselves as black may seem no more valid than Trujillo's decree that they are Indians. Yet Blas Jímenez's argument that the Dominican Republic must confront its African roots is shared by a post-Trujillo generation of Dominican intellectuals who have reexamined their history, reassessed their culture, and tried to get Dominicans to accept that they are a mulatto people with *both* European *and* African roots.

Outside intellectual circles, their efforts have had only a modest impact in the face of an official ideology that continues to promote an image of the Dominican Republic as Spanish and white, but there are some signs of change. Some of them are symbolic steps—the addition of a black statue to the Indian and European outside the natural history museum, or the inclusion of black and mulatto Roman centurions in the Santo Domingo Good Friday procession, where "a generation ago . . . those selected had to possess certain physical characteristics similar to those of the old Romans."[9] Hairstyles, too, have begun to change. "In the last ten years it has been accepted that women should wear their hair naturally," said Tatika, and men's hairstyles increasingly reflected "the latest fashions from American stars and baseball players."

Perhaps the biggest change in the Dominican Republic is not the fashions that arrived from the United States, but the one million Dominicans who now live there and what they bring home when they return. Carlos Pérez had not experienced racism in the Dominican Republic, where as a light mulatto "I don't have any limitations, because I get treated as a white." But in the United States he experienced "what it's like to be treated as a black. That's when you feel: 'It's lousy when there's racism in a country,' and you start hoping that racism is eliminated." But "on this island," he cautioned, "it has been present for five centuries."

In 1992, with an enthusiasm unmatched in the rest of the hemisphere, the Dominican Republic celebrated the five hundredth anniversary of "the Discovery and Evangelization of America" that had begun on its shores.

The Dominican celebration was presided over by its octogenarian chief executive, Joaquín Balaguer. To commemorate the occasion, the blind Balagúer sank much of his budget into the construction of the Columbus Lighthouse, a cruciform tomb for the explorer's reputed bones. In its side rooms, each of the American republics had exhibits paying homage to Columbus's legacy, as did Italy, his birthplace, and Spain, "the Dominican motherland." Yet, despite the fact that five out of six Dominicans have African ancestry, this background was ignored, and no African nation participated in the exhibition. It was symbolic of this mulatto nation's attitude to its African roots and its black citizens.

A Racial Democracy?

In 1988, Brazil commemorated the centenary of its abolition of slavery. Yet, unlike the more recent Columbus Quincentenary, it was not regarded as an opportunity to take a hard look at the historical treatment of blacks or the state of race relations in Brazil. On the contrary, the centennial of the "Golden Law" granting slaves their freedom was officially celebrated as an example of Brazil's genius in creating a racial democracy that abolished slavery without a civil war and has escaped the racial tensions that have haunted the United States and other multiracial societies in slavery's aftermath. Brazilians were even treated to a television spectacle that seemed more like an allegorical painting out of the past than a portrait of contemporary life: a group of deferential blacks and mulattos thanking the heir of Princess Isabel, the Brazilian monarch who signed the "Golden Law," for their delivery from bondage.

Yet, in Salvador, the old colonial capital, pressure from black cultural groups forced the cancellation of any celebration. The only commemoration was a black protest march in which Princess Isabel was burned in effigy. These contradictory images symbolize the experience and consciousness of people of African descent in Brazil.

Brazil was the last nation in the Americas to abolish slavery, and today has its largest population of African descent, perhaps seventy-five million out of its one hundred fifty million inhabitants. With a population only three fifths that of the United States, Brazil has roughly three times as many people with African roots. "We are a mixed race nation," President José Sarney, himself a member of Brazil's white elite, proclaimed to the U.S. Congress in 1986, "and the world's second largest black nation after Nigeria."[10]

In reality, Brazil is a country of many racial and ethnic strands—Amerindian, European, and Asian in addition to African. But although half its people probably have African ancestors, most of them do not think of themselves as "black," nor does Brazilian society impose a black racial identity upon them. On the contrary, Brazil's self-image is that of a racial rainbow. If the Dominican Republic has defined itself as a white nation and Haiti as a black republic, Brazil has embraced the image of itself as a multiracial country shaped by the mixing of races and cultures.

Together with this celebration of Brazil as a multiracial society has come the larger claim that Brazil is a racial democracy, free from the prejudices of Anglo America, a society that has embraced Afro-Brazilian culture as a central feature of its national identity. Unlike the Dominican Republic, Brazil is a country where the African roots of the national dance, the samba, are celebrated, not denied. Vianna Moog is only one of many Brazilian intellectuals who have maintained that "the highest, most significant, and most edifying aspect of our culture is racial brotherhood."[11]

The roots of Brazil's racial democracy, such influential figures as sociologist Gilberto Freyre argued, were to be found in the uniquely tolerant character of Brazilian slavery. Its rigors, he maintained, were softened in the master's bedroom, where the lascivious Portuguese planters, without Anglo-American racial "prejudices," preferred their black and brown slave mistresses to their white wives, often freeing them and their mulatto children. The result was a fusing of Africa with Europe in America. As a consequence of this Portuguese "plasticity," Freyre argued, Brazilians became a new "race." Historians have questioned Freyre's beatific vision of Brazilian slavery, and feminists his celebration of Portuguese "sexuality," but this has done little to alter Brazil's vision of itself.

"Every Brazilian male needs three women in his life" runs a common saying that manages at once to be sexist, elitist, and racist: "A white woman to bear his heirs, a black woman to cook for him, and a *mulata* to make love to." This embrace of the *mulata*—the daughter of miscegenation—as the sexual ideal lies at the heart of Brazil's self-image as a racial democracy. It suffuses the fiction of Jorge Amado, Brazil's most successful living writer, whose best-selling novels, such as *Gabriela, Clove and Cinnamon,* and *Dona Flor and Her Two Husbands,* have been made into movies and TV soap operas seen around the world.

"There exists only one solution to the racial problem and that is the mixing of the races," Amado said recently. "Anything else . . . leads irrevocably to racism."[12] There *is* something softer about race relations in Brazil than in North America, yet even among mulattos, a subtler racism often surfaces. Alma and Julia are highly educated sisters of a racially mixed marriage, yet from childhood they have been viewed and treated differently. Alma, a *morena,* who has "light brown skin and delicate nose and lips," has not been "discriminated against or labeled as black." Julia, a *sarará,* with a thin nose, but a darker skin, "thick lips and kinky hair," was "not seen as white," Alma attested. "People never believe we're sisters," she related. "Despite all the miscegenation in this country, people don't openly admit it." Even within their family, "it created problems between us," Julia recalled, "because I was considered the little black girl and she was considered white. . . . They used to joke that I was found in a garbage can." Alma agreed: "There's an idealized image of this country as an ideal experiment in heavy miscegenation that's widely peddled to this day." But she said, "those of us who live within this culture know that deep traces of discrimination exist."[13]

In Brazil, it is not enough not to be black. As in the Dominican Republic, it is also important not to *look* black. Mulattos do enjoy an acceptance in white society that they would not have in the United States, but only if they are light-skinned mulattos with white physical features.

By the time slavery was abolished, there were almost as many mulattos in Brazil as whites. Yet, at a time when white supremacists in the United States were reacting with alarm to a numerically insignificant miscegenation as threatening the "mongrelization" of the "white race," the Brazilian elite, which also believed that "white is better," was advocating racial mixing as a strategy for "whitening" Brazil, along with European immigration, which the government promoted. In Brazil, there would be no Ku Klux Klan, no legal segregation or racial discrimination. Instead, Brazilian "sexuality" would eliminate racial difference. Miscegenation was equated with assimilation. In 1911, one Brazilian anthropologist predicted that in a century the entire population would be "white."

In time, this ideology of "whitening" became an article of faith among Brazil's elite. It created a context that favored mulattos over blacks and enabled light mulattos to pass for whites. It also set the rationale for the appropriation and whitening of Afro-Brazilian culture by the national society: The samba was slowed into the jazzy bossa nova; in religion, "black" Macumba was transmuted into "white" Umbanda. No studies were done to test the ideology's validity. Instead, the military regime censored television programs challenging the racial line and removed questions about race from the 1970 census. In the absence of hard data, discussion was reduced to the anecdotal evidence of Gilberto Freyre, and Brazilian elites continued to celebrate their country's freedom from racism.

Yet, when the census of 1980 restored race to its categories, it found that during the preceding two decades the percentage of Brazilians identifying themselves as white had dropped from 61 percent to 55 percent, while mulattos had grown by a similar proportion. The implications were clear: Instead of becoming whiter, Brazil was becoming browner. If racial differences disappeared in the next millennium as a consequence of miscegenation, the result was likely to be a mulatto—not a white—nation.

The racial inequality implicit in the ideology of whitening was reinforced, yet obscured, by the hierarchical character of Brazilian society. It was a society of domination and deference, of patrons and clients, with an overwhelmingly white elite at the top and largely nonwhite manual laborers at the bottom. The lack of any black or many mulatto faces at the top of Brazilian society was not ascribed to racial discrimination. In 1977, the head of the Congress affirmed that Brazil was a country without racial prejudice, in which success "depends on individual effort, intellectual ability, and merit."[14]

By then there was growing evidence that this was not true. The government's own surveys showed that on the average, blacks earned little more than one third of white incomes and even mulattos received only half. Moreover, the disparity in earnings increased with the level of education and occupational status, although elite ideology predicted it should diminish. Scholars concluded that one third of this difference in economic rewards was the result of a racial discrimination that was no less real for not being legal. In addition, as nonwhites had less access to education and were concentrated in low-status jobs, they were caught in what one sociologist called a cycle of cumulative disadvantage.

This was something that blacks and mulattos in Brazil had known for a long time, yet generally were reluctant to protest. For many mulattos, the largest group of nonwhites in Brazil, there remained the hope that they—or their children—would pass for white. Successful blacks preferred to avoid discrimination rather than confront it. "I don't insist on going where I don't fit," admitted Mário Américo Castro, a former São Paulo city councilman. "I'm not going to upset a situation which, for better or worse, is good."[15] But among poor blacks as well, the impact of the national myth of racial democracy has been pervasive, even when it is contradicted in their own lives. Blacks are more likely to attribute their problems to poverty or a lack of education than to racism. The lack of overt discrimination, moreover, makes racism in Brazil more difficult to combat. In the United States, explained popular singer Caetano Veloso, blacks knew "what they had to fight against, because there limitations were defined and clear-cut. But in Brazil, because these things are ambiguous, racism has a more solid base." Although the ambiguities of race relations had enabled Brazil to avoid the bitter racial conflict that has plagued the United States, for many people, Caetano concluded, "this is the worst kind of racism."

During the transition from military rule that began in the 1970s a growing number of blacks did protest, joining organizations such as the Unified Black Movement (MNU), which tried to mobilize blacks to fight discrimination and inequality. Its members were mostly middle-class blacks, whose numbers had grown during the economic "miracle" of 1968 to 1974, but who had run up against the informal barriers of racial solidarity in their efforts to ascend the social and occupational ladders. Many were inspired by the U.S. civil rights movement and the independence movements in Portuguese-speaking Angola and Mozambique. They were attacked by conservatives as racists who were importing U.S. notions of Black Power to disturb Brazil's unique racial harmony. Worse, their efforts evoked little response from Brazil's poor blacks, who were skeptical of all politicians and more worried about poverty than racism. "Brazil," Luiza Bairros, the MNU's national coordinator, concluded bitterly, "is the most successful racist system in the world."[16]

But the efforts of black activists did have an impact on the Catholic church, which began to examine its own internal racism—with only one black bishop out of 350 prelates. The black consciousness movement also influenced the political parties of the center-left, who nominated more black candidates for public office and pressed successfully for an article prohibiting racism in the new 1988 constitution. Efforts to elect more blacks to public office, however, were rarely successful. With few exceptions, poor blacks as well as whites failed to vote for black candidates, although in a country where most poor people still vote for candidates of a higher class and status they believe can help them, race may not be the sole explanation.

Benedita da Silva, the first black woman elected to Brazil's Congress and one of only five black federal deputies in 1989, is one of the exceptions. "I know that racial democracy is a lie in Brazil from my own life. I encounter racism every day," she said. "Everywhere I go, I am reminded that this is how things are, and I adjust to it." Even being a member of Congress is no guarantee of equality, although she is aware that "when they know I am a deputy I get treated far better than when they just think that I am a black woman." As a federal deputy, she has tried to get Congress to address the problem of racism but found little support. As a poor black woman, Benedita da Silva does her best to represent all three constituencies. "In Brazil, it is even harder to get people to confront the problems of

blacks than it is to get them to confront those of women and poor people,"
she said. "Anyone who still thinks that Brazil is a racial democracy is
looking at a picture postcard."

There have been signs of change, even among poor blacks, although
these stirrings owe more to Afro-Brazilian popular culture than to electoral
politics. One sign of the times has been the revival of interest in Zumbi, the
legendary king of Palmares, the famous seventeenth-century *quilombo,* or
community of fugitive slaves, who symbolized black resistance to oppression. Jorge Ben's 1974 hit song "Zumbi" celebrated the black leader and
prophesied his return. And the star black singer-songwriter Milton Nascimento began to speak out about racial prejudice in Brazil, writing a
"Quilombo Mass" in 1982 that celebrated the "*quilombos* of yesterday, today,
and tomorrow" and envisioned "making Palmares again" in Brazil.[17]

But it was in the most popular form of Afro-Brazilian culture, the
Carnival pageant, that a new black consciousness was emerging with greatest force. As 1988 approached, Carnival samba schools focused on the theme
of the centennial. In Rio de Janeiro, the prize-winning samba was entitled
"One Hundred Years of Freedom: Reality or Illusion?"

> *Can it be . . .*
> *The Dawn of Liberty,*
> *Or was it all just illusion?*
> *Can it be . . .*
> *That the dreamed-of Golden Law,*
> *Signed so long ago,*
> *Was not the end of slavery?*
> *In the real world of today,*
> *Where is freedom?*
> *Where is it? I don't see it.*[18]

For a growing number of Brazilians of African descent, racism had
replaced slavery as the force that kept them in chains. This was even true
in Bahia, the heart of black Brazil and the land of Jorge Amado. In Salvador,

its capital, four out of five residents are black or mulatto, but thirty-two out of thirty-five city council members are white. Yet, in Salvador, the center of Afro-Brazilian religion and culture, a new black consciousness was emerging in the city's poorest neighborhoods.

As military rule loosened in the 1970s, a new kind of Carnival group, the *bloco afro,* was born. The *blocos* were a reaction to the commercialization of Carnival by white entrepreneurs. Instead, they promoted a revitalization of Afro-Brazilian culture and Carnival pageants with African themes and social messages. The first was Ilê Aiyê, which was founded in 1974 with the goal of building black pride. Today, it has three thousand members and sponsors a black beauty festival, in addition to an annual Carnival pageant. In Bahia, Ilê Aiyê's chief rival is Olodum.

On a Sunday in Pelourinho, Salvador's oldest black district, the insistent beat of African drums announces the presence of Olodum. Already, thousands have gathered in the main square where slaves were auctioned during the last century. The African drummers of Olodum march to a different beat.

To most of the world Olodum is a backup band on Paul Simon's 1990 hit album *The Rhythm of the Saints.* But back in Pelourinho, Olodum is much more than a band. It is the most important of Bahia's *blocos afros* and the most ambitious of them as well. "Olodum is a cultural group, not a music association," stressed director Guilherme Arguimimo. Its goal is to "create a culture of resistance." Its new Pelourinho "house" is a focus of activities throughout the year, including lectures on African and Afro-Brazilian history and classes in languages, music, dance, and theater. "We felt that we had to do something for our own people, here in Pelourinho," one of Salvador's poorest areas. "Particularly the street children," Arguimimo explained. "We had to offer them an orientation, an education, a goal." Olodum also set out to change the ambience of Pelourinho, notorious for prostitution and street crime. "We turned our house into a community center and got people involved." Now, hundreds take classes. On Sundays five thousand people turn out to watch Olodum rehearse, and on Tuesdays, another two thousand show up for their "African Bar" debuts and tryouts.

Africa is a theme that runs through Olodum. Its drums are striped gold, green, and black, the colors of African liberation. Its costumes are inspired by the shapes and stamped textiles of Africa. Its name means "The Supreme God" in Yoruba. Its Carnival pageants often celebrate Africa's past glories and present struggles. And although Olodum is proud of Brazil's African roots, unlike Ilê Aiyê it is open to whites and mulattos as well as blacks. "When we started Olodum, we decided that Olodum would be open to everyone," Arguimimo recalled. *"We* would not practice apartheid."

The struggle of Nelson Mandela and South African blacks against apartheid is a theme of many of Olodum's songs. They even named their auditorium for Mandela, whose visit in 1991, Arguimimo said, "was like a dream come true." It is not just solidarity that motivates this South African focus, but Olodum's search for examples that convey its message: "We need to struggle together for freedom and equality."

It was Olodum's assessment of the situation of blacks in Brazil, not South Africa, that led them in 1983 to transform the group from a music association into a cultural group. "Black people were ashamed of themselves, of being black, when we began," the Olodum director recalled, "because they were told that anything black was inferior." Young blacks were also "losing their culture," through the impact of radio and rock music. "We decided that we had to make black people believe in themselves." A decade later, progress has been made, although there is still a long way to go, Arguimimo felt. "Today, many blacks in Bahia have a different view of themselves. They are proud of being black, proud of their African culture, and they believe that they are as good as white people," he said. "They are changing their mentality, and if we keep on working, it will be even better in the future."

It was an optimism based on activism on the part of a proudly black cultural group that thinks of itself as political but not partisan and as revolutionary but not violent. In 1988, Olodum played an important part in pressuring the state and municipal governments to cancel celebrations of the centennial of abolition. Their vision was clear in their Carnival song for that year:

Is it Utopia
Or pure truth
The beat of the drums
Free the world
Free me Olodum
From the evils
Of false abolition
From this apartheid world.
Build Olodum
A world of equality
Where liberty
Shall be liberty.[19]

Massa Day Done?

Carnival is also the central event of the year in Trinidad, the largest island of the eastern Caribbean, where the steel band and calypso were invented. Carnival groups practice for months, and the weeks to Lent are dominated by their preparations. The calypsos sung are often topical, with pungent yet humorous allusions to political foibles or social mores. The pageants are elaborate, costumed fantasies on historical or mythological themes.

In 1970, Carnival was different. On its first day, protest bands appeared with calypsos about Black Power and pageants on the "The Truth About Blacks—Past and Present." They not only portrayed the slaves and "massas" of the colonial era, but also the alleged "stooges of the massas" of postcolonial Trinidad. This was no fantasy; it was history in the service of politics. Within a month a group of radical black intellectuals—the National Joint Action Committee—had detonated a "revolution" from below that fused anti-imperialism with black nationalism and demands for "food, shelter, employment, dignity [and] a place in the political structure" for the overwhelmingly black urban poor.[20] Before the "February Revolution" was over it had galvanized the unemployed youths of ghettos like the aptly named Shanty Town, mobilized a coalition that included labor unions and steel band associations, the U.S.-influenced Black Panthers, and the uniquely Trinidadian Afro-Turf Limers. At its height the Black Power movement proved strong enough to put 30 thousand to 100 thousand people in the streets and threatened to shut down Trinidad with a general strike. The government was forced to declare a state of emergency in order to contain the crisis.

On the surface, Trinidad seemed an unlikely place for a successful Black Power movement. After all, it had been ruled by an overwhelmingly black party, the People's National Movement, since it was granted independence from Britain in 1962. The PNM was led by Eric Williams, one of the preeminent black West Indian intellectuals of his generation, a charismatic political leader who had written trenchantly about slavery and race relations in the Caribbean and was supported by the black middle and working classes. It was Williams who had won election on the eve of independence with the slogan "Massa Day Done," promising "the disinherited and dispossessed" that with his election they were "taking over this country from the Massa's hand," and urging them, as a popular calypso put it, "to clear the way, and let the people play."[21]

Trinidad, moreover, was a multiracial society, with an Anglo white and French creole elite, a colored and black middle class, and nearly as many people of East Indian as of African descent. Most of the East Indians were laborers on the sugar plantations where their forebears worked as contract laborers imported after abolition to replace freed black slaves. Although the Black Power leaders made an effort to appeal to these Indian workers, even including them in their definition of "black people," they underestimated the tensions between the two communities, and the racism in a society where, as V. S. Naipaul, Trinidad's most celebrated and acute writer, put it: "The Indian despises the Negro for not being an Indian; he has, in addition, taken over all the white prejudices against the Negro."[22] Indian businesses were among those attacked by poor blacks during the demonstrations, and many Indians were insulted at "being called black."[23]

Even to many Trinidadians of African descent, "Black Power" seemed "unsuitable for application to the requirements of this multi-racial, multi-coloured society."[24] It also seemed both dangerous—a threat to Trinidad's "racial harmony"—and unnecessary. Although Eric Williams

Dieudonné Cédor's 1948 Haitian Naïve-style painting, *Ceremony at Bois Caïman, 1791*, pays homage to Boukmans, the escaped slave and Voodoo priest who presided over the August 1791 rites that began the Haitian revolution, and the slaves who swore loyalty to their cause: "For Liberty! Victory or Death."

Throughout Latin America, Indians
have been organizing themselves
to defend their common interests.
In Ecuador, such efforts culminated
in the formation of a national confederation of indigenous peoples
and the "Indian Uprising" of
1990. Modern technology helps a
political organizer promote popular
participation in the highland
community of Atausi.

The performance of La Diablada, the Devil Dance, at the Carnival of Oruro, attests to the survival of Bolivia's ancient Indian cultures. But the sign for Coca-Cola, "the official soda of the Carnival," shows the impact of international consumer society.

At Rio de Janeiro's pre-Lenten Carnaval, dancers move to the syncopated rhythms of the samba, derived from the Afro-Brazilian religion Candomblé. Samba schools, often based in rural slums, spend much of their energy and resources creating the elaborately costumed and choreographed pageants on historical or mythological themes for the annual competition.

At Saut d'Eau, a spectacular water-
fall in Haiti's interior, ecstatic Voodoo celebrants gather each year on
July 16 to worship the goddess of
love, Ezili Freda, who is said to have
appeared here as the Virgin Mary
on that date in 1843 and 1881.
Thousands of Haitians make annual
pilgrimages to such sacred sites.

During Augusto Pinochet's dictatorship, *arpilleras*, or appliquéd tapestries, became a form of political protest sewn by Chilean women whose families were victims of the military's human rights abuses. This one depicts the security forces burning alive teenagers Rodrigo Rojas and Carmen Gloria Quintana during a 1986 demonstration. Rojas died, but Quintana survived and her disfigured face became a national symbol.

In Jinotepe, Nicaragua, demonstrators at the 1978 funeral of a teenage activist killed by dictator Anastasio Somoza's National Guard hold aloft her larger-than-life photograph. Young people such as the victim and her mourners, filled with a spirit of outrage and hope, formed a central part of the Sandinista rebellion.

Deep in the rain forest stands the Amazon Theater in Manaus, Brazil. Completed during the rubber boom in 1896—with furnishings, painters, and opera stars imported from Europe—it was abandoned when boom turned to bust. Now restored, it is a monument to the pretensions of the rubber barons who built it.

always maintained a multiracial rhetoric, and the PNM included Indian Muslims in their leadership, at bottom it remained a party of Afro-Trinidadians. Williams himself, said Anthony Maingot, a Trinidad-born sociologist, "spoke of Indian Trinidadians as if they were still an immigrant group."[25] Williams had opposed Hindi as the language of instruction in Indian schools and won power over the party of the Indians in a 1961 campaign characterized by intimidation, violence, and accusations by Indian leaders of gerrymandering, unfair rules, and electoral fraud. If any group had cause for complaint at its exclusion from a proportional share of power, it was Trinidad's East Indians, not its blacks.

But control of Trinidad's economy and high society remained in the hands of foreign whites and local creoles, lending credence to Black Power accusations that the PNM were "Afro-Saxons" who were "stooges of the massas," rather than representatives of the descendants of their slaves. Even black workers and professionals complained of discrimination in employment. Moreover, the benefits of Trinidad's independence had not reached its urban slums, whose unemployed poor blacks transformed an intellectual movement into a "revolution." The correlation between class, color, and culture was sufficiently strong to create a coalition united by a black fist.

The Black Power movement illuminated the cross-cutting divisions within Trinidadian society. It also exacerbated the tensions between its ethnic communities and set the course of politics along racial lines for over a decade. During the fifteen years that followed, the Afro-Trinidadian PNM continued to hold power, under Eric Williams and his successor, George Chambers. Although it did not endorse Black Power in principle, in practice the PNM used its control of the government to compensate blacks for the growing numbers and economic strength of Asian-Trinidadians, who moved into the commercial vacuum created by the gradual withdrawal of Anglos and French creoles.

In 1985, amid an economic crisis caused by the collapse of Trinidad's oil economy, the PNM was ousted by a multiracial coalition that included both Asians and some of the black intellectuals who had inspired the Black Power movement of 1970. Although this coalition proved no more successful in dealing with the country's economic problems and eventually broke up into its component parts, to observers like Anthony Maingot, its 1985 victory "showed that racial politics could be defeated in Trinidad."

There was little improvement in the living conditions and prospects of the black urban poor during the two decades that followed the Black Power movement. Yet in 1990 a Black Muslim attempt at an armed coup evoked little popular support. Still, the looting of Indian businesses that accompanied the unrest frayed ethnic tempers on both sides, laying bare the resentments that lie just below the surface. "Them Indians—them already got all the business," complained Anthony Skarret, a resident of a black slum rife with unemployment. "If they take over the government, we're going to have war."[26] But there has been no racial war in Trinidad, where the PNM was returned to power in a quiet 1992 election. Despite continued ethnic tensions, there was no recurrence of the communal violence that plagued election campaigns three decades before.

"West Indians have learned from experience that tolerance is necessary in multiracial societies," explained Derek Walcott, the celebrated West Indian poet who lived for many years in Trinidad. "Somebody who becomes racially intolerant is no longer West Indian," he affirmed, "because the whole point of the West Indian is racial tolerance."

Race, class, and culture are all human inventions, which are shaped and reshaped over time and space. The black and white North American conception of race is penetrating Latin America and the Caribbean, carried by returning migrants and popular culture. Racism does exist in the other Americas, even if it takes different forms and racial tensions often lurk beneath a seemingly harmonious surface. Yet the fluidity of racial identities in Latin America and the Caribbean, and the growing acceptance within its nations that they are multiracial and multicultural societies, offers hope that the region's racial and ethnic tensions can be transcended. The challenge is to assure equal opportunities for all Americans, regardless of the color of their skin, the texture of their hair, or the ethnicity of their parents. "But to end racism, the mentality of society has to change," said Carlos Pérez, "and *that* takes a long time."

Faced with civil codes that legalized male supremacy in most of Latin America, educated women have organized to fight for equal rights. In Chile, feminists formed the Movement for the Emancipation of Chilean Women (MEMCH) in 1937, which spearheaded the struggle for female suffrage that won women the vote in 1949.

Chapter 9

In Women's Hands

Women have often led the struggle for human rights under the brutal military regimes of the past two decades, turning their traditional private roles as mothers and wives to new public purposes. In Argentina, "Las Madres" of the Plaza de Mayo became the conscience of their nation, carrying photos of their disappeared relatives.

In Chile, "Women for Life" created new ways of dramatizing the struggle to restore democracy. During the 1988 plebiscite campaign they used life-sized "shadows" of General Augusto Pinochet's victims to remind Chileans why they should vote against the dictator.

During the economic crisis of the 1980s, poor women pooled their meager resources in communal kitchens to help feed their families. In Lima, Peru, an estimated 20 percent of the population depended on communal kitchens in 1992, when these "Glass-of-Milk" mothers demonstrated against increased food prices.

Spanish Americans traditionally divided the social universe between the male world of the *calle,* or street, and the *casa,* or home, the women's sphere. But even in rural areas such as Chile's Aconcagua Valley, necessity and opportunity have now led women to enter the work force, as fruit packers in the new export plants.

Although prejudice has kept women in the Americas from a fair share of political power, several women have become heads of government. In the West Indies, with its tradition of strong and independent women, Eugenia Charles has been prime minister of Dominica since 1980.

9   *In Women's Hands*

*I*n October 1988 the largest political demonstration in the history of
Chile capped a successful campaign for the restoration of democracy after
fifteen years of dictatorship. Prominent among the hundreds of thousands
of Chileans flooding the Pan-American highway south of Santiago were the
faces of women. Some marched with their university or factory contingent.
Others carried signs identifying their shantytown workshop or communal
kitchen. A mother held the photograph of her disappeared son with the
poignant lettering: "Where are they?" Women gathered under the flag of
their political parties, of the right, left, or center, and others marched
behind the purple banner of the feminist movement. Among the speakers
they cheered were women professionals and politicians. Some were with
their husbands and some brought children, but many were not accompanied by a man. The signs they carried, the slogans they shouted, the songs
they sang made it clear that these were not passive victims of history but
protagonists of their own destinies.

Our myths about Latin America and the Caribbean die hard, and our
images of women south of the border are no exception. In our media and
our minds they assume stereotypical, if contradictory, forms: They are
long-suffering and all-forgiving madonnas, dedicated to lives of self-sacrifice; exotic sexpots, Carmen Miranda dancing with a tropical fruit headdress, or Evita Perón, predatory and threatening; powerless wives or

companions, subordinated to macho men; or unskilled workers or maids, poor and illiterate. Their passions are the private affairs of the heart, not the public affairs of the nation.

There may be individuals who match these images and fulfill these myths, but such stereotypes fail to prepare us for the more complex realities of women's lives in Latin America and the Caribbean. Women today are presidents as well as mothers, workers as well as wives, artists as well as models. They publish newspapers, manage businesses, and operate in hospitals. Some may still be subordinated to their husbands, but many are themselves heads of households. They are also guerrilla commanders and labor organizers, community leaders and religious prophets.

Although the stereotypical Latin American woman was always more mythic than real, during recent decades the region's women—by choice and necessity—have come to play new roles, and to develop new organizations and ways of thinking, that have altered their lives and changed their societies. Migration has dislocated their families and placed them in a struggle for survival in alien surroundings. Global economic forces and national policies have shaped their belated entry into a changing wage-labor force, presenting them with opportunities and problems. Political whirlwinds have reached deep down into the region's societies, sundering families and prompting women to assume new responsibilities in their homes and communities and to fulfill old ones in new ways.

Some of these challenges, such as internal migration and economic crisis, have confronted poor women in countries such as Mexico, Peru, and Chile with particular urgency, often leading them to join together to cope with problems that are beyond their individual resources. Political upheavals—whether in revolutionary societies like Cuba and Nicaragua, or in countries ruled by repressive military regimes, such as those of Argentina, Brazil, and Chile—however, have affected women of all classes, creating a basis for women's movements that transcend class lines. As a result, Latin American feminism has differed from its North American and European models, embracing broader social and political concerns.

The economic roles of women have also been transformed in recent decades, as women increasingly left their homes to enter the work force in response to both new opportunities and new necessities. Between 1950 and 1980 the percentage of women in the wage-labor force grew by nearly half, from 18 percent to 26 percent. In revolutionary Cuba, by 1990, two out of five workers were women. In Peru and Mexico migration to city slums and border assembly plants has provided women with new opportunities to earn a living but forced them to take on new responsibilities and risks in return; in Chile, a boom in export agriculture has created a similar pattern in rural areas as well.

Although domestic service is still the most common type of job open to women, others have proliferated as industry expanded in countries such as Brazil and as the informal economy grew throughout the region. Increased educational opportunities have also multiplied the number of women in the "helping" professions—teaching, medicine, and social work—and in white-collar jobs such as secretary and receptionist. By 1990 more than half the urban professionals and technicians in both Cuba and Chile were women, although mostly in lower-level positions, and in Chile at salaries only half those earned by men with comparable education. Throughout the region, moreover, working women put in a "double day," saddled with responsibility for housework in a society where men consider caring for home and children to be "women's work."

The changes affecting women in Latin America and the Caribbean have also altered their private lives. *Marianismo,* an ideal of female conduct based on the Virgin Mary, affirming women's moral superiority but pre-scribing a life of humility and self-sacrifice, has been a myth few could afford to live by, while machismo, with its aggressive assertion of male domination and chauvinism, has been all too real. In recent decades, moreover, confronted by powerlessness in the workplace and political arena, many men have sought to assuage their anxieties and affirm their identities by intensifying their control over their women and children.

Increasingly, however, women have been challenging this machismo in their public and private lives. Dramatic declines in fertility and increases in education have freed women to participate more fully in the economic and political life of their communities and nations. Their growing eco-nomic roles outside the home have given them greater autonomy and often made them their family's principal breadwinner. Their participation in neighborhood social organizations and national political movements has increased their self-confidence and at times given them greater influence outside their home than their men. In several countries, feminists who were active in the restoration of political democracy have demanded "democracy in the home" as well as in the nation.

These changes have called into question the traditional balance of power and division of responsibilities within the family. They have also led to painful confrontations and adjustments as relations between men and women are renegotiated. Reports of physical and sexual abuse have increased in several countries, along with divorce and desertion. In Brazil "violence against women is the issue of the 1990s," said Benedita da Silva. In Nicaragua more than half the households are headed by women, a pattern common as well in the Caribbean. "In Colombia," noted labor leader Tulia Camacho, "the family means a mother and her children." Increasingly it is women who bear the burden of cushioning their families against the shocks of economic crisis, social violence, and political repression.

Throughout the region, the worlds of women have multiplied and expanded, and the lives of both women and men have been transformed as a result. Chile is a striking example of these far-reaching changes. There the dramatic events of the past three decades have prompted women of all classes to embrace new responsibilities and to play new roles in their home and neighborhood, workplace and nation.

Scraps of Life

The women who sat around the plain table in a church basement sewing their "scraps of life" onto burlap were of many ages and backgrounds. What they shared was their grief, for all had lost close relatives—husbands, fathers, children—to the political repression of the Pinochet dictatorship. But they also had in common a determination to transform their grief into a "cry of rebellion" that, as one of them put it, "expressed the whole experience of having a dear one arrested and disappeared."

Arpilleras (the word means burlaps) are appliqué landscapes that Chilean peasant women traditionally embroidered with bucolic scenes of rural life. During the military regime, however, they became a form of political protest, as well as a means of self-support and a way for women to express on cloth the traumas they had witnessed and experienced. Although unique in its artistry, the *arpillera* workshop was emblematic of the way in which the dramatic events that have buffeted Chile have impelled women of all classes to transform their lives and increase their impact on the society around them.

Middle- and upper-class women have long been prominent in Chilean arts and professions. Poet Gabriela Mistral (1889–1957) was Latin America's first Nobel laureate, winning the prize for literature in 1945. She was notable not only for the elegance of her verse, but also for tackling the public themes once thought of as the male domain. Her work in rural education, her career as a Chilean consul, and her commitment to the victims of Franco's fascism marked her as a woman deeply engaged in the world outside the home. Mistral's prose is as evocative and public as her poetry and life, celebrating her country's varied landscape as a "synthesis of the planet."

> *It starts in the desert, which is like beginning with a sterility that loves no man. It is humanized in the valleys. It creates a home for living beings in the ample fertile agricultural zone. It takes on a grandiose sylvan beauty at the end of the continent, as if to finish with dignity, and finally crumbles, offering half life, half death, into the sea.*[1]

Chile has also been described less poetically as a "geographic madness," a narrow strip of land twenty-six hundred miles long, rich in metals and minerals, farms and forests. During its first century of independence Chile styled itself "the England of South America" and took particular pride in its democratic politics and rule of law. But if Chile was a democracy, it was an oligarchic democracy, an elite club of male lawyers and landowners, miners and merchants. Even in the 1920 elections, Chile's first experience of mass politics, only 5 percent of the adult population voted. This low electoral participation reflected many factors, including low levels of literacy, but most important was the restriction of the franchise to men. Women, half the nation, were not allowed to vote, no matter how advanced their education.

Yet Chilean women were among the first in the region to win access to education and the professions. In 1877, Chile was the first country in Latin America to admit women to its universities. "And it was the first country to have women professionals," recalled the octogenarian lawyer Elena Caffarena in 1990. "The first female doctor in Latin America was from Chile . . . then we had lawyers and later dentists. The cultural situation was good, but the legal situation was not."

Chile's nineteenth-century civil code, like others in the region, gave men control of their wives and children. It also barred women from many areas of public life. The result was often paradoxical. A woman could become a lawyer, but not an executor of a will. She could defend a client in court, but needed her husband's consent to testify herself. She could become an expert on the country's constitution, but could not participate in politics. Gabriela Mistral might represent her country abroad and receive Chile's first Nobel prize, but she could not vote in the presidential elections held a few months later.

The 1946 election marked the end of the era of the Popular Front, center-left reform coalitions that first came to power in 1938. This era had also witnessed the formation of the Movement for the Emancipation of Chilean Women (MEMCH), Chile's first national feminist organization, which spearheaded the campaign for female suffrage. "It was a long struggle," Caffarena recalled, because of cultural prejudices and partisan fears of how women would vote. Finally, in 1949—the same year as in Argentina— women won the right to vote in national elections, although feminists were soon disappointed in its results. Chile's women bypassed the budding Feminine Party for the established political parties, which formed "women's fronts" to attract their votes yet did little to press women's issues. The feminist movement withered on the vine, but it left a legacy of activism that would inspire a later generation of women searching for beacons to guide them through the uncertainties of a traumatic era.

Decades of Upheaval

The years from 1960 to 1990 were unprecedented in Chilean history. They were decades in which the political spectrum shifted from the center to the left, before the pendulum swung abruptly to the far right, where it remained for sixteen years, and then moved decisively back to the center. They were years of reform, revolution, and counterrevolution, of deepened democracy and repressive dictatorship. Before they were over, women of all ages and classes, political views and ideological visions would participate in the politics of Chile and the shaping of their country's history. Their ideas about society and images of themselves would be altered and Chilean women would emerge from this trial by fire with new roles, responsibilities, and goals that challenged traditional notions of a woman's place.

From 1964 to 1970 Christian Democrat Eduardo Frei led a center-left "revolution in liberty" that began an agrarian reform and the nationalization of the U.S.-owned copper mines. It also promoted grassroots organization but raised popular expectations that it could not fulfill. In response, Chileans voted narrowly in 1970 for Socialist Salvador Allende's "democratic road to socialism," a program of even more radical reform that promised to extend what Frei had started and prepare the way for a future transition to democratic socialism.

Many women shared this experience of reform and radicalization. Daughters of aristocratic Catholic families such as María de la Luz "Marilú" Silva began as supporters of Eduardo Frei's Christian Democratic reforms and ended as activists in Salvador Allende's revolution. "My family were all rightists, but my husband was a leading Christian Democrat and that was what I became," she said. "A trip that we took to China in 1968 was important in my political evolution. It opened my eyes to another political reality. On the way home, we stopped over in Paris. It was May 1968 and there was revolution in the air. I read everything I could get my hands on. I was soon a convinced Marxist." In 1970 she left the Christian Democrats—and her husband—to support Salvador Allende.

Other Christian Democrats were radicalized by their frustrating experience of trying to improve the lot of poor women in urban shantytowns or peasant villages. Silvia Alvarez began doing such political social work under Frei. By 1971 she was dissatisfied with the Christian Democrats and helped form the Christian Left, a small party that joined Allende's Popular Unity coalition.

Still others attended university as socialists and committed their training and talents to that cause. Marisa Matamala graduated from medical school with a specialization in social medicine. During the Allende era, Dr. Matamala worked in "mother-child health programs in the north of Chile," in shantytowns and mining camps. She still recalls it as a time of idealistic if naive commitment. "We all . . . expected to build a beautiful socialist future full of happiness. . . . With the professional work, we did social work in the shantytowns and political work in the unions."

It was a time of ferment at all levels of society, but particularly at the broad bottom of the social pyramid, where peasants, workers, and shantytown dwellers saw Allende's "revolutionary process" as the opportunity to realize their historic aspirations for land, equality, participation, and a decent living standard. In poor urban neighborhoods, women like Ube Torres helped to organize their communities and press for housing, schools, paved streets, and jobs. Ube headed a health committee that supervised sanitary conditions in Santiago's New Havana shantytown—itself the outgrowth of an Allende-era land seizure. In different ways, women of varying educational and social backgrounds participated in *los cambios,* or "the changes," of the era.

But most Chilean women did not commit themselves to Allende's program of radical reform. Among his opponents were upper-class women like Viena Frugone who were appalled by a social revolution in which it seemed "the poor were seizing the streets" and "the communists were taking over the government." She became active in one of the many rightist women's groups.

Still others were educated middle-class women who may have opposed Allende's "democratic road to socialism" on political grounds, but were driven to translate this feeling into active opposition by growing consumer shortages and political violence. Alicia Romo recalled not being able to knit clothes for her baby daughter "because there was no yarn in the markets, and I had to take apart old things to make new ones." Diapers were hard to obtain, as were cotton and alcohol. "To get a little sugar, we would have to stay in line all day. We didn't have meat or milk. And on top of all of this we were worried, because life was not stable. There was violence in the streets, bombs at night . . . and we thought maybe our families would not return at the end of the day." Rightist paramilitary groups were responsible for most of this violence, and increased consumer buying power for much of the shortages, but many women blamed the leftist government for both problems.

Opposition women "began to mobilize," Romo said, in a series of escalating protests that began with the "March of the Empty Pots" in December 1971, by mostly middle- and upper-class women and their maids banging empty pots to protest the first food shortages. "On the day of the March of the Empty Pots, I found myself with women whom I had never seen before, from all areas and neighborhoods . . . women of different ages," Romo recalled. Some were members of the center and right opposition parties, which promoted these protests. "But the majority were independent," Romo claimed. It "was not a question of ideology, but of being practical. We wanted security and tranquillity, that's all."

What was unique and powerful in the march was that for the first time, women of the middle and upper class were taking to the streets in political protest. Although many were supporters of opposition parties, most were protesting as mothers and wives who were concerned that the government was threatening the welfare of their families. During the years that followed, Chilean women of sharply contrasting views would translate their traditional roles into radically new forms of political activity, "motivated by fundamental concerns like the protection of life and security, and the need to provide their family with food and a good future," explained Alicia Romo. "This moves women of all ages—young, old, everyone."

The Allende government had hoped that the concrete benefits of increased incomes and medical, housing, and other social programs would win the support of poor housewives for its democratic road to socialism. But by 1972 the resources for these programs were exhausted. Poor and middle-class women were particularly affected by the consumer shortages and inflation that undermined Allende's "revolution process" with accelerating force in 1972 and 1973, and receptive to opposition radio programs designed to exploit their anxieties—part of the CIA's covert campaign to "destabilize" the Allende government. A "consumer psychosis" gripped many Chilean women, bringing even normally apolitical women into the streets to protest against the government they held responsible.

By mid-1973 Chile's economy was disintegrating, its society was deeply divided, and its politics were polarized. "Feminine Power," a shadowy organization of the right, began sponsoring protest marches demanding Allende's ouster. "Women asked the military for direct intervention," Romo said. Viena Frugone was less restrained: "We asked, we pleaded, we demanded that the military take command, and they listened to us."

In August the wives of senior military officers took part in an unprecedented demonstration outside the house of the army commander, General Carlos Prats, a "constitutionalist" who favored maintaining the armed forces' political neutrality. They accused him of weakness and demanded his resignation; the humiliated Prats stepped down shortly thereafter. General Augusto Pinochet replaced him, and a fortnight later, on September 11, 1973, Allende died in a bloody military coup. Women claimed a major role in his overthrow.

"The participation of women was decisive in the success of the coup," Viena asserted proudly nearly two decades later. "We all went out into the street demanding that we didn't want a Marxist government." As in Brazil in 1964, the model for many Chilean opposition leaders, this endorsement by women voting with their feet "to defend that cornerstone that is the family" was of great symbolic importance to the military, who shared the same conservative social values.

Yet Chilean women had differing reactions to the military coup and the dictatorship that followed. "During the military intervention I cried," recalled Alicia Romo, who would soon become a senior official in the Pinochet dictatorship. "Because democracy, something important, in which I had always believed, something we Chileans were tremendously proud of, was being broken." But the coup "was what we had struggled hard for all that time, and was what I wanted." Viena Frugone was less ambivalent: "On the day [Allende's] Popular Government was inaugurated I felt as if the ceiling of my room had fallen on me and I was trapped. On September eleventh, I felt that everything opened up and I was free again."

For many Chilean women, however, the coup represented not the end of anxiety, but the beginning of a tragedy. To leftist activists like Marilú Silva, the coup meant the "defeat of our dreams." For many it also represented a threat to their lives and liberty. Thousands of suspected leftists were killed or detained, many of them in outdoor stadiums or in concentration camps in the northern deserts or Antarctic islands. Ube Torres's New Havana shantytown was raided by the military and many of her friends and neighbors were taken away.

Men were more likely to be targeted by the military, whose machismo sometimes worked to a woman's advantage. Silvia Alvarez held a much more important political post in Allende's Popular Unity coalition than her husband, a senior official in the ministry of agriculture. When a police officer arrived at their Santiago apartment to arrest him after the coup, she tried to intervene, insisting: "It's *me* you want, not him." The officer turned on her in a voice filled with anger: "Shut up, woman! This is a man's business!" She was left free to work for her husband's release and their exile in the United States.

Other women who had been active in leftist causes were less fortunate. Some were killed, others imprisoned. Marisa Matamala went underground, but was captured and sent to Villa Grimaldi, one of Pinochet's most dreaded torture chambers, which had once been an elegant restaurant in an Italianate villa complete with swimming pool and manicured grounds.

The reports of human rights organizations are filled with testimony of the special punishments suffered by women prisoners. So are the memories of the women who survived the horrors visited on them in secret "interrogation centers" such as Villa Grimaldi, where Marisa and her friend Nubia Becker once shared a tiny cell. "Torture became commonplace, almost routine," Marisa recalled with horror. "Men and women alike were tortured," but women were tortured in ways that revealed there was sexual politics involved as well as political ideology.

The military "rejected the fact that women were involved in politics, because women should be at home . . . looking after the family," Nubia explained. "To them it was very offensive that women should be involved in other things, a break with the past. That made them very angry. . . . They wanted to make us feel like prostitutes." So while male prisoners "might be beaten more," women were subjected to special humiliations. "We were totally naked, which puts one in a very helpless position," Marisa revealed. Many were raped. But worst of all, she recalled, were the electric shocks of "the grill": "They made you lie in these metal beds and they applied currents to the most sensitive parts of your body—your vagina, your mouth, your nipples," Dr. Matamala related. "They wanted to impose their power and diminish you." The goal, she said, was to get their female victims "to play the part of the weak woman. That brings out the *machista* counterpart, which is at the same time deprecating and protective." Her experience of machismo in the torture chamber helped make Marisa Matamala a strong feminist.

But even women who had not been active politically became victims of the military repression. Doris Meniconi was the mother of thirteen children, who had taken pride and joy in the rich family life she had created in a modest Santiago neighborhood. Although she was not herself a political person, several of her children had been active during the Allende period, and her son Miguel Angel had become a leftist student leader. She had been worried about his involvement. After the coup, her fears proved justified. Miguel Angel went underground, but was captured in November 1974 and never seen again, joining the thousands of "disappeared"—an experience Chilean women shared with mothers in Argentina and Brazil.

As in Brazil, it was the churches that took the lead in aiding the victims of the dictatorship. In 1975 Catholic archbishop Raúl Silva Henríquez created the Vicarate of Solidarity, which provided a wide range of services, from legal aid and personal counseling for the families of victims to soup kitchens and temporary shelter for the hungry and homeless. Behind its religious shield were sheltered such human rights groups as the Association of Relatives of the Detained and Disappeared, founded in 1974. Most of its members were women: mothers and grandmothers of the detained, wives and sisters of the disappeared. They remained a backbone of the human rights movement in Chile throughout the dictatorship, demanding an end to torture and arbitrary arrest and imprisonment and an accounting of the fate of their relatives. They held private vigils and public meetings, sent letters and signed petitions, testified before international commissions and organized demonstrations in the streets and squares of Chile. In 1979 they pinned photos of their missing relatives to their clothes, chained themselves to the iron fence around the closed Congress building, and declared a hunger strike. Although they were occasionally beaten by soldiers and arrested by police, what gave them a relative immunity from the repression that had engulfed their family members was that they were acting as anguished mothers and wives in their traditional female roles as protectors of the family, not as political activists.

The Vicarate of Solidarity also helped women like Doris Meniconi form *arpillera* workshops, providing them with space and supplies and selling the tapestries in its shops. The messages they sewed into their *arpilleras* were direct and powerful. Some are very personal, like Doris's *arpillera* showing her broken home and outside it the Christmas tree that symbolizes "the last Christmas I spent with my children." The angel in its branches is her disappeared son, Miguel Angel. A typically Chilean landscape, with the snowcapped Andes in the background and the Pacific Ocean in the foreground, expresses her untiring search for her missing son: "From the mountains to the sea, from the country to the city."

Other *arpilleras* were more public, depicting such events as the women's chaining in front of the Congress. Still others went beyond their own experience to a more general denunciation of human rights violations: helicopters dropping bodies into a ravine in the mountains of Paine, peasants being burned in ovens or buried in a field while their relatives hold a silent vigil. As the women's skills and confidence grew, so did the scope of their concerns.

The *arpilleras* served many purposes. They were therapy for women traumatized by the disappearance of their loved ones and their own powerlessness to protect them. They were a source of income, sold throughout the world. They were a new form of artistic expression, exhibited to acclaim even in North America and Europe. But most of all, they were an innovative way to act politically where traditional politics were banned. The military could repress a street demonstration, but they didn't know what to do with this resistance movement in textiles. "During the sixteen years of dictatorship, our group played a very important role," one *arpillerista* affirmed. "It helped to publicize the violation of human rights at a national and international level. . . . Besides, it showed women here in Santiago how to unite and form groups."

Stirring the Common Pot

Some of the groups Chilean women formed during the decade that followed the 1973 coup were human rights groups, but others were "popular economic organizations," neighborhood self-help groups whose goal was to enable poor women and their families to survive hard times by banding together. Many of these were *talleres productivos,* or "productive workshops," which embroidered tapestries, knitted sweaters, or baked meat pies for sale on the street or through church stores. Others were communal kitchens where destitute families pooled their meager resources and women who had never before worked outside their homes cooked meals for hundreds of people. Each elaborated on the notion of women's work, but in an innovative way. By the mid-1980s there were thousands of these groups, not only in Chile, but also in Peru and other countries of the region gripped by economic crisis. In 1990, one out of five Lima families depended on communal dining rooms for their sustenance.

The economic crisis of the 1980s led growing numbers of women throughout Latin America and the Caribbean to enter the work force and to experiment with mechanisms of collective survival. But in Chile political upheaval and government policies added an additional economic burden for many. In the aftermath of the coup, political persecution claimed the lives, liberty, or jobs of hundreds of thousands of Chileans. To these political firings, the deep recession that followed the government's freeing of prices and freezing of wages added economic layoffs. They were compounded after 1977 by neoliberal economic policies that decimated Chilean industry, leading to a wave of bankruptcies, and to drastic reductions in personnel by the enterprises that survived. When the newly deregulated banks crashed in the global recession of 1981, the Chilean economy plunged into its deepest economic crisis since the Great Depression, taking large numbers of firms and jobs with it.

Although the rash of bankruptcies and layoffs affected Chileans of all classes, they struck with particular severity at poor Chileans, those least able to bear its costs. Families now found themselves without any income. Men who had been used to fulfilling their roles as providers now found themselves without jobs—or realistic prospects of getting them. Moreover, the military's regressive social policies had destroyed the "safety net" of the prior era: There were few welfare programs for poor people to fall back on, except for a make-work program that paid a dollar a day.

In this familial economic crisis, women were forced to assume new responsibilities, particularly where their men were absent, unemployable, or took refuge from their inability to support their families in alcohol or desertion. Feeding their families was a traditional female concern. Now it meant increasingly desperate efforts to find the means of putting bread on the table. In the shantytowns of Santiago, where four out of five men were unemployed by 1983, women increasingly became breadwinners. "If the man couldn't find work," Ube Torres explained, "it was easier for the woman to go out and beg, or go out and clean streets." Others cooked food to sell on the streets, or sold their bodies on dingy downtown corners or in dark suburban traffic circles.

Still others, too burdened with children to be able to work far from home, sought imaginative ways to make ends meet, often by turning traditions of mutual assistance into popular economic organizations. They were women like Elba Vargas, whose squat body and swarthy skin revealed an Indian ancestry that identified her as lower class to other Chileans. Her lined face and stooped shoulders betrayed a lifetime of work and worry that had aged her far more than her thirty-odd years. She carried her youngest child close to her breast, and when she spoke there was a bitterness in her voice. "My mother had twelve children and everyone was happy. Who can afford to raise twelve children today? You would have to be a millionaire!"

There were no millionaires in Elba's Santiago shantytown whose tin-roofed shacks, unpaved streets, and stunted children belie its stunning site at the foot of the snowcapped Andes. Instead, there was the daily struggle for survival that brought poor women to join forces, pooling their poverty in an effort to find together the livelihood that had eluded them alone. These survival strategies took many forms. Women formed "workshops" that took in laundry. Others set up communal kitchens that would assure their own families a nutritious meal.

The *olla comun* ("common pot"), or communal kitchen, had long been a tradition of organized labor in Chile. Striking workers would set up a big cauldron opposite their factory and solicit solidarity in the form of food contributions, which would be cooked up for the strikers. What was new after the coup was the establishment of permanent communal kitchens in residential neighborhoods by women searching for a way to feed their families. Each family contributed a few pesos, and the women went around soliciting contributions of food and wood, sometimes with help as well from the Church. Then they would spend the afternoon cooking the ingredients they had collected into a simple but nutritious soup or stew. For many families, this might be their only meal.

Yet participating in the communal kitchen was a difficult decision for proud people accustomed to being self-supporting. It was a statement to your neighbors that your husband could not provide for his family, which was so humiliating that even women whose families were hungry shrank from joining *la olla,* and those who did often hid it from their neighbors. In New Havana, there was a woman "who didn't have food for her children for a whole week. She wanted to kill herself and her children out of despair," said Ube Torres. "I heard about it and brought her to *la olla*, explaining that she wasn't the only one with that problem." Ube was convinced that the communal kitchen she and her neighbors formed had saved many women from prostitution and alcoholism, even suicide. "That is why we are proud of *la olla.*"

The women of New Havana also had to hide the location of their communal kitchen because the military regarded it as politically subversive. On the day after Christmas 1975 the armed forces surrounded the shantytown at dawn, took their men away, and then advanced on *la olla*. "The military found where *la olla* was located . . . so we all got together around the place [and] we didn't let the soldiers come in. We said it was our children's food, and if they threw it away we would fight them." Faced with this show of desperate resistance by enraged women in their role as mothers, the soldiers backed off. "Despite all that repression," Ube reflected, "we became strong—by acting as *women.*"

In a sense the military were right: *la olla was* subversive, both of the military's pretensions to control Chilean society and the traditional sexual politics that they supported. The *olla* became an informal support group, helping women to stand up to physical and verbal abuse from men who often took out on their wives their own embarrassment at not being able to support their families. "Women now have more strength," Ube testified. "Before they allowed themselves to be hit, and they would stay quiet, and go to their rooms and cry, and no one would realize that their husband was treating them badly. Now they arrive at *la olla* and say: 'He hit me because I arrived late and didn't give him dinner . . . and I didn't even have any food.' " In response, "We all say to the women: 'Answer him back. Don't let him hit you. Don't let him say that to you. Don't stay quiet. Don't let him humiliate you, because you have the same rights as him.' So we give them courage . . . courage to answer their husbands back, courage to defend themselves."

While popular economic organizations such as the communal kitchens and laundry workshops were created as collective survival strategies by poor women in urban shantytowns, over time they also became social circles and the base of a broadening range of community organizations such

as literacy and theater groups. They also changed the worldview and
behavior of the women involved. In part, it was because when women
"began to liberate themselves from the four walls of their home . . . they
began to see another reality," Ube explained. In part, as the women of
Elba's laundry workshop concluded, it was because as they learned to
support themselves, they also "learned to have confidence in themselves."
To Ube, the difference all this made in women's behavior was clear:
"Women act with greater liberty now." Women also became more active
politically and assumed greater leadership roles in their community. "In
the marches you see more women than men," Ube affirmed. "And in our
neighborhood social organizations most of the directors are women." Often
what began as a communal kitchen or artisanal workshop eventually generated a women's support group as well. These organizations remained
"feminine" rather than "feminist," but they justified the confidence of
feminists such as Marilú Silva that "once women realize their power they
will never again allow men to push them around."

Democracy in the Country and the Home

While poor women were banding together for economic survival during
the decade that followed the 1973 coup, middle-class women were reviving
a feminist movement that had declined after helping women to secure the
vote in 1949. It was the trials and tribulations of the 1970s that produced a
renewal of feminism among a new generation of political activists and
intellectuals. These new feminists were mostly women of the left who had
previously accepted its insistence on subordinating the concerns of gender
to the conflicts of class. They came to feminism in their prison cells,
underground hideouts, or places of exile, or else through their work with
poor women or study of the historic relationship between Chilean women
and their political parties.

     For most, a feminist consciousness emerged out of their reflections on
their own past experience and current situation. Marilú Silva began to
wonder why her work with women had been disparaged during the Al-

lende era as "not revolutionary." María Antonieta Saa, at the time a young leftist activist, recalled that as the only woman at a national labor confederation meeting, her miniskirt had caused a stir, but the men "really didn't pay proper attention" to what she said. After the coup, she continued to work "semiclandestinely, writing and distributing newspapers. [Then,] suddenly I began to think of myself. What's happening to me as a woman? What is my role?" She found that other leftist women were going through the same process of introspection. "We began to meet with other women to discuss these issues." Many had returned from exile in Europe and the United States with their consciousness altered by contact with First World feminism. Marisa Matamala was among those who concluded "that we had to start a new road and had to understand that our struggle as women was part of the class struggle, but that the women's struggle could never be replaced by the class struggle." Out of these reflections and discussions a new Chilean feminism began to emerge.

Most feminist activists remained committed to leftist causes and many tried to reconcile their dual commitments through the elaboration of a "socialist feminism." As elsewhere in Latin America, this fusion of socialism with feminism has given Chilean feminism a stress on the problems facing poor and working women generally absent among their North American sisters.

From their years of political activism, they brought an experience in organization and an ability to mobilize a mass movement of women around issues that ranged from human rights to economic survival, but infused now with gender perspectives. These socialist feminists were influential in the formation of women's consciousness-raising groups even in Chilean shantytowns. Over time, a varied and broad-based women's movement emerged, based in the neighborhood as well as the workplace, and led by women who shared both feminist and social concerns. This movement flourished during an era when other social movements were repressed.

In 1983 the feminists formed an umbrella organization, MEMCH '83, which linked up with the feminism of the past in its appropriation of the name of its first federation—MEMCH—and in the participation of veterans of that earlier feminism such as Olga Poblete and Elena Caffarena.

Within it were grouped women's labor unions, shantytown workshops, and human rights groups, but also the feminist research institutes and study circles that had been created during the previous decade of dictatorship. Olga Poblete and Elena Caffarena were honored as "foremothers," founding matriarchs of the MEMCHs of 1938 and 1983, living links with a feminist tradition that had been broken by decades of subordination to the priorities of political parties. The slogan—"Democracy in the country *and* in the home"—summed up the twin goals of Chilean feminism. By late 1983 MEMCH's leaders were ready to join with other prominent women to launch a broad-based movement "for democracy."

Women for Life

In November 1983 Sebastián Acevedo set himself aflame in the main square of the southern city of Concepción to protest the disappearance of his children at the hands of Pinochet's secret police. His traumatic sacrifice punctuated an era of renewed upheaval. The regime's policies had plunged Chile into a grave economic crisis. More than a third of the labor force was unemployed; the national income was plummeting. Desperation helped poor Chileans to overcome their fear of repression. The shantytowns rose in rebellion, symbolized by the burning barricades with which enraged youths kept the dictatorship's soldiers at bay. Yet the opposition political parties seemed incapable of transcending their partisan rivalries and ideological differences to give effective leadership to this rebellion from below.

It was in this dramatic moment that "Women for Life" was founded. A group of women activists from the center and the left decided to set aside their own differences and work together *"Por la Vida!"*—"For Life!" Teresa Valdés, a sociologist from an elite Chilean family, was one of the group's founders. "We chose the name 'For Life' because we were fighting against death represented by unemployment, hunger, drugs, exile, torture, and repression," she said. "Unity appeared to be essential to change things. The crisis had run too deep and the efforts of other social sectors had been insufficient. We were critical of our political leaders and convinced that, as women, we would be capable of going a step further, proving that it is possible to work together." They announced the formation of "Women for Life" at a press conference called to express their "horror and outrage, as women, at the conditions" responsible for the suicide of Sebastián Acevedo, "whose sacrifice deeply shocked the consciousness of Chileans."

"As an initial action we invited all the women of Santiago to join us in a rally at the Caupolicán Theater," the largest in Santiago—with a capacity of ten thousand—"to seal our agreement and commitment to work together actively 'For Life,'" Valdés said. "We invited all the women's organizations to work with us in the preparation of the rally." The 1983 Caupolicán meeting would be the first open political rally since the coup. "No men were allowed in. Women handled the press, the microphones, even security," Marilú Silva recalled. "It was an extraordinary scene: Ten thousand women, rich and poor, Christian Democrats and Communists, university graduates and illiterates, united in their defiance of the dictatorship."

The rally was "one of the most significant opposition events [and] a large step forward for Chilean women as a political force," Teresa Valdés concluded. "A sequence of presentations and testimonies reflected on ten years of women's activities under the dictatorship—in human rights organizations, in workshops to support family income, at the universities, as professionals in the fields of education, health . . . and in the political parties." It was at once a watershed in Chile's struggle for democracy and in the evolution of its women's movement.

It was also an auspicious debut for Women for Life, which emerged as a key umbrella organization in the struggle for democracy that followed. "We became aware of our potential and realized that it was possible to work together for democracy," explained Valdés. "The outcome of the rally is what we call 'the spirit of Caupolicán': an active commitment to the struggle for democracy aimed at unifying women from the opposition and including women of all sectors, taking into account our own problems as women and our own styles, respecting each other's points of view and the work of the different organizations." "The great virtue of Women for Life," Marilú Silva said, "was to respond to a political moment, but without relying on any of the established political forces."

For Olga Poblete, who had participated in half a century of women's movements, Women for Life was also striking in its creativity. "They changed the logos and the language of politics." At Caupolicán, "they created a new format. They used the big screen, and while some appeared painting on the stage, others were showing testimonies . . . they did not give speeches. They *demonstrated* what had to be done."

A flair for the dramatic and an ability to find the common denominator that would attract the largest possible movement of women would be the hallmark of Women for Life during the years that followed. It continued to protest the regime's injustices with highly visible actions: silent vigils, collective fasts, poster campaigns, street actions. "When the state of siege was finally lifted in October 1985, we organized the largest women's march in twelve years of military rule," Teresa Valdés said. "Our slogan was '*Somos Mas*'—'We Are the Majority' " and the goal was the restoration of democracy. When police attacked the women with water cannons, they held up their palms and chanted, "*We* have clean hands."

Such demonstrations kept the flame of resistance alive, but could not by themselves bring the dictatorship to an end. As the struggle for democracy evolved, the political parties resumed their leadership role, and Women for Life found it increasingly difficult to maintain their immunity from partisan political divisions over strategy and tactics. The group began to lose its unity and its power "to mobilize large numbers of women," said Marilú Silva, because "we no longer could find the common denominator." It was emblematic of the divisive impact of the resurgent political parties on the women's movement as a whole.

The General's Women

By 1988 the campaign for democracy was moving from the streets to the voting booth. General Pinochet had agreed to hold the plebiscite on his fifteen-year dictatorship stipulated in his own 1980 constitution, confident that he could win eight more years in power through ballots instead of bullets.

What persuaded Pinochet that he could extend his reign at the polls was the restoration of economic prosperity—and his belief that Chile's women strongly supported his rule. To the Chilean military, who saw themselves as defenders of the traditional family, women were their natural allies. The role women had played in calling for the military coup had confirmed them in this conviction. In its wake, the military regime had tried to consolidate female support, even among the poor women whose families had been hurt by the regime's economic and social policies. The military called on their women supporters to do their part.

Many conservative women responded to this call. Following Chilean elite tradition, Viena Frugone volunteered to work with poor women in CEMA-Chile, the network of Mothers' Centers run by Lucía Iriarte, General Pinochet's wife. By 1988 Frugone was its head in Valparaíso, the nation's chief port and second largest city. CEMA had been a paternalistic charity that handed out sewing machines in exchange for political support since 1964. Under General Pinochet, CEMA-Chile retained this character, but also propagated conservative values—"the values of Western Christian society," Viena Frugone affirmed. "To us the main things were God, country, and family." The materials distributed by Lucía Iriarte de Pinochet's office added other qualities close to the heart of the military: order, prudence, discretion. These were very different ideals than those of equality, justice, autonomy, and democracy that were being disseminated by the women's groups competing with CEMA-Chile for the hearts and minds of Chile's poor women.

CEMA-Chile was also more top-down in its structure and methods. It was organized along military lines, with uniforms for its ten thousand volunteers. Many of them were the wives of military officers, and their performance in CEMA-Chile became part of their husbands' service records. It was also against women in politics, encouraging them to center their lives in the home, not in the public sphere.

Yet Pinochet did appoint a few women to high positions in his government. Mónica Madariaga, a lawyer with a reputation as an iron lady, became minister of justice, the highest cabinet post ever occupied by a woman in Chile, and presided over the transformation of the military dictatorship into an authoritarian regime, complete with constitution and legal codes. Today she is head of a private university.

So is Alicia Romo, whom Pinochet appointed director of industry and commerce, a rare woman among the U.S.-trained "Chicago boys," whose doctrinaire free-market economics transformed Chile more profoundly than Pinochet's authoritarian politics, although at an elevated social cost. Romo still defends the economic "shock treatment" she helped implement: "We had to reduce the size of the state and make people understand that they were responsible for managing their own finances, not the state through fixed prices. We had to break a lot of myths held by Chileans."

Although these policy shifts contributed to the crisis, they eventually spurred the investment of money and expertise in such new export lines as fruits. As a result, the economic changes that Alicia Romo helped implement had a major impact on rural women, drawing them out of their homes and into new economic roles.

Grapes of Wrath

Traditionally, rural Chilean women did not work outside the home. They did not infringe on their husband's status as the family's breadwinner. They rose at dawn to make his breakfast, took care of the garden, children, and house while he worked, and had dinner waiting when he came home at dusk. They certainly were never out alone late at night. Now, four out of five Chilean rural laborers are temporary workers, and most of these 350,000 seasonal workers are female *temporeras.* This has provoked a dramatic change in women's roles and family dynamics.

Santa María, in the beautiful valley of Aconcagua north of Santiago, is today the heart of Chile's grape industry. Where there once were self-sufficient family farms, now there are only vineyards and fruit orchards. "When the packing houses came into the valley a decade ago, everything began to change," Leontina explained, with a toss of her graying black hair. She smoked a cigarette nervously as she recounted the transformation of Santa María. Peasant families like her own were expelled from their land and forced to live on the edge of town or up in the barren hills. Some men continued to be hired at minimum wage to tend the plants and pick the fruit, but it was their wives and daughters—whom the new "bosses" thought had "softer hands [and] greater patience"—who found work at the new packing plants that processed the grapes, apples, and kiwis for export to North America and Europe.

The work was hard and the conditions inside the packing houses harsh. The women were paid by the box they cleaned or packed, a piece-rate system that encouraged self-exploitation. Although the pay was *"una miseria"*—four U.S. dollars to clean fifty boxes of grapes—women who pushed themselves could earn as much as four times the minimum wage that their husbands brought home. "That's why we do it, because we are poor and need the money to make ends meet," Leontina said. "And the packing season is very short, so you have to make as much as you can during those four months."

"It was better before," Josefina said in the dramatic valley of Elqui, some two hundred miles north of Santa María. "There wasn't as much money before, but one planted more . . . each couple had their little plot and they planted and harvested what they ate—carrots, lettuce, everything. Now, every little bit of land is taken up with grapes, so people don't plant and have to buy everything." From self-sufficient farmers, her people had become ill-paid consumers at the mercy of the market. Even with their increased earnings, their family income "didn't reach." The windfall she had anticipated when she started working in *el packing* had proved an illusion.

What made it worse was that this minimal economic gain was purchased at a high personal cost. The grapes were harvested by the men during the morning, and the women entered the packing houses in the early afternoon. Because of the quality controls needed for foreign markets, all the fruit picked that morning had to be cleaned and packed the same day. This meant that the women worked shifts of twelve to sixteen hours each day. "We enter *el packing* at one or two in the afternoon," Leontina explained, "and often don't get home until dawn."

The personal costs paid by the *temporeras* did not end at the packing-house door. Once they arrived home, after an exhausting fifteen-hour shift, they were likely to be confronted by a recently awakened husband who wanted his breakfast made—or worse, by no husband at all "and the kids left to themselves," Leontina complained bitterly. That is what had happened to her. "My husband doesn't drink, but his vice is other women, and with my working all night, he didn't wait around for me." It was a common complaint. Leontina was one of many *temporeras* whose marriages disintegrated under the pressure of their work shifts.

But even those families that survived often went through painful adjustments. "It was hard for my husband to understand why I was too tired to make breakfast for him when I came home, and he felt that he was too macho to take care of the children," Angelica said. It is the children who suffer most. "You just have to leave your kids with whomever you can—with a neighbor, with a family member, or just leave them alone," said Yolanda. "My daughters cry when I leave because they're all alone."

Still, working outside the home was often an eye-opening experience for rural women in Chile. The money they earned gave them greater self-confidence and control over their lives. It also led them to insist on greater equality inside their homes. "Though my husband didn't want to get his breakfast and take care of the children at first, in the end he began to understand," Angelica affirmed. For Amanda, working in *el packing* "was like a liberation, because I had known nothing else but my home, and my husband drank a lot and beat me and the children." Her work gave her the courage and confidence to stand up to him and eventually to leave.

It had also given some of the women in Santa María the courage to form a union and stand up to their employers. Leontina and Olga had even led a work stoppage and won their demands, although at the cost of their own jobs. By 1990 they were union officers, part of a rare female majority in the leadership of a rural workers' union. Their experience had raised both their consciousness and their confidence. When they were sent to a meeting of mostly male rural union leaders in Santiago, "we had to fight with the national leaders," Leontina related, "because they are very *machista* and they didn't like it that women arrived as national delegates and spoke as much as the men." Like labor leaders throughout the region, Chilean unionists saw women as temporary workers whose special needs took second place to those of male workers. But, Leontina recounted, "Olga told them that they had to understand our reality—the reality of the valley of Aconcagua: 'We women workers are a majority and our work is a double day.'"

Chile's experience of the new export industries was typical of the region. In much of Latin America and the Caribbean, neoliberal economic policies that stressed exports have created agriculture and industries that offer women badly needed jobs, but at low wages and high personal costs. Throughout the region, moreover, women continue to work a double day. Yet it was on the basis of this economic "success" and the women who "benefited" from it that General Pinochet hoped to win a renewed political mandate at the polls.

Will the Circle Be Unbroken?

In July 1988 Women for Life inaugurated "Chile Creates," the first cultural festival since the military coup, with a chilling performance of larger-than-life shadow puppets representing the disappeared. Even a year before, such an event would not have been possible. But now Chile was about to begin its first election campaign since 1973, the long-promised plebiscite on General Pinochet's fifteen-year dictatorship. It was a symbolic act that underscored the human rights issues that would play a large role in the campaign that followed.

The plebiscite of 1988 was the decisive event in Chile's restoration of democracy, even though General Pinochet was the only candidate on the ballot and the voters' only choice was to vote "Sí" or "No" on another eight years of his rule. Women were active in both the "Sí" and "No" campaigns, playing particularly key roles in the house-to-house canvassing that the "No" supporters relied upon to overcome fears and get out the vote. Both

sides identified women, half the electorate, as a critical swing group and
targeted them in its campaigning.

In Pinochet's plebiscite strategy, women occupied a central place.
Historically, women had always voted more conservatively than Chilean
men, and ·they had played a key part in the ouster of Allende that had
brought the military to power. Moreover, Pinochet had made defense of
the traditional family a tenet of his ideology, even though his policies had
often undermined it in practice. He expected Chile's women to reward him
with a large majority of their ballots, offsetting male votes against him.

But the new social and economic roles that Chile's women had been
thrust into during his dictatorship had altered their politics as well. When
the ballots were counted on October 5, 1988, a majority of women had cast
them for the "No." Their votes assured Pinochet's plebiscite defeat and the
election of an opposition leader, Patricio Aylwin, as president the following
year.

When General Pinochet reluctantly handed over his presidential sash
to Aylwin in March 1990, Chilean women could look back on three decades
of intense change and activity with a mixture of satisfaction and frustration.
They had increased their participation in the work force, created new
social organizations, and become the conscience of the nation in matters of
human rights. They had formed female networks that had enabled their
families to survive difficult economic times, expanded their political participation in innovative ways, and played a leading role in the resistance
against the dictatorship and the restoration of democracy. These varied
activities had increased their self-confidence and raised their consciousness
as well, leading many women to demand "democracy in the home" as well
as in the nation.

Yet these gains for women as a group had come at great personal cost
for individual activists, a reflection of the traumas and transformations of
three decades of intense change. "We have paid a high price for participating in the women's movement," concluded Marilú Silva. "I know of few
women active in the movement who are still with the same man as in 1970."
Although she was aware that these relationships might not have lasted
anyway, Teresa Valdés agreed: "Many of us have lost our marriages, or our

companions, because the paths taken are different and incompatible. . . . This also happened at the popular level." Ube Torres's marriage had survived, but she reported that in her shantytown "almost all the members of the communal kitchen are separated." In part, this was because the more conscious and confident women would no longer accept the abusive relationships of the past; in part, because their men were unable to accept the new roles of their women—or their own inability to support their families. Social and political activism, therefore, was not the only source of marital tensions. Many men were unable to cope with long-term unemployment or their women working. In the valley of Elqui, a conservative rural society, the new economic roles of women meant that "the majority of marriages have conflicts, and many of them break up," said Josefina.

Many of the gains of Chilean women, moreover, seemed incomplete in 1990. Women still filled lower-echelon jobs that were ill-paid and offered few opportunities for promotion. Despite their increased self-confidence and self-consciousness as women, their inequality before the law remained. And though the Aylwin government was committed to the protection of human rights and to clarifying the fate of the disappeared, it was not prepared to anger the army—still headed by an intransigent General Pinochet—by punishing their persecutors.

Women were also disappointed when the top positions in Chile's restored democracy went to established male political leaders. When the first elected president in two decades announced his cabinet, there were no women among his ministers. Only one female mayor was appointed by President Aylwin. In the new Congress, where there were just two elected women senators and seven deputies, the situation seemed little better. Nor were women given many leadership posts within the traditional political parties. After their prominent role in the struggle against the dictatorship, "we had expected more," Marilú Silva commented bitterly. "And we deserved more."

Potentially the situation was better than it appeared. The National Women's Service (SERNAM), a new women's agency within the government, was created in 1990, and a year later accorded ministerial rank. It was led by feminists with excellent political connections and a reform agenda. Marilú Silva became a senior advisor in the ministry of education, with responsibility for eliminating sexism from the curriculum, a key to sensitizing the next generation of Chileans to gender issues. María Antonieta Saa, the one woman appointed mayor, was using her powers to pioneer new programs for women and to publicize such feminist concerns as violence against women. She was a popular mayor and a likely congressional candidate.

Within the Congress, moreover, there were also signs of hope. The handful of female deputies included dynamic young women of varying views and parties who had the ability and ambition to make major political careers. The two female senators were both potential presidents. One of them, Christian Democrat Carmen Frei, owed her career in part to the name recognition provided by her father, Eduardo, the popular former president.

The other was Laura Soto, who first came to public attention as a courageous human rights lawyer defending political prisoners in the wake of the coup in the coastal district around Valparaíso, Chile's main naval base. "It was very dangerous work," but she persisted, in the face of death threats and attempts to kidnap her young daughter. She emerged as a local leader of the movement for the restoration of democracy and a founder of the Party for Democracy (PPD), a center-left party with a modern image, imaginative policies, and capable leaders.

In 1989, Soto was nominated for the Senate but was given little chance of election as an underdog running against well-known and well-funded political veterans. But "Laurita" was the candidate of the women of the region and that would make all the difference. "It was the young women in particular who identified with my candidacy and pushed my campaign," she said proudly. They plastered the walls of Valparaíso with posters, and painted them with murals. They were not only colorful but inventive, making up slogans that appalled the political pros but appealed to the ordinary people who constituted the bulk of the electorate. By the time *Abuelitas para Laurita*—Grandmothers for Laurita—was formed, it was clear that a grassroots revolt of women who had never before participated in electoral politics was taking place. When the votes were counted, Laura

Soto had been elected senator by "an overwhelming majority," with a candidacy and a campaign that represented the triumph of the new female-led social movements over the old male-dominated party politics. In 1990, she capped this success by being elected first vice president of her party, with good prospects of becoming its head in the future. Could a woman be elected president of Chile? "Yes," Soto replied, "but not for another fifteen years." That first female chief executive might well be Laura Soto.

But Laura Soto is aware that she is the exception, and that "Chilean women have a long way to go in their struggle for equality." At the other end of the political spectrum, Alicia Romo shared these concerns, but took a more philosophical view: "Our women have played an important role in the life of the country and they have changed the direction of society. However, our participation has been like that of a Greek chorus—which appears and disappears. At times of profound crisis, when the country faces dramatic situations, women appear and act with great strength and conviction."

Yet women in Chile have not pressed with equal determination for a reversal of the laws and biases that discriminate against them. Once the crisis passed, most returned to their private lives and left the public sphere to their men. If Chilean women are to gain the equal opportunities that both Alicia Romo and Laura Soto agree they deserve, they must transform their intermittent political participation into a permanent political presence. Their rich experience of recent decades should help them win the battles that remain to be fought.

Women's New Worlds

Much of this recent experience of Chilean women was shared by women elsewhere in Latin America and the Caribbean, although each country has its own history and each woman her own story. In much of the region women pioneered new grassroots organizations—human rights groups, mutual aid workshops, popular economic organizations, feminist study circles, and consciousness-raising groups.

In countries as diverse as Guatemala and Argentina, women have also taken the lead in protesting human rights violations and demanding an accounting of the fates of their disappeared relatives. In Buenos Aires, "the Mothers of the Plaza de Mayo" became the conscience of their nation and an international symbol. In Colombia, a country wracked by social as well as political violence for nearly half a century, marches of "Women for Life" echoed Chile's but took on an even broader meaning.

In Lima shantytowns, such as Villa El Salvador, women began with self-help groups and then went on to form a neighborhood "women's federation," which reflected their new identities and self-confidence as women. The cumulative impact of this experience of organization and struggle is also evident internationally in the growing attendance at the periodic meetings of the region's feminists.

The bittersweet political experience of Chilean women was also shared in other countries of the region. In Argentina, Uruguay, and Brazil women also played leading roles opposing dictatorships and demanding the return of democracy. Yet when democratic government was finally restored, there were fewer women in Uruguay's Congress than before. In Argentina, where the last president before the military takeover had been a woman, none occupied prominent positions once democracy was restored.

By comparison, the political gains of women in Brazil's restored democracy seemed considerable. There, a woman was named finance minister, the most important cabinet post, in the first directly elected national government, and women were elected mayor in several key cities, including São Paulo, Brazil's largest metropolis, one of the most prominent political positions in the country. Brazil's active women's movement also secured the creation of governmental councils on women's rights at national, state, and municipal levels and the establishment of special police stations to deal with violence against women. They won a major legal victory in 1991 when the nation's supreme court, led by a new woman justice, outlawed the "honor" defense that men had used successfully in the past to excuse their murder of unfaithful wives. They were also successful in winning "virtually all our demands for reform of the civil codes" in the new constitution, asserted feminist activist Rosiska Darcy de Oliveira. As a result, she said, "In Brazil today, women have won equality before the law." But the legislation to implement many of these new constitutional principles has yet to be enacted. It also remains to be seen whether the new government councils on women's rights can resist the pulls of Brazil's patronage politics and still conservative society. As in Chile, moreover, Brazil's elites and voters have yet to choose a woman to lead their nation.

But if Laura Soto ever does become president of Chile, she will not be the first head of state in the region. Women have led governments in countries as diverse and distant as Dominica and Bolivia, Haiti and Argentina. But it is in revolutionary societies such as Nicaragua that women have played the most prominent political roles. Women composed a third of the Sandinista forces during their rebellion against the Somoza dictatorship and accounted for an even larger share of the FMLN insurgents in El Salvador and the Shining Path guerrillas in Peru. Yet in revolutionary Cuba, where women have won equal pay and an egalitarian family code, there were few women among the nation's leaders after thirty-three years of revolutionary rule. "And even among women, images of the ideal political leader are almost universally male," sociologist Elena Díaz reported. "It is difficult to change the prejudices of three centuries in three decades," she reflected ruefully. "Even with a revolution."

In the past, a Catholicism that drew on both European and Indian beliefs satisfied the intense religiosity of Latin Americans like these pilgrims at Mexico's shrine of the Virgin of Guadalupe. Over 90 percent of Latin Americans remain nominally Catholic, but many ceased to attend church when they moved from rural homes to city slums.

Chapter 10

The Power and the Glory

Liberation theology, which urged the Church to adopt a "preferential option for the poor" and to encourage grass-roots organizations, was the theme of this 1989 São Paulo discussion featuring theologian Leonardo Boff, Cardinal Paulo Arns, and labor and political leader Luis Inácio "Lula" da Silva.

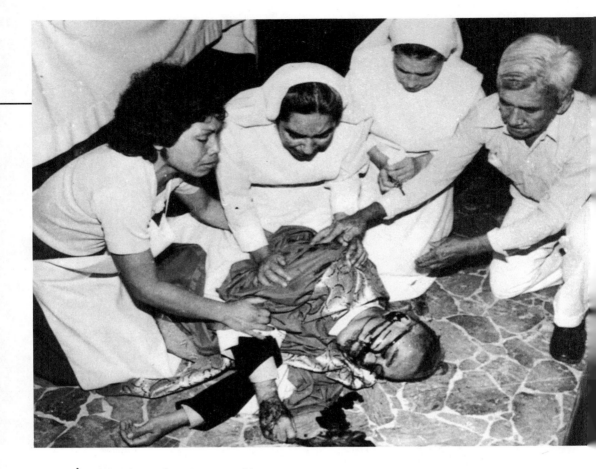

In many Latin American countries, progressives within the Church took the lead in struggles for human rights and social justice, and over eight hundred churchpeople became martyrs for these causes. The most famous was El Salvador's Archbishop Oscar Romero, who in 1980 was murdered by a rightist death squad while saying mass.

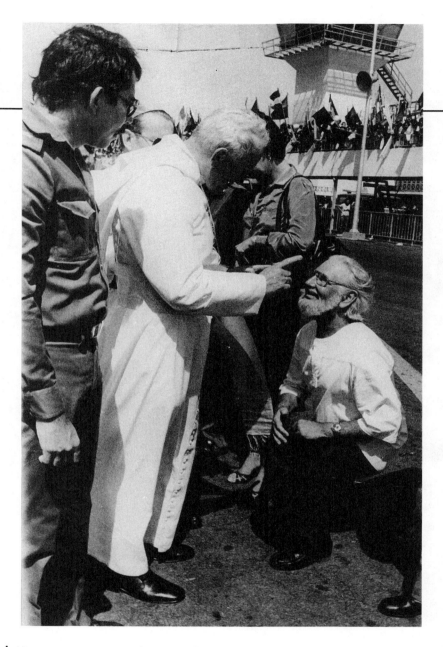

In Nicaragua, progressive clergy even became involved in the Sandinista revolution and several priests were appointed to high positions. Their presence in a "Marxist" government worried Pope John Paul II, who publicly reprimanded Father Ernesto Cardenal in 1983 for remaining culture minister despite papal orders to resign.

Today the Vatican seems more concerned about the inroads of evangelical Protestantism, led by Pentecostals
such as "Bishop" Edir Macedo—
shown here "laying on hands"—whose
Universal Church of the Kingdom of
God, which stresses faith healing and
exorcism, is one of Brazil's fastest-
growing denominations.

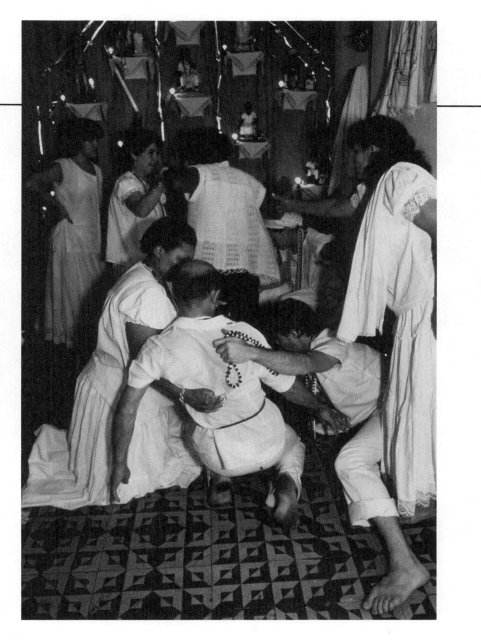

The other rapidly growing religion in Brazil is Umbanda, a uniquely Brazilian synthesis of European and African Spiritism that appeals to both the urban white middle class and the black and mulatto lower class. In this São Paulo center, a medium possessed by a spirit is helped by assistants.

The dramatic changes in Latin America's Catholic Church have also had a profound impact on North American Catholics, from missionary orders such as the Maryknolls to middle-class laity who risked jail in cities such as Chicago to offer sanctuary to Salvadoran refugees denied asylum by the U.S. government.

10   *The Power and the Glory*

*I*N October 1991, Pope John Paul II paid his second visit to Brazil and his tenth to Latin America and the Caribbean in little more than a decade. He met with Indian chiefs in the Amazon and bishops in their urban sees, and talked with landless peasants in the Northeast and elite politicians in Brasília. Even for so well-traveled a pontiff this was unusual attention, which underscored the importance to the Vatican of Brazil in particular— and Latin America in general.

More Catholics live in Latin America and the Caribbean than in any other region on earth. By the end of the century it will be home to three Catholics out of five. Brazil has the world's largest national Church, with more than 110 million believers and 350 bishops.

But it was not just the huge numbers of the faithful that persuaded the pope to make a tiring ten-day journey through the continent's biggest country. It was also his concern over the millions of believers lost to religious rivals: Where nineteen out of twenty Brazilians belonged to the Church fifty years ago, its bishops estimate that only three out of four do now. Within the Catholic church as well, Brazil is where the Vatican has faced the most important challenge to its authority from advocates of more democracy inside the Church and greater social activism and political involvement in the world outside. The self-styled "country of the future"

353

may well be where the future of the Catholic church in Christianity's third millennium is decided.

Like much of Latin America and the Caribbean, Brazil is experiencing a revival of religiosity. Brazil's remarkable explosion of spiritual renewal, social activism, and theological debate displays a richness and creativity that reflects its diverse cultures. But throughout the region, people have questioned old religious beliefs and institutions and created new ones. In Jamaica, poor blacks have embraced the neo-African rites of the Rastafarians; in Guatemala, middle-class *ladinos* and Indian peasants have converted to evangelical Protestantism. In Nicaragua, many Catholics joined a Marxist revolution and formed a so-called "people's church" opposed by the hierarchy. This ferment has underscored the continuing importance of faith in Latin America and the Caribbean while pushing churches into uncharted terrain.

That these other Americas would be regarded in 1992 as a land of religious innovation would have surprised most observers fifty years ago. For most of five centuries, the Catholic church has dominated the region's religious life and been regarded as a conservative pillar of the status quo. In 1915, Brazil's bishops told the country's priests to "inculcate the spirit of obedience and submission to those who govern in civil society . . . to lead the faithful to accept their proper situation and the conditions in which they were born."[1] But during recent decades, the Latin American Church has been at the storm center of change—and been transformed in the process. It has seen revolutionary priests killed in combat and liberal bishops martyred for their defense of the oppressed. It has opened up its cathedrals to forbidden meetings of labor unions and its offices to victims of human rights abuses. It has helped peasants to organize land seizures and Indians to defend their communities. It has promoted popular participation within the Church and political democracy in the nation. And it has carried on an intense internal debate over the nature of the Church, the character of its mission, and the methods it should employ to pursue these goals.

This extraordinary ferment within the Latin American Church has been prompted by the profound changes taking place within the society and politics of Latin America and the Caribbean. Massive migration from the countryside to the cities—in search of economic and educational opportunities, or in flight from rural violence and civil war—was one cause of concern, as "cultural Catholics" drifted away from the Church of their childhood. People whose families for generations had attended the same rural church were uprooted and resettled in urban shantytowns hundreds of miles away. In many cases, in these sprawling new communities there were few churches or priests and they often had difficulty responding to the special needs of these poor migrants. Increasingly, the Catholic church was losing the loyalties of these former faithful to religious or secular competitors—Protestant evangelicals, Spiritist cults, Marxist movements—who seemed to offer more definite answers to the problems in their lives and a supportive community to help them deal with their unfamiliar environment. This disaffection reflected many factors, but the common denominator was the perceived irrelevance of the Church to people's lives and needs.

The postwar decades were also a time of intellectual and political ferment in much of Latin America and the Caribbean. Within the Church, many priests and nuns who worked with the poor and oppressed—whether in the Indian highlands of Guatemala or Peru, the migrant slums of San Salvador or Port-au-Prince, or the rain forests of Brazil or Ecuador—were politicized by that experience and opened to new ways of analyzing the region's inequalities and the Church's role in combating them. Some were influenced by Marxist critiques and by the example of social revolution set by Cuba after 1959. In Colombia, Father Camilo Torres, a prominent priest, even took up arms and died as a leftist guerrilla in 1966, after his efforts at peaceful reform were frustrated by entrenched interests. During the past three decades the Latin American Church has lost more than eight hundred Church martyrs to the cause of nonviolent social change. During the 1960s and 1970s, a period of revolutionary upheaval and rightist repression in much of the region, progressive Catholics developed a new "theology of liberation" and prescribed a new political and pastoral practice for the Church.

Toward a Theology of Liberation

"We have an evangelical commitment to make a preferential option for the poor," said Dom Adriano Hypólito, the progressive bishop of Nova Iguaçú, a sprawling working-class city near Rio de Janeiro. "So how are we going to realize this option? It's not enough just to talk and pray. As a Christian and as a pastor, I feel I have a duty to support movements that work for the good of the people."[2] One of the innovations that Dom Adriano supported were the Christian Base Communities, grassroots groups that studied the Bible and related it to their daily lives, often with transforming effects. As one base community leader in Nova Iguaçú attested: "I was always a very religious person and was active in the Church. But before coming to Nova Iguaçú, I had experienced only the closed Church of Rio. It didn't get involved in politics, or if it did, it was on the government's side. For them, the Bible isn't linked to life," she claimed. What had changed her vision and her life was that "we moved to Nova Iguaçú. That's when I started to develop a political consciousness. I participated in the base community and learned a different understanding of the Bible, committed to the poor and social justice."[3]

Ever since the mistreatment of the Indians during the Conquest shocked Bartolomé de las Casas into becoming a Dominican crusader for indigenous rights, there have always been voices within the Church concerned with protecting the poor and promoting social justice. In 1891, Pope Leo XIII made such concerns part of the social doctrine of the Church. This was reflected in such organizations as Catholic Action, which, beginning in the 1920s, mobilized lay activists from the middle and working classes under Church direction. In Brazil, Catholic Action influenced such future Church leaders as Dom Hélder Câmara, teaching them the importance of linking faith with social reform. During the 1950s the Vatican encouraged the creation of national bishops' councils to increase the responsiveness of local Churches to the problems of their flocks. The National Council of Brazilian Bishops (CNBB) was founded in 1952 under Dom Hélder's leadership as the first episcopal council in Latin America. It played a central role in the innovations of the decade that followed, including educational reform and grassroots organizing.

But it was Vatican II, the extraordinary conference of Catholic prelates summoned by Pope John XXIII to Rome in 1962, that catalyzed the quantum leap in doctrinal debate, social activism, political involvement, and popular participation of recent decades. The Vatican was responding to the diffuse but dramatic changes of increasingly industrial, urban, and secular societies, while affirming the Church's need to assert a strong moral authority lacking in its muted and tardy response to fascism and the Holocaust. At the same time, as a global institution it was called upon increasingly to deal with the issues of poverty, inequality, and political repression.

In an effort to meet these challenges, Vatican II initiated a dramatic reform of Catholic doctrine and practice, and a revamping of the structures and decision-making of the Church. It committed the Church to a social doctrine that more explicitly stressed the obligation to speak out in defense of human rights—using the "prophetic voice of the Church"—and to promote peace and justice in this world as well as the next. Vatican II also encouraged those who favored a more democratic Church in which collegiality would be the watchword and the magisterium, or teaching function of the Church, would be shared by episcopal councils nationally by the bishops in their sees and by priests and laity at the local level. Behind this ferment lay the notion that the Church was not just the Catholic hierarchy but "the people of God," a community of believers sharing Christ's legacy and united in a struggle for the common good. By the time Vatican II ended in 1965, John XXIII was two years dead. His successor, Paul VI, was a more cautious pope, but he advanced the main lines of his predecessor's reforms, particularly where Third World areas such as Latin America were concerned.

Vatican II built upon ideas and initiatives pioneered in several countries, including Brazil, but it was also central to legitimating them and promoting others. Gustavo Gutiérrez, a young Peruvian cleric, was inspired by his experience of Vatican II, but found that the translation of its principles into terms relevant to his poor and exploited parishioners in a

Lima slum demanded a new theology. For Gutiérrez, liberating Peru's poor majority from its "bondage" to the wealthy entailed an "Exodus" that the Church had a responsibility to lead. In his rethinking of Catholic doctrine, the structure of societies such as Peru's were "sinful" in oppressing the country's peasants. Salvation required a commitment to social justice, not just to good works, and a communion of people with each other, not just with God.

Gutiérrez's theology offered to the poor a Christ whose "Good News" was their liberation on earth as well as in heaven. His was a call to political activism from the pulpit. Silence would mean complicity with unjust structures and "institutionalized violence." The Church had to help the poor to understand their situation and to overcome their powerlessness and oppression. Only then would true Christian reconciliation be possible. The hour was late, the plight of the poor desperate. The intervention of the Church was both a social necessity and a moral obligation.

Gutiérrez's ideas helped shape the discussions at the 1968 Conference of Latin American Bishops (CELAM), which met in Medellín, Colombia, to apply the conclusions of Vatican II. In a region where poverty was extreme, inequalities glaring, and repression harsh, the translation of Vatican II required an active involvement of the Church in the struggles of the poor, the exploited, and the oppressed. The result was a commitment at Medellín to "a preferential option for the poor" as the way to secure peace, social justice, and human rights, and an endorsement of such new forms of popular participation as the base communities, as a way of reaching the faithful and increasing their involvement in the Church and their community.

Medellín, therefore, reflected not only the reforms of Vatican II, but also the beginnings of grassroots innovations in pastoral practice and the emergence of a specifically Latin American theology, which drew on Marxist critiques of capitalism but above all reflected the region's unique history and conditions. In the wake of Medellín, this "theology of liberation"—in reality a diverse set of ideas by an equally varied group of theologians—would be elaborated by churchpeople of many nationalities, backgrounds, and beliefs into an alternative vision of salvation and church that would reverberate around the globe.

In Brazil, the leading theologian of liberation was Leonardo Boff, a scholarly and sophisticated Franciscan intellectual whose primary concern is the application of liberation theology within the Catholic church. His work is imbued with a vision of Jesus as "liberator of the poor" and of the early Christian church as a community of believers struggling together for salvation, whose clergy were concerned with service not power. Boff strongly supported the new grassroots organizations—which he saw as "reinventing the Church"—and the sharing of the Church's teaching function with laypeople as part of the democratization of the Church that he advocated.

His ideas would influence clerics in his own country. During the decade that followed Medellín, within a frame of reference created by its conclusions and liberation theology, but impelled as well by their own experience, Brazil's bishops would promote a pastoral revolution that would make the Brazilian Church one of the most progressive in the world.

Miracles Are Not Enough

At the time of the Medellín meeting, the Brazilian Church seemed one of the more conservative in the continent, its earlier reformist thrust blunted by the fear of communism and the military coup of 1964. The progressive leadership of the CNBB had been replaced by conservatives who supported the military regime and policies that ignored the plight of the poor. The most salient exception was the Northeast, Brazil's most impoverished and underdeveloped region, whose extreme inequalities of wealth and power generated conflicts its clergy could not ignore.

The decade that followed the military coup was an era of economic growth and political repression. The regime trumpeted its economic successes and silenced its political opponents. Increasingly, the Brazilian Church spoke up for the victims and criticized the costs. The Northeast's

poverty and social conflicts had impelled its clergy to promote both popular education and land reform before the coup. With the foreclosure of
reform and the repression of popular movements under the military regime, the Church stepped in to fill the gap and defend the powerless.

In the escalating conflict between the military and the Church that
followed, the principal victims were local priests and laity; but the chief
target was Dom Hélder Câmara, the reform-minded archbishop of Recife.
During these years, the diminutive but fiery prelate kept up his impas-
sioned defense of human rights and advocacy of social justice, despite
repeated attempts to intimidate him into silence. Faced with the killing and
jailing of clergy and attacks on bishops, the Brazilian Church closed ranks,
with even conservative bishops criticizing the military regime. Dom
Hélder, by the late 1960s an international celebrity, led the way, but other
bishops accompanied him on a journey to increasingly progressive positions that led the military to label many of them "subversives."

The Church's preferential option for the poor prompted the region's
bishops to advocate land reform and—using the prophetic voice of the
Church—to protest "the abandonment of our brothers, the peasants, who
are subjected to chronic injustice and permanent exploitation." By 1973, the
bishops of the Amazon were also condemning the "Brazilian model" responsible for the economic "miracle" as producing a "development that
enriches only a small minority. . . . For the poor, the system offers a future
of increasing marginalization. For the Indians, it offers a future of death."[4]

In the north, where the poor had no access to health care, education,
or legal advice, the Church went beyond protest to create the institutions
that could provide concrete assistance. One was the Indian Missionary
Council (CIMI), which stressed the need to respect the Indians and help
them defend their way of life. Another was the Pastoral Land Commission
(CPT), which was formed to link the Church with isolated rural populations, advise them in their struggles, and act as a catalyst for rural reform.
With its staff of lawyers and social scientists, the CPT documented human
rights abuses and offered legal aid. It also promoted grassroots organizations such as rural unions, and "accompanied" the poor in their struggles

for land and social justice, an activist stance that placed the CPT in the front line of rural conflicts.

But poverty and repression were not confined to the less developed north of Brazil. Nor were the innovations within the Catholic church. If anything, the denial of human rights and social justice were more glaring in the Center-South, where political and economic power were concentrated and experiments with grassroots groups were most intense. In Nova Iguaçú, death squads killed over two thousand people, and Bishop Adriano Hypólito was kidnapped and beaten. This violence created more martyrs for the progressive cause, but it did not halt the spread of these popular organizations.

The most widespread and innovative of these organizations were the Christian Base Communities, neighborhood or village groups of twenty to fifty people who met weekly, fortnightly, or monthly to pray together, study the Bible, and discuss its implications for their own lives. Most base communities in Brazil were created at the initiative of priests or other local pastoral agents, in part to compensate for the shortage of priests. During the two decades following Medellín, an estimated eighty thousand were formed, with a membership of perhaps two million. Although base communities stress popular participation and lay leadership, they are linked to the Church by regular visits by priests, brothers, and sisters, and by courses, writings, and cassettes distributed by the diocese.

Some of the most active base communities were in the new working-class suburbs on the periphery of São Paulo, settled by the flood of rural migrants who flocked to Brazil's industrial capital in search of jobs after 1970. São Miguel is typical of these São Paulo communities, an area of respectable houses and impoverished shantytowns, where many people spend up to four hours a day commuting to and from work in other parts of the city. To ask them to attend a meeting after so exhausting a day is to ask a lot.

Yet some fifty people gathered in an unheated community center on a cold June night in 1991 to discuss the Christian family, the theme for the year chosen by Brazil's National Council of Bishops. Most were leaders of the sector's base communities—male and female, young and middle-aged, workers and middle class. Their metal folding chairs were arranged in a circle to emphasize the democratic character of the meeting. There were two priests present, but neither one wore a cassock, and their leadership was exercised in indirect, subtle ways. Most of the delegates were articulate and poised. "It is by participating" in the base community, Waldo explained, "that I gained this self-confidence."

Waldo is a metalworker with a wife and children. He joined the base community in the early 1980s when his union was on strike and his personal life was in turmoil. It had helped him to surmount those problems and to better understand "the true message of Christ, the liberator of the poor." For Waldo, the base community had revitalized his religious commitment and his links to the Church. It had also given him the opportunity to emerge as a leader and to develop the skills and self-confidence that then enabled him to become a leader in his union and a political activist as well. Waldo's base community is regarded as one of the most successful in the sector, and Waldo's leadership is a major reason for this success.

Waldo's story is not unique. Most members of base communities join for personal or religious reasons. Many become politically aware from participating in the group and some go on to become active in their neighborhood or workplace or party. But base communities are fundamentally religious groups and not all are political in their concerns or progressive in their orientation. Much depends on their leaders and the local priest. Padre David is a North American, one of the many foreign priests brought to São Paulo after 1970 to deal with the enormous problems of ministering to the needs of its millions of poor parishioners. He was one of the foreign priests praised by his bishop of many years for "living lives of true sacrifice." Today, roughly half of Brazil's priests are foreigners, a reflection of the crisis of vocations within the country, but also of the impact of liberation theology in Europe and North America.

Much has changed in Padre David's sector of São Miguel since he began to live and work there over a decade ago, and the church groups he helped organize and orient deserve much of the credit for these improvements. He recalled urging people to talk about their needs: "First one and then the others talked about how when a child fell sick there was no way to get medical care. 'What do you think should be done about this problem?' I asked. 'We need a hospital here or at least a clinic,' they said. I then met with other groups, who said the same thing. So, they began to work together and today there is a modern hospital a few blocks away."

But not all of Padre David's work with grassroots groups is oriented to community action. Many of the residents of São Miguel are recent migrants from rural areas, whose spiritual needs are particularly great. "They arrive here from a village in the Northeast or Minas Gerais, where they knew everyone, and the church was the center of the community, and they are lost, completely lost," he said. "They go to church and they don't know anybody. Even the base communities are too large. So we formed small street groups to meet their needs."

And I remember one night we were reflecting upon the Exodus and the Israelites' forty years of wandering in search of the promised land in the book of Genesis. . . . So I had the people just talk about themselves and their parents, how they got here. . . . It was wonderful. They loved telling their story: how they moved first from the Northeast to Minas Gerais and then to São Paulo, a real journey . . . and why they came to São Paulo, because at that time it was the promised land where they could get jobs . . . and it was marvelous, because they could make the connection between Exodus and their own lives and it was a great help to them, and helped them connect with each other as well. . . . Now you can't do that in a parish church with five hundred people on a Sunday morning! That is why these grassroots groups—the base communities, the street groups, the Bible circles, the workers' commissions—are so important.

Leaders of those grassroots groups credit Padre David and the sisters who work with him for much of their success. "Padre David opened our eyes to the fact that the roots of our problems were in Brazil's unjust society," Waldo said. But to the North American priest, the credit for promoting these grassroots organizations and encouraging the work he did with them went to his Brazilian superiors, particularly Cardinal Paulo Evaristo Arns, the archbishop of São Paulo, and Dom Angélico, the bishop of São Miguel for most of Padre David's years there. "It was Dom Angélico who inspired and oriented our work."

Angélico Sandālo Bernardino was one of nine children born to a metalworker and union activist in the interior of São Paulo State. In 1975, after he had spent fifteen years as a worker-priest in the provincial town of Ribeirão Prêto, Cardinal Arns brought him to São Paulo as bishop of São Miguel. Dom Angélico's predisposition in favor of the poor came from his family background and his practice from his early training in Catholic Action, but his vision of the Church was shaped by liberation theology, which took "our reality in Latin America as its point of departure." It informed the "new road of the Church" in Brazil, the grassroots organizations which were central to the success of a "people's church," and their members, who "were taking possession of the Word of God and mixing it with their lives. Out of this mixture is emerging a new force," asserted Dom Angélico, with whom the Church should share its teaching function, traditionally a clerical monopoly. "There are laity, men and women, who are called to be ministers of the word, ministers of baptism . . . animators of groups, animators of communities," he emphasized. "Within the base communities, there has been a true ministerial explosion."

The neighborhood base communities, moreover, were not the only grassroots organizations promoted in São Paulo. "We also work with groups that have a more acute perception of reality," Dom Angélico explained. "Some from the world of labor or the land, who feel called to work for labor reforms, for agrarian reforms; and others who feel more called to work for health or human rights." Dom Angélico himself felt called to work closely with industrial workers. He had played a leading role in the Pastoral Workers' Commission introduced to Brazil's industrial center by its archbishop, Dom Paulo Evaristo Arns.

Under Cardinal Arns, what had been a conservative diocese became one of the most progressive in the continent. As head of the Church in Brazil's industrial heartland, Arns promoted the Pastoral Workers' Commission to help workers at a time when unions were repressed, strikes banned, and labor leaders persecuted. As leader of an archdiocese that contained one thousand slums, he also encouraged the formation of base communities and other neighborhood organizations, hundreds of which proliferated in the São Paulo area. Although Cardinal Arns modestly affirmed, "The base communities came from the grassroots. All I did was support the pastoral agents who had already started something new,"[5] his bishops and priests stressed how important such "support" from their archbishop had been to their work. It was the combination of international mandate, episcopal support, local priest initiatives, and grassroots leadership that made São Paulo a model of progressive Catholicism and the Brazilian Church a leader in applying the principles of Vatican II and Medellín to the concrete realities of helping the poor to help themselves.

But Cardinal Arns's work was not limited to reforms within the Church. If anything it was his bold public stands on the larger issues confronting Brazil, and his role in opposition to the military dictatorship, that made Dom Paulo one of the towering figures of that traumatic era.

When he became head of the world's largest archdiocese in 1970, Arns was known as a scholarly Franciscan and a diplomatic moderate. But in January 1971 the new archbishop was confronted by the military's imprisonment of a priest and an archdiocesan social worker. Arns personally intervened, but was treated rudely himself and shocked by their appearance and their story: Both had been brutally tortured. Arns responded with a denunciation that he ordered nailed to "the doors of all the churches" of São Paulo and, with CNBB support, circulated nationally, defying the military censors. His elevation to cardinal in 1973 placed the papacy behind his bold human rights stand. "In a public audience in St. Peter's Square," Arns recalled with pride, Pope Paul VI "called me to his side, saying, 'This man defends human rights and so prevents the deaths of innocent people.' "

What further enhanced Cardinal Arns's immense moral authority was that he went beyond protecting clerics and Catholics to defending the human rights of *all* Brazilians. He formed the Peace and Justice Commission mandated by Vatican II and turned it into a human rights commission with a large staff of lawyers and social scientists who investigated, documented, and denounced human rights violations, in addition to assisting the victims and their families. In 1975, the universality of Arns's defense of human rights was underscored by his response to the imprisonment and death by torture of the prominent Jewish journalist Vladimir Herzog, a turning point in Brazil's political opening. Arns not only denounced Herzog's murder, but invited the head rabbi of São Paulo to join him in an ecumenical service in the cathedral. "The stance of Dom Paulo Evaristo was of critical importance," Dom Angélico stressed. "He made it legitimate to defend human rights." To Arns, however, the significance of the Herzog case went further: "For me, Vladimir Herzog was the beginning of the end of torture, of censorship, and of arbitrary imprisonment and disappearances."

Arns also became one of Brazil's most trenchant critics of an economic model that increased inequality even in the industrial heartland of the economic "miracle" and left São Paulo's poverty unsolved. "He has really been a second St. Francis of Assisi," Dom Angélico said, "a man profoundly committed to the poor of God, to the cause of social justice and human rights." Under Dom Paulo, moreover, the São Paulo Church served as an umbrella for the new social movements that would play central roles in the struggle to restore democracy. In that elongated transition, Cardinal Arns also played a leading part, opening his churches for forbidden union meetings and allowing his clergy and laity to help the charismatic labor leader Lula form the Workers' Party, a democratic socialist party imbued with progressive Christian ideals. "By working with the most socially conscious politicians and the most responsible parties," argued Dom Angélico, "we were changing the country."

They were also changing Brazil's Catholic church. By 1978, the Brazilian Church had won an international reputation as one of the most innovative and progressive in the world. This was symbolized that year by the possibility that Cardinal Aloíso Lorscheider, archbishop of Fortaleza, would succeed Paul VI as the supreme pontiff, before the ailing Brazilian discouraged his own candidacy. Later that year, after the brief papacy of John Paul I, the puff of smoke over the Vatican signaled the election of John Paul II, a Polish prelate with a very different historical experience, cultural background, and political orientation than Lorscheider. His accession would have a profound impact upon the divided Latin American Church.

Not all the Latin American bishops were as open to change as Brazil's.

In Argentina, only four out of eighty defended the cause of human rights during the "dirty war" that followed the military coup of 1976, despite the record number of "disappeared." Colombia's hierarchy remained as closed to the new currents within Catholicism as its elite was to demands for social reform and political participation.

Four years after the Medellín conference, the city's conservative archbishop, Alfonso López Trujillo, became secretary-general of CELAM by a narrow margin, determined that the next regional bishops' conference, set for Puebla, Mexico, in 1978, would be different. During the decade between Medellín and Puebla, López Trujillo purged the CELAM staff of progressives and prepared the way for a document that would repudiate liberation theology. Before the key conclave, he sent a letter to conservative bishops urging them to "prepare your bombers, get some of your delicious venom ready. . . . May your blows be on the mark."[6]

Yet despite his efforts and the presence of a new, more conservative pope, Puebla would be different than López Trujillo envisioned. In part, this was because many progressive prelates were selected by their colleagues to attend; in part because the Brazilian Church, the largest and best organized, under the leadership of Cardinal Lorscheider, who presided over the Puebla conference, mobilized the region's progressive and moderate bishops to modify conservative designs. But John Paul II also shaped the outcome of Puebla. This was his first encounter with the poverty of Latin America, and it so shocked him that he endorsed the Church's "preferential option for the poor," while warning against the involvement of priests in politics or any embrace of Marxism.

The result was a set of conclusions sufficiently general and ambiguous to allow both progressives and conservatives to claim "victory." The principles of Medellín and Vatican II, committing the Church to the promotion of peace, justice, and human rights, were reaffirmed, but the debate on how best to promote them—by evangelization or politics, reform or revolution, ballots or bullets, capitalism or socialism—remained unresolved.

Even as the bishops at Puebla were congratulating themselves at their success in forging a consensus in increasingly complex circumstances, the events that would create problems for this consensus were beginning to unfold. In the mountains and shantytowns of Nicaragua, the guerrilla war and popular rebellion that would oust the Somoza dictatorship and inaugurate the Sandinista revolution was entering its final phase. In July 1979, Anastasio Somoza would flee and a leftist revolutionary government would take over in Managua.

At the end of the year, a reformist coup in El Salvador detonated a decade of repression and civil war that would soon claim a martyred archbishop as its most prominent victim. There a few priests even embraced the guerrilla cause and endorsed violence as the only way to change "unjust structures" in the face of an intransigent elite determined to hold on to its privileges and security forces prepared to kill those who demanded reforms. Together, these Central American upheavals would challenge Puebla's consensus.

The Red and the Black

In the heat of an August morning in 1984, the men whirled and danced outside the hilltop suburban basilica of Santo Domingo to honor Managua's patron saint, whose image they had borne on their shoulders from the distant city center. They had been up all night dancing, singing, and praying. Their hands held crosses, but they moved to a more ancient rhythm in trances that evoked the vision quest of their Indian forebears. Their faces were masklike, painted red and black, colors identified not with the saint but with the Sandinista revolution. They would dance until Archbishop Obando y Bravo came to give a sermon sharply critical of the Sandinistas and of those clergy who supported their revolution. With its diversity and conflict, spirituality and politics, Nicaragua represented the divisions and ferment within the Latin American Church in their most extreme form.

In 1979 Nicaragua was a country where most people were poor, land was unequally distributed, and economic progress had been purchased at a high social cost. Like Brazil, which also had an authoritarian government,

Nicaragua had witnessed the emergence of a progressive clergy and grass-roots organizations in the wake of Vatican II and Medellín. Yet, as citizens of a small nation that has experienced dictatorship for most of its history, U.S. hegemony for most of this century, and revolutionary upheaval for most of the past decade, Nicaraguans have also had to struggle with issues that Brazilians have not had to face, such as the relationship between revolutionary politics and Christianity. These issues made tiny Nicaragua a big symbol for both progressives and conservatives within the Catholic church.

Nicaraguans are an intensely devout people, but in 1979 most of them saw no contradiction between being Christians and being revolutionaries. The overwhelming majority of Catholic priests and laity supported the Sandinista-led rebellion against the corrupt, brutal, and exploitative Somoza dictatorship. The growing opposition of the Catholic hierarchy to the Somoza regime culminated in June 1979 in an unprecedented pastoral letter that legitimated the popular rebellion then under way. This step identified the Church with the Sandinista-led rebellion, as did the prominent roles played by base communities and priests within the Sandinista movement.

When Somoza fled in July 1979 and a coalition "government of national reconstruction" replaced him in Managua, several priests were named to cabinet positions, while others headed its economic planning and its literacy campaign. Here at last was a revolution that had come to power with the support of the Church, under leaders who professed their faith, a revolution free from the anticlericalism of the Cuban and Mexican revolutions.

Yet, four years later, relations between the Church hierarchy and the Sandinista state were tense, the pope was demanding that priests leave the government, and Archbishop Miguel Obando y Bravo, the primate of the Nicaraguan Church, had become a leading critic of the Sandinista revolution. What had gone wrong in this partnership between Catholic revolutionaries and their Church?

For the most part, the trajectory of church-state relations in revolutionary Nicaragua paralleled the breakdown of the coalition that had brought the Sandinistas to power. The euphoria that followed Somoza's fall soon gave way to a growing concern among the Sandinistas' centrist partners that their revolution was a Marxist wolf in Christian sheep's clothing. Archbishop Obando y Bravo shared these concerns. He had opposed Somoza, but he did not share the social radicalism of Nicaragua's progressive clergy or their openness to Marxist analysis of Nicaragua's problems. Nor did he accept the legitimacy of their efforts to create what he viewed as a "people's church" sympathetic to the Sandinistas and largely autonomous of episcopal control. On the contrary, he was a staunch anticommunist who worried about the Sandinistas' ideology and the progressives' theology.

Obando y Bravo's opposition was encouraged by the United States, which sought to reverse the Sandinista victory. Washington viewed the Church as the Nicaraguan institution that could lead the internal political opposition to the Sandinistas that would complement its own economic pressures and Contra guerrillas. It looked to the archbishop to legitimate this opposition, and to Pope John Paul II to restore order and orthodoxy to a divided Nicaraguan Church.

For a Polish pope who had spent his life confronting a Communist regime, the triumph in Nicaragua of a Marxist-led revolution with the help of the local Catholic church was a disturbing development. His concern deepened with the Sandinista promotion of the "people's church" advocated by some progressive clergy, which identified "the kingdom of God" with their revolution and challenged the authority of the Catholic hierarchy by drawing on arguments from liberation theology and the conclusions of Vatican II and Medellín. Within this context, the presence of priests in high office within the Sandinista government was a red flag to the former Cardinal Wojtyla. In 1981 the pope ordered the priests to leave their government positions.

Yet only one of the priests had obeyed his directive when John Paul II landed at Managua airport on his first trip to Central America in March 1983. Father Ernesto Cardenal, the minister of culture and Nicaragua's leading poet, was on the tarmac to greet the pontiff. But as Father Cardenal knelt to kiss the pope's hand, John Paul II wagged a finger with the admonition: "You must straighten out your position with the Church."[7]

It was a sign of conflicts to come in a papal visit that was filled with confrontations. The most dramatic took place at an historic outdoor mass in Managua attended by an estimated half-million Nicaraguans, including the nine-member Sandinista Directorate, in a setting dominated by murals of revolutionary "martyrs" and a giant billboard proclaiming: "THANK GOD AND THE REVOLUTION." When the pope seized the occasion to criticize the government for dividing the Church by promoting "unacceptable ideological commitments," organized Sandinista supporters drowned him out with chants of "Popular Power" and other revolutionary slogans. A furious John Paul II tried to silence them, but the confrontation between contrasting visions of the proper relationship between Catholic church and revolutionary state was not so easily suppressed.

Despite his appeals for dialogue and reconciliation, which the Vatican continued to reiterate during the months that followed, the pontiff's visit seemed to harden Nicaragua's political lines and the divisions within its Catholic church. Father Cardenal and the other priests remained in the government and a minority of committed Catholic revolutionaries continued to support the Sandinistas and a "people's church" centered on grassroots groups such as shantytown base communities. A vocal conservative minority, led by Bishop Pablo Vega before his expulsion in 1986, increasingly opposed the Sandinistas, and some even supported the armed Contra resistance to their rule. Archbishop Obando y Bravo himself, at the urging of the Vatican, became less aggressive in his opposition to the regime, but he questioned the legitimacy of the Sandinista draft in their civil war against the Contras, for whom he held a Miami mass in 1985 after his elevation to cardinal. A majority of Nicaraguan Catholics, including moderate bishops, preferred reconciliation within the Church, a negotiated resolution to the civil war, and peaceful reforms within society. In Nicaragua, the Catholic church was as divided as the rest of society and along very similar lines. Yet, by the end of the decade, moderation would prevail both in the pulpit and at the polls—in an election that was the result of a negotiated settlement in which Cardinal Obando y Bravo would himself play a mediator's role.

The impact of the pope's 1983 visit to Central America was not restricted to Nicaragua. In war-torn El Salvador and Guatemala, John Paul II's promotion of a middle way between "rightist authoritarianism" and "leftist totalitarianism" fell on more receptive ears, as did his urging the Church to promote a dialogue between warring extremes.

John Paul II apparently left Central America persuaded that a lasting peace could be achieved only if human rights and social justice were secured, although he urged the faithful to pursue those goals by nonviolent means. But the pope's experience of Sandinista Nicaragua seems to have persuaded him that he had seen the future of liberation theology and the "people's church," and did not like it. In its wake, he reaffirmed his ban on priests in politics and elaborated his own "theology of reconciliation," which held that personal conversion, not class struggle, was the solution to "social sin," and that "spiritual mobilization," not armed revolution, was the way to transform oppressive structures.

Nor was John Paul II willing to accept a democratization of the Church that could call into question his own supreme authority, or those of bishops within their dioceses or priests within their parishes. During the years that followed, he backed efforts to contain the influence of liberation theology, beginning with the largest and most independent of the region's Churches—Brazil.

A New Catholic Counterreformation?

The value placed on consensus and the ascendancy of the National Council of Bishops within the Brazilian Church enabled it to avoid the polarization of a Nicaragua. But during the 1980s, a battle was waged for the soul of Brazil's Catholic church, one in which the pope played a major role.

Tensions between the Vatican and the Brazilian Church had been growing since John Paul II's first visit, in 1980, as the pope sought to limit the autonomy of the world's largest national Church, and they intensified after his 1983 trip to Central America. Equally important, the situation in Brazil had changed as well. After 1980, Brazil's gradual transition to democracy accelerated, and in 1985, the last military president was replaced by a civilian leader elected by the Congress. In the political context of a transition to democracy, most moderates agreed with Dom Eugênio Sales, the conservative archbishop of Rio de Janeiro, that "a new period for the Brazilian Church is beginning. The Church had a very active role in the period when Brazil was becoming a closed society. It was the 'voice of those who had no voice.' Today the parliament, press, and parties are functioning fully. They should speak, and the Church should take care of its own affairs."[8] Moreover, many moderates felt uneasy at the extent to which progressives had become identified with leftist labor unions and political parties. In São Paulo, Cardinal Arns had allowed clerics to promote Lula's Workers' Party and base communities to help in its campaigns. This made some moderates more receptive to the message of conservatives within the Church hierarchy, led by Cardinal Sales.

Sales accepted the decisions of Medellín and Puebla, but sharply criticized the way they were implemented by progressives. Dom Eugênio did not oppose the preferential option for the poor, but he interpreted it to mean "an evangelical option that includes all the poor in any sense of poverty, material and spiritual. The poor," he stressed, "are all those who need God's greatness."[9] In practice, this meant a deemphasis on the economically deprived and a stress on the spiritual needs of the middle class and educated youth. Sales and his top aide, Swiss-born Bishop Josef Romer, did not oppose liberation theology outright, but they damned it with faint praise. "The intentions of liberation theology are good," affirmed Romer, "because it is impossible for the Church in Latin America to live with such great poverty." But "liberation theology also has a big demerit: using Marxism instead of the Gospel and talking of class struggle as if it were a biblical postulate."

Sales and Romer were also accepting in principle, yet critical of practices of Brazil's Christian Base Communities. Here, too, Bishop Romer argued, "the idea and the intentions were good, a way for the priests to share with the people their anguish, fears, and suffering, and to offer them solidarity," but the results had been problematic. "Many people began talking of the base communities as if they were a new church, a *people's* church," he explained.

But, Dom Eugênio insisted, the communities were part of the Church and they required close supervision by the hierarchy. "Their mission is not determined by the people," he stressed.[10] For Cardinal Sales, the mission of the base communities is not social and political action, but deepening the religiosity and promoting the personal transformation of their members. Although many progressives might endorse these goals, they would also insist that for Brazil's poor such personal transformations also required reforming the structures of society, and that entailed social and political action.

"The base communities have great potential to help the poor to help themselves," Romer argued, "but in Brazil they have sometimes been distorted by political interests." That was not the case in Sales's archdiocese. "Here in Rio de Janeiro, we do not allow base communities to be used as a vehicle for a political party, as has happened in other places in Brazil," Romer asserted, with a swipe at Cardinal Arns. "Here in Rio . . . we do not confuse politicization with evangelization. We stress that we want to promote political participation in the name of the Gospel, but not evangelization in the name of a politician."

When the Vatican decided to move against the autonomy of the Brazilian Church and the power of the progressives within it, Cardinal Sales became its chief local spokesman and his archdiocese the showcase for an alternative model of Catholicism than that identified with the progressives. It also promoted the conservative movements of European Catholicism—Opus Dei and Communion and Liberation—which progressives point out were also actively involved in politics. Moreover, where the most progressive of Brazil's prelates stressed that all members of the Church could participate in deepening its teaching function, Sales took a narrower view. Sales stood as well for a more traditional Church in which consultations might occur but the bishop's word was supreme in his diocese and papal authority was unquestioned in the Catholic world.

Beginning in 1984, the Vatican stepped up its attacks on liberation theology. The pope publicly condemned its Marxist elements, Gustavo Gutiérrez was criticized by the Vatican, and Leonardo Boff was officially "silenced."

Increasingly, Pope John Paul II used his power to appoint and transfer bishops to dilute the power of progressives within the Brazilian Church. The most dramatic reversal came in Recife, in the impoverished Northeast, a bastion of liberation theology under the inspired leadership of Dom Hélder Câmara—for decades "the prophetic voice of the Brazilian Church," stressed Dom Angélico. When Dom Hélder retired in 1985, John Paul II nominated a combative conservative as his successor. The result was an undeclared ecclesiastical war in which many priests refused to meet with the new archbishop, who closed two seminaries, fired eight priests, purged the local Pastoral Land Commission, and phased out the Peace and Justice Commission.

But even in São Paulo, where Cardinal Arns remains archbishop, John Paul II has curtailed his power and limited his influence. In 1989, Dom Paulo's huge archdiocese was divided into five independent sees, leaving Arns with the mostly middle-class center of the city, but without authority over many of the working-class suburbs that were the sites of his most progressive innovations. Arns had favored restructuring the world's largest archdiocese, but not along these lines, and his twelve recommendations for the prelates whose authority would replace his own were ignored by the Vatican.

In São Miguel, this meant the replacement of Dom Angélico by a new bishop, who was less supportive of base communities and worker commissions, and more interested in reaching the middle class and talking about the family. Progressive priests like Padre David continued to promote grassroots organizations and democratic participation, while trying to reconcile their concerns with those of a more conservative bishop, but it was a difficult task, and in 1991 there was a sense that the base communities and street groups were in decline.

Part of the problem was "burnout" within the communities, after two decades of intense activity, along with the loss of the most able and committed leaders to political groups such as Lula's Workers' Party within the altered political context of Brazil's restored democracy. But the character and concerns of the new bishop had also played a role. "The energy is gone," Padre David lamented. "Without the support of your bishop, you feel like you are out there on your own."

The priorities of the new bishop had also led to a greater attention to the needs and concerns of the middle class who had bought houses in São Miguel during the past decade. As a result, one lay missionary worried that the shantytown dwellers whom she had cultivated for more than a decade were feeling increasingly ill at ease in the base communities and were participating less. At a 1991 meeting of base community leaders to discuss the family, the theme for the year, a group of workers were openly critical of the new priorities. One asked angrily: "What has happened to *our* concerns?"

Yet, in Vila Brasilândia, on the other side of São Paulo, an area similar in character to São Miguel where Dom Angélico was now bishop, those concerns still claimed priority, and progressive priests and laity spoke of continued support from above and dynamism below—although Arns himself recognized that many CEBs were floundering after "twenty years of existence." Within the archdiocese of São Paulo, Cardinal Arns pressed on with the elaboration of his progressive vision of the Church. After a year-long process that included consultations with non-Catholics as well as Catholics and a vote by a council composed of both clerics and laity, the archdiocese decided in mid-1991 that its priorities for the next three years would be work, health, and housing, "the three main problems of the people," one priest underscored. In the Brazilian Church, much still depended on the local bishops—and they spanned a broad spectrum of views.

The result was a mixed picture of conservative advances and progressive continuity within a national context of moderation set by Brazil's National Council of Bishops. By 1991, one half of Brazil's 298 active bishops had been appointed by John Paul II, giving the CNBB a more conservative cast. But the majority of Brazilian bishops remained moderates, balancing articulate conservative and progressive minorities with their own desire for consensus and concern for the autonomy and unity of Brazil's Catholic church.

By 1991, moreover, progressives themselves had shifted their stand, sometimes as a tactic, more often as a result of their own rethinking or the new concerns of their flocks. Liberation theology, always a diverse body of opinion that reflected the society and era in which it was created, changed over time, as did the stance of its advocates. Dom Angélico talked of "doing the same thing as before, but in a different way."[11] But he also agreed with Bishop Romer that "it is not the function of the Church to get involved in party politics." Significantly, as the political preoccupations of base communities and other grassroots organizations receded—in part out of disillusionment with party politics—spiritual concerns have taken center stage. Dom Angélico's Workers' Commission now organizes pilgrimages and several of Padre David's base communities have constructed chapels around which their activities now revolve. Today few Brazilian bishops favor identifying the Catholic church with a particular labor union or political party. Fewer still condone violence as a political tactic or social strategy.

Yet most back the Pastoral Land Commission, which continues to support Brazil's landless peasants and poor squatters in their struggles to acquire land in a country where 2 percent of the landowners hold 57 percent of the arable land, struggles that cost seventy-five lives in 1990. The Land Commission, with its support for rural unions and land seizures, remains an anathema to conservatives such as Bishop Romer, who criticizes it for "provoking conflicts instead of resolving them." But the CNBB continues to back the Land Commission as fulfilling the Church's preferential option for the rural poor, and both conservatives and progressives accept the CNBB's authority.

Progressive Catholics may be on the defensive in the final decade of the millennium, but they have made their mark on the world's largest national Church. As a result, there is a consensus in Brazil in favor of a strong Church stand on human rights and democracy, and even conservatives talk of the need for social justice and a special concern for the poor. Moreover, as the pope himself stressed on his 1991 visit to Brazil, the Church also endorses land reform and indigenous rights, while opposing policies that have created "two Brazils: one poor and one rich."

Within the Church, the CNBB has established itself as a national force with a capacity to innovate and shape a Brazilian Catholicism. Grassroots organizations such as the base communities have proliferated throughout the region and established a popular participation that the

Vatican may want to redirect into more exclusively spiritual channels but is reluctant to reverse.

Progressive theologians might trim their sails to accommodate the changed winds from Rome, but "people have been touched by the message of liberation theology and *that* is consolidated," one lay missionary stressed, reflecting on her São Miguel experience. "They themselves tell us that, and you can see it in the connections they make between life and faith—even in what they sing." She smiled at the memory: "They love to sing that song about the Exodus that goes: 'We are the People of God'—and, when they reflect on that line, they say: *'We too* are the people of God.' Now *that* won't go away!"

Is Latin America Turning Protestant?

In Ipanema, the beautiful beach community of Rio de Janeiro, Sunday is a special day. Along the broad strand of golden sand one half of the coastal road is closed to traffic, and filled with joggers and exercisers toning their half naked bodies for the weekend ritual. By midmorning the beach is filled with sun worshipers spread-eagled on the altar of hedonism, living witnesses to the Brazilian cult of the body beautiful.

A few blocks away, in the main square of Ipanema, a different ritual is being enacted. In the church of São Francisco, a Catholic mass in Portuguese is being intoned by the parish priest. The church is full, mostly with wealthy couples, many of whom seem more interested in who else is there than in the words of the sermon echoing through its neo-Gothic space. But there are also people of intense religiosity, like the beautiful adolescent girl with long blonde hair and eyes welling with tears, who burns a candle and kneels in prayer at a side altar of the Madonna, oblivious to the larger ceremony around her, then crosses herself and slips silently out a side door.

Across the square, in a plain upstairs hall filled with electronic synthesizer music an equally large number of people are gathered, listening intently to a young man preaching with a hand-held microphone like a religious rock star. Most are poor women, many of whom work in the homes of the wealthy attending the Catholic mass across the square or in the shops and restaurants that line the commercial district of Ipanema. They have come for a prayer meeting of the Universal Church of the Kingdom of God, one of the largest of the Pentecostal sects that are the fastest-growing religious groups in Brazil.

There are now more Protestant preachers than Catholic priests in the world's largest Catholic country and estimates of "born-again" Brazilians range as high as thirty million. They are the most dramatic evidence for the recent inroads of evangelical Protestantism in many of the countries of Latin America, inroads that have led to claims of forty million converts and brought observers to ask: "Is Latin America Turning Protestant?"[12]

The conventional wisdom is that Latin America is Catholic territory, with some 95 percent of its population born into the Church. Until recent decades, Protestant penetration of this Catholic preserve was restricted to Caribbean basin areas colonized or influenced by Protestant nations such as Britain, Holland, and the United States, or else to regions of Protestant immigration, such as the German Lutherans of southern Brazil. But since World War II, Protestants have emerged as a serious challenge to Catholic hegemony in a continent that Rome has long considered its own.

Today roughly half the region's Protestants live in Brazil. The dislocation of rural migrants that posed new problems for the Catholic church created new opportunities for Protestant rivals—such as the Pentecostals, who took off from Methodism's theology and Baptism's recipe for salvation but stressed conversion through direct experience of the Holy Spirit. In 1930, Pentecostals represented only one in ten Brazilian Protestants (aside from the German Lutherans); by 1964, they accounted for seven of eight.

The oldest and largest of these Pentecostal churches is the U.S.-based Assemblies of God. Their Brazilian church was founded in 1911 by two Swedes who received "the call" to spread the word in Pará, at the mouth of the Amazon, while attending a revival meeting in South Bend, Indiana. Their preaching won the support of many of Pará's Baptists and the Assemblies of God expanded from there. In the countryside, they captured the disillusioned followers of a failed local messiah. In the villages, they won converts to their chapels among migrant laborers. In the towns and cities, they held open-air prayer meetings and established "mother churches" that spread a network of satellite churches through urban neighborhoods and surrounding communities. Their stress on the capacity of ordinary people filled with the Holy Spirit to become church leaders turned every member into an evangelist and the Assemblies of God into Brazil's fastest-growing denomination. By 1964 the Assemblies of God claimed one million Brazilian believers, and by 1984, six million, half their Latin American members and roughly half of Brazil's Protestants.

Though the largest, the Assemblies of God were just one of many Pentecostal groups in Brazil to experience a rapid increase in membership during these decades. Some had only a handful of believers meeting in a *favela* shanty or a storefront; others claimed hundreds of thousands of members and boasted ample, modern facilities and access to the mass media. Prominent among the latter were such homegrown churches as "Brazil For Christ," founded in 1956 by Manoel de Mello. He began with the Assemblies of God but formed his own church after becoming a successful evangelist. By 1964, Brazil For Christ claimed three hundred thousand members, recruited largely from the migrant urban lower and working classes, and it was the fourth largest Protestant group in Brazil. Today it has four hundred fifty thousand members. It boasts the biggest religious temple in Latin America, a huge São Paulo mother church that twenty thousand people attend each week, and a media arm that broadcasts nearly three hundred radio programs daily over 250 stations.

The emulation of U.S. media evangelists is even more apparent in the spectacular rise of "Bishop" Edir Macedo and his Universal Church of the Kingdom of God. Macedo began preaching in a Rio funeral home to a few followers and during the 1970s formed his own Universal Church, which today has temples throughout Brazil, a membership estimated in the millions, and a publishing house of its own. Recently, Macedo bought control of Rede Record, a radio and television network, for an estimated forty-five million dollars, a sign of his understanding of the power and potential of the "electronic church" pioneered by such U.S. televangelists as Jimmy Swaggart and Pat Robertson, both of whom have had a major impact on evangelicals in Latin America and the Caribbean. Macedo's ability to accumulate that kind of money is testimony to the hold that he has over his mostly poor followers. Their willingness to reach into their shallow pockets and share their meager earnings was as evident in Ipanema on Sunday morning as their readiness to raise their arms in praise of the liberating power of the Holy Spirit.

Instead of a theology of liberation from worldly evils, Macedo offers a cult of liberation from evil spirits, which he sees as his divine mission: "By the work of the Holy Spirit, our church was raised up for a special task: Liberating people possessed by demons."[13] He calls his church the final stage in the development of Protestantism that began in Europe but will culminate in Brazil:

We have already passed through the era of Protestant prayer with Luther, of revivalist prayer with John Wesley and now we have to go beyond merely Pentecostal prayer, which is in fashion, to the complete prayer that distinguishes us. We have to go beyond saying that Jesus saves [like the Baptists], and baptizing with the Holy Spirit [like the Pentecostals], in order, above all, to liberate people who are oppressed by the devil.[14]

Churches that practice exorcism like Macedo's Universal Church now occupy a significant place in Brazil's broad religious spectrum.

The proliferation of Protestant churches in Brazil is as astonishing as their rapid growth. There are many reasons for this Protestant explosion, and only some are religious. Most boast charismatic preachers, like Manoel de Mello or Edir Macedo. Their enthusiastic practices, including possessions by the Holy Spirit, exorcisms of evil spirits, and speaking in tongues, offer a powerful and immediate religious experience, which brings the believer into direct contact with the divine. Their faith healings are today's miracles, testimonies of grace and substitutes for the modern medicine that the poor cannot afford and rural migrants do not trust.

But there are also more secular reasons for the dramatic success of Pentecostals among the poor migrants to Brazil's burgeoning urban slums. Their informal meetings of small prayer groups are congenial to those intimidated by the anonymous city. Many Pentecostal groups cut their converts off from the surrounding society, creating comprehensible communities comparable to the rural villages they had left. At the same time, these congregations function as support groups that help the new arrivals adjust to urban life and find jobs and housing. They also act as escalators of personal advancement. Stressing sobriety, thrift, and self-help, these groups confer an enhanced sense of self-worth and self-confidence on their members, who are encouraged to participate actively in the life and leadership of the congregation even if they are poor, black, or illiterate. This egalitarian promotion of lay leadership offers the poor the exhilaration of empowerment.

Though many of these features are also characteristic of the Catholic base communities, much of this Pentecostal expansion seems to be at Catholic expense. Claims that Brazilian Catholics were converting to evangelical Protestantism at the rate of six hundred thousand a year may be exaggerated, along with projections that show Latin America becoming Protestant territory early in the next millennium. But the stress that Pope John Paul II laid on the Protestant challenge during his 1991 visit to Brazil and the extent to which the Vatican has retooled to combat it—including plans for its own electronic church, Lumens 2000—underscores the seriousness with which this Pentecostal expansion is regarded within the Catholic church.

Catholic conservatives and progressives may disagree on other issues, but both share a concern with the inroads of evangelical Protestantism among the faithful. Where there is less agreement is over *why* Brazilians are leaving the Catholic church for these Protestant sects. Conservative clerics like Bishop Romer stress the Church's failure "to meet the spiritual needs of the people." At the Rio prayer meeting of Macedo's Universal Church, believers agreed with this diagnosis. Carlos, the teen preacher, told how he had been brought up as a Catholic, but left the Church because it was "spiritually dead." Margarethe, a woman in her thirties with two young children, stressed that she had become a "believer" because in the Catholic church "you worship a dead god and here I found the living God."

In response, the Church has promoted Catholic charismatic movements, with many of these same characteristics, including speaking in tongues and possession by the Holy Spirit. Their rapid spread, with more than one million adherents in Brazil by 1991, suggested that such movements were responding to a real spiritual need. Even progressives were willing to concede that "we have stressed the historical Christ too much and neglected the Holy Spirit," as one catechist in São Miguel put it. The recent spiritual focus of many base communities reflects this realization. Dom Angelico, who claimed to be "concerned about the quality of belief, not the quantity of believers," also recognized a need to improve the evangelical work of the Church. His solution was to create more base communities and street groups, ones small enough to offer the intimate community of the Protestant sects and with a similar degree of participation and shared prayer and self-help.

But to conservatives like Bishop Romer, progressive base communities were part of the problem, not its solution, because they offered "sociological support," not the "human support" that the Protestant sects provided. Romer might be correct, but for different reasons than he claimed. The problem was not the social concerns of the base community, but the character of its members and the burdens of its theology. The base communities, with their stress on Bible reading and analysis of the written word, emphasized a literacy that many poor Brazilians did not possess. In one Rio shantytown, an illiterate woman who left a base community to become a Pentecostal, explained that

I used to be a Catholic. But when these Bible circles came, all they did was read, read, read. There was no more prayer. I felt they only liked those who could read. The Assembly of God is a place of prayer. They know that the Word kills, but the Spirit revives.[15]

But in another Rio *favela*, a teacher who had no literacy problem had also left a base community for an evangelical congregation because of the difference in the people. "Here I found peace and love and a community of help. Elsewhere there is a lot of egotism, but here people always help you with your problems," Cecilia explained after an upbeat prayer meeting

at the local Universal Church. "When I first came here I had many problems—especially family problems. But with the help of the Holy Spirit and
the pastor and the people here, I overcame these problems." In her local
base community, Cecilia had been reluctant to discuss her family problems
in front of neighbors who might gossip about her. The Universal Church
congregation, composed of people who had themselves come seeking help,
was more supportive as a community. "Many people come here desperate
because of their problems, but they leave here feeling peaceful."

Community support might be one reason, but an absolution from
personal responsibility embedded in Macedo's theology was another reason for this inner peace. "I learned that many of my problems were caused
by evil spirits," Cecilia said. In the Catholic church individuals are responsible for their sins. But in the Universal Church, if your husband left you
or your child was unruly or you fell ill, evil spirits are to blame, and prayer,
exorcism, or the laying on of hands could solve the problem.

The return of democracy in Brazil brought Pentecostal leaders into
the political limelight. Most were drawn to a right of center politics and
many supported the military regime of 1964–85. But this identification of
Pentecostals with the political right is not universal, as is often claimed.
One of the largest and most flamboyant evangelical churches—Brazil For
Christ—shared with progressive Catholics their opposition to the military
and espousal of liberal causes. Benedita da Silva, the Rio slum-dweller and
federal deputy, belongs to the generally conservative Assemblies of God,
but represents the same leftist Workers' Party as many progressive Catholics. As a teenager in a Rio shantytown, Benedita had developed leftist
views and leadership skills participating in Dom Hélder Câmara's youth
movement, but she later joined the Pentecostals out of "a need for greater
intimacy with God." Yet Benedita's conversion to a Pentecostal church
with a reputation for conservative views has not altered her politics. She
is as known for her progressive stands in the Assemblies of God as in the
Brazilian Congress: "I belong to a minority there too," she said. "They're
always talking about life after death. I say, fine, but let's not forget life after
birth."[16]

Benedita's family was as much involved in Afro-Brazilian religion as in the Catholic Church. The explosive growth of Brazilian Pentecostalism is not only a response to the Catholic failure to meet the spiritual needs of poor rural migrants, but is also an alternative to the expansion of Spiritist religions of African origin among these newly urban populations.

In Copacabana, Rio's most famous beach suburb, a pastor in the Universal Church of the Kingdom of God is carrying out public exorcisms of evil spirits with the support and praise of his congregation. But these are not just any demons. The names by which the pastor calls them are those of the spirits worshiped by the Afro-Brazilian cults that are the Pentecostals' chief rivals for the adherence of the country's urban poor. The exorcisms are part of "a holy war" declared by Bishop Macedo on the gods of Africa that the slaves brought with them to America. Using a microphone and a powerful speaker system, the pastor commands the spirits to leave the body of an ailing *mulata*. Soon she is rolling on the floor in agony and ecstasy while the congregation condemns the exorcised Afro-Brazilian spirit "to burn in the Holy Fire of Jesus of Nazareth."

Houses of the Spirits

Outside a large building in a prosperous residential neighborhood in Brasília, the parking lot is filled with late-model cars and old jalopies. It is Friday night and inside the white-walled structure an Umbanda ceremony is taking place. The devotees sit on plain wooden benches waiting their turn to consult the spirits. They seem a racial and social cross-section of Brazilian society—white and mulatto, black and Asian. There are poor people with shabby clothing, but most are middle-class and some are stylishly dressed. Mariana is a social worker, Sebastião a construction worker, Herminia a housewife, and Sergio a government bureaucrat. All are members of the same "Spiritist center."

These are but a few of the millions of Brazilians who practice Umbanda, a uniquely Brazilian religion that combines the rites of Brazil's enslaved Africans with the séances of European pseudoscience. "Most Brazilians may be nominally Catholic," asserted anthropologist José Jorge de Carvalho, "but Spiritism is the real religion of Brazil."

Belief in communication with the unseen spirit world has a long history in Brazil. It already existed among indigenous peoples when the Portuguese arrived in 1500. During the centuries of slavery that followed, Africans brought with them to the New World their own rites of spirit possession and divination. But the story of contemporary Brazilian Spiritism begins in France in 1855, when a Parisian spiritualist began to receive messages through a medium from a "Druid" spirit who identified himself as Allan Kardec. These seance "psychographs" formed the basis of "Spiritism," which combined the evolutionism of nineteenth-century Positivism with Christian ethics and Hindu notions of reincarnation. "Kardec's" *Book of the Spirits* reached Brazil in 1857 and within three decades Brazil had become the most important center of Spiritism in the world—a title that it has retained ever since. By 1990 the number of Brazilian Spiritists was estimated at seven million, while those who consulted one of Brazil's fifty-five hundred Spiritist centers in times of need was calculated at twenty million.

In France, Spiritism remained a scientistic philosophy on the margins of polite society. In Brazil, Kardecism was transformed into a mystical religion of the educated middle classes. Its seances centered on miraculous cures through spiritual healing by the laying on of hands, *pases*, and spiritual vibrations designed to draw out evil fluids and infuse beneficial ones, and around moral instruction from "evolved" spirits—including such philosophers and political leaders as Confucius and Abraham Lincoln—intended to free mortals from suffering caused by the errors of their past lives.

Afro-Brazilian and Amerindian deities were recognized as real, but were rejected as "ignorant" spirits whose lack of culture and uncouth behavior barred them from Kardecist rituals, which were carefully controlled by specially trained mediums. Socially, Brazilian Kardecists distinguished themselves from the mostly black, lower-class devotees of Afro-Brazilian religions, such as Candomblé and Macumba, which they referred to disparagingly as "low Spiritism." Yet it was through its fusion with these Afro-Brazilian beliefs that Kardecism would have its greatest Brazilian impact, in the cults of Umbanda.

Umbanda is an urban twentieth-century religion centered on the Brazilian spirits excluded by Kardecism. It was founded in Rio de Janeiro during the 1920s by middle-class whites who had become dissatisfied with an overly refined Kardecism. They were attracted to the drama and power of Candomblé and Macumba, but repelled by their blood sacrifices, black magic, and lower-class settings. Their solution was to synthesize European and African Spiritism into a uniquely Brazilian religion that would satisfy the spiritual needs of the educated white middle class, within whose ranks Umbanda expanded rapidly during the decades that followed World War II.

Umbanda devotees today number in the tens of millions and its cults span a broad spectrum of rites and society. At one end are the thousands of Umbanda centers, often in lower-class neighborhoods, that remain close to its Afro-Brazilian roots. Its *chefes,* or chiefs—Pais or Mães de Santos (Fathers or Mothers of the Saints)—may lead Umbanda ceremonies one day and Candomblé the next. One of the most noted is José Paiva de Oliveira, president of a Brazilian federation of Candomblé and Umbanda, and a faith healer of repute. The walls of his center are decorated with photographs of the politicians and other famous people who have consulted him at his suburban "farm" in Luiziania near Brasília, where Pai Paiva presides over Afro-Brazilian rites that run from "light" Umbanda to "heavy" Candomblé. Each rite has its place in the calendar and space within his compound. There are rooms for each of the West African *orixás,* or deities, of Candomblé, where the initiated celebrate their cults.

Umbanda, on the other hand, is celebrated in the open courtyard of his compound, around a table strung with colored lights on which the symbols of the spirits to be called have been placed. Chief among them are the proud, unconquered Indian Caboclos and the passive but wise Preto Velho slaves from Brazil's past. Here Umbanda's material symbols seem kitsch Candomblé. Its Pretos Velhos are minstrel-show blacks, tourist figurines of pipe-smoking Uncle Toms. Its Caboclos are cigar-store Indians, whose appearance owes more to movies than to anthropology. They might have Brazilian names like Tupinambá, but their feathered head-dresses recall the Comanches of the U.S. plains as imagined by Hollywood Westerns, not the naked, painted bodies of Amazon Indians. These images of Indian and African spirits reflect common myths of Brazil's past, but as visualized by popular culture in the age of global mass media.

Brazilian Candomblé, like Haitian Voodoo, is at bottom the religion of African villages transported to American plantations. Umbanda, on the other hand, is a translation of African beliefs for Brazilian city dwellers, many of them white, middle-class, and upwardly mobile. For Pai Paiva, Umbanda is a simplification of Candomblé, a lesser truth within the same Afro-Brazilian tradition for a broader public. Its songs are simpler—and sung in Portuguese, not Yoruba—and its dances less complex. In Candomblé, he explains, the African *orixás* themselves possess their worshipers; in Umbanda they are usually distant astral figures who are too evolved to descend to earth. Instead, they send spirit intermediaries, most of whom are pseudohistorical figures from Brazil's distant or recent past: Indian chiefs and black slaves, or bandits and prostitutes transmuted into Exus, the unruly messengers of the deities. It is also "lighter" than Candomblé, demanding less of its devotees and restricting its scope to socially accept-able forms of desire and benevolent "white" magic. Its ceremonies do not use liquor or drugs; their stress is on charity and good works; its offerings are honey and grains, not blood sacrifices. "Candomblé is African," said Pai Paiva. "Umbanda is *Brazilian*."

This identification with Brazilian nationalism was a source of Um-banda's broader acceptance after World War II, but there are more pro-found reasons as well for its spectacular leap in recent decades. Pai Paiva's claim that "one third of Brazil's 150 million people are devotees" may be exaggerated, but no one doubts that tens of millions have sought the aid of its *chefes*. Many are rural migrants trying to cope with unaccustomed lives in anonymous cities. Some converted to Protestantism, but more turned to Umbanda, which was closer to their cultural heritage and re-quired less change in their lives, even allowing them to remain nominally Catholic. For these migrants, Umbanda provided both a supportive com-munity directed by benevolent human and divine patrons and an explanation of the difficulties that they faced in their daily lives. Pai Paiva stressed that "Umbanda is a very practical religion," whose rituals are designed to solve the problems of the faithful—their lack of work, money, or love—through the advice dispensed by the spirits, the support network created through the center, and the charity of the *chefe*.

It is this concrete, problem-solving character of Umbanda that many devotees cited when asked why they were Umbandistas. João, a recent migrant from the Northeast, had become an ardent follower when his Pai had arranged for him to work at a factory managed by another member of his local center. Sebastião, a black construction worker, had become a convert when his Mãe had cured an illness with herbs and purification after medical doctors had not helped him. Herminia, a middle-aged *mulata* housewife, had turned to Umbanda when other methods had failed to restore her husband's fidelity. Pomba-Gira, the brazen Exu of aggressive sensuality, had revealed to her that her problems were the result of a spell cast by her rival and showed her how to get her husband back. All had become firm believers in Umbanda because of the concrete benefits they had received.

There are also urban centers of "Pure" or "White" Umbanda throughout Brazil that cater to an educated, middle-class clientele. Brasília's Spiritist Center of Our Lady of Glory—associated with Yemenjá, the Yoruba goddess of the sea—is located on a large lot in a comfortable neighborhood, its identity announced by a discreet sign and the concentration of cars in its ample parking lot. The temple is adjacent to an old-age home supported by the center, a symbol and incarnation of its commitment to the Kardecist ideal of charity. Its decor is austere. The temple walls are pure white, on which the abstract signs of *orixás* have been drawn. In the front is the ritual sector where the *chefe* and mediums receive the spirits, presided over by a statue of a beneficent Madonna. The rectangular hall is divided in half by a fence with gates leading to a back waiting area with simple benches, where the clients wait to consult the spirits. The mediums and their assistants are dressed in white uniforms, like hospital orderlies, but there is an otherworldly quality to the scene and an almost monastic air to the ritual that is accentuated by the a capella singing of hymns.

The Umbanda ceremony begins with an invocation of Jesus, its link to Christianity. A reading from Allan Kardec suggests its other European source of inspiration. The invocation of God the Father initiates the shift to African ritual, as the creator invoked is not the Hebrew Jehovah but the Yoruba Oxalá. The major African *orixás* are then honored in turn, but not called upon to appear. It is with the calling of the spirits, by songs and clapping, that the main part of the ceremony, the possessions and consultations, begins. At irregular intervals, the mediums go into trances and take on the personalities of the spirits. One is visited by the Caboclo Tupinambá, a proud warrior spirit who demands a cheroot and staggers around emitting war whoops. He is known for his herbal remedies. A Preto Velho, Rei Congo, comes next, greeting the *chefe,* telling his story, and offering counsel. His medium is a woman whose voice suddenly drops in register and calls for a pipe.

The petitioners who wish to consult the spirits remove their shoes, enter the ritual sector of the hall, and approach the possessed medium, who embraces them. They are then cleansed by a laying on of hands that draws the evil forces that are afflicting them out of their bodies. This is accompanied by a rhythmic finger clicking that contrasts with the irregular cries of the possessed. Tupinambá bathes his client with cigar smoke and the consultation begins. What had been an orderly ceremony seems to disintegrate into anarchy, as devotees come forward to consult the spirits and some of them are also possessed. But the appearance of dissolved order is an illusion. When all those waiting have been served, the *chefe* comes out of his trance and leads a brief hymn to Yemenjá and a final song of thanks to Oxalá, bringing the ceremony to a close. The devotees genuflect as they leave, as in the Catholic church many attend on Sundays.

Public ceremonies are usually held two or three times a week, although on other nights Umbanda *chefes* may hold personal consultations. But their responsibilities include more than spiritual mediation. They also devote time and energy to the organization of their center, although the larger and more prosperous centers have administrators and boards of directors. Pure Umbanda *chefes* are often middle-class professionals, even military officers or government bureaucrats, who generally do not depend on their Umbanda earnings, and may donate more to their center than they receive from its members.

Their clients, however, often see Umbanda as a source of material as well as spiritual fulfillment. In another Brasília Spiritist center on a Friday night in late June of 1991 more than two hundred petitioners lined up to ask the spirits for the material goods—money, cars, houses—they desired. They had taken numbers earlier in the evening and bought foods such as flour and honey from the center to offer the spirits when their turn came. To the repeated chant of "Now that Exu Two Winds has arrived, life will be better," the consultations begin. The clients wait for their number to be called, then make their offerings to the spirits and line up for the opportunity to consult the Mãe de Santo, an old black woman who has been possessed by the Exu Two Winds, known for his power to grant material wishes.

Despite the chanting, the atmosphere seems less sacred than mundane, with the devotees talking among themselves about what they will ask the Exu for when their turn comes. Many of them are educated and sophisticated, like Mariana, a government social worker, and her teacher friend Katia, who sit next to me so that they can practice their English. They stress that this center also offers Kardecist sessions and "study groups" on other religions. It is an eclecticism common in Umbanda, which has few fixed dogmas and is continually creating new spirits. This has allowed Umbanda to absorb influences from theosophy and Rosicrucianism, as well as aspects of Kardecism, Candomblé, and popular Catholicism. "Umbanda is like Brazil," declared Katia. "It takes in everything, mixes them together, and then makes them into something all its own."

The Center of the World

Brazil's syncretic religious creativity is particularly in evidence at the Valley of Dawn, a cult center of twenty thousand near Brasília. It was founded some three decades ago by Tia (Aunt) Neiva, who was a truck driver until she picked up a "divine hitchhiker" who revealed that she was destined to found the religion for the third millennium—a recurring theme in the "country of the future." Valley of Dawn, the Spiritist religion that she established, is extremely complex, combining Christianity, Umbanda, and theosophy with an imagined re-creation of religions from other geographic areas and historical eras. Today there are Inca, Greek, Egyptian, Islamic, and Tibetan rites among those celebrated at the Valley of Dawn. Most involve "historical" role-playing by costumed acolytes—saris for the Indian rites, jaguar masks for the Aztec—in "sets" whose religious aesthetics almost border on camp, as in a "Temple of Isis" that owes more to Cecil B. DeMille than to Egyptology. And Tia Neiva's theology allows for the revelation of still other rites in the future. To the unbeliever, Valley of Dawn's religious celebrations often look more like Carnival pageants than divine revelations, but it is all done with total seriousness by devotees who may be educated civil servants by day, yet find in its nocturnal rites the satisfying spiritual experience missing in their lives.

If the Valley of Dawn is the ultimate cult of Spiritist syncretism, the Temple of Good Will is the last word in ecumenical mysticism, a New Age pyramid for a futuristic capital. "To many of us, Brasília is not only the capital of our country, but also the center of the world," explained Anselmo. He is studying economics, but even that most rational of social sciences is no barrier to mysticism in Brasília. This modern capital built on an imperial scale at the geographic midpoint of Brazil is also thought of by many of its residents as a New Age global navel constructed over the planet's biggest crystal formation. "An American astronaut confirmed that looking down from outer space," said Antônio Haroldo Franco da Rocha, administrator of the Temple of Good Will, which advertises itself as the ultimate in "unrestricted ecumenicism." It is certainly the ultimate New Age pyramid, constructed of seven slabs of luxurious white marble joined at the top by "the world's largest crystal," a self-styled "conjunction of Superior Spirituality, Culture, Art & Ecology."[17]

Inside the circular sacred space, meditating worshipers follow a stone spiral to the exact center of the pyramid under the great crystal, where they receive its healing energy. Once purified they pray "in their own way" at the altar near the "throne of God," a modern construction representing the four elements—air, earth, fire, and water—before exiting on the far side of the sanctum, in a spatial analogue to their search for spiritual perfection. In a side chamber, a photograph of the founder of the Legion of Good Will, Alziro Zarur, a Brazilian radio personality of Christian Arab descent, is flanked by a picture that groups Jesus, Mohammed, and Buddha with Allan Kardec and Karl Marx. The Legion promises to "inaugurate the Kingdom of the Love of God on earth for all creatures, religious or atheist."[18] It already has groups in North America and Europe, confided administrator Franco da Rocha, but its only temple was in Brasília, "the center of the spiritual world."

The religious imagination of Brazilians seems inexhaustible. There are space-age cults that worship UFOs and others such as Orion, whose mediums contact spirits from other galaxies. There are messianic movements and religions of Japanese origin. Brazilians seem open to a variety of religious experience that belies their Catholic orthodoxy and underscores their social disquiet and cultural diversity. Nor is there any sign of this religious ferment slackening. On the contrary, as a new millennium approaches, there is every reason to believe that the number of new religions will multiply in the "country of the future."

The rise of popular participation within the Catholic church, the explosion of Protestant sects, the expansion of Spiritist cults, and multiplication of new religious experiences all bear witness to a religious revival of unprecedented proportions in Latin America and the Caribbean. Miracles may not always be enough and worshipers may be motivated by the concerns of this world, but this religious ferment is at bottom a testament to the region's intense religiosity. The question that this poses, mused José Jorge de Carvalho, is "how to pass from the world of the spirits—to the world of the Spirit."

Latin American artists and writers have sought to create a "people's art" that would be at once modern and nationalistic. In revolutionary Mexico, muralists like Diego Rivera led the way, with wall paintings celebrating the pre-Hispanic past, such as this depiction of the Aztec market of Tlatelolco.

Chapter 11

The Magical and the Real

Women writers have been increasingly prominent in Latin America and the Caribbean. One of the first to win recognition was Chilean poet Gabriela Mistral, who was awarded the region's first Nobel Prize for literature in 1945.

Political engagement has been another hallmark of the region's artists and writers during this century. Pablo Neruda, Chile's other Nobel laureate, recited his poetry to rapt audiences of workers. He was also a Communist senator and his party's presidential candidate.

Writers and artists have long played prominent public roles in Latin America and the Caribbean, but they have not spoken with one voice on social or political issues. Mario Vargas Llosa, Peru's foremost novelist, has criticized Indian activists and ran for president in 1990 as the candidate of the right.

The blurring of the lines between elite and popular culture and the fusion of genres is characteristic of recent Latin American and Caribbean art. Derek Walcott, the West Indies' leading poet, has also turned his talents to musicals celebrating Jamaican reggae and Trinidadian steel bands.

Brazilian music is a multicultural synthesis that is also truly popular, sung
and danced by ordinary Brazilians, and
not just at Carnival time. Here, Caetano Veloso, one of Brazil's foremost
singer-composers, listens to street kids
sing one of his songs on a corner in
Salvador, Bahia.

The Magical and the Real

M

any years later, as he faced the firing squad, Colonel Aureliano Buendía was to remember that distant afternoon when his father took him to discover ice. At that time Macondo was a village of twenty adobe houses, built on the bank of a river of clear water that ran along a bed of polished stones, which were white and enormous like prehistoric eggs. The world was so recent that many things lacked names, and in order to indicate them it was necessary to point.[1]

With these words, Gabriel García Márquez drew readers into the magical world of *One Hundred Years of Solitude*, the novel that would place Latin America on the literary map of a world that had generally ignored its existence for far more than a century. It was 1967, a watershed year for Latin American writers—the year in which Miguel Angel Asturias became the first Latin American novelist to be awarded the Nobel Prize. In short, it was the year Latin American literature was finally recognized as one of the world's great contemporary literatures and the publishing "Boom" in Latin American writing that had begun a few years before with the appearance of Julio Cortázar's dazzling novel *Hopscotch* reached its peak.

Individual Latin American writers had won acceptance on the world stage of letters before. Gabriela Mistral, the Chilean poet, had been awarded the region's first Nobel Prize in literature in 1945. But never before had so many Latin American writers commanded so large an international

audience and such worldwide acclaim. By 1992, three more writers—
García Márquez, Pablo Neruda, and Octavio Paz—would become Nobel
laureates.

During the 1960s, a literary world that had always regarded Latin
America as a cultural backwater was taken by storm. A new generation of
virtuoso writers burst upon the scene with a literature that was distinctively Latin American, yet experimentally modern. Although they were
socially committed and politically engaged, they were very different from
the social realists who had preceded them. They claimed a liberation of the
imagination from the tyranny of realism and the right to invent new
narratives, a new language, and a new history.

They also were acutely conscious of the unique experience of Latin
America as a region on the edge of "civilization," whose history of uneven
development belied the West's easy faith in the inevitability of progress.
Brazilian novelist João Guimarães Rosa was aware that in the shadows of
the futuristic towers of Brasília was another Brazil in which the Knights of
the Round Table lived in the stories sung by traditional *cantadores,* who
were themselves heirs of medieval troubadors and African griots. García
Márquez conjured up a world in his native Colombia where magic was as
real as money and ice as magical as dragon's eggs. These time warps of
uneven development might be an economic nightmare and a political
problem, but they were a cultural resource for writers ready to mine their
rich lode of myth, history, and paradox.

This new generation of writers was also influenced by the modern
mass culture penetrating their region with the technological revolution.
Many utilized cinematic techniques in their novels and some wrote film
scripts and criticism as well. Manuel Puig wrote novels about the shaping
impact of Hollywood movies and Argentine tangos on the lives of ordinary
people, while Mario Vargas Llosa created a plot around the life of a radio
soap opera writer.

To readers in New York and Paris, this brilliant group of Latin
American writers had come out of nowhere. But the writers themselves
were aware of their debt to the generations before them, as well as to the
rich popular cultures of their homelands. Just as one of their central

subjects was the history of Latin America reimagined, that history also contained the roots of the literary imagination that flourished in the Latin American "Boom" that began in the 1960s.

For Latin American writers, "history" begins with the European "discovery" and conquest of the region, the founding myths that were the subject of the region's earliest literature. "Latin America is the invention of writers," affirmed Puerto Rican novelist Luis Rafael Sánchez. "It was invented first of all by the chroniclers. Those first Latin American artists recognized as writers—Mexico's Sor Juana Inés de la Cruz, "El Inca" Garcilaso de la Vega from Peru—took as a starting point the differences from the [European] world that was trying to assimilate them. . . . The invention of the continent was the first assertion of of our identity." Much of colonial literature was written in praise of the New World, its marvels and uniqueness, ranging from the chronicles celebrating the European "discoveries" and conquests to the praise poems and histories of creole authors. By the late eighteenth century, such works had helped create a sense of their separate identity among Spain's American colonists, a step toward the independence movements of the early nineteenth century.

Independence brought much new writing, although little great literature before the brilliant ironic novels of Joaquim Machado de Assis in late-nineteenth-century Brazil. But these early works—essays, poems, histories—had a value as "founding fictions" that shaped an identity for new nations, inventing "Argentina" as their forebears had invented "America." Nonfiction was often written with the passionate intensity of fiction and with an equally subjective view of its characters. Domingo Sarmiento's *Facundo: Civilization and Barbary,* which denounced the insular caudillos and mestizo gauchos for condemning Argentina to barbarism and identified progress with European culture and values, was a classic of this genre, but there were others. Whatever their literary qualities, they were exercises in persuasion, part of the public debate over the character and destiny of the region's republics and the policies its governments should pursue. They underscore the public role of Latin American intellectuals and artists as the conscience of their societies and in the politics of their nations, enduring characteristics to this day.

By the late nineteenth century, the nations of the region were established and the export boom helped create cosmopolitan cities such as Buenos Aires and a literate elite who looked to Paris for its cultural models. This same era saw the emergence of Modernism, the first literary movement to originate in Latin America. Influenced by French Romanticism and Symbolism, Modernism stressed art for art's sake and staked the claim of Latin America's writers to participate in the international avant-garde. Rubén Darío, the great Nicaraguan Modernist, celebrated the ivory tower of art in his poems, many of which are filled with images of classical sculpture. Yet Darío was drawn to socialism and late in his career was moved by fears of U.S. expansion and his country's tortured history to a growing concern with Latin American realities.

Painting for the People

Latin American painters were the first to try to bridge the gap between art and life, with revolutionary Mexico in the lead. Before the revolution of 1910, painting had been dominated there by conservative fine arts academies whose Beaux Arts styles had been overtaken by the avant-garde in their European countries of origin. But they continued to reflect the conservative tastes of the region's Europhile elites. Diego Rivera (1886–1957) had learned to paint in the Mexican Academy of San Carlos, which in 1907 awarded him a scholarship to study in Europe. There he experimented with different styles, painted with Picasso and Mondrian, and became a significant contributor to synthetic Cubism, before he abandoned abstraction for a neoclassical realism influenced by Cezanne, Picasso, and Giotto. David Siqueiros (1896–1974) also studied in Europe during this era, absorbing the impact of Futurism as well as Cubism.

The Mexico that Diego Rivera returned to in 1921 was a very different country from the one he had left. In the interim Mexico had experienced a revolution, the first great mass upheaval of the century, which had swept away the old order but not yet replaced it with a new one. For José Vasconcelos, the education minister in the government of revolutionary general Alvaro Obregón, it was a unique opportunity to educate his largely mestizo people and to reshape their ideas about their country and its history. In a nation where the vast majority were at best semiliterate, art could substitute for the written texts that most Mexicans could not read.

During the revolution Mexican artists had begun to talk about a mural art for the masses that would be distinctively Mexican. Vasconcelos gathered these young artists around him, lured Rivera and Siqueiros back from Europe, and offered them the walls of his own ministry as a place to begin. Rivera had studied Renaissance frescos in Italy, but it was on a trip to the Yucatán with Vasconcelos in 1921 that he discovered the art that had once adorned the walls of pre-Columbian cities. This new interest in Mexico's indigenous heritage reinforced the revolutionary political aesthetic adopted by the newly formed Union of Technical Workers, Painters, and Sculptors. "We repudiate so-called easel painting," proclaimed their manifesto, which viewed it as "bourgeois" art unsuited for a revolutionary era. They embraced mural painting, declaring: "Art must no longer be the expression of individual satisfaction, but should aim to become a fighting, educative tool for all."[2]

Although Siqueiros, the most political—and polemical—of the group, wrote the manifesto, it also reflected the views of Rivera, who had been impressed by the Italian Renaissance frescos that he saw as "visual books" for an illiterate people. Rivera had returned home with the goal of creating a Mexican Renaissance whose murals would serve a similar pedagogic purpose. One of the lessons he sought to teach with his murals was a positive revaluation of Mexico's indigenous culture, for centuries demeaned by a Europhile elite, a goal that echoed Vasconcelos's own promotion of *indigenismo*. It was taken up by the new union's Declaration of Principles, with its ringing rejection of centuries of imitation of European aesthetic models. "The noble work of our race, down to its most insignificant spiritual and physical expressions, is native (and essentially Indian) in origin," the 1922 manifesto affirmed. "With their admirable and extraordinary talent to create beauty . . . the art of the Mexican people is the most wholesome spiritual expression in the world, and our greatest treasure."[3]

Rivera began assembling his own collection of pre-Columbian treasures, which served as models and inspiration for his forms and themes during the decades that followed. He immersed himself in the study of pre-Hispanic cultures; painted watercolor illustrations for the *Popol Vuh,* the Quiché Maya sacred book, that echoed the original hieroglyphs; and even experimented with indigenous techniques in his painting. His masterful National Palace mural, which depicts the history of Mexico in one giant panel, emulated the serpentine screenfold and pictographs of pre-Conquest Mexico. But for the most part, Rivera's *indigenismo* was expressed in his idealized vision of the pre-Hispanic past as Mexico's golden age and its Indian and mestizo masses as the suffering servants of subsequent Mexican history, with Spanish conquistadors and Yankee capitalists as its villains. "For the first time in the history of art," stressed Rivera, "Mexican mural painting made the masses the hero of monumental art."[4]

Although Rivera pioneered a recognizably "Mexican" style of painting, he shared Siqueiros's grounding in European Cubism and stress on "the magnificent geometrical structure of form," as well as the latter's insistence that "we must absorb the constructive vigor" of Indian culture, but "live our marvellous dynamic age." Siqueiros pressed for an art that would be at once Mexican and modern.[5] Mexico's revolutionary art would be public, readable, nationalist, revisionist—and avant-garde.

Many artists contributed to the Mexican mural movement, but it was dominated by the "three greats"—Rivera, Siqueiros, and José Clemente Orozco (1883–1949). Although the three differed in personality, politics, and styles, they shared a social commitment and political engagement, as well as formidable creative gifts. Of the three, Orozco was arguably the most profound and Siqueiros the most experimental, but Rivera was the most readable and his work came closest to the goal of an "art for the people." His widely reproduced images—such as a heroic Zapata leading his white horse and peasant guerrillas—became revolutionary icons. "The Mexican muralists are the best example of popular art in Latin America," asserted Fernando Botero, the celebrated Colombian artist. "Their influence goes beyond mere plastic values and their importance beyond the works themselves," affirmed Mexican intellectual Luis Cardoza y Aragón. "These artists created in the Mexican people a consciousness of nationality. This dimension of their work is what makes them 'founders' of a truly [Latin] American art."[6]

Mexico's muralists became an inspiration for Latin American artists, from contemporaries in South America to the recent wall paintings of Sandinista Nicaragua and Chicano Los Angeles. In the United States, the impact of Mexican art was also seen in the mural movements of the 1930s and on artists as diverse as Thomas Hart Benton and Jackson Pollock.

Within Mexico itself, the influence of the great muralists was so pervasive and their definition of "Mexican art" so powerful that the problem for later artists was how to escape it in order to create a Mexican art of their own. Rufino Tamayo, who rejected mixing politics with painting and blended European styles with the indigenous mythology of his native Oaxaca, won an international reputation that outlived the muralists and had an impact on many younger artists. But it was Diego Rivera's wife, Frida Kahlo (1907–1954), who showed them the way, with her embrace of a Mexican popular art that was very different from her husband's neoclassical "art for the people."

Kahlo shared Rivera's political commitment in her life, but it did not influence her art, which is as private in its themes and concerns as Rivera's was public. Disabled from a bus accident at age eighteen, Frida Kahlo turned her powerful gifts inward. Her penetrating self-portraits, often with her parents or husband included in ways that reveal their relationships to her, speak to us today with a self-awareness that bridges the gap between eras and cultures. "I paint myself," she explained, "because I am so often alone. Because I am the person I know best."[7]

The Frida she knew was a person who longed to possess the elusive Diego Rivera yet knew that she never could—except in her paintings. In her masterpiece, *Diego on My Mind*, Rivera stares out of her forehead as the "third eye" of wisdom. In *The Love Embrace of the Universe, Mexico, Diego, Me, and Mr. Xolotl*, Rivera is pictured as the baby Diego Kahlo never had, a benign Buddha sitting on her lap, while she in turn is perched in the lap of a half-brown, half-green Mexican earth goddess, supported by a more

abstract universe. Although the painting is filled with witty allusions, at
bottom they are a Mexican Madonna and child transported to a pre-
Columbian paradise.

Frida Kahlo was instinctively a surrealist, whose colors and fantastic
subjects express an inner truth that often seems more profound than the
painterly surfaces of Diego Rivera. Yet Frida Kahlo remained faithful in
her own way to the ideal of *mexicanidad.* But where Rivera looked to the
pre-Columbian past, Kahlo found her inspiration in Mexican popular
culture and in popular forms like the devotional *retablos* painted to thank
the Virgin or a saint for a miracle accomplished or a wish granted. Yet, for
Frida Kahlo, whose life was filled with pain and unable to bear the child
she desired, these painterly devotions took on a bitterly ironic air. There
are no inscriptions of thanks in her *"retablos"* for the divine intervention that
never occurred. "My painting carries with it the message of pain," she
wrote to a friend in the year she died, but "painting completed my life. I
lost three children. . . . Painting substituted for all of this."[8]

Yet despite the intensity of Kahlo's pain—the pain of artistic creation
as well as the pain of her tortured body and psyche—she was a strong and
courageous woman who overcame her private agony to put her unique
artistic vision on canvas. Many of her works are vibrant with sexually
symbolic Mexican fruits and ironic social commentary, as in *The Bride Who
Is Horrified to See Life Opened,* a still life showing a tiny wedding-cake bride
overwhelmed by the lush melons and papaya cut open on a yellow table
bursting with phallic bananas and two hairy coconuts. It is this Frida
Kahlo—the unconventional painter and the bisexual, the celebrant of
Mexican popular culture and fearless explorer of her own identity—who
has inspired a younger generation of Mexican artists trying to escape the
shadow of "the greats" of the mural movement.

Nahum Zenil has taken her ironic use of popular religious painting
one step further, in a series of paintings presenting himself as saint and
sinner. He also uses Kahlo's penetrating examinations of her psyche as the
point of departure for making his own homosexuality, a taboo subject in
macho Mexico, the central theme of his work.

Frida Kahlo's influence has been particularly strong on women artists like Dulce María Nuñez, who has embraced both her psychological family portraits and her celebration of Mexican myth and popular culture. But there are also postmodern touches—a bit of kitsch consciously thrown into a religious painting of the grieving Madonna, or a *Dutch Huitzilopochtli*, a blonde Aztec sun-god who personifies the European misunderstanding of Mexico since its discovery and conquest almost five centuries ago. The heads in her *Tzompontli*, her pop culture "Aztec" skull rack, are not those of sacrificed enemy warriors, but rather photos of criminals, culled from the police blotters of tabloid newspapers, painted in the style of photorealism. "I like to include a disturbing element," she explained, "which is ripped out of context and forces people to see things a new way."

In that Dulce María Nuñez is typical of the current generation of Mexican artists. The young painters are a diverse group who, unlike the muralists, do not form a cohesive generation with a common program. As in the rest of the region, in an age of high technology most are aware of artistic fashions in Europe and the United States, and many are influenced by them. Nuñez herself began as an abstract expressionist before turning to figurative painting. But despite their differences and incorporation of foreign influences, contemporary Mexican artists are heirs to a tradition that stretches back through the muralists of the postrevolutionary era and the popular religious painting of the past century to the images of the Conquest and the sculptures and pictographs of the ancient Aztecs and Mayas. They have made their own synthesis of these disparate elements, creating an art that is personal yet at the same time Mexican.

"My goal is to express the values of the Mexican people," said Dulce María Nuñez. Although she paints on canvas, not walls—"that era was a golden age but it came to an end"—in her own way she embraces the muralists' goal of reaching out to popular audiences. "I paint images from the everyday lives of the people. I am always interested in asking ordinary people for their reactions to my work, and their responses are very rich in meaning for me," she said. "Their understanding of my paintings is often very close to what I want to say, and when I hear their reactions, then I know that I have not erred in what I have expressed in my art."

In Latin America, even artists such as Fernando Botero who rejected the muralists' model as "overly political" were inspired by their revaluation of the region's pre-Columbian culture, creation of an authentic Latin American art, and appeal to popular audiences. For Botero, the renowned Colombian painter and sculptor of volumetric forms, his stay in Mexico was seminal to the development of his own distinctively Latin American style. "I went to Mexico because I had been living in Europe but dreaming of Latin America, and Mexico is the most Latin American country in the region," he said. "I went there in search of Latin American reality." In Mexico, Botero not only encountered the reality of his region and the muralists' portrayal of it, but also discovered pre-Columbian art, which he believes is a "common heritage" of Latin Americans. "My own art not only portrays Latin American themes and subjects, but also reflects my interest in pre-Columbian art," he said, "and it is through my love for this art that something appears in my work that is identifiably Latin American." Botero believes that "if you are a Latin American artist, your artistic language too should be touched by Latin America." It is not something that Botero does "consciously or systematically, [and] it is difficult to define," he said, "but my roots are reflected in my work, and when you look at it, you see immediately that there is something identifiably Latin American about it."

Not all Latin American artists would agree with Botero's concerns with creating a "Latin American" art. Many have looked outside the region for inspiration—before World War II to Europe and since then to the United States—and prided themselves on the internationalism of their abstract artistic language. Roberto Matta, the respected Chilean Surrealist, always refused to identify himself or his art with the continent of his birth. Like Matta, Joaquín Torres-García, the noted Uruguayan Constructivist, lived most of his life in Europe before returning to his native Montevideo in 1933 to found a journal and a school. But Torres-García incorporated Andean influences into his art and affirmed that "our geographical position seals our destiny."[9]

Botero is critical of "the many Latin American artists whose work is derivative of the schools of Paris or New York. . . . I believe that art should have deep roots in the country or continent of your birth," he said. "It gives honesty to your work and a sense of belonging to the place you and your art come from. Egyptian art was Egyptian, Greek art was Greek." Yet they were also universal, and the same, he hoped, was true for his Latin American art. "It is something that belongs to a place, to a continent, even while it belongs to the frame of culture of the Western world in the twentieth century, which we also cannot ignore," he said. "I am not an Indian. I am not living in the twelfth century. I am a Latin American in the twentieth century, where we know everything that has been done in New York or Paris, but, at the same time, we have a different view of it. I try to express this difference in my work, and that is what gives it authenticity."

This difference is also what led Botero's work to be ignored when he first came to New York in 1960. "I was doing the opposite of the abstract expressionism that everyone was doing at the time and they accused me of being provincial," he recalled. "It was very difficult to get galleries interested in my work." Today, Botero's paintings sell for millions and are bought by museums and collectors around the world. But he is most proud of the fact that in his native Colombia "my work is known by everybody, even the lower classes. You can go to a little café or bar anywhere in Colombia and on its walls will be a reproduction of my work. You can ask anybody in Colombia about the painter Botero and they will say: 'The man who paints fat people.' " Despite his international reputation, it was this popular recognition in his own country that he found particularly satisfying, "because art is the expression of a people, and when people identify with the voice of an artist, then that art has succeeded in expressing their reality." It was what made the role of the artist "so unique in Latin America." In the United States, he said, "ordinary people don't care about the work of even the best-known artists." In Latin America, by contrast, "people are waiting for you to say something, and when you do they understand it and come together around it." It meant a far wider audience and a far greater artistic responsibility. "In Colombia, ordinary people are touched by my work."

The Boom

At hundreds of rallies, in places remote from one another, I heard the same request: to read my poems. They were often asked for by title.... And if I have received many awards, awards fleeting as butterflies, fragile as pollen, I have attained a greater prize, one that some people may deride, but not many can attain. I have gone through a difficult apprenticeship and a long search, and also through the labyrinths of the written word, to become the poet of my people.

—*Pablo Neruda,* Memoirs[10]

After painters, poets were the next artists to seek a wider popular audience and a more explicit political engagement in Latin America. Pablo Neruda had first encountered poets reading to mass audiences in Spain during the Civil War, where poets read their work to rapt audiences of troops facing death in the fight against fascism. When he was writing his monumental *Canto General* during the 1940s, Neruda began to read his poems to mass meetings of Chilean workers, most of whom had never read poetry and many of whom were at best semiliterate. "My reward," he wrote, "is the momentous occasion when, from the depths of the Lota coal mine, a man came up out of the tunnel into the full sunlight on a fiery nitrate field, as if rising out of hell, his face disfigured by his terrible work, his eyes inflamed by the dust, and stretching his rough hand to me, a hand whose calluses and lines trace the map of the pampas, he said to me, his eyes shining: 'I have known you for a long time, my brother.' That is the laurel crown for my poetry."[11]

It was a crown that also motivated poets elsewhere in Latin America, such as Cuba's Nicolás Guillén and Nicaragua's Ernesto Cardenal. When revolutionary movements triumphed in their countries they helped shape a "cultural revolution," which began with literacy campaigns and a stress on education that created millions of new readers, and culminated in the formation of "poetry circles" that created thousands of new writers. Cardenal, in particular, became famous for his public readings, which, like

Neruda's, made poetry a mass political event. As minister of culture, he promoted what he termed "an enormous cultural renaissance. Now laborers, artisans, members of the armed forces . . . write poetry—very good, modern poetry," he boasted in 1981. "With the triumph of the revolution," Nicaragua had become "a nation of poets."[12]

Guillén, like Neruda a longtime Communist, went further in advocating a poetry written *for* the masses, not just an elite poetry read to the masses. Guillén criticized writers who surrendered themselves "to sheer games of the imagination, to inconsequential verbalisms, to hateful polychromes, to amusing crossword puzzles, to deliberate obscurities."[13] Guillén's concerns were shared by the social-realist novelists of the postwar era, but not all Latin American writers agreed with him, or with the public voice and social function of poetry. For Octavio Paz, Mexico's leading poet and essayist, poetry was a transcendental experience, not a political act. Yet Paz also embraced the responsibility of writers to act as the conscience of their societies. In his famous essay "The Labyrinth of Solitude" (1950), Paz stripped away the masks that hid the elusive Mexican character, which he criticized as a source of his country's underdevelopment. This literary search for national failings reflected the sense of crisis that beset the region during the years that led up to the Cuban revolution of 1959.

By then, moreover, a growing number of gifted Latin American novelists, including many who embraced a leftist politics and social commitment, had begun to write in innovative styles that were both Latin American and modern. Among them was Guillén's compatriot Alejo Carpentier, who shared Guillén's commitment to Afro-Cuban culture but rejected his insistence on social realism as inappropriate for writers who wanted to capture the reality of Latin America and the Caribbean, a region where the fantastic was also the real. In the prologue to his 1949 novel of the Haitian revolution, *The Kingdom of This World*, Carpentier spoke of the "marvellous real" as its defining characteristic:

> *Given the virginity of its landscapes . . . the challenging presence of the Indian and the Black, the Revelation caused by its recent discovery, the fertile Mestizo*

cultures it has produced, America is far from having exhausted its stream of mythologies. . . . But what is the whole history of America if not the chronicle of a marvellous reality?[14]

Carpentier's view of Latin America's reality as magical, and the writer's task as finding a language to convey it, was shared by the Guatemalan Miguel Angel Asturias. That same year he published *Men of Maize*, arguably the first novel of what would become known as "magical realism," today an overused term that has lost much of its meaning, but then a striking new vision. Both Carpentier and Asturias had traveled in surrealist circles and knew André Breton's view that Mexico was inherently magical. They also shared Neruda's commitment to articulate the collective experience of their people in their work. Asturias had already published *El Señor Presidente* (1946), a pioneering "dictator novel" that introduced a revolutionary new language in which to express the need for a social revolution. He went further in *Men of Maize*, combining surrealist techniques with Maya myth to create a magical realism capable of conveying Maya resistance to the advance of capitalism in their own terms. Other Latin American writers of fiction, such as Peru's José María Arguedas and Brazil's João Guimarães Rosa, also experimented with new narrative techniques to translate oral traditions into literary prose.

Yet the writer who would have the greatest influence over the Boom generation was the Argentine Jorge Luis Borges, the master of cryptic "fictions" who was a conservative in his politics and a universalist in his themes. Borges was an early Modernist who sought to separate reading from reality by writing stories that were distant in time or space, and he insisted that what was magical about Latin America was not its collective consciousness but the refraction of its reality in the mind of the individual writer. In his fantastic, labyrinthine plots, playing with words and ideas, and his assertion that Latin America's marginality entitled it to borrow freely from the world's cultural heritages, Borges set an example of verbal liberation and literary universality that would inspire the generation of virtuoso writers who came to maturity in the Boom.

This liberation would also be made possible by the emergence of a new, enlarged audience for their works, itself a reflection of the expansion of Latin America's cities and the extension of its educational opportunities. Of particular importance for the Boom generation were the new urban, university-educated middle class, mostly students and professionals, who would eagerly await their next book. These new readers allowed writers like Carlos Fuentes, Mario Vargas Llosa, or Gabriel García Márquez to publish in previously inconceivable editions of hundreds of thousands. Writers were now accorded a star status once reserved for matinee idols, with an adoring public listening to their opinions on everything from love to politics. Within Latin America, they found a readership that transcended national boundaries and underscored the creation of a regional culture. Their works were translated into many foreign languages and became best-sellers in countries as distant and diverse as Japan, Germany, and the United States.

Like Borges, the writers of the Boom were critical of the "primitive" and "provincial" novels of Latin American realism. Instead, they embraced a literary experimentation that vaulted them into the world's avant-garde. Julio Cortázar's *Hopscotch* (1963) was designed so that it could be read either straight through in the conventional manner or by jumping numbered chapters in a prescribed pattern, as in the children's game of its title. Vargas Llosa's complex literary architecture in *The Green House* (1966) and Fuentes's exploration of the divided self in *The Death of Artemio Cruz* (1962) were as contemporary as any European or North American author. García Márquez's formal inventiveness rivaled that of any living writer.

Unlike Borges, a central theme of their works is the history of Latin America and a critique of its society and politics. Many were national allegories and often they took the form of family chronicles that extended over several generations. García Márquez's *One Hundred Years of Solitude* (1967) can be read as an allegory of Colombian history seen through the story of the Buendía family of Macondo. In *The House of the Spirits* (1982), Isabel Allende, one of a growing number of women writers to take on the public themes that were once a male preserve, used a similar generational structure to explore the contemporary history of Chile. The story is told from the perspective of its women, the novel's central protagonists, whose visionary powers sustain their family—and their country—in this turbulent century.

The resolutions of their novels stood in stark contrast to the unresolved problems of the histories they related. García Márquez's magical Macondo is protected by its isolation from the outside world for a time. But once that isolation is breached, and both capitalism and class conflict appear, it is doomed "because races condemned to one hundred years of solitude did not have a second opportunity on earth."[15] What is lost with the Macondos of this world is the popular memory that is often the reverse of official histories, with their national perspective and evolutionary bias. The novelist must replace the traditional storyteller and act as scribe for this "lost" view from the backlands. This "last storyteller" celebrates a disappearing popular culture as it fades into and from memory.

Beginning in the mid-1970s, paralleling the fashions in literary criticism, Latin American novelists began to deconstruct history itself. Historical novels like Fuentes's *Terra Nostra* (1975) critiqued the transformation of history into myths that create a usable past whose hidden ideology legitimates an unjust present. Augusto Roa Bastos's towering novel, *I, The Supreme One* (1974) explored the figure of José Gaspar de Francia—the singular caudillo of postindependence Paraguay, who cut off his country from the outside world for over two decades—and dissolved history and its heroes into different kinds of discourse. García Márquez himself, in his novel of the last days of Simón Bolívar, *The General in His Labyrinth* (1989), reduced the mythic Liberator to a mere mortal while humanizing the romantic hero who withdraws from the public sphere into the twilight of his private life. The historical novel became a revisionist history, researched by a team of historians and transformed into a worldwide bestseller by the master of fiction.

In their most recent works, moreover, Fuentes, Vargas Llosa, and García Márquez all seem to have abandoned literary experiments for a more realistic and readable style. To some, this is a sign that they have moved away from their earlier affirmations of the responsibility of writers to their national publics, and have begun instead to write for an international audience, as literary superstars in a global culture.

Yet the region's writers retain the political engagement that was a salient characteristic of the Boom of the 1960s, even where their politics, like Vargas Llosa's, have changed in the interim. This politics was reflected not only in their works, but also in their frequent public pronouncements, themselves a reflection of their new status as cultural stars with large followings of new readers. Vargas Llosa proclaimed that "literature is a permanent insurrection" and turned his 1967 Gallegos Award ceremony for the best novel in Spanish during the preceding five years into a platform for his manifesto on the writer's obligation to act as a critic of their unjust societies—"paradises of ignorance, of exploitation, of blind inequalities, of misery, of economic, cultural, and moral alienation." The region's writers, he concluded, were "rebels with cause."[16] Fuentes likened writers to "sharpshooters," while Cortázar compared them to "guerrillas," and took pride that his "guerrilla novel," *A Manual for Manuel* (1973), was the favorite camp-fire reading of Venezuelan guerrillas. García Márquez, a friend of Fidel Castro and the Cuban revolution, used his 1982 Nobel Prize acceptance speech to appeal for European support of Latin America's revolutionary "attempts at social change." He argued that "the immeasurable violence and pain of our history are the result of age-old inequities and untold bitterness," and that in Latin America the "social justice sought by progressive Europeans [required] different methods for dissimilar conditions."[17]

But their common agreement on the public role and social responsibility of the artist did not mean that the Boom generation of writers shared the same political views. After an initial period in the 1960s, when they all supported the Cuban revolution and opposed military dictatorship and U.S. hegemony, they went their separate ways and ended at different points on the political spectrum, with the Cuban revolution a litmus test.

At first, the Cuban revolution seemed hospitable to artistic experiment, declaring that "within the revolution everything" was allowed, and creating the Casa de las Americas, whose international prizes promoted such new genres as testimonial literature. But as the revolution's difficulties grew, its definition of what was "within the revolution" contracted—and so did its circle of international artistic supporters. The Heberto Padilla affair of 1971—in which a talented but contentious Cuban poet was detained and forced to write a "confession" of his alleged literary political errors—was the turning point. But the relationship between the Cuban revolution and culture was complex, and writers would differ in their judgments—and in their political trajectories. Cortázar and García Márquez retained their leftist loyalties, but Vargas Llosa became a presidential candidate of the right, while Fuentes and Paz positioned themselves to the left and right of the liberal center.

Even within these political camps there have been differences and debates. Paz and Vargas Llosa might share a vehement opposition to the Cuban revolution, but when Vargas insisted at a 1991 symposium in Mexico organized by Paz that "the perfect dictatorship . . . is not the Cuba of Fidel Castro" but "Mexico, because its dictatorship is so camouflaged that it does not appear to be a dictatorship, yet it has all of a dictatorship's characteristics," Paz disagreed sharply. When the Peruvian writer went on to assert that "no other dictatorial system in Latin America has been as efficient or subtle in recruiting intellectuals, by giving them public positions and commissions," and asking them "not for a systematic adulation" but rather "a critical attitude as the best way to guarantee its permanence in power," Paz took offense. Vargas left Mexico the next day, an ironic comment on a symposium about "The Experience of Liberty"—and on a session called "Toward the Open Society."[18]

By 1991 a growing number of Latin American writers agreed with the acclaimed Puerto Rican author Luis Rafael Sánchez that Latin America was "a continent that is complex, diverse, and above all, plural," where "there are one thousand ways to write, just as there are one thousand writers who try to portray the faces of our countries in different ways." In Mexico alone these possibilities ranged "from the testimonial novel of Elena Poniatowska, who looks for the face of Mexico in the voices and faces of the dispossessed, to the literature of Carlos Fuentes, who works with the luxuriant, rich, brainy worlds of the bourgeoisie, and sees the Hispanic American world as a metaphor for the whole universe." In Brazil, Nelida Piñon, one of a remarkable group of women writers who have come to the fore in the wake of the Boom, has "created a literature which takes opera as a starting point," explained Sánchez, whose own new narratives have drawn on the forms and stars of popular music, while adding a postmodern concern with criticism. His compatriot Edgardo Rodríguez Juliá has used parody and pastiche in his apocryphal "chronicle" of a colonial slave revolt. This literary diversity, Sánchez argues, makes it "very simplistic to think that all of this continent writes under the label of magical realism."

A Nation of Artists

"García Márquez is an African author, not a Spanish writer. He may be Colombian, but he comes from the Caribbean [coast]," claimed Derek Walcott, the celebrated West Indian poet, offering a minority view. "Magical realism," he added, "is just another term for the Caribbean imagination." To Walcott, who joined García Márquez as a Nobel winner in 1992, this reflected the African storytelling traditions of the lands that border on this "cultural Sargasso Sea, a fertilizing lagoon of culture."

Walcott grew up with these griot traditions in his native St. Lucia, a small British island in the eastern Caribbean with a French colonial past. "All around me was a rich oral tradition of poetry," he said. "St. Lucia has the *comte,* a story told in couplets in French Creole, and the ballad singer, who sings narrative songs with a lot of tragic wit, a favorite throughout the islands." This tradition is clear in his prize-winning epic poem, *Omeros,* where the black St. Lucian fisherman, Achille, returns to Africa in a dream. There he meets his dead father and hears "the griot muttering his prophetic song of sorrow that would be the past"—the story of his ancestors sold into slavery:

> *We were the colour of shadows when we came down*
> *With tinkling leg-irons to join the chains of the sea,*
> *for the silver coins multiplying on the sold horizon,*

> *and these shadows are reprinted now on the white sand*
> *of antipodal coasts, your ashen ancestors*
> *from the Bight of Benin, from the margin of Guinea.*[19]

But *Omeros* is no celebration of "back to Africa," which Achille imagines "like the African movies he had yelped at in childhood." Derek Walcott sees himself "not as an Africanist," but as a "West Indian," heir to the many cultures that together have made "the Caribbean a multimelodic region." He grew up speaking English and French Creole, "and a third language which is a mixture of the other two." In his island school he studied Greek and Latin, and "learned to recite great poetry" in several languages. At home his mother used to recite "passages from Shakespeare, Gray's 'Elegy' and Wolsey's 'Farewell,' which she knew by heart." These were all part of his West Indian cultural inheritance, Walcott argued: "What composer who with all those melodies around would say: 'I'll just choose one?'"

Yet *Omeros* is much more than just a medley of melodies. Walcott has written a brilliant epic poem in an age when most poets believe it is impossible to write epics. It is an extremely ambitious work, which adapts Homer's *Iliad* to the lives of black fishermen on his native St. Lucia, while reflecting on the history of the Americas, Europe, and Africa. What made this task especially difficult was that Derek Walcott wrote *Omeros* in Dante's *terza rima*—rhymed three-line stanzas—in a language that lacks Italian's easy rhymes. Moreover, he sustained this form for more than three hundred pages of luminous verse. These are extraordinary achievements, which won Walcott awards on both sides of the Atlantic.

Despite its European forms and universal themes, Walcott stresses the Caribbean origins and character of *Omeros*. "Caribbean reality is an epic framework," he said, and the very scale of the poem reflected "the huge experience of the Caribbean," the "oldest part of America," where "scale is related to the sea not the land." St. Lucia might be a small island, but "when you hear the sound of the wind coming across a valley you know that it's coming from clear across the world," he said. "When you think of the next port—it's Dakar in Africa." *Omeros* might be long by contemporary poetic standards, but it "is like a fleabite compared to the immensity of the Caribbean."

Most of Walcott's poems are not epics. In fact, many are brief "praise poems," although they share with *Omeros* a celebration of the Caribbean's natural beauty and rich popular culture. In the Caribbean, he argued, "people talk like poetry, with an instinct first of all to rhythm, not meaning." As a result "the poet is not a freak in the Caribbean: My melody, my syntax is exactly the way my friends speak." Yet, for Derek Walcott, poetry is something that he writes for other poets, not to be read aloud to mass audiences, although as he writes he "hears the echoes on the line."

Still, Walcott has reached out to popular audiences. Helped by his belief that "poetry is music—melody and rhythm"—something he has accused North American poets of forgetting—he has turned his hand to musicals. "In simultaneous cultures like the Caribbean," he asserted, "where people don't just like one thing—they like everything—it was natural for a person to think of poetry and theater as the same art."

In 1991 Derek Walcott was hard at work on *Steel,* a musical set in Trinidad about the creation of the steel band, and based upon the calypsos for which that island in the sun is famous. In *Steel,* Walcott explained, he "was trying to create a new form, by writing one line at a time with a chorus, then another, with the whole thing designed as a poem, as in the Greek or Japanese theater." The test of its success, as in the Greek theater, would be the response in the arena: "if a Caribbean audience, which may include illiterates, is emotionally moved by it."

Caribbean popular culture is also what his musical celebrates. The story revolves around the postwar creation by poor Trinidadians of the steel drum or "pan," which Walcott claimed was "the only new instrument of the twentieth century." It was "one hell of an achievement," he declared, that somebody cut the top off an empty oil drum and "made it into an instrument that was utterly new: What an emblem for a culture!" It was a story filled with ironies, including the creation of a new national culture out of the waste products of the industrial age brought to Trinidad by British colonialism and foreign companies. "The drum, the main symbol of the thing, is an industrial garbage bin that contains Trinidad oil," Walcott explained. "But if it is empty, it also contains Trinidad music."

Steel celebrates that music, beginning with the steel band itself, which Trinidadians have now developed into a sophisticated instrument "that can play anything, even symphonies," marveled Walcott. At the center of Trinidad's music scene was calypso, which Walcott called "a great literary form in music," whose masters, like The Mighty Sparrow and Attila the Hun, were popular poets. They were also "the conscience of the people," whose critiques of social ills and corrupt politicians "preserve the integrity and honesty of the nation," a theme in *Steel.*

But the real heroes of *Steel* are the people of Trinidad. "They are a nation of artists," Walcott affirmed. "During Carnival everyone becomes a performer, dancing or singing." Trinidad is also a nation of critics, whose aesthetic sense and artistic judgments Walcott compared to the ancient Greeks. But it was "not derivative," he stressed. "The Greeks didn't have a steel band: They had a Pan but no pans; they had a Calypso but no calypsos." It all came together around Carnival, the annual pre-Lenten festival that is the focus of the year in Trinidad. The judges of the best calypso bands and costumes are "ordinary Trinidadians." It is a "competition that is judged like the ancient Greek theater." A few weeks before Carnival, "up in the savannah, the best bands compete in the semifinals and the finals on the basis of orchestration. They play the same music," he explained, "and the forty to fifty thousand people who are judging with their applause are not applauding the music. They are applauding the arrangements, and people quarrel about a passage of orchestration," Walcott recounted. "Where else does that happen in the world?"

Musical Missions

"Each year we ask the best songwriters to compose music for us on the theme we have chosen for our Carnival pageant," explained Olodum director Guilherme Arguimimo. "Then we let the people decide." Thousands gather in the main square of Pelourinho to hear the competition and vote with their applause for the song that will become Olodum's anthem for Carnival, when it will be sung and danced by thousands more in the streets of Salvador, Bahia, Brazil's first capital. Among them will be Caetano Veloso.

Veloso is one of Bahia's leading singer-composers, with an international reputation that takes him far from the sparkling blue waters of its Bay of All Saints. Yet, for Caetano, Carnival in Salvador is "an annual event," for which he always returns. "It is such an intoxicating sensation to be in the street—so many people, so disorganized, so alive," he explained. "Many times I cry out of emotion. For me it's the great Dionysian festival. It's like a Greek tragedy. It's primordial times."

Veloso is heir to the rich popular music tradition of Brazil, to many the most varied in Latin America and the Caribbean. It includes the African rhythms brought to Brazil by slaves and incorporated into Afro-Brazilian religions such as the Candomblé of his native Bahia. But it also includes the melodic lines of Portuguese songs and the narrative ballads of the rural Northeast where Caetano was born. The European guitar, African drum, and Amerindian percussion of Brazil's ensembles symbolize the elements in the nation's cultural mix. They all come together in the samba, Brazil's national dance—as much the basis of its famous Carnival as calypso is of Trinidad's. It is this music to which the samba schools stage their annual pageants, with their allegorical themes, sumptuous costumes, and elaborate choreography, South America's match for Trinidad's pre-Lenten festival.

Foreigners who have experienced Rio de Janeiro's Carnival might be aware of this rich musical heritage, but samba first became well known in North America in a virtual self-parody: Carmen Miranda's notorious television romps of the early 1950s dressed as an exotic vamp with a headdress of tropical fruits. To North Americans, she confirmed their image of Brazil as exotic and sensual, but not a country to be taken seriously. For Brazilians, Caetano has written recently, Carmen Miranda was a "cause for both pride and shame."[20] She was the musical emblem for a nation still dependent on "an economy of desserts."

The late 1950s brought President Juscelino Kubitschek's new vision of an industrial Brazil, the country of the future, symbolized by Brasília, his modern new capital. In popular music, this new vision was expressed by the bossa nova, a slowed-down samba that offered an idealized Brazil in its sophisticated nostalgic lyrics and jazz-influenced music. With the sensual Astrud Gilberto as "The Girl from Ipanema," and Stan Getz adding his haunting saxophone to João Gilberto's lyrics and Tom Jobim's music, the bossa nova became Brazil's second postwar international popular music craze.

A decade later, the Brazil of the bossa nova seemed spent and so did the popular culture it had produced. Kubitschek's populist democracy had been replaced by a military dictatorship and its nationalistic industrial policy by an openness to foreign technology and investment. In popular music, too, there was a sense that the old—the elegant bossa nova, the modern Brazilian music of the 1950s—was exhausted, and that a new music which reflected Brazil's new realities was needed. In São Paulo, Chico Buarque de Hollanda, son of one of Brazil's leading historians and intellectuals, created music prized by the middle-class students who opposed the dictatorship, turning Brazil's musical traditions into protest songs against the military regime. In Rio de Janeiro, Milton Nascimento, with his rich tenor and melodic lyricism, made popular a "new samba," which took off from Jobim's jazzy bossa nova, but added the rural rhythms and troubador tradition of his native Minas Gerais and the complex black jazz of Charles Mingus and John Coltrane.

Ironically, it was from Bahia, the historical heartland of Brazilian culture, that the most raucous challenge to the old popular music and the new military vision of Brazil would come. It was called Tropicalism and its leading protagonists were Gilberto Gil, a black singer with a taste for the Beatles, and Caetano Veloso, a singer with European features, hair like Bob Dylan's, and a love of "English neo–rock-and-roll."[21] They were also young men with a musical mission. "Tropicalism was our answer to the prejudices of the time," Caetano explained. "There were people who wanted to dilute and crystallize the bossa nova—a movement of organized beautiful forms—and we wanted to get from the bossa nova what was still alive in it." The way they did this was "to turn the bossa nova inside out, bringing out the guts of Brazilian music. And within those guts," he recounted, they stuffed "everything that Brazil could eat from the outside. In there were all the influences, everything that had happened in the past, everything that was happening then. So you could see pieces of the Beatles, pieces of movies of Godard, the most disparate things from the whole world—Argentine tangos, Portuguese fados, songs played in the whorehouses of Brazil—all this showed up in the middle of our songs." Significantly, Caetano's 1967 hit "Tropicalia" ended "with the exhortation 'Carmen Miranda-da-da-Dada.'"

There were also two other nonmusical inspirations for Tropicalism. One was the 1920s' literary movement of Brazilian Modernism known as Cannibalism. Its key text was Mario de Andrade's novel *Macunaíma* (1928), with its carnival of pastiche and its Brazilian Indian hero, whose consciousness got "left behind on the island of Marapata," so he "grabbed the consciousness of a Spanish American, stuffed it in his head, and got on just as well."[22] Cannibalism's ideologue was poet Oswald de Andrade, who "was inspired by the Brazilian Indians, who had inaugurated this country when they ate Bishop Sardine," Caetano said. "It's true, the bishop's name was Sardinas, and Oswald de Andrade said, 'This is the day that Brazil started.'" In the heterodox vision of Cannibalism, which turned the cultural theories of the day inside out, Brazil developed by incorporating foreign influences and digesting them into a synthesis that was uniquely Brazilian, and thus a form of cultural nationalism rather than cultural imperialism. "The idea of Cannibalism," said Caetano, "was more or less in our minds."

It was also in the minds of Brazilian filmmakers such as Joaquim Pedro de Andrade, who during this same era filmed *Macunaíma,* and Nelson Pereira dos Santos, director of the witty send-up of colonialism, *How Tasty Was My Little Frenchman,* both standard-bearers of the "Cannibalist-Tropicalist" phase of Brazil's celebrated New Cinema. But it was Glauber Rocha, the magical realist of the Cinema Novo, who inspired Caetano Veloso. "The movie *Terra em Transe* [Land in Anguish] by Glauber Rocha was one of the starting points of the idea of Tropicalism, in my head anyway," Caetano recounted. "I saw this movie in 1966 and I was very impressed with the first images of people on the beach. There was a guy with Carnival garb from the municipal theater, another one with a cross in his hand, and that first mass done like an absurd opera." For Caetano, Glauber Rocha presented "an image of Brazil, with a very violent and terrible commentary" that responded to "the violence of the dictatorship." With Tropicalism he set out to express "that violent feeling of oppression" in music.

"Caetano exploded with two concepts—rock music and the whole counter-cultural movement," explained Nelson Motta, himself a songwriter and journalist who "baptized" the Bahia movement with the name Tropicalism. "The idea of Tropicalism was to take all Brazilian values— the trashy ones as well as the good ones, the ugly ones as well as the beautiful ones—and incorporate them into its art," Motta said. When asked what Brazilian music he liked best, Gilberto Gil replied: "There are various ways of making Brazilian music: I prefer all of them." This became a slogan for Tropicalism—and a hallmark of Caetano's music. Veloso sang boleros, sambas, and rock; he composed pop music, classically influenced music, and traditional Brazilian music. For Nelson Motta, "Caetano Veloso was a liberator of the arts in Brazil. He made it possible for each generation to follow its own path," Motta emphasized. "Today you can do what you want without asking anyone for permission. In Caetano's time this was difficult."

In 1967, Veloso and Gil were attacked by the traditional left as agents of cultural imperialism. "There was a great upheaval in Brazil in 1967 as in the whole world, and a student revolt that was latent," Motta recalled. "The greatest form of expression was the music festivals promoted by the TV stations. It was in one of these festivals in '67 that Caetano Veloso and Gilberto Gil introduced their new creations, which provoked an enormous scandal. The music of Gil was very Brazilian, but with arrangements similar to the pop symphonies that George Martin did for the Beatles, which was enough to cause a scandal, and Caetano because he appeared with a rock-and-roll group was seen as a traitor to Brazilian music, as someone who had sold out."

Caetano had intruded the electric guitar into Brazilian music and that was enough to arouse the ire of the artists and students of the left. "They thought that Brazilian music could only be acoustic, with the traditional voice and guitar, as in the bossa nova," Motta explained. "They even went into the streets of São Paulo on a parade with signs saying: 'Down with the electric guitar!' 'Down with imperialism!' 'Viva Brasil!' "

The following year Caetano and Gil were jailed by the rightist military dictatorship. Even afterwards, they were uncertain why, although they had their suspicions. "Caetano was jailed as a subversive because he had long hair or lipstick or danced like Carmen Miranda. All of this was transgressive behavior which provoked indignation. That was enough in Brazil during those times to send someone to jail," Nelson Motta said. In addition, "Caetano had his own way of thinking, his reasoning was complex, and he spoke in metaphors." The military might not understand him, "but they felt that he was dangerous to the youth, a bad example to chastity, against the values of national pride, against religion, against work. They felt he was a threat to the Brazilian family."

Once Veloso and Gil were in jail, the military didn't know what to do with them, so they shaved off Caetano's long hair, kept the two incommunicado for a few months, and then exiled them. For Caetano, "it was a trauma," but also an opportunity to see Jimi Hendrix, the Rolling Stones, and other musicians he had heard only on recordings. "We didn't lose our vision," he said, "nor the fundamental desire that moved us at the time."

When Caetano and Gil returned from exile in Britain after almost three years, they took up where they had left off. "Since we came back from London, I have continued making music, although faced with a different reality, we have tried different things," Caetano said. "And I have tried to maintain the vision of Tropicalism, keeping watch over what is happening in popular music, and keeping alive the flame that inspired Tropicalism, the flame of strong cultural creation. This is my responsibility, my commitment."

In the process, Caetano Veloso has gone from being the enfant terrible of Brazilian popular music to becoming one of its acknowledged masters and most respected authorities. "He always surprises. He has a great capacity to renew himself. He became an artist who is at the same time a classic and from the avant-garde. And his opinion about any artist in Brazil has been decisive for the last twenty years," asserted Nelson

Motta. "Any musician who wants to be a great artist has to have the approval of Caetano." Not all the Brazilian musicians of today do. "There are a lot of interesting creators, but there is a trend toward low-quality products," Caetano observed. "Songs called 'romantic'—low-grade senti-mental songs—are covering the country in a way unseen since the 1950s." The rock-and-roll of the 1980s, which he had welcomed for its "rigor, radicalism, and sophistication," had given way to a worrying "wave of indifference" which Caetano associated with Brazil's economic crisis and loss of confidence. Even Caetano, who has stood for the absorption of foreign influences, was worried that "cultural syncretism can be dangerous now, if it is carried along in this indifference, this lack of self-respect. Syncretism does imply the danger of losing your soul."

Perhaps that was why he had become a strong supporter of the revolution in popular music taking place in Bahia, led by *blocos afros* like Ilê Aiyê and Olodum, which had begun as neighborhood Carnival groups but evolved into a force for musical innovation as well as a movement to promote Afro-Brazilian consciousness. The *blocos* had begun in response to the commercialization of Carnival and its domination by "electric trios," whose amplified sound trucks drowned out the street groups. "Carnival is still the main activity of Ilê Aiyê," affirmed Antônio dos Santos Vovo, its founder and director. "Here in Bahia, you can do a thousand activities, but music is the strongest thing, and everything here ends up in samba. The music is very strong and very beautiful. And with music we say everything. Any information we want to get across we put to music."

There had been changes in Salvador's Carnival since the *blocos* emerged. Ilê Aiyê's pageants today include over twenty-five hundred sing-ers and dancers, and 150 percussionists. Each year there is not only a new song but also a new dance, most of them derived from Candomblé. Now the electric trios quiet down when the *blocos* come through Salvador's Castro Alves Square, "because the people want to sing our songs," said Vovo. Caetano had helped the *blocos* gain respectability by performing "When Ilê Aiyê Goes By," in which a lover says: "You can take me, you can kiss me, you can crush me, but let me go when Ilê Aiyê goes by." Olodum then consolidated their fame with their 1987 Carnival hit "Pharoah." Now the *blocos* are celebrated throughout Brazil and the best song-writers vie for their favor.

They have also acquired an international reputation through their association with such superstars as David Byrne and Paul Simon. Byrne has rekindled an interest in the samba with his recent recordings and world tour with a Brazilian band featuring Margareth Menezes, the sultry young Bahian singer who is revolutionizing Brazilian rock by incorporating Caribbean rhythms and other foreign influences in the tradition of Caetano Veloso and Gilberto Gil. Paul Simon used Olodum as the drum band in *Rhythm of the Saints* and helped Bahia's most dynamic *bloco* to raise funds for a Carnival costume factory by giving a benefit concert for them in late 1991. For Olodum's Guilherme Arguimimo it was "a collaboration with mutual benefits," because "we are making our music known to the whole world." Other Brazilians were more critical. In Vovo's view, "it's only working for one side," because "they still see Brazil as the Third World." For Caetano, the problem is that the collaboration suggests an international relationship "which could be alive but generally isn't." To a North American audience, Paul Simon might seem a daring pioneer, bringing Third World music into the U.S. mainstream. But to Caetano, artists such as Paul Simon didn't take enough risks. "It is done in such a way that they preserve themselves. So you hear those crystalline sounds, with Olodum underneath, and nothing really happens to anyone," he insisted. "When you hear those filtered international versions, you don't really feel what was promised."

Brazilian music critic José Ramos Tinhorão was even more out-spoken in his judgments. "Paul Simon and David Byrne are doing their work," he argued. "They are artists of the colonizing countries, the indus-trial countries, who come here to use the Brazilian sound as raw material in the same way as Americans buy our minerals and then sell us the automobile engines. That's their job." It was up to the Brazilians not to become culturally dependent, as they had become economically depen-dent. Caetano agrees on the importance of "Brazil affirming itself as a nation. There is a need for a cultural identity."

The Importance of Being Luis Rafael Sánchez

If Brazilian intellectuals, in the region's largest and most independent country, were worried about "U.S. cultural imperialism," was it any wonder that this was an obsession of intellectuals in Puerto Rico? A U.S. possession since 1898, Puerto Rico still has only limited self-government, and remains a country that has never been an independent nation, a small Spanish-speaking island subject to the powerful influence of the English-speaking mainland, which is now home to two out of five Puerto Ricans.

The central concern of Luis Rafael Sánchez, the island's foremost writer, is Puerto Rico's Spanish American identity. It is a concern symbolized by the *roqueros,* Puerto Rican teenagers who wear Van Halen T-shirts and listen to North American rock-and-roll, which he dismisses as "an empty music whose lyrics they can't even understand." He takes solace in the fact that the current enthusiasm for salsa among young Puerto Ricans "has served to withstand the invasion of American music." But to Sánchez, this passion for U.S. rock music is emblematic of "one of the big problems in Puerto Rican culture"—the language problem. "This is a Hispanic country. We are precariously bilingual and try to get by in English because we have to," he argued. "But when we reach our inner world, our affections, our feelings, that which moves us, then that's when we go to our boleros, to our *danzas,* to our literature in Spanish," the writer insisted. The *roqueros* might "get carried away by the music, by the beat. But when they need to get into the lyrics, they have to go back to the bolero."

It was this notion that the essence of the Puerto Rican identity lay in its popular culture, and that its own popular music was the best defense against "the excessive Americanization of culture" on the island, that led Sánchez to write his acclaimed novel *The Importance of Being Daniel Santos* (1988), celebrating one of the great Puerto Rican bolero singers of the previous generation. Sánchez had chosen Daniel Santos as the hero of his novel because "he is very Puerto Rican" and was "acknowledged and applauded because of his patriotic fervor. His greatest compositions were

dedicated to the nation, and they celebrated the beauty of our country."
Equally important for Sánchez was that Daniel Santos's songs "addressed
the fact that this is a Hispanic American nation, independent of its size or
particular political situation. Daniel sang to the nation."

Yet, for Luis Rafael Sánchez, the importance of Daniel Santos was not
just that he was a proudly Puerto Rican artist, but also that he was an artist
of that larger Spanish-speaking region which José Martí called "Our America." "Daniel is a great man in Spanish America," Sánchez declared. "In
Mexico, he's known as *el jefe*. In Venezuela, he's an idol. People go to the
stadiums, the ballparks to hear him sing." But for Sánchez, the importance
of *being* Daniel Santos was his personal style as well as his artistic performance. "He's still remembered as an idol, because in his life, although there
was hardship, he liked raising hell, he liked rum, sunrises, and several
women," Sánchez said. "Daniel would stay up all night, and he would begin
his day by drinking again. His legend is not only that of a great artist, but
also the legend of a sentimental prototype. It is the legend of the man with
whom the great mass of the lower class identified."

Sánchez fervently believes that writers are "biographers of their
nationalities." Their "invention of the continent was the first expression of
this Hispanic American identity," and their assertion of this "identity was
a form of resistance." The same was true today, he said. "If we forsook our
identity as a people, our spiritual identity, our roots, we would stop being
what we are and would become just one more minority integrated into the
North American world. We are a people," he insisted. "We are a country.
We are a nation."

Builders of Images

The urgent nationalism of Luis Rafael Sánchez and his concern about the
corrosive impact of foreign cultural penetration on the identity of Spanish
Americans is shared by intellectuals at the other end of the continent and
in other genres. In Argentina, a nation that has long thought of itself as

superior to the rest of the region and regarded Puerto Ricans as scarcely Spanish American, it is a central theme in the work of Fernando Solanas, the country's leading filmmaker over the past three turbulent decades.

Argentina was one of the first nations in the region to develop its own film industry, beginning in the 1930s with popular tango movies starring Libertad Lamarque, inspired by the films made in Paris and New York by the legendary Carlos Gardel. It also produced one of the first Latin American directors to receive international recognition, Leopoldo Torre Nilson, whose *House of the Angel* (1957), an avant-garde film influenced by Ingmar Bergman, about the corruption of innocence in a decadent society, was lauded in Europe. Eva Perón's own film career made Peronists aware of the power of celluloid images, but, ironically, what Argentines now think of as "Peronist" cinema was a product rather of the military dictatorships that kept Perón from political power after 1955.

Solanas's *The Hour of the Furnaces* (with Octavio Getino as codirector) was a response to the military coup of 1966 and the regime's repression of artistic freedom and political liberties. It was a four-hour cinematic polemic in three parts: The first, "Neocolonialism and Violence," critiqued Argentina's economic and cultural dependency and denounced its "foreignizing" elite for selling out the nation. It became an icon of the era's Third World "cinema of liberation." The second and third parts are sectarian in their politics and openly political in their goals: to place film at the service of politics and to mobilize the audience into political action. "Every spectator is a coward or a traitor," part two begins, quoting Frantz Fanon; part three ends with an appeal for insurrection. *The Hour of the Furnaces* was not just an "underground" film, it was an artistic weapon of a political underground. "It was shown in apartments, people's homes, unions, student centers. The screenings were clandestine," critic Josefina Ludmer recalled. *"The Hour of the Furnaces* was an incredible political, intellectual, and artistic event."

For Solanas, *The Hour of the Furnaces* was also an effort to "provide an image of my people," one that replaced the Europhile elites' vision of a cosmopolitan Argentina with that of an impoverished and provincial people struggling for their rights. The value of artists is that "only they can convey their people's sensibility," he explained. "People who can't build their own images are oppressed people, colonized people."

In 1976, another military coup ousted another Peronist government, and another military regime targeted filmmakers and other artists in their "dirty war" against "subversives." Many "disappeared" into the new junta's torture chambers and unmarked graves. Solanas, like many South American artists in that decade of brutal dictatorships, fled into exile, in his case to Paris. For him, as for Caetano Veloso, it was a traumatic yet liberating experience. "Exile is a machinery of emotional destruction," he recounted. "It's a melancholy, nostalgic life. You try to grab hold of things from the homeland, the affections, the memories." Music proved to be "the most emotional language" of his nationalism, and the tango the sound of his nostalgia. "I never consumed so many tangos in my life as in those years of exile." The result was *Tangos: The Exile of Gardel* (1985), a film about Argentine exiles in Paris, which celebrates the tango as the country's authentic popular culture, through which it can be renewed. Solanas used a new cinematic style that showed he had learned film needed to be beautiful as well as didactic in order to engage its audience.

On his return to Argentina after the ouster of the military regime, Fernando Solanas began work on *Sur* (1988), which tells the story of the military dictatorship, its repression, and the traumas of those who resisted, as well as the betrayal of popular expectations of change under Argentina's restored democracy. The title, Spanish for "south," is a metaphor of many meanings. It is the part of Buenos Aires that gave birth to the tango, and houses the working-class barrios that form the base of Peronism. Patagonia, the windswept south of Argentina, with its prison camps but open landscapes, symbolizes the country's choice of paths. In the film, the café "Sur" is where four old men sitting at a "table of dreams" imagine an alternative history—and future—for Argentina. The south is also where Argentines encounter an "American destiny" and discover their country's identity in a world order defined by the opposition between the developed "North" and the underdeveloped "South." It symbolizes both the neocolonial dependence of Argentina's past and the possibility of an independent nation in the future.

Sur built on Solanas's earlier films, but also utilized magical realist juxtapositions and Brechtian techniques to force its audience to confront its political questions. Yet *Sur* is also a hauntingly beautiful and moving film, with evocative images and emotionally engaging characters, which integrates tangos seamlessly into its structure and soundtrack. Two decades after *The Hour of the Furnaces,* Fernando Solanas had finally created an Argentine cinematic masterpiece, for which he was awarded the best director prize at Cannes.

After *Sur,* Solanas set out to make a film about the entire region, although one that shares the concerns of his earlier work. *El Viaje* (1992) chronicles the journey through Latin America of a young Argentine in search of his—and its—identity. But the controversy the film has provoked in Argentina has less to do with its continental concerns than with its national politics. In a particularly surrealistic segment, Solanas presents a vision of a Buenos Aires with flooded streets that are revealed to be open sewers on which a cynical population makes its way in boats. "The metaphor of Buenos Aires as a sewer is closely linked to the current political situation in the country," Solanas explained. "Here, I'm trying to express a world of absolute corruption, of great decadence." It was also a world in which the government was selling off national assets to foreign investors, a "selling of the fatherland" that was an old Peronist accusation against Argentina's elite. Only this time the government in question was a Peronist government Solanas had voted for and supported, adding a bitter note of betrayal to his critique. In a sequence laced with black humor, President Carlos Menem appears as a well-dressed frog-man interviewed by a sycophantic press on the ornate steps of the Congress building leading down to the sewer streets of his capital.

JOURNALIST: *Dr. Frog, what's the reason for your visit?*

    DR. FROG: *The extension of Buenos Aires's sewer system with the support of foreign investors.*

JOURNALIST: *But haven't we hit bottom?*

    DR. FROG: *Not at all. We're sailing full steam ahead.*

JOURNALIST: *Have the waters come down?*

DR. FROG: *The waters will be only slightly above the tabulated values.*
JOURNALIST: *Anything else?*
DR. FROG: *Boys, don't make waves! I'd like to ask you to have faith. You'll come out afloat. Argentines! Dive in and swim!*

An enraged Menem sued Solanas, who had accused him of corruption, for slander and defamation, but the filmmaker stood his ground and repeated his charges. "Generations of Argentines have accumulated the nation's wealth, and these gentlemen have no mandate to give it away," he told the press on the courthouse steps. The following day Solanas was shot by unknown assailants, most likely of Peronist persuasion. "When I'm opening up my car, one of them comes up from behind and shouts at me: 'Now you're going to shut up, you son of a bitch!' " Solanas related. But if that was their goal, the attempt to intimidate him was a failure. Although in great pain, Solanas remained defiantly outspoken, proclaiming, "We Argentines are not going to shut up . . . despite all the intimidation and bullying from the Mafia that is plundering the country! We Argentines are going to defend our patrimony with our nails and teeth." In this struggle, Solanas maintained, the responsibility of the artist remains the same. "The central protagonist of my films is my country" and his subject has always been "the history of my country, which I've told in every way—from documentary, poetic, and fictional viewpoints," he said. "The necessary task of Latin American artists is to rescue images of ourselves"—and "to build images of ourselves."

It was a task that other Latin American filmmakers have also embraced, although not always with Solanas's concern for a new cinematic language with "the utopia of a look that can invent a world."[23] In Argentina, more conventional directors stretched the existing codes of the family drama and melodrama to explore the human rights abuses of the military regime in ways that the broad public would accept. María Luisa Bemberg mesmerized an audience of two million with *Camila* (1984), the story of an aristocratic woman who is executed by the nineteenth-century dictator Juan Manuel de Rosas for having an affair with a priest. The parallels to the more recent repression of the military regime of 1976–83 were clear to the tearful moviegoers who saw this historical melodrama. Luis Puenzo's *The Official Story* (1985) won an Academy Award for its revelations of the reality of the disappeared to supporters of the military regime who had always denied its human rights abuses.

Hector Babenco, an Argentine-born director working in Brazil, also won an Academy Award for *Pixote* (1981), a poignant film about another forgotten casualty of military rule, the millions of street children ignored by Brazil's economic "miracle." Its success made him an international draw and enabled him to adapt *Kiss of the Spider Woman*, Argentine Manuel Puig's novel about the power of movies and love, for Hollywood, with an all-star cast that included William Hurt and Raúl Juliá.

In the 1960s, Brazil's New Cinema had been among the most innovative and acclaimed in the region. It produced such masterpieces as Glauber Rocha's apocalyptic vision of the impoverished Northeast, *God and Devil in the Land of the Sun* (1963), which used surrealistic techniques and operatic pastiche to attack social inequality and the manipulation of the poor by oppressive landowners, social bandits, and religious messiahs. During Brazil's post-1974 political opening, a state agency dominated the film industry, promoting and subsidizing films, including those by critics of the regime. Carlos Diegues, its subdirector, punctured the balloon of Brazilian *grandeza* with his comic *Bye Bye Brazil* (1979), the "Miracle" seen through the eyes of a traveling circus seeking its country of the future in the Amazon. His *Xica da Silva* (1976), about a slave mistress of a colonial mining millionaire who converted her sexuality into a moment of power, subverted official history with its carnivalesque send-up of Brazil's myth of racial democracy as flowing from the concubinal bed. Eight million people flocked to *Xica* and more than ten million saw Bruno Barreto's adaptation of Jorge Amado's sexual comedy, *Dona Flor and Her Two Husbands* (1976), which also won over foreign audiences. By 1980 Brazilian cinema had doubled its audience and market share, drawing nearly one third of the country's moviegoers.

The decade of democratic restoration that followed produced some notable Brazilian films, by both old New Cinema directors and a new generation of filmmakers. Nelson Pereira dos Santos—who in the 1960s had translated Graciliano Ramos's realist novel of the impoverished Northeast,

Barren Lives, into a powerful film promoting social change—made Ramos's autobiographical *Memories of Prison* into a cinematic masterpiece in 1984, transforming the novelist's experience of 1936–37 in dictator Getúlio Vargas's prisons into a critique of the military repression of 1967–73. For Pereira dos Santos, prison was "a metaphor for Brazilian society," a "prison in the broadest sense of the term, the prison of political and social relations which keep the Brazilian people captive."[24]

Among the new directors, women stood out, as they did among the region's new novelists. Suzana Amaral's *The Hour of the Star* (1985), a subtle adaptation of Clarice Lispector's acclaimed feminist novel of 1977 about the closing of women's minds in a chauvinistic society, augured well for the future of the Brazilian cinema at the moment when democracy was restored. Yet, by the end of the decade, Brazil's economic crisis had brought its film industry to a halt, except for those few directors able to secure foreign funding. By then it was clear that television had replaced the cinema as the screen on which the dreams of Brazil's 150 million people were projected.

To Cry Is a Pleasure

I was in Havana in 1984 to make a PBS documentary and Cubans seemed eager to give me their often opposed points of view. Everyone from government officials to dissident intellectuals told me the same thing one day: They would be happy to have dinner with me, but they had to be home by 10:00 P.M. At first I thought it was a curfew, but as I walked the streets of Havana at that hour on a balmy summer night, the open windows revealed lit TV screens pouring forth the same dialogue like some giant sound system. All of Havana seemed tuned to one television channel. But this television event that commanded the rapt attention of the entire population of Communist Cuba was not a Fidel Castro speech or a revolutionary epic by Cuba's own noted filmmakers. It was an historical soap opera by Rede Globo, Brazil's largest commercial television network. Hurrying back to my hotel, I caught the twenty-third episode of "La Esclava"—"The Slave"—which traced the efforts of a beautiful, light-skinned Brazilian slave to find her father and her freedom. The following day that was all people talked about. Reinaldo González, a writer and film critic, confirmed my conclusion. "Liberated Cuba," he declared, with more than a hint of irony, "is enslaved to 'The Slave.'"

Television first emerged in postwar Latin America as a status symbol of the wealthy. By the 1970s it had become a staple of the middle class, and by 1990, urban workers and even slum-dwellers and peasants had access to television in many countries. In Brazil, where popular culture had been local and even radio had been regional, the military regime spurred the creation of a national television network with its advertising; the migration of thirty million people from the rural Northeast to the cities of the south during the 1970s helped create a national audience. Brazil was the world's seventh largest television market by 1990, and Rede Globo the fourth largest commercial network. By then, the *telenovela,* as Latin American soap operas are known, dominated its prime-time programming.

At first Latin America's television programs were mostly imported from the United States. Reruns of "Bonanza" or "Lassie" dubbed into Spanish or Portuguese became hemispheric TV hits. As late as the 1970s, television was viewed by many in the region as a form of U.S. cultural imperialism, projecting North American political ideologies and social values. Yet, by then, programs produced in Latin America itself and tailored to its cultural traditions had begun to appear throughout the region, led by Brazil and Mexico, its two largest countries, whose *telenovelas* became national passions. Between 1972 and 1983, the share of national programs on Brazilian television doubled, from 30 percent to 60 percent, with *telenovelas* leading the way. Significantly, these *telenovelas* were not imitations of U.S. soap operas or movies, but rather adaptations of older forms of Latin American popular culture. In both countries, the first *telenovela* produced was "The Right to Be Born," a 1960s adaptation of a 1948 Cuban radio serial, itself embodying a long tradition of melodrama celebrated by Reinaldo González in his evocative *To Cry Is a Pleasure* (1988). Soon, both Brazil and Mexico were creating their own *telenovelas.*

In Brazil, the roots of the *telenovela* go back still further. Scholars have traced its origins to the oral traditions of storytelling, from the narrative folktales to the topical songs of the traveling *cantadores* of the Northeast. Ironically, the form of oral tradition most similar to the *telenovela* is one of the most ancient, the *cantoria,* in which two poets vie for public favor in a narrative verse contest accompanied by guitar that may go on for several hours or several days, telling stories that range from epic tales of Brazilian social bandits and religious messiahs to mythic marvels, medieval Iberian romances, and current news.

As millions of Brazilians moved from the rural Northeast to towns and cities, so did the *cantadores.* Today they can even be found in the squares of São Paulo, the continent's largest city. Once their audiences learned to read, they had their verses printed up in cheap, brown-paper *folhetos,* hung on a *cordel,* or string, and sold to their listeners. This "literature on a string" idealizes rural values and criticizes the corrosive impact of "progress," but many poems also attack the social inequities of rural Brazil and comment on current events, often with bitter humor. "I used to read romances," said São Paulo *cantador* João Cableira. "Somebody would call me and I sang the poem. I am semiliterate, but *cordel* gave me a broad vision."[25]

Today, leading *cantadores* can be found on records and on the radio, which limits the form but assures the survival of the tradition and represents the transformation of a regional popular culture into a national mass culture. In Brazil, this oral tradition was first reflected in the *radionovela* and then in the *telenovela,* which continued the tradition of complex plots stretched over seemingly endless episodes, and an opposition between good and evil characters, but gradually evolved its own themes, including a focus on contemporary social problems.

In Brazil, the soaring popularity of *telenovelas* during the military dictatorship recalled the political censorship that Vargas Llosa argued conferred a social role on literature in the nineteenth century, when "fiction became a substitute for social science." Under Brazil's post-1964 military rule, with its censorship and managed news, the *telenovela* became a substitute for journalism. "Every night on the national news, we were presented with an idealized false image of our country, an official version," explained Teresa Pinheiro, herself a journalist and a fan of *telenovelas.* "So, all of Brazil waited for the news to end and the *telenovelas* to begin. The *telenovelas* were the only place we could see our social reality reflected back at us."

By the 1980s, Brazilian *telenovelas* had so captured their national audience that they were more popular than such blockbuster U.S. imports as "Dallas," which "was regarded by Brazilians as a curiosity," said Pinheiro, reflecting a "North American reality very different from our own." By contrast, Brazilian *telenovelas* by such masters of the genre as Gilberto Braga "captured the Brazilian reality perfectly, its language, its conflicts over abortion and domestic violence, everything." At the same time, Rede Globo created a series of historical *telenovelas* that "began to define our history epoch by epoch, with a fine eye for historical detail, like good literature, like Balzac," but for a far wider audience. "The *telenovelas* have created characters that symbolize what Brazil was—and is—experiencing," she explained. "That is why we watch them."

By 1991, Globo's rivals were importing Mexican *telenovelas* in an effort to make inroads on its market share, and Brazilians were debating the relative merits of the two leading Latin American producers of this most popular of contemporary genres. Although some Brazilian critics argued that the Mexican *telenovela* was "more realistic," because it incorporated a broader range of social types, Teresa Pinheiro dismissed this as "elitism," pointing out that most Brazilians did not share this view: "Even the best of the Mexican *telenovelas* has a Brazilian audience half the size of the worst of Globo's *telenovelas.*"

The Brazilian claim that Mexican *telenovelas* were more "realistic" would have surprised Mexican critics who have attacked the *telenovelas* of Televisa—Mexico's dominant private network—as unrealistic for their rags-to-riches plots. One of Televisa's harshest critics is Jesusa Rodríguez, a performance artist whose theater group is on the cutting edge of the Mexican avant-garde. She has excited and divided reviewers in Europe and the United States with an all-female *Donna Giovanna* and scandalized audiences in Mexico with a seminude production of Oskar Panizza's *The Council of Love,* in which she plays a lascivious devil hired by the Holy

Family. In Rodríguez's adaptation, Panizza's banned 1894 play about sy-phillis becomes a contemporary commentary on AIDS and self-censorship.

One of her most commented-on recent productions is *To Reach an Orgasm, II,* a parody of the popular Televisa *telenovela,* "To Reach a Star, II" and a send-up of the whole genre. Jesusa uses her *"telenovela"* to criticize the Mexican "everyday family, in which the husband rapes the maid and gets her pregnant, which happens a lot in Latin America, and at the same time gets his wife pregnant." But she also takes on abortion and Mexico's social inequalities: "The wife, who is rich, will go to a good clinic to have an abortion, and the maid will die from a badly performed abortion, as usually happens." In Jesusa Rodríguez's skit, the maid is aborted with a drill on top of the photocopier of a corner store, while the audience squirms with discomfort—a discomfort they do not feel watching a Televisa *telenovela,* in which such a plot would never occur and such visual language would never be allowed.

Jesusa's broader cultural concern is with the homogenization of mass culture imposed by a dominant national television network such as Televisa, whose taste and politics exercises an implicit media censorship in tacit collaboration with the government. She insists on maintaining a self-supporting theater, because "it means that you don't have to work for Televisa," which, for her, is the mass media enemy. Similar concerns have been voiced in Brazil, where Rede Globo dominates the mass media.

Beyond the comparison between Brazilian and Mexican *telenovelas* lies the fact that both are now shown widely in other Latin American countries, and that these foreign markets are taken into consideration by Globo and Televisa in designing their programs. It is part of a larger cultural phenomenon: Contemporary Latin American and Caribbean cul-ture is no longer contained within national boundaries.

There was always a "Latin American" audience for literature, but popular culture was traditionally local or at most regional. The creation of a national popular culture is itself the recent product of new communica-tions technologies, such as film, radio, audiocassettes, and television, and of migration to the cities and increased mass literacy. These same changes in technology and society have also been responsible for the more recent creation of a "Latin American" popular culture. Dance crazes, such as tango, rhumba, and mambo, were the first to travel across borders, although they were mostly urban elite events. Luis Rafael Sánchez has underscored the extent to which bolero singers of the previous generation such as Daniel Santos were stars throughout the region. But now the international character of popular culture is far more pervasive. In Chile, Mexican *rancheras* are now so popular that when a rural grape pickers union in provincial Aconcagua held a song festival in 1990, the winning songs were all *rancheras,* not *cuecas,* the traditional music of rural Chile.

Also new is the appearance of cultural hybrids, even in the most unlikely places. In the shantytowns of Lima, Indian migrants from the highlands have created *chicha* music, which combines Andean melodies with Afro-Caribbean rhythms and electric instruments, creating a cross between salsa and the Indian *huayno.* Salsa itself is an international hybrid, a mix of danceable music that is identifiably Hispanic Caribbean, yet not from any one country in the region. There are even signs of popular music crossing the more difficult cultural barriers between Latin America and the non-Hispanic Caribbean. Today, reggae is danced in Brazil and lambada in Jamaica. Recently, Jamaican singing star Jimmy Cliff spent six months in Bahia developing samba-reggae. "We were pleased to help him," said Olodum's Guilherme Arguimimo. "Our music may sound different, but we share the rhythms of the same ancestors."

Nor are cultural hybrids that cross the borders of genres and the frontiers of nations confined to popular culture. This blurring of lines is a characteristic of the "postmodern" era, in the written word as well as the celluloid image, and Latin America and the Caribbean are no exception to this trend. In *The Importance of Being Daniel Santos,* Luis Rafael Sánchez uses the sentimental music and irreverent lyrics of the bolero to mock elite culture and to erase the lines between high and popular culture, transforming the novel into a cultural hybrid. For Sánchez, this is an explicit goal of his book. He even argues in a section entitled "The Method of Discourse" that *"The Importance of Being Daniel Santos* is a hybrid frontier narrative, exempt from the rules of genre."

For Argentine writer Manuel Puig, movies were the last refuge of the romance. The transformation of his novel on that theme, *Kiss of the Spider Woman,* into a Hollywood film completed the circle. His *Betrayed by Rita Hayworth* (1968) explores the poignant gap between the idealized world on the screens of provincial Argentina and the lives of its audience—the motivation for Eva Duarte to become Evita Perón. Puig's *Heartbreak Tango* (1969) takes the form of a popular serial and includes tangos, radio soaps, and other forms of popular culture. Puig even wanted to publish it as a serial.

Today, the phenomenal success and pervasive influence of the *telenovela* is having a major impact on Latin American writers. In Mexico, one recent soap opera, "Cradle of Wolves," reached an audience of forty million, half the country's population. This has prompted Gabriel García Márquez, the region's best-selling novelist, to go even further than incorporating popular culture in his novels. Confronted with the evidence that one episode of a popular *telenovela* reached more people than all the copies of all his novels published in Spanish, the Nobel laureate decided to write a *telenovela* himself. García Márquez, who began as a journalist and still practices that profession, now works mainly on television and films. "I was always very interested in visual storytelling," he said, "but recently it has become the thing that involves me most."[26]

Writers and artists throughout Latin America and the Caribbean are mixing their media and blurring the lines that traditionally separated high and popular culture. In the process, they have produced a rich and vibrant modern culture that has spread not only throughout the region but into the First World as well. In today's global village the dynamic and diverse culture of Latin America and the Caribbean commands a growing audience.

Despite the differences in their genres and views, styles and agendas, the creators of this varied culture would probably agree with Gabriel García Márquez that:

We, the inventors of tales, who will believe anything, feel entitled to believe that it is not yet too late to engage in the creation of . . . a new and sweeping utopia of life, where no one will be able to decide for others how they die, where love will prove true and happiness be possible, and where the races condemned to one hundred years of solitude, will have, at last and forever, a second opportunity on earth.[27]

The symbols of sovereignty have a deep resonance in Latin American and Caribbean nations whose independence has been limited by more powerful states. In Panama, which began its independent life as a U.S. protectorate, efforts by nationalistic students to raise the Panamanian flag in the U.S. Canal Zone led to bloody clashes in 1964.

Chapter 12

Endangered States

In Chile, Socialist Salvador Allende's 1971 expropriation of U.S.-owned copper mines helped justify a C.I.A.-led "destabilization" of his elected government. Such covert forms of U.S. interference in the internal affairs of "sovereign" nations were more common during the Cold War than military intervention.

Jamaica's Michael Manley (above, left) challenged U.S. bauxite companies by raising their taxes and Washington with his independent foreign policy, leading to international tensions and internal conflicts. Reggae star Bob Marley was a Manley supporter, but in 1978 he brought Manley together with his rival Edward Seaga (right) in an effort to end political violence. Manley's promotion of a Jamaican nationalism based on the popular culture of its poor blacks helped Jamaicans create a new pride in their identity. Mutabaruka (left), a Rasta "dub" poet who recites his work backed by a reggae band, performs in chains as a reminder of slavery and a symbol of the continued subordination of blacks.

In 1982, an unpopular Argentine military regime invaded the Malvinas, or Falkland Islands, ruled by Britain since the 1830s, in an effort to recapture support. The slogan "The Malvinas Are Argentine" served to unify a deeply divided nation, until military defeat shattered the illusion.

In Colombia, leftist guerrillas and cocaine cartels have both challenged the authority of the state. In 1985, M-19 guerrillas seized the Supreme Court, which burned down in the confrontation that followed, leaving many dead. Here, a surviving hostage, face blackened by smoke, flees the scene.

Endangered States

*I*N December 1989 twenty-four thousand U.S. troops invaded Panama and ousted its government. Its ruler, General Manuel Noriega, having surrendered, was spirited out of the country in violation of Panamanian and international law to stand trial in the United States. Its new president, Guillermo Endara, was inaugurated on a U.S. army base and kept from the press and his people until the military operation was over. In its wake, the U.S. military arrested Panamanian labor, political, and community leaders, detaining many for months without charges or trials in defiance of legal norms. U.S. "advisers" placed in government ministries instructed their Panamanian heads on what to do and how to do it. Pentagon psychological warfare experts spread pro-U.S. propaganda throughout the country. The Panamanian Defense Force was reduced from an army to a police force, leaving the U.S. military garrison to defend the "independent" nation and its vital canal. Most Panamanians supported the U.S. intervention as a way to get rid of a hated dictator, but many worried about its implications. "The message was clear," stressed Panamanian sociologist Marco Gandásegui. "Panama was once again a U.S. protectorate."

Although most of the region's leaders wanted an end to Noriega's tyranny, virtually all Latin American nations condemned the U.S. invasion as a violation of Panama's sovereignty. The defense of national sovereignty has great resonance in the other Americas, where many leaders consider sovereignty a basic concept.

It is also an ambiguous and elusive one. Webster's dictionary defines sovereignty as both "supreme power" and "freedom from external control." But like race and ethnicity, sovereignty is a notion that has changed with time and place. In the modern era, sovereignty—supreme power within a territory—became an attribute of the nation-state. Popular sovereignty, where a government's right to rule rests on a mandate from its citizens, became a defining characteristic of democracies. The new nations of Latin America spent the first century of their independent life trying to consolidate their territories and create modern nation-states. Most have spent the past half century wrestling with demands for popular sovereignty in nations where elites have often ruled with scant concern for the majority of their people.

In the Americas, whose nations are all former colonies, there has also been a stress on sovereignty as freedom from external control. Initially, this autonomy was understood in purely political terms, but in recent decades economic and even cultural sovereignty have become causes of concern and political banners around which people in Latin America and the Caribbean have rallied. In the United States, an American nation that is also a former colony, sovereignty is not a salient issue, which sometimes makes it difficult for us to understand Latin American and Caribbean sensitivities on this score. For Carlos Lemos, who had to uphold Colombia's sovereignty as that country's minister of government, the reasons for these different attitudes toward sovereignty are clear. "When you're born as a country in the beginning of your history, like Britain, then sovereignty is something you take for granted. When you're very powerful, like the United States, you do not have to think about sovereignty," he said. But "when you have a small or middle-size country like Colombia, which used to be a Spanish colony, with a weak military and a fragile economy, we have to assert our sovereignty."

As the stress on sovereignty among the new nations of the former Soviet Union has dramatized, it is an issue particularly where weaker states historically have been dominated by larger neighbors. In Latin America and the Caribbean, European colonial powers posed the initial threat to the sovereignty of new nations. But during the past century, the hegemony of an expanding United States, "the Colossus of the North," has been regarded as the most serious challenge. This concern has sparked outbursts of anti-Americanism and played a role in the revolutionary movements that have shaken the region. It is reflected in the culture of the other Americas and in hemispheric diplomacy. Yet this stress on the U.S. threat often obscures the many dimensions of sovereignty, the ambiguities of its challenges, and the complexity of its defense in today's world.

Contemporary threats to the sovereign authority of Latin American and Caribbean states have taken a variety of forms. Panama, where recent U.S. military intervention underscored the limits of a national sovereignty already restricted by the presence of a U.S. military garrison in a U.S.-governed Canal Zone, is the clearest case. Jamaica, where efforts to exert national control over foreign-owned natural resources and assert an independent foreign policy ran into a U.S. opposition that fell short of overt intervention, is a more ambiguous example. Colombia, where a state of questionable legitimacy from the standpoint of popular sovereignty has faced threats to its supreme authority from internal challengers such as guerrillas and drug traffickers, as well as from external powers such as the United States, illustrates other dimensions of the issue. The changing character of the special relationship between the United States and the other American republics, in an age of regional economic integration and concerns over environmental protection and human rights, reveals that the continued relevance of national sovereignty itself is being called into question.

Between Two Seas, Within Two Empires

"Panama is a country whose history has been shaped by its geography," said Vice President Ricardo Arias Calderón in May 1991. Geography granted Panama the boon and burden of being the shortest land bridge between the Atlantic and Pacific oceans. During the colonial era, this made it a center of international commerce, where the silver of Peru was exchanged for the manufactures of Europe. "From the start, Panama has been a country of [goods in] transit," said Arias Calderón. "This has produced an economy oriented to services, not agriculture or industry." It also made Panama "a country with a special relationship to a metropolitan power"—first Spain and now the United States.

Panama became a focus of U.S. interest during the California gold rush, when railroads were built across its narrow isthmus to speed miners and goods to the Pacific coast, avoiding the long sea journey around Cape Horn. Even then it was clear that a canal would be better than a railroad, and an 1850 treaty between England and the United States assured both equal power over a future waterway. Panama had become a neglected department of Colombia, a nation jealous of its sovereignty. In 1878, Ferdinand de Lesseps, the builder of the Suez Canal, won a Colombian concession to repeat his performance in Panama, but he gave up the project a decade later in the face of financial and technical difficulties, leaving a French company to sell his concession to the highest bidder. Although a sea-level canal through Nicaragua would have been easier and cheaper to build, lobbyists persuaded the U.S. Republican party to make a Panama canal part of its 1900 election platform and the U.S. Congress to pay forty million dollars for the French concession. But in 1903, the Colombian Congress refused to ratify the Hay-Herrán Treaty, which gave the United States a one hundred-year lease on a ten-kilometer strip on both sides of the canal.

Teddy Roosevelt was president, and he was not a man to take no for an answer or wait patiently for a negotiated solution. Instead, he encouraged the small Panamanian independence movement, which rebelled in November 1903. U.S. warships blocked Colombian forces sent to suppress the revolt, and three days later Washington recognized Panama's "independence." The payoff came only twelve days later, when Phillippe Bunau-Varilla, the French company's agent—"neither Panamanian nor a diplomat"[1]—put on his new hat as Panama's envoy to Washington and agreed to the permanent cession of a ten-mile-wide canal zone that the United States would control "to the entire exclusion of the exercise by the Republic of Panama of any sovereign rights." The Hay-Bunau-Varilla Treaty and Panama's 1904 constitution further eroded the new nation's sovereignty by empowering the United States to appropriate other lands and waters it deemed necessary to construct and maintain the canal; to police the cities at either end of the waterway; and to intervene anywhere in the country with its troops "to reestablish the public peace and constitutional order." The Panamanian army was downgraded to a police force and the United States undertook to "maintain the independence of the Republic of Panama." The new republic began its national life as a U.S. protectorate.

The Hegemonic Presumption

For many in Latin America, Panama—with its U.S. garrisons and proconsuls—symbolized the North American threat to the sovereignty of the nations of the region. Nor was it their only cause for concern. Since 1823, when the Monroe Doctrine declared the hemisphere off-limits to new European colonization, Latin Americans have worried that Washington's real goal was to transform the region into a U.S. sphere of influence. The U.S.-Mexican War of 1845–48, and the forced cession of half of Mexico that followed, fueled these fears south of our borders, as did the ideology of Manifest Destiny, with its assertion of a God-given U.S. right to appropriate the territory of others in pursuit of its divinely ordained continental expansion.

By midcentury, the United States had achieved naval parity with Britain in the Caribbean. But the United States could not yet compete in economic terms with its European rival for the trade and investment of Latin America and the Caribbean.

By the end of the nineteenth century, the situation had changed. The United States was a budding industrial and military power that was beginning to look beyond its own "last frontier." It was the age of imperialism and the United States was a latecomer to the race for overseas colonies. Africa and Asia had already been carved up, leaving Latin America as the remaining site for a U.S. place in the sun. Increasingly, Washington did advance a vision of the Americas as a U.S. sphere of influence. This "hegemonic presumption" was asserted in the Olney Doctrine of 1895, which declared that "the United States is practically sovereign on this continent and its fiat is law." Three years later Washington declared war on Spain and took over Madrid's remaining Caribbean possessions, transforming Cuba into a protectorate and Puerto Rico into a colony. Then came Panama, and Latin American fears of an expanding U.S. empire grew more pronounced, as U.S. troops occupied the strategic waist of the hemisphere and Britain recognized U.S. control over the canal.

Concern turned to alarm in 1904, when Teddy Roosevelt seized the occasion of a dispute between the Dominican Republic and its foreign creditors to claim a U.S. "police power" in the internal affairs of American republics where "chronic wrongdoing or an impotence . . . results in a general loosening of the ties of civilized society." Because of the Monroe Doctrine, he concluded, "in the Western Hemisphere, the United States cannot ignore this duty." It was the language of the New Imperialism, the "white man's burden" as a rationale for empire. This Roosevelt Corollary to the Monroe Doctrine justified three decades of U.S. military intervention in the Caribbean basin. The United States occupied Haiti, Nicaragua, and the Dominican Republic for years at a time, and sent troops into Mexico and Cuba for briefer stays. Sovereignty had become a relative concept in the Americas.

An aggressive "dollar diplomacy" assured U.S. businessmen favorable concessions and a good investment climate even in countries where U.S. troops never landed. Taking advantage of European weakness after the First World War, the United States replaced Britain as the region's principal banker, foreign investor, and trading partner by 1930.

Latin Americans did not accept this U.S. expansion with equanimity. In Nicaragua, between 1927 and 1933, Augusto César Sandino led a successful guerrilla resistance to the U.S. marines occupying his country and became a hemispheric hero. As the Caribbean Sea turned into a U.S. lake, nationalists who had once looked to the United States for support against European colonial powers voiced fears that the Colossus of the North would prove an even greater threat to the independence of their countries. Their prophet was José Martí, the Cuban poet and patriot, who had organized Cuba's late-nineteenth-century independence movement from a U.S. exile, but came to consider the struggle against "Yankee imperialism" as the great task of his generation and its successors. He admired the energy and creativity of the United States, but feared the greed of its businessmen and the jingoism of its politicians. "I have lived in the belly of the monster," Martí said, "and I know its entrails."[2]

In southern South America, a region of European influence distant from the United States, responses to U.S. expansion were more measured but equally strong. One was an aristocratic anti-Americanism that stressed the superiority of Latin American spirituality over the materialism of the United States. Its classic statement was *Ariel,* by José Rodó, a Uruguayan lawyer for British enterprises. Drawing an analogy to Shakespeare's *The Tempest,* Rodó compared Latin Americans to the blithe spirit Ariel, the United States to the brutish Caliban, and Europe to the wise and cultivated Prospero. He urged Latin Americans to remain loyal to Europe, the source of their culture and values, and to resist the physical force and materialism of the United States.

A more pragmatic reaction to the U.S. threat was to learn from Yankee ingenuity how to resist it. The Argentine merchant Carlos Bunge spoke for many Latin American businessmen who admired North American entrepreneurial drive and technological facility, but feared the political hegemony that might result from its economic expansion. His advice was to emulate the U.S. example as a way of defending the region against U.S. encroachments.

A more formal response on the part of many Latin American nations was to reject the legitimacy of the Roosevelt Corollary and to try to use international law and organizations to limit U.S. expansion and halt its unilateral intervention in the Americas. Their rejoinder was Argentina's Drago Doctrine, which insisted that debt collection should not be an excuse for foreign intervention. It was accepted as part of international law in the Hague Conference of 1907. During the years that followed, Latin Americans continued their efforts to bring U.S. interference to a halt, using the League of Nations to devise a collective security system and the periodic inter-American conferences to press demands for an end to unilateral military intervention on a resistant United States.

During the 1920s, these pressures and the reluctance of the U.S. electorate to shoulder the costs of empire led Washington to retreat from the imperial rhetoric and Big Stick policies of the Roosevelt Corollary, and to seek ways to end U.S. occupations of Caribbean Basin republics. But it was left to another Roosevelt—Franklin Delano—to open a new era in inter-American relations with his proclamation of the Good Neighbor policy in his 1933 inaugural address. With FDR's renunciation of unilateral intervention in 1936, Latin Americans celebrated the diplomatic victory they had sought for so long. By then, however, U.S. economic and military strength had assured it a hemispheric ascendancy that was no less real for being less visible. Within this new context, the United States was prepared to renegotiate its relationship with Panama.

The U.S. protectorate came to an end in 1939, but U.S. dominance remained, along with fourteen military bases, thousands of troops, and the Canal Zone on which Panama's economy depended. But for Panama's tiny commercial elite, who spoke English and were lighter skinned than the country's mulatto majority, the change in status had significance. It established "Panama's national identity," which Ricardo Arias Calderón argued was "expressed in knowing how to negotiate and to take advantage of a favorable international conjuncture to achieve our own agenda." For the next three decades, this elite ruled Panama in close collaboration with Washington. "The great task of this era was to transform a republic into a nation-state," said Arias Calderón, "and each Panamanian into an active citizen." The U.S. presence impeded the first goal but promoted the second.

There was growing Panamanian resentment of continued U.S. control, particularly around the Canal Zone. U.S. residents there enjoyed higher wages and living standards than Panamanian workers, who also resented the racism of the Zonians. The conflict over raising the Panamanian flag in the Canal Zone came to symbolize its restriction of Panamanian sovereignty, sparking rising anti-Americanism and violent riots that claimed twenty-seven lives in 1964. Panama's U.S.-trained security forces kept these protests under control, and ousted the nationalistic Arnulfo Arias three times from the presidency.

The military coup of 1968 was different. It brought to power General Omar Torrijos, a charismatic officer influenced by the Third World nationalism of the era, including Nasser's success in gaining control of the Suez Canal for Egypt. Although he was a dictator who did not respect the rights of his opponents, Torrijos was also a populist who ousted the old political elites and promoted land reform, social programs, and popular organizations. He was a nationalist as well, who created a foreign policy independent of Washington, forging links with Fidel Castro and supporting Nicaragua's Sandinista revolution against Somoza. Torrijos tried to lessen Panama's economic dependence on the canal by transforming Panama into an international banking center and encouraging agriculture, mining, and even industry.

Most of all, he was determined to regain the canal for Panama. His efforts finally bore fruit in 1977, with the signing of a new treaty with President Jimmy Carter providing for the canal's return to Panamanian sovereignty in the year 2000. Although the accord contained loopholes through which the United States could continue to drive its tanks, two out of three Panamanians approved of the treaty, and Torrijos himself is remembered by many as "the defender of Panama's sovereignty."

Torrijos died in 1981, in a suspicious airplane crash, and was succeeded by General Manuel Noriega, a clever but unscrupulous intelligence officer with ties to the CIA and Fidel Castro, the Nicaraguan Contras and the Colombian drug cartels. Noriega had few of Torrijos's virtues and many more vices. "Under Torrijos, the armed forces were an instrument of the nation," said sociologist Marco Gandásegui. "With Noriega the nation became an instrument of the armed forces." Under Noriega's corrupt and repressive rule, popular organizations atrophied and political opposition multiplied. Increasingly, he was a military dictator without popular support. In 1989, Noriega's halting of a presidential election that Guillermo Endara, as candidate of a broad opposition alliance, was winning by a landslide, revealed the dictator's political weakness. By then, the United States had also soured on Noriega, and begun to use economic sanctions in an effort to drive him from power. When those did not work, and two coup attempts failed, Washington turned once again to the unilateral military intervention it had forsworn half a century before. At midnight on December 20, 1989, U.S. troops moved out of the Canal Zone into the "sovereign" Republic of Panama with the goal of ousting its ruler and sending him back to the United States for trial on drug charges. Operation Just Cause had begun.

For Panamanians, the invasion may have had a "Just Cause," but its results were disappointing. In four days of fighting, the United States had used far more force with far less precision than seemed necessary to oust and apprehend Noriega. Several hundred to several thousand lives were lost; the exact number is buried in the mass graves in which many victims were interred. Panama also suffered an estimated two billion dollars in property damages, on top of the estimated one to eight billion dollars in losses from U.S. sanctions during the two years leading up to the invasion. Within this context, the U.S. reconstruction aid of one billion dollars was woefully inadequate, and most of it had to be spent for arrears payments on Panama's four-billion-dollar foreign debt.

By mid-1991, foreign capital and economic growth were returning to Panama, but one out of five Panamanian workers was out of a job and robbery was so common that downtown Panama City was unsafe in broad daylight. José Gallardo was one of many public employees fired in the new government's budget cutting. Now he drives his aging car as a taxi and tries to make ends meet. "It is not easy, because people are poor," he explained. "The invasion freed us from Noriega, but if Torrijos were alive, he would be elected."

Faith in democracy was another invasion casualty in Panama. The Endara government proved to be weak, incompetent, and corrupt. Its coalition unraveled and its popular support plummeted. "The people feel defrauded," said Gallardo. "We wanted a change but all we got was politicking, as in the past." The invasion brought back to power the neocolonial political elite that Torrijos ousted in 1968, an elite with a very narrow social base—and even narrower concerns. "They are only interested in serving themselves, the rich, and the United States," said sports trainer Franklin Bedoya. Roberto Troncoso, president of Panama's Committee for Human Rights, agreed: "This government hasn't been able to put the word 'democracy' back in our dictionary."[3]

It also had been unable to restore Panama's sovereignty or sense of national identity. Admittedly, these are difficult tasks in a country where the national currency is the dollar, the national territory is cut in two by a de facto foreign colony, and the old colonial power maintains a large military garrison within a short tank drive of the capital. When former Noriega soldiers rebelled one year after the invasion, U.S. troops were called in to defeat the coup attempt. From the perspective of Panamanian sovereignty, the country has taken a giant step backward.

The invasion also meant a return to the past psychologically. It undermined the belief Torrijos had nurtured that Panamanians were a sovereign people who could decide their own destiny. Instead, said Gallardo, it reinforced "the old belief of Panamanians that they need the United States to protect them and get things done."

For the United States, too, the results of its invasion of Panama have been largely disappointing. A central stated objective of Operation Just Cause was to stop Panama from being used to transship Colombian cocaine and launder its profits. Yet, two years later, drug traffic through Panama had increased. Ironically, without Noriega's strong—if corrupt—hand on the tiller of state, Panama was wide open to the cocaine cartels.

If the real U.S. motivation was to retain control of the Panama Canal into the next millennium, however, the invasion could be considered a success. With Panama's security force reduced to police functions and its government dependent on U.S. support, the defense of the canal has once again devolved onto the U.S. military forces based in the Canal Zone.

"Even Torrijos left a door open for U.S. troops to remain after the year 1999," said Ricardo Arias Calderón, who had left the Endara government in 1991, but might well be president in the year 2000. Panama was a "small country that could not afford an army." Arias was opposed to maintaining the U.S. bases into the next millennium, *provided* that democracy was consolidated, the Panamanian state and police were modernized, and an alternative source was found for the two to three hundred million dollars per year that the bases earned Panama. Still, the end of military rule coinciding with the end of the Cold War created a unique opportunity for a demilitarized Panama, in which a neutralized canal "would not be just a utopian dream. If we continue to live in a world without confrontations among great powers, there will be no reason for the United States to maintain its troops in Panama," Arias Calderón argued. "And there will be even less reason for Panamanians to want them there."

Foreign troops are only the most visible threat to the sovereignty of the nations of the other Americas. Since World War II, overt U.S. military intervention has been rare—confined to the Dominican Republic in 1965, Grenada in 1983, and Panama in 1989—but its covert interference has been common. The Cold War framed these interventions and was used to justify the assassination of foreign leaders and the "destabilization" of elected governments, as well as the sponsorship of military coups and insurgent armies. On the global chessboard of the Cold War, Latin America and the Caribbean was a U.S. sphere, and any decline in U.S. hegemony there was viewed as a loss for Washington and a gain for Moscow.

Although Moscow also viewed the Americas as a U.S. sphere, fated by geography to U.S. domination, the threat of "international communism" was the rationale for the formation of a collective security system under U.S. command in 1947. The United States became the principal trainer and supplier of the region's armed forces, who were viewed in Washington as bulwarks against communist subversion. Many Latin American military officers were trained in the Canal Zone, which became the headquarters for the Pentagon's Southern Command—whose mission covers South America, not the southern United States.

This was the heyday of U.S. economic ascendancy in the region as well. World War II had weakened its European and Japanese rivals. By 1950, the United States accounted for half of Latin America's imports and almost as large a share of its exports. During the two decades that followed World War II, U.S. investment in the region increased fivefold, consolidating its preeminent position in the economies of the other Americas. The prominence of U.S. enterprises in the region meant that economic national-ism would be conflated with anti-Americanism and demands for reform with threats to U.S. interests.

These mutually reinforcing concerns informed the CIA covert opera-tion that overthrew the left-leaning Guatemalan government of Jacobo Arbenz in 1954. They motivated the secret organization of the exile inva-sion against revolutionary Cuba that came to grief at the Bay of Pigs in 1961, and the failed efforts to assassinate Fidel Castro—using everything from poisoned milkshakes to exploding cigars—during the years that followed. They justified U.S. support for the Brazilian military takeover of 1964 and the Uruguayan coup of 1974. They also led President Richard Nixon to mount a covert war in Chile after 1970, which "destabilized" the elected government of socialist Salvador Allende and helped set up the violent military coup of 1973. Allende's expropriation without compensation of large U.S. copper mines added economic interest to an anticommunist covert action begun even before Allende was inaugurated. The revelation of this undercover operation and its bloody outcome shocked the U.S. public and confirmed Latin American suspicions.

Even without such active U.S. interference, sovereignty was often difficult for a small American nation to sustain in the face of Washington's pressures and the claims of giant corporations whose economic leverage exceeded that of their host. Jamaica, the largest of the English-speaking Caribbean islands, but still a ministate of 2.5 million, was a case in point.

Get Up! Stand Up!

> *Get up! Stand up!*
> *Stand up for your right!*
> —*Bob Marley*

On October 16, 1968, a group of poor youths from Kingston's slums who had never been to college joined students in protesting the Jamaican govern-ment's ban on the return from Canada of a young Guyanese historian at the University of the West Indies. When the government also tried to bar the protest, with its "Black Power" banners and chants, the demonstration turned into a day-long riot in which automobiles, store windows, and government buildings were damaged, two people were killed, and a score or more injured. What had Walter Rodney done to justify being declared persona non grata in his country of residence? Why had uneducated ghetto youths taken to the streets to "stand up for *his* right"?

Rodney's lectures on African history had instilled new pride in "people brainwashed for centuries in a sense of their own worthlessness,"[4] while his public lectures on "Black Power" had forged a link between his university followers and poor blacks. But Rodney's stress on African achievements was neither new nor surprising in the land of Marcus Garvey, whose back-to-Africa movement had made similar points half a century before. It was Rodney's situating the condition of Jamaica's black majority within an "Imperialist World" where "every country in the dominated colonial areas has an overwhelming majority of nonwhites [but] power . . . resides in the white countries,"[5] that seemed so "dangerous" to Jamaica's rulers. So was his argument that as a result blacks remained both poor and powerless in independent Jamaica. Equally explosive was his insistence that Black Power entailed breaking with a "white racist imperialism," "the assumption of power by the black masses in the islands," and "the cultural reconstruction of society in the image of the blacks."[6]

The Black Power riots of 1968 punctured the myth of Jamaica as a model of race relations, giving a hollow ring to the new nation's proud motto: "Out of many, one people." They also called into question the significance of the independence in which Jamaica's leaders took equal pride. Jamaica might have become politically independent in 1962, stressed Rodney, but it remained economically dependent: Its economy was still controlled by the old colonial power, Britain, and the new imperial power, the United States. It was a neocolonial society whose elites did not challenge this continued foreign domination because they had been shaped by the colonial power's educational system and were given a small share of the profits as its stewards. "A black man ruling a dependent state within the imperialist system," argued Rodney, "is simply an agent of the whites in the metropolis."[7] Jamaica might not be as economically dependent on sugar as in the past, but psychologically it remained a plantation.

Most of Jamaica's light-skinned and British-educated political elite preferred to bar Rodney from reentering the country rather than hear his message, despite its evident appeal to Jamaica's poor black majority and educated youth. "The real aim of Black Power is to overthrow the government,"[8] charged Finance Minister Edward Seaga.

An exception was Michael Manley, political heir to the People's National Party (PNP), the more liberal of Jamaica's two major parties. The PNP had been founded in 1938 by his father, then a distinguished lawyer and later a popular prime minister. Norman Manley enjoyed strong support among urban workers. Like his father, Michael Manley had studied in England and been influenced by the Fabian socialism of the British Labor Party and the winds of change blowing through the Third World in the 1960s. By 1972 the younger Manley was ready to transform the style and content of Jamaican politics.

Manley reached out from his father's working-class base to the poor unemployed blacks who lived in fetid slums such as Kingston's Trenchtown, a very different Jamaica from the elegant mansions and beautiful beaches of the tourist trade. He embraced the language, music, and symbols of the Rastafarians, the religion and culture of many of Jamaica's poor blacks, with its roots in Marcus Garvey's back-to-Africa movement and its worship of Ethiopia's emperor Haile Selassie as a living God. His 1972 election campaign moved to the hypnotic beat of reggae, Rasta music transformed into popular music and then into political music, its message of liberation given a secular twist and a Jamaican setting. Manley presented himself as Joshua, the prophet who would lead his people from the Egypt of neocolonial Jamaica to the promised land of freedom, peace, and justice. He even brandished the "Rod of Correction" that Haile Selassie had given him as a symbol of his mandate to reform Jamaica.

For poor blacks who rallied to Manley's standard, his campaign was a revelation. As Bob Marley, an emerging reggae star from the Trenchtown ghetto, put it in his powerful anthem: "Get Up, Stand Up!":

You can fool some of the people some times
But you can't fool all the people all the time
So now we see the light
We gonna stand up for our right.

The content of Manley's campaign was as shocking to many Jamaicans as his political style. "In 1972, there were two main challenges," Manley recalled. "We were falling behind very badly in the whole area of human resource development and social justice, which had never really been seriously addressed in Jamaica." The second challenge was equally difficult: "We had not come to grips with the problem of a very dependent and fragile economy, which we had really brought from colonialism."

Manley, a brilliant campaigner, was able to translate these concerns into terms that all Jamaicans could understand. "I myself believe first of all in a society of equality," he told cheering crowds. "I believe secondly in a society of social justice, and I believe thirdly that a society of equality and justice has got to rest on a foundation of the personal spirit of self-reliance."

For leading Rastas like Mutabaruka, a "dub" poet who recites accompanied by a reggae band, Manley seemed to be embracing their values—like self-reliance—and making them into a national economic strategy. "Manley felt that true self-reliance meant a certain sovereignty as an independent nation," Mutabaruka recounted. "So he said that we must import less and grow more food, and the people moved toward that." Jamaica's poor blacks also moved toward Manley politically. "He had a lot of Rastas sympathizing with him and his political party, because they were going to change Jamaica."

Manley summed it all up in the title of the reggae song that became his campaign slogan: "Better Must Come." It was a message of good news that swept him into power.

If better were to come, Manley had to find a way of financing his ambitious social programs. The natural candidate was Jamaica's most valuable resource—bauxite, the raw material for aluminum. "Bauxite had been very important for the Jamaican economy even before independence," recalled Carlton Davis, head of the Bauxite Institute created by Manley and a top Manley adviser at the time. "It became even more important now that we were on our own . . . one of the major earners of foreign exchange." During the 1970s, said Robert Honiball, an executive for Kaiser Aluminum, "the bauxite industry was Jamaica's *most* important industry, and at one time it represented as much as sixty percent of export earnings and eighteen percent of gross domestic product." By 1970, after a decade of heavy investments by the six large multinational corporations with Jamaican mines, bauxite was a ten-billion-dollar industry. But, before 1972, Jamaica's revenues from its bauxite exports were limited to only a shilling for every ton sold. "The royalty paid by the bauxite companies to Jamaica was actually *nothing,*" said one outraged worker at the Clarendon mines, where the red earth slag heaps dominate the landscape. "We were just *giving* away our raw material!"

It was OPEC that inspired Manley's decision to raise the bauxite levy. At the end of 1973 the oil cartel had quadrupled the price of oil. "To an economy like Jamaica that was a very serious development for which we were not prepared," Carlton Davis said. "So that was a driving factor, because the oil had to be paid for. In a modern economy there was just no alternative." Yet to Manley, OPEC's example also offered Jamaica a solution to the problem the oil cartel had created. He led the way in forming the International Association of Producers of Bauxite with other exporters such as Guinea and Australia. It was the era in which Third World nations were asking for a more equitable New International Economic Order. Manley demanded a renegotiation of the bauxite contract his father had signed in 1957, which still had several years to run. For Manley, there were also broader considerations behind this move. "Bauxite represented two things," he explained. "One was a wasting resource, and therefore something you have to use to national advantage while it lasts. We were very anxious to have bauxite make a serious contribution to the resources of the country and to the resource base of the government." The other was an issue of sovereignty: "We tried to experiment with the problem of how does a very small country, that is one link in the chain of multinational corporations, assert the interest of that link against a chain that's so complex and worldwide."

Negotiations with the mostly U.S. companies—including such major corporations as Alcoa, Reynolds, and Kaiser—failed to reach agreement on a new levy. So Manley's government made a calculation of what they felt was "a fair share," taking into account "rising prices in the aluminium market," and imposed a new royalty rate of 7.5 percent on its own. "Naturally, the companies were upset, because it represented the unilateral imposition of the tax," Honiball recalled. Yet, "after the initial shock, they felt that it would be in their interest to arrive at an agreement with the government." Kaiser broke ranks and agreed to the increase, and the others followed, Carlton Davis said. "So, we were no longer regarded as a pariah in our relationships with major multinational corporations."

Jamaica may not have been regarded as a pariah by foreign corporations, but it certainly was not viewed as having a good investment climate. During the years that followed, foreign investment dried up, beginning with the bauxite industry. The solidarity that Manley had counted on from the other bauxite producers proved unreliable. Guinea had encouraged him to impose the higher levy, but then failed to follow his lead. When Reynolds pulled out of Jamaica it was because they had "got an offer from Australia, which they could not refuse," recalled Hector Wynter, editor of *The Daily Gleaner,* Jamaica's leading newspaper. The companies that stayed in Jamaica recouped their heavy investments of the 1960s but did not reinvest. Moreover, "there was a certain contraction of production," recalled Manley, which he attributed to "changing energy costs in the aluminium industry" and "the stagflation of the middle seventies," but he admitted, "it has been said it was because of the bauxite levy." Delroy Lindsay, a Jamaican businessman and former diplomat, was far blunter. "Manley tried to play the economic game by his own rules. He started this New International Economic Order thing and reneged on an agreement with major American companies. But bauxite didn't have the same blackmail potential as oil did," Lindsay stressed. "So, internationally, Michael's initiative came to naught."

Within Jamaica, however, Manley's imposition of a higher bauxite royalty over company objections was widely applauded. In part it was the increased revenues themselves—"two hundred million dollars the first

Social criticism and political engagement are common to much of modern Latin American art. Fernando Botero's 1967 *Presidential Family* includes a military officer and a bishop, portraying the interlocking character of the Colombian elite, whose bloated wealth and self-image are suggested by the artist's volumetric style.

Zapatistas (1931) by José Clemente Orozco, one of the "three greats" of the Mexican mural movement, is an enduring image of the Indian and mestizo soldiers of Emiliano Zapata, the legendary peasant leader of the Mexican revolution. The repeated ranks of guerrillas and their women *soladeras* suggest the anonymous masses who fought for land of their own.

In *Diego on My Mind,* Frida Kahlo's 1943 self-portrait, the Mexican painter reveals her obsession with her artist husband, Diego Rivera, here imbedded in her forehead. Kahlo is dressed as a Tehuanta, a costume favored by Rivera, who shared her love of Mexican popular culture but not her surrealist artistic style.

Dutch Huitzilopochtli (1990), with its blonde Aztec war god, is Dulce María Nuñez's ironic comment on the long-standing "European misunderstanding of America." The vibrantly phallic bananas suggest an exotic Mexican sexuality—and a celebration of popular culture seen as well in the artist's *Fruitstand* paintings.

Evangelista (1989), Nahum Zenil's send-up of the European imposition of Christianity on his Indian ancestors, shows the artist as a beatified friar in the manner of colonial portraits, but with an obsessive repetition that reflects his narcissism and today's technology—as well as offering a wry postmodern commentary on traditional Mexican religious painting.

350.000 MEXICAN AMERICANS DEPORTED

The North American plutocrat and victimized Mexican masses in this section of Judy Baca's *Great Wall of L.A.* (1990), installed in a Chicano barrio, draw on the Mexican muralist tradition of painting a "people's history" on public walls. But its style also reflects the new syncretic "border culture" of today's Mexican-American community.

For most of Latin America, the 1980s were "the lost decade," an era of economic crisis. But for Peru's Indians it was the *Decade of Chagwa,* or chaos, in which the war between Shining Path guerrillas and the armed forces drove Indian peasants to flee their highland homes for city slums. Here the refugees themselves turn their trauma into art.

In Brooklyn, New York, the annual West Indian Carnival has all the color and excitement of the original, and monsters all its own. It reflects the heritage of the more than half a million people from the non-Hispanic Caribbean in New York City, adding to the rich cultural mix of the "New New York."

year, nearly eight times the year before," recalled Carlton Davis, who calculated that since 1974 the royalty has netted Jamaica $2.5 billion. "We were able to meet our oil bill and do a number of the economic and social programs the government had promised when it won power in 1972." But beyond those quantitative gains lay an equally important benefit that was more difficult to calculate. "It developed self-confidence among all classes, because it gave the country a self-esteem it had not seen since independence," Davis emphasized. "In fact, these were the years when Manley was at the peak of his popularity because he was seen as the figure that had led this defiance." Even the conservative *Daily Gleaner* praised him "for an act of imposing sovereignty for a newly independent country." Seventeen years later, Eddie Evans recalled his own feelings of pride and elation when he heard of Manley's bauxite tax. He was a hotel worker in Montego Bay, where "you had to spend all day bowin' and scrapin' to these American tourists." Manley's "standin' up for Jamaica [was] like that Bob Marley song say: 'Stand up for your right!' "

The increased revenues and popularity were a heady triumph for Manley. He was reelected in 1976 in a landslide on a far more radical program of bringing democratic socialism to Jamaica. His spending on economic infrastructure and social programs such as education multiplied. His foreign policy took on a bolder and more militantly Third World stance. Manley had "met Fidel Castro in 1973 on the way to the nonaligned summit that was held in Algiers that year," the Jamaican leader recalled, and had been "impressed by his immense personality, his warmth, and his intellect." In 1975, Manley accepted Castro's invitation to visit Cuba.

Castro pulled out all the stops. "Here he was a Third World leader of a small country going to Cuba, and he's met with banners: FIDEL Y MIGUEL SÍ, IMPERIALISMO NO! CAPITALISMO NO, SOCIALISMO SÍ! VENCEREMOS JUNTOS! WE SHALL OVERCOME TOGETHER! This went to his head," Hector Wynter claimed. Manley responded in kind, with a speech that used the language of Martin Luther King, Jr., to affirm his commitment to Third World solidarity between a democratic socialist Jamaica and its nearest neighbor, a communist Cuba. "We face a long hard road. We face tremendous problems, but our eyes are fixed on the mountaintop of a dream," he affirmed. "And one day we will stand together on that mountaintop and we will look back down that road and we shall say together: 'We Shall Overcome!' "

Washington might live with Manley's nationalistic bauxite policy, but not with his embrace of their closest enemy and endorsement of Cuba's intervention in the Angolan civil war. Moreover, the United States was maintaining a policy of isolating Castro in the hemisphere and Manley had broken that quarantine. If his bauxite levy alienated Wall Street, his support of Fidel Castro outraged Washington. "It got the United States angry," Manley admitted. Looking back, he regretted that "the whole dynamics of the thing seemed to sweep everybody along into a totally unnecessary hostility." His party stood for "democracy, the rule of law, and respect for private capital. Everybody just overreacted." But beyond these dynamics, Manley argued, lay a more profound conflict—"the problem of sovereignty. I remember feeling pressure from this great and respected neighbor to the north, because of what was just a Third World friendship," he recounted. "I resented it and felt that it was an invasion of Jamaica's just right to pursue an independent path . . . an invasion of Jamaica's sovereignty."

United States hostility also had practical consequences. "It definitely slowed down the flow of economic cooperation that you get through U.S. aid, which is very important for young countries in this hemisphere," Manley said. "Doors did not seem as wide open," recalled Winston Davis, then Jamaica's ambassador to the Organization of American States. "The number of tourists from the United States began to go down." Even worse for Jamaica "was that in creating an atmosphere of suspicion and hostility, they virtually guaranteed that no private capital would invest in Jamaica," Manley said. "Not that they told companies not to invest. But the mood made it unlikely that anybody would." An ex-diplomat, Delroy Lindsay could afford to be more frank: "Once the Americans started to put the pressure on, Jamaica was dead."

With bauxite production dropping, tourism on the decline, and foreign investment at a standstill, Jamaica began to experience increasing economic difficulties. They were compounded by a flight of domestic capital, which Hector Wynter blamed on Manley. "On his return from Cuba in July 1975, he held a big meeting in Montego Bay in which he made a statement which then led to the ruin of Jamaica," the *Daily Gleaner* editor claimed. Manley reaffirmed his commitment to socialism and "declared that if there were Jamaicans who wished to become millionaires overnight, there are five flights a day to Miami. Let them take them and go!" Many wealthy Jamaicans did just that during the years that followed, taking their capital with them. The money for Manley's ambitious social and economic programs dried up and his popularity plunged. The second oil price rise of 1979 completed the economic debacle, and the conservative opposition moved in for the political kill.

In the 1980 elections the Jamaica Labor Party's Edward Seaga—who as finance minister in 1968 had accused Rodney's followers of being "not members of the Black Power movement, but rather of Red Power"[9]—won decisively. Seaga's campaign platform promised a return to orthodox economics and the U.S. alliance, which, he argued, would bring back foreign investors and tourists. To many Manley supporters, the loss was more than just a partisan political defeat. "When Michael Manley lost the election in 1980, I was disappointed," recalled former ambassador Davis. "Because an experiment that I believed in and a path that I thought a small Third World country had to walk to be able to provide some hope for its people was going to come to an end."

Davis's intuitions were correct. An era had come to an end, and the future looked suspiciously like the past. Soon after Seaga became prime minister, ads began to appear in the United States showing a deferential black waiter encouraging North American tourists to "Come back to Jamaica—the way things used to be." Tourism did gradually recover during Seaga's eight years in power, but neither tourism nor Reaganomics proved a cure for Jamaica's economic ailments or social ills. In 1989, Jamaicans reelected Michael Manley, expecting that better would come once again.

It was a sadder but wiser Manley who took over the reins of government. Although he still espoused the old goal of social welfare, the means that he now embraced seemed closer to those of Seaga than to the old Manley. "We have to create the institutions and the training to support the spirit of wanting to do business," he argued in 1991. Privatization of state-owned firms, the free market, and an open economy were the solutions and "competition . . . the key to efficiency and creativity in business." Where he had spent freely on social welfare before, Manley now imposed an austerity plan whose goal was a balanced budget. Where he had sought to build democratic socialism, he now sold off indebted state enterprises. Where he had been the target of U.S. hostility, Manley was now the example held up by George Bush as the model for other Caribbean leaders to follow.

For businessmen like Delroy Lindsay, now head of a multimillion-dollar financial services group that had made a fortune after buying a bankrupt state bank, the new Manley is a realist. "Jamaica is next door to the United States, the largest capitalist economy in the world. Now that is a reality. That is our geography. We can't change that," he emphasized. "We are 2.5 million people, the United States is 250 million people," he continued. "That is the reality. You've got to accept it." The implications were clear for Lindsay: "It is for us to try and forge an economic relation-ship which can extract reciprocal benefits. . . . That is the challenge to our leaders."

But Manley's second coming was a disappointment to many. "He is not the same Manley that I used to idealize in the seventies," asserted Winston Davis. "He once championed the cause of the poor man, but now he has embarked on hard economic measures that hit those same people who live in the lowest social order."

In the ghettos of Kingston, where Manley had once been hailed as a political prophet, unemployed black youths now talked of hunger and hopelessness. "It's rough. . . . You wake up in the morning [and] you don't know where your tea's comin' from, you don't know where your lunch's comin' from, you don't know where your dinner's comin' from," one member of a street corner group recounted. "It forces the youth to do the wrong things . . . because there's not enough work, and the youth don't want to live in poverty."

"There's a lot of disappointment in this society about the line Manley take now," said Mutabaruka in 1991, a year before Michael Manley announced his resignation because of ill health. Manley's "selling our black people, our poor people to foreign interests" confirmed his view that despite the frequent praise for Jamaica's two-party democratic system, a British colonial legacy, "over the years none of the two parties had ever truly represented the people."

To Manley, however, his new line was an effort to correct "some serious mistakes we made in the seventies." It was not so much that Manley's ideals had changed as his sense of the possible. "It is an illusion to think that any country enjoys sovereignty in a pure theoretical sense. . . . Nobody has the freedom to do whatever you like," he reflected. "But small countries are that much more so constrained by economic dependence. They are fragile. They are smaller. They have less capacity to influence the movement of economic trends in the world," he concluded with a weary air. "There are severe limits in practice on this thing called sovereignty."

Even those who had opposed the old Manley or were disappointed in the new Manley praised what he had meant for them and for Jamaica. "What Manley meant for a 'rural boy' like me in the seventies was providing opportunities for bridging the gap between rich and poor through education," affirmed Ambassador Davis. "Had it not been for Michael Manley's radical changes, a person like me who had the faculties but not the economic means to go through university would not have made it." For Delroy Lindsay, Manley "provided a lot of people with a perception of an opportunity because there was a feeling that the social structure was changing and you could achieve in society." As a businessman, "what Manley did for me in the seventies was to provide an opportunity for Jamaicans of African descent like me to go into business, because a lot of the traditional business class vacated Jamaica." For Manley, this was not just an economic issue, Lindsay stressed: "The whole concept of social equality was very high on his agenda."

So was the consolidation of Jamaica as a sovereign nation. To Hector

Wynter, one of Manley's sterner critics, he not only "gave to every Jamaican the feeling that 'You are equal to any other Jamaican,'" but also gave
them a sense that "Jamaica as a whole was equal to any other country."
Manley may have failed to achieve his ambitious goal of economic sovereignty, but he succeeded in getting Jamaicans to create a positive new
image of themselves and their young nation. This new national identity
was shaped not only by his policies, but also by the vibrant popular culture
that he embraced—and promoted.

    "Emancipate yourselves from mental slavery/None but yourselves
can free your mind," urged Bob Marley in "Redemption Songs." During
the 1970s, many Jamaicans did "emancipate" themselves from Jamaica's
neocolonial elite culture. The result was the formation of a new Jamaican
identity, which celebrated the African heritage of 90 percent of Jamaicans.
Politics and popular culture were mutually reinforcing. Manley made
respectable what had been the pariah culture of reggae and Rastas, which
the elites had disdained as the culture of "Congos"—ignorant and uncivi-
lized. Within the political context of the Manley era, it became fashionable
to wear dreadlocks, like reggae, and adopt an "African" identity. "In the
seventies we had an upsurge of black awareness, of trying to identify with
Africa," Mutabaruka recounted. "It moved from the ghettos of Jamaica into
the political mainstream, where the music played a great part in culturizing
all of Jamaica."

    The new cultural fashion may have begun in the urban slums of
Kingston, but it soon spread to middle-class youths in schools and universities, shaping the new generation of Jamaica's professionals in a very different cultural mold than their parents. The dreadlocks and other badges of
this culture have been adopted throughout the Anglophone West Indies by
young people who do not necessarily share Rasta religious beliefs. As one
upwardly mobile black parent complained: "You send them off to university and they come back with dreadlocks as if they had been brought up
in Trenchtown."

    In the end, though Manley's dependent Jamaica was unable to sustain
its full political and economic sovereignty, it did create a new Jamaican

identity. Moreover, in the vibrant popular culture of reggae, Jamaicans also forged a cultural sovereignty which projected their new nation onto the world stage, with Bob Marley, their first universal pop icon, as a cultural ambassador before his premature death from cancer in 1981.

In Mandela Green, an outdoor "entertainment center" near Montego Bay, an audience of poor blacks waiting for Mutabaruka to start his show were vocal in their disappointment at Manley's second coming. "He is no Joshua, man," declared Eddie Evans. For Donald Livingstone, "the dreams of the 1970s are gone"—self-reliance, equality, independence. "But," he reflected, "we still have the music. They can't take that away from us." In the background, Bob Marley's pensive "Redemption Songs" filled the night:

> *That's all I ever had,*
> *Redemption songs,*
> *These songs of freedom . . .*
> *Songs of freedom.*

Perils of the State

"For a country like Colombia, sovereignty is a basic concept," argued Carlos Lemos, a former minister of government. "We want to be respected by other countries. We want to have our own rules. We want to be able to stand on our own, to have our borders respected." The United States had violated Colombia's sovereignty and shown little respect for its borders in 1903, when Teddy Roosevelt engineered the secession of Panama, until then Colombia's northernmost department.

Yet foreign intervention is not the only peril facing nation-states in Latin America and the Caribbean. In recent years, the chief threats to Colombia's sovereignty—the "supreme power" of its government—have been internal. Once known for its coffee, Colombia is now notorious for its cocaine—and its drug lords for their ruthless use of violence and creation of a virtual state within the state. The government's monopoly of coercive force, a key attribute of sovereignty, has been lost, and Colombia's political system and rule of law have been threatened by the assassination of ministers, judges, and presidential candidates.

The political history of Colombia is a paradox. Colombia claims the longest-lived democracy and two-party system in South America and takes pride in its long tradition of the rule of law and constitutional rights. But its history has been marked by some of the highest levels of violence in the region. Its first century of independence was punctuated by eight national civil wars between Conservatives and Liberals and fourteen regional conflicts, a reflection of the country's fragmented geography and weak national identity.

During the past half century, Colombia has been in a state of "near permanent war," stressed Arturo Alape, a leading analyst of the era. It began with "La Violencia" of 1948–57, and continued with Latin America's longest guerrilla war. It culminated in the overlapping violence of narco-terrorists, rightist paramilitary groups, armed forces, and guerrillas that brought the country to the edge of anarchy during the 1980s.

La Violencia began with a political murder, the assassination in Bogotá of the charismatic Liberal populist Jorge Gaitán. He had challenged the elite's political dominance by mobilizing excluded sectors of the population around his political star. The result of Gaitán's killing in 1948 was the urban riot and rebellion known as the Bogotazo, in which the enraged populace of Colombia's capital went on a rampage, leaving an estimated forty thousand dead—and detonating an even deadlier conflict in the Colombian countryside.

Some two hundred thousand Colombians lost their lives in La Violencia during the decade that followed, a complex struggle that is still imperfectly understood. Recent research has revealed a web of social conflicts over land and labor associated with the postwar coffee boom beneath the partisan political surface of La Violencia. Alape argued that the elites who controlled the traditional parties decided to end the fighting by a power-sharing agreement when the emergence of a peasant war of growing intensity began to threaten their social control.

Although La Violencia ostensibly ended with the formation of this National Front in 1957, the peasant war and social banditry went on for another decade, and Arturo Alape is only one of many analysts who stress "that the fighting has never ended." Out of these peasant rebellions leftist guerrilla "republics" emerged in outlying regions, showing the limits of both government authority and democratic politics in Colombia.

The most important limitation of Colombia's democracy has been its exclusion of alternatives to the two traditional parties. As a result, a large portion of the electorate have felt disenfranchised. This was particularly clear in the decades after La Violencia, when the warring Liberals and Conservatives agreed to alternate in the presidency and share power. This National Front pact reduced elections to a ritual act in which fewer and fewer Colombians bothered to participate.

This choreographed two-party system was challenged by ANAPO, a populist party headed by a former military strongman, General Rojas Pinilla. Its apparent election victory on April 19, 1970, was denied by fraud and its protests were silenced by intimidation. It was a lesson that led many ANAPO leaders to give up on Colombia's rigged democracy and to join with veteran leftists in 1972 to form the April 19 Movement (M-19), named after the day of the electoral fraud. "The M-19 is the only guerrilla movement to emerge out of an election," stressed Everth Bustamante, one of its few surviving founders. "Our demand was democracy and our goal was to open up the political system."

The M-19 entered a complex political landscape that already included several other guerrilla movements. The largest was the Colombian Revolutionary Armed Forces (FARC), today the oldest guerrilla army in the hemisphere. It had emerged out of La Violencia's social war under legendary peasant leaders like Manuel Marulanda. The FARC was heir to the guerrilla "republics" destroyed by the army in the mid-1960s, and had localized strength on the frontiers of settlement. Its threat to the supreme authority of the Bogotá government was its "armed colonization" of a growing number of frontier zones in different parts of Colombia, a country with large unsettled areas divided by three Andean ranges. The FARC was oriented to Moscow, but the other major leftist tendencies also had their "armed forces" and "zones of influence." The National Army of Liberation (ELN) was a pro-Cuban group from the 1960s, while the People's Liberation Army (EPL) was a Maoist movement of the same era. Although the guerrilla groups differed in their ideologies, they agreed in their analysis of why their recourse to arms was necessary and why the peasants in their zone supported them.

"In our country, guns are what give you power," said Bernardo Gutiérrez, leader of the EPL. "Because the state was unable to govern in these regions, the armed groups took over and began to carry out governmental functions." But there were political and social dimensions to the guerrillas' support among the peasants as well. "In Colombia, we have a two-party system, but the two parties do not represent the interests of the majority," he explained, "so the guerrillas were able to provide them with an alternative." Guerrilla groups like the EPL also provided the peasants with protection from local landowners like Fidel Castaño, a rancher whose death squads had terrorized the Caribbean zone of Santa María La Antigua and frustrated peasant hopes for land of their own.

Although the Colombian government denied both the guerrillas' legitimacy and the need for violence, Rafael Pardo, who has dealt with the guerrilla issue as both defense minister and national security adviser, agreed with Gutiérrez that the peasants support the guerrillas because "the Colombian state has concentrated its resources and interest in the development of urban areas and the Andean areas of commercial agriculture." These policies, he admitted, "for many years . . . left a number of areas in the country abandoned." It was because "the state was not there to solve the problems of the people," he argued, "that the guerrillas pretend to substitute for the state."

By 1980, large areas of Colombia were zones where the national government's writ did not reach and guerrillas "taxed" local landowners and foreign oil and banana companies, and in some areas even provided such "governmental services" as education and security. Colombian governments sought to end this secession, both by attacking the guerrilla strongholds and by negotiating their reincorporation into the nation's political life. These efforts faltered after guerrillas who laid down their arms were attacked by the army and their leaders were assassinated by rightist death squads in a "dirty war" that undermined presidential peace initiatives. In 1985, the M-19 denounced the "peace process" as a farce and seized the Palace of Justice with the Supreme Court justices inside, a bold bid for public attention that backfired when the army stormed the building, killing judges and guerrillas alike.

Many of the death squads were linked to the armed forces or to local landowners, whose "self-defense forces" the military promoted. But other killings were the work of the private armies of the drug lords of Medellín, who emerged during these years as violent new contenders for wealth and power, providing money and weapons for the "dirty war."

Colombia had long been a producer of marijuana, and it became a significant exporter of the narcotic weed to the United States during the turned-on seventies. It was the emergence of cocaine as the new U.S. recreational drug of choice toward the end of that decade that turned a modest illicit traffic into a major illegal export boom and transformed Colombia's drug lords into international cocaine kings.

As cocaine became fashionable in Europe and North America, Colombia's drug traffic boomed. By 1990 it was a five-to-six-billion-dollar-a-year business, more than three times as valuable as coffee. From an economic viewpoint, the cocaine boom was the latest in a long line of Latin American export booms, with the exception that this time Latin American "entrepreneurs" controlled much of the processing and international marketing as well. They bought coca leaves from poor peasants in isolated areas of Colombia, Peru, and Bolivia, processed them in secret jungle labs, and then sent the cocaine by plane or boat to European and U.S. markets.

Since time immemorial, coca leaves have been a prized Andean crop, valued for their medicinal and narcotic qualities in work and in ritual. For poor farmers eking out a living in isolated valleys, growing coca leaves for the traffickers, peasants stressed, "is the resource of the poor" in areas "the government abandoned." Most of the profits from this immense but illegal traffic were monopolized by a small group of drug lords organized into loose "cartels" identified with Colombia's major cities. During the 1980s, the Medellín cartel was the wealthiest, as well as the most ostentatious and the most violent. Its bosses, men from modest backgrounds like Pablo Escobar and petty criminals like Carlos Lehder, became instant billionaires, nouveaux riches who flaunted their wealth in flashy cars and opulent residences complete with private zoos—and private armies.

As was traditional in Colombia for men of new wealth trying to make their way into the elite, the drug lords invested money in land, acquiring vast estates through purchase and intimidation. Traffickers owned roughly one of out of every thirteen acres cultivated in Colombia by 1990. Many of them were in frontier areas such as the Magdalena Medio, where guerrilla groups were active in defending peasants and "taxing" landowners. There, the "security" interests of the drug barons merged with those of other local landowners: Their private armies added their firepower and ruthlessness to the already complex alliance of the army and landlord death squads responsible for peasant massacres and escalating clashes with the guerrillas. Drug lords emerged as local leaders of landed elites in contested frontier zones where the national government was weak. By 1990, the overlapping violence of army, landowners, guerrillas, and drug barons had created a climate of fear that had traumatized Colombia and called into question the sovereignty of the national government over the territory it claimed to rule.

It was not just in outlying rural zones that the government's writ had ceased to run. In Medellín, Colombia's second city, there were large areas where the authority of the government was all but absent. Medellín is the capital of Antioquia, a region famous for its enterprising citizens and economic drive. It is also the country's industrial heartland, and until recently was better known for its textile barons than its cocaine kings. But in the recession of the 1980s, textile mills laid off workers, and the number of unemployed was swelled by rural migration to the shantytowns that ring Medellín, like so many other Latin American cities.

The cocaine cartel picked up the slack, during the enormous expansion of the cocaine trade in the 1980s, when it became fashionable among both rich and middle class in the United States and crack swept through the ghettos. Cocaine revenues, estimated at $3.5 billion a year by 1990, financed nearly a third of Colombia's imports, kept its currency strong, its debt low, and its economic growth the region's highest. Cartel profits helped fuel Medellín's dynamic underground economy and accounted for some 250,000 jobs, 3 percent of Colombia's labor force. By 1990, drug money was an integral part of Colombia's economy.

The drug lords also used their enormous wealth to corrupt the government and to turn themselves into a virtual parallel political power. Pablo Escobar even built housing projects and won popular support among the poor by posing as a benevolent patron. His word was more respected— and his coercive force more feared—than that of the government authorities. He financed political campaigns and ran for Congress himself as the candidate of the most traditional of Liberal party factions. Nor was Escobar the only one. Carlos Lehder even formed his own political party, which won local elections. "There were few politicians in Colombia untouched by drug money," Arturo Alape asserted.

At first the spread of cocaine use seemed more a U.S. than a Colombian problem. But by 1990, inexpensive forms of cocaine, like *basuco,* an even cheaper and rougher derivative than crack, had created more than 250,000 addicts in Colombia itself, making drug addiction into a Colombian social problem as well, particularly among the urban poor of cities like Medellín. The situation was compounded by the failure of Colombia's governments to invest in education or jobs for the poor, or even to police their shantytowns.

This abandonment of the urban slums created a vacuum that was filled by the *sicarios,* or "killer kids," "because there is no good education available for the youth and there are no other economic resources here,"

Elizabeth Lievano, a local judge, explained. There are not enough jobs and there is job discrimination against kids from these poor neighborhoods. "So these drug traffickers came and told them, if you go and kill somebody, I'll give you two hundred, three hundred, even a million pesos," she said. "Killer kids exist in Medellín because they get paid a lot of money for it." Between 1980 and 1991 the murder rate in Medellín soared from 730 to 7,081, more than three times as many as in New York City, which had more than four times as many people.

In much of Medellín the government is invisible, and power literally comes out of the barrel of a gun. The killer-kid gangs even seem better organized than the government. "Gangs here work in different ways," one teenage *sicario* explained. "Some of them are small-timers who just steal from taxis or steal people's chains and rings, watches and stuff. They live in the poorer neighborhoods high in the hills." But this was just the bottom of the hierarchy. "Others are more organized. They have cars and motorcycles; they have good guns. And then there are the guys who have offices. They get the big jobs, for which they get paid several million pesos. They're the ones who kill the big politicians. They're very well organized," the killer kid said with evident admiration. Within this hierarchy there is a pecking order and a system of patronage. "Sometimes the guys who are very well organized . . . they give jobs to other people. And then those people give jobs to other people," he explained. At the very top were the cocaine kings of the Medellín cartel. "That's how it works."

By 1991, very little else seemed to work in Medellín, a city "ruled by the law of silence and the law of revenge," one judge confessed. By then, however, a new force—local Popular Militias—had emerged to contest control of the slums of Medellín with the killer kids. "We fulfill the wishes of the community and they tell us through their [councils'] actions," one ski-masked militia leader stressed. Some of the leaders, like him, seem to be former leftist guerrillas who are continuing their old struggles against an unjust regime. "We are a self-defense organization for the masses . . . created because the state abandoned these areas," he said. Before the militia arrived, he claimed, "there was total chaos here. The people who ruled here were the gangs. People lived in fear because of those delinquents." Yet within two years, "with the support of the people, we have been able to pacify this community. We have given life back to this community. . . . Now you don't see shut schools. You see kids playing in the streets till late at night." He was proud of his militia's achievements. "The government has been here for a century and they have not been able to do what we have done in only two years," he boasted. "We have become our own government." It was a claim based on a rough notion of popular sovereignty: "Our existence depends on the people, who are the most sovereign of all."

Judges like Elizabeth Lievano insist that "the militias are not the solution," but Colombia's weak system of justice has been unable to provide answers to the widespread violence. In Medellín the state itself is no more than a symbolic presence. Judges attend the removal of the bodies from the scene of the crime and conduct pro forma investigations into the victims' deaths. The Colombian government has no solutions to the violence that its own policies and priorities have spawned. "There are no resources for the system of justice, because governments here keep spending money on everything else," Lievano complained. There was too little spent on education and development for the poor, she stressed. Even judges "feel abandoned by the government because it seems more interested in things other than justice."

By 1990, the more direct threat to Colombia's system of justice stemmed not from its budget priorities or its inability to control the killings in Medellín's slums, but rather from its efforts to combat Medellín's drug cartel, under pressure from the United States—their biggest market. As cocaine use spread in the United States without Washington being able to stem the "epidemic," the U.S. government began to press Colombia to solve a U.S. problem by stopping the drug traffic at its source. But the drug lords' power to corrupt and intimidate soon made it clear that Colombia's judicial system could not be relied upon to apprehend, prosecute, or punish them. The Medellín cartel was the most powerful and ruthless, ready to buy or kill anyone who stood in its path. In 1984 it even assassinated Colombia's top law officer, Justice Minister Rodrigo Lara, who had led Colombia's drug war.

In 1980, Colombia had signed a treaty with the United States providing for the extradition of criminals. After Lara's murder, President Belisario Betancur began to apply this provision to drug traffickers wanted in the United States. Although most of those extradited were minor figures, in 1986, Carlos Lehder, the most flamboyant of the Medellín kingpins, was captured and extradited to the United States, where he was given the life sentence that does not exist in Colombia. Extradition soon became the issue around which the Colombian conflict revolved, with the drug lords offering to pay off Colombia's thirteen-billion-dollar foreign debt if extradition were ended, but threatening to kill public figures who supported the policy. At bottom, they sought to buy or shoot their way into Colombia's elite. "Using their immense economic power, they tried to take over the state, not directly but through fear and intimidation," argued Carlos Lemos. "They wanted the state to do whatever they wanted. So, even though sovereignty is formally there, because we haven't been invaded by another country, it's being attacked internally."

During the years that followed, "the Extraditables" murdered judges, journalists, and ministers with impunity. Their reign of terror intensified in 1989, after President Virgilio Barco embraced extradition as a response to the Medellín cartel's attack on Colombia's political elite—and heavy U.S. pressure. It was symbolized in August 1989 by the assassination of Liberal senator Luis Galán, the leading candidate to succeed Barco, as he campaigned on an antidrug platform. The day after Galán's murder, President Barco declared "war against the drug traffickers," and his final year in office witnessed an "all-out war" on both sides. The government confiscated the properties of the Medellín cartel, which resorted to terror bombings in public places that claimed hundreds of innocent victims. By the time Barco left office in 1990, an estimated eleven thousand Colombians had lost their lives in the nation's drug wars, and most Colombians had wearied of its toll. Public opinion was expressed in a popular song, "We Want Peace":

The news is spreading.
The war is everywhere.
Everyone knows.
Everyone is confused.
The war is killing us civilians.
In the mountains and in the countryside,
The enemy is everywhere.
Under the blue skies there are many dead.
The war is killing brothers.
We want peace!

Cesar Gaviria was elected in 1990 on a platform opposed to drug trafficking but pledged to peace. Once in office the young Liberal president opted for a new approach to the threats to his authority represented by both the drug lords and the guerrillas: negotiation and compromise. If the Medellín cartel would turn themselves in and cooperate with the prosecutors, his government would not extradite them to the United States. This promise was codified in the new 1991 constitution, and by 1992, Pablo Escobar and the Ochoas, the most powerful heads of the Medellín cartel, had surrendered and were in jail awaiting trial by Colombian courts on reduced charges punishable by a maximum of fifteen years in prison. Gaviria's gamble seemed to have paid off.

Although the human and political costs of the drug war were uppermost in Gaviria's mind, his decision to opt for a "Colombian" solution to the problem of narcoterrorism also reflected a growing concern over the external threat to the authority of his government. If the drug lords' direct challenge to the state comprised one threat to its supreme power, the efforts of the United States to shape Colombia's drug war constituted a menace to their nation's sovereignty that worried many Colombians. The U.S.'s insistence on extradition, Judge Lievano asserted, "made us feel inferior, saying that extradition was better because we weren't able to administer justice—knowing that we were a sovereign country." She was equally incensed at the result of U.S. pressures: "Instead of helping us, the United States created a war."

For Colombia, it has been a very costly war. "Many people have died: government leaders, judges, wonderful journalists, ministers of state, and ordinary civilians," mourned Carlos Lemos. "They have blown up planes, put bombs in supermarkets. A whole generation in Medellín, which was the most industrious city in Colombia, has been corrupted." Carlos Jiménez, who had been Betancur's attorney general but resigned because he believed extradition "was going to fill the country with blood," underscored a further cost: a weakening of institutions like the judicial system. "The United States had demanded military repression as the solution of our problems," he charged, and the result was "we nearly finished off our country." He much preferred Gaviria's solution for its "sensibility and rationality," and acted as lawyer for the Ochoas in negotiating their surrender, the first under the new policy. The Gaviria government, despite "pressures from the U.S., has applied *Colombian* solutions to our problems," stressed Jiménez. "It has sought a dialogue."

Gaviria applied a similar strategy of dialogue and negotiated deals to end the threat to the supreme power of Colombia's government posed by the guerrillas. In 1991 a special assembly was convened to write Colombia's first constitution since 1886. Aware that the exclusion of dissident groups from Colombia's political process was a fundamental reason for its loss of legitimacy and for the guerrilla movements, Gaviria made certain that the constitutional assembly included representatives from outside the traditional parties and elites. This assured that the new constitution would reflect a popular sovereignty long absent from Colombia's "democracy." Even guerrilla leaders were impressed. "Here is the old political class representing the elite alongside the new political forces and those who represent the popular forces," Bernardo Gutiérrez marveled in mid-1991. "The workers and the Indians are represented. There are the traditional parties and the new parties. . . . The assembly reflects the whole of Colombia today!"

Gaviria even offered the guerrillas guaranteed seats in the assembly if they negotiated an end to their rebellion. By 1992, four of the six guerrilla groups had laid down their arms and participated in the constitutional assembly, with the M-19 playing a leading role, and its leader, Antonio

Navarro, talked of as a possible successor to Gaviria as president. For Bernardo Gutiérrez, who led his EPL guerrillas out of the hills and into the constitutional assembly, the decision to lay down arms was a response to changing times and indecisive battles. "It was no longer legitimate to fight for political goals with arms, because the Colombian people want peace," he explained. "In Colombia, we've reached a negative draw. The army couldn't beat the guerrillas, nor could the guerrillas beat the army. But this draw was negative because in the middle of it was a civilian bloodbath, a political violence which got deeper all the time."

As a result, Gutiérrez and his EPL guerrillas took a leap of faith and "carried out the most beautiful madness," he said. "We laid down our guns in a country where there is so much political and social violence [and] bet everything on peace." As the Columbus Quincentenary year began, his bet seemed to be paying off. The new constitution was one of the most progressive in the region and Gutiérrez himself had become a senator in the first legislative elections held under the new rules. Equally significant was a ceremony he officiated over in the EPL's former Caribbean stronghold of Santa María La Antigua. There, in mid-1991, Gutiérrez negotiated another peace, this one with his old enemy, landowner Fidel Castaño. The EPL guerrillas laid down their guns and Castaño disarmed his death squads. Then, on a hot summer's day, Gutiérrez assembled his peasant supporters to receive land titles to forty-acre farms from the local bishop. By late 1991, "Don Fidel" had distributed forty thousand acres of his lands to peasants whose aspirations for land of their own he had once fought to the death.

By then, a mood of optimism had swept over Colombia, replacing the despair of two years before. The heads of the Medellín cartel, the godfathers of narcoterrorism, were either dead or in prison, and the level of drug-related violence had dropped dramatically. Moreover, the United States had accepted President Gaviria's "Colombian solution" to the problem of narcoterrorism, including the end of the extradition that Washington had insisted on in the past. The threat to Colombia's sovereignty posed by an escalating U.S. drug war was receding. So was the guerrilla threat. Not only had four of the six guerrilla groups laid down arms, but the two remaining groups had begun to negotiate their reincorporation into the nation's political life.

Yet, in mid-1992, there were signs that the euphoria might have been premature. By then, negotiations had stalled with the two guerrilla groups that remain in rebellion—the FARC and the ELN—the two largest, with the biggest territorial bases and the least incentive to end their insurrection. The assassination of some of the M-19 and EPL guerrillas who had lain down their arms had not helped the government's cause. This was not the only sign of the fragility of Gaviria's solutions to Colombia's conflicts. Fidel Castaño might make peace with the peasants of his zone, but a massacre in another region underscored that the recourse to violence in land conflicts had not come to an end.

Nor had the challenges posed by the cocaine cartels. Although most Colombians applauded the negotiated imprisonment of the Medellín drug lords, critics worried that they were still running their narcotics operations from their comfortable jails and charged that the plea bargaining that put them behind bars represented less a victory for the government than a triumph for the cocaine kings. Pablo Escobar's escape from prison in July 1992 underscored how tenuous even this compromise was. Moreover, if narcoterrorism had declined, drug trafficking had not. If anything, there were signs that it was expanding in Colombia, through the addition of heroin made from locally grown poppies, applying the lessons learned and networks created in the cocaine trade to a similar streamlining of the heroin traffic. The jailing of the Medellín cartel bosses may have hampered their operations, but as a result the rival Cali cartel moved into the vacuum and increased its market share.

"Unless the drug trafficking problem is solved," argued former Medellín mayor Juan Gómez, "threats to our sovereignty will continue to exist, because countries affected by the [drug] business will try to influence our policy towards it." Colombians like Gómez cite Peru, with its U.S. firebases in coca-growing areas, and Bolivia, where U.S. agents fly on antidrug missions, as examples of restrictions on the sovereignty of independent nations as a result of the U.S. drug war. The July 1992 U.S. Supreme Court decision legitimating the kidnapping in foreign countries of alleged criminals wanted for trial in the United States underscored this threat, while the role of U.S. planes in the hunt for the escaped Escobar revealed that Colombia was still vulnerable to U.S. pressures if its own solutions failed.

Although criticisms of Gaviria for "giving in to the narcoterrorists" have grown, most Colombians have backed his "national solution" to the problem. The young president himself was clear about what he had achieved and what remained to be accomplished.[10] He had ended narcoterrorism, which he termed "a purely Colombian phenomenon" that had traumatized his nation of thirty million people. Gaviria was under no illusion that his measures had ended the cocaine traffic, but *that*, he stressed, "is a *global* problem."

By 1992 it was evident that drug trafficking was not the only problem confronting the nations of the Americas that could not be solved within their own boundaries. Increasingly, the dilemmas they faced required international solutions, which in turn raised new fears of a loss of sovereignty.

Heightened global concern about environmental problems—from the hole in the ozone layer over Chile to the destruction of the rain forest in the Amazon—was one such issue. In Brazil, it led to growing fears of a move to "internationalize" the Amazon as a global trust, which united leftist and rightist nationalists in defense of Brazilian sovereignty—and prompted President Collor to seize the initiative and host the Earth Summit in June 1992.

Nor was ecology the only political issue that has made strange bedfellows in Latin America and the Caribbean during recent decades. In the past the region's leftists were among the strongest upholders of national sovereignty as a defense against the intervention of the United States. Successful revolutionary movements in Mexico, Cuba, and Nicaragua benefited from their association with an anti-U.S. nationalism. But when military regimes in Central and South America violated the human rights of leftist loyalists, and no political or judicial recourse was possible within their nations, Latin

American leftists became partisans of international pressure. Many who had attacked the Nixon administration's "destabilization" of Allende's government during the early 1970s applauded Jimmy Carter's policy of sanctions against Pinochet's Chile and other "flagrant violators of international standards of decency"—an assertion of a U.S. moral police power different in its motives and methods, but similar in its rationales, to the Roosevelt Corollary.

Some Latin Americans went further, pressing the United States to take the lead in forcing the region's military regimes to restore civilian rule. Largely for reasons of its own, Washington responded with initiatives that ranged from diplomatic pressure to the creation of the National Endowment for Democracy, a group of private political organizations with public financing that openly supported forces deemed democratic in Latin America and the Caribbean, providing expertise and assistance in registration drives, campaigning, and ballot counting, as well as international observers to discourage electoral fraud.

In Chile, such international pressure and assistance was credited with playing a significant role in the plebiscite defeat of the Pinochet dictatorship in 1988 and in the restoration of democracy that followed. U.S. Ambassador Harry Barnes was even praised for his active role in Chile's transition to democracy by socialists who had condemned U.S. diplomats for interfering in Chile's internal politics against the Allende government. European forces long absent from the hemisphere, such as the democratic Socialist International and its Christian Democratic equivalent, played an active role as well. During the 1980s, such external interference in the internal politics of sovereign states to defend democracy and human rights gained a new legitimacy in a region long jealous of national sovereignty and wary of foreign intervention in the name of higher values.

The ambivalence of the other Americas on this score was heightened when the United States cited the restoration of democracy as a rationale for its invasion of Panama in 1989. Yet in 1991 and again in 1992, the Organization of American States itself imposed economic sanctions on the Haitian military regime that had ousted the first democratically elected president in that country's violent history, and it took the lead in seeking a negotiated solution that would restore Jean-Bertrand Aristide to Haiti's presidency. It also endorsed the principle of multilateral intervention to protect democratic governments against such dictatorial seizures of power.

For their supporters, these restrictions on national sovereignty in the interest of higher values, embodied in such international accords as the United Nations Declaration of Human Rights, is a form of empowerment of silenced majorities. But they represent new challenges to the sovereignty of the nation-states of Latin America and the Caribbean. To many, however, the most serious challenge to national sovereignty today comes from the seismic shifts within the world economy.

A Special Relationship?

"Sovereignty is an outdated concept," argued Ricardo Arias Calderón, vice president of Panama, a country that has had particular difficulty sustaining its full independence. "It is no longer relevant in a world shaped by international economic forces. Even Mexico is integrating its economy with that of the United States." The Panamanian vice president's comment might be self-serving, but it underscored a new challenge to the sovereignty of the nations of the Americas.

Throughout Latin America and the Caribbean, regional integration is regarded as the new economic panacea. It is a startling development for both the United States and the other Americas, one likely to reshape the hemisphere in the next century, if not the next decade.

Most surprising of all, as Arias Calderón underlined, Mexico was leading the way. Mexico is not only the largest Spanish American country, but also one of the most nationalistic, a reflection of its revolution of 1910 and its proximity to the United States. Mexico's 1917 constitution limited foreign ownership of Mexican resources and during the 1930s Mexico nationalized U.S.-owned oil wells and railroads. After World War II, Mexican governments encouraged foreign investment, but as part of a strategy of promoting import substitution industries. In the 1970s Mexico led Third World nations in demanding a New International Economic Order, which would give them a larger share of the benefits of foreign trade and investment. It was also the decade of the Mexican oil boom, in which Mexico used its petrodollars to fuel its dreams of joining the ranks of the industrial powers. This dream vanished with the falling price of oil and the debt crisis of the 1980s. Mexico defaulted on its eighty-billion-dollar foreign debt in 1982, and boom turned rapidly to bust. As in most of the region, the "lost decade" of the 1980s ended Mexico's infatuation with protected inefficient industries and dreams of economic autonomy. By 1990 Mexico was prepared to sacrifice its aspirations for economic independence on the altar of economic realism.

Carlos Salinas de Gortari, a U.S.-educated economist, took over Mexico's powerful presidency in 1988 and began to open up its economy. Tariffs were lowered, government spending was reduced, and state industries were sold to private investors. Central to Salinas's economic strategy was attracting foreign investment, and the booming assembly plants in the free zone along the U.S. border seemed the model most likely to succeed. At first he tried to woo Japanese and European investment, but he had limited success. By 1990, Salinas had come to the conclusion that economic integration with the United States was Mexico's best bet. His proposal that Mexico join the North American Free Trade Association (NAFTA) formed the year before by the United States and Canada fell on receptive ears in Washington and an agreement was announced in August 1992.

For the United States, the decision to create a regional common market would itself have been a surprise to analysts fifteen years ago. The 1970s had witnessed a shift away from the traditional idea of a "special relationship" with Latin America and the Caribbean to the "globalism" of the Trilateral Commission, with its stress on worldwide markets and resources, and the joint "management" of global "interdependence" by the United States, Western Europe, and Japan. Within this context, the Carter administration moved toward establishing bilateral relationships with Latin American and Caribbean nations that reflected their economic roles, not their geographic locations. Significantly, the U.S. share of the region's exports and foreign investment declined considerably from 1960 to 1979, with Europe and Japan expanding their economic relations with Latin America and the Caribbean.

During the 1980s, the Reagan administration became obsessed with the Caribbean basin, but for political, not economic, reasons. The Caribbean Basin Initiative of 1983 allowed twenty-two Caribbean and Central American states duty-free or reduced tariff access to the U.S. market for their manufactures, but it was informed by fears of revolution, not by a vision of economic integration. Yet by the end of the decade, the declining ability of U.S. industries to compete with Asian and European rivals in world markets and the prospect of a division of the world into warring trading blocs had led Washington to refocus its attentions on markets and sources of raw materials and cheap labor closer to home. In 1989, the Bush administration agreed to a North American Free Trade Association with Canada, and a year later was talking about an "Enterprise of the Americas," which would create a common market from Alaska to Argentina.

Mexico was not the only Latin American nation to be thinking along similar lines. Chile signed a free-trade agreement with Mexico, and by mid-1992 was viewed by Washington as next in line for one with the United States. Venezuela was leaning in a similar direction, and had proposed a lowering of tariff barriers to the islands of the English-speaking Caribbean community. As the final decade of the century began, regional economic integration was in fashion throughout the hemisphere. Argentina, Brazil, Paraguay, and Uruguay were negotiating a Southern Cone common market, the MERCOSUR, that would unite their 190 million people and $450 billion gross domestic product by 1995 in a free trade zone stretching from the Amazon to Antarctica, one that might eventually include Chile and Bolivia and lead to a South American common market. Even the ministates of the Anglophone Caribbean were talking about the need to more fully integrate their tiny economies, already united in the Caribbean Community (CARICOM), with Michael Manley's Jamaica in the lead. The Caribbean Basin Initiative became permanent in 1990, and by 1992 Bush's

Enterprise of the Americas initiative was more than just a rhetorical gleam in some speechwriter's eye.

Although this new interest in regional integration was in part a reaction to the painful economic crisis of the 1980s, it also reflected efforts to adapt to a changing global economic order. By 1990, Latin America's hopes of economic autonomy and the United States' expectations of industrial hegemony had both been swamped in debt and dashed by Asian and European rivals. The collapse of communism, moreover, meant that Eastern Europe and the republics of the former Soviet Union were absorbing a growing share of world attention and resources. Significantly, it was after attending a 1990 World Economic Forum meeting in Davos, Switzerland, that was supposed to focus on Mexico, but instead concentrated on Eastern Europe, that Carlos Salinas decided integration with the United States was Mexico's only real option.

In 1992, an increasingly unified Europe was turning inwards and raising tariff barriers against Latin American exports in favor of those from former European colonies in Africa. Behind the renewed interest in regional integration in the Americas lay the prospect of the division of the world into hostile trading blocs. "We are talking here of facing the tremendous competition from Europe and from Japan and Asia," emphasized Salinas. "The main argument of the negotiations" for a North American Free Trade Association, he said, was "having the capacity to cope and compete with the regional blocs that are being formed around the world."

Paradoxically, the willingness of American countries like Mexico that once stressed their economic nationalism to integrate their economies with that of the Colossus of the North is likely to lead to an *increasing* stress on other dimensions of sovereignty, such as independent foreign policies. It was Mexico's Salinas who invited Fidel Castro to attend the first meeting of Ibero-American heads of state in 1991 and then hosted a private conclave with Castro and the presidents of Venezuela and Colombia a few months later, over U.S. objections. When asked about Cuba by the editors of *Newsweek* in early 1992, Salinas took the opportunity to stress that Mexico disagreed with Castro's policies, but "*we* are very respectful of *their* sovereignty."[11] Implicit was a message for his North American audience: And we hope that the United States will be very respectful of ours.

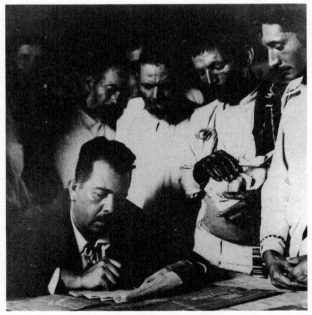

Mexico's epic revolution of 1910 cost some two million lives during a decade of fighting. Pancho Villa (shown above leading his "Golden Cavalry") and Emiliano Zapata, both legendary popular leaders, lost the struggle for power, but their concern for the rural poor eventually triumphed.

Although the Mexican revolution was a diverse movement without a common ideology or program, it became known throughout the Americas for its land reform. Between 1934 and 1940, President Lázaro Cárdenas distributed land to more than eight hundred thousand peasants, such as those watching him sign an agrarian reform decree.

Chapter 13

Making Revolution

The Cuban Revolution inaugurated a
new revolutionary era in 1959, when
the charismatic young Fidel Castro
took power after a guerrilla war
against the U.S.-backed Batista dictatorship. Castro embraced socialism
and a Soviet alliance and appealed to
young rebels elsewhere in the region
to follow his example.

Although many revolutionaries imitated Castro's strategy of guerrilla warfare, Chile's Salvador Allende pursued a "democratic road to socialism" after being elected president in 1970. Pressure from workers such as these demonstrators from the nationalized "Ex"-Yarur textile mill radicalized his nonviolent revolution.

In 1979, Nicaragua's Somoza dictatorship was overthrown by a broad coalition led by the Sandinistas, a
revolutionary movement inspired by
both Cuba and Nicaragua's Augusto
Sandino. The Sandinistas mobilized
urban youths, whose popular insurrections helped defeat Somoza's National
Guard.

A "crusade" that virtually eliminated adult illiteracy in one year and the creation of a nationalistic popular culture were Sandinista achievements during a decade in power mostly spent fighting U.S.-backed Contra insurgents. Here poor women pose with a larger-than-life Sandino at the Museum of Heroes and Martyrs.

In El Salvador, the FMLN, an alliance of five revolutionary movements, gained control over large rural areas but was unable to win national power. The military stalemate led FMLN military commander Joaquín Villalobos—shown here broadcasting over the clandestine rebel radio—to support a negotiated end to the twelve-year civil war in 1992.

In Peru, the Maoist Sendero Luminoso, or Shining Path, has defied post–Cold War trends by expanding its "People's War" into a serious revolutionary threat. In Lima's women's prison, captured Senderistas show their discipline and loyalty to their leader, "President Gonzalo." An army attack in April 1992, which killed over one hundred prisoners, ended Senderista control of their cell blocks.

13 *Making Revolution*

*I*n the cold clear morning of the Andean highlands, the peasant partisans of the Shining Path were drawn up in ranks against an azure sky. Their faces were brown and weather-beaten, their features and clothing marked their Indian ancestry. Their weapons were primitive, in many cases just sickles attached to long sticks. To the historian, they seemed an evocation of revolutions in China or Russia whose time had come and gone. Yet, here they were, in April 1992, after the collapse of communism on other continents, chanting its slogans, talking with confidence and determination about the inevitable triumph of their revolution under the banner of their Communist party and the Maoist ideology of the leader they idolized as "President Gonzalo." "The old society was unjust. There were landlords who oppressed and exploited the people," asserted Commissar Francisco. "We have learned much from the Party. With the People's War we have swept away the landlords, using a broom of steel as taught to us by President Gonzalo."[1] The fire of communism may have gone out elsewhere, but in the Peruvian Andes the flame of socialist revolution burns brighter than ever.

Viewed from North America, Latin America and the Caribbean seem lands of social unrest and political turmoil, where bullets are more common than ballots and revolutionaries are always waiting in the wings. Rebellions have been common in the region, but successful revolutions—

499

the seizure of power in order to transform politics and values, restructure economies, and redistribute wealth, status, and opportunity—have been rare. Between the Haitian revolution of 1791 and the Mexican revolution of 1910, more than a century went by without a profound social revolution shaking the Americas. Another half century would elapse before the Cuban revolution of 1959 would successfully challenge the hemispheric status quo, inaugurating three decades of revolutionary upheaval that would bring the Sandinistas to power in Nicaragua and guerrilla movements to much of the region. Today, with the disintegration of the Soviet Union, the electoral defeat of the Sandinistas, the peace process in El Salvador, and the economic crisis in Cuba, this cycle of revolution seems to be coming to an end. But the emergence of the Maoist Shining Path as a contender for power in Peru raises the question: Is a new revolutionary cycle about to begin?

Predictions of imminent revolution have been frequent in Latin America and the Caribbean during this century, in response to conditions that afford ample justification for rebellion. Certainly, if poverty and oppression, economic inequality and unrepresentative government were sufficient causes for revolution, it would be far more common in the Americas. But revolutionary upheavals have generally required something more. Paradoxically, the roots of revolution have often been nourished by economic progress. The integration of the region into the world order has also generated vulnerable economies, social dislocations, and political tensions, while raising popular aspirations and democratic expectations. The costs of this "progress" and the frustration of these expectations contributed to the success of revolutionary movements in Mexico, Cuba, and Nicaragua—and to revolutionary ferment throughout the region.

In all three successful revolutions, the identification of the old regime with foreign interests added the flag of nationalism to the banner of rebellion. This helped persuade some members of the elite and middle classes to lead the rebellions and others to support them. Its narrowed base of support weakened the old order, and this weakness was as important to the rebels' victory as their own strength.

But the overthrow of the old regime and the destruction of its army did not end the struggle for power. Revolutionary movements are often coalitions, united in their opposition to the status quo, but divided by varying visions of the new order to erect in its place. The fall of the old order has often led to new conflicts over power and policy, which were won by those who mobilized the greatest military and political support. In these contests, foreign powers also played a role, as backers of revolutionary factions or as symbols of external interference used by revolutionary leaders to rally popular support.

The resolution of these power struggles—and the promises made during their course—shaped the character of the revolutions that followed. Despite their differences, the Mexican, Cuban, and Nicaraguan revolutions all redefined the language of politics and altered their countries' economic and social policy agendas. Moreover, revolutionary regimes in all three countries conferred on their citizens an enhanced sense of national pride and personal self-worth by promoting a nationalistic popular culture and by standing up to the United States.

Revolutions in the Americas pose special problems for the United States, the hemisphere's principal power. Challenges to the status quo in its sphere of influence are unwelcome in Washington, particularly as U.S. dominance in the region often gives revolutionary nationalism an anti-American cast. The stirrings of radical unrest in the region have often led the United States to intervene in defense of its perceived strategic, economic, and political interests. They have also focused the attentions of the United States on a region that it has often taken for granted, impelling it to rethink its policies and even to recast its hemispheric relations. Viewed from the United States, revolutions in Latin America and the Caribbean carry the special urgency of revolutions in its sphere.

The Mexican, Cuban, and Nicaraguan revolutions have also had a major impact on the rest of the region. They have been viewed as models to be emulated and as symbols to be sustained by nationalists elsewhere in Latin America and the Caribbean. But what does it mean to be a revolutionary in the 1990s? It is a question being answered in El Salvador, where an armed struggle is now taking an electoral course, and in Peru, where a very different revolutionary movement is mounting a violent challenge to the old order.

Revolutionary Echoes

"Better to die on your feet than to live on your knees," a dying Mexican rebel is said to have scrawled with his blood on a Cuernavaca wall. It might have been the motto for his country's epic revolution. In 1910, landless peasants, dispossessed ranchers, and ill-paid laborers rose up against General Porfirio Díaz's oppressive regime, which had forced them to pay the social costs of Mexico's integration into the global economy, with its stress on exports and foreign investment, while excluding them from a fair share of its economic benefits and political participation. The Mexican revolution was the century's first mass upheaval, and it would have a major impact on the rest of Latin America.

Viewed from up close, the Mexican revolution seemed an unlikely model to emulate. Its factions exhibited little social or ideological coherence and fought each other with a ruthlessness that belied their once common cause. Its leaders ranged from dissident oligarchs, frustrated entrepreneurs, and provincial teachers to labor organizers, village chiefs, and cattle rustlers. During the years that followed their military triumph in 1920, the ruling "northern dynasty" of revolutionary generals seemed more concerned with consolidating power than with transforming their society—though Education Minister José Vasconcelos did promote rural literacy and a nationalistic popular culture that reevaluated Mexico's Indian heritage. The Depression of the 1930s did bring to power Lázaro Cárdenas, a revolutionary populist who delivered on the revolution's long-delayed promise of land reform, backed labor unions in their struggles with foreign-owned corporations, and expropriated U.S. oil companies and utilities. Cárdenas also promoted a "Mexican socialism," a nationalistic blend of socialist ideas with images of an idealized pre-Hispanic past such as the *ejido,* or agrarian reform community, whose beneficiaries, peasants like María Luz Ojeda in Zacatecas, still venerated Cárdenas half a century later. But after World War II the revolutionary pendulum swung back to the right, with a corrupt and repressive regime promoting industry and export agriculture in partnership with Mexican entrepreneurs and U.S. corporations. By 1991, when President Carlos Salinas buried its last vestige, the agrarian reform—by allowing *ejido* lands to be sold and large estates to be formed—the Mexican revolution was long dead. In Zacatecas, angry peasants protested that this meant a "return to the old hacienda system, with a few large landowners" and that "the peasant will go back to being a slave, like before the revolution."

Yet, for revolutionaries elsewhere in the region, the Mexican revolution has been a source of inspiration. Mexico's labor unions might be corrupt, but Augusto César Sandino, who worked in the Tampico oil fields during the 1920s before returning to Nicaragua to take up arms against U.S. intervention, came away from Mexico excited by its favoring the rights of workers in their struggles with foreign companies. Nor was Sandino alone in seeing solutions to his country's problems in Mexico's revolutionary model. Land reform, the transformation most associated with the Mexican revolution, became an obligatory banner of every subsequent revolution in Latin America and the Caribbean. Mexico's commitment to its Indian peoples may have been more rhetorical than real, but its ideology of *indigenismo* resonated in other countries with large indigenous populations, such as Peru, Bolivia, and Guatemala. Vasconcelos's faith in popular education as the solution for his country's poor would also find imitators elsewhere, while the legacy of the nationalist popular culture that he promoted would be painted on the walls of Allende's Chile and Sandinista Nicaragua long after Mexico's own revolutionary murals had become largely tourist attractions.

But it was Cárdenas's bold economic nationalism that made the deepest impression on the rest of the Americas. After the Mexican revolution, neither foreign investment nor private property seemed sacrosanct in Latin America, and the issue of nationalization was on the political agenda of the revolutions that followed. Moreover, after World War II, Mexico's rulers compensated for the freezing of revolution at home by a prorevolutionary stance in their foreign policy. Fidel Castro was one of many Latin American revolutionaries who found a refuge in Mexico. From there he set sail in 1956 for Cuba on a voyage that led to a revolution whose radicalism, evangelical fervor, and hemispheric impact would exceed Mexico's own.

Revolutionizing Cuba

It was 1985 and Fidel Castro's beard was flecked with gray. The once young
guerrilla leader was now pushing sixty and he no longer smoked his
trademark Cohiba cigars, but the Comandante's energy and enthusiasm
were still unflagging and his charisma was much in evidence. It was after
midnight, the hours in which he read, wrote—and gave interviews. "Revolutionaries are not born, they are made," he stressed, "by poverty, inequality, and dictatorship."

Like the Mexican revolution, the Cuban revolution of 1959 was a
seismic historical event. It not only transformed the Caribbean's largest
island, but also had a major impact on the rest of the Americas, revealing
the new limits of U.S. hegemony and catalyzing a reshaping of hemispheric
relations. As in Mexico, the roots of Cuba's revolution were nourished by
the island's reincorporation into the world order that began in the late
nineteenth century. A Spanish colony until 1898, Cuba—like Panama—
became a republic under U.S. auspices, which limited its independence but
assured its modernization. With Washington guaranteeing political stability and a good investment climate, U.S. capital poured into the island,
ensuring Cuba's position as the world's leading sugar producer.

Enormous sugar mill complexes were created, factories in the field
that consumed huge quantities of land and labor, converting Cuban landowners into dependent farmers and peasants into proletarians. Cuba's
prosperity came to depend on sugar, which accounted for 80 percent of its
export earnings, but was vulnerable to fluctuating world prices. The result
was a dizzying pattern of boom and bust—such as the "dance of the
millions" in 1920–21, when sugar prices soared over twenty-two cents a
pound only to plunge below four cents a pound—in which fortunes were
made and lost, while U.S. control of sugar production and processing grew.
Cuba's sugar industry never recovered its dynamism after the Depression
of the 1930s, and by the 1950s depended on its privileged access to a
subsidized U.S. market. At the same time, the sugar industry's monopoliza-
tion of land and labor made it difficult for Cuba to feed itself, creating the

paradox of a fertile island living on foodstuffs imported from Florida at an inflated cost.

This was not the only Cuban paradox. National statistics showed Cuba to be one of the wealthiest countries in the region—whether the measure was income, doctors, or telephones—but these benefits were unevenly distributed socially and geographically, with poor rural Cubans the most deprived. Fidel Castro was not the only critic to charge that Cuba was "a rich country with too many poor people."

The overweening U.S. presence in Cuba was another source of resentment. By 1928, U.S. investors controlled three quarters of Cuba's sugar, as well as strategic sectors from banking to utilities. Three decades later they accounted for 85 percent of all foreign investment, and the United States for two thirds of Cuba's exports and three quarters of its imports. It was little wonder that "Cuba for the Cubans" was a cry of reformers from the 1930s to the 1950s and would prove a popular revolutionary goal in the 1960s.

This economic dominance was reinforced by a political ascendancy that had begun with the Spanish-American War, which freed Havana from Madrid but turned Cuba into a U.S. protectorate. Under the notorious Platt Amendment of 1901 that Washington imposed on the new republic, the United States had the right to intervene in Cuba's internal affairs. During the two decades that followed, it landed troops four times and sent proconsuls on other occasions. A flicker of reform in 1933 was snuffed out by U.S. opposition. The Platt Amendment was finally renounced in 1934, but U.S. hegemony remained. Earl Smith, the last U.S. ambassador before Castro's revolution, described himself as "the second most important man in Cuba"—after the dictator, General Fulgencio Batista.

If Cuba's stagnant economy and unequal society provided the kindling for Castro's revolution, and U.S. domination the flame of resentment, it was Batista's dictatorship that sparked the conflagration. The extended U.S. political tutelage had aroused Cuban expectations of democracy without laying the foundation for its consolidation. From the 1920s on, Washington supported pro-U.S. strongmen over nationalistic democrats. Our final man in Havana was General Batista, who seized power for the last time in 1952 in a military coup that prevented an election he was sure to lose and reformers were favored to win. This frustration of democratic aspirations would ignite the revolt.

Among the leaders of this rebellion was a young lawyer named Fidel Castro, who led a quixotic attack on the Moncada army barracks, the country's second largest, on July 26, 1953; it was a military failure but a political success, capturing the popular imagination and founding a revolutionary movement. At his trial, Castro turned the tables on his accusers, placing the regime on trial for violating Cuban civil liberties and political rights in an electrifying courtroom defense that concluded: "Condemn me, it does not matter. History will absolve me."[2] He was sentenced to prison, but released in a 1955 amnesty and exiled to Mexico. There he prepared the rebel force that landed in eastern Cuba in December 1956. Plans to coordinate this landing with a popular insurrection in Santiago, Cuba's second city, went awry, but a few survivors made their way to the nearby Sierra Maestra, where they began guerrilla warfare. Two years later they would enter Havana in triumph.

Castro's victory was based on a growing mastery of guerrilla warfare, increasing peasant support, and a strong urban underground. But most of all, Castro's success stemmed from Batista's weakness: his lack of committed support. When victory eluded the dictator, his troops deserted, his civilian backing faded, and the United States abandoned him. As rebel columns streamed toward Havana in late 1958, Batista's army disintegrated and the "strongman" fled the country.

The rebellion was over, but the revolution had just begun. When Fidel Castro and his bearded young guerrillas descended from the Sierra Maestra and made their way across Cuba to Havana in January 1959, few among the millions who cheered their triumphal procession could be certain what their victory portended. Within the rebel ranks were varying visions of the path that their "revolution" should take. Many were middle-class moderates, like Mario Llerena, a rebel emissary abroad, whose notion of revolution was confined to the establishment of political democracy and some mild social reforms, and who believed that "there was no desire, no expectation, and no need for a radical revolution."[3] Others, including some of Castro's closest companions, such as his brother Raul and the Argentine Ernesto "Che" Guevara, were Marxists who equated revolution with socialism. Still others, including Castro himself, were influenced both by the revolutionary humanism of José Martí, Cuba's independence hero, and by their own experience of Cuba's underdevelopment and inequalities. Their ideology might not be fixed, but they were determined "to revolutionize Cuba from the bottom up." The contest among these factions was at once a struggle for power and a battle between rival revolutionary visions.

It was a struggle that Castro and the radicals won easily, a victory that reflected Castro's own ascendancy within his movement and control of the rebel army. It also stemmed from his ability to rally the overwhelming majority of Cubans to his side. They responded to Castro's charisma and they identified their revolution with him: "If Fidel is Communist, then so are we" became the refrain. But they also responded to the radical thrust of his revolution, which implemented an agrarian reform, raised real wages, eliminated illiteracy, promoted social programs, and stood up to the United States, eventually expropriating more than one billion dollars in U.S. properties. Many Cubans opposed Castro's radicalism. Over 10 percent of the population of six million went into exile, most to the nearby United States, but many to other countries of the Americas. Their departure eased Castro's path to power.

Castro won the struggle for power in increasingly close alliance with Cuba's Communist party, which had opposed Castro initially and played little part in the rebel victory, but which enjoyed sizable support among organized labor. For the Communists, Castro offered access to power and the opportunity to make the socialist revolution they themselves had never been able to win. For Castro, the Communist alliance provided disciplined working-class support at a time when his radicalism was alienating his original middle-class political base. It also helped him secure the backing of the Soviet Union, which he needed in order to survive his growing confrontation with the United States.

For the United States, Castro's increasing Communist ties were as worrying as his agrarian reform, whose major targets were U.S. sugar companies. By mid-1959, the *Wall Street Journal* was warning that "the

Revolution may be like a watermelon. The more they slice it the redder it gets."[4] As actor and as symbol, the United States played a central part in Cuba's internal power struggle. This reflected the traditional U.S. role as the ultimate arbiter of Cuban politics, plus Washington's distrust of Castro and his revolution. Though the United States had pressured Batista to leave office in late 1958, it had also tried to prevent Castro from assuming power by arranging a military alternative. When this failed, Washington threw its support to the moderates within Castro's own movement, which the Cuban leader used to discredit them. Their defeat left the United States with the stark choice of accepting Castro's victory and coming to terms with his radical vision of a new Cuba, or else trying to overthrow him. Predictably, with a revolution on its doorstep, Washington chose confrontation over compromise.

But the emergence of the Soviet Union as a rival superpower and alternative patron for Cuba meant that the economic and diplomatic pressures that had persuaded Havana to follow the U.S. lead in the past were no longer sufficient. Washington's final option was force. Covert intervention had undermined the leftist Arbenz government in Guatemala in 1954, and the CIA was given a chance to repeat that success. The CIA recruited and trained an exile army, confident that its landing would detonate a popular rebellion against the man the U.S. viewed as a Communist dictator. But this strategy came to grief in April 1961 at the Bay of Pigs, "a perfect failure," which revealed Castro's political support and military strength to be far greater than Washington had believed.

In the wake of his Bay of Pigs victory, Castro consolidated both his personal power and his revolution's socialist definition, wrapping both in the mantle of nationalism. On the eve of the invasion, one million Cubans gathered in Havana's Revolution Square to hear Fidel declare their revolution socialist. As a mock coffin of Uncle Sam was passed from hand to hand, Castro asked the crowd to "vote" for or against socialism. A thunderous roar of approval gave him the answer he wanted: Cuba was now in the socialist camp. The missile crisis of the following year only confirmed that reality. President John F. Kennedy may have faced down Soviet Premier Nikita Khrushchev and forced Moscow to withdraw its offensive missiles from Cuba, but in return the U.S. gave assurances that it would not invade the island. At the time, Castro was outraged at Khrushchev's failure to consult him, but he later admitted that "Khrushchev was right." The resolution of the missile crisis meant the consolidation of his revolution.

But revolution is a process that unfolds over time. During the next three decades, Castro steered his revolution on a gyrating course. A 1961 campaign based on student volunteers that succeeded in virtually wiping out illiteracy in one year underscored for Castro the power of revolutionary consciousness and mass mobilization to overcome seemingly insurmountable obstacles. He followed the same strategy in his drive to develop Cuba economically while creating a heterodox utopian socialism based on moral—not material—incentives, which would refute both U.S. laws of capitalist economics and the Soviet model of socialist stages. Its proof was to be a ten-million-ton sugar harvest by 1970, almost double Cuba's previous record, and Castro mobilized his nation to meet this symbolic goal. When that harvest failed to reach ten million tons, and led to widespread economic dislocation and political disillusionment, Castro took personal responsibility for the debacle. Years later he excused these mistakes of his youth as "errors of idealism: we wanted to build communism without first passing through socialism."

For much of the 1960s, Cuban economic strategy followed Fidel Castro's changing enthusiasms—for and against sugar and industry, cattle and coffee—and the joke was that "his checkbook was Cuba's budget" in a system of "unplanned planning" with "more checks than balances." Beginning in the 1970s, Castro embraced Communist orthodoxy, moved closer to Moscow, and adapted Soviet institutions and models to Cuban conditions. By 1989, a synthesis of Soviet and Cuban experience seemed consolidated in Cuba, and a postrevolutionary society had emerged. A balance of three decades of revolution could be drawn up.

Revolution had created far greater changes in Cuba than in Mexico. Few private enterprises remained and the economy was guided by central planning. A one-party Communist state had been established with unprecedented power to mobilize resources and reshape society. The old class structure had been leveled and Cuba claimed the most equal society in the Americas, although new status distinctions had emerged, based on revolutionary roles and political connections. Literacy and education were universal, along with free medical care, and life expectancy approached U.S. levels.

Rural Cuba had benefited most. Bayamo, the Sierra Maestra province where Castro had established his guerrilla headquarters, was one of Cuba's poorest and least developed regions in 1959. Twenty-five years later, its modest rural homes sprouted television antennas and pastel-painted schools dotted its hillsides, including innovative coeducational boarding schools where students worked half the day in the fields. In the provincial capital, where a Nestlé dairy had been the sole industry, thirty-five factories provided employment, and local citizens prided themselves on their medical clinics and cultural centers. Unlike many rural areas in Latin America and the Caribbean, Bayamo had held its population in the interim, as the revolution's heavy investment in the countryside stemmed the tide of migration inundating cities in the rest of the region. People spoke of the difference that the revolution had made in their lives and in those of their better fed, better dressed, and better educated children.

Yet, for all the dramatic changes, some of the salient features—and problems—of prerevolutionary Cuba remained, albeit in new guises. Industry had made significant strides, but sugar still accounted for the bulk of the country's exports. The revolution had recorded impressive gains in education and public health, but their quality was debatable and many Cubans found their material aspirations unfulfilled. Mass organizations and local "popular power" institutions gave Cubans greater political participation than before the revolution, but not the Western-style democracy and civil liberties that many Cubans desired. The seamy side of the Cuban revolution was hidden behind the prison walls where political dissidents languished. Social conformity was enforced by revolutionary block committees and shoddy Soviet goods were part of the price for Cuba's dependence on Moscow's trade and aid.

Although Castro's Cuba was no longer dependent economically on the United States in 1989, it seemed to have exchanged that dependency for a niche in COMECON, the Soviet bloc common market. This was the source of Cuba's comparative prosperity during the 1980s crisis that hit other countries in the region, but a far cry from the young guerrillas' dreams of economic autonomy and industrial development. Since 1989, moreover, the collapse of communism and disintegration of the Soviet Union have revealed just how vulnerable revolutionary Cuba remains to foreign events beyond its control. By mid-1991, COMECON was history, the Cuban economy was in deep trouble, and even a Cuban Communist who stressed his strong support for the revolution reflected ruefully in Havana that "dependency is bad, no matter what side of the river it's on." By 1992, Moscow's new anti-Communist leaders were unwilling to subsidize the Cuban economy and unable even to meet their trade commitments to their erstwhile ally in such vital areas as oil, grain, and spare parts for Cuba's largely Russian machinery. Although a defiant Castro vowed "to go back to plowing with oxen" before he surrendered his socialist dream, the future of his revolution was in doubt.

Yet, whatever the ultimate fate of the Cuban revolution, its impact on the Americas is incontrovertible. For some, Cuba was a model to emulate, for others a threat to combat, but there were few neutrals where Castro's revolution was concerned.

The Guerrilla Decade

"The duty of revolutionaries is to make revolution," Fidel Castro proclaimed in February 1962.[5] Throughout the hemisphere and across the political spectrum there was the hope—or fear—that Latin America was ripe for revolution, and that the Cuban revolution would sweep over the region as the French revolution had once swept across Europe, ending oppressive old regimes and replacing them with a new egalitarian order.

The dream of another Cuba inspired young revolutionaries throughout the region to exchange their books for rifles and to head for the hills in the expectation of repeating Fidel Castro's success in their own countries. None triumphed until the Sandinista victory in Nicaragua in 1979, but their efforts to do so made the 1960s the "Guerrilla Decade."

It also made "No More Cubas" the priority of U.S. policy in the region. Within this context, President Kennedy promoted the Alliance for Progress, a program of ambitious social and economic reforms designed to deprive Castro's imitators elsewhere in the region of the social base for revolution. "All people of this hemisphere are entitled to a decent way of life," he warned. "Those who make peaceful revolution impossible will make violent revolution inevitable." But the Alliance soon ran aground on the rocks of anticommunism and self-interest, and then lost its way as Washington placed increasing priority on military assistance to counter guerrilla insurgencies. When Lyndon Johnson replaced Kennedy in the White House in late 1963, backing for democratic reformers withered in Washington and support for anticommunist dictatorships grew.

The fear of another Cuba at first motivated some Latin American and Caribbean elites to carry out economic and social reforms from above in the hope of forestalling a revolution from below. But it also led the middle classes—whom the Alliance envisioned as a repository of democratic values—to support authoritarian regimes and harsh military measures to deal with real or imagined revolutionary threats. One way or another, the shadow of Cuba's 1959 revolution shaped the hemispheric history of the decades that followed as a contest between revolutionary movements and their opponents.

In this continentwide struggle, Venezuela emerged as a key battleground. Fortunate to possess the region's largest oil fields, Venezuela also had its second largest per capita income. But this wealth was unevenly distributed, as were its fertile lands. In the democratic wave that followed World War II, a reform movement led by Acción Democrática (AD), a social democratic party, came to power in 1945. But it was overthrown by a military coup in 1948, and replaced by the corrupt and repressive dictatorship of General Marcos Pérez Jiménez. He was ousted in 1958 after a popular rebellion spread to the armed forces, bringing AD's Rómulo Betancourt to power at roughly the same time as Fidel Castro, on seemingly similar platforms after the defeat of strikingly similar dictatorships. Castro visited Caracas in 1959 and received a warm welcome. But, as they consolidated power, the two leaders moved in opposite directions, with

Betancourt moderating his once radical reform stance, while Castro radicalized his reformist agenda. By 1962, Castro and Betancourt were sworn enemies and leftist guerrillas had taken up arms against the Venezuelan president.

Many of them were middle-class students, youthful former members of AD like Moses Moleiro, who had become disillusioned with Betancourt's declining commitment to radical change and inspired by Castro's revolutionary example: "We saw that while our leaders had been talking about revolution for thirty years, in Cuba the revolution triumphed in two years of fighting; while Rómulo Betancourt had been talking about agrarian reform for thirty years, and governed twice without doing anything about it, in Cuba a far-reaching agrarian reform was taking place."[6] In response, they left Acción Democrática, formed the Movement of the Revolutionary Left (MIR) in 1960, and began preparing for "armed struggle." Other guerrillas were Venezuelan Communists who had taken part in the rebellion that ousted Pérez Jiménez and were impatient with their own party's preference for democratic reform in a situation that they believed was ripe for revolution. In the view of Fabricio Ojeda, a leader of these revolutionary Communists, "Venezuela was an erupting volcano."[7]

Militant strikes and slum riots and a 1962 uprising by sympathetic army units underscored the possibilities of urban insurrection. Venezuelan guerrilla leaders followed Castro's example and headed for mountainous rural zones to begin rural guerrilla warfare, reducing the cities to rear bases of support.

The Acción Democrática government countered by accelerating its agrarian reform, jailing leftist political leaders, and intensifying its military counterinsurgency with U.S. assistance. By 1969, when the opposition Christian Democrats elected Rafael Caldera president, Venezuela's guerrilla movements were no longer a threat, the left was deeply divided, and some of its most important advocates of armed struggle were now arguing for accepting Caldera's offer of amnesty and returning to electoral politics. In a democratic Venezuela, the need for "armed struggle" was less clear than in Batista's Cuba. Moreover, in a country where two out of three people lived in urban areas, "guerrilla action depends on developments in the town," argued Teodoro Petkoff, a Communist leader whose brother was a rural guerrilla commander.[8] When Petkoff left the Communist party in 1970, it was not to join his brother in the mountains, but rather to found the democratic Movement to Socialism (MAS), with the goal of forming a broad leftist electoral alliance and formulating a "Venezuelan road to socialism."

Although the guerrilla movements in each country had their own histories, and some were more successful than others, the problems experienced in Venezuela—military mistakes, political divisions, and a weak social base—were common throughout the region. In response to these defeats, the Cubans published Regis Debray's *Revolution in the Revolution?* as a how-to manual of guerrilla revolution based on the Cuban model, and formed OLAS—the Organization of Latin American Solidarity—as a regional revolutionary international to provide the political support lacking from local Communist parties and their Moscow patrons.

In 1967, Che Guevara himself—the prototype and theorist of the rural guerrilla—began guerrilla warfare in Bolivia with the goal of "turning the Andes into the Sierra Maestra of South America" and aiding the global revolutionary struggle by creating "two, three, many Vietnams."[9] A year later he was dead at the hands of U.S.-trained troops. Guevara was the victim of the same combination of strategic and tactical errors, feuds with local Communists, and lack of a sufficient peasant base that had doomed other Latin American efforts to emulate Cuba's example. In the wake of Guevara's death, Havana seemed to give up on the possibilities of Cuban-style revolution in the Americas. Instead, Castro supported the wide array of "revolutionary" movements that emerged in countries with differing conditions and traditions—from urban guerrillas such as Uruguay's Tupamaros to Salvador Allende's "democratic road to socialism" in Chile.

The blocking of these varying revolutionary roads by U.S.-backed armed forces—and in particular the 1973 military coup in Chile—persuaded Castro that Washington would not allow even a democratic revolution to succeed in the Americas. In the mid-1970s, Castro redirected his revolutionary hopes and Cuban efforts to Africa, while seeking a rapprochement in the Americas with regimes he had once sought to overthrow. High on his list was Venezuela, led by Carlos Andrés Pérez, who had been a tough interior minister during the successful counterinsurgency campaign against Fidelista guerrillas of the mid-1960s. As president from 1974 to 1979, however, Pérez led efforts to reintegrate a more restrained Cuba into the inter-American system. Although the United States succeeded in blocking these initiatives within regional organizations such as the OAS, several Latin American and Caribbean nations renewed diplomatic relations with Cuba. It was a sign of the growing determination of the region's countries to shape a hemispheric policy independent of Washington's dictates, which would surface with far greater force with the Nicaraguan revolution of 1979.

The Revolution of the "Muchachos"

The convoy of jeeps wound its way through the jungle-covered mountains of northern Nicaragua, with soldiers deploying up the hillsides at turns in areas where Contra guerrillas were active. It was January 1983, and Sandinista vice president Sergio Ramírez was leading a group of cabinet ministers in a whirlwind weekend tour of the provinces.

Each stop revealed another facet of the revolution they led and the problems it faced. At a Matagalpa farm, committed students spending their Christmas vacation picking coffee beans worried about recent Contra attacks that had claimed several lives not far from where they were gathering the vital harvest, on which Nicaragua depended for badly needed export income. In another production center, a grimy migrant worker embraced "Comandante Lea" Guido, the minister of health, and reminded her of the time they fought together against Somoza's National Guard in León, one of the Sandinistas' "hero cities." Nearby, teenage teachers at a school empty of equipment complained of the lack of resources with which to follow up their successful literacy campaign. At an isolated estate that had once belonged to a Somoza general, a group of resettled Miskito Indians stood in stony silence listening to Vice President Ramírez, an accomplished writer, deliver a speech in elegant Spanish, a language they didn't understand. The day ended at a rural retreat, but there was no respite for the weary ministers from the dilemmas they faced. Local land-owners came to drink coffee with them—and to complain about low government prices for agrarian products, which were responsible for declining production levels and the increasing smuggling of cattle across the border into Honduras.

Over glasses of white rum, youthful ministers talked of how they had left school to join the Sandinista revolution; how they had spent their college years learning instead how to defeat the Somoza dictatorship. "We had no time to learn how to govern," explained Comandante Mónica Baltodano, who had become minister of regional affairs, responsible for an ambitious decentralization program. "But we thought that defeating Somoza was the hard part, that the revolution itself would be easy. Now we know we were wrong."

The Sandinistas were the first to follow Castro's guerrilla path to power. What made the Sandinista success particularly striking was that it took place in the Central American country under U.S. influence for the longest time, a nation ruled by a second-generation dictator educated at West Point and commanding a modern U.S.-armed and -trained National Guard.

In Nicaragua, as in Mexico and Cuba, economic modernization and political dictatorship bred the conditions for social revolution. Coffee exports had led Nicaragua's integration into the international economy after 1870, but they had lost their dynamism in the Depression of the 1930s. After World War II, a cotton boom compensated for the stagnation of coffee exports, but this economic success came at a high social cost. Subsistence farming gave way to commercial agriculture and some two hundred thousand peasants were forced off their newly valuable lands. Some joined the ranks of ill-paid migrant laborers. Many more swelled the tide of migration to Managua, Nicaragua's burgeoning capital. There they eked out a living in urban shantytowns where most residents were unemployed and most families impoverished. These displaced peasants and desperate slum-dwellers would be prime recruits for the Sandinista rebellion.

Dictatorship had been a central issue in modern Nicaragua since the

1930s, when National Guard commander Anastasio Somoza arranged the murder of Augusto Sandino and then took over the government. By the 1970s, three Somozas—Anastasio (1936–56) and his sons Luis and Anastasio—had ruled Nicaragua, imposing a corrupt dictatorship more long-lived than Porfirio Díaz's and more ruthless than Fulgencio Batista's. By then the Somoza family controlled a quarter of the country's arable land and twenty-six of its largest corporations. They had also used their power to undermine the position of dissident elites, to create a new elite of their own cronies, and to repress the protests of workers and peasants who had paid the price of the Somozas' vision of modernity. In imposing a dynastic dictatorship, the Somozas had personalized Nicaraguan politics. This made it possible for the rebels to unite a socially diverse alliance against the regime: the Somoza dictatorship was the central issue in the revolt.

As in Mexico and Cuba, nationalism reinforced the demand for revolutionary change and gave it an anti-U.S. cast. Nicaragua had been the first Central American country to be invaded by North Americans in 1855—when Tennessee adventurer William Walker made himself Nicaragua's president—and the first to be occupied by U.S. Marines, in 1908. The United States intervened repeatedly during the early twentieth century in an effort to reshape Nicaraguan politics, and was responsible for both the creation of the National Guard and the selection of Somoza to command it. Successive U.S. administrations of both parties backed the Somoza dictatorship and armed the Guard, despite complaints about both. When Franklin D. Roosevelt was asked "how he could support that son of a bitch Somoza," he is said to have replied: "Somoza may be a son of a bitch, but he's *our* son of a bitch." During the Cold War, the Somozas' anticommunism was sufficient to assure Washington's support, and the Somozas played their U.S. cards with skill, cultivating Washington politicians and envoys. North Americans made large profits as Somoza business partners and the United States dominated Nicaragua's trade and finance. Small wonder that Nicaraguans identified the United States with the Somoza regime and blamed Washington for their economic, social, and political ills.

In 1970, few countries in the region seemed as ripe for revolution as Nicaragua, yet as unlikely to have one. The Sandinista National Liberation

Front (FSLN) was inspired by Sandino's example, but it emulated Castro's. Founded by radicalized students in 1961, it was one of the less successful of the many Latin American guerrilla groups that followed Cuba's lead during the 1960s. But new political and military strategies and tactics—urban organization and peasant mobilization, broader social alliances at home and support abroad, dramatic armed actions and popular insurrection—would bring the Sandinistas to power in 1979.

Equally important were the errors and unpopularity of the Somoza regime. When an earthquake devastated Managua, the nation's capital, in 1972, Anastasio Somoza profited from the reconstruction, pocketed relief funds, and used these monies to enter economic sectors previously reserved for other members of the Nicaraguan elite. Somoza's cynical corruption in the face of national disaster embarrassed the educated middle class and alienated business elites whose interests were prejudiced by his new ventures. His actions also scandalized the Catholic church: in Nicaragua, unlike Mexico or Cuba, the Church would support the rebellion, culminating in 1979 in an unprecedented episcopal endorsement of armed overthrow of the dictatorship.

In 1977, a group of twelve prominent professionals and clerics was formed to bridge the gap between the Sandinistas and the elite opposition to Somoza led by Pedro Joaquín Chamorro, a charismatic publisher and political reformer. Chamorro's assassination in January 1978 released a national outrage that transcended class lines and set the stage for the insurrection that followed.

During the next eighteen months, strikes by dissident business elites led by Alfonso Robelo and popular insurrections led by the Sandinistas brought the Nicaraguan economy to a halt and the dictatorship to its knees. In this *revolución de los muchachos,* or Kids' Revolution, spontaneous urban rebellion by young slum-dwellers was as important as planned Sandinista offensives. When Somoza's intransigence undermined U.S. efforts to arrange a transfer of power to Robelo's moderates, and when Latin American opposition blocked Washington's proposal for hemispheric intervention, the Sandinistas completed their defeat of Somoza's National Guard, a personal army that disintegrated when the dictator fled the country in July 1979.

In Nicaragua, as in Cuba, the course of the rebellion determined the outcome of the struggle for power that followed, establishing the Sandinistas as both the people's choice and the sole military force. Their business allies were relegated to a minority position in the revolutionary government headed by Sandinista commandante Daniel Ortega, whose policies they were powerless to influence. In April 1980, Robelo and Violeta Bárrios de Chamorro, Pedro Joaquín's widow, resigned from the revolutionary junta and joined an opposition that included business elites and disillusioned Sandinistas and clerics.

As in Mexico and Cuba, the triumph of the Sandinista revolution meant the transformation of rebels into rulers, the creation of a dominant revolutionary party, and the extension of state power into new realms. A literacy "crusade" based on the Cuban model made impressive gains against great odds, and an increase in political participation through Sandinista mass organizations occurred as well. Fidel Castro urged the Sandinistas not to make the same mistakes he had made, and they tried to shape their revolution in a distinct mold. Unlike Cuba, opposition parties and newspapers were permitted and competitive elections were held, although opponents complained of restrictions on the press and their political freedoms. Land reform, a central focus of Nicaragua's revolution, as it was in Mexico and Cuba, was an eclectic showcase for Sandinista pragmatism, combining private ownership and state farms with an expanding cooperative sector. Large landowners remained in control of most of Nicaragua's export crops, but the country's capitalists lost their political influence and complained that government policies prejudiced their interests. They provided strong support for the internal political opposition to the Sandinistas and to the U.S.-backed Contra guerrillas whose efforts to overthrow them increasingly dominated Sandinista concerns, along with a tightening U.S. economic squeeze with the same goal.

By January 1983, Health Minister Lea Guido was reduced to handing out toys donated by U.S. solidarity groups to rural children in the northern border zone, "because the policy of the U.S. government makes it impossible to give them the medicines that they really need." Eventually, over 60 percent of the Sandinista government's expenditures would be devoted to defense. If the Nicaraguan revolution accomplished less than its predecessors, it was in large part due to the need to devote a growing portion of its more limited resources to fighting a Contra force of sixteen thousand recruited, trained, armed, and directed by the United States. In the end, perhaps the biggest achievement of the Sandinista revolution was its survival for a decade in the face of unremitting U.S. hostility that ranged from a virtual economic embargo to Washington's largest and most overt covert war.

In response, the Sandinistas moved closer to Moscow and radicalized their revolution, accelerating their agrarian reform to give Nicaragua's peasants something to fight for. In the cotton fields of León, along the Pacific Coast, this strategy seemed a success. Looking at his cooperative's first cotton crop, Luis Mayorga talked in 1983 of how its previously landless members had gotten together at a meeting of the local Sandinista peasant organization and decided to take advantage of the government's offer of land by forming a cooperative, which also made them eligible for government credits, an imported tractor, and technical assistance. A year later, their cooperative was prospering and its members were talking about adding livestock and building a school for their children. Many of the peasants involved had been apolitical before, Mayorga recounted, "but we are all Sandinistas now."

But not all Nicaraguan peasants reacted positively to Sandinista attempts to organize them into cooperatives. Many were individualistic farmers in less populated zones who resented such governmental interference. So did the Miskito Indians of the Atlantic Coast, who considered themselves a nation apart from Spanish-speaking Nicaragua and demanded both political autonomy and control over the resources in the third of Nicaraguan territory that they considered their homeland, demands that the Sandinistas, with their nationalist ideology, were unwilling to grant. It was in these regions that the Contras found significant rural support and recruits.

In the short run, the result of the U.S. covert war was to stiffen Sandinista resolve and enable them to rally support under the banner of nationalism. Most Nicaraguans, with a new pride at their country's ability to stand up to the Colossus of the North, viewed the Contras as a continuation of the Somoza National Guard, complete with U.S. arms and backing. Over time, however, the costs of the fratricidal conflict in blood and treasure undercut Sandinista resources and popularity.

Together with errors born of inexperience and ideology, bureaucratic mismanagement and political infighting, a heavy debt burden inherited from Somoza and Moscow's reluctance to assume the responsibility for financing "another Cuba," the Contra war and U.S. economic squeeze restricted the Sandinistas to a struggle for survival that they won on the battlefield but lost at the polls. In 1990, weary of sacrifice and disillusioned with the Sandinistas' inability to deliver on their promises of a better life, Nicaraguans voted them out of office. They elected the opposition leader Violeta Bárrios de Chamorro, a conciliatory elite figure whose family includes both Sandinistas and Contras. She promised an end to the fighting and the hope of U.S. aid in solving the country's economic problems. The Sandinista revolution became the first revolution to be ended by ballots after taking power with bullets. In a way, that was as much of a revolution as the Sandinistas' partly successful efforts to transform Nicaragua during a decade of revolutionary rule.

Yet, the fact that many Sandinista initiatives survived their ouster, and that the Sandinistas themselves remain Nicaragua's strongest political force, with a good chance of recapturing power in the next elections— although as social democrats whose policies seem closer to capitalism than socialism—owed itself to a far quieter revolution in inter-American relations, which deprived the United States of the Contra military victory that Washington sought. It was a diplomatic revolution begun by regional powers such as Venezuela and Mexico, but one in which the tiny Central American nations themselves were the chief protagonists and the diminutive president of demilitarized Costa Rica was the conquering hero.

A Quiet Revolution

From the White House, Honduras and Costa Rica may have looked alike in 1981, small Central American nations whose economies were dependent upon U.S. aid and trade. Seen from Central America, they were polar opposites, and so were their responses to U.S. efforts to make them fronts for Washington's war against the Sandinistas.

Honduras, a largely mestizo nation of four million, was the poorest country in Central America. It was the last of the banana republics, with a corrupt military, a weak political system, and a fear of its neighbors that left it open to U.S. blandishments. *"La Embajada,"* as the U.S. embassy in Tegucigalpa was known, soon became the regional command center for Washington's covert war, and Honduras's rugged Nicaraguan border area a sanctuary for the Contras.

Costa Rica, on Nicaragua's southern frontier, was a country whose two million people were largely of European descent, with the highest levels of income, education, and equality in Central America. It was also the one nation in the region with a strong democratic tradition, a welfare state, and no army, the result of a post–World War II social democratic "revolution" led by José Figueres and his Liberation party. Convinced that "war is not a natural human condition" and that "poverty and armies" constituted the "biggest threats to democracy in Latin America," Figueres set out to eliminate both from Costa Rica. His success made Costa Rica an oasis of peace and democracy in a region notorious for violence and dictatorship.

Four decades later, falling coffee prices and rising welfare costs had taken the shine off the Costa Rican model, but the "Ticos' " pride in their country and its democracy remained. Costa Rica had supported the Sandinista struggle against Somoza, a longtime enemy, but turned sour on Nicaragua's revolution when it went beyond the bounds of their own social democracy—and the moderate stance of former Sandinistas and their allies, men like Edén Pastora and Alfonso Robelo, who found a friendly exile in Nicaragua's southern neighbor. But Costa Ricans clung to their neutrality in the middle of the Central American storm and resisted U.S. pressures to remilitarize their country and turn it into the "southern front" against the Sandinistas. Yet, without an army of their own the Ticos were ill-prepared to police their frontiers. They had become a combat zone between Sandinistas and Contras by 1986, when Oscar Arias was elected president as the Liberation party standard-bearer, over a more conservative candidate who favored an active Costa Rican involvement in the U.S.-backed Contra war.

Arias was a political scientist with degrees from U.S. and British universities and a clear understanding of his country's uniqueness—and vulnerability. Even before becoming president, he was convinced that being dragged into the Contra war would be fatal for Costa Rica's proud democracy and possibly for its sovereignty as well. His inaugural address stressed the need for "an alliance for liberty and democracy," language that he shared with Ronald Reagan, but interpreted very differently. Arias also proclaimed "nonintervention" to be a "sacred right" of the nations of the Americas.[10]

As president he moved decisively to reassert Costa Rican sovereignty over its own territory, closing down a Contra airstrip and arresting the reputed head of the CIA operation in his country. But Arias believed that unless peace was restored in Nicaragua, Costa Rica's neutrality and democracy remained at risk and its economic prosperity a receding dream. A December 1986 visit to Washington persuaded him that the Reagan administration would fight until the last Central American to roll back the Sandinista revolution. It was this conviction that brought Arias to take the lead in creating a Central American peace process that transformed even U.S. client states into protagonists of their own destiny. It was the culmination of a long process of change in inter-American relations.

Historically, the United States had been the ultimate arbiter of the region's affairs. Washington had renounced the right of unilateral intervention in 1936, but was instrumental in the creation of mechanisms for multilateral intervention through the mutual defense provisions of the Rio Pact of 1947 and the formation of the Organization of American States (OAS) the following year. Under heavy U.S. pressure, the OAS in 1954 defined the political control of any American country by "the international Communist movement" as a threat to hemispheric peace that justified collective intervention. The resolution was directed against Guatemala, where a left-leaning coalition that included the small local Communist party had undertaken a set of land and labor reforms prejudicial to important U.S. economic interests, and served to justify the covert CIA intervention that overthrew the Arbenz government later that year. Similar considerations would be invoked to justify both the OAS's expulsion of an avowedly Communist Cuba in 1962, and the 1965 U.S. intervention in the Dominican Republic to forestall a popular insurrection aimed at restoring the ousted constitutional president, reformer Juan Bosch, where the alleged Communist threat was difficult to demonstrate. During the two decades that followed World War II, the OAS served to legitimate a U.S. policy of intervening to contain or reverse perceived revolutionary threats in Latin America and the Caribbean.

Fourteen years would pass before another threat of revolution in the U.S. sphere—in Nicaragua—would lead Washington to turn to the OAS once again to rubber-stamp U.S. intervention. In 1979, however, the OAS rejected Washington's appeal to intervene in Nicaragua. Clearly, much had changed in the interim.

The economic bases of U.S. hegemony had weakened, as Latin American nations industrialized and Japanese and European rivals cut into the U.S. share of the region's trade and investment, and the capacity of Latin American countries for autonomous action had increased. In addition, the moral authority of the United States had declined with its covert war against the democratically elected Allende government and U.S. support of military regimes in the region. The Carter administration had won credit for its human rights stand, but its insensitivity to Latin America's economic aspirations and its vacillating Nicaragua policy robbed its OAS initiative of credibility.

Latin American perceptions of the threat of regional revolution were also different in 1979 than in the 1960s. Fears that the Cuban revolution would sweep over the region had faded, and few governments in the OAS saw a Sandinista Nicaragua as posing a threat of regional revolution, while many saw the Nicaraguan revolution as a justified response to decades of oppressive dictatorship and U.S. domination. In opposing U.S. requests for an OAS "peacekeeping force" in Nicaragua, moreover, Latin American nations were expressing their defense of national self-determination against the Colossus of the North. As a consequence, when the Carter administration asked the OAS to sanction the creation of a peacekeeping force, it was decisively defeated. For the first time in history, the OAS had served to block a U.S. intervention, not to legitimate one. The Nicaraguan revolution not only challenged U.S. hegemony in its own backyard; it also provided an opportunity for other American republics to assert their autonomy.

In the wake of the U.S. defeat in the OAS, Washington discounted it as a policy instrument and looked instead to more malleable subregional groupings. In 1983, when an internecine struggle in Grenada provided an excuse for the United States to intervene and put an end to that island's socialist revolution, the Reagan administration turned not to the OAS, but to the association of eastern Caribbean ministates for endorsement. Similar considerations governed U.S. strategy in Central America, where Washington bypassed the OAS and presented the other Central American states as the regional judge of any Nicaraguan peace accord. It was a strategy that reflected U.S. distrust of the Latin American majority in the OAS and dismay at the emergence in 1982 of informal but highly visible Latin American efforts to broker a compromise peace agreement that would deprive the U.S.-backed Contra war of legitimacy—and leave the Sandinistas in power.

Beginning in 1982, the Contadora group—Colombia, Mexico, Panama, and Venezuela—of regional powers pressed for a negotiated solution to the linked Central American conflicts, an approach which Washington could not openly oppose. Instead, it used its influence with Central American client states such as Honduras and El Salvador to block successive Contadora initiatives. In 1986, the Contadora group was strengthened by the creation of a South American support group, but continued U.S. opposition stalemated their efforts to broker a peace. Still, a meeting of the region's foreign ministers reaffirmed that the overwhelming majority of

Latin American nations opposed U.S. intervention and favored a negotiated settlement.

Oscar Arias built on these Latin American initiatives, but launched
his own *Central* American peace plan, in which its leaders would themselves resolve the conflicts plaguing their region through a linked process
of negotiations and elections. "Only democracy," he affirmed, "can end
wars between brothers."[11] Washington still wanted a military victory in
Nicaragua, not a negotiated settlement that left the Sandinistas supervising
their own elections, and Reagan deemed the Arias plan to be "fatally
flawed."[12] But his ability to block Arias was now weakened by the Iran-
Contra scandal and the congressional opposition to continued funding of
the Contras that had provoked Colonel Oliver North's illegal efforts to
secure Asian financing for the U.S. covert war against the Sandinistas.
When the Costa Rican president persuaded his fellow Central American
heads of state—including Nicaragua's Daniel Ortega—that peace and
elections were in their best interests, the road was open to the Esquipulas
accords of August 1987, which provided for a peace process centered around
negotiated settlements of the region's conflicts and respect for democracy
and human rights, including amnesties for insurgents and new elections in
which all parties could participate.

It was with justice that Oscar Arias was awarded the Nobel Peace
Prize in 1987, and it was significant that it was a Central American—not a
United States—initiative that ended Nicaragua's long and bitter civil war.
"Let Central Americans decide the future of Central America," Arias used
his Nobel award ceremony to tell the United States, urging it to "support
the efforts for peace instead of the forces of war in our region." The goal,
he stressed, was not "peace alone" but "peace and democracy, together,
indivisible, an end to the shedding of human blood, which is inseparable
from an end to the suppression of human rights."[13] Although Washington
remained fixated on Nicaragua until the Sandinista defeat in February 1990,
Arias's words seemed equally applicable to El Salvador, where a revolution
of similar longevity was also entering its final phases, although in radically
different circumstances.

War Without End

"In the case of El Salvador, ideology was not the principal generator of armed conflict," argued Rubén Zamora, a democratic reformer with a degree in political science and two decades' experience of Salvadoran politics. "Here the civil war began because there was no political space. First we tried the electoral route, but all the elections were marred by fraud and repression. We also tried the so-called extra-parliamentary politics route of demonstrations. But the response to these street demonstrations was to shoot people, and each demonstration became a massacre," he recounted. "People like myself who were opposed to armed struggle even tried something that was against our principles—an alliance with the military—participating in the '79 junta with the young officers. But all those roads were systematically blocked and closed." The other cause of the Salvadoran conflict, he asserted, was "the problem of social injustice. In economic and social terms, El Salvador may be the most polarized country in Latin America." This combination of "great polarization and constant repression," concluded Zamora, was "the recipe for civil war."

It was a conflict of incredible ferocity, which claimed some seventy-five thousand lives and one million displaced persons and lasted for twelve years. The 1980s may have been a decade of revolutionary change in Nicaragua, but for revolutionaries in nearby El Salvador, they were years of endless war.

El Salvador has the second smallest territory in Central America, but the region's second largest population. In 1979, its high population density was compounded by an unequal distribution of land that gave 2 percent of its people 60 percent of its land, and left hundreds of thousands with no land at all. Many eked out a living as tenants or migrant laborers; others crossed into Honduras in search of land or a living; still others swelled the slums of San Salvador and sought urban jobs.

It was the coffee boom of 1870–1930 that prompted this concentration of landholdings and people. During this era, an entrepreneurial elite composed of *ladino* landowners and foreign merchants—the so-called "fourteen families," although their number was closer to two hundred—coalesced, and a polarized class structure emerged, along with Central America's most radical labor movement and most dynamic Communist party.

The Depression of the 1930s brought the coffee boom to an end, along with the oligarchic democracy that had given El Salvador political stability during the preceding decades. In 1932, a rural rebellion was organized by the Communists, led by Farabundo Martí, whose memory and cause would be invoked by the rebels of the 1980s, who named their "national liberation front" the FMLN in his honor. The revolt was crushed by the army, which massacred thousands of peasants and Indians, a model of social control that has appealed to sectors of the Salvadoran elite and military ever since: One of the most notorious death squads of the 1980s was named after the general who ordered the massacre. In El Salvador, both sides saw the civil war of the 1980s as the continuation of a conflict that stretched back to the 1930s.

For most of the next half century, the military ruled El Salvador in close alliance with the country's elite, which expanded its activities from coffee to cotton after World War II and then into industry with the formation of the Central American Common Market in 1960. This economic growth, however, did little to ameliorate the poverty in which most Salvadorans lived, or modify the rigid class structure into which the country was divided. "The fourteen families were practically the owners of El Salvador," emphasized peasant leader Miguel Alemán, "the owners of the governments, of all the money and all the production. This is what generated great poverty in the middle of great wealth in our country, and that has been the fundamental problem of us peasants, who have been denied education, health, housing, and the respect that we deserve as human beings." Efforts at reform, even when led by Christian Democratic moderates, were systematically repressed by the military in the name of anticommunism, while the United States ignored these violations of human rights.

In El Salvador there was no Somoza against whom a coalition that crossed class lines could unite. Instead, there was the rigidity of a society divided by class, whose inequalities were sustained by an intransigent elite and a repressive military. As a result, Salvador's civil war would be a class war, waged with a brutality that reflected the country's social tensions—and political polarization.

In 1972, reformers José Napoleón Duarte and Guillermo Ungo were running mates on a Christian Democrat–Social Democrat ticket that was winning decisively until the military intervened to stop their electoral triumph. When Duarte protested, he was jailed, tortured, and sent into exile, along with Ungo. A decade later, Duarte would rule El Salvador in alliance with its armed forces, while Ungo headed the Democratic Revolutionary Front (FDR) in alliance with leftist guerrillas.

During the 1970s, five revolutionary movements were formed, reflecting a broad spectrum of leftist views, from orthodox Communists and Trotskyists to those influenced by liberation theology or Castro's Cuba. They mobilized peasants and urban workers into popular organizations of increasing strength in the face of a fierce repression that prevented them from opening up the political system before 1979.

The Sandinista victory in nearby Nicaragua in July of that year altered Salvadoran politics as well. In its wake, a Washington that had taken Central America for granted worried that it was ripe for revolution. El Salvador's repressive politics and social inequities marked it as a target of opportunity for leftist revolutionaries, and the United States believed that it was next on their list. These concerns led the Carter administration to back the ouster of the hardline president, General Carlos Romero, in October 1979 by a group of reforming younger officers anxious to avoid Somoza's fate, and the formation of a civil-military junta pledged to agrarian, banking, and political reforms. At bottom, Washington opted to support reform from above out of fear of revolution from below.

But the political space created by the junta was soon filled by leftist popular organizations, which jammed the streets of the capital with tens of thousands of demonstrators. The reaction of Washington was to shift its support to the more conservative military officers in the governing junta and to the right-wing Christian Democrats under Duarte. The response of the Salvadoran elite and their security forces and death squads was murder: the cold-blooded massacre of demonstrators, the killing of thousands suspected of leftist sympathies, and the assassination of their civil and political leaders. Among the most prominent victims were San Salvador Archbishop Oscar Romero, an advocate for the poor and human rights who was assassinated while saying mass, and Rubén Zamora's brother Mario, a Christian Democrat who as Attorney General for the Poor in the new government sought to promote social reform.

Increasingly, the reformers—who united in April 1980 to form the FDR, which allied itself with the FMLN the following year—were forced underground by an unremitting repression that made it impossible to engage in politics openly in the cities of El Salvador. By 1981, the Salvadoran left had come to the conclusion that armed struggle was their only option and that the countryside was their best bet. The repressive response of an intransigent elite had transformed reformers into revolutionaries and political cadres into guerrillas. "We were left with only one choice," explained Rubén Zamora, who had been the junta's civilian chief of staff, "go home and cry—or armed struggle." Zamora, who left the Christian Democrats out of disillusionment, became the FDR's chief spokesperson abroad, but many in the Salvadoran left exchanged the city streets for the country's jungle-covered mountains and the mass meeting for the guerrilla ambush. By 1981, the FMLN felt strong enough to call for a "final offensive" that they believed would bring them to power before Ronald Reagan became president on January 20.

Reagan had campaigned on a platform blaming the advance of "Communist" revolution in Central America on the liberal policies of the Carter administration, and advocating an interventionist U.S. policy that would roll back the revolutionary tide in El Salvador and Nicaragua before it reached the borders of the United States. "The government of El Salvador," asserted Reagan, "is on the front line in a battle that is really aimed at the very heart of the Western Hemisphere, and eventually us."[14] Top Reagan officials also saw El Salvador as the place to put an end to the "Vietnam syndrome" by demonstrating that the United States could defeat leftist guerrillas at an acceptable cost. The Salvadoran army halted the FMLN "final offensive," and during the decade that followed, over five billion dollars in U.S. aid allowed the armed forces to modernize their weapons and tactics and quadruple in size. Washington was less successful in getting them to change their repressive ways.

With a rightist government in Washington willing to ignore abuses in El Salvador in its war against communism, violations of human rights multiplied. Rightist leader Roberto D'Aubuisson—whom U.S. Ambassador Robert White held responsible for the assassination of Archbishop Romero—vowed to stop communism in El Salvador no matter what the cost in lives, and the nation's security forces seemed to take the former military officer at his word. North Americans were shocked by the cold-blooded murder of four U.S. women missionaries one month after Reagan's election and angered at the inability or unwillingness of the Salvadoran military to bring their killers to justice. But viewed from El Salvador, the U.S. missionaries were just four of the thousands of victims of its bitter civil war, most of whom were civilians, many of them women and children.

The same was true of two U.S. agrarian reform advisers shot in San Salvador a fortnight before Ronald Reagan's inauguration, whose fate symbolized that of the land reform they had promoted. In the Reagan years, agrarian reform made little progress in the face of the fierce opposition of rightist landowners like Oscar Calvo, who considered the U.S. advisers "socialists" and the agrarian reform "robbery," which illegally "confiscated" lands "that ought to be in the hands of those who know how to make them produce," one of "the three reforms"—together with the nationalization of banking and foreign trade—"that destroyed the Salvadoran economy." Landowners backed D'Aubuisson, and their death squads joined the security forces in terrorizing the countryside, making membership in an agrarian reform cooperative hazardous and election as a peasant leader risky.

The exception was in the territories controlled by the FMLN, where "peasants supported the FMLN's struggle as just and necessary," according to Miguel Alemán, "because there was no other way to solve the social problem." By 1983, the FMLN had consolidated strongholds in El Salvador's mountainous northern regions and begun to expand its area of influence toward the coast. As the combatants on both sides grew in numbers and their weapons in firepower, the fighting escalated. The Salvadoran military pursued a Vietnam-style counterinsurgency, complete with U.S. helicopters and advisers. The guerrillas countered with a "war of movement" and attacks on provincial towns and military barracks. Although the tide of battle seesawed throughout the decade, by late 1989—when a powerful FMLN offensive in the nation's capital shocked San Salvador but failed to ignite a popular insurrection—it was clear that neither side could win El Salvador's endless war. It was a realization that led both government and guerrillas to the peace table called for by the Esquipulas accords of 1987.

By 1990, much else had changed as well, both in El Salvador and in the world outside. By then, the Salvadoran right, united in the National Republican Alliance (ARENA) founded by D'Aubuisson, had won political power by defeating the Christian Democrats in both presidential and legislative elections, converting many in its ranks to the gospel of democracy now being preached by Washington. President Alfredo Cristiani, moreover, represented the country's business elites, who were convinced that El Salvador's crippled economy could not be cured so long as the fighting continued, and that the war could not be won on the battlefield. The United States was also growing weary of El Salvador's interminable war and the U.S. Congress was increasingly reluctant to bankroll a Salvadoran military whose continued violations of human rights were underscored by the murder of six Jesuit priests in November 1989.

There was also less reason for Washington to support a costly war in El Salvador. The collapse of communism in Eastern Europe and the accelerating disintegration of the Soviet Union heralded the end of the Cold War that had framed U.S. policy toward El Salvador. The Sandinista defeat at the polls meant that there was no longer a credible revolutionary threat in Central America and persuaded many in Washington that ballots—not bullets—were the best way to counter leftist advances. Within this context, the United States was willing to accept the principle of a negotiated settlement in El Salvador.

By then, moreover, the Salvadoran left had also shifted its stance. The civilian reformers of the FDR, such as Rubén Zamora, had always been in favor of a negotiated settlement, and in 1987 had formed the Democratic

Convergence to participate in elections "and plant the idea of a political solution." By January 1990, the revolutionary movements that formed the FMLN had come to a similar conclusion, after an internal debate over the implications of changes in the "socialist world" for El Salvador's revolution between Marxist-Leninists, who believed in a broad-based revolution led by a political vanguard that would transform their society from above, and less ideological leftists, who saw force as a way of opening up the political space for popular movements to change Salvadoran society from within. The debate was won by the more pragmatic faction headed by Joaquín Villalobos, commander of the People's Revolutionary Army (ERP), militarily the strongest of the FMLN's five guerrilla movements. Villalobos, a brilliant if ruthless tactician with a disarming baby face, had been influenced by liberation theology as an economics student at university and contrasted his own views with "the dogmatic ideological elements who dominated the FMLN when it started." The ERP, he stressed, had been founded by radicalized "university students and Christian groups" who had never been Communists, and influenced by the Sandinistas, with their "open model of revolution."

The Sandinista electoral defeat in February 1990 was a shock to the FMLN, increasing their sense of isolation—and bringing home the impermanence of military victory. Latin American leaders in Mexico and elsewhere urged the FMLN to seek a political settlement. President Cristiani signaled the ARENA government's readiness to negotiate when he "offered a process of dialogue with clear objectives, such as to promote democracy and respect for human rights and reconciliation within Salvadoran society, and then to put an end to the conflict itself," asserted Oscar Santa María, the president's cabinet chief. The FMLN accepted Cristiani's offer.

After two years of difficult negotiations between deadly enemies who had little reason to trust each other, the United Nations helped broker the accord signed at the beginning of 1992. It was a political compromise that allowed both sides to claim victory, while leaving the future in doubt. The FMLN secured a promise that human rights and the land reform carried out in its areas of influence would be respected, but few concrete commitments. It also won agreement on proposals for "purifying" a reduced armed forces, for a new police force under civilian control into which its fighters could be integrated, and for democratic reforms that might open up the political system and give the left a better chance of winning power through elections. In return, the government got the FMLN to agree to end the twelve-year insurgency, to recognize its legitimacy, and to accept its constitution.

For Santa María, the minister closest to President Cristiani, this meant that "the FMLN would now submit itself to the democratic system" and transform itself from "a guerrilla force into a political force." For Rubén Zamora, the significance of the accords was that "for the first time since 1930 there is a real chance to demilitarize and democratize the country." On February 1, 1992, FMLN guerrillas joined their supporters in a peace celebration in the main square of San Salvador. This was the revolutionary left's first public demonstration in the country's capital in more than a decade. "When we went into the plaza, it was like a triumph," one guerrilla fighter affirmed. For the FMLN, claimed Villalobos, "this is a revolution."

Not all Salvadorans were as pleased with the peace accords or as satisfied with their outcome. Ultrarightists like Oscar Calvo viewed the accords as the equivalent of "a pact between the police and a thief," which robbed the government of its "legitimacy" and "authority, . . . lowering it to the level of the guerrillas . . . the new Attilas," whom the government had now allowed to shoot their way into the parliament. Landowners like himself were organizing to oppose the accords, he claimed, because "our governments have been too soft."

Peasant leaders like Miguel Alemán were supportive of the peace process in principle, but remained skeptical of them in practice. For him, the accords had changed little: "The shooting war may have ended, but in a nation where eighty percent of the population is now below the poverty line, the war of hunger, misery and exploitation continues," he asserted. In the countryside, "the only change was that with the ceasefire there are no longer military operations and forced recruitment. But the government has still not given the peasants so much as a flea! So the fruits of the accords have been minimal."

In San Salvador, a shopkeeper in a food cooperative was also skeptical. He talked about continued insecurity and his "fear of speaking openly. . . . There has been so much blood spilled, but the people are even poorer than before," he lamented. "The world thinks that the war in El Salvador is over, but here nothing has ended. The situation is dangerous and could explode at any moment, because the people have hope with the peace process, but we still have the same problems and the same fear," he stressed. "This could be an even more dangerous time bomb than before."

Clearly, the peace accords had not by themselves resolved El Salvador's social inequities or transformed its basic institutions. "All we have done," argued Rubén Zamora, in mid-1992 vice president of the legislature, "is bought some time." Much remained to be done, moreover, before the accords could be fully implemented and the peace consolidated. But leaders on both sides expressed confidence that El Salvador's long civil war was coming to an end. Perhaps the most optimistic sign was that both sides now regarded democracy not just as a tactical instrument to achieve other goals, but as an important end in itself. Even FMLN military leaders like Villalobos were now willing to affirm that they had learned that "the principal problem is not to fight to take power, but to fight for structural changes that establish new rules of the game." The Salvadoran armed forces, whose commitment to democracy has also been questioned, claimed to have learned its significance from twelve years of costly combat. "We have understood that the democratic system is the best one for this society," asserted General Ernesto Vargas, who negotiated the peace accords for the military, "and that the authoritarianism within our society has to totally disappear."

Only time will tell whether this new commitment to democracy will last and whether the Salvadoran left can secure through the ballot box the revolutionary changes that they failed to win on the battlefield. What is clear, however, is that one phase of their struggle has ended and a new one with different characteristics has begun.

By 1992, with the Soviet bloc consigned to the dustbin of history, the Sandinistas transformed into a parliamentary opposition, the Salvadoran civil war ending in a negotiated settlement, and most of the once revolutionary left in South America sounding like social democrats, the cycle of revolution in Latin America and the Caribbean that had begun in Cuba in 1959 seemed to be coming to an end. It was an issue with which the Cubans themselves were trying to grapple. "It may be that a small cycle of revolution is ending, but that had happened before, with the death of Che Guevara, only for a new cycle to start with the Sandinistas," argued Luis Suárez, a leading Cuban analyst of the region's revolutionary movements. "So long as the conditions that require revolution—poverty, oppression, exploitation, inequality, injustice—exist, revolutionaries will appear to challenge them. Those conditions are more acute in most of Latin America and the Caribbean now than a decade ago," he claimed, "and today's neoliberal policies of will make them even worse."

In Peru, Hernando de Soto, a noted advocate of free market policies, agreed, because neoliberal policies "created opportunities for the upper crust of the population—probably no more than ten to twenty percent—but the situation remains the same for the lower eighty to ninety percent." For Peru's Shining Path, it was a recipe for revolution.

Peru's Shining Path

"We are in the decade of triumph of 'People's War' " in Peru, a diminutive guerrilla affirmed in April 1992, with a conviction that belied her imprisonment in a Lima cell block that was run by its political prisoners until their massacre by security forces a month later.[15] In the men's part of the prison, her comrades were equally emphatic. The crisis of communism in other parts of the world did not deter them from insisting that "revolution is the principal political tendency in the world," as one declared. "Here in Peru we have developed 'People's War' for twelve years under the direction of our party headed by our beloved and respected President Gonzalo. We will take power in the entire country this decade and then continue the socialist revolution with successive cultural revolutions to reach Communism, which is the goal of all humanity."[16]

The cycle of socialist revolution might be coming to a close in

Central America, but in Peru, the heartland of the ancient Inca empire, a tiny provincial faction of a small Maoist party has transformed itself into the biggest revolutionary threat in the Americas. By mid-1992, Sendero Luminoso, or the Shining Path, was making front pages around the globe with its bombing campaign in the country's capital and alleged control of the world's largest coca-growing region. How had Sendero Luminoso achieved such "success" and who was this "President Gonzalo," so revered by his followers that his leadership sustained them even in the shadow of death and his teachings even after his capture in September 1992?

In North America, Sendero might be a new headline, but in Peru it was an old story. On June 24, 1969, the "revolutionary" military regime of General Juan Velasco proclaimed a sweeping land reform and the transformation of "Indians" into "peasants." In the national furor that followed, few in Peru noticed that two days earlier thousands of outraged Indian peasants had taken over the center of the highland town of Huanta to protest the military government's decree depriving their children of the right to a free education. The previous day, in the departmental capital of Ayacucho, the same issue had mobilized high school students and shantytown dwellers in a militant demonstration that left at least four dead and thirty-seven arrested. Among the detained were the mestizo leaders of the People's Defense Front, including eight professors from Ayacucho's University of San Cristóbal de Huamanga, headed by Abimael Guzmán, a philosophy teacher who wrote his thesis on Immanuel Kant and considered "prison . . . an occupational hazard."[17] A few months later, Guzmán formed his own "Communist Party of Peru," better known as "the Shining Path," which would transform these young demonstrators into political cadres and fanatical soldiers of a millenarian revolution.

The Shining Path—the name refers to José Carlos Mariátegui's term for the proletariat's role in the Communist revolution—emerged out of the successive splits in the Peruvian Communist party that Mariátegui founded in 1928. These divisions produced several Maoist factions during the 1960s, a decade that also saw the rise and fall in Peru of Trotskyist peasant organizations and guerrilla groups inspired by Cuba. Guzmán had been trained in Mao's China and spent time there during its 1960s Cultural

Revolution, for him an inspiring experience decisive in his political formation. He would remain an unrepentant Maoist long after Maoism had gone
out of fashion in China.

By 1970, Guzmán had lost the battle for national leadership of Peru's
Maoist party, but consolidated control over most of its organization in
highland Ayacucho, one of Peru's poorest and most neglected departments.
It was also a region much of whose society and values were shaped in a
hierarchical and authoritarian mold by centuries of semifeudal relations.
"Ayacucho," Guzmán would later affirm, "helped me understand the peasantry."[18]

The social conflict out of which Sendero emerged in Ayacucho was
not over land—which the economic decline of the region's elite and the
guerrillas of the mid-1960s had helped them acquire by purchase or seizure—but over access to free education. In this struggle, the Indian peasantry and rural migrants to the shantytowns of the region's capital were
often led by mestizo advisers, provincial intellectuals of lower-middle-
class origin resentful of their own exclusion from power by the creole elite.
"Abimael Guzmán himself," recalled Carlos Iván Degregori, a Peruvian
anthropologist who was his colleague at Ayacucho's University of San
Cristóbal de Huamanga, "was the image of the typical provincial Peruvian
intellectual: a mestizo properly dressed in a collar and tie, with glasses," a
formal person "who insisted on being addressed as 'Professor.' "

The future revolutionary leader accumulated power within the self-
governing university as its personnel chief. By 1970, Guzmán and his
comrades controlled the university's basic education curriculum, which
they transformed into a course of indoctrination in their party's Maoist
ideology and a recruiting ground for its cadres among the new generation
of students from rural communities who entered the university in growing
numbers after 1969, many of whom were products of the movement for free
education that they identified with Sendero Luminoso. After graduation,
these cadres returned to their rural communities as teachers and recruited
their own students for Sendero's revolutionary cause. This stress on hierarchical organization, ideological indoctrination, and the recruitment of educated mestizo youth as cadres has shaped Sendero to this day.

When Sendero was bested in the competition for control of Ayacucho's mass organizations and university by political rivals—many the heirs of the revolutionary New Left of the 1960s, who became leaders of the new social movements of the 1970s and would form the United Left party of the 1980s—it withdrew into itself, stressing internal cohesion and ideological purity, defining itself not as a mass party, but rather as a revolutionary vanguard for the "masses," who, Guzmán stressed, "have to be taught through overwhelming actions so that ideas can be pounded into them." It is the language of the authoritarian mestizo teacher of Indian peasants whom he regards as inferior, even as he dedicates his life "to serve them."[19] In mid-1992, when its power touched millions, by most accounts Sendero's cadres numbered only a few thousand—and Abimael Guzmán, its unquestioned leader, was portrayed on its posters as a teacher carrying the book of ideology whose "all-powerful truths" justify his political pedestal.

With the defeat of Maoism in China in 1976, Sendero claimed its mantle and Guzmán—who took the nom de guerre "President Gonzalo"— was transformed into "the fourth sword of Marxism," the successor to Marx, Lenin, and Mao. His "Gonzalo-Thought"—"the application of Marxism-Leninism-Maoism to our concrete conditions"—became increasingly schematic and millenarian, defining communism as "the society of 'great harmony' . . . toward which 15 billion years of matter in motion . . . has necessarily and uncontainably been heading."[20] Sendero now projected itself as *the* leader of global revolution in an era of violence that would culminate in "world-wide 'People's War.' "[21] In this new era, revolution would center on violence and war would be the central task of revolutionaries.

On the eve of the 1980 elections that signaled Peru's restoration of democracy after twelve years of military rule, Guzmán went underground and launched his "People's War." With a ringing denunciation of "false revolution" and "false democracy" he proclaimed to "our heroic and combative people" that "today . . . your finest children, flesh of your flesh, steel of your steel, have unleashed the red wind and the flaming banner of rebellion" in order to "forge a new world with weapons in hand."[22]

Sendero would have remained an obscure footnote to the fractious history of the Peruvian left had it not been for its surprising success during the decade that followed. From a small underground Maoist faction in a forgotten region of Peru, it grew into a revolutionary movement that dominated much of Peru's Andean highlands and extended its reach to the coca-producing valleys above the Amazon rain forest and the coastal shantytowns of Lima.

How did a small provincial Maoist group become so serious a revolutionary threat? It is a question that has provoked many answers, few of them verifiable, many of them uninformed. Where so secretive an organization as Sendero Luminoso is concerned, information is a weapon and controversy the norm.

Part of the explanation lies in its stress on efficient organization and the careful recruitment and indoctrination of disciplined young cadres, who accept Guzmán's simplified view of Peru's complex realities as "scientific" truth and are totally dedicated to Sendero's cause, vowing not only to die for it, but also to kill for it—paying what Guzmán has called "the quota" of blood needed to win his revolution. This glorification of violence and martyrdom has led some experts to regard it more as a religious cult centered around Guzmán's powerful personality than as a political party. "President Gonzalo" himself underscored that "leadership is key" and attacked critics of his growing cult of personality as "revisionists."[23] The unquestioning obedience and self-sacrifice of his young followers have been one of Sendero's greatest sources of strength.

Empowerment was another Sendero theme, from its slogan—"Everything Other Than Power Is an Illusion"—to its promise to its educated mestizo cadres that they would "conquer" the national power denied them by Peru's creole elites. Carlos Iván Degregori recalled a conversation with Sendero cadres in Ayacucho who told him: "Look, it's 1981. By 1985, Ayacucho will be a liberated zone; by 1990 Peru will be an independent country. Wouldn't you like to be a minister? Wouldn't you like to be a military chief? . . . The revolution is going to triumph, and those of us who have been in the party the longest will be the bosses."[24]

For the most part, however, Sendero's success reflects Peru's failures, as well as the Shining Path's capacity to understand and exploit the faultlines within Andean society. Particularly important has been Sendero's ability to manipulate the resentments and aspirations of Peru's poor, largely Indian majority.

Although the military "revolution" led by General Juan Velasco proclaimed a sweeping agrarian reform in 1969, its implementation was uneven and it failed to solve the problem of landlessness in the highlands or to resolve the land claims of many indigenous communities. During the decade that followed the restoration of democracy, moreover, much of the land belonging to the agrarian reform cooperatives was reprivatized. In areas where the military's agrarian reform had not restored lands taken from indigenous communities in the past or where the breakup of cooperatives had created new resentments, Sendero organized land invasions to win the local peasantry to its cause. But even within indigenous communities where private landholdings had generated lesser inequalities, Sendero attacked "the landlords" and appealed to the poor peasants who owned no land and had to work the fields and tend the flocks of their richer neighbors. Aided by its informants within rural communities, Sendero also utilized ancient rivalries between villages and valleys and old enmities within rural communities to establish a base and undermine local leaders.

In regions where land was not an issue, as in its original base in Ayacucho, Sendero focused instead on the failure of the Peruvian state to deliver social services such as education, or to remedy the poverty of the local population. In striking this note, it played on the longstanding dissatisfaction of highland regions with their neglect by the governments in Lima.

Throughout the Peruvian Sierra, moreover, Sendero was able to take advantage of what U.S. Ambassador Anthony Quainton called "the sense of profound cultural grievance in the Indian peoples of the highlands."[25] In a region that the creole elite still refers to as *la mancha india*, or the Indian Stain, racism is pervasive—and resented. An unequal social hierarchy based upon color and ethnicity was a colonial legacy reinforced after independence by Peru's ruling creole elites. Velasco's agrarian reform undermined the power of the old rural elite, but the administrators of the new agrarian cooperatives often ran them with a similar disdain for their

Indian peasant members. The return of democracy, moreover, often meant the restoration of the old elites in the guise of political power brokers. But even where the agrarian reform succeeded in displacing the old elite, it left a local power vacuum that Sendero's cadres could fill.

Although Sendero's rigidly Maoist ideology, with its stress on class, left little room for ethnic nationalism, and its own hierarchy—with light-skinned leaders, mestizo cadres, and dark-skinned soldiers—replicated Peru's, Sendero cadres appealed to the Indians of the highlands in Quechua and exploited their resentment at centuries of discrimination, oppression, and neglect by the country's creole elites and mestizo middlemen. More-over, there was sufficient ambiguity in its critiques and appeals for alien-ated Indians to imagine that Sendero might offer Peru policies "that would have its roots in our ancestors," as one Indian migrant put it, "a policy based on our own idiosyncracies."[26]

In extending its influence to zones that were both distant and differ-ent from its original highland base, Sendero has also demonstrated a surprising political pragmatism at odds with its ideological rigidity. In the Huallaga Valley, a zone of recent colonization above the Amazon rain forest in northern Peru that has become the world's largest producer of coca leaves, Sendero set aside its moralistic antidrug stance to offer protec-tion to peasant growers against both the Colombian cocaine cartels and the corrupt Peruvian military and U.S. drug agents sent to combat the illegal narcotics traffic. In return, the Shining Path has received an estimated $250 million in "taxes," which could purchase the modern weapons that it will need to defeat the Peruvian armed forces—and the U.S. intervention Guzmán predicts—in the final stage of its insurrection. Yet, in effect, the U.S. cocaine market is financing Sendero's "People's War."

Sendero itself attributes its advances to "the support of the masses." But Sendero's opponents, who range from right to left, ascribe them to the Shining Path's "terrorism," the "revolutionary violence" that Abimael Guzmán defended as "a universal law" and glorified as "the river of blood" across which Sendero will lead Peru to the Maoist promised land.[27]

Sendero has used violence both as a political strategy and as a mili-tary tactic. Where its appeals proved unpersuasive and rural communities remained loyal to political rivals or their own autonomy, Sendero has responded with an intimidation that has ranged from peasant massacres to the "selective liquidation" of local notables and community leaders— whether they were associated with the government, with other leftist parties, or just with the rotational grassroots democracy that has ruled Andean communities for centuries. In Ayacucho, such exemplary violence led to the massive resignation of terrified local officials, and their replacement by "People's Committees" controlled by Sendero cadres. In a community near Mayobamba in the western highlands, the execution of village elders who had participated in a government rural development project sent the message that involvement with foreign aid agencies or the government could be a death sentence.

The response of Peru's civilian governments to Sendero's challenge to their authority was to militarize the affected regions, by declaring a state of emergency and bringing in the army and special forces to conduct a counterinsurgency campaign. But the military shared the racism of Peru's elites and lacked Sendero's precise information about the Andean communities they policed. Massacres, disappearances, and strip searches devastated the lives of peasants and townspeople. The reign of terror in the highlands claimed many innocent victims and made Peru one of the region's worst human rights violators. In classic guerrilla fashion, Sendero provoked a governmental repression that proved its political points and created the polarized situation it sought. Youths whose families had suffered military abuses were ripe for recruitment by the Shining Path.

Moreover, the government security forces sent to combat Sendero often attacked the leftist grassroots organizations best able to accomplish that task. "The security forces are part of the problem, not its solution," argued Juan Rojas, secretary-general of the Peruvian Peasant Confederation, a Sendero rival. The result was that Sendero often emerged as the only alternative to a repressive and racist military and was able to appear as the "protector of the people against the abuses of the soldiers."

It is hard to judge how much of Sendero's growth is due to the attraction of its appeals and how much to its use of intimidation and violence. But it is clear that the government's militarization of areas where

Sendero has been active has been counterproductive, creating more Sendero sympathizers than it killed—and a flood of refugees fleeing the conflict.

Caught in a crossfire between state security forces that violated their human rights and an equally ruthless revolutionary army, many in the highlands have voted with their feet and opted out of the conflict by migrating out of the area. Today there are zones of rural Ayacucho that are virtually depopulated, their inhabitants fled to Lima, where neighboring shantytowns are peopled by refugees from Huanta—one by victims of the army, the other by victims of Sendero. But even in highland areas closer to Lima, such as the region around Mayobamba, Sendero's "selective liquidations" have generated a selective migration—which one expert estimated at 10 percent of the population—of people threatened by Sendero: local landowners or merchants, community leaders it views as rivals, or youths it has tried to recruit.

It is a far more pessimistic migration than the earlier movement of enterprising young men and women—like Mayobamba's Carlos or Concepción—looking for better economic or educational opportunities, encouraged by families seeking to extend their networks from the highlands to the coast. Instead, it is an exodus of desperate refugees fleeing the violence that has killed their kin and destroyed their communities, "leaving only orphaned children and the aged who have no relatives left" behind.[28]

By 1992 an estimated quarter of a million Peruvians had fled their rural homes for the comparative safety of garrison towns or coastal cities, the largest group of displaced persons in South America. By then it was clear that the conflict had followed them, as the Shining Path expanded its operations in Lima, the site of more than half of Sendero's actions in 1991.

Although Sendero had long had a presence in Lima, announced by periodic electricity blackouts or other dramatic but largely symbolic acts—what it called "propaganda through action"[29]—its initial focus was on recruiting and training cadres, with a stress on the poor students similar to those who had formed its initial recruits in Ayacucho. In Lima's venerable University of San Marcos, Peru's oldest university, Sendero's critique of Peruvian society and promise of empowerment found a resonance in the resentful mestizo and *cholo* students who had "made it" to San Marcos, only to find that their hard-won university degrees do not translate into job opportunities in Peru's failing economy or into respect from the country's creole elite. Equally important was Sendero's ascendancy over Lima's teachers' college, whose graduates were sent to staff the new schools created in its rapidly expanding shantytowns—repeating the recruitment strategy that had served Sendero so well in Ayacucho.

During the final years of the 1980s, Sendero began to expand its bases from the rural communities and provincial towns of the highlands to the Lima shantytowns peopled by migrants from those provincial communities and towns, many of them fleeing the violence that Sendero's People's War had provoked. Sendero did not participate in the leftist-led social movements that made these shantytowns bastions of grassroots democracy, preferring "generated organisms" subservient to party orders. But Sendero penetrated neighborhood assemblies, intimidated opponents, and established its "People's Committees" and web of informants. In 1987, moreover, the Shining Path took control of *El Diario*, a Lima newspaper known for its labor reporting, which enabled Sendero to reach a wider and more literate audience with its positions as Peru's 1990 presidential elections approached.

By then Sendero's progress was aided by the failures of Peru's democratic political system, the collapse of its economy, and the shrinking power of its state. The restoration of democracy in 1980 raised popular expectations that Peru's civilian leaders were unable to fulfill. As in other South American countries, they inherited a heavy foreign debt burden from the military regime, which was soon compounded by rising international interest rates and a severe global recession. In Peru, populist policies, a debt default, and an ecological disaster deepened the crisis, which culminated in the collapse of the economy under President Alan García's populist government (1985–90), in which inflation soared to an incredible 3500 percent, while the economy contracted and living standards plunged.

To the failure of Peru's elected governments were added the failings of their opponents within the democratic left. Although the left had begun the 1980s with optimism as leaders of the new social movements—from unions to women's groups—that played a prominent role in the restoration of democracy, the "United Left" ended the decade in disunity and disarray, a medley of squabbling personalist parties, with no answers to Peru's deepening crisis and with declining popular support. By 1990 Peruvians were disillusioned with the entire spectrum of parties and politicians, whom they regarded as both corrupt and incompetent.

It was this economic crisis and antiparty sentiment that enabled Alberto Fujimori, a political novice without strong party backing or a detailed program, to win an upset victory over Mario Vargas Llosa, Peru's most famous writer, in the presidential elections of 1990. This antipolitics mood also allowed Fujimori to win initial public approval in March 1992 for his bloodless coup and closing of a Congress he accused of corruption and obstruction. Fujimori's neoliberal austerity plan curtailed inflation but caused increasing unemployment and destitution in a country where a majority of the population lives below the poverty line, while his coup eliminated democratic alternatives to an authoritarian government—and an authoritarian revolution.

The real target of Fujimori's coup was not a do-nothing Congress, but an all too effective Sendero Luminoso, which also tapped into this deep vein of discontent and despair of alternatives. Sendero expanded its support and activities into labor unions and urban shantytowns, recruiting workers and migrants with its disciplined organization and self-sacrificing cadres, its simplified analyses of Peru's problems and confident assertion that Communism was the answer, along with its image of efficacy in a country where nothing else seemed to work. As in the region's other revolutions, Sendero's greatest strength may be the weakness of the old order it wants to overthrow.

In Canto Grande, a vast slum near a Lima prison where captured Senderistas are interned, a carpenter explained Sendero's appeal: "The people are tired of so many problems and the ideologies that used to move them. Now many people are talking about Sendero as a good alternative. They say that in the jails they are well disciplined, and that Sendero could lead us to a better life." The evidence for this was in the changes wrought by Sendero since its cadres took over the community. "In Canto Grande there was a lot of street crime," he related, "but because of Sendero now you can walk in peace."[30]

By 1992 an estimated 40 percent of Peru's territory and a third of its population was beyond the control of its elected government—although estimates of Sendero's control within that large area varied widely. Sendero's leaders now spoke of preparing the urban encirclement and insurrection that would bring Lima to its knees and Sendero to power. "We are convinced," affirmed a Lima guerrilla leader, "that victory is already ours.

"Only the masses can conquer power," he underscored. But, in mid-1992, Sendero's Lima commanders exuded confidence that they were "conquering power with the help of the masses, because they help us with everything from a glass of water to their own blood." The Shining Path had reached "strategic equilibrium," a new more aggressive phase of their "People's War," moving from guerrilla attacks to large force confrontations, and now expected to take power in Peru "in a few years."[31]

To win their People's War, Sendero will need the active support of the majority of Peru's people. But *do* the Peruvian "masses" support Sendero and its People's War? The evidence is mixed.

As early as 1982, the massive turnout for the funeral of slain Sendero leader Edíth Lagos in her native Ayacucho, where her father is a leading merchant, underscored that Sendero did have significant popular support in areas of the highlands, although some studies suggest its violence has cost Sendero peasant support since then. Yet the Shining Path's ability in later years to extend its bases to other areas makes it clear that Sendero's appeals are not confined to the region where it was born.

But Sendero's efforts to extend its sway over Peru's northern highlands have been stopped by peasant *rondas,* or community-organized self-defense forces. And, in Puno, on the high plateau near Lake Titicaca, Sendero offensives were twice repelled by local peasant militias. In Lima, too, Sendero has found its way barred, by the grassroots social movements that had been defending the interests of shantytown dwellers with success for more than a decade in *pueblos jóvenes,* or new towns, such as Villa El Salvador, which began in 1971 as a handful of shacks in the desert sands to the south of Lima, but today is a sprawling self-governing community of more than 350,000 people.

Sendero's response to this popular rejection was terror. On February 15, 1992, María Elena Moyano, who had been elected deputy mayor of Villa El Salvador by 80 percent of its eligible voters, was killed in cold blood by a Sendero "liquidation squad" at a fundraiser for a local soup kitchen. Then, as her children watched in horror, her body was blown to bits by dynamite, leaving no corpse to be venerated. Yet, despite this brutal attempt at intimidation, thousands of mourners followed Moyano's casket to the grave—in a popular repudiation of Sendero as striking as Edíth Lagos's funeral had been of Sendero support. María Elena Moyano had emerged out of the communal kitchens of Villa El Salvador to become a founder of its women's federation. As a leader of its social movements in their struggle against hunger, disease, and governmental neglect, her commitment and integrity earned her the nickname "Mother Courage" and international attention—and her public advocacy for democracy and peace Sendero's enmity. Despite the public outcry at her assassination, a Sendero leader in Lima defended it as a "selective liquidation" of a "proven agent of imperialism who has trafficked in the poverty of the exploited class."[32]

It was not a view with much support in Villa El Salvador. "True revolutionaries do not direct terror at the people and do not attack their popular organizations," charged Carlos, a human rights activist from Villa El Salvador. He had worked with María Elena Moyano to bring schools and teachers to a lower-class community that today boasts one of the highest rates of school attendance in Peru. "Sendero wants to destroy the social movements in Villa because we are a threat to them," he charged, "because we are an example of how grassroots democracy can succeed in Peru. They want there to be no alternative between them and the government. Sendero knows that they cannot win over the people of Villa El Salvador, so their goal is to intimidate them. They are terrorists, not revolutionaries."

Carlos is determined to continue to fight for his vision of grassroots democracy, but intimidation does work in a country where the state security forces seem unable to protect their citizens from the terrorism they urge them to oppose. The day after a 1991 Sendero "armed strike," a taxi driver confessed to me that he had stayed home even though he was "one hundred percent against Sendero. If I didn't stay home they would bomb my taxi and kill me." A year later, a similar Sendero "strike" stopped most of Lima's trade and transport. In Huaycán, an impoverished Lima shanty-town, a dynamite attack on the marketplace discouraged even its street vendors from earning their meager daily bread. Sendero's show of strength made a deep impression on Pascuala Rosado, Huaycán's elected leader: "It was as if they had total control." Rosado herself was under armed guard in July 1992, following a Sendero threat of a fate similar to that of María Elena Moyano. She had sent six of her seven children away, she said, because "I don't want them to kill *me* in front of my children."[33]

Sendero Luminoso is the most controversial revolutionary movement in Latin America and the Caribbean today, seen by its supporters as selfless liberators of the poor and by its opponents—from the left to the right—as the Khmer Rouge of the Andes, with its implications of another Cambodian "killing fields" should it take power. In mid-1992 it was not clear whether Sendero Luminoso would become the first revolutionary movement since Nicaragua's Sandinistas to win national power—and even less clear what such a victory would portend for Peru or the rest of the region. The capture and life sentence of Abimael Guzmán and other Sendero political leaders in the fall of 1992 added more question marks to the future of the Shining Path and Peru. What is evident from Sendero's growth in recent years is that the collapse of communism in Eastern Europe and the Soviet Union and the crisis of the Cuban model in the Caribbean and Central America do not mean the end of revolution in the Americas.

But they do mean that the revolutions of the future are likely to be different from those of the past. "There are no paradigms anymore," stressed Colombian analyst Arturo Alape, who has followed Latin America's revolutionary movements for the past three decades. "Each country has to create a model of revolution that reflects its own history and conditions."

Mexican-Americans are the oldest and largest community of Latin American and Caribbean origin in the United States. But it was only in the 1960s, when the struggles of Chicano farmworkers such as these demonstrators captured national attention, that they began to raise their political profile. During the last few decades Mexican-Americans have become increasingly urban, by 1990 constituting more than a third of the population of Los Angeles. Only recently have they begun to translate their numbers into political power, as in the 1990 election of Gloria Molina (left) to the Los Angeles County Board of Supervisors.

Chapter 14

North of the Border

The arrival of over half a million exiles
from Castro's Cuba turned much of
Miami into a "Little Havana," where life
resembled the prerevolutionary original. Their concentration in Miami
helped Cubans retain their identity,
while incorporating elements of North
American popular culture.

U.S. popular culture has been enriched by the presence of Latin American and Caribbean communities. Gloria Estefan, "the Latin Madonna," and her Miami Sound Machine have become crossover pop-music stars.

Latin American and Caribbean communities in the United States are trying to exert increasing influence over Washington's policies toward their homelands. In 1991, Haitians in Boston protested the ouster of President Jean-Bertrand Aristide in a military coup and demanded U.S. action to restore him to power.

The 1980s saw the century's biggest
wave of immigrants to the United
States, most of them from Latin America and the Caribbean. At P.S. 19 in
Queens, New York, half the kindergarten classes are bilingual in Spanish and
students come from all over the Americas to live in the "New New York" and
become "Americans."

North of the Border

"Give me your tired, your poor, your huddled masses yearning to breathe free," wrote Emma Lazarus in 1883. Inscribed on a bronze plaque at the base of the Statue of Liberty at the entrance to New York Harbor, these lines expressed the promise of "the land of liberty" for generations of immigrants to the United States.

During the 1980s, more immigrants arrived in the United States than in any other decade in history. Yet, unlike millions of their predecessors, few of them were welcomed by Lady Liberty and few came from Europe. Most were migrants from Latin America and the Caribbean who had traveled north, not west, to reach the United States, and crossed borders, not oceans, to arrive at its shores.

How this nation of immigrants deals with this new wave of immigrants from the south may well shape its domestic history and hemispheric relations during the twenty-first century. It may also force the United States of America to rethink what it means to be "American."

These new immigrants have made the United States the fifth largest Spanish-speaking country in the world. Today, it has the hemisphere's largest Puerto Rican city, second largest concentrations of Cubans, Salvadorans, Haitians, and Jamaicans, and fourth largest Mexican metropolis. During the next century, people of Latin American origin will surpass African-Americans as the nation's largest minority group. Their concentrations in such large states as California, Florida, New York, and Texas—and in some of the country's biggest cities—will increase their social and political impact still further. Already, more than half of Miami is of Latin American descent, and the same is true for nearly 40 percent of Los Angeles and a quarter of Houston and New York. Increasingly, "Anglos"—a term that "Hispanics," people with Spanish American cultural roots, apply to all white English-speaking North Americans—will have to come to terms with the fact that they not only share the Americas with their Latin American and Caribbean neighbors, but that they also share their own country with growing communities of "Latinos," people of Latin American descent.

The 1990 census revealed that there were more than 22 million Hispanics living in the continental United States—a 53 percent increase over 1980 and a sixfold rise over 1950 estimates. By 1992 there were some 25 million living on the mainland. If current trends continue, there will be more than 30 million Hispanic-Americans by the year 2000. They are already the largest non-English-speaking immigrant group, and some projections predict that as much as a third of the U.S. blue-collar labor force may regard Spanish as its mother tongue during the twenty-first century.

These figures only confirm what many North Americans knew already. The concentration of Hispanics in major urban areas has made them more visible and increased public awareness of their presence and problems. Nor have Hispanic-Americans been content to remain a silent minority. Increasingly, they are participating in politics and speaking out, electing representatives to defend their interests, and demanding bilingual education for their children and a say in U.S. policy toward their countries of origin.

Some Hispanic-Americans are new neighbors, the result of the waves of recent immigration—legal and illegal—that have multiplied the populations of Latin American and Caribbean origin in cities around the country. But others are descended from Hispanic colonists who had settled in what is today California and the Southwest long before those territories became U.S. possessions. The Anglocentric history of the United States, which begins with the arrival of English colonists in the early seventeenth century, is misleading: Hispanics had been living in what is today the United States for decades before the Pilgrims landed at Plymouth Rock and exploring its lands for a century before John Smith set foot in Jamestown.

The Other Side

Mexicans were the first Hispanic-Americans, residents of territories forcibly incorporated into the United States in the wake of the "Mexican War" of 1845–48. By the Treaty of Guadalupe Hidalgo of 1848, which transformed northern Mexico into the U.S. Southwest, some eighty thousand Mexicans lived in the ceded territories, three quarters of them in New Mexico, a state that is still nearly 40 percent Mexican-American, despite receiving little of the massive Mexican immigration since then.

During the nineteenth century, the flow of Mexicans across the untended border reflected the drift of people in search of land or jobs. By 1910 Mexican migrants were crossing the border in large numbers in search of work, drawn by the far higher wages in the United States, the one constant in a changing relationship. By then Mexican laborers were a major presence in the fields of Texas and the mines of Arizona and Colorado. The demand for agricultural labor in an expanding southwestern economy during the years that followed led U.S. growers to recruit labor inside Mexico, offering free transportation and advances on their wages in an often intense competition for Mexican workers.

Before 1917 migration across the border with Mexico was largely unregulated, and even the creation of the Border Patrol in 1924 was mostly directed at Asians excluded by the National Origins Immigration Act of that year. By then Mexicans had replaced Asians as the low-paid menial labor force of California and the Southwest, whose employers used their political influence to keep the sluice gates of migration open.

In the decades that followed, Mexican labor migration ebbed and flowed with the U.S. economy, expanding in eras of prosperity and contracting in times of trouble—often with an assist from the U.S. government. During the Great Depression hundreds of thousands of Mexicans—including many born in the United States—were deported as scapegoats for the high levels of unemployment. World War II meant a renewed need for labor and a new U.S. recruitment policy, the Bracero program, which brought roughly fifty thousand Mexican workers per year to the United States between 1942 and 1964 to work mostly as agricultural laborers. A growing flow of illegal Mexican migration developed alongside this legal, if temporary, labor migration and increased when the Bracero program came to an end after 1964. Most of the illegal migrants also crossed the border to work for a season and then return home with the money they had saved. Increasingly, however, both legal and illegal migrants stayed in the United States, joining Mexican-American communities that swelled in size, and began to appear in U.S. regions distant from the border zone. By 1990, there were more than thirteen million people of Mexican descent living in the United States.

By then they had ceased to be predominantly rural laborers and had come to occupy a major place within the urban working class of the western states. Some have made it into the middle class, as owners of small businesses or as professionals, although Mexican-Americans graduate from college at a rate that is only one quarter of the national average.

Mexican-Americans have also emerged as a political force that is courted by politicians of both parties and is producing its own elected leaders. For many this political activism was a new departure. Until recent decades Mexican-Americans had been noted for their political passivity. Many did not become citizens. Others fought bravely for the U.S. flag in foreign wars but were not active in its domestic politics—a reflection both of their subordination within the United States and their continued identification with nearby Mexico. Those who did participate in U.S. politics tended to be Democrats, but their special needs and interests were generally neglected by both major parties.

For Mexican-Americans, as for African-Americans, the 1960s were a political watershed. Inspired in part by the civil rights and Black Power movements, "Chicanos"—as the most politicized Mexican-Americans now called themselves, from a corruption of "Mexicanos"—extended their activities from moderate civil rights organizations such as LULAC (the

League of United Latin American Citizens) to radical political parties such as La Raza Unida, or the United (Indo-Mexican) Race, to redress their grievances and promote their interests. La Raza won local elections in Texas and LULAC fought discrimination in California, but both failed to win their more militant demands. Still, they did succeed in training a generation of Chicano political leaders, and LULAC remains an important Latino organization.

Yet, it was not Chicano electoral politics, but Mexican-American labor politics that made their struggles part of the consciousness of the larger nation. The efforts of César Chávez, a charismatic leader inspired by Martin Luther King, Jr., and the civil rights movement, to organize the exploited Mexican-American agricultural laborers of California for his United Farm Workers captured the conscience of the United States for "La Causa"—and made Chicanos realize the possibilities of political action. As they became increasingly urban, they faced different problems—substandard housing, inadequate schools, police brutality—and found that the solutions to these problems required local political power.

By 1980 Mexican-Americans numbered over ten million. By then they had begun to turn their numbers to political account, by electing representatives who were themselves Chicanos, or else pledged to promote their cause. Henry Cisneros, mayor of San Antonio from 1981 to 1989, symbolized this new generation of Chicano politicians. An attractive leader to both Anglos and Hispanics, Cisneros was considered a potential vice-presidential candidate before he withdrew from electoral politics.

Recently, a new Mexican-American political star has risen in Los Angeles, where Hispanics constitute nearly two fifths of the population yet have not exercised much political influence. Gloria Molina is the California-born daughter of an immigrant Mexican laborer. She began her political career as a community activist, and went on to serve in the California State Assembly and the Los Angeles City Council. In 1991 she became the first Chicano elected to the five-member Los Angeles County Board of Supervisors, one of the most important local government offices in the country, making her the highest ranking Hispanic-American woman in U.S. politics. Molina now represents the country's largest Latino constituency and shares responsibility for overseeing a county of nine million residents and a budget of twelve billion dollars.

In her new role, Gloria Molina has been a vocal and effective board member who has been called an "anarchist" by its chair, but she has been successful with most of her initiatives for social programs such as health care and pro-Hispanic measures such as allowing people to testify in Spanish before the board. "The most important thing," stressed Sergio Muñóz, editor of *La Opinión*, Los Angeles's major Spanish-language newspaper, "is that she has truly been the voice of a community that didn't have any access to the Board of Supervisors—and it's a loud gutsy voice."[1]

Gloria Molina's next political stop may be a run at becoming mayor of Los Angeles, which would make her the most important Latino officeholder in the United States. In 1991 Hispanics constituted 9 percent of the U.S. population but accounted for only 3 percent of elected officials, including ten U.S. representatives and 131 state legislators, but no senators or governors. "I think she is going to be one of a handful of people who really shines," said Harry Pachon, director of the National Association of Latino Elected and Appointed Officials. "The Latino community in California has a tremendous influence on the Latino community nationwide, simply because one of three Latinos nationwide lives in California."[2]

Gloria Molina's rise from neighborhood activist to political prominence in the country's second largest city may well be a harbinger of things to come. But more typical of the present is the accelerating political participation of Mexican-Americans at the grassroots level in communities such as Bell Gardens.

The Taking of Bell Gardens

Today Bell Gardens is an urban community sandwiched between two freeways in Southeast Los Angeles. But not long ago, its name reflected its reality. Bell Gardens, like other communities in southern California, has been transformed during the past half century from an area of rural plots to one of urban lots.

Claude Booker was one of the original residents of Bell Gardens, back in 1935 when it was "gardens and animals" and "about four thousand people . . . spread around the whole area," he recalled. "It was just a typical Midwest-type town, settled by people from the South and the Midwest"— and it was "a hundred percent Caucasian."

Like most of Los Angeles, both the rural character and ethnic composition of Bell Gardens underwent dramatic changes during succeeding decades. After World War II, building on subdivisions began, and after 1970 "you began to see the transition" from a sparsely populated rural community to a densely populated urban community, Booker related. This was followed during the 1980s by the "real heavy transition from Caucasian to Hispanic." In 1990 the population of Bell Gardens was 90 percent Hispanic.

Most of them were of Mexican descent. Some were middle-class property owners like María Chacón, who had come to Los Angeles from Chihuahua, where her mother still lives. She was among those "who had come to build a dream here in Bell Gardens—to build a house or establish a business and to accumulate wealth." By 1990 she and her husband had built five rental houses on their Bell Gardens property. Their tenants, like most of the Hispanic residents of Bell Gardens, are "humble people, working people, most of them Mexicans who have just finished fixing up their residency papers or hadn't really decided to become citizens," Chacón explained. "Here you feel like you're in Mexico with your people; you feel very comfortable here in Bell Gardens."

But the Mexican-Americans of Bell Gardens felt far less comfortable when they ventured into its City Hall. Virtually all its City Council members were Anglos, and Claude Booker, its city manager, ran its government. Frank Durán, a local businessman, was only one of many Mexican-Americans who complained of the "arrogance" with which the city's Hispanic majority was treated, "especially people that didn't know how to speak English."

This lack of representation and respect had rankled with many Hispanic residents, but it had never moved them to action until María Chacón "got wind of the change in zoning" planned by the City Council—which prohibited the building of more than two housing units on a lot and mandated the removal over time of those that already existed, a measure that could eventually affect most of the city's forty-two thousand residents. The result was a grassroots movement that led to a revolution in local politics whose implications transcended the Bell Gardens city limits.

According to Claude Booker, the goal of the rezoning ordinance was "to stop runaway growth" so as "to not have so much high-density development in future years." To Mexican-American property owners like María Chacón, however, such rhetoric masked a "land grab" by the City Council in which they were the victims. For years they had been hassled by city inspectors who cited their properties for building code violations as minor as broken screens or cracked cement. As soon as they cured one violation, they received notice of others. Since 1987, when the rezoning plan was first drawn up, Bell Gardens was issuing notices of substandard conditions "at ten times the rate of the city of Los Angeles," recounted Alan Gross, a lawyer who is today Bell Gardens' city attorney. "The main point is that none of them were ever terminated," he explained, which created problems in mortgaging or selling the property. Instead, city inspectors began to harass tenants and the city manager began to press Mexican-American property owners to sell their parcels to the city—at the lowered valuations to which these "substandard notices" had caused their properties to fall. Between 1987 and 1991, the city had spent forty million dollars buying up properties. For Gross it was a classic case of urban removal masked as urban renewal.

"They themselves said that twenty-five thousand people were going to be affected," recounted María Chacón, who had taken the lead in getting property owners together, most of them modest Mexican-American landlords like herself. For them, the rezoning ordinance was the last straw, lowering the value of their property and their ability to sell it. Her friend Sophie's parcel dropped in value from $850,000 to $250,000 as a result. "If you came with the dream that if you bought your house when you were young and you worked and sacrificed and saved you could have something, and then they destroy it just so people can come build townhouses and condominiums—that's not justice," Chacón charged. For María Chacón it would mean the death of her American dream, and she was determined to fight the rezoning—and the Anglo power brokers of Bell Gardens who had "abused us Latinos" all these years.

For behind the issue of rezoning lay the larger questions of racial prejudice and ethnic conflict. María Chacón was convinced that the reason the City Council pushed this rezoning was because "a majority of us were Mexicans and the council people thought we weren't going to do anything. Because the city manager said, 'All Mexicans are ignorant and irresponsible.'" Chacón bristled at the remark. "I thank God that I am not that irresponsible," she said, "and that I am always searching for justice." María Chacón united some seventy-five angry property owners, but none of them had any political experience. So they went to someone in a nearby town who did.

Rudy García had been born in Arizona, but was raised in Mexico. He returned to the United States in the 1950s and enlisted in the army. It was only then that he became conscious of racial discrimination. "In Texas . . . we got thrown out of a restaurant because we didn't see the sign that said: 'No dogs or Mexicans allowed.' They want me to go fight for them, but I can't even eat at their restaurants!" After he was discharged, Rudy García moved to Los Angeles, where he found work in Huntington Park. But he was unable to live there "because they weren't renting to Hispanics." Experiences like those were one reason that he got involved in LULAC. The other was "the need to do something for our kids" because of their 54 percent high school dropout rate. To García, "this is a different type of discrimination . . . a revolving door" that kept Mexicans from progressing. Rudy García became active politically "because if we don't change this, we are going to fail as a people."

In Maywood, a town near Bell Gardens, LULAC's efforts to organize the Hispanic community in the face of a similar zoning problem a few years before had failed to stir it to action. So when María Chacón and her group came to García for advice, he leaped at the opportunity, which he saw "as a very important political movement for the community." For Rudy García, the underlying issue was representation. "I said to myself, 'This is it. The Southeast will never be the same again. First, we get our people elected there in Bell Gardens and then the rest of the Southeast cities will go.' Throughout the Southeast areas we're from 88 to 95 percent, and look at the representation—there's *none!*"

García provided the nascent Bell Gardens movement with the political leadership they lacked, and brought in Alan Gross, an Anglo lawyer who had taken part in the Maywood effort, to furnish legal advice and assistance. They formed a "No Rezoning Committee," opened an office, installed phones, and the complaints started to roll in. "People all over town who now had a place to vent their frustrations and send their complaints were calling and coming in," Gross recounted, "and we were hearing all kinds of complaints, focusing in large part on the arrogance of the people who ran the city government."

The committee decided to organize a recall drive to force a new City Council election. The problem was that many of the Hispanic residents of Bell Gardens were not U.S. citizens, and among those who were, few registered to vote and fewer still cast their ballots. As a result, Claude Booker admitted, "in a town of forty thousand, six or seven hundred votes would elect a person."

In response, the No Rezoning Committee decided on a two-pronged strategy. One goal was to convince Mexicans to become U.S. citizens and to register to vote, because when Rudy García asked a meeting packed with one hundred angry Mexicanos, "How many of you here can vote?" only four or five raised their hands. So, García said, "Okay, we are going to get each and every one of you to become a citizen." First, he helped them overcome artificial barriers created by interviewers who failed Mexican applicants for not knowing President Reagan's favorite food. Then he established "citizenship classes" and got four to five hundred people to become citizens.

The second problem was to get the Hispanic community to vote. A registration drive turned passive citizens into eligible voters, while an innovative strategy of getting people unlikely to come to the polls to vote by absentee ballot addressed the problem of low Hispanic voter turnout. When the recall ballots were counted on March 10, 1992, "it was a landslide," Rudy García related. "We beat them by sixty-two percent." A second vote one month later confirmed this shift in political power, electing a Hispanic majority to the City Council that included Rudy García and Frank Durán. In Bell Gardens, Mexican-Americans were no longer a political minority.

The rezoning and recall movement was an important learning experience for all concerned, although people active in it extracted different meanings. For Frank Durán, a neophyte city councilman, it was "the start of an education" and the beginning of opening up the political system to Mexican-Americans in his community. "We'll probably be getting more people coming in to the council meetings and start getting involved—and then that person will talk to someone else and it will mushroom."

Alan Gross, the Anglo lawyer and activist, took a longer view. What impressed Gross was that "over the year the inhibitions against speaking out have worn away." At the start, Mexican-Americans had been afraid to speak their mind and challenge the Anglo authorities who controlled their community, but by late 1991 "they would go to the City Council meetings and stand up there and vent their frustrations and tell the council what they thought of them—older people, younger people, women, men, high school students, priests, everybody." He recalled going home to Beverly Hills and telling his friends: " 'You would pay money to go and see this.' It was a fantastic lesson in democracy!"

It was also a lesson in the value of citizenship and political participation. María Chacón had lived in the United States for twenty years but had never become a U.S. citizen because she "never thought it was necessary" and "always thought that [she] wanted to be a Mexican and to go back," she explained. "I had to suffer and go so low as to have my rights taken away before I finally said—Enough!" Chacón had become a citizen during the recall drive and it was a transforming experience. "We have rights, and if they don't give them to us, then we have to take them. The Constitution of the United States is there for everybody," María Chacón affirmed. "Latinos need to fight because we have a very bright future, but we have to unite and we have to show people that we can take the reins of government."

For Rudy García, too, the lesson was empowerment, but he saw it in a larger frame. He now uses the Bell Gardens movement in his citizenship classes, to demonstrate that "each and every one of you that is here studying for citizenship . . . you're going to be part of the process. You're going to be able to participate. You're going to be able to tell somebody: 'Hey, wait a minute. You don't shine me off like that. I voted for you, Mister'—something we never had the opportunity to say before." But it was the implications of the Bell Gardens victory for other Los Angeles communities that was its greatest significance for him. "I look at Bell Gardens as a first domino," he explained. "It went down . . . and I will make sure that it continues to go from one city to the next city." They would use rezoning, recalls, "whatever it takes, because whether we go over, under, around, or through it, we're going to do it. This is going to happen." For García, Bell Gardens marked the end of an era for Southeast Los Angeles's Mexican-Americans: "We are tired of being victims and second-class citizens. We no longer want to get on the bus and sit in the back. Now we want to drive the bus—hell, we want to *own* the bus. Why not? We're the majority, right?"

But Latino empowerment through elections is not the only thing that is happening in Los Angeles, as the dramatic riots of April 1992 underscored. While transfixed Americans watched South-Central Los Angeles burn on their television screens, commentators presented it as an outburst of African-American rage in the wake of the acquittal of white police officers accused of beating a black motorist, Rodney King.

Yet in a city in which nearly two out of five people are of Hispanic descent, their invisibility was striking as Anglos rushed to define the issue in the familiar terms of black-white racial conflict. Only gradually did it become clear that many of the rioters and victims—one third of those killed and arrested and 40 percent of those who suffered property damage—were not blacks but Hispanics. "Latinos actually got the brunt of this," argued demographer Dr. David Hayes-Bautista, head of U.C.L.A.'s Chicano Studies Research Center. "They got beat up, burned out, and arrested. Yet it is still being looked at as a black-white issue."[3]

Equally surprising to many was that in large part, the Hispanics involved were not Mexican-Americans—the established Chicano barrios of East Los Angeles remained mostly quiet during the riots—but Central Americans, recent immigrants who peopled decaying South-Central neighborhoods where there are today as many Hispanics as blacks. The influx of Central Americans during the 1980s has added hundreds of thousands of Hispanics to Los Angeles's ethnic mix and made it the world's second largest Salvadoran city. Most of these recent residents are illegal immigrants, whose fears of being deported make them vulnerable to exploitation and abuse. Many of them work in jobs in domestic service, sweatshops, and agriculture where they get paid less than the minimum wage, receive no benefits, and run greater risks of injuries. In South-Central Los Angeles, one third of the Hispanics live below the poverty line and many sleep in crowded rented garages. These people had little reason to defend their neighborhood stores—though many of them were owned by enterprising members of their own community—and every incentive to participate in the looting.

Many were also refugees who brought with them memories that shaped their behavior. Salvadorans often "looted" food and diapers. "We've been through things like this in El Salvador, so the first thing you do is to be sure that there will be enough food to feed the family," explained Francisco, a Salvadoran in South-Central. "Unconsciously many people acted as if they were still back there."[4] As far as the U.S. government was concerned, they ought to be back in Central America. Illegal migrants who were arrested were immediately deported, and Central Americans complained that police were using house searches for looted goods to identify people for deportation.

Yet, in the face of such abuses of authority, the Central Americans of South-Central had little recourse. Unlike the Mexican-Americans of Bell Gardens, they had no political representation—and as illegal immigrants little prospect of electing representatives. When Hispanic political and community leaders met in Chicano East L.A. after the riots to chart a common course, they were unable to identify a single leader from South-Central to invite. "At a time when we really needed to reach out there, we found that we were not as informed as we could have been about who the

Latino leaders were in that area," Gloria Molina confessed. "All of us have a lot of work to do to learn about the changing demographics of South-Central Los Angeles."[5]

But Los Angeles is not the only city in the United States whose demographics have been transformed during recent decades by the flood of migrants from Latin America and the Caribbean. In 1959, Miami was a city of southern whites, retired Jews, and aspiring blacks that styled itself a winter resort for the northern United States. Today it has a Cuban mayor, a Hispanic majority, and a sizable Haitian minority, and regards itself as the capital of the Caribbean.

A Little Havana, A Cuban Metropolis

In Miami, Eighth Street is now known by its Spanish name, Calle Ocho. The main street of Little Havana, it is the core of a Cuban community that dominates the city. It is also the heart of South Florida's large and growing Hispanic population, which comes together once a year in the Calle Ocho Festival, the biggest Latino street fair in the United States. In 1992, more than a million people attended this annual event, where they ate Latino food, listened to Latino music, and danced to Latino rhythms. Most of them were Cuban, but many were from Central or South America, members of the more recent immigrant wave to South Florida that has diluted the Cuban character of Miami's Hispanic community even while confirming its ascendancy. Today Miami is the largest Latino-led city in the United States and the first major North American city to undergo such a radical transformation of its ethnic character. But first and foremost, it is a Cuban city, the largest aside from Havana, and one more prosperous than Cuba's capital some ninety miles away.

Like Mexican-Americans, Cuban-Americans have been in the United States for more than a century. But the origins of the Miami community are more recent, and the bulk of the Cuban immigrants arrived in the United States after 1959. Moreover, from the start, the Cuban community in the United States has been composed of exiles whose migration was shaped by political events rather than economic processes.

The first Cubans to settle in the United States were émigrés fleeing Spanish repression of the Cuban independence movement that rose in rebellion in 1868 but did not triumph until three decades later with U.S. assistance. José Martí, the Cuban poet and patriot, was only one of many independence leaders who took refuge in the United States and stayed to organize the struggle for Cuban independence from its shores, relying on the resources of the Cuban communities concentrated in New York and in Florida's cigar-making centers of Tampa and Key West. But the size of the Cuban-American community remained small before the Cuban revolution, probably not exceeding thirty thousand people in 1959.

During the two decades that followed, over eight hundred thousand Cubans fled their island, more than 85 percent of whom settled in the United States and Puerto Rico. The impact of this intense immigration was magnified by the concentration of Cubans in the Miami area, which despite U.S. government efforts to disperse them, was home to three out of five Cuban-Americans in 1980.

This Cuban emigration wave began during the early days of Castro's revolution with the supporters of defeated dictator Fulgencio Batista at the start of 1959 and continued with upper- and middle-class opponents of the revolutionary regime. During the four years of increasingly radical revolution that followed, over 200,000 Cubans came to the United States— landowners and industrialists whose properties had been expropriated, managers whose enterprises had been nationalized, and professionals and small businessmen who saw no future for themselves in a Communist Cuba.

Luis Botifóll came in this first wave of Cuban exiles. "I left Havana in August 1960," he related, because "I was a lawyer and I didn't see how I could survive under a Communist regime in which there were no rights, no free enterprises. So I decided to come to this country with my family, just for a short time, because I didn't think that the situation would last for a long time. Thousands of Cubans like me came under those conditions."

Botifóll was also typical of that first wave of Cuban émigrés in that he arrived in Miami with the intention of taking part in reversing the revolution he had fled. This was encouraged by the U.S. government, which treated the exiles as "freedom fighters" and recruited heavily in the exile community for the CIA's secret army against Castro. "We came here with the purpose of going back to Cuba. We came as exiles. We didn't come to stay. We didn't come just because we thought we could get a better life here than we had in our country. We came here because of circumstances in Cuba that we thought would not last long—and that in the meantime being here we could help to overthrow Castro."

It was the failure of the CIA's exile army at the Bay of Pigs in April 1961 and of the U.S. efforts to oust Castro that culminated in the missile crisis of October 1962 that turned a group of refugees into a community of immigrants. More than half a million Cubans would arrive in the United States during the two decades that followed, but this first group of exiles defined the community they joined, charted its course, and shaped its character.

"When I first came here, I didn't expect to stay, so I didn't want to engage in anything," recalled Luis Botifóll. "I just wanted to survive, waiting for the day of going back to Cuba." Once they realized that they were in the United States for the long-term—and possibly forever—Cuban exiles like Botifóll began to adapt to their new country and to make their way. They were helped in starting out by their status as political refugees, which gave them legal residence in the United States and access to government assistance denied other migrants from Latin America and the Caribbean. But, above all, they were helped by the capital, skills, credentials, and experience that they brought with them to Florida, the site of $150 million in Cuban real estate investments even before the revolution. Botifóll began at the top, in the Republic National Bank, which was taken over by wealthy Cuban exiles. "I got involved with this bank that was changed from being a community American bank to a Cuban bank. I started as a member of the board of directors. Eventually I became chairman."

Cuban-run financial institutions like the Republic National "played a very important part in the development of this community," Botifóll asserted, "because . . . in those days, the Cubans who came here didn't have a financial statement that could support a loan. But since we knew them from Cuba, and knew their abilities and how honest they were, we took a chance with them and gave them what we call a 'character loan'—a loan based on their character, not on their collateral. Fortunately, these people were very successful, they paid us back and continued to be our clients. And that made this bank not only the biggest spending bank in the United States but also the biggest local bank, with over a billion dollars in assets."

Among Republic National's clients "from the beginning," was Felipe Valls, today one of Miami's most successful entrepreneurs. Valls also came to the United States in 1960, but unlike Botifóll, he came without capital or connections, and with two children and a pregnant wife to support, so he "started working in a restaurant equipment business in Miami Avenue." Valls was typical of the middle-class Cubans who constituted the bulk of that first wave of exiles. "Most of the Cuban businessmen who came here in that year had small businesses in Cuba," he explained. Once in Miami, "most of them went to work and then opened their own businesses." Valls worked in a restaurant equipment business for two years and "then I opened a very small place, importing espresso coffee machines from Italy. . . . That was my start." It was a rocky one, because "no Cuban had any credit here" so "I had to give credit to my own customers. So I had no money and it was a big struggle because the profits here were big but not enough to finance the equipment." From there Valls branched out into restaurants, including the Versailles, today one of the most popular Cuban restaurants in Miami's Little Havana, but at first "a very small place with a seating capacity of sixty people. Now it's over three hundred." Today he owns fourteen restaurants and a glass factory, as well as shopping centers and other real estate. Valls employs more than one thousand people, most of them Cuban—as are the food in his restaurants and the customers who eat there.

It is this enclave character of Miami's Cuban community that gave it an autonomy and strength lacking in other Hispanic-American communities without comparable capital, education, and business experience. "The Cubans who came here were lawyers, bankers, businessmen," stressed

Botifóll, contrasting them with immigrants who came to the United States to "make a better living based only on their hands." As a result, the Cubans "had the know-how . . . the ability, and if they had a little help and they had a market—which was created by ourselves—they could succeed."

Felipe Valls was not the only Cuban exile to begin his business career in Miami with a small café or restaurant in the 1960s and end as a manufacturer three decades later. In prerevolutionary Cuba U.S. enterprises had dominated the industrial sector, limiting Cubans to the role of managers and redirecting Cuban entrepreneurs into services and real estate. It was to these sectors that they gravitated when they first settled in Miami, before broadening out into manufacturing. Together these dynamic Cuban entrepreneurs created an economic enclave with low-cost labor provided by more recent Cuban émigrés from working-class and lower-middle-class backgrounds. As each wave of Cuban exiles found its bearings and began to work its way up into the middle class, it was replaced by newer arrivals both directly from Cuba and from other areas of the United States. The last sizable Cuban wave was the more than one hundred twenty-five thousand Mariel refugees of 1980. Since then, the smaller groups of Cubans arriving in Miami have not kept pace with the labor needs of its expanding economy. As a result, the bottom rungs of Little Havana's labor force—such as the unskilled jobs in Valls's restaurants—are now filled by Central Americans, who arrived during the 1980s from Nicaragua or El Salvador, as refugees from leftist revolution or rightist repression.

Few Miami Cubans are wealthy and many are poor, but most are middle class, and the average income of Cuban-Americans is now as high as the national average for all U.S. citizens, the only community of Latin American and Caribbean origin to have reached that plateau. As Cubans made it into the middle class, many of them moved out of Little Havana into the Miami suburbs, where they have flavored their American dream with a Spanish accent and a Caribbean style.

Businessmen such as Botifóll and Valls have done far better than the national average. Today Cubans own a disproportionate share of the nation's largest Hispanic-owned businesses. They have also been hired by U.S. corporations as their intermediaries with Latin America and can claim one of the nation's most respected and highly paid corporate executives, Roberto Goizueta, the chairman and chief executive officer of Coca-Cola since 1981. His services were valued so highly by the company's board of directors that he was offered a package of bonuses and stock options worth an estimated eighty million dollars to *not* retire until 1996. Under Goizueta's direction Coca-Cola has not only grown and profited—its shares have risen 900 percent in value—but it has also become a more international company, with Latin America and the Caribbean accounting for much of its lucrative overseas expansion. Coca-Cola's new international orientation reflects Goizueta's own background. It also parallels the increasingly international orientation of Miami's Cuban-led economy.

With Cubans who spoke their language and understood their culture running Miami's financial institutions, Latin American capital—flight capital looking for a safe harbor or drug money in need of laundering—poured into South Florida. Its banks became some of the nation's busiest and most profitable—Republic National went from some ten million dollars in deposits in 1967 to over one billion dollars by 1992—and Miami became the financial capital of the Caribbean Basin.

It also became the U.S. commercial gateway to Latin America. Miami's port surpassed New Orleans in its Latin American trade, and its airport bested Atlanta's in its international traffic. "We are responsible for making Miami a center of commerce with Latin America," claimed Luis Botifóll. "Because even though Miami has a very good geographical position, in order to succeed in attracting people from Latin America you have to speak their language," he stressed. "So we provided the language. And the multinational companies started using Cubans as representatives in Latin America. So these Cubans were more or less ambassadors of goodwill for Miami. And the people in Latin America realize if we have to do something in the United States we better go to Miami where we can make ourselves understood. So we created that relation between Miami and Latin America which is in certain part the reason why Miami has grown so much," Botifóll asserted. "Castro was a blessing for Miami!"

In recent years, Miami's Cuban community has begun to flex its political muscles as well as its economic strength. At first, Cuban exiles concentrated their economic energies on making it in Miami, while focusing their political efforts at the national level on trying to influence U.S. policy toward Castro's Cuba. Right-wing exiles grouped in semiclandestine organizations such as Alfa-66, many of whose members had been trained by the CIA, made politics their priority. Their goal was to overthrow Castro and they were willing to use intimidation, even terrorism, against those who did not share this objective.

As the years passed and Castro consolidated power, Miami's Cuban community also began to focus on local politics. At first, Miami's Cubans were content to support a Puerto Rican, Maurice Ferré, for mayor. Ferré, a diplomatic moderate, shared their Hispanic Caribbean background, but as the representative of one of Miami's smaller ethnic groups, and one with affinities to Miami's African-American community, he was not a threat to either established Anglo interests or disadvantaged blacks. But as their numbers and citizenship grew, Cubans pressed for a comparable share of political power. By 1990 Cubans were a majority in Miami and they deserted Ferré to elect one of their own, Harvard-educated Xavier Suárez, as the first Cuban mayor of a major U.S. city.

They have been equally successful in national politics. Unlike Mexican-Americans, the wealthier and more conservative Cuban-American community linked itself to the Republican party, which it helped to break the Democrats' domination of Florida politics. In return, successive Republican administrations in Washington gave its Cuban constituents, led by the right-wing Cuban National Foundation, virtual control over its policy toward Castro's Cuba, rewarding them with the creation of Radio Martí, a powerful station run by conservative Cubans and beamed to Cuba, over the strong objections of its Communist government. By 1992 Cuban-Americans had become the first community of Latin American and Caribbean origin to gain the kind of leverage over U.S. policy toward their country of origin exercised by Jewish-Americans or Greek-Americans.

With economic and political power have come resentments—from the former Anglo majority they displaced, from the African-American minority whose hopes of progress they dashed in the process of securing their own success, and from other immigrant groups that have fared less well.

Haitians, for example, have bristled at the special treatment that Cubans have received, which they ascribe to racial discrimination. The most dramatic difference has been in the reception of would-be immigrants from Cuba and Haiti, neighboring islands with very different populations and politics. Cubans have been welcomed as political refugees from a "totalitarian government . . . while the Haitians also were coming from an authoritarian government but were still not accepted in this country," charged Rolande Dorancy, an attorney at Miami's Haitian Refugee Center. To her, this proved that "it's a racial problem. The Cubans are considered to be white and the Haitians are black." As a result, she claimed, instead of the open-arms welcome that Cuban refugees received, the Haitian "boat people" fleeing their country's brutal military dictatorship have been intercepted at sea by the U.S. Coast Guard and, as "economic migrants," returned to their country, where many have suffered persecution. In fact, many Haitian refugees are fleeing political persecution, while many Cuban immigrants are looking for better economic opportunities.

But even those Haitians who have made it to Miami complain that they have been discriminated against by the U.S. government. "If you walk through Little Haiti and Little Havana, you will see there's a big difference," Dorancy underscored, contrasting Haitian poverty with Cuban prosperity. "The Haitians who are coming don't have a way of supporting themselves economically. But the Cubans do, because the U.S. government gave them their patronage," she charged. Haitians also face job discrimination from Cubans in Miami, she claimed, and not "only because we don't speak Spanish, because we do have Haitians speaking Spanish. It is because of the color of our skin."

Many African-Americans in Miami feel even more resentful. "Before the influx of Cubans in the early 1960s, blacks felt that with the civil rights movement, we were in the process of really energizing our community economically and politically," recounted African-American attorney H. T. Smith. "Now, since so much is based upon Latin America and speaking

Spanish, African-Americans blame Cubans for taking away their jobs and political empowerment . . . at least 90 percent of black Miami" does.

African-American community leaders like Smith argue that local Anglos still "have the money and the real power" in Miami. He contends that they have manipulated these tensions to play off "the African-American community and the Cuban-American community against each other in the typical divide-and-conquer type approach to maintain its power."

To many Anglos, however, their concern is not retaining power in Miami, but "becoming foreigners in their own country." Philip Thomas, a leader of Miami's "English only" movement, was willing to acknowledge that Cuban immigrants had "given a great impetus to the city," but contended that "the quality of life has suffered" in Miami. "Whereas before we had a fairly homogeneous community and things were quiet and peaceful, now you have a great deal of ethnic tension that we didn't have before. Nearly two thirds of the people living here now have come from other parts of the Americas, bringing in a wide variety of cultures and a spectrum of other languages, Spanish more than any other." Thomas's daughter had had to learn Spanish before she could land a job in a local bank. "Spanish has become so much a dominant language here, that if you're not conversant in Spanish, you are pretty much frozen out of a great many opportunities."

It was this growing predominance of Spanish in Miami that persuaded the *Herald,* the city's leading newspaper, to begin publishing a Spanish-language edition in 1976. For the *Herald,* a venerable daily confronted by dramatic changes in the character of the community it served, it was a business decision, as was its creation in 1987 of a full-fledged Spanish newspaper, *El Nuevo Herald.* Its Anglo publishers sought "to meet the needs of more people coming in from different parts of Latin America—Central Americans, Colombians, Puerto Ricans," explained *El Nuevo* editor Carlos Verdecia. "The Cuban exodus stopped, but that made the Hispanic community more diverse and we needed to address that." Today only half of this Spanish-speaking community is Cuban, and *El Nuevo Herald* has become "not a Cuban paper" but rather "a paper for all Hispanics in South Florida."

Despite its efforts to adapt to its changing demographics, the *Miami Herald* has had to confront serious differences in political culture. When *El Nuevo Herald* published charges of corruption leveled against Jorge Más Canosa, the leader of the Cuban National Foundation, Carlos Verdecia was accused of being a "Communist" and received death threats. "The Cuban-American National Foundation," Verdecia asserted, "is a group that has been very successful in changing the approach to the Cuban issue in the political system of the United States. They created PACs, they created lobbying arms. They've been very influential in Washington." But "they have not been as successful in learning how to deal with a free press in a democratic system." In a Miami dominated by Cuban exiles, a hard line on Castro—and unquestioning support of his enemies—is still a political litmus test.

Yet as the generation that fled Cuba ages and passes from the scene, their obsession with overthrowing Castro and support of rightist politics may fade as well. The generation of Cubans raised in the United States has other concerns and priorities, more similar to those of their Anglo peers than their Cuban-born parents. They have gone to college in similar proportions and acquired the professional degrees that are passports to success in the United States.

They have also integrated into U.S. society much more than their parents and absorbed far more of Anglo culture, while infusing it with their own unique contribution. Their stance is symbolized by the crossover success of Gloria Estefán, the "Latin Madonna," and her Miami Sound Machine, whose fusion of Anglo-American pop lyricism with Caribbean rhythms has made her a national star. Estefán, the daughter of a Batista bodyguard who was captured at the Bay of Pigs, lacks his political commitments and stresses the difference between her generation and Cuban exiles like her parents. "Cubans who've grown up in the United States have the best of both worlds," she affirmed, "because we've been inspired by the business mind and the unbelievable freedom of the Anglo world, but we have a lot of our own ethnic flavor, especially in Miami."[6]

Unless the collapse of Castro's Cuba refocuses the attentions of Miami's Cubans on returning to Havana—or another massive wave of refugees fleeing the crisis of communism reinforces their preoccupation with the island to the south—Miami's Cuban community is likely to continue its successful integration into North American society on its own terms.

To some, this Cuban success story—sticking together and using their numbers, language, and culture to obtain their American dream—is a formula for other Latino groups to follow. To others, the Cuban success was a product of a time and place that are difficult to replicate. Luis Botifóll himself stressed the uniqueness of the Cuban experience in Miami, with its large numbers of professionals and businessmen. He was also aware that the peculiar advantages of Miami were not confined to its geographical location. "Coming to Miami had the advantage that Miami was a little place, so our presence here could be important," Botifóll explained. If "we had gone to New York or Chicago, I'm sure we would not be successful, because we would get mixed up in that big metropolis."

Puerto Rican and Proud

June 14 is Flag Day in the United States, and in New York, red, white, and blue flags were everywhere on a hot Sunday in 1992. Yet the flags were not the stars and stripes of the United States, but the lone-star banner of Puerto Rico. Pride was the watchword for the day, along with an insistence that with education and persistence Puerto Ricans, too, could share the American dream, despite increasing poverty, unemployment, drug use, street crime, and school dropouts.

It was the largest march in the Puerto Rican Day parade's thirty-five-year history, with some one hundred thousand marchers and more than a million spectators, making it the year's biggest demonstration of ethnic pride in New York City. The high turnout was reflected in the political importance of the event, as candidates of all ethnic backgrounds and ideological persuasions used the occasion to woo a potentially decisive voting bloc, although one that, like Mexican-Americans, too often has not registered and shown its political strength at the polls.

It was a joyous occasion and a vibrant parade, with drum majorettes dressed like Middle Americans but moving to syncopated Caribbean rhythms exemplifying the mix of North and Latin American that is today's "Nuyoricans," or New York Ricans. As the marchers made their way up Fifth Avenue past Rockefeller Center, little girls in red, white, and blue waved Puerto Rican flags from their fathers' shoulders in time to the salsa beat. "We are here to show our pride in being Puerto Rican and to celebrate our culture," one man in the crowd explained as others nodded agreement. "We are *both* Americans *and* Puerto Ricans."

After Mexican-Americans, Puerto Ricans are the largest group of Hispanics on the U.S. mainland. What makes this remarkable is that Puerto Rico has a population—a little over 3 million in 1990—that is roughly one quarter the size of Cuba's. There are nearly as many Puerto Ricans on the mainland—some 2.7 million—as on the island. Part of the explanation for this proportionally larger Puerto Rican presence is that they are not foreign immigrants but, since 1917, U.S. citizens by birth, who need no visas to make the journey and no green cards to remain or work.

Like Cuba, Puerto Rico came within the U.S. orbit as a result of the Spanish-American War of 1898, which transformed a Spanish colony into a U.S. possession. Capital from the mainland flooded the island, turning self-sufficient farms into export plantations and their displaced peasants into rural migrants to burgeoning cities. The Depression of the 1930s hit Puerto Rico with particular severity. New Deal reformers responded with the creation of a self-governing "commonwealth" and a program of industrial development known as "Operation Bootstrap," which modernized the island but failed to provide jobs for most of the migrants flooding its cities.

When their expectations of jobs in the industries they saw around them and of participating in the consumer society they saw on television were disappointed in San Juan and Ponce, Puerto Ricans sought to fulfill them on the mainland, aided by inexpensive postwar air fares and aggressive labor recruiting for expanding U.S. industries in need of unskilled workers. In 1945 there were fewer than one hundred thousand Puerto Ricans living on the mainland, but their numbers multiplied rapidly during the decades that followed.

Most of them settled in the New York City area, where Puerto Rican men found jobs in factories, hotels, and restaurants, while women worked as seamstresses and domestics. As with Mexicans in the Southwest, Puerto Ricans filled the need for low-wage menial labor in the expanding economy of the Northeast. Over time, the concentration of mainland Puerto Ricans in New York fell from 80 percent in 1950 to less than 40 percent by 1980. They branched out into New England, where Hartford, the insurance capital, with its service jobs, became their second largest mainland city and the mill towns of Massachusetts offered factory work. They also headed west to Chicago, where the Puerto Rican and Mexican migration streams met and mingled. In New York, Puerto Ricans settled in decaying neighborhoods vacated by earlier immigrant groups who had made it into the middle class and moved out to the suburbs, turning Italian East Harlem into Spanish Harlem and the Jewish Lower East Side into Loisaida. By 1980 New York had become the world's largest Puerto Rican city.

By then the light industries of the Northeast had begun to decline in the face of competition from lower-wage areas of the U.S. South and the Third World. Moreover, the Puerto Rican hold on unskilled jobs in New York was being contested by newer immigrants—many of them illegal— from other countries of Latin America and the Caribbean who were willing to work for less and in conditions that Puerto Ricans, as U.S. citizens and union members, would no longer accept.

But escalating unemployment in Puerto Rico itself combined with the presence of relatives and the availability of social services in New York to sustain the flow of migrants despite the decline of job opportunities. The result by 1992 was an enlarged but impoverished Puerto Rican population, which was in danger of joining poor African-Americans as a permanent underclass, with similar income and education levels, drug problems and crime rates.

But many Nuyoricans are neither poor nor drug pushers. They have made it into the middle class and become educated professionals, who offer their community political and cultural leadership. Nearly 10 percent of mainland Puerto Ricans are college graduates, double the rate of Mexican-Americans, although only half the national average. Geraldo Rivera and

Raúl Julia are only two of the Puerto Rican success stories who have become household names in Anglo as well as Puerto Rican homes.

Even in areas like the South Bronx that have become national by-words for poverty and urban blight, Puerto Ricans have struggled to retain their dignity and culture. Lacking the political strength of California's Chicanos or the economic resources of Miami's Cuban community, Puerto Ricans have turned to their culture as a source of community, identity, and pride. In burned-out neighborhoods whose empty lots were filled with garbage and industrial wastes and whose streets had been taken over by drug dealers, community gardens began to appear, along with *casitas,* little frame houses that served as cultural centers and places for children to play and teenagers to hang out.

For José Rivera, who was born in Puerto Rico but raised in the Bronx, the *casitas* are also an affirmation of his community's continuity, of its links to its island legacy and culture. "The *casitas* go back to Puerto Rico, where people would build little houses by the rivers that they could move from place to place when the government forced them to relocate," he explained. But few of the Puerto Rican migrants who moved into the apartment buildings of New York City thought that the time would come when they would once again build their *casitas*—in the Bronx.

"In the late 1960s we had a lot of problems in the Bronx with fires," Rivera recounted. "Landlords were benefiting from the destruction of their buildings for the insurance, and you had fires that would burn down five or six complete blocks." His own neighborhood "turned into a desolate area" of demolished buildings and empty lots. "And people got tired of seeing them used to dump garbage and abandoned cars and industrial wastes, so people got together and planted community gardens and built these *casitas* . . . so that they would have a place to hang out," he explained. "People would come to the *casita* to play music or to celebrate holidays together."

The *casitas* have defied the efforts of an uncomprehending city bureaucracy to tear them down and emerged as oases of hope and symbols of the survival of New York's Puerto Rican community even amid the squalor and violence of the South Bronx. They also began the renewal of

José Rivera's neighborhood. The communities organized themselves around the *casitas,* but then went on to bring the gangs and drug problems of their barrios under control. This demonstration that they could fight urban blight was recognized by the city, and Rivera's neighborhood is now "being remodeled and becoming a good place to live, with lots of smaller houses, which are less vulnerable to vandalism"—and more Puerto Rican, he asserted, "because many of us are from the country. So it's really like bringing Puerto Rico here: The *casitas* are Puerto Rico in New York."

They are also cultural centers, where Puerto Ricans like José Rivera maintain their heritage. Rivera is a full-time musician, lead singer, and drummer with Los Pleneros de la '21, a group "dedicated to the preservation of Puerto Rican culture and Afro-Caribbean folk music," he explained. It was organized in 1983 by a group of musicians whose parents had known each other on the island. Today they keep alive the traditional music of Puerto Rico—the Hispanic *plena,* with its topical lyrics, and the Afro-Caribbean *bomba,* with its evocation of plantation culture and Spiritist rites of possession.

But the Pleneros do more than just preserve the old songs. They also create new ones, itself an old tradition. In Puerto Rico, explained Rivera, *plenas* "were like a newspaper—people would write *plenas* about what was happening and take them from town to town." The Pleneros de la '21 maintained this tradition as well. "Two days after the Rodney King trial verdicts" in Los Angeles, he related, "we had a song about it."

"This is our music, the music of our parents," Rivera stressed, adding that the Pleneros' role was to bring it to their own children, even in the heart of New York City. On a steamy June Saturday in Central Park, Puerto Ricans of all ages formed an enthusiastic audience for the Pleneros, including teenagers who looked more likely to be singing salsa than *plena.* For Nelly Tanco, one of the group's featured singers, this enthusiasm was understandable. "I used to be into salsa myself, but I feel that in this more traditional music I am more into my country," she explained. "When you talk about salsa, it is a mix of everybody's music, but when you are talking about traditional music like *plena,* you are talking about something as

Puerto Rican as rice and beans," she affirmed. "Put it this way: We cannot live without rice and beans—and the same is true for our music."

But for many Nuyoricans, who grew up in the ghettos of Manhattan and the Bronx with African-Americans and are often regarded as "blacks" by a North American society that does not recognize mulattos, rap—itself a child of Jamaican reggae—is a more natural musical outlet than *plena* or even salsa, the popular music of today's Puerto Rico.

"We were raised in the ghetto, and all our friends was all into hip hop. Every street corner there was a jam. So we just got influenced by that and began to rap, because it was there," explained Rick "Puerto Rock" Rodríguez, lead singer of Latin Empire, a dynamic Nuyorican rap group. "If we would have been raised in Puerto Rico, we'd probably be singing salsa." Although they had been bored as children by the sentimental boleros of a Daniel Santos that their parents loved, "we don't dislike salsa or anything—we love it and we include it into our raps." This mix was a natural one for Nuyoricans like Latin Empire's Anthony "Krazy Taino" Boston, who "started off speaking Spanglish. I mean Spanish at home, then all of a sudden I began speaking English at school, and then I started to adapt to both, and I found myself mixing them both." The result was "street jams with a Spanish flavor," said Rick, describing the creation of "bilingual rap," which mixes rhymes in both languages.

Yet, now that they are "older and wiser," they are proud of the songs of their parents, which also show up in their raps. Because "if you lose your culture," stressed Tony, "then you gonna be lost in the sauce." Latin Empire sees their own raps as a continuation of the Puerto Rican *plena* tradition, but in a different context and with a different beat. Rap is like *"plena,* saying the story of something that happened in one pueblo," Rick explained. It was one reason "the older people give us R-E-S-P-E-C-T," affirmed Tony, but it also made the younger Nuyoricans "feel proud of their culture," Rick stressed. "Like yeah, that's right, I'm Puerto Rican and *proud."*

Puerto Rican artists and community activists have taken the lead in this effort to preserve and promote their unique culture in an urban environment where Nuyoricans are subject to the dual lures of mainstream Anglo culture and African-American ghetto culture—the first a passport to assimilation and ascent into the middle class, the second a reflection of the racism, poverty, and urban problems that both communities share. The Puerto Rican Traveling Theater—a mobile troupe that offers free performances at community centers and schools around the city—has satirized the willingness of upwardly mobile Puerto Ricans to deny their cultural heritage as the price of assimilation. In *The English-Only Restaurant* no Spanish is spoken, and a ghetto macho who refuses to play by these rules is ostracized—until a police raid reveals them to be all "just Puerto Ricans" in the eyes of Anglo society and their heritage reasserts itself.

Ecuelecuá is a community-based performance group in Manhattan's Loisaida, or Lower East Side, which creates plays on themes of everyday concerns such as domestic violence, which they develop through community informants and then present as part of a strategy of community empowerment. "The role of culture in addressing the issues that Puerto Ricans face in New York is a key one," argued director María Mar. "It goes back to the role that the arts have played in Puerto Rican and Latin American history, which is that of education and bringing people together to analyze their problems and to celebrate their own power." Her codirector, Ben Soto, agreed. "Puerto Ricans are one of the most assimilated of the Latino groups, yet still you're always an outsider," he emphasized. Culture is "fundamental to the issue of political power, because the way people see themselves is essential to their feeling capable of doing things, to feeling that they can move forward."

But it is not just Puerto Rican artists who are maintaining their cultural traditions and community in New York's concrete jungle. Ordinary Nuyoricans share their fierce pride in being "Boricuas" (after the Taino Indian name for the island) and in their culture and ethnic identity—"even Puerto Ricans that don't speak Spanish and aren't into Spanish music," underscored Rick Rodríguez. It is why June 14 is an annual occasion for an outpouring of ethnic pride.

On Manhattan's Upper West Side, an area shared by Anglo professionals, African-Americans, and Latinos, the celebrations started the night before, as Puerto Rican flags sprouted out of the basement apartments of supers and syncopated Caribbean rhythms took over Broadway. Around the corner from my house, a super had set up a stand selling "I am Proud to be Puerto Rican" buttons and homemade *pasteles de bacaláo,* pastries stuffed with codfish. Behind him his friends sat in his doorway—as their fathers had sat in front of their *casitas* in Puerto Rico—with their guitars and maracas and bongo drums, playing "the old songs," breaking into rakish harmonies, while their wives talked and their children danced on the sidewalk. "We are proud to be Puerto Ricans," he explained, "and we want everyone in this neighborhood to know that."

Quisqueya Heights

The plane for Puerto Plata was late and we were the only ones waiting in the empty airport lounge at Port-au-Prince, so conversation came naturally. José was heading home for a visit to San Francisco. "No, not California," he laughed, "the Dominican Republic." I should come and visit, he said. They had everything there one could want—swimming pools, restaurants, discos—and he had just built a new house for his mother with the money he had made in New York. It turned out that he lived in Washington Heights, my old neighborhood, so we talked about *el barrio* and how it had changed: "It's *Quisqueya* Heights now, man," he crowed, invoking the ancient Indian name for his native island of Hispaniola. I didn't ask him what he did for a living, although his flamboyant clothes, expensive jewelry, and streetwise style gave me a clue: Most of the Dominican cocaine dealers in northern Manhattan come from the little town of San Francisco de Marcorís overlooking the rich Cibāo Valley. Their remittances had transformed it from a poor hill town into a repository of riches.

They had also given its sons an unsavory reputation. In 1991, 160 of them returned home in closed coffins, victims of New York's drug wars. The shooting death by police of José "Kiko" García, an alleged cocaine dealer, in disputed circumstances, had set off days of rioting in Washington Heights that one Dominican resident called "a mini–Los Angeles." It had not attracted the same national attention or caused comparable losses, but the Dominican riots of July 1992 revealed to many New Yorkers for the first time the existence of a community that constitutes the city's largest group of recent immigrants, yet one that had remained largely invisible—except for headlines about crack houses and drug wars. There *are* narcotics traffickers in the Dominican community of Washington Heights, although much of their business is in selling to Anglo users in cars from suburban New Jersey who cross the nearby George Washington Bridge.

But few of the estimated half million Dominicans in New York are drug dealers. Some are entrepreneurs who have opened supermarkets in neglected ghetto areas. Many more are small businessmen, owners of stores, bars, and restaurants throughout the city. Most are manual workers in sweatshops and factories where they earn the minimum wage or less. They are hardworking immigrants whose remittances to their families in the Dominican Republic now constitute that island nation's largest source of dollars. They are also New York's fastest-growing ethnic group, accounting for upward of four out of five people in areas of Manhattan and Queens.

Like other immigration from the Caribbean Basin, the growing tide of migrants from the Dominican Republic reflects U.S. involvement in its internal affairs. It began during the 1960s, a decade of U.S. military intervention, economic expansion, and political interference. It accelerated during the 1980s, and today Dominicans are the seventh largest immigrant group in the United States. It is also one of most concentrated, but in New York, not in South Florida, unlike their Caribbean neighbors from Cuba. By 1985 Dominicans had become the largest foreign-born group in New York.

Unlike the Puerto Rican migrants, the new Dominican community in New York is largely composed of middle-class people whose educational and financial resources are greater than those of most of their compatriots. Many are children of small landowners from the countryside who were seeking ways to supplement their family incomes or to save the money with which to expand or modernize their family farm. Others had owned businesses in Santo Domingo and looked to set up their own enterprises in

New York, or else to accumulate the capital to establish a business back home. Most were forced to accept work that was beneath their occupational status in the Dominican Republic, jobs they left as soon as they had accumulated the capital to open their own business.

Today, Dominicans own *mamí y papí bodegas*—mom and pop grocery stores—throughout New York, and some have gone on from there, filling the niche left vacant by the withdrawal of mainstream businesses from ghetto areas. C-Town, an expanding chain of owner-operated supermarkets, is a good example of this Dominican success. It was created by Krasdale Foods, a large grocery wholesaler, in 1975 to replace their customers in the chain stores that had abandoned New York City for the suburbs. Today, C-Town is a "voluntary association" of 167 franchised stores with one billion dollars in sales a year. Roughly half of these stores are owned by Dominicans, who impressed Krasdale president Charles Krasne, himself the son of an immigrant Russian grocer, with their willingness to work hard and take risks: "They are very industrious and they stick their necks out," he asserted. "They came to New York to get rich, and they succeeded."[7]

Mariano Díaz, who came to New York fifteen years ago without any capital and today earns a six-figure income from his store, is a case in point. Díaz began by working in his uncle's *bodega* in Queens, saving the money for his own store. In 1982 he bought a *bodega* on 100th Street in Manhattan, which he sold in 1987 to help finance the C-Town store that he leased on the ground floor of a building at the northwest corner of Central Park, on the edge of Harlem. Dominican owner-operators like Mariano Díaz manage the stores themselves, work six-day weeks and twelve-hour days and double the normal profit margins. Today Díaz's store sales exceed four million dollars a year, part of the more than one billion dollars in groceries sold by Dominican storeowners in New York annually. Yet he is already thinking of the future, his gaze fixed on the American dream that has brought so many immigrant entrepreneurs to North American shores. "If my kids pursue this kind of work," he mused, "we will do something together."[8]

Bodegas and supermarkets may be emblematic of the Dominican road to riches, but they are not the only route. Inwood, at the northern tip of

Manhattan, is honeycombed with stores and services whose names and owners reveal their Dominican origins. Tucked in between Rosa's Bar and a pool hall in the shadow of the elevated subway line, El Lina looks from the outside like so many other small Latin American restaurants in New York—a space divided between a counter and a table area, clean but modest, with plastic flowers and tablecloths and tile floors. But to Onésimo Quesada and his brother Santiago, it is the start of their American dream. Following in the footsteps of an elder brother who had migrated in 1981, they came to New York from Santiago, the Dominican Republic's second largest city. There they had trained under their father, the head chef in El Pez Dorado, or the Golden Fish, honored in 1991 as the country's best restaurant. But after sixteen years, they had little to show for their labors except the skills they had learned, and little chance of going further in their own country. So they decided to come to the United States to open a restaurant of their own. "There is more opportunity here," Onésimo, the head waiter, explained as he served plates of rice, red beans, and fried plantains that the *New York Times* has described as "an essay in Caribbean aesthetics."[9] He served us with a flourish learned in more elegant surroundings, but with a pride in his food and a confidence in his future. "This restaurant is just a beginning," he confided. "Someday we will have a restaurant in New York like El Pez Dorado." For recent immigrants such as the Quezadas, the United States of America remains the land of opportunity.

Latinos

The United States attracted more immigrants during the 1980s than in any previous decade. They came from all over the world to "the land of liberty," but almost half came from Latin America and the Caribbean. Mexico accounted for nearly half of these 3.5 million legal immigrants, with the Dominican Republic providing the next largest American contingent, followed by El Salvador and Jamaica, Cuba, Haiti, Colombia, and Guyana.

But many of those who settled in the United States did so illegally and a count of their numbers would increase these official totals.

In New York, a city that historically has been the gateway to America for immigrants, these recent arrivals have transformed its neighborhoods, creating a "New New York" very different from the old. The 1990 census documents a "Hispanic" population of New York City of nearly 1.8 million, but this is an underestimate. Many of the New Yorkers from Latin America and the Caribbean entered the United States illegally and are reluctant to be counted for fear of being deported. Guestimates, moreover, are part of a political numbers game that makes any statistic suspect, as the distribution of both power and resources depends upon the numbers that are accepted.

Today New York has over 900,000 Puerto Ricans, twice as many as San Juan, but there are also an estimated half a million Dominicans, almost as many as in Santo Domingo, along with at least 85,000 Colombians and 80,000 Ecuadorians, perhaps 60,000 Mexicans and Cubans, and smaller but still substantial numbers of Central Americans. Moreover, in addition to these Spanish Americans, New York is today home to a growing community of Brazilians, more than 100,000 Haitians, and an estimated half million West Indians, most of whom are Jamaicans but with all of the smaller islands represented as well. Together they have made New York the world's largest Caribbean city, not only turning Washington Heights into Quisqueya Heights, but also transforming Brooklyn's Crown Heights into a West Indian "island." Leading Haitian newspapers are now printed in Brooklyn and Colombian politicians raise campaign funds in Queens's Jackson Heights.

It is in the borough of Queens that the New New York is most on display. Here, Koreans and Cambodians, Russians and Jamaicans live cheek by jowl with Latinos in neighborhoods where an elementary school like Corona's P.S. 19 may have children from forty-seven countries, including virtually all the Latin American republics. "We are a little OAS," quipped the school's principal, Dr. Barbara Miles, herself the daughter of West Indian immigrants.

This multicultural mosaic is visible in the street signs and audible in
the accents of passersby. It is also savored in the great variety of foods and
restaurants available in Queens. "You can see the melting pot in the
restaurants—Argentine and Uruguayan, Colombian and Dominican,
Peruvian and Ecuadoran," explained actor John Leguizamo, who lived in
Jackson Heights during the 1980s. Today, the best Argentine chorizo sau-
sages and meat pies in New York are to be found in Jackson Heights, home
to the largest Argentine community in North America, most of them white
middle-class professionals.

But Argentines are only one of the many groups from Latin America
and the Caribbean who have made Queens their new home and the New
New York an inter-American mosaic. There is a five-block stretch along
Roosevelt Avenue in Jackson Heights that contains no fewer than ten
Colombian restaurants. Underneath the elevated subway tracks, storefronts
advertise delivery services to the families left behind in Bogotá and Baran-
quilla, Cali and Medellín. A few blocks farther into Corona, the neighborhood becomes Dominican and the sound of the Spanish and smell of the
food changes. Here, a *botánica* selling herbal remedies and statues of Afro-
Caribbean *santos* competes for attention with Blockbuster Video. In the
other direction are polyglot neighborhoods, with Jamaicans and Koreans,
Peruvians and Filipinos mixed with Mexicans and Ecuadorians, in addition
to older groups of Greeks and Italians. It was in such a multicultural
neighborhood that Leguizamo spent his teenage years in the 1980s. "School
was like Benetton," he recalled. "You'd look around the class and there
were so many different colors and faces."

Most of those faces were from Latin America, but "it was different
growing up in Queens than in Miami, where there is one big group of
Hispanics—the Cubans," he underscored. "I grew up in a mixed neighborhood—even among the Latinos. There were a lot of Puerto Ricans and
Colombians, but there were also Salvadorans and Argentines, and some
Hondurans and lot of Ecuadorians. And now there are many Dominicans
and Mexicans as well." Though these groups all spoke Spanish, within
Latin America they stressed their separate national identities, with their
racial differences and claims of superiority. In Queens, on the other hand,

"you saw the differences, but it didn't matter. In Queens, we all felt drawn to each other and there was an instant bond, because of this language and culture that we share," he explained. "People started to identify not as Colombians or Puerto Ricans but as *Latinos.*"

The result was the emergence of a new synthetic Latino identity and a new syncretic popular culture. Leguizamo's friends danced to reggae and rap, as well as to cumbia and tango, merengue and salsa. It is salsa, which cannot be identified with any one country of the Hispanic Caribbean but draws on the musical traditions of all of them, plus the diverse Hispanic communities in the United States, that best expresses this new "Latino" culture.

Leguizamo, the child of a Puerto Rican father and a Colombian mother, exemplifies this Latino identity, which he explores in performance pieces, like his prize-winning *Mambo Mouth,* with its focus on the working-class and street people of his Queens adolescence, or its successor, *Spic-O-Rama,* which examines the middle-class Latinos of today. *Mambo Mouth*—*Salsa Mouth* might have been a better title for his wide-ranging and pungent skits—satirizes a rogues' gallery of Latino types, from an older generation Cuban talk-show host bragging about his sex appeal to a teenage Puerto Rican street kid looking for his first sexual encounter, and from a failed Colombian "Inca God Dad" to a successful Latino "Crossover King" who offers seminars on how to assimilate—and become Japanese.

But his most poignant and explicitly political skit is the confrontation between an illegal Mexican immigrant and an I.N.S. official of Dominican origin who is implementing Anglo laws and deporting him. To the Anglo majority in his audience, Leguizamo has his Pepe Vásquez proclaim in Spanish-accented English: "Come on . . . it's not like I'm stealing or living off you good people's taxes. I'm doing the shit jobs Americans don't want . . . *Who* the hell wants to work for $2.25 an hour picking toxic pesticide-coated grapes?" But his message to the large Latino minority watching his show is expressed in Vásquez's appeal in Spanish to his Dominican interrogator: *"Somos de la misma sangrita. Los latinos debemos ser unidos y jamás seremos vencidos"*—"We are of the same blood. Latinos ought to be united and if we are, we will never be defeated."

"And I truly believe that," Leguizamo told me after his performance. "The characters in my show are representatives of the community. They are prototypes." Leguizamo explained: "America may not realize it yet but Latin prototypes are being created right now—and not just by me. It is these mambo kings and salsa queens, Aztec lords and Inca princesses, every Hernández and Fernández, whom this country will one day come to understand and respect."

John Leguizamo's one-man show not only won critical praise, it also played to sold-out theaters and was featured on HBO. It is only one of the signs that Latino culture is coming of age within the United States and winning increasing appreciation among non-Hispanics as well. In 1990, Oscar Hijuelos won a Pulitzer Prize for his novel *The Mambo Kings Play Songs of Love,* with its nostalgic evocation of the world of the first Latin crossover dream, the Cuban musicians of the postwar era, modeled after the television success of Desi Arnaz in "I Love Lucy."

The risks—as well as the richness—of multicultural fusion is the central subject of Mexican poet-performance artist Guillermo Gómez-Peña, whose many Mexican masks reveal the ambiguities of North-South cultural tensions that are at once destructive and creative. More self-consciously intellectual than Leguizamo, Gómez-Peña focuses on the border as a metaphor for U.S.–Latin American relations, as an obstacle for Mexican immigrants like his family, and as an opportunity for the United States. "There is a great new fusion taking place," he argued, "and I think that syncretism is as much a part of U.S. culture as it is in Latin America."[10] Along both sides of the two-thousand-mile U.S.-Mexican frontier, a new "border culture" has emerged, a fusion of both cultures into a new popular culture that will enrich both countries. Los Lobos, the award-winning Chicano band from Los Angeles that plays everything from rancheras to rhythm and blues, is one example. The murals of East L.A. artist Judy Baca, which draw on both the Mexican muralists and the W.P.A. populist tradition while adding something uniquely Chicano, are another. Gómez-Peña's innovative performance art is already having an impact on U.S. experimental theater. But his goals are not limited to artistic innovation. "The real wound in contemporary America is a matter of race and identity," he maintains, the result of the "misunderstanding between cultures" which has become a "bleeding wound" in U.S. cities where recent immigrants have concentrated. "The overriding concern of my work is to articulate the complex relationship between the North and the South in the hope that I can contribute to a better understanding between the cultures."[11]

For the self-proclaimed "Warrior for Gringostroika," part of this task is for Latinos to "rediscover" their America and for Anglos to understand the Latino experience of North America. It is a goal that brings his border art into the mainstream of the U.S. debate over bilingualism and multiculturalism and what it means to be an "American" in 1992.

Americans

When I was growing up in the Inwood section of Washington Heights at the north end of Manhattan Island during the postwar years, it was an ethnic mosaic of Irish and Jews, Germans and Greeks, Italians and Armenians. Most of my schoolmates were children or grandchildren of immigrants, who were trying to make it into the middle class and fulfill their American dream in New York City.

Today my old neighborhood seems changed. The language heard most frequently on the streets is Spanish, as are the signs on the stores. Most residents are from the Dominican Republic, part of the complex wave of migration, legal and illegal, from south of our borders that has transformed New York City—and the United States—during recent decades.

Below the Hispanic surface, though, much about my old neighborhood remains the same. Most of these new neighbors are also hardworking immigrants determined to make good in the United States. The Irish bars now have Spanish names and the insistent rhythms of merengue have replaced the lilting strains of Celtic harps in their jukeboxes, but they remain local watering holes whose music defines their ethnicity. The kosher grocery stores are now *bodegas* selling "tropical products," but they still lend immigrant tables a nostalgic taste of home. The neighborhood still functions as a way station of integration for immigrants on the way up into the lower middle class, and my old elementary school is still seen as their children's first step in that direction. Much has been written about the new wave of immigrants from Latin America and the Caribbean, but how different are they from the earlier waves of European immigrants?

Until recently, the "making of the United States" out of a "land of immigrants" was a linear story of progressive "Americanization," in which the immigrants' acquisition of English-language skills and educational credentials were their passports to success. Its popular counterpart was the ideology of the "melting pot," in which immigrants lost their ethnic characteristics and identities and emerged as "Americans."

In the wake of the ethnic revival that followed the black consciousness movement of the 1960s, historians are questioning whether assimilation was ever as linear a process as an earlier generation wanted to believe and arguing that the melting pot was always more ideal than real. Notions of "ethnic resilience" now shape scholarly studies, while the "multicultural mosaic" has replaced the "melting pot" of assimilation as the dominant metaphor of public policy and political debate.

Although this revolution in conventional wisdoms reflects a reevaluation of the experience of earlier immigrant groups, the seeming resistance to assimilation by the new wave of immigrants from Latin America and the Caribbean has become a driving force. Among Latinos, the first ideological statement of this alternative vision emerged from Chicanos influenced by the civil rights movement, but the notion of "La Raza"—a Mexican fusion of Spaniard and Indian—was more a reaction to failure than a recipe for success.

Among Latinos it was Miami's Cubans who first demonstrated that success in the United States could be a product not of assimilation but of banding together and resisting its lures. In South Florida they created an ethnic enclave in which a knowledge of Spanish and an understanding of Latin American culture became central to economic and political achievement—and it was English speakers who felt disadvantaged. "There's a good bit of bad feeling about that," Philip Thomas asserted. This "bad feeling" found an expression in Thomas's Dade Americans United, which a decade ago succeeded in making English the sole legal language of Miami's Dade County. But legislation has done little to alter Miami's bilingual and multicultural character.

Thomas blames the *Miami Herald*'s Spanish-language newspaper for "encouraging people to retain their own language and culture almost to the exclusion of English." For him it was a case of American institutions adjusting to immigrants where it ought to be the other way around, as had been the case in the past. For the *Herald*, it was an effort "to be responsive and sensitive to what the community needs," according to Carlos Verdecia. "Everybody thought that Cubans would assimilate, that they would start reading in English and there would be no need for a Spanish-language publication," the editor recounted. What happened was "quite the opposite. *El Nuevo* had to be launched as an expanded newspaper in 1987 to meet the needs" of a new wave of immigrants who "were more comfortable in Spanish." It is this continual flow of new immigrants that sustains Miami's Spanish language and culture—as it does that of Los Angeles and New York.

For Anglos such as Philip Thomas, this is a sign that Hispanics are refusing to assimilate. Carlos Verdecia disagrees: "Hispanics and Cubans feel that they are as American as apple pie," he insisted, and despite Anglo fears, second-generation Cubans speak English well. "In fact, we are the ones to worry," argued Verdecia, "because our children lose their Spanish." Thomas's concern was misplaced, he concluded. "I don't think there should be a fear of Miami losing its English language, but I do think that it is so much richer for having so many different cultures and so many different languages."

The Cuban success in a bilingual and multicultural Miami may be too much a product of a particular time and place to serve as a model for other immigrant groups. Elsewhere, the demand for bilingual education and advocacy of a multicultural mosaic reflect frustration at the powerlessness of even sizable Latino populations and the failure of schools to stem the alarming dropout rates of Latino children, which augur ill for their future in a society stratified by education.

Yet Anglos like Philip Thomas are not the only ones worried about the multicultural trend. Linda Chavez, a director of the U.S. Civil Rights Commission under President Ronald Reagan, has attacked bilingual education and multiculturalism and argued for assimilation out of a concern for both Hispanic success and U.S. unity. Chavez sees bilingualism as an understandable response to high Latino dropout rates, but argues that "the results are counterproductive and lead to increased segregation and prejudice." She is concerned that Hispanic youngsters spend "their entire school lives" in bilingual programs, leaving them unprepared for the English-speaking society outside. She also worries that there are communities in the United States where no English is spoken and criticizes Spanish-language ballots for U.S. citizens who are supposed to know English, transforming these communities into political enclaves as well. Chavez defends the older notion of assimilation, which she recognizes "has become a dirty word," arguing that Hispanics can assimilate "and still celebrate their own traditions within their families." She warns that "if we persist in emphasizing our separateness rather than our sameness, then we can only expect that race and ethnicity will be a major source of conflict in coming decades."[12]

Dr. Barbara Miles, the principal of New York's P.S. 19, in a city where bilingual education is mandated for all children who lack the fluency to learn in English, strongly disagrees. The great majority of the students in her Queens elementary school come from Latin America and half of the kindergarten classes are bilingual, with children learning thematic units in both Spanish and English. She had received angry phone calls demanding to know: "Why are we accommodating the needs of the Spanish-speaking children?" But Dr. Miles argued that "research demonstrates quite clearly that children need to be taught in their native language first and then we can transfer those skills to English." She was convinced that bilingual education worked: At P.S. 19, by fifth grade only one bilingual class remained to serve recently arrived older children. All the other children were now able to learn in English. "That is our focus," Miles stressed. "We want them to become English-speaking because they live in an English-speaking country."

Like their parents, few of whom are U.S. citizens, the children in P.S.

19 are proud of the country they came from, a pride that P.S. 19 encourages through activities that "celebrate the diversity" of its student population. In one bilingual class, students provided a living geography lesson with a choreographed and costumed play in which they presented information about their countries of origin. "We celebrate the independence day of the Dominican Republic," where most of the school's children come from, related Dr. Miles. The children "told us about the history of the Dominican Republic, and it was very heart-warming when they sang the national anthem of the Dominican Republic."

Yet, for Miles and her staff, "another aim is for all of the children to be aware that they are or will be U.S. citizens. We pledge allegiance to the flag every day," she stressed, "and every assembly begins with the singing of 'America the Beautiful.' " The fifth-grade graduation, the culminating event for P.S. 19 students, featured patriotic songs sung by a United Nations of young voices.

Even the kindergarten graduation celebrated the children's first steps toward becoming "Americans," yet without losing their identities as Dominicans or Colombians. Watching their children create a ceremony in both English and Spanish, Adolfo Avila was proud that his daughter had "learned a lot at school," but also "proud that she speaks both languages." So was Silvia Balz, who was not yet a U.S. citizen, but was "very proud to live in this country" and felt "one hundred percent American. And," she stressed, "all my children feel totally American."

The presence of a large and growing group of immigrants who speak a foreign language, take pride in their distinctive culture, and insist on bilingualism and a multicultural society has sparked alarm among many in the United States—as was the case with nativist reactions to previous immigrant waves. Former Colorado governor Richard Lamm articulated these fears when he wrote in *The Immigration Time Bomb: The Fragmenting of America:* "Increasingly, the political power of more than fifteen million Hispanics is being used not to support assimilation but to advance 'ethnic pride' in belonging to a different culture. The multiplication of outsiders is not a model for a viable society."[13]

There *are* some special characteristics of the recent wave of immigrants from Latin America and the Caribbean. There is more return migration or recycled migration, a reflection of shorter distances and low air fares. These new neighbors also arrived during the era of the "new ethnicity," a time of revived ethnic awareness among all hyphenated-Americans. There is a greater demand for bilingual education, and educators are more receptive to the need of immigrant children for special programs to ease their integration into U.S. society. There has been more integration than assimilation among first-generation immigrants, and greater reluctance among some groups to become citizens.

But Governor Lamm's concerns—and the more widespread fears that lay behind them—are misplaced. Bilingual education accelerates both integration and assimilation. Moreover, as in the past, assimilation has been a gradual process, but the second generation of recent immigrants, U.S. citizens at birth, speak better English and are more assimilated than their parents. There is every reason to believe that succeeding generations will continue the pattern of progressive assimilation—though with a greater complexity and ethnic pride than may have been true for immigrants who arrived in an era when such ethnic retention seemed less legitimate.

Even the new Hispanic ethnic pride and politics that Lamm warns against have both precedents in the past and a different meaning than he lends them. In the past, such reaffirmation of ethnic identities was a step toward the social and political integration of European immigrant groups, many of which still vote for candidates of their ethnic origin. There is every indication that the same is true of the new ethnic politics within communities of Spanish American origin, who are learning the value of citizenship and democracy by using them to defend their interests. In Los Angeles, experiences of the power of the vote have persuaded Mexicans in Bell Gardens to become U.S. citizens. In New York, where only one of five Dominican immigrants is a U.S. citizen and most maintain a binational identity, the key role of José Linares, the first Dominican City Council member, in representing his community during the July 1992 conflict may have a similar impact. Few communities have learned to play the U.S. political game as well as Miami's Cuban community, but Chicanos and Haitians have tried to repeat their success in influencing U.S. policy toward their countries of origin and more recent immigrants. The doubling of Hispanic-majority congressional districts in 1992 will advance this process. In many ways the newer immigrants are following in the footsteps of the old, who learned to use their numbers and political influence to promote the interests of their communities.

What is perhaps new is the question posed by these Latin American communities to the larger U.S. society: Why do we have to give up our culture in order to become "Americans"—in a melting pot that never really melted? It is a question that this nation of immigrants would do well to ponder. In the century of the global village, in which international distances are shrinking but economic competition is increasing, an insistence on "English Only" seems both anachronistic and self-defeating. Miami's Cuban community has demonstrated how a bilingual and multicultural environment can be an economic advantage in a new world order of mobile capital and global sourcing. Within the proposed "Enterprise of the Americas" hemispheric free-trade zone, a knowledge of Spanish and Portuguese and an understanding and appreciation of the cultures of Latin America and the Caribbean will be indispensable for North Americans. It is an argument for promoting a bilingual and multicultural society within the United States instead of insisting on assimilation as the price of acceptance.

The vibrant cultures that these immigrants bring with them can only enrich the culture of the United States. The strong arms, needed skills, and feisty entrepreneurship of immigrants from Latin America and the Caribbean have already contributed to this country's economic progress, helping to rejuvenate decaying cities and to maintain declining industries. Latinos have participated increasingly in this country's politics and contributed their artistic traditions and talents as well. There is every reason to believe that their children and grandchildren will play increasing roles in this country's future, just as the children and grandchildren of European immigrants have done.

On Ellis Island in New York Harbor, a "Wall of Honor" bears the names of hundreds of thousands of European immigrants who entered the United States through this gateway to the "land of liberty" during the late nineteenth and early twentieth centuries and helped to make this country the land of opportunity. The recent wave of immigrants from the Americas have arrived by more diverse routes—they have landed at airports, traversed dangerous straits in small boats, and crossed porous frontiers—and the site for their monument is less clear. Yet, a century from now they too should merit a monument to their courage in immigrating and to their contribution to their new country.

The United States has always prided itself on being a land of immigrants, but historically its citizens have also been ambivalent about the most recent immigrant wave. In the next century, people of Latin American and Caribbean origin will become the largest minority in the United States, which will have to come to terms with the fact that they are not immigrants but "Americans"—citizens of both the country and the hemisphere that we all share.

Notes

1: A View from the South

1. Quoted in Rachel Weiss with Alan West, *Being America: Essays on Art, Literature, and Identity in America* (Freedonia, N.Y.: White Pine Press, 1991), pp. 123–24.

2. Joseph Conrad, *Heart of Darkness,* 2nd edition, ed. Robert Kimbrough (New York: W. W. Norton, 1971), p. 34.

3. Quoted in *Time,* September 18, 1989, 77.

4. Quoted in the *New York Times,* July 30, 1991.

5. Quoted in Luis Carlos Benvenuto, *Breve história del Uruguay* (Montevideo: ARCA, 1967), p. 88.

6. Gabriel García Márquez, *One Hundred Years of Solitude,* trans. Gregory Rabassa (New York: Harper & Row, 1970), p. 383.

2: Legacies of Empire

1. Reprinted as "Columbus's Letter on His First Voyage," in Samuel E. Morison, *Christopher Columbus, Mariner* (Boston: Atlantic Monthly Press/Little, Brown, 1942), p. 206. I have partly retranslated the quote.

2. Bernal Díaz del Castillo, *The True History of the Conquest of Mexico,* trans. Maurice Keatinge (Congleton, England, 1800), pp. 130–31.

3. Bernal Díaz del Castillo to Emperor Charles V (Santiago de Guatemala, February 22, 1552); reprinted in *Letters and People of the Spanish Indies: Sixteenth Century,* eds. and trans. James Lockhart and Enrique Otte (New York: Cambridge University Press, 1976), p. 78.

4. Fray Antonio de San Miguel, Bishop of Michoacán, quoted in John Lynch, *The Spanish American Revolutions, 1808–1826* (New York: W. W. Norton, 1973), p. 298.

5. Quoted in Magnus Mörner, *Race Mixture in the History of Latin America* (Boston: Little, Brown, 1967), p. 69.

6. Quoted in John Chance, *Race and Class in Colonial Oaxaca* (Stanford: Stanford University Press, 1978), p. 178.

7. Quoted in Mörner, *Race Mixture*, p. 64.

8. Reprinted in Irving Leonard, *Baroque Times in Old Mexico* (Ann Arbor: University of Michigan Press, 1959), p. 178. I have partly retranslated this quote.

9. Translation by Robert Graves, in *Chicano Literature: Text and Context*, eds. Joseph Sommers and Antonia Castañeda Shular (Englewood Cliffs, N.J.: Prentice-Hall, 1972), pp. 10–11.

10. Quoted in Leonard, *Baroque Times in Old Mexico*, pp. 126–27.

11. Quoted in Robert Ricard, *The Spiritual Conquest of Mexico*, trans. Lesley Byrd Simpson (Berkeley: University of California Press, 1966), p. 16.

12. Quoted in Ibid., p. 187.

13. Quoted in Rachel Beauvoir-Dominique, *L'Ancienne Cathédrale de Port-au-Prince: Perspectives d'un Vestige de Carrefours* (Port-au-Prince: Henri Deschamps, 1991), p. 42.

14. Quoted in John Hemming, *The Conquest of the Incas* (New York: Harcourt Brace Jovanovich, 1970), p. 408.

15. Quoted in Charles Boxer, "Brazilian Gold and British Traders in the First Half of the Eighteenth Century," *Hispanic American Historical Review*, XLIX (August 1969): 454.

16. Quoted in Stuart Schwartz, *Sugar Plantations in the Formation of Brazilian Society: Bahia, 1550–1835* (New York: Cambridge University Press, 1985), p. 144.

17. Quoted in Hubert Herring, *A History of Latin America*, 3rd ed. (New York: Alfred A. Knopf, 1967), p. 214.

18. Quoted in John L. Phelan, *The People and the King: The Comunero Revolution in Colombia, 1781* (Madison: University of Wisconsin Press, 1978), pp. 71–72.

19. Quoted in Herring, *Latin America*, p. 280.

20. Quoted in Lynch, *Spanish American Revolutions*, p. 298.

21. Quoted in Herring, *Latin America*, p. 276.

3: *The Perils of Progress*

The sources for this chapter include the writings of Peter Smith and producer Elizabeth Nash's interview with Torcuato Di Tella, Jr.

1. José Hernández, *The Gaucho Martín Fierro*, bilingual edition, trans. C. E. Ward (Albany: State University of New York Press, 1967), pp. 9, 23.

2. W. H. Hudson, *Far Away and Long Ago* (London: Everyman's Library, 1967), p. 2.

3. William Walton, *Present State of the Spanish Colonies*, 2 vols. (London, 1810), 1:349.

4. Quoted in John Lynch, *Argentine Dictator: Juan Manuel de Rosas, 1829–1852* (Oxford: Oxford University Press, 1981), p. 125.

5. Henry Southern, British Minister to Buenos Aires; quoted in Ibid., p. 171.

6. Quoted in James R. Scobie, *Argentina: A City and A Nation*, 2nd ed. (New York: Oxford University Press, 1971), p. 78.

7. Dr. Manuel Pizarro, quoted in Ysabel F. Rennie, *The Argentine Republic* (New York: Macmillan, 1945), p. 186.

8. Reprinted in *One Family, Two Worlds: An Italian Family's Correspondence Across the Atlantic, 1901–1922*, eds. Samuel L. Baily and Franco Ramella, trans. John Lenaghan (New Brunswick, N.J.: Rutgers University Press, 1988), pp. 190–91.

4: A Second Independence?

In addition to the published sources cited below, this chapter draws on Peter Smith's work on Argentine politics and Daniel James's research on Berisso, and on interviews conducted in Argentina by producers David Ash, Elizabeth Nash, and Andrés Di Tella.

1. Quoted in Thomas C. Cochran and Rubén Reina, *Capitalism in Argentine Culture: A Study of Torcuato Di Tella and S.I.A.M.* (Philadelphia: University of Pennsylvania Press, 1962), p. 110.

2. *La Reforma* (Santiago), May 6, 1933.

3. Quoted in Joseph Page, *Perón: A Biography* (New York: Random House, 1983), p. 53.

4. Quoted in Ibid., p. 70.

5. Quoted in Ibid., p. 67.

6. Quoted in Ibid., p. 72.

7. Quoted in Ibid., p. 99.

8. Quoted in Ibid., p. 96.

9. Quoted in Ibid., p. 96.

10. Quoted in Ibid., p. 98.

11. Quoted in Ibid., p. 108.

12. Quoted in Ibid., p. 118.

13. Juan Caserta, quoted in Cochrane and Reina, *Capitalism in Argentine Culture*, p. 197.

14. For an insightful analysis, see Daniel James, *Resistance and Integration: Peronism and the Argentine Working Class, 1946–1976* (Cambridge: Cambridge University Press, 1988), pp. 32–33.

15. Quoted in Ibid., p. 33.

16. Quoted in Ibid., p. 33.

17. Quoted in John Barnes, *Evita—First Lady: A Biography of Eva Perón* (New York: Grove Press, 1978), p. 49.

18. Quoted in Page, *Perón*, p. 144.

19. Quoted in Ibid., p. 144.

20. Quoted in Ibid., p. 149.

21. Quoted in Ibid., p. 149.

22. Quoted in Cochran and Reina, *Capitalism in Argentine Culture*, p. 166.

23. Quoted in George I. Blanksten, *Perón's Argentina* (Chicago: University of Chicago Press, 1953), p. 239.

24. Quoted in Winthrop R. Wright, *British-Owned Railways in Argentina: Their Effect on the Growth of Economic Nationalism, 1854–1948* (Austin: University of Texas Press, 1974), p. 249.

25. Quoted in Blanksten, *Perón's Argentina*, p. 242.

26. Antonio Sudiero, quoted in Cochran and Reina, *Capitalism in Argentine Culture*, p. 197.

27. Eva Duarte de Perón, *Evita By Evita*, English ed. of *La razón de mi vida*, Buenos Aires, 1953 (London: Proteus Books, 1978), p. 7.

28. Quoted in Blanksten, *Perón's Argentina*, pp. 101–2.

29. Antonio Sudiero, quoted in Cochran and Reina, *Capitalism in Argentine Culture*, p. 197.

30. Quoted in James, *Resistance and Integration*, p. 29.

31. John Dos Passos, "Visit to Evita," *Life* (April 11, 1949), 31. For an insightful account of Evita's "gift of giving," see Marysa Navarro and Nicholas Fraser, *Eva Perón* (New York: W. W. Norton, 1981), pp. 114–33.

32. Navarro and Fraser, *Eva Perón*, p. 134.

33. Quoted in Blanksten, *Perón's Argentina*, p. 109.

34. Quoted in Navarro and Fraser, *Eva Perón*, p. 179.

35. Quoted in Arthur P. Whitaker, *Argentina* (Englewood Cliffs, N.J.: Prentice-Hall, 1964), p. 137.

5: Capital Sins

This chapter draws in particular on the work of Albert Fishlow, Thomas Skidmore, and Alfred Stepan on Brazil, and on interviews conducted in Brazil by producers Rachel Field and Rebecca Marvil.

1. *The Economist* (July 31, 1976), p. 43.

2. Ralph Della Cava, "The 'People's Church,' the Vatican and Abertura," in *Democratizing Brazil*, ed. Alfred Stepan (New York: Oxford University Press, 1989), p. 145.

6: Continent on the Move

This chapter incorporates ideas from the writings on migration of María Patricia Fernández Kelly and Alejandro Portes, and interviews conducted in Mexico by producers Ray Telles and Marc de Beaufort.

1. For a full account of Adelaida's story, see Patrick Oster, *The Mexicans: A Personal Portrait of a People* (New York: William Morrow, 1989), pp. 21–35.

2.   Quoted in Maria José de Mattos Taube, *De migrantes a favelados: estudo de um processo migratório,* 2 vols. (Campinas: Editora da Unicamp, 1986), 2:16.

7: *Children of the Sun*

Kay Warren's work on ethnicity and identity is reflected in much of this chapter, which also draws on the research of Melina Selverston on Ecuador and Jeffrey Himpele on Bolivia, and on interviews conducted in Bolivia by producers Lourdes Portillo and Jane Regan with Patricia Romero, Felix Zorilla, and the Mamani family.

1.   Quoted in Henry E. Dobyns and Paul L. Doughty, *Peru: A Cultural History* (New York: Oxford University Press, 1976), p. 251.

2.   Mario Vargas Llosa, "Questions of Conquest," *Harper's Magazine* (December 1990), 51–52.

3.   I have drawn the Mayobamba story from the work of Susan C. Bourque and Kay B. Warren summarized in their *Women of the Andes: Patriarchy and Social Change in Two Peruvian Towns* (Ann Arbor: University of Michigan Press, 1981).

4.   See Jürgen Golte and Norma Adams, *Los caballos de Troya de los invasores: estrategías campesinas en la conquista de la Gran Lima,* 2nd ed. (Lima: Instituto de Estudios Peruanos, 1990).

5.   Michael J. Harner, *The Jívaro: People of the Sacred Waterfalls* (New York: Doubleday/Natural History Press, 1972), p. 21.

6.   Quoted in Ernesto Salazar, *Indian Federation of Ecuador,* Cultural Survival, International Working Group on Indigenous Affairs, Paper No. 28 (1987): 144.

7.   Quoted in *La Hora* (Quito), June 7, 1990.

8.   For my account of San Andrés and the new Mayan studies, I have drawn on Kay B. Warren's "Integrating La Violencia: Shapes of Mayan Silence and Resistance in Guatemala," in *The Violence Within: Culture and Political Opposition in Divided Nations,* ed. Kay Warren (Boulder, Colo.: Westview Press, 1992), chap. 1, and on her "Transforming Memories and Histories: The Meanings of Ethnic Resurgence for Mayan Indians," in *Americas: Essays,* ed. Alfred Stepan (New York: Oxford University Press, 1992).

8: *A Question of Color*

In addition to the published sources cited below, this chapter draws on reflections by Anthony Maingot and Thomas Skidmore about race relations in the Caribbean and Brazil respectively, and on interviews conducted in Haiti and the Dominican Republic by producers Lourdes Portillo and Jane Regan.

1.   Eric Williams, *The Negro in the Caribbean* (Westport, Conn.: Negro Universities Press, 1942), pp. 63–64.

2.   David Nicholls, *From Dessalines to Duvalier: Race, Colour and National Independence in Haiti* (Cambridge: Cambridge University Press, 1979), p. 156.

3. Quoted in French in Ibid., p. 210. Author's translation.

4. Quoted in H. Hoetink, *El pueblo dominicano (1850–1900): apuntes para su sociología histórica,* 3rd revised ed. (Santiago, Dominican Republic: Universidad Católica Madre y Maestra, 1985), p. 255. Author's translation.

5. Joaquín Balaguer, *La isla al revés: Haïti y el destino dominicano,* 6th ed. (Santo Domingo, Dominican Republic: Editora Corripio, 1990), p. 63.

6. Quoted in Franklin Knight, *The Caribbean: The Genesis of a Fragmented Nationalism* (New York: Oxford University Press, 1990), p. 225.

7. See, for example, Balaguer, *La isla al revés,* p. 32.

8. Bandleader Luis Senior, quoted in Deborah Pacini Hernández, "The Merengue: Race, Class, Tradition, and Identity," in *Americas: An Anthology,* eds. Mark B. Rosenberg, A. Douglas Kincaid, and Kathleen Logan (New York: Oxford University Press, 1992), p. 171.

9. Camilo Yaryura, "El santo entierro," *Suplemento Listín Diario* (Santo Domingo), June 4, 1983; quoted in translation in H. Hoetink, " 'Race' and Color in the Caribbean," in *Caribbean Contours,* eds. Sidney Mintz and Sally Price (Baltimore: Johns Hopkins University Press, 1985), p. 65.

10. President José Sarney, speech to Joint Session of the U.S. Congress, Washington, D.C., September 11, 1986.

11. Moog's comments, addressed to the Escola Superior de Guerra, Brazil's influential armed forces academy of higher learning, were reported in *Jornal do Brasil* (Rio de Janeiro), August 3, 1972, and quoted in translation in Thomas Skidmore, "Race and Class in Brazil: Historical Perspectives," in *Race, Class and Power in Brazil,* ed. Pierre-Michel Fontaine (Los Angeles: Center for Afro-American Studies, University of California, Los Angeles, 1985), p. 12.

12. I am grateful to Thomas Skidmore for this quote.

13. From *Brazilian Women Speak,* ed. and trans. by Daphne Patai (New Brunswick, N.J.: Rutgers University Press, 1988), pp. 12–13.

14. Petronio Portella, reported in *O Globo* (Rio de Janeiro), April 6, 1977; quoted in Skidmore, "Race and Class in Brazil," p. 12.

15. Quoted in George Reid Andrews, *Blacks and Whites in São Paulo, Brazil, 1888–1988* (Madison: University of Wisconsin Press, 1991), p. 176.

16. Quoted in the *New York Times,* September 24, 1991.

17. Quoted in Andrews, *Blacks and Whites in São Paulo,* p. 218.

18. Quoted in Ibid., p. 219.

19. I am grateful to Guilherme Arguimimo for making these lyrics available to me, together with his translations.

20. Quoted in Herman L. Bennett, "The Challenge to the Post-Colonial State: A Case Study of the February Revolution in Trinidad," in *The Modern Caribbean,* eds. Franklin Knight and Colin Palmer (Chapel Hill: University of North Carolina Press, 1989), pp. 136, 141.

21. Quoted in Selwyn D. Ryan, *Race and Nationalism in Trinidad and Tobago: A Study*

of Decolonization in a Multiracial Society (Toronto: University of Toronto Press, 1972), p. 280.

22.   V. S. Naipaul, *The Middle Passage: The Caribbean Revisited* (London: André Deutsch, 1962), p. 80.

23.   Ganesh Hall, letter to the editor, *Trinidad Guardian,* April 8, 1970; quoted in Bennett, "The February Revolution in Trinidad," p. 139.

24.   R. K. Richardson, letter to the editor, *Trinidad Guardian,* March 26, 1970; quoted in Ibid.

25.   Quoted in Hoetink, " 'Race' and Color in the Caribbean," p. 75.

26.   Quoted in the *New York Times,* September 24, 1990.

9: In Women's Hands

This chapter incorporates the reflections of Cornelia Flora, Marysa Navarro, and Helen Safa on women in Latin America, and interviews conducted in Chile by Rachel Field and Juan Mandelbaum.

1.   Gabriela Mistral, "My Country," *UN World,* May 1950, p. 51.

10: The Power and the Glory

In addition to the published sources cited below, this chapter draws on the work of Margaret E. Crahan and Ralph Della Cava, and on the interview with Cardinal Paulo Evaristo Arns conducted by producers Veronica Young and Tanya Cipriano.

1.   Quoted in Arthur F. McGovern, *Liberation Theology and Its Critics: Toward An Assessment* (Maryknoll, N.Y.: Orbis Books, 1989), p. 227.

2.   Quoted in Scott Mainwaring, *The Catholic Church and Politics in Brazil, 1916–1985* (Stanford: Stanford University Press, 1986), p. 196.

3.   Quoted in Ibid., pp. 198–9.

4.   Quoted in Ibid., pp. 88, 94.

5.   Quoted in Ibid., p. 109.

6.   Quoted in Ibid., p. 244.

7.   *New York Times,* March 5, 1983.

8.   Quoted in Mainwaring, *The Catholic Church and Politics in Brazil,* p. 240.

9.   Quoted in Ibid., p. 240.

10.   Quoted in Ibid., p. 250.

11.   Quoted in *Veja,* September 9, 1991, p. 54.

12.   See, for example, David Stoll, *Is Latin America Turning Protestant? The Politics of Evangelical Growth* (Berkeley: University of California Press, 1990).

13.   Edir Macedo, *Orixás, caboclos e guias—deuses ou demônios,* Coleção Reino de Deus (Rio de Janeiro: Universal Produções–Indústria e Comércio, 1982), p. 13; quoted in Mariza de Carvalho Soares, "Guerra Santa no país do sincretismo," in *Sinais dos tempos:*

diversidade religiosa no Brasil, ed. Leilah Landim (Rio de Janeiro: Instituto de Estudos da Religião, 1990), p. 81.

14. Quoted in Ibid., p. 84.

15. Quoted in John Burdick, "Who Are the 'People' in 'The People's Church'?" in *Churches and Change: Contemporary Latin America,* ed. Margaret E. Crahan (forthcoming).

16. Quoted in the *New York Times,* February 19, 1987.

17. Legião da Boa Vontade, "Templo da Boa Vontade" (Undated pamphlet available at Brasília temple).

18. Ibid.

11: *The Magical and the Real*

This chapter draws heavily on the work of Jean Franco on literature and popular culture in Latin America, and incorporates interviews conducted by producers Juan Mandelbaum and Andrés Di Tella with Josefina Ludmers, Nelson Motta, Jesusa Rodríguez, Luis Rafael Sánchez, Fernando Solanas, Caetano Veloso, and Antônio Dos Santos Vovo, and by producer Rachel Field with José Ramos Tinhorão.

1. Gabriel García Márquez, *One Hundred Years of Solitude,* trans. Gregory Rabassa (New York: Harper & Row, 1970), p. 11.

2. David Alfaro Siqueiros, "A Declaration of Social, Political and Aesthetic Principles," in *Art and Revolution,* trans. Sylvia Calles (London: Lawrence and Wishart, 1975), p. 25.

3. Ibid., p. 20.

4. Quoted in Luis Cardoza y Aragón, "Diego Rivera's Murals in Mexico and the United States," in *Diego Rivera: A Retrospective* (New York: W. W. Norton, 1986), p. 187.

5. David Alfaro Siqueiros, "Three Appeals for a Modern Direction to the New Generation of American Painters and Sculptors," *Vida Americana,* no. 1 (Barcelona) May 1921; reprinted in Dawn Ades, *Art in Latin America* (New Haven, Conn.: Yale University Press, 1989), p. 323.

6. Cardoza y Aragón, "Diego Rivera's Murals," p. 187.

7. Quoted in *Mexico: Splendors of Thirty Centuries* (New York: Metropolitan Museum of Art, 1990), p. 683.

8. Quoted in Ibid., p. 683.

9. Quoted in Ades, p. 144.

10. Pablo Neruda, *Memoirs,* trans. Hardie St. Martin (New York: Farrar, Straus & Giroux, 1977), pp. 170–1.

11. Ibid., p. 171.

12. Ernesto Cardenal, "Closing Address," Meeting of Intellectuals for the Sovereignty of the Peoples of America, Managua, Nicaragua (September 7, 1981); reprinted in *Lives on the Line,* ed. Doris Meyer (Berkeley and Los Angeles: University of California Press, 1988), p. 209.

13. Nicolás Guillén, "Words of Greeting," Fifth Conference of Soviet Writers, Moscow (1971); reprinted in Ibid., p. 107.

14. Alejo Carpentier, *The Kingdom of this World (El Siglo de las luces)*, trans. Harriet de Onis (New York: Alfred A. Knopf, 1957), prologue.

15. García Márquez, *One Hundred Years of Solitude*, p. 383.

16. Mario Vargas Llosa, "La literatura es una forma de insurección permanente," acceptance speech on receiving the Rómulo Gallegos Award, Caracas, Venezuela (1967).

17. Gabriel García Márquez, "The Solitude of Latin America," Nobel Prize acceptance speech, Stockholm (December 1982); reprinted in translation by Marina Castañeda in the *New York Times*, February 6, 1983.

18. *La experiencia de la libertad*, vol. 1, *Hacia la sociedad abierta* (Mexico City: Vuelta, 1991), pp. 157–63.

19. Derek Walcott, *Omeros* (New York: Farrar, Straus & Giroux, 1990), pp. 148–9.

20. Caetano Veloso, "Caricature and Conqueror, Pride and Shame," *New York Times*, October 20, 1991.

21. Ibid.

22. Quoted in Gerald Martin, *Journeys Through the Labyrinth: Latin American Fiction in the Twentieth Century* (London: Verso, 1989), p. 144.

23. Quoted in John King, *Magical Reels: A History of Cinema in Latin America* (London: Verso, 1990), p. 96.

24. Quoted in Ibid., p. 121.

25. Quoted in William Rowe and Vivian Schelling, *Memory and Modernity: Popular Cultures in Latin America* (London: Verso, 1991), p. 88.

26. Quoted in the *New York Times*, August 21, 1991.

27. García Márquez, "Solitude of Latin America."

12: Endangered States

This chapter incorporates the reflections on sovereignty of Franklin Knight and Peter Smith, as well as Mark Chernick's work on Colombia and interviews conducted in Colombia and Jamaica by producers Marc de Beaufort and Elizabeth Nash.

1. John Weeks and Andrew Zimbalist, *Panama at the Crossroads: Economic Development and Political Change in the Twentieth Century* (Berkeley: University of California Press, 1991), p. 12.

2. Quoted in Alonso Aguilar, *Pan-Americanism from Monroe to the Present: A View from the Other Side*, revised Eng. ed., trans. Ada Zatz (New York: Monthly Review Press, 1968), p. 122.

3. Quoted in the *New York Times*, February 11, 1991.

4. Norman Girvan, "After Rodney," quoted in Colin A. Palmer, "Identity, Race,

and Black Power in Independent Jamaica," in *The Modern Caribbean*, eds. Palmer and Franklin Knight (Chapel Hill: University of North Carolina Press, 1989), p. 117.

5. Walter Rodney, *The Groundings with My Brothers*, 1st U.S. ed. (Chicago: Research Associate School Times, 1990), p. 18.

6. Ibid., p. 28.

7. Ibid., p. 18.

8. Quoted in Palmer, "Independent Jamaica," p. 120.

9. Quoted in Ibid., p. 121.

10. Quoted in the *New York Times Magazine*, October 13, 1991.

11. Quoted in *Newsweek*, February 3, 1991, p. 41. Italics added by author.

13: Making Revolution

This chapter draws on many sources, including writings done for the *Americas* project by Cynthia Arnson, Margaret E. Crahan, and Peter Smith, and interviews conducted in Mexico, El Salvador, and Peru by producers Marc de Beaufort and Yezid Campos. The producers' Peruvian interviews are indicated in the notes below, but it should be emphasized that the interpretations and opinions expressed in the Peru section of this chapter are either mine or those of other scholars.

1. From an interview by Marc de Beaufort and Yezid Campos, March 1992.

2. Fidel Castro, "History Will Absolve Me," in *Revolutionary Struggle, 1947–1958: Selected Works of Fidel Castro*, eds. Rolando E. Bonachea and Nelson P. Valdés (Cambridge, Mass.: MIT Press, 1972), p. 221.

3. Mario Llerena, *The Unsuspected Revolution: The Birth and Rise of Castroism* (Ithaca, N.Y.: Cornell University Press, 1978), p. 198.

4. *Wall Street Journal*, June 24, 1959.

5. Fidel Castro, "Second Declaration of Havana," in *Fidel Castro Speaks*, eds. Martin Kenner and James Petras (New York: Grove Press, 1969), p. 104.

6. Quoted in Richard Gott, *Rural Guerrillas in Latin America*, rev. ed. (London: Penguin Books, 1973), p. 168.

7. Quoted in Ibid., p. 181.

8. Quoted in Ibid., p. 262.

9. Ernesto "Che" Guevera, "Letter to the Tricontinental" April 1967, in *Vencerermos*, ed. John Gerassi (New York: Simon and Schuster, 1968), p. 423.

10. Oscar Arias, *El camino de la paz* (San José, Costa Rica: Editorial Costa Rica, 1989), pp. 117, 177, 198, 319–20.

11. Ibid., p. 107.

12. Quoted in Eldon Kenworthy, "Promoting Democracy and Peace: Comparing U.S. and Costa Rican Discourse on Nicaragua." Paper presented at the XVI Congress of the Latin American Studies Association (Washington, D.C.: April 4–6, 1991), p. 13.

13. Oscar Arias, Nobel Peace Prize address, reprinted in the *New York Times*, December 11, 1987.

14. Quoted in Raymond Bonner, *Weakness and Deceit: U.S. Policy and El Salvador* (New York: Times Books, 1984), p. 234.

15. From and interview by Marc de Beaufort and Yezid Campos, March 1992.

16. Beaufort and Campos interview, March 1992.

17. Abimael Guzmán, quoted in Carlos Iván Degregori, *El surgimiento de Sendero Luminoso: Ayacucho, 1969–1979* (Lima: Instituto de Estudios Peruanos, 1990), p. 13.

18. Abimael Guzmán, *Interview With Chairman Gonzalo*, trans., Committee to Support the Revolution in Peru (Berkeley, Calif.: Committee to Support the Revolution in Peru, 1991), p. 101.

19. Abimael Guzmán, quoted in Degregori, "Return to the Past," in *Shining Path of Peru*, ed. David Scott Palmer (London: Hurst, 1992), p. 40.

20. Communist party of Peru–Sendero Luminoso, quoted in Degregori, *Sendero Luminoso*, p. 209.

21. Guzmán, *Interview*, p. 53.

22. Quoted in Gustavo Gorriti Ellenbogen, *Sendero: História de la guerra milenaria en el Peru*, 2 vols. (Lima: Editorial Apoyo, 1990), I, p. 143.

23. Guzmán, *Interview*, pp. 14, 22–3.

24. Degregori, "Return to the Past," p. 43.

25. Beaufort and Campos interview, March 1992.

26. Beaufort and Campos interview, March 1992.

27. Quoted in Orin Starn, "New Literature in Peru's Sendero Luminoso," *Latin America Research Review* 27: 2 (1992), p. 219.

28. From an Artes de Sarhua painting reproduced on the cover of Robin Kirk, *The Decade of Chaqwa: Peru's Internal Refugees* (Washington, D.C.: U.S. Committee for Refugees, May 1991).

29. Quoted in Michael L. Smith, "Shining Path's Urban Strategy: Ate Vitarte," in Palmer, *Shining Path*, p. 131.

30. Beaufort and Campos interview, March 1992.

31. Beaufort and Campos interview, March 1992.

32. Beaufort and Campos interview, March 1992.

33. Quoted in the *New York Times*, July 27, 1992.

14: North of the Border

This chapter draws on the writings and ideas of Alejandro Portes, Rubén Rumbaut, and Marta Tienda, and incorporates interviews conducted by producers Peter Bull and Joseph Tovares in Los Angeles, Miami, and New York.

1. Quoted in the *New York Times*, October 11, 1991.

2. Quoted in Ibid.

3. Quoted in the *New York Times*, May 11, 1992.

4. Quoted in "All Things Considered," National Public Radio, May 17, 1992.

5.   Quoted in the *New York Times,* May 11, 1992.

6.   Quoted in *Elle* (June 1992), 42.

7.   Quoted in the *New York Times,* January 1, 1992.

8.   Quoted in Ibid.

9.   *New York Times,* May 27, 1992.

10. Quoted in the *New York Times,* October 13, 1991.

11. Quoted in Ibid.

12. Linda Chavez, "Multicultural Society: Mosaic or Melting Pot," *Worldlink* No. 2 (1992), 60 and 63.

13. Richard Lamm and Gary Imhoff, *The Immigration Time Bomb: The Fragmenting of America* (New York: Dutton, 1985), p. 123.

Illustration Credits

122   UPI/Bettmann Newsphotos
155   Alberto Bravo/La Nación
156   © Rick Reinhard, 1983, Impact Visuals
157   © Nair Benedicto, N-Imagens
158   © Zeka Araujo, N-Imagens
200   © Helen Hughes
201   © Terry Moore, 1986, Woodfin Camp & Assoc.
202   © Terry Moore, 1986, Woodfin Camp & Assoc.
203   Don Bartletti, *Los Angeles Times*
204   Don Bartletti, *Los Angeles Times*
234   Bolivian Photo Agency, La Paz
235   *(top)* © 1989 Vera Lentz, Black Star; *(bottom)* Jane Regan
236   © 1991 Milton Gurán, Impact Visuals
237   © Stephen Ferry, Gamma Liaison
238   Andrew Cooper, The Rainforest Foundation
271   © Carole Devillers
272   AP/Wide World Photos
273   *(top)* © Alex Webb, Magnum Photos; *(bottom)* Jane Regan
274   Ronaldo Kohn, Azul Press
275   Rejane Carneiro, N-Imagens
276   AP/Wide World Photos
307   Courtesy of Elena Caffarena and Olga Poblete
308   © Enrique Shore, Woodfin Camp & Assoc.
309   © Helen Hughes
310   Yezid Campos
311   © David A. Harvey, Woodfin Camp & Assoc.
312   AP/Wide World Photos
346   © Victor Englebert
347   Delfim Martins, Pulsar
348   Arzobispado de San Salvador, El Salvador. Courtesy Publicationes Pastorales del Arzobispado/Orbis Books
349   AP/Wide World Photos
350   Nair Benedicto, N-Imagens
351   © Juca Martins, Pulsar Imagens E Editora
352   Art Walker, *Chicago Tribune*
394   Courtesy of CENIDIAP (Centro Nacional de Investigación, Documentación e Información de Artes Plásticas)/INBA (Instituto Nacional de Bellas Artes, Mexico)
395   *(top)* Courtesy of Museo Gabriela Mistral, Dirección de Bibliotecas, Archivos y Museos, Vicuña, Chile; *(bottom)* © Sara Facia
396   © Diana Walker, Gamma Liaison
397   R. Feldman, American Repertory Theatre

398 Bauer Sá
442 UPI/Bettmann Newsphotos
443 La Nación
444 *(top)* Everybody's Magazine; *(bottom)* Shanachie recording artist
445 © Owen Franken, Sygma
446 AP/Wide World Photos
492 *(top)* Library of Congress; *(bottom)* Archivo General de la Nación—Mexico/ Archivo Histórico Central Archivo Fotográfico Diáz, Delgado y García. Impresión: Caja 3: 100/1
493 Lee Lockwood
494 Peter Winn
495 © Susan Meiselas, Magnum Photos
496 Antonio Turok, Mexico
497 Katy Lyle/The Traveling Museum, © Panateca
498 Yezid Campos
550 *(top)* © Stephanie Maze, Woodfin Camp & Assoc.; *(bottom)* © Douglas Burrows, Gamma Liaison
551 © Randy Taylor, Sygma
552 AP/Wide World Photos
553 © Jerry Berndt, all rights reserved
554 Peter Bull

Color Section (between pages 144 and 145)
1 © Stephen Ferry, JB Pictures
2 © Victor Englebert
3 © Robert Frerck, Woodfin Camp & Assoc.
4 © Rogério Reis, Pulsar Imagens
5 © Juca Martins, Pulsar Imagens
6 *(top)* © Jacques Jangoux, 1976, Peter Arnold Inc.; *(bottom)* © Adam Woolfit, 1980, Woodfin Camp & Assoc.
7 *Lienzo de Castas,* Anon., 18th century, Museo Nacional del Virreinato, Tepotzotlan/INAH/CNCA, Mexico, photo by Bob Schalkwijk
8 Bolivian Photo Agency, La Paz

Color Section (between pages 304 and 305)
1 Painting by Dieudonné Cedor, 1948, *Ceremony at Bois Caïman,* 1791, Musée d'Art Haitien, Port-au-Prince, Haiti, courtesy of Selden Rodman
2 © Sebastiao Salgado, Magnum Photos
3 Bolivian Photo Agency, photo by Pedro Cote
4 © Stephanie Maze, Woodfin Camp & Assoc.
5 © Carole Devillers

6   © Marcelo Montecino
7   © Susan Meiselas, Magnum Photos
8   © Claus C. Meyer, N-Imagens

Color Section (between pages 464 and 465)

1   Botero, Fernando, *The Presidential Family*, 1967, oil on canvas, 6'8⅛" × 6'5¼". Collection, The Museum of Modern Art, New York, gift of Warren D. Benedek. Photo © 1992, The Museum of Modern Art, New York

2   José Clemente Orozco, *Zapatistas*, 1931, oil on canvas, 45 × 55". Collection, The Museum of Modern Art, New York, given anonymously. Photo © 1991, The Museum of Modern Art, New York

3   Frida Kahlo, *Self-portrait as Tijuaná (Diego on My Mind)*, 1943, from the collection of Natasha Gelman, photo by Martha Zamora

4   Dulce Maria Nuñez, *Huitzilopochtli Holandés*, 1990, courtesy Galería OMR

5   Nahum Zenil, *Evangelista*, 1989, courtesy Galería de Arte Mexicano

6   © Judith F. Baca, SPARC

7   ADAPS (Asociación de Artistas Populares de Sarhua, Ayacucho, Peru)

8   © Ken Ross, Gamma-Liaison

Map on endpaper overleaf   Model by Yeorgos N. Lampathakis, photo by Skolos Wedell, design by Gaye Korbet and Hisako Matsui, WGBH Design

Maps on pages 6 and 7   "Turnabout map," after Jesse Levine 1983; Mercator and Peters projections, design by Gaye Korbet and Hisako Matsui, WGBH Design

Index

PETER WINN is academic director of the PBS series "Americas: Latin America and the Caribbean," a seven-year project that gave rise to this book. Born in New York in 1942 and educated at Columbia College and Cambridge University, Mr. Winn has taught history at Yale and Princeton and was the Barnette-Miller Professor of International Relations at Wellesley College. He is a professor of Latin American history at Tufts University and a senior research associate at Columbia University's Institute of Latin American and Iberian Studies.

Mr. Winn is the author of *Weavers of Revolution,* a critically acclaimed oral history of contemporary Chile, and has published widely on Latin America and United States–Latin American relations in the *New York Times,* the *Los Angeles Times,* and the *Christian Science Monitor,* among other periodicals. He has served as advisor to two prize-winning documentary films—*Against Wind and Tide: A Cuban Odyssey* (which was nominated for an Academy Award) and *Cuba: In the Shadow of Doubt* (winner of a Golden Hugo), for which he also coauthored the script. He is a recipient of the Latin American Studies Association's Citation for Distinguished Contribution to Public Understanding of Latin America. Mr. Winn lives in New York with his wife and two children.